Madrid

timeout.com/madrid

Published by Time Out Guides Ltd, a wholly owned subsidiary of Time Out Group Ltd.
Time Out and the Time Out logo are trademarks of Time Out Group Ltd.

© **Time Out Group Ltd 2004**
Previous editions 1995, 1997, 1999, 2000, 2002

10 9 8 7 6 5 4 3 2 1

This edition first published in Great Britain in 2004 by Ebury
Ebury is a division of The Random House Group Ltd,
20 Vauxhall Bridge Road, London SW1V 2SA

Random House Australia Pty Limited, 20 Alfred Street, Milsons Point, Sydney, New South Wales 2061, Australia
Random House New Zealand Limited, 18 Poland Road, Glenfield, Auckland 10, New Zealand
Random House South Africa (Pty) Limited, Endulini, 5A Jubilee Road, Parktown 2193, South Africa

Random House UK Limited Reg. No. 954009

Distributed in USA by Publishers Group West
1700 Fourth Street, Berkeley, California 94710

Distributed in Canada by Penguin Canada Ltd
10 Alcorn Avenue, Toronto, Ontario, Canada M4V 3B2

For further distribution details, see www.timeout.com

ISBN 1-904978-26-6

A CIP catalogue record for this book is available from the British Library

Colour reprographics by Icon, Crowne House, 56-58 Southwark Street, London SE1 1UN

Printed and bound by Cayfosa-Quebecor, Ctra. De Caldes, KM 3 08 130 Sta, Perpètua de Mogoda, Barcelona, Spain

Time Out Guides Limited
Universal House
251 Tottenham Court Road
London W1T 7AB
Tel + 44 (0)20 7813 3000
Fax + 44 (0)20 7813 6001
Email guides@timeout.com
www.timeout.com

Contributors

Introduction Harvey Holtom. **History** Nick Rider (*The Family of Charles IV* Clayton Maxwell). **Madrid Today** Nick Lyne. **Seeing the bulls** Robert Elms (*Where and how* Alex Leith). **Flamenco** Rob Stone. **Where to Stay** Helen Jones, Danny Wood. **Sightseeing** Harvey Holtom, Sally Davies, Madeleine Knights (*Room 56-A* Richard Schweid; *Defining the indefinable*, *No peace for the gifted* Michael Jacobs; *Watch this space* Clayton Maxwell; *Sainted love* Annie Bennett; *The garden of unearthly delights* Nick Rider). **Restaurants** Clayton Maxwell. *Additional reviews* Sally Davies. **Tapas** Sally Davies (*Doing vermouth* Clayton Maxwell). **Cafés & Bars** Sally Davies (*Tertulias* Michael Jacobs; *A vine romance* Clayton Maxwell). **Shops & Services** Harvey Holtom, Simon Hunter (*Material world* Helen Jones). **Festivals & Events** Harvey Holtom (*Burial of the Sardine* Clayton Maxwell). **Children** Andrew Wallace. **Film** Rob Stone. **Galleries** Clayton Maxwell. **Gay & Lesbian** Barry Byrne, Pablo Espinoza, Jimmy Shaw. **Music** *Classical & Opera* Delaina Haslam; *Rock, Roots & Jazz* Simon Hunter (*Sounds of the City* David Oancia). **Nightlife** Simon Hunter. **Sport & Fitness** Alex Leith (*Getting steamy* Clayton Maxwell). **Theatre & Dance** Delaina Haslam. **Trips out of Town** Sally Davies (*Toledo* Nadia Feddo, *The recycled cathedral* Annie Bennett). **Directory** Nathalie Pédestarres

Maps page 306 Mapworld, 71 Blandy Road, Henley on Thames, Oxon RG9 1QB; pages 262, 272, 307 JS Graphics (john@jsgraphics.co.uk); pages 308-315, 319, 320 supplied by the Consorcio de Transportes de Madrid.

Photography by Venetia Dearden, except: page 10 Hulton Getty; page 24 Corbis; pages 27, 241 Getty Images; page 241 Hadley Kincade; pages 29, 253, 254, 255, 258, 260, 261, 263, 264, 267, 268, 274 Sally Davies; page 257 Jonathan Cox.

The following images were provided by the featured establishments/artists: pages 13, 15, 18, 23, 61, 62, 65, 67, 68, 70, 82, 127, 192, 217, 225, 230, 245, 246.

The Editor would like to thank

Laura Cuenca at the Patronato de Turismo de Madrid, Juan Peiro at Paradores de España, Olga Viñas and Concha Bentura at TurMadrid, Botoa Lefe at the Thyssen, Mercedes González Amezúa at the Real Academia de San Fernando, Teodoro García at the Reina Sofía, José María Ambrona at the Prado, the stationmaster at Tablada, Bob & Lourdes González Steane, Sarah Guy, Delaina Haslam, Ella & Sebastián Holtom, Sam Le Quesne, Clayton Maxwell, James Mitchell, John O'Donovan, Maggi Riach. Special thanks to Simon Hunter.

Contents

Introduction

People who come to Madrid do so for any number of reasons. Some are lured by the three celebrated palaces of art – the Prado, the Thyssen and the Reina Sofía – and end up being seduced by the ramshackle and idiosyncratic museums that pepper the city. Others come in search of *la marcha*, that indefinable good-time spirit, be it gay or straight. Others are simply here to eat and drink, and are drawn equally to the ancient down-at-heel taverns and the new breed of creative restaurants. Some come here to live.

Not all are aware, though, that they are visiting a city in the throes of enormous change. Those who speak little Spanish may not notice that the person serving them food or drink speaks in a singsong Andean accent; the Italianate tones of the River Plate or the shushing sounds of Eastern Europe. Not everybody notices just how many North and sub-Saharan African men are employed on building sites, and it might not be obvious that the guttural sounds of Arabic heard in Lavapiés, or the dazzling garments sported by the African women there, are relatively recent phenomena.

Economic prosperity has brought about many other changes, as well as immigration. The chic boutiques and designer powerhouses once contained within the upmarket neighbourhood of Salamanca have now spread into the old city. The Armani-clad *madrileño* tucking into chicken satay or sushi is nowadays just as much a part of the scene as the cloth-capped, *cocido*-eating *castizo*.

Ah yes, *castizos*. Go to any of Madrid's popular fiestas, like San Isidro or La Paloma, and you will see blokes in dogtooth-check jackets, neckies and flat caps, accompanied by women in long, frilly, tight dresses, with headscarves and carnations in their hair. These modern-day descendants of the 18th-century *majos* and *majas* painted by Goya are living proof that, though much has changed, much also remains the same.

Locals still hang on to many things they have always held dear. Going out and having a good time is considered as much a right as voting. And party they still do, despite a succession of conservative, kill-joy local governments that have tried their damnedest to smother nightlife. Bars may close earlier nowadays, the city may be more European, some might even say boring, but there is still a strain of that rebellious attitude that visitors found so refreshing back in the days of La Movida. Not for nothing are *madrileños* nicknamed *gatos* (cats), a moniker that owes much to nocturnal wanderings. People here still go to bed an hour or two later than their counterparts in Paris, London or Berlin. And despite superficially thick-skinned attitudes, certain human qualities remain intact also; witness the spontaneous generosity and solidarity displayed by so many ordinary citizens on that terrible 11 March.

Change may be the order of the day, but many facets of life here that have always attracted visitors are, seemingly, eternal. Enjoy them.

ABOUT TIME OUT CITY GUIDES

Time Out Madrid is one of an expanding series of travel guides produced by the people behind London and New York's successful listings magazines. Our guides are all written and updated by resident experts who have striven to provide you with all the most up-to-date information you'll need to explore the city, whether you're a local or first-time visitor.

THE LOWDOWN ON THE LISTINGS

Above all, we've tried to make this book as useful as possible. Websites, telephone numbers, transport information, opening times, admission prices and credit card details are all included in our listings. And, as far as possible, we've given details of facilities, services and events, all checked and correct at the time we went to press. However, owners and managers can change their arrangements at any time. Before you go out of your way, we'd strongly advise you to call and check opening times, dates of exhibitions and other particulars. While every effort has been made to ensure the accuracy of the information contained in this guide, the publishers cannot accept responsibility for any errors it may contain.

PRICES AND PAYMENT

We have noted whether venues such as shops, hotels and restaurants accept credit cards or not but have only listed the major cards – American Express (AmEx), Diners Club (DC), MasterCard (MC) and Visa (V). Many businesses will also accept other cards, including Switch/Maestro or Delta, JCB, Discover and Carte Blanche. Some shops, restaurants and attractions may accept euro travellers' cheques issued by a major financial institution (such as American Express or Thomas Cook).

The prices we've supplied should be treated as guidelines, not gospel. Fluctuating exchange rates and inflation can cause charges, in shops and restaurants particularly, to change rapidly. If prices vary wildly from those we've quoted, ask whether there's a good reason. If not, go

elsewhere. Then please write and let us know. We aim to give the best and most up-to-date advice, so we always want to know if you've been badly treated or overcharged.

THE LIE OF THE LAND

Mail addresses in Spain include a five-digit postcode, which for Madrid always begins 28 and is written before the name of the city (as in 28014 Madrid). We have given these codes for organisations or venues you might need to write to, such as hotels. We have also divided the city into areas – simplified, for convenience, from the full complexity of Madrid's geography – and the relevant area name is given with each venue listed in this guide (for an overview of areas used, see p307). And there's a series of fully indexed colour street maps, a map of the surrounding countryside and two transport maps at the back of the guide, starting on p308.

TELEPHONE NUMBERS

It is necessary to dial provincial area codes with all numbers in Spain, even for local calls. Hence all normal Madrid numbers begin 91, whether or not you're callling from outside the city. From abroad you must dial the international code, followed by 34 for Spain, then the 91.

To dial numbers as given in this book from abroad, use your country's exit code (00 in the UK, 011 in the US), followed by the country code for Spain (34), and then the 91.

ESSENTIAL INFORMATION

For all the practical information you might need for visiting the city (including visa and customs information, disabled access, emergency telephone numbers, a list of useful websites and the lowdown on the local transport network) turn to the Directory chapter at the back of this guide. It starts on p277.

MAPS

We've included a series of fully indexed colour maps to the centre of the city at the back of this guide – they start on p305 – and, where possible, we've printed a grid reference against all venues that appear on the maps.

LET US KNOW WHAT YOU THINK

We hope you enjoy *Time Out Madrid*, and we'd like to know what you think of it. We welcome tips for places that you consider we should include in future editions and take notice of your criticism of our choices. You can email us on guides@timeout.com.

> There is an online version of this book, along with guides to over 45 other international cities, at **www.timeout.com**.

In Context

History

Ignored and insignificant shanty town makes good.

In the 17th century, after Madrid had become capital of the Spanish Empire on the whim of Philip V, an attempt was made to construct an ancient past for it, and writers developed the story of its descent from a Roman city called Mantua Carpetana. Though there were Roman towns nearby at Alcalá de Henares (Complutum) and Toledo (Toletum), and Roman villas along the valley of the Manzanares, there is no real evidence that there was ever a local Mantua, or that any of these settlements was the origin of modern Madrid. The story of Mantua Carpetana, however, served to obscure the insignificance of Madrid before Philip II moved his Court here in 1561, and above all the embarrassing fact that it was founded by Muslims. Specifically, in about 860, during the reign of Mohammed I, fifth Emir of Córdoba.

ARABIAN SIGHTS

Following their eruption into the Iberian peninsula in 711 the Arab armies did not occupy the inhospitable lands north of the Sierra de Guadarrama, but established a frontier more or less along the old Roman road linking Mérida, Toledo and Saragossa. The original *qasr* (a word absorbed into Spanish as Alcázar) or fortress of Madrid was one of a string of watchtowers built north of this line in the ninth century, as Christian raids into Al-Andalus became more frequent. The rocky crag on which it stood, where the Palacio Real is today, was ideal for the purpose, since it had a view of the main tracks south from the Guadarrama. It also had excellent water, from underground streams within the rock. Madrid's original Arabic name, Mayrit or Magerit, means 'place of many springs'.

Mayrit became more than just a fortress, with an outer citadel, the eastern wall of which ran along the modern C/Factor, and a wider town or *medina* bounded by the Plaza de la Villa and C/Segovia. A section of wall, the Muralla Arabe on Cuesta de la Vega, and the remains currently being excavated next to the Palacio Real are the only remnants of Muslim Madrid visible in the modern city. Both citadel and *medina* consisted of a mass of narrow alleys, like the old quarters of North African cities today.

Mayrit was attacked by Christian armies in 932 and 1047, and in the 970s was used by the great minister of Córdoba, Al-Mansur, as a base for his celebrated 100 campaigns against the north. By the 11th century it had a population of around 7,000, among them Abul-Qasim Maslama, mathematician, astronomer, translator of Greek literature and experimenter in magic.

CHRISTIAN CONQUEST

In the 11th century the Caliphate of Córdoba disintegrated into a mass of petty princedoms called *taifas*, and Mayrit became part of the Emirate of Toledo. In 1086 Alfonso VI of Castile was able to take advantage of this situation to conquer Toledo, and with it Madrid. The town's main mosque became the church of Santa María de la Almudena, which would survive until the 19th century. For many years, however, Madrid would remain on the front line. In 1109 it was again besieged, by a Moorish army that camped below the Alcázar in the place ever since known as Campo del Moro (Field of the Moor). A new wall was built, enclosing the area between the Alcázar and Plaza Isabel II, Plaza San Miguel and Plaza Humilladero.

> ### 'Isabella ordered the expulsion of all Jews and the forcible conversion of the Mudéjar Muslims.'

Christian Madrid was a very rural town, and most of the population who worked did so on the land. Madrid did acquire some large religious houses, notably the Friary of San Francisco, where the church of San Francisco el Grande stands today, supposedly founded by Saint Francis of Assisi himself in 1217. Madrid was still not entirely Christian, however. Many Muslims, known as Mudéjares, had stayed in the conquered areas, retaining their own laws and religion, and were prized by the Castilian monarchs for their skills as builders and masons, still seen today in the towers of San Nicolás de los Servitas and San Pedro el Viejo. In Madrid they were confined to the area known as the Morería. Medieval Madrid also had a smaller Jewish population, concentrated outside the walls in Lavapiés.

Madrid did finally begin to play more of a role in the affairs of Castile in the 14th century. In 1309 the Cortes or parliament met here for the first time. Medieval Castile did not have a fixed capital, but instead the Court followed the king around the country, and the Cortes met in many different towns at different times. In the 14th and 15th centuries Castile was dogged by a series of social revolts and civil wars, between monarchs, the nobility, and rival claimants within the royal family itself. Against this backdrop Madrid began to gain popularity as a royal residence, as a country retreat more than as a centre of power.

Political instability did not prevent there being substantial economic progress in 15th-century Castile, which enabled Madrid to become a reasonably prosperous trading centre for the first time. Its trade outgrew the old market in Plaza de la Villa, and in the 1460s an area east of the 12th-century wall was built up as a ramshackle new market square, origin of the Plaza Mayor. A new town wall was built, not for defence but so that taxes could be levied on people living in the new parts of the town. Its eastern entrance was a new gate, the Puerta del Sol.

THE CATHOLIC KINGS

At the end of the 15th century a new era was opening up in Castilian and Spanish history. In 1476 Enrique IV's sister Isabel and her husband Fernando of Aragon succeeded in bringing the civil wars to an end. Through their marriage they united the different Spanish kingdoms, although each retained its own institutions for another two centuries. Within Castile they established an absolute monarchy and a professional army that enabled them to intervene in the wars of Renaissance Italy. The devout Isabella was also one of the instigators of the militant sense of religious mission that would mark imperial Spain. Detesting the religious coexistence of medieval Spain, she ordered the expulsion of all Jews in 1492 and the forcible conversion of the Mudéjar Muslims in 1502, with a reinforced Inquisition to police these measures. Also in 1492 came the conquest of Muslim Granada, which won Ferdinand and Isabella the title 'Most Catholic Kings' from the Pope. In this same year, they also sponsored Columbus's first voyage to America.

Madrid retained a degree of royal favour, helped and continued its modest growth, and at the end of the Middle Ages had a population of around 10,000-12,000.

On 11 May 1561 the small-time aristocrats who ran the town of Madrid received a letter from their king, Philip II, warning that he, the entire royal household and all their hundreds of hangers-on would shortly be coming to stay. They immediately set about panic-buying food from surrounding towns, using the money set aside for the fiesta of Corpus Christi, much to the irritation of the local population. No one quite realised, though, that this visit was intended to be a permanent stay.

THE EMPIRE STRIKES OUT

In the previous 50 years the Spanish monarchy had been transformed. Ferdinand and Isabella were succeeded by their grandson Charles of Habsburg (1516-56). Through his father, Philip, Duke of Burgundy, Charles also inherited Burgundy (the Netherlands and large parts of eastern France) and the Habsburg lands in central Europe, and would in 1519 receive the title Holy Roman Emperor, as Charles V. He would also acquire ever-larger territories in America. Thus Spain became part, and increasingly the centre, of a worldwide empire.

When he first visited Spain in 1517 Charles appointed French speakers to many state posts. This led in 1520 to the revolt of the Comuneros, in which the towns of Castile, Madrid among them, rose up against foreign influence and the encroachment of royal power on their traditional freedoms. However, after this had been suppressed in 1521, Charles came to value Spain – above all Castile – more and more, as the most loyal part of his empire.

Charles and his successors had an immense sense of the greatness of their dynasty and their imperial mission, believing that their vast territories had come to them through providence and that it was their right and duty to defend both them and the Catholic faith. This would involve continual and ever more costly wars, against the French, the Muslim Turks and the northern Protestants. This idea of mission combined perfectly with the crusading, military spirit already imbued in the Castilian Church, army and aristocracy.

Charles V made no attempt to give Castile a capital. However, on his visits to Spain he spent considerable time in Madrid, hunting at El Pardo and giving the town another grand title, Imperial y Coronada (Imperial and Crowned).

A CAPITAL IS CREATED

In 1555 Charles abdicated and the title of Holy Roman Emperor went to his brother Ferdinand, but Spain and Burgundy were passed to Charles's son, Philip II (1556-98). The fundamental figure in Madrid's history, Philip was a deeply pious, shy, austere man. His father had travelled incessantly about his many dominions, and led his armies into battle. Philip, in contrast, ruled his inheritance from behind a desk, as a kind of king-bureaucrat, sometimes dealing with over 400 documents a day. This extraordinary exercise in paperwork naturally required a permanent base.

Moreover, in the 1540s Charles V had introduced Burgundian state ritual into the relatively informal Court of Castile. Every appearance of the monarch followed a set ceremonial order, with a ritual etiquette that became ever more elaborate in succeeding generations as the Habsburgs amplified their idea of their own grandeur. The number of Court attendants mushroomed, making an itinerant Court all the more impractical.

Why Philip chose a town without a cathedral, college or printing press as capital remains unclear. The fact that Madrid was near the centre of the Iberian peninsula probably appealed to Philip, who was fascinated by geometry and Renaissance ideas of a king as the 'centre' of the state, but his choice made no economic sense at all, since it gave Spain the only major European capital not on a navigable river. Madrid – which for centuries would normally be referred to in Spain as 'La Corte', the Court, never as a city in its own right, which indeed it wasn't – would be a capital of the monarchy's own creation, a pure expression of royal power.

Having established his ideal capital, Philip did little to build or plan it. He had extended the Alcázar when he was still crown prince, then his attention shifted to El Escorial, where he increasingly spent his time. Royal piety was demonstrated by the endowment of new houses for religious orders, such as the Descalzas Reales. Philip II founded 17 convents and monasteries in Madrid, Philip III 14 and Philip IV another 17, and they would cover a third of the city until the 19th century. A wider city wall was put up in 1566, and the Puente de Segovia in the 1580s. Philip's favourite architect, Juan de Herrera, planned the rebuilding of the Plaza Mayor, but the only part built during his reign was the Casa de la Panadería in 1590. Philip's idea of a capital seemed more like a collection of royal establishments than a living city.

Reality, however, was more powerful than this rudimentary concept. The establishment of the Court and aristocracy in Madrid – the great centres of consumption and patronage – made it a magnet for people from all over Spain and abroad. The population went from under 20,000 in 1561 to 55,000 in 1584 and close to 85,000 by 1600. Building did not keep up with the influx, and a law decreed that in any house of more than one storey, the upper floor could be requisitioned to house members of the Court. In response, people simply put up houses with only one floor, and much of the new Madrid grew as a mass of shabby, low buildings slapped together out of mud.

This improvised capital did not impress foreign visitors. Lambert Wyts, a Flemish aristocrat who arrived in 1571, said that it was 'the foulest and filthiest town in Spain'. Thick mud made it impossible to ride a horse down the main streets in winter until a few cobbles were put down in the 1580s. There were no drains of any kind, and the streets were full of

Philip II, portrayed by Rubens. *See p11*.

waste thrown out of the houses every night, producing an 'unbearable stench'.

Madrid had taken on a characteristic that would stay with it to this day – that it was a city of outsiders, in which at least 50 per cent of the population was from somewhere else. Another trait for which Madrid would be repeatedly condemned was that it was a city that consumed but did not produce anything. The trades that did develop in Madrid – carpentry, shoemaking, jewellery-making, fan-making, laceworking – were overwhelmingly oriented to servicing the Court and aristocracy.

The economic frailty of Madrid reflected that of Castile as a whole. The gold and silver of Mexico and Peru seemed to give the Habsburg kings limitless potential wealth. The demands of their wars, however, were immediate, and could only be met by loans from foreign bankers. The result was soaring, uncontrollable debts, which not even American gold could service. Also, the country's political hierarchy had been built on the basis of giving the aristocracy, the *hidalgos* or lesser gentry and the Church immense privileges, including exemption from taxation. This meant that the ever-increasing war taxes hit precisely and only the few productive sectors of the population. Young men of working age were also continually being drawn off for the army.

For a country with the social system of Castile, constant imperialism was near suicidal; in time, it would lead to the eradication of the growth visible under Ferdinand and Isabella, and a catastrophic decline in the rural population.

IN DAYS OF GOLD

One aspect of Spain during its 'Golden Century' was its intense Catholic faith. This was also, though, the golden age of the *picaro*, the chancer, the figure living on his wits as seen in the picaresque novels of the period. In a society that valued aristocracy, status and military or state service over productive activity, and in which the real economy was rapidly dwindling, their numbers naturally multiplied.

The mecca for all *picaros* was Madrid, the one place where ex-soldiers, landless peasants and drifters would be most likely to find a niche, as servants or bodyguards, or by gambling, pimping, thieving or many other means. The great poet and satirist Quevedo wrote a whole book cataloguing the varieties of Madrid's low life and how they acquired cash. Madrid also contained a great many of the very poor, living off the charity provided by the huge number of religious houses in the city.

Picaros were not only found among the poor. Madrid also drew in thousands at the other end of society, often *hidalgos* with estates run to ruin, who came hoping to attach themselves to some lordly patron and so break into the circles of the Court. For them, maintaining appearances, presenting an image of aristocracy, was everything. In 1620 Madrid acquired its first guidebook, the 'Guide and advice to strangers who come to the Court, in which they are taught to flee the dangers that there are in Court life', by Antonio Liñán y Verdugo, a lawyer from Cuenca. He warned provincials who might have to do business in Madrid that in 'this Babylon', 'of every four things one sees, one cannot believe even two', for everything was just 'fabulous appearances, dreamed-up marvels, fairy-tale treasures, and figures like actors on a stage'.

This volatile mass naturally needed entertainment. One source was the theatre, the focus of the extraordinary literary vitality of the city at this time. There were also fiestas and royal ceremonies, and even foreigners who complained about the mud and the stink were impressed by the variety of luxuries that could be had in Madrid, from Italian lace to fresh fish, brought caked in ice from the Basque coast.

THE COURT ADJOURNS

In 1571 came the greatest success of Philip II's reign with the defeat of the Turkish fleet off Lepanto in Greece. In 1580, he also became King of Portugal. He appeared to be at the height of his strength. However, suspensions of payments on his debts were becoming frequent occurrences, and in the 1560s a rebellion had broken out in the Netherlands that would develop into a morass into which Spanish armies and wealth would disappear without trace. His dispute with England – leading to the catastrophe of the Armada – and interventions in France's religious wars, were equally costly.

As problems mounted without ever being resolved, a gnawing frustration spread through Castilian society, and scapegoats were sought. The former Muslims, nominally converted to Catholicism in 1502, were put under increasing pressure and then expelled from Spain in 1609, and the Inquisition – if not the all-pervading force of Protestant caricatures – was given great powers to investigate any deviations from Catholic orthodoxy.

Philip II died in 1598 at El Escorial, aged 71. His son Philip III (1598-1621) and grandson Philip IV (1621-65) had neither the intelligence, confidence or normally the motivation to carry on with the awesome burden of work he had set as an example. Philip III began the practice of ruling through a favourite or *valido*, in his case the Duke of Lerma. Spain's impoverished state, aggravated by a devastating plague in 1599, was impossible to ignore, and Lerma responded by making peace with England and the Dutch.

He also committed the ultimate injury to Madrid by moving the Court to Valladolid, in 1601. The main stated reason was that this would help revive the economy of northern Castile, although Lerma also stood to benefit personally. He also argued that Madrid, in any case, was so overrun with undesirables that it had become intolerable. The monarchy's purpose-built capital was out of control and it would be best to write it off and start again.

Within a few months Madrid was so deserted that 'it appeared as if the Moors or the English had sacked and burnt it'. By 1605 the population had fallen back to just 26,000, little more than before Philip II's arrival in 1561. However, the Valladolid experiment did not work, and it became evident that Madrid had acquired a momentum that was difficult to disregard. In 1606 the Court returned, amid huge rejoicing, and only a year later the population was already back to 70,000.

POMP AND CIRCUMSTANCE

It was after the definitive establishment of Madrid as capital, with Philip III's brief declaration *Sólo Madrid es Corte* (Only Madrid is the Court), that more was at last done to give it the look of a grand city. The Plaza Mayor was finally completed in 1619, followed by the Ayuntamiento or city hall and the Buen Retiro

palace. The aristocracy, too, began to build palaces around the city once they were assured they would not have to move on again, and Madrid acquired several much more elaborate baroque churches.

The Plaza Mayor was the great arena of Habsburg Madrid. Able to hold a third of the city's population at that time, it was the venue for state ceremonies, bullfights, executions, *autos-da-fé* (the ritual condemnation of heretics), mock battles, circus acts and carnival fiestas, as well as still being a market square. Particularly lavish entertainments were staged in the plaza in 1623 for the Prince of Wales, the future King Charles I, who arrived in Madrid under the alias of 'Tom Smith' in a fruitless attempt to negotiate a marriage with the sister of Philip IV.

Habsburg Madrid functioned rather like a giant theatre, a great backdrop against which the monarchy could display itself to its subjects and to the world. On either side were royal estates, which determined the shape of the city left in the middle and its peculiar north-south pattern of growth. Several times a year royal processions took place, with stops for various ceremonies in the Plaza Mayor and High Masses in various churches. For the occasion, buildings were covered in garlands, and temporary arches erected along the route with extravagant decoration extolling the virtues of the dynasty. As the Spanish monarchy slid towards economic collapse the lavishness of these ceremonies only increased, maintaining an illusion of power and opulence.

Away from this ceremonial route, the Habsburgs built few squares and no grand avenues, and old Madrid continued to develop along the tangled street plan it retains today. Even so, the opulence of the Court – and the poverty outside the capital – still attracted more people into the city, and in about 1630 Madrid reached its maximum size under the Habsburgs, with possibly as many as 170,000 inhabitants. In 1656 it was given its fifth and final wall, roughly surrounding the area now considered 'old Madrid', which would set the limits of the city for the next 200 years.

THE PRICE OF WAR

For many years the centre of all the Court pomp was King Philip IV. Throughout the 1620s and 1630s, while the Court maintained its image of grandeur, his *valido,* the Count-Duke of Olivares struggled to maintain the Spanish empire against threats on every side. In the 1620s Spain won a series of victories, and for a time it seemed the rot had been stopped. In 1639, though, a Spanish fleet was destroyed by the Dutch, and in 1643 the French crushed the Spanish army at Rocroi in Flanders. Naval

In the frame The Majas

In the 18th century, the appearance of ordinary people in European cities became increasingly similar, with more or less the same three-cornered hats, breeches and mop-caps appearing everywhere. Not so in Madrid, however, where this era saw the appearance of the *majos* and *majas*. A *majo* wore embroidered shirts, a short jacket with a swathe of buttons, their hair held in a net, and always carried a knife. *Majas* wore short, mid-calf skirts with a mass of petticoats, pearl-white stockings, embroidered bodices, an intricately braided hairstyle and, on top, a dramatic lace mantilla. They were drawn from trades such as coach-driving, dressmaking, cigarette rolling or market trading and most often from Lavapiés. *Majas* especially were known for their wit, grace and verbal ferocity. In a capital that was still to a great extent a city of servants, but whose servants were renowned for talking back, they were not deferential to anybody.

They were most seen in all their finery at fiestas such as the Romería de San Isidro. Goya depicted them often. Also, their cocky elegance led to them being taken up by the upper classes, so that even *grandes dames* like the Duchess of Alba would dress up as *majas*, which is what probably gave rise to the story that Goya's nude and clothed *majas* are portraits of the Duchess herself.

A theory that has been discredited by art scholars in recent years, it still has many subscribers, and the woman depicted does bear a startling resemblance to the Duchess, and the large bow around her waist had featured in several of Goya's portraits of her. And, yes, it is possibly true that the Duchess had an affair with the painter, with whom she holed up for several months, on one of her country estates, after the death of her husband. It is unlikely, however, that she would allow herself to be painted in such a way, given her standing in society and the certain exposure of the works. Some critics have put forward the idea that the head was in fact painted on to the body later, and this is certainly the visual effect.

What is irrefutable, however, is that Goya was obsessed with Alba, and a more likely explanation for the likeness is simply that he tended to project her image on to an idealised form of female beauty. *Goya's* **Clothed Maja** *and* **Nude Maja** *are found at the Prado (see p63).*

defeats made it ever more difficult for Spain to import gold and silver from America. Olivares sought to extend taxation in the non-Castilian dominions of the crown, which led in 1640 to revolts in Portugal and Catalonia. Portugal regained its independence, and the Catalan revolt was only suppressed after a 12-year war.

By mid-century the effects of endless wars on Castile were visible to all, in abandoned villages and social decay. Even Madrid went into decline, so that by 1700 the city's population had fallen back to about 100,000. In the 1660s, the total collapse of the Spanish empire seemed an immediate possibility. Castile, the first world power, had been left poorer than many of the countries it had tried to dominate.

END OF THE HABSBURG LINE

In the Court, meanwhile, life became ever more of a baroque melodrama. Of Philip IV's 12 legitimate children by his two wives, only two girls had survived into adulthood – the youngest the Infanta Margarita, the little princess in Velázquez's *Las Meninas*. In 1661, however, when Philip was already prematurely aged, the queen, Mariana of Austria, had a son, conceived, the king wrote to his friend the nun Sister María, 'in the last copulation achieved with Doña Mariana'. Philip IV died in 1665, leaving as regent his widow Mariana.

The new heir, the future King Charles II, chronically infirm from birth, provided the dynasty with scant consolation. The Habsburgs' marked tendency to ill-health had been accentuated by their habit of marrying cousins or nieces. The Habsburg jaw, the growth of which can be followed through family portraits, had in Charles become a real disability. He was unable to eat solid food. Because of this – or more likely, due to the endless cures he was subjected to for his many ailments – he suffered from uncontrollable diarrhoea, which detracted from the stately dignity of Court ceremonies.

In the meantime, the economy and government continued to slide. Concern centred again on the need for an heir, and Charles was married off twice, despite a general belief that he was both impotent and sterile. As it became evident that the throne of the Spanish empire would soon become vacant, the Court was overrun with bizarre intrigues, with different factions and the agents of European powers all waiting on Charles' final demise. In 1695 the French Ambassador reported that the king 'appeared to be decomposing', and could barely walk without assistance. Even so, Charles hung on until the age of 38. In 1700, though, with the pathetic last words, '*Me duele todo*' (It hurts everywhere), he finally died, and the Spanish Habsburg dynasty came to an end.

BOURBON MADRID

Philip V (1700-46), first Bourbon King of Spain, secured his throne in 1714, after the 12-year War of the Spanish Succession. He was the grandson of Louis XIV of France and María Teresa, daughter of Philip IV of Spain. Castile, abandoning its more usual francophobia, gave him complete support. The alternative, Archduke Charles of Austria, was supported by Catalonia and the other Aragonese territories, to whom he had promised a restoration of their traditional rights. Twice, in 1706 and 1710, Charles' British, Dutch, Portuguese and Catalan army took Madrid, but was unable to hold it.

Once victorious, Philip reformed his new kingdom along lines laid down by his illustrious grandfather in France. In 1715 the remaining rights of the former Aragonese territories were abolished, so that it is from this date that Spain can formally be said to exist.

A French king brought with him other innovations. Philip V, raised at Versailles, and his Italian second wife Isabella Farnese were not taken with Madrid or its gloomy Habsburg palaces, and so built their own Franco-Italian villa at La Granja. They were not overly upset when the entire Alcázar burnt down in 1734, and a new Palacio Real was commissioned from Italian architects. Philip V and his administrator of Madrid, the Marqués de Vadillo, also sponsored many buildings by a local architect, Pedro de Ribera.

Reform led to economic recuperation and a recovery in Madrid's population. People still came and went, but it also acquired a more stable resident population, with a merchant community and an artisan and working class. Even so, in many ways Madrid had changed little. Its main function was still to serve the Court, whose ceremonies set the calendar. They were as lavish as ever: until the 1770s the amount spent annually by the Crown in Madrid was greater than the entire budget of the Spanish navy.

Fernando VI (1746-59) was a shy but popular king who gave Spain its longest period of peace for over 200 years. Childless, he was succeeded by his half-brother Charles III (1759-88). Previously King of Naples for 20 years, he too was unimpressed by Madrid. However, more than any of his predecessors he set out to improve the city, becoming known as Madrid's Rey-Alcalde or 'King-Mayor'.

ENLIGHTENMENT STRIKES

Charles was fascinated by Enlightenment ideas of progress, science and the applied use of reason. No democrat, he sought to bring about rational improvement from the top. Reforms were undertaken in the bureaucracy and armed forces, and to improve trade with Spanish America. He challenged the privileges of the religious orders, and expelled the Jesuits from Spain in 1767 for their refusal to co-operate.

In Madrid, Charles first undertook to do something about the mud in winter, suffocating dust in summer and foul smells at all times – which were noted by every visitor to the city. A 1761 decree banned the dumping of waste in the streets, and Charles' Italian engineer-architect Francesco Sabatini began building sewers and street lighting. A string of major buildings was erected, of which the Casa de Correos in Puerta del Sol and the Puerta de Alcalá are the best-known. A later queen of Spain remarked that it sometimes seemed as if all the monuments of Madrid had been built by Charles III.

Charles III's grandest project was the Paseo del Prado (*see p100* **Watch this space**). He sent scientific expeditions to every corner of his empire, and planned to exhibit the fruits of their varied researches in a Museum of Natural Sciences – now the Museo del Prado – and the adjacent Jardín Botánico.

Popular reaction to the king's improvements was mixed, some of them being resented as foreign impositions. A decree of Charles III's Italian minister Squillace provoked one of history's first fashion revolts. In 1766 he banned the traditional long cape and wide-brimmed hat and ordered the use of the international three-cornered hat, with the argument that the capes were used by criminals to conceal weapons. In what became known as the Motín de Esquilache (Squillace Riot), a mob marched on the Palacio Real, and forced the repeal of the decree.

Reform and improved trade did create a feeling of well-being in late 18th-century Madrid. Nevertheless, Spain was still a very feudal society, and the real economy remained backward and frail. And, in an absolute monarchy, a great deal depended on each monarch. Charles IV (1788-1808), whose rather dozy face was immortalised by Goya (*see p18* **In the frame**), had none of his father's energy or intelligence. Also, he chose as his minister the corrupt Manuel Godoy. After the French Revolution, Spain joined other monarchies in attacking the new regime; in 1795, however, Godoy made peace and then an alliance with France, leading to an unpopular war with Britain. Then, in 1808, when Godoy was vacillating over changing sides once again, he was forestalled by anti-French riots that proclaimed Charles IV's son Fernando as king in his place. Napoleon sent troops to Madrid, assuming this decrepit state would be as easy to conquer as any other. It was not to be, at least not initially, and the consequences were horrific (*see p22* **In the frame**).

Once victory was his, Napoleon made his brother, Joseph Bonaparte, King of Spain. In Madrid he tried in a well-meaning way to make improvements, among them some squares for which the city has since been very grateful, notably the Plaza de Oriente and the Plaza Santa Ana. However, this did nothing to overcome the animosity around him. In 1812 the Duke of Wellington and his army arrived to take the city, in a battle that destroyed much of the Retiro palace. The French were finally driven out of Spain in 1813. As well as the fighting itself, the year 1812 brought with it a catastrophic famine, which in Madrid killed over 30,000 people.

'In 1812 a Cortes had met in Cádiz and given Spain its first-ever constitution.'

The shock of this upheaval initiated a period of instability that continued until 1874, although it could be said that the instability only really ended with the death of Franco in 1975. Spain withdrew into its own problems, with one conflict after another between conservatives, reformists, revolutionaries and other factions. Each struggled to impose their model on the state and create a political system that could accommodate, or hold back, the pressures for modernisation and some form of democracy.

In 1812 a Cortes had met in Cádiz and given Spain its first-ever constitution. This assembly also gave the world the word 'liberal'. However, when Fernando VII (1808-33) returned from French captivity in 1814, his only thought was to cancel the constitution and return to the methods of his ancestors. His absolute rule, though, was incapable of responding to the bankruptcy of the country. The regime was also struggling to hold on to its American colonies, by then in complete rebellion. In 1820 a liberal revolt in the army forced Fernando to reinstate the constitution. He was saved three years later, ironically by a French army, sent to restore monarchical rule. Meanwhile, defeat at Ayacucho in Peru (1824) left Spain with only Cuba, Santo Domingo and Puerto Rico of its former American empire.

In 1830 Fernando VII's wife María Cristina gave birth to a daughter, soon to be Queen Isabel II (1833-68). Previously, the most reactionary sectors of the aristocracy, the Church and other ultra-conservative groups had aligned themselves behind the king's brother Don Carlos. When Fernando died in 1833, Carlos demanded the throne, launching what became known as the Carlist Wars. To defend her daughter's rights, María Cristina,

In the frame The Family of Charles IV

It is not a pretty picture. Charles IV, King of Spain from 1788-1808, was known as a simple fellow of mushy intellect, and his wife, María Luisa, a nymphomaniac. The pair, primarily the Queen, took a fancy to the young Manuel Godoy, a royal guard about half her age. They appointed the handsome playboy to chief minister and he promptly became the Queen's lover. Unperturbed by playing the cuckold, Charles turned a blind eye to his wife's wanton ways, and María Luisa, happy with having her cake and eating it, called the relationship – King, Queen, chief minister – 'the earthly trinity'. Godoy was in a good position. A lusty, simple fellow himself, he had his wife, a mistress, and the Queen.

as Regent, had no choice but to look for support from liberals, and so was obliged to promise some form of constitutional rule.

OLD ROMANTICS

For the next 40 years Spanish politics was a see-saw, as conservative and liberal factions vied for power, while the Carlists, off the spectrum for most people in Madrid, occasionally threatened at the gates. Madrid was the great centre for aspiring politicians, and the problems of Spain were discussed endlessly in its salons and new cafés, which multiplied around this time. This was the era of Romanticism, and writers such as the journalist Larra and poet José Espronceda were heavily involved in politics. Similarly, many of the politicians of the day were also writers.

Much of the time, though, these reformers were shepherds in search of a flock, for there were no true political parties. The only way a faction could hope to gain power was with the support of a general with troops at his disposal.

The *pronunciamiento*, or coup, was the main means of changing governments, and soldiers identified with particular sides – Espartero, Serrano and Prim for the progressives, Narváez and O'Donnell (a descendant of Irish soldiers) for the conservatives – were the heroes of their followers. Later, many from either side had monuments or streets named after them. The clashes were never decisive, and it was later said that Spain had gone through 70 years of agitation without ever experiencing a revolution.

This political instability did not mean that life in Madrid was chaotic. Visitors in the early 1830s found a small, sleepy, shabby city, which seemed sunk in the past. Convents and palaces still occupied nearly half its area. It was around this time that Spain acquired its romantic aura. A growing number of foreigners visited, drawn by Spain's timeless, exotic qualities. One was the French writer Prosper Mérimée, who in 1845 wrote his novel *Carmen*, later put to music by Bizet, who himself never visited Spain at all.

The royal couple showered him with gifts and titles, and grandly named him the Prince of Peace. However, the ruling threesome did not sit well with either the commoners or the aristocracy, and the Queen's son, crown prince Ferdinand, was particularly disgusted. A bitter rivalry grew between Ferdinand and Godoy, who was suspected of plotting to rob Ferdinand of the future crown, on top of bedding his mother.

But no one should feel too sorry for Ferdinand. In 1808, Napoleon's troops, on their way to occupy Portugal, decided to stop over in Spain and conquer Castile as well. Ferdinand, however, had entered into secret negotiations with Bonaparte, hoping to overthrow his mother and father. In a plot line worthy of *Hamlet*, Charles came upon a mysterious note in his prayer book revealing his son's alleged plot against him. Ferdinand was summarily imprisoned for high treason, with his own mother calling him 'a spiked vine of cowardice'.

The 'earthly trinity' was unsettled by these events of familial betrayal and invading Frenchmen. Smelling trouble, they decided to make a run for it, but didn't get far, and Charles eventually abdicated the throne in favour of his plotting son. Ferdinand was to become one of the most malevolent kings in all of Spanish history – he would go on to re-establish the Inquisition and publicly draw and quarter his enemies.

Goya's masterful painting, only thinly veils the Shakespearean familial tensions brewing. It is a menacing, unflattering family portrait. The painting has famously been described as that of 'a corner baker and his wife after having won the lottery'. Hemingway called it a 'Masterpiece of loathing'. Lascivious María Luisa dominates the canvas, much taller here than in life. She is the figure of control, both in the painting and in the government of Spain. The children at her sides are María Isabel and Francisco de Paula, both of whom were rumoured to be Godoy's children. Poor Charles stands to her left, dwarfed by the presence of his wife; he stares blankly from the canvas, looking like a distracted, rounder version of George Washington. Behind him is his epileptic brother, Don Antonio. Beside Don Antonio is the small face of Doña Carlota, the King's eldest daughter, who was deformed in a hunting accident and inherited the same nymphomania as her mother. On the left side of the painting, hidden in shadows, is the King's senile sister, Doña María Josefa, a dark haggard face in the back. And in front of her, the scheming Ferdinand. Godoy is conspicuous by his absence.

Goya's **The Family of Charles IV** *is found at the Prado (see p63).*

EXPANSION AND TURMOIL

The 1830s, however, also saw the single most important change in Madrid during the 19th century. In 1836 the liberal minister Mendizábal took advantage of the church's sympathy for Carlism to introduce his Desamortización or Disentailment law, which dissolved most of Spain's monasteries. In Madrid, the church lost over 1,000 properties. Most were demolished remarkably quickly, and an enormous area thus became available for sale and new building.

Some urban reformers saw this as an opportunity to build broad, airy avenues, following the always-cited example of Paris. Some major projects were undertaken, the most important being the rebuilding of the Puerta del Sol, in 1854-62. However, most of the local traders who benefited from Desamortización lacked the capital to contemplate grand projects, and built separate blocks without challenging the established, disorderly street plan. The districts of old Madrid took on the appearance they have largely kept until today, with great numbers of tenement blocks. They allowed Madrid to grow considerably in population, without going outside its still-standing wall of 1656.

A few factories had appeared in the city, but for the most part the Industrial Revolution was passing Madrid by. Constitutional governments expanded the administration, and the ambitions of the middle class were focused on obtaining official posts rather than on business ventures. Two more major changes arrived in the 1850s. In 1851 Madrid got its first railway, to Aranjuez, followed by a line running to the Mediterranean. Railways would transform Madrid's relationship with the rest of the country, opening up a realistic possibility of it fulfilling an economic function. Equally important was the completion of the Canal de Isabel II, bringing water from the Guadarrama, in 1858. Madrid's water supply, still part-based on Moorish water courses, had been inadequate for years. The canal, inaugurated with a giant spurt of water in Calle San Bernardo, removed a crippling obstruction to the city's growth.

Madrid's population was by this time over 300,000. Steps were finally taken for it to break out of its old walls, and in 1860 a plan by Carlos María de Castro was approved for the Ensanche (extension) of Madrid, in an orderly grid pattern to the north and east. However, as with earlier rebuilding, the plan came up against the chronic lack of large-scale local investors. The only major development undertaken quickly was the section of C/Serrano bought up by the flamboyant speculator the Marqués de Salamanca, whose name was given to the whole district. Moreover, even the marqués was unable to sell many of his properties to Madrid's conservative-minded upper classes at a viable price.

Meanwhile, the political situation was deteriorating once again, after a long period of conservative rule begun in 1856. Isabel II had become deeply unpopular, surrounded by an aura of sleaze and scandal. In September 1868, yet another military revolt deposed the government and, this time, the queen as well.

There followed six years of turmoil. The provisional government invited an Italian prince, Amadeo of Savoy, to become king of a truly constitutional monarchy. However, in December 1870 General Prim, strongman of the new regime, was assassinated. Carlist revolts broke out in some parts of the country, while on the left new, more radical groups began to appear. At the end of 1868, a meeting in Madrid addressed by Giuseppe Fanelli, an Italian associate of Bakunin, led to the founding of the first anarchist group in Spain. The Cortes itself was riven by factions, and Amadeo decided to give up the struggle and go back to Italy.

On 12 February 1873 Spain became a republic. Rightist resistance became stronger than ever, while many towns were taken over by left-wing juntas, who declared them autonomous 'cantons', horrifying conservative opinion. To keep control, Republican governments relied increasingly on the army. This proved fatal, and on 3 January 1874 the army commander in Madrid, General Pavía, marched into the Cortes, sent its members home, and installed a military dictatorship.

THE BOURBONS RETURN

At the end of 1874 the army decided to restore the Bourbon dynasty, in the shape of Alfonso XII (1874-85), the son of Isabel II. The architect of the Restoration regime, however, was a civilian politician, Antonio Cánovas del Castillo. He established the system of *turno pacífico,* or peaceful alternation in power (thus avoiding social tensions), between a Conservative Party, led by himself, and a Liberal Party which was

made up of former progressives. The control of these 'dynastic parties' over the political system was made secure by election-rigging and occasional repression.

In the late 1870s the wealthy of Madrid set out on a building boom. They finally overcame their reluctance to leave the old city, and the Salamanca area became the new centre of fashionable life. Most of the district's new apartment blocks had lifts, first seen in Madrid in 1874. In earlier blocks upper floors had been let cheaply, so that rich and poor had often continued to live side by side. With lifts, however, a top floor could be as desirable as a first, and this kind of class mixing faded.

> ### 'The 1880s saw the beginning of a housing crisis, with the growth of shanty towns around the city.'

Government and official bodies, too, undertook a huge round of new building. The Banco de España, the Bolsa and the main railway stations are all creations of the 1880s. Madrid meanwhile acquired a larger professional middle class; it also attracted intellectuals from around the country.

At the same time, Madrid was receiving an influx of poor migrants from rural Spain, with over 200,000 new arrivals between 1874 and 1900. Economic growth was reflected in the appearance of yet more small workshops rather than factories. There were also many with next to no work, and the 1880s saw the beginning of a housing crisis, with the growth of shanty towns around the outskirts of the city.

The established order seemed in little danger in the first decades of the Restoration. The events of 1868-74 had discredited the old Romantic idea of the unity of the people in pursuit of democracy. In 1879 the Spanish Socialist Party, the PSOE, was founded, but for a long time the level of agitation in the capital was very limited.

THE EMPIRE STRIKES BACK

Just before the end of the century, however, the preconceptions on which Spanish political life had been based received a shattering blow. The Restoration regime presented itself as having returned the country to stability and some prestige in the world. In the 1890s, however, Spain was involved in colonial wars against nationalists in Cuba and the Philippines. In 1898, the government allowed itself to be manoeuvred into war with the United States. In a few weeks, almost the entire Spanish navy was sunk, and Spain lost virtually all its remaining overseas territories. Known simply as 'The Disaster', this was a devastating blow to Spain's self-confidence. The regime itself was revealed as decrepit and incompetent, based on a feeble economy. Among intellectuals, the situation sparked off an intense round of self-examination and discussion of Spain's relationship with the very concept of modernity. Politically, it signalled the beginning of the end of the cosy settlement of 1874.

Although the intellectual debates of this time centred on Spain's apparent inability to deal with the modern world, the problems of the regime were not due to the country being backward. Rather, they spiralled out of control because after 1900 the country entered an unprecedented period of change.

BRIGHT LIGHTS, BIG CITY

Sudden economic expansion was set off by three main factors. One, ironically, was the loss of the colonies, which led to large amounts of capital being brought back to the country. Most important was World War I, which provided unheard-of opportunities for neutral Spain in the supply of goods to the Allied powers. Then, during the worldwide boom of the 1920s, Spain benefited hugely from foreign investment.

Within a few years Spain had one of the fastest rates of urbanisation in the world. The economic upheaval caused by the world war led to runaway inflation, spurring a huge movement into the cities. Madrid did not grow as rapidly as industrial Barcelona, which had become the largest city in the country. Nevertheless, after taking four centuries to reach half a million, it doubled its population again in just 30 years, to just under a million by 1930. Only 37 per cent of its people had been born in the city.

The most visible manifestation of this growth was a still-larger building boom. Bombastic creations such as the Palacio de Comunicaciones were symptomatic of the expansive mood. Most important was the opening of the Gran Vía in 1910, a project that had first been discussed 25 years previously, which would transform the heart of the old city with a new grand thoroughfare for entertainment, business and banking.

Another fundamental innovation was electricity. The city's trams were electrified in 1898, and the first metro line, between Sol and Cuatro Caminos, opened in 1919. Electricity allowed Madrid, far from any other source of power, finally to experience an industrial take-off in the years after 1910. It was still far behind Barcelona as an industrial city, but was much more important as a base for major banks. Larger companies and new industries brought with them more aggressive styles of working, and a more industrial working class. Many lived in shabby slum districts in the outskirts, or 'misery-villes' of shanties that mushroomed around the city. At the same time, expansion in banking and office work was also reflected in the large number of white-collar workers.

Madrid was also, more than ever, the mecca for intellectuals and professionals from around the country. This was the background to the enormous vigour of the city's intellectual life at this time, the 'Silver Age' of Spanish literature. From writers of 1898 such as Antonio Machado and Baroja to the poets of the 1927 generation, Rafael Alberti and García Lorca, the city welcomed an extraordinary succession of literary talent, and painters, scientists and historians. From the 1910s onward, Madrid's cafés were full of talk, forums for discussion multiplied, and any number of newspapers and magazines were published. The sheer range of activity was remarkable.

In politics, this urban expansion made it impossible for the 'dynastic parties' to control elections in the way they were able to do in small towns and rural areas. In 1910, a Republican-Socialist coalition won elections in Madrid for the first time. Tensions came to a head in 1917, with a general strike throughout the country. In the following years the main focus of conflict was in Barcelona, where virtual urban guerrilla warfare broke out between the anarchist workers' union the CNT and employers and the state. In 1923 the Captain-General of Barcelona, General Primo de Rivera, suspended the constitution and declared himself Dictator, under King Alfonso XIII.

In Madrid, this was first greeted with relative indifference. However, by his action Primo de Rivera had discredited the king and the old dynastic parties, without putting anything in their place. A widespread movement against the monarchy developed in the '20s, based in a sentiment that a society that felt increasingly mature should not have a ramshackle, discredited government imposed upon it.

In 1930 Primo de Rivera resigned, exhausted. The king appointed another soldier, General Berenguer, as new prime minister. In an attempt to move back towards some form of constitutional rule, the government decided to hold local elections on 12 April 1931. They were not expected to be a referendum on the monarchy. However, when the results came in it was seen that republican candidates had won sweeping majorities in all of Spain's cities.

THE SECOND REPUBLIC

On 14 April 1931, as the results of the local elections became clear, the streets of Spain's cities filled with people. In Madrid, a jubilant mass converged on the Puerta del Sol. It was these exultant crowds in the streets that drove the king to abdicate and spurred republican politicians into action, for they had never expected their opportunity to arrive so soon.

The second Spanish Republic arrived amid huge optimism, expressing the frustrated hopes of decades. Among the many schemes of its first government, a Republican-Socialist coalition, was a project for Madrid, the Gran Madrid or 'Greater Madrid' plan, intended to integrate the sprawling new areas around the city's edge. A key part of it was the extension of the Castellana, then blocked by a racecourse above C/Joaquín Costa. The racecourse was demolished, and the Castellana was allowed to snake endlessly northward, forming one of the modern city's most distinctive features. Also completed under the Republic was the last section of the Gran Vía, from Callao to Plaza de España, site of Madrid's best art deco architecture.

Possibilities of further change and renovation, however, were to be entangled in the accelerating social crisis that overtook the Republic around this time. The new regime aroused expectations that would have been difficult to live up to at the best of times. Instead, its arrival coincided with the onset of the worldwide depression of the 1930s. Moreover, Spain's own – partly unreal – 1920s boom had exceeded the real capacity of the country's economy. Activity slowed down, and unemployment spread.

At the same time, labour agitation and republican legislation brought wage increases for those in work. This caused panic among many employers, who became easy fodder for a belligerent, resurgent right. Levels of tension were even more intense in the countryside, where agrarian reform was bogged down by conservative opposition.

In the frame The Third of May

Nearly 200 years old, this remains one of the world's most modern paintings. It marked a complete transformation in the portrayal of war. Previously, with very few exceptions, war paintings had presented war as a noble contest, and served to glorify heroic deeds, and celebrate kings and commanders – a prime example hangs nearby in the Prado, Velázquez' *Las Lanzas*. In Goya's war images, in contrast – whether the *Tres de Mayo* or the *Desastres de la Guerra* – there is no glory, only misery, brutality and chaos. Death, mutilation and casual savagery are more prominent than victories. There are no generals or famous heroes, only faces in the crowd. There is heroism – again anonymous – but it seems wild, desperate, ultimately futile. It is this searingly honest, unblinking sense of the truth and horror of violence that makes the *Tres de Mayo* so permanently contemporary.

The events portrayed were very real. On 2 May 1808 Madrid awoke to learn that Napoleon had kidnapped the Spanish royal family, and that French troops were taking over the country. They expected little resistance beyond skirmishes and manageable grumbling. Instead, uncoordinated Spanish army units and, above all, the people of Madrid fought the invaders street by street, using knives or their bare hands. In the Puerta del Sol, the crowds hurled themselves against the Mamelukes, the Arab mercenaries

Napoleon had acquired during his invasion of Egypt in 1798. As the day wore on, though, the French gradually won control of Madrid, and in the early morning of 3 May – enraged that they had had to fight so hard against a mere street mob, rather than real soldiers – they set out to teach the city a lesson. Captured 'insurgents' were disposed of in mass executions on the hill of Príncipe Pío, which is now at the southern end of the Parque del Oeste.

Goya painted his *Dos de Mayo*, of the struggle in the Puerta del Sol, and *Tres de Mayo* in 1814, just after the French had been driven out of Spain. How much personal observation went into them is an unanswered question. Goya was in Madrid during those days, and one of his gardeners later claimed the artist had watched the executions through a telescope. However, this is impossible to confirm.

With its pared-down style foreshadowing 20th-century expressionism, the *Tres de Mayo* is the first truly modern image of war. Its resonances do not end there. The French were genuinely surprised as well as infuriated by the resistance they met in Spain. Napoleon's empire saw itself as carrying a systematised version of the French Revolution around Europe: in return for obedience, countries like Spain that had been ruled by backward monarchies were offered rational administration, new roads, education – in short, progress. Goya himself,

THE POLARISATION OF POLITICS

As frustration grew among workers, calls for the end of republican compromise in a second, social, revolution increased, especially from the anarchist CNT and the Communist Party. Even the Socialist Party was radicalised. On the right, similarly, the loudest voices – such as the fascist Falange, founded in 1933 by José Antonio Primo de Rivera, son of the former dictator – demanded authoritarian rule as the only means of preserving social order. The vogue for extremism was fed by the mood of the times, in which Nazism, Italian Fascism and Soviet Communism appeared as the most dynamic international models.

In 1933 the coalition between Socialists and liberal republicans broke up. With the left split, elections were won by conservative republicans backed by the CEDA, a parliamentary but authoritarian right-wing party. Reform seemed to come to a dead halt. In October 1934 the CEDA demanded to have ministers in the government, and a general strike was called in response. It was strongest in the mining region of Asturias, where it was savagely suppressed by army units commanded by a rising general called Francisco Franco.

Left-wing parties were subjected to a wave of repression that radicalised their supporters still further. In new elections in February 1936, however, the left, united once again in the Frente Popular (Popular Front), were victorious. In Madrid the Front won 54 per cent of the vote.

A liberal-republican government returned to power, with Manuel Azaña as president. By this time, however, the level of polarisation and of sheer hatred in the country was moving out of control. Right-wing politicians called almost openly for the army to save the country. The military had already laid their plans for a coup.

as a liberal, had been suspected of being an *afrancesado*, a French sympathiser, but was disgusted by the brutality with which the French imposed their power. Most ordinary Spaniards opposed the invasion almost instinctively. The *Dos de Mayo* and *Tres de Mayo* capture all the mad, savage chaos of a mass uprising and, in the *Tres*, of its terrible consequences. As has often been noted, the insurgents about to be executed have individual faces and expressions, whether defiant, terrified or lost in despair. The French soldiers form a faceless, uniformed line. As such, they can represent every anonymous power that has tried to impose its own idea of progress at gunpoint.

Goya's **The Third of May 1808 in Madrid** *is found at the Prado (see p63).*

The **Civil War** took a heavy toll on Madrid's spirit.

REVOLUTION AND WAR

On 18 July 1936 the generals made their move, with risings all over Spain, while German and Italian aircraft ferried Franco's colonial army from Spanish Morocco to Andalucia. In Madrid, troops failed to seize the city and barricaded themselves inside the Montaña barracks, the site of which is now in the Parque del Oeste.

The coup was the spark for an explosion of tension. The workers' parties demanded arms. On 20 July, as news came that the army had been defeated in Barcelona and many other cities, the Montaña was stormed and its defenders massacred, despite the efforts of political leaders to prevent it.

With the right apparently defeated, Madrid underwent a revolution. Among left-wing militants the mood was ecstatic: factories, schools, the transport system and other public services were all taken over, and, although the government remained in place, it had little effective power. Ad-hoc militias and patrols were the only power on the streets, and, amid the paranoia and hatred that were the other side of revolutionary excitement, summary executions of suspected rightists were common.

Meanwhile, the war still had to be fought. Franco's regular troops were advancing from Seville preceded by stories of reprisals more terrible than anything done by the 'red terror' in Madrid. The militias seemed powerless to stop them. Defeat for the Republic seemed inevitable. German planes bombed the city. On 6 November, as Franco's advance guard arrived, the government left for Valencia, a move widely seen as desertion.

CITY UNDER SIEGE

Without a government, however, a new resolve was seen in the city. In the southern suburbs the troops were resisted street by street. Women, children and the elderly joined in building trenches and barricades, and comparisons were immediately drawn with 2 May 1808. On 9 November the first foreign volunteers, the International Brigades, arrived, doing wonders for morale. Madrid had become the front line of international democracy. After savage fighting Franco halted the frontal assault on Madrid in November 1936.

Madrid saw little more direct fighting. From the Casa de Campo, where the remains of trenches and bunkers still exist today, the army settled in to a siege. Attempts to push them back north and south of Madrid were unsuccessful. The city was regularly bombed, and bombarded by artillery, who took their sights from the Gran Vía, 'Howitzer Avenue'.

People adapted to the situation. You could go to war by tram, and combatants were taken their lunch on the line along the Gran Vía. Right-wingers were scarcely harassed after the first few months. The siege, however, ground down the spirit of November 1936. Shortages were acute; particularly terrible was the severe winter of 1937-8, when doors and furniture were burnt for fuel. The powerful role established by the Communists, won through the Republic's dependence on the Soviet Union as its only source of arms, alienated many who were not Party supporters.

General Franco, meanwhile, was advancing on other fronts. During 1937 his forces overran the Basque Country and Asturias, and in March 1938 they reached the Mediterranean near Castellón. In January 1939 they finally conquered Catalonia. In Madrid, fighting broke out behind Republican lines between the Communists, committed to fighting to the end, and groups who wanted to negotiate a settlement with Franco. Those in favour of negotiation won, but found Franco had no intention to compromise. On 28 March the Nationalist army entered Madrid.

THE LONG DICTATORSHIP

Madrid emerged from the Civil War physically and psychologically battered. Throughout the city, hundreds of buildings stood in ruins. Buildings, however, could be rebuilt fairly quickly; healing the damage done to the city's spirit would take decades.

The Madrid of the 1940s was the sombre antithesis of the expansive city of ten years previously, or its current outgoing, vivacious self. A great many *madrileños* had lost someone close to them, to bombs, bullets, firing squads or prison camps. The black market rather than art and literature dominated café conversation, and the figures of earlier years were mostly in exile, or keeping indoors.

The existence of 'two Spains' (right–left, traditional–liberal, rich–poor) was all too apparent. As the victors marched in, they wasted no time in rounding up members (or just suspected sympathisers) of 'enemy' groups, anarchists, Communists, union members and liberals. Some were turned in by neighbours, which created a sordid atmosphere of bitterness and distrust. During the early '40s, while the rest of the world was wrapped up in World War II, thousands were executed in Spain. Others paid the price of defeat by serving as forced labour on fascist landmarks such as the Valle de los Caídos, Franco's vast victory monument and tomb.

Madrid's loyalty to the Republic almost led to it losing its capital status, as voices were raised calling for a more 'loyal' city to represent the country. Tradition and financial interests bore more weight, however, and the capital stayed put. The Falange, official party of the regime, produced extravagant plans to turn Madrid into a Spanish version of Imperial Rome, but a dire lack of funding and galloping inflation scotched most of these nouveau-Imperialist notions. The economy was in a desperate state, and Spain went through a period of extreme hardship, the *años del hambre* or 'hunger years'. Many people remember not having eaten properly for ten years after 1936. This poverty also led to the phenomenon that would most shape the face of Madrid in the post-war decades: massive immigration from Spain's rural provinces.

Madrid has grown faster than any other European capital this century. A 'big village' of just over half a million at the turn of the century, and 950,000 in 1930, it passed the three million mark by 1970.

> ### 'Franco was saved by the US government's 'our son-of-a-bitch' policy in choosing allies.'

Until the 1950s, migrants arriving in Madrid found few real opportunities for work, in an economy that was internationally isolated and excluded from Marshall Aid and the other reconstruction packages of post-war Europe. After 1945 many in Spain and abroad assumed that the Franco regime would shortly go the way of its former friends in Germany and Italy.

Most European countries continued to shun the regime, at least in public, but in 1953, as the Cold War intensified, Franco was saved by the US government's 'our son-of-a-bitch' policy in choosing allies. A co-operation treaty gave the regime renewed credibility and cash in exchange for air and sea bases on Spanish soil, and later President Eisenhower flew in to shake the dictator's hand.

For those not devoted to the regime, life under Franco was often a matter of keeping one's head down and getting on with things. Football and other forms of escapism played an enormous part in people's lives.

The national Stabilisation Plan of 1959 gave the fundamental push to Madrid's development, and brought Spain definitively back into the Western fold. The plan revolutionised the country's economy, and especially that of the Madrid region. In the 1960s, tourism began to pump money into Spain, and Madrid trebled in size to became an industrial powerhouse. Quiet tree-lined boulevards were widened to make way for cars, and elegant Castellana palaces were replaced by glass-sheathed monoliths. Madrid took on much more of the look, and feel, of a big city.

LIFE AFTER FRANCO

The 1960s also saw the revival of opposition to the regime in the shape of labour unrest, student protests, and the rise of the Basque organisation ETA. The oil crisis of 1973 coincided with the assassination by ETA of Franco's prime minister, Admiral Carrero Blanco, when a bomb planted beneath a Madrid street launched his car right over a five-storey building. The regime, already challenged by political opposition, now had to deal with rising unemployment, inflation and a moribund Franco. The transition to democracy had begun.

Franco died in November 1975, closing a parenthesis of nearly 40 years in Spanish history. A new age, uncertain but exciting, dawned. In July 1976 King Juan Carlos, chosen by Franco to succeed him, named a former Falange bureaucrat, Adolfo Suárez, as prime minister. Nobody, however, knew quite what was going to happen.

To widespread surprise, Suárez initiated a comprehensive programme of political reform. Clandestine opposition leaders surfaced, parties were legalised and famous exiles began coming home. The first democratic elections since 1936 were held in June 1977, and a constitution was approved in late 1978. Suárez' centrist UCD (Centre-Democratic Union) won the national elections, but local elections in Madrid in 1979 were won by the Socialists, led by Enrique Tierno Galván as Mayor.

The 'other' Spain, though, had not disappeared, and was getting nervous. Hard-core Francoists were horrified at the thought of Socialists and/or Communists coming to power. Many of the 'old guard' still held influential positions in the armed forces, and were not inclined to give them up easily.

On 23 February 1981 democrats' worst nightmares appeared to come true when a Civil Guard colonel called Tejero burst into the Cortes with a squad of men, firing his pistol into the air. Tanks were in the streets in Valencia, and there was uncertainty everywhere. In Madrid, however, troops stayed in their barracks. A little after midnight, King Juan Carlos appeared on TV and assured the country that the army had sworn him its allegiance and that the coup attempt would fail. The next day,

people poured on to the streets to demonstrate support for freedom and democracy.

The wolf had shown his teeth, but they were not as sharp as had been feared. Moreover, the coup attempt significantly helped to win Felipe González and the socialist PSOE their landslide victory in the elections of November 1982.

SOCIAL REVOLUTION, CITY RENOVATIONS

The late 1970s and early '80s saw the arrival of democracy and free speech, the loosening of drug laws and the breakdown of old sexual conventions. Long-repressed creative impulses were released. The compulsorily staid Madrid of earlier years gave way to an anything-goes, vivacious city: an explosion of art, counter-culture and nightlife, creativity and frivolity known as the Movida – very roughly translatable as 'Shift' or 'Movement'.

The Socialists used control of Madrid's Ayuntamiento – led by the very fondly remembered Tierno Galván – to renovate the city's infrastructure, with long-overdue facelifts in squares and parks. Mayor Tierno also provided unprecedented support for all sorts of progressive causes and the arts, and launched a whole string of new festivals.

If Tierno Galván's local administration was happy to be regarded as godfather to the Movida, the national government of Felipe González was still more eager to be seen as leaders of a reborn country. Decades of isolation ended with Spain's entry into the EU in 1986. This had a near-immediate effect on the economy, and in the late '80s the country was the fastest-growing member of the EU. The González governments achieved major improvements in some areas – health, the transport system – but frustrated the expectations of many of their supporters, often giving the impression they believed modernisation would solve all Spain's problems more or less by itself.

The apotheosis of the country's transition was the 'Year of Spain' in 1992, with the Barcelona Olympics, Expo '92 in Seville and, with a somewhat lower profile, Madrid's year as Cultural Capital of Europe. Afterwards, a different mood became apparent. Spain's pre-'92 boom had postponed the effects of the international downturn at the end of the '80s, but it hit Madrid with a vengeance in 1993. Breakneck growth had created its own problems, and land speculation sent property prices spiralling. Meanwhile, the Socialists inseparable from the boom, began to be dragged down by a staggering stream of revelations of corruption.

Disenchantment with the Socialists and a newly cautious mood that followed the brash overconfidence of the boom years were major factors behind the rise of the re-formed right of the Partido Popular (PP). Even before Spain's great year, in 1991, the PSOE had lost control of the Madrid city administration to the PP.

THE POPULAR VOTE

The 1990s in Spain were markedly different in feel and content from the preceding decade. Led by the deliberately bland José María Aznar, the Partido Popular ably connected with the groundswell of discontent provoked by the later years of Socialist administrations. In the 1993 election Felipe González, long the great survivor of Spanish politics, lost his overall majority, but staggered on for another three years by means of a pact with Catalan nationalists. Next time, however, in 1996, the winners were the PP, even though they too still had to rely on pacts with minority parties to be able to form a sustainable government. The PSOE was sent into opposition for the first time in 14 years.

In Madrid the PP had already made its mark on local life. Having rallied voters by denouncing the sleaze and corruption that overwhelmed the PSOE, and the Socialists' irresponsible – as many saw it – spending of taxpayers' money, the PP felt it had a clear mandate to cut back and balance the books. In Madrid, this meant cuts in budgets for arts festivals, a tightening up on licences for new bars and clubs and a general attack on the supposed excesses of the nightlife scene.

Despite harsh criticism for its perceived philistine approach to culture, its decidedly un-liberal stance on issues such as immigration or gay rights or its Francoist origins, the PP managed an absolute majority in the 2000 general elections thanks mainly to its practical, managerial approach to the economy and the disarray of the opposition.

The PP's second term in office was a different story. From mid 2002 onwards, several major events took place that would eventually lead to their downfall. The first warning was the 2002 general strike, closely followed by the sinking of the *Prestige*, Spain's worst-ever ecological disaster. Aznar's flirtation with Bush and Blair led to Spain participating, albeit in a small way, in the Iraq war, against the wishes of 94 per cent of the Spanish people. The death, in mid 2003, of 62 Spanish military personnel in an air crash in Turkey while flying home from Afghanistan in a sub-standard Ukrainian plane provoked criticism that the Defence Ministry was doing things on the cheap. More than the events themselves, it was government bungling, and Aznar's angry-bull-in-a-china-shop stance, that seriously undermined the PP.

The 11 March bombings, and the subsequent media manipulation, were the last straw. The Socialists, under the mild-mannered José Luis Zapatero, had been carefully rebuilding and were now seen as a preferable, honest and decent alternative. They now face many complex questions: the regeneration of democracy, the redefinition of Spain's 'autonomous regions', immigration, terrorism – ETA may be on the ropes but is still there, joined now by Al-Qaeda – and Spain's role in Europe and the wider world.

In Madrid itself, the PP still controls both city and region, under Alberto Ruiz Gallardón and Esperanza Aguirre respectively. Though they belong to the same party, they represent radically different styles and are widely thought to hate each other. They managed to put all differences aside, however, as Madrid received a fillip with the wedding of Crown Prince Felipe and commoner Letizia Ortiz – a diplomatic and financial success for the city and a morale booster for most of its people. But they will have to learn to see eye to eye in the longer term if Madrid is to face up to its own challenges, namely the city's unbridled growth, the regeneration of the central area, transport issues, immigration, growing crime and the Olympic bid.

Prince Felipe marries Letizia Ortiz.

Key events

c860 AD Madrid founded during the reign of Emir Mohammed I of Córdoba.
1085-6 Alfonso VI of Castile conquers Toledo and Madrid.
1109 Madrid besieged by Moorish army.
1212 Battle of Navas de Tolosa: decisive defeat of Muslims in Spain.
1309 First Cortes (parliament) held in Madrid.
1476 Isabella becomes unchallenged Queen of Castile after battle of Toro.
1492 Conquest of Granada; expulsion of Jews from Spain; Discovery of America.
1520-1 Madrid joins Comuneros revolt.
1547 Birth of Cervantes, in Alcalá de Henares.
1561 Philip II moves Court to Madrid from Toledo.
1563-84 Building of El Escorial.
1566 Beginning of Dutch Revolt.
1574 First permanent theatre opened in Madrid, the Corral de la Pacheca.
1588 Defeat of the Armada against England.
1599-1600 Plague and famine in Castile.
1601-6 Court moved to Valladolid.
1605, 1615 *Don Quixote* published.
1609 Expulsion of former Muslims from Spain.
1617-9 Completion of Plaza Mayor.
1632-40 Buen Retiro palace built.
1640 Revolts in Portugal and Catalonia.
1643 Battle of Rocroi: Spanish army in Flanders decisively defeated by the French.
1665 Philip IV succeeded by Charles II, aged four.
1700 Charles II dies without an heir.
1702-14 War of the Spanish Succession: Philip V, first Bourbon King of Spain.
1715 Decree of Nova Planta; Spain created as one state.
1734 Alcázar of Madrid destroyed by fire.
1761 Charles III bans waste dumping in Madrid streets.
1778 Goya moves to Madrid from Aragon.
1808-12 Madrid under French occupation.
1812 Cortes in Cádiz agrees first Spanish constitution; disastrous famine in Madrid.
1814 Fernando VII abrogates constitution.
1810-24 Latin American Wars of Independence.
1820 Military coup begins three years of liberal rule.
1823 French army restores Fernando VII to full power.
1833 Carlist Wars begin on death of Fernando VII; constitutional government established in Madrid, with limited powers.

1836 Main decree on Disentailment of Monasteries; University of Alcalá de Henares moved to Madrid.
1851 Railway line to Aranjuez inaugurated.
1858 Canal de Isabel II water system inaugurated.
1868 Revolution overthrows Isabel II.
1871 Amadeo of Savoy becomes king of Spain. First trams in Madrid, drawn by mules.
1873 Amadeo abdicates; Republic declared.
1874 January: Republic becomes military dictatorship after coup. December: Alfonso XII declared King.
1879 Spanish Socialist Party (PSOE) founded.
1898 Spanish-American War: disaster for Spain. Madrid's tramlines electrified.
1910 Building of Gran Vía initiated.
1917 General strike in the whole of Spain.
1919 First Madrid metro line opened.
1923 Primo de Rivera establishes dictatorship.
1930 Fall of Primo de Rivera.
1931 Proclamation of Second Republic.
1934 General Strike against the entry of right-wing ministers into government; strike is bloodily suppressed in Asturias by General Franco.
1936 February: elections won by Popular Front; July: military uprising against left-wing government; November: Francoist forces launch assault on Madrid.
1939 1 April: Franco declares war over.
1946-50 UN imposes sanctions on Spain.
1953 Cooperation treaty with USA.
1959 Stabilisation Plan opens up the Spanish economy.
1961 First violent attack by Basque nationalists of ETA.
1970 Juan Carlos declared as General Franco's successor.
1975 20 November: Death of Franco.
1977 15 June: Spain's first democratic general election.
1979 April: Enrique Tierno Galván elected Socialist Mayor of Madrid.
1982 Socialists win national elections.
1986 1 January: Spain joins the EEC.
1991 Popular Party (PP) takes over Madrid city council.
1992 Madrid, European City of Culture; Barcelona Olympics; Expo '92 in Seville.
1996 Partido Popular win national elections.
2004 Socialist victory in general elections, three days after March 11 terrorist attacks kill 192.

Madrid Today

The terrorist attacks, and their aftermath, put politics back on the agenda.

In the ten years since the first *Time Out Madrid* was published, the Spanish capital has regularly been the target of bomb attacks by the Basque separatist group ETA. Then, on 11 March 2004, just three days before the general election, the capital's commuter rail network was hit, killing 192 people and injuring hundreds more. This was carnage on a new scale.

THREE DAYS THAT SHOOK A NATION
The initial assumption was that ETA had struck again. But it soon became clear to many that ETA's denial, together with its lack of the necessary resources, suggested that Al-Qaeda was responsible. The government's refusal to admit the possibility, and its manipulation of the media – even pressuring the United Nations and the international diplomatic community in the process – simply aroused suspicions that it was covering something up.

Finally, on the Saturday night before the election, José María Aznar's Popular Party

(PP) administration admitted the 'possibility' that the killings might have been the work of Islamic extremists. The next evening, a stunned prime minister appeared on television to concede a humiliating electoral defeat. Prior to the blasts, discussion in the media had extended only as far as whether the PP would be able to hold on to its absolute majority.

In early 2003, more than a million people had demonstrated in the capital against José María Aznar's decision to support the United States and Britain in invading and occupying Iraq. A year later, on a rainy Friday evening the day after the Atocha bombings, an even greater number trudged in quiet anger along the Paseo de la Castellana. Many were unsure why they were there. It was partly a mark of respect for the dead and the injured; but it was also a warning to the government that the time for being lied to, and perhaps lying to themselves, was over. Could it be that *madrileños* were recovering political consciousness?

The following evening, the Saturday before the election, thousands of mainly younger people gathered outside the headquarters of the PP to protest the lack of information about progress in the investigation. The government blamed the opposition Socialists for organising it, and made veiled threats that the electoral process was in jeopardy. The police refused to break up the protest. On Sunday morning, tens of thousands of previously disillusioned left-leaning voters who presumably had stayed at home in previous elections, woke up to the reality that they could change things and headed to the polling stations.

TIME TO GROW UP

If the 1980s was a time to party amid the experimentalism and excesses of the post-Franco Movida, then the 1990s saw many from that generation settle down to a job and a mortgage. Spain's political system has never encouraged grassroots activity anyway, and

Racial awareness

The perpetrators of the attacks on 11 March may have been Muslim extremists, but by targeting one of the capital's poorer areas they also killed eight Muslims, and injured a further 40. Of the dead, some 47 were non-Spaniards. The bombers were so effective largely because they attracted less attention in the south and east of the capital, which is home to 50 per cent of the more than half a million foreigners resident here.

Two decades ago, there were barely 190,000 non-Spaniards in the entire country. A decade ago, that number was living in the capital alone. At present, one in eight of the population of Madrid is non-Spanish; by 2020 that figure is expected to have risen to one in five. The rate of growth has, to say the least, been rapid: in 1991, 67 foreigners were applying each month for residency in the capital; by 2004, that figure had risen to 7,000.

In the aftermath of the attacks, the media generally avoided coverage of the 'enemy within' variety, instead offering plenty of space and airtime to moderate representatives of the Muslim community. Nevertheless, Spanish perceptions of the Moroccan community, particularly, seem increasingly negative. Polls show that they are the least liked of the immigrant population, and are largely associated in many people's minds with rising levels of street crime. Following the attacks, polls showed that large numbers of people believe that their Moroccan cousins support Al-Qaeda. Inevitably, there were incidents in the aftermath of the bombings: mosques were pelted with eggs, and shop windows smashed.

In fact, the largest immigrant community in Madrid by far is Latin American – comprising more than 300,000 people. Moroccans make up less than ten per cent of the capital's total immigrant population. The fact that a higher percentage of Moroccans are here as family units means they have a disproportionate presence in schools, where their inability to speak the language (along with east European children) makes it tougher for them to integrate.

To date, no political party has emerged as able to garner support by playing the race card, but during its 1996-2003 term of office, the conservative Popular Party government of José María Aznar played up to fears associating crime with foreigners, and changed the immigration law, effectively making it more difficult for those already in the country to attain legal status, while reducing their civil rights. During this time the media was full of stories of the growing numbers of Moroccans and sub-Saharan Africans arriving in rickety boats across the Strait of Gibraltar – while most immigrants actually arrived under quota systems from Latin America, usually to work in the hotel trade and agriculture.

In a country with a falling birth rate, Latin Americans, east Europeans and Moroccans are going to have to pick up the slack to keep afloat an unproductive economy that relies on low wages to maintain any semblance of competitiveness. In recent years, it has been immigrants who have contributed up to a third of new social security contributions.

It remains to be seen how the Socialist government will deal with the pressures that the rapid increase in immigration has put on society in terms of education, housing, health and jobs. Spain has been flung into the realities of multiculturalism in a very short period, and while traditionally a tolerant society, it is only a question of time before people start looking round for scapegoats.

after the scandals associated with the Socialists, many voters identified the PP with the grown-up business of making money.

Ten years ago, a survey by leading daily *El País* showed that interest in current affairs was lower than in the early 1960s – having reached a peak in the late 1970s. The Popular Party had no difficulty holding on to City Hall throughout this time, despite a universally ridiculed mayor – despised even by the city's legendarily reactionary taxi drivers.

Those ten years have seen a property boom. A decade ago, the monthly rent on a typical two-bedroom apartment in the city centre was around €450. Today that figure has doubled. To buy the same property would have cost between €50,000 and €80,000; the figure today would be at least three times higher. Meanwhile, many parts of the city centre, such as Chueca, Malasaña, Lavapiés, Embajadores and Atocha, were run down, with an ageing population. Today, Chueca's gay population has revitalised the area, but sent prices there spiralling, and Malasaña is fast catching up.

Since 1996, some two million houses have been built, helping to fuel the speculation boom, which has been threatening to collapse for some time now. But at the same time, huge numbers of properties are empty, with owners wary of entering into rental contracts that bind them for a minimum of five years, preferring instead to inflate the speculative bubble by selling them on. Demand for rented accommodation has been made more acute by the capital's growing number of immigrants, who are often obliged to share to cover rent on small, badly maintained properties (*see p30* **Racial awareness**).

One of the Socialists' campaign promises in the recent election was to provide low-cost housing to young people and the capital's growing numbers of immigrants, unable to find a foothold on the property ladder.

MORE BORING THAN OSLO?

The city's passion for partying has evidently cooled. Quite simply, *madrileños* have less time and money for staying out late and misbehaving. Aside from which, bar closing hours are strictly enforced – with most places shut by around 2am. The streets of Lavapiés were once thronged with late-hour revellers seven nights a week; they are quieter now than under Franco. Meanwhile, the municipal police continue to crack down on the *botellón* – impromptu open-air drinking sessions by the under-20s. Takeaway alcohol sales are now forbidden after 10pm.

Spain's best-known film-maker, Pedro Almodóvar – a figurehead of the Movida – is concerned that at this rate, Madrid will soon be 'as boring as Oslo'. But Madrid has never aspired

to be hip in a way that, say, its distant cousin and eternal rival Barcelona has. It is a city where style and appearance are everything, and where City Hall has long subsidised, or tamed, popular culture. In the heady Madrid of the 1980s, the Socialist administration pumped money into culture. Over the last ten years, however, the autumn festival has seen its budget cut by the Popular Party, and this three-month dance, drama, and music event now simply passes most people by. Meanwhile, on Gran Vía, Spanish-language versions of Broadway and West End hits continue to pack 'em in.

The city has blithely refused to produce a cultural scene that reflects its status as capital. It has no decent grassroots music scene, for example (unlike Oslo – currently the centre of European techno jazz), lacking both decent venues, and more importantly, appreciative and knowledgeable audiences. The important thing in Madrid has always been, first and foremost, to simply be out and about with friends, and first-time visitors are still enchanted by the crowded late-night good humour of its streets. There has never been any shortage of bars, and failing the money to bar crawl, the *botellón* still offers an immediate, if risky solution. Some might say Madrid retains the mindset of a provincial capital, looking in on itself; unlike cosmopolitan Barcelona – a port, close to the French border, and long keen to distance itself from all things Spanish. Madrid's city council is belatedly, and in some cases rather heavyhandedly, trying to curb its denizens' taste for the night, but this is still a city that takes on a life of its own after dark, cheerily offering up its often shabby pleasures in a way that Barcelona, say, has long since moved on from.

SCRUBBING UP WELL

Partly prompted by its bid to host the 2012 Olympics, the authorities will continue cleaning up the city centre. But the 80,000 or so sex workers in the capital continue to function through classified ads, via out-of-town clubs, or by walking the streets of Villaverde, a rough district on the south side of town.

This guide has sometimes bemoaned Madrid's loss of innocence. But it is, after all, the capital of a country that, after a brief and disastrous flirtation with Atlanticism, has again committed itself to a key role in the European Union, and at a critical time. It's a more expensive, populous, anonymous, and competitive place than it was a decade ago and will obviously become more so. The events of March 2004 marked a watershed, arguably sparking off an awareness of Madrid's place in the wider world. Some might say *madrileños* are finally growing up.

Seeing the Bulls

Love it or loathe it, but at least try to understand it.

For many visitors to Spain the bullfight is a barbaric anachronism, a preening blood sport that is dying out in this modern land. Well, they're right about it being bloody: this is not a fun day out for the squeamish. But they're wrong on every other count. First off, it isn't a sport. The essence of sport is an even contest where the end result is unpredictable. The events in the arena are not a competition, and the end result is always the same – the bulls will die. The harsh reality is that you are watching the ritual slaughter of six animals for sheer entertainment. Closest perhaps to opera, and reviewed in the culture section of most newspapers, this is a theatrical performance, a tragedy, involving a truly wild animal and men in *trajes de luces*, 'suits of lights'. Of course it isn't fair; it isn't supposed to be.

And it is certainly isn't dying out. Over the last few years the number of events held throughout Spain – and the number of people attending them – has been rising to record levels. Television has taken the top stars of the ring to new heights and the leading matadors are among the highest-paid performers in the world. That young boy in tight trousers might

well be earning €120,000 (£80,000) a day for his murderous work. Therefore a great ticket for an important fight can set you back a good deal of money, if, that is, you can get one. On the big days in the big rings, every seat is sold and the atmosphere at this highly social event is electric, with the whole city seemingly hanging on every pass.

And it isn't really a bullfight either – that's a clumsy English mistranslation of *la corrida*, the bull-running. Any man foolish enough to fight a wild bull would die in seconds. The Iberian fighting bull is arguably the most dangerous animal in the world and the idea is to control it and then dance with it before dispatching it; to create a fleeting but sometimes profound beauty out of the act of slaughter. To the Spanish this is a celebration of death, which in other countries is hidden away, as countless animals die in ignominy in abattoirs. The bull, which has lived a minimum of four years of absolutely natural existence, on the finest pasture Spain can provide, then gets his chance for a day of destiny and maybe even glory in the sun. 'We are going to see the bulls,' they say.

At heart, the Spanish attitude to the *corrida* comes from a profoundly different view of nature. In Britain, for example, a temperate country, long urbanised and industrialised, nature is a distant green and fluffy thing that has to be protected. In Spain, a land still tied to agriculture, where the sun is too hot and the soil too poor, nature is a powerful, noble adversary, which has to be fought. And the fighting bull is its greatest champion. Day after day Spain sends her young men (and the occasional woman) out on to the sand (*arena* simply means sand) to enact this elaborate metaphor of man's continuing struggle with nature, to prove that beauty can still be summoned from the beast.

'Then the moment of truth arrives and the great beast should be felled with a single blow from the sword.'

If this all sounds preposterously poetic, that's because it is. Artists and writers as diverse as Picasso and Hemingway, Orson Welles and García Márquez have been attracted to the bloody arenas, because at best the bullfight is a profound lyrical and visceral exploration of the meaning of both death and life. Lorca, the great Andalucían poet, so enamoured of the bulls, called *la corrida* 'the last serious thing'. And the Spanish certainly take it seriously.

But that doesn't mean that if you go and see one it will be any good. Even the superstar matadors don't come with a guarantee, and what they are attempting is a difficult and dangerous business with a genuinely wild and unpredictable animal. The ideal is that the various prescribed stages of this highly technical ritual are played out fluently and smoothly, all grace and style. The bull should be brave and noble and the men controlled and artistic. The emotional high point should be the *faena*, when the matador is in the ring alone with the bull and the true dance of death occurs. This is where man and animal become almost as one as they pass each other time and again, closer and closer, in a heart-stopping blur of crimson and gold. Then the moment of truth arrives and the great beast should be felled with a single blow from the sword. That's how it should be.

But of course it isn't always, and what is supposed to be elegant and honest can end up brutal and clumsy, unworthy of the poetry and the art. Sometimes the bulls are flawed and weak, other times the matadors cowardly and sloppy. There are tricks, too, to fool all but the

most ardent eye, and horns can be shaved to reduce the danger. This is a serious business and it can be a dodgy one.

But then, one blazing afternoon under an unforgiving southern sun, all the fates will fall into place. A bull, fierce and swift and handsome, will come racing out into a packed *plaza*, hear the crowd gasp, and see the matador straighten. He will charge and charge and the men will work with valour and honour to make sure that his death, and therefore his life, is a memorable one. The extraordinary emotion transmitted from the matador, the man in the gleaming gold, charged with the terrible task of dealing death, will infect the crowd. As he connects and cavorts with the bull, *olés* soft and long will start to emerge, a collective exhalation, as a single man takes the primeval power of this beautiful adversary and slows it to a dream with a few sublime swishes of his cape. Then, finally, in frozen silence he will leap over the horns, his sword straight to the heart and his place in the annals assured.

On such, all too rare, days, the dreadful danger and the awesome artistry will touch every soul present. I've seen grown men sob on such days. I've seen and felt and known why Spain still clings to this ancient and terrible entertainment, as the very soul of its identity, *la fiesta nacional*. If you dare to see for yourself, you may possibly witness such a rare and wondrous afternoon.
Robert Elms is a broadcaster, travel writer and inveterate Hispanophile.

Where and how

The 25,000-capacity Las Ventas bullring holds *corridas* every Sunday from March to October, as well as on various public holidays and festivals. The traditional starting time is 7pm, though some kick off as early as 5pm.

Tickets for Sunday bullfights can be obtained at the *taquillas* (ticket windows) near the main entrance of the bullring or online at the official website (see details below). Prices vary greatly. As a rule of thumb the nearer the seat is to the arena, the pricier the ticket. Any equivalent ticket is cheaper in *sol* (in the sun) than in *sombra* (in the shade). Thus a front row seat in *sombra* for a *corrida de toros* will cost you €108, while a seat in the gallery in *sol* for the same fight only costs €3.80. Prices are halved for *novilladas* (fights with young bulls and young matadors).

If you can't get a ticket at the *taquillas*, there are plenty of authorised agents in Madrid, though they charge 20 per cent commission. Try La Oreja de Oro (C/Victoria 9, 91 523 16 53), La Taurina (C/Pasaje Matheu s/n, 91 522 92 16), Galicia (Plaza del Carmen, 1, 91 531 27 32) or Localidades (Plaza de Santo Domingo, 91 559 50 28). There is also an independent online booking service, www.ticketstoros.com, with pages in English. Tickets can then be collected at the TEYCI kiosk, just a few metres from the main *taquilla*, an hour before the *corrida* begins. You'll need to show your passport, or confirmation email if you booked online.

Plaza de Toros de Las Ventas

C/Alcalá 237 (91 726 35 70/www.las-ventas.com). Metro Ventas. **Open** Box office Mar-Oct 10am-2pm, 5-8pm Fri, Sat; from 10am on fight days. Closed Nov-Feb. **Tickets** €1.90-€108. **Credit** MC, V.

LAS FERIAS

The best time to watch a top-quality *corrida* is during the Feria de San Isidro. For 20 consecutive evenings from mid May to early June, bullfights are held at 7pm, including *novilladas*, *rejones* (on horseback) and *Goyescas* (in period costume). It is, however, difficult to get tickets for what is the highlight of the season for bullfighting aficionados. Most tickets for the San Isidro are snapped up way in advance by season-ticket holders. Any that are unclaimed are put on sale five days before the corresponding fight; by law 1,000 tickets for each fight must be put up for sale

at 10am of the day of the fight, though huge queues form for these. San Isidro is preceded by the Feria de la Comunidad, which has a number of *novilladas* and a major fight on 2 May. Fights are also held daily during the Feria de Otoño, beginning in late September.

THE CULTURE

A good introduction to bullfighting is Ernest Hemingway's often brilliant account of this most Spanish of spectacles, *Death in the Afternoon*. You can find reviews and forthcoming line-ups in the local press and in weekly magazines such as *6 Toros 6* and *Aplausos*. You can mix with aficionados before and after fights, in bars and restaurants near Las Ventas such as Los Timbales (C/Alcalá 227); Donde Leo and El Albero, both at C/Pedro Heredia 22; or Taberna de Sierra on C/Villafranca 11. In May, before San Isidro, you can inspect the bulls, which are on public display in the Casa del Campo near Batán Metro. The bulls can also be seen at Las Ventas on the morning of each fight.

OUTSIDE MADRID

Many towns within easy reach of Madrid stage *corridas* on some Sundays during the season and on their annual saint's day. Many also hold bullfights, with daily bullfights, during their annual fiestas. These small-town fairs often include an *encierro*, in which young bulls are run through the streets first thing in the morning, as in, Pamplona's San Fermín. But be warned: bull-running requires a deal of acquired skill, and untrained tourists should be aware that joining in is extremely dangerous. Several have died doing so.

The first bullfights of the year take place in freezing February in **Valdemorillo**, to the north-west of Madrid. **Aranjuez** holds important bullfighting *ferias* on 30 May and in early September. But August is the cruellest month for the bulls: **Chinchón** has *novilladas* in its historic Plaza Mayor, and a smaller event takes place in **Manzanares el Real**. The most spectacular *encierro* close to Madrid is in **San Sebastián de los Reyes**, while the most prestigious fair is the one in **Colmenar Viejo**; both in late August. **Toledo** holds a bullfight on Corpus Christi day.

There is more information on these towns in the **Trips Out of Town** chapter (*see pp253-75*). For dates and details of transport, *see p294* **Tourist information**.

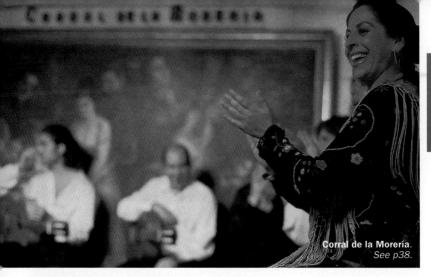

Corral de la Morería.
See p38.

Flamenco

Hold on to your skirts.

The Gypsy *cantaor*, the singer of flamenco *cante jondo*, or 'deep song', is the voice of his race and the keeper of its myths. Although flamenco is commonly perceived and exploited as a joyful and colourful form of song and dance, it is really about suffering and anguish. Its origins lie in the language and traditions of the Andalucian Gypsies, whose beliefs and fears are expressed in a performance style that employs a complex mythology to recount the suffering of their ancient exile, the history of their marginalisation, and the existential anguish that results.

Members of a lowly Indian caste once attached themselves to Arabian armies moving west into North Africa, serving them as blacksmiths, cooks and entertainers. They moved on through Egypt, from where they took their name ('E-gypti-an'), before arriving in southern Spain. The first organised group of Gypsies reached Spain in 1462 pretending to be pilgrims to the Catholic faith, and were consequently afforded protection and provisions by the Spanish nobility. By the end of the 15th century, these nomads had outstayed their welcome. Racism was stirred up by clerical propaganda that accused Gypsies of witchcraft and cannibalism, and in 1499 the kingdoms of Castile and Aragon ordered Gypsies to settle within 60 days or be banished.

Persecution intensified under Charles V, when Gypsies were hunted and enslaved in the galleys. In 1619 all Gypsies were sentenced to death if they refused to settle, inter-marry and live like good Christians. This enforced sedentariness resulted in concentrated settlements in Andalucía, when a national rout of Gypsies in July 1749 caused them to flee towards the south and led to an inevitable deterioration in living conditions in the overburdened areas of Seville, Granada and Cadiz. The brutality of this measure had the desired effect and by 1763 conditions were peaceful enough for Carlos III to declare an amnesty for Gypsies with the objective of transforming them into useful citizens. Fortunately, Andalucía, with its warm climate and fertile earth, was much to their liking and they prospered by smithery, fortune-telling and musicianship. This last skill was especially appreciated by the Catholic church, which employed Gypsies to perform at religious festivals and ceremonies.

Gypsies maintained cordial working relationships with the local populace while preserving their customs, language, song, dance and oral traditions in the privacy of their own homes. On the foundations of Indian traditions of performance, Gypsy musicians, singers and dancers constructed a style that overwhelmed traditional folksong. By the mid 19th century, professionals were performing for public audiences on the stages of *cafés cantantes* (theatre-bars) and *tablaos* (restaurants with a stage). During the Franco years there was an effort to disenfranchise the Gypsies from a song and dance that had become identified with Spanish culture, but when flamenco and folksong proved inseparable, this policy was adapted to claim that flamenco had been indigenous to Spain all along.

Post-dictatorship, authentic flamenco underwent a revival thanks to the growing clusters of migrant Gypsy camps on the outskirts of Madrid and the emergence of such figures as the legendary *cantaor* Camarón de la Isla and the guitarist Paco de Lucía. A pop-rock type of flamenco became ubiquitous, but at the other extreme from the wine-bar muzak of the Gypsy Kings and the kitsch spectacles of Joaquín Cortés there are plenty of innovative and exciting performers. Today's flamenco fan can keep up to date with what's happening by visiting the specialist shop El Flamenco Vive (C/Conde de Lemos 7) near the Palacio Real, or by looking at www.flamenco-world.com.

CD-wise, for traditional *cante* there is nobody better than Camarón de la Isla (try *Camarón: Antología*, 1996) but since his death in 1992 the more contemporary Enrique Morente (*Lorca*, 1998) has become the reigning *cantaor*. For an equivalent female voice, try the traditional Carmen Linares (*Carmen Linares en antología*, 1996), the decidedly Moorish Estrella Morente (*Mi cante y un poema*, 2001) or the infectious rhythms of Niña Pastori (*Eres Luz*, 1998). For an innovative fusion of flamenco with Cuban rhythms, try Bebo & Cigala (*Lágrimas negras*, 2003) and for the ancient Arabic sounds of *flamenco andalusí* choose Lole y Manuel (*Nuevo Dia: Lo mejor de Lole y Manuel*, 1994), who are so hip they feature on the soundtrack to Quentin Tarantino's *Kill Bill Vol. 2*.

VENUES

Time was that theatres such as the Teatro Real and Teatro Pavón were the equivalent of Carnegie Hall for flamenco artists. Nowadays the big stars play for big money to bigger audiences in concert halls and even stadiums, but you can still see unknowns imitating the legends and trying out new trends in pursuit of *duende*, the somewhat malevolent spirit-guide that is said to possess the greatest performers.

The most authentic flamenco inhabits a closed world and is proud of it; but if you know where to go and are lucky on the night you might be granted a peek. Madrid's original *cafés cantantes* are long gone but visitors can still catch a feel by crawling the bars around the

Las Carboneras. *See p38*.

district of Huertas and the Plaza Santa Ana, where a lucky dip of extravagantly nicknamed performers can sometimes yield a future star. These shows are mostly spontaneous so don't expect them to be advertised. The best way to see flamenco is to bar-hop in streets that live and breathe it, such as C/Echegaray. Rule of thumb: the more the punters look like the performers, the more chance there is that you're in the right place.

Where people are most likely to see Spanish dance, though, is at a *tablao*, of which there are several in Madrid; below is a selection of those with more genuine performances. As well as the show, you can dine or just drink; both are appallingly expensive, but if you stay till closing time you may get your money's worth of flamenco dance and music. The fun really starts around midnight, when most tourists go off to bed and the major artists appear; until then you may just get the kitsch jollity of the *cuadro de la casa* (the house musicians and dancers). Flamenco purists are notoriously snobbish about what's on offer in Madrid, but even they are thrilled by the performances at **Casa Patas**, where guitarists are skilled, dancers ooze power and grace, and singers are as they should be – bloody terrifying.

Also, as well as watching a Spanish dance show, you can join in, by heading to a *sala rociera* or Andaluz dance club for a bout of *sevillanas* and the odd rumba. For some prior preparation, many schools offer classes in these and other popular Spanish dances (*see p249*).

FESTIVALS

A great way of experiencing flamenco dance is as part of the city festivals in honour of **San Isidro** and the summertime **Veranos de la Villa** (for both, *see p246*), while the **Festival Flamenco Cajamadrid** is held in February and March in the **Teatro Albéniz** (*see p246*), and the Colegio San Juan Evangelista takes up the challenge with its **Festival Flamenco** in April. **Madrid en Danza** runs May-June and features many of the best flamenco dancers.

How to make a *jaleo*

Audiences who sit in respectful silence and applaud politely at the end of a performance of flamenco *cante* (song) and *toque* (guitar) might actually be insulting the performers. That's because audience participation – *jaleo* – is an essential part of authentic flamenco, and no truly great performance is ever given or witnessed without it. So this is no time to be shy: give as good as you get and you'll get as good as you give.

Watch and listen to how the guitarist bullies the *cantaor*, the singer of flamenco 'deep song', into giving the utmost performance. The guitarist plucks around the first murmurings of the *cantaor* until he hears the right tone being struck by his partner's voice, whereupon his sudden *rasgueo* (strum) alerts the *cantaor* to the fact that this is the direction to be taken. When you hear these single *rasgueos*, you'll know the performance is warming up. Listen closely to the guitarist and the experts around you in the audience. They will start to goad the singer with phrases such as '*Ezo e*' ('*Eso es*' – 'That's it'), '*Vamos ya*' ('Let's go') and '*Anda ya, chiquillo*' ('Go with it, man'). Any *cantaor* worth his salt will respond by digging deeper.

A rhythmic rapping will begin, soft at first as these complicit torturers tap their palms flat against table-tops. Gradually you'll become aware of their rings and bracelets rapping on the wood and the sound will become sharper.

Some will turn their fingers in, forming fists that will punch up the rhythm. When the tattoo is solid and inescapable, the guitarist shows the way to go by tearing off on his own before returning quietly for the *cantaor*, who should by now be humming in time with the rhythm, nodding his head, eyes closed, tapping a foot and summoning up the true voice of deep song as if it were a mix of phlegm and bile, which it is. The audience pushes him to the edge with the calls and rapping and if he needs an extra shove the clapping (*palmas*) will start, leaving him no place to turn. Now wait. Wait for it.

The sound you'll hear is that of a man falling into the abyss of human existence and landing in a spiritual wasteland that is floating in an indifferent cosmos. If he's any good, that is. Growls, howls and a great range of guttural vocalisations of pain and despair are the true language of the authentic *cante* and the words are not so important as the tone of the performance. How many times will the guitarist scoop up the *cantaor* and make him fall again? How cruel will the audience be in forcing the martyrised *cantaor* to face the pain of their shared existential suffering? It depends on the night and the skill of the performer, for whom alcohol is not just a vice but an anaesthetic. Bruised knuckles, teary eyes and a headache? Okay, now you can applaud.

Al Andalús

C/Capitán Haya 19, Chamartín (91 556 14 39). Metro Cuzco. **Open** 9.30pm-6am Mon-Sat. **Performances** 10.30pm, 11pm, 1.30am. **Admission** €18. **Credit** AmEx, DC, MC, V.
With *sala rociera* decor of the most kitsch kind, this place offers a raucous live show, but the very best part of it all is watching the mainly middle-aged public throw themselves into *sevillanas* till dawn. The admission price includes one drink.

Almonte

C/Juan Bravo 35, Salamanca (91 563 25 04). Metro Diego de León. **Open** 9pm-5am daily. **Admission** minimum consumption 1 drink. **Credit** AmEx, MC, V. **Map** p311 K2.
This 'flamenco disco' attracts a much younger crowd than Al Andalús. Beautiful youths flaunt it freestyle before *sevillanas* prompt a free-for-all. The evening is for dancing, the night is to be seen dancing. Try to work your way downstairs, where the most attention-grabbing dancing can be admired and – go on – attempted.

El Arco de Cuchilleros

C/Cuchilleros 7 (91 364 02 63). Metro Sol. **Open** 9pm-3am Tue-Sun. **Performances** 11pm-2am. **Admission** (incl 1 drink) €14 Tue, Wed; €6 Thur-Sun. **Credit** AmEx, DC, MC, V. **Map** p313 D8.
An expensive tourist trap that provides a pre-packaged thrill for the undemanding. The generic flamenco show alternates with the weekend spectacle of *rocieros*: groups of frilly, folklore-drenched performers, whose song and dance originate in the pilgrimage to the Virgen del Rocío in Huelva.

Café de Chinitas

C/Torija 7, Sol & Gran Vía (91 547 15 01/ www.chinitas.com). Metro Santo Domingo. **Open** 9pm-2am Mon-Sat. **Performances** from 10.30pm. **Admission** (incl dinner) €69; (incl drinks) €31. **Credit** AmEx, DC, MC, V. **Map** p313 D6.
An indulgent evening's entertainment for those who like to play at being 19th-century aristocrats – and don't mind paying 21st-century prices. At least this self-styled 'Cathedral of Flamenco' makes an effort, with sumptuous decor that contributes to the

Casa Patas.

experience. The food and floorshow are expensive, yes, but at least it means the owners can afford to pay top euro for flamenco stars, who may not break a sweat but will still send you reeling into the night.

Candela

C/Olmo 2, Lavapiés (91 467 33 82). Metro Antón Martín. **Open** 11pm-5.30am Mon-Thur, Sun; 10pm-6am Fri, Sat. **No credit cards. Map** p313 F9.
An atmospheric place, though performances aren't scheduled and will only take place after hours when you've gone. Still, this in-the-know watering hole for professional musicians and amateurs is welcoming to knowledgeable and respectful aficionados.

Las Carboneras

Plaza del Conde de Miranda 1, Los Austrias (91 542 86 77). Metro Sol. **Open** 8.30pm-midnight Mon-Sat. **Performances** 9pm Mon-Thur; 8.30pm, 9-11pm Fri, Sat. **Admission** (incl 1 drink) €22. **Credit** AmEx, MC, V. **Map** p313 D8.
Packed with tourists, this bar-restaurant still offers value for money, with an energetic, passionate show performed by enthusiastic dancers. The set menus comprise typical fare, and diners are exempt from the admission charge. Highly polished flamenco for that inauthentic but unashamedly fun night out.

Casa Patas

C/Cañizares 10, Lavapiés (91 369 04 96/ www.casapatas.com). Metro Antón Martín. **Open** 1.30-4.30pm, 8pm-2am Mon-Sat. **Performances** 10.30pm Mon-Thur; 9pm, midnight Fri, Sat. **Admission** (incl 1 drink) €27 Mon-Thur; €30 Fri, Sat. **Credit** AmEx, DC, MC, V. **Map** p313 E8.
This is a plush and somewhat pricey place to savour traditional or *nuevo flamenco*. Recent topliners have included Chaquetón, Remedios Amaya and Niña Pastori. A highly prized venue with a reputation to maintain, Casa Patas is deservedly proud of its standing and treats its loyal, knowledgeable and sometimes intimidating audience with mutual respect. Feast on traditional *rabo de toro* (bull's tail) for that authentic edge.

Corral de la Morería

C/Morería 17, Los Austrias (91 365 84 46/www. corraldelamoreria.com). Metro La Latina. **Open** 9pm-2am daily. **Performances** from 10.30pm. **Admission** (incl dinner) €72; (incl drinks) €32. **Credit** AmEx, DC, MC, V. **Map** p312 C8.
More serious and exacting than Las Carboneras, this long-standing *tablao* sports seemingly authentic Arab decor and an atmosphere to match. A relaxed mix of tourists, fans (Hemingway, Che Guevara and Picasso have all paid a visit) and professionals enjoy a solid, expensive and sometimes exhilarating show.

Corral de la Pacheca

C/Juan Ramón Jiménez 26, North of centre (91 353 01 00). Metro Cuzco. **Open** 9pm-midnight daily. **Performance** 10.30pm. **Admission** €30 (incl 1 drink). **Credit** AmEx, MC, V.
This grand centre of popular and traditional flamenco boasts a history of star performers and even starrier punters. Built on the site of a 17th-century theatre, it began life as a *tablao* but grew into an imposing venue with a large auditorium and stage.

La Soleá

C/Cava Baja 34, Los Austrias (91 366 05 34). Metro La Latina. **Open** 10pm-6am Tue-Sat. **Credit** MC, V. **Map** p313 D8.
This small but amiable bar boasts a constant babble of flamenco aficionados and a roster of in-house performers who alternate with spontaneous (and extremely variable) songs from the clientele.

Torres Bermejas

C/Mesonero Romanos 11 (91 532 33 22/www.torres bermejas.com). Metro Callao. **Open** 8.30pm-2am daily. **Performance** 9.30pm. **Admission** (incl dinner) €65; (incl drink) €29. **Credit** AmEx, DC, MC, V. **Map** p313 E6.
Modelled somewhat kitschly on the Alhambra, this bar plays hosts to authentic Gypsy flamenco and a faithful in-crowd, managing to absorb the tour parties without spoiling the mood. The paella and the Rioja veal are, like the flamenco, rich and satisfying.

Where to Stay

Where to Stay

Pillow talk.

For a compact city, Madrid has an unusually large number of hotels. In fact, so many new properties have opened in the past few years that there are concerns that there are too many, in the centre at least. For visitors, of course, this can only be a good thing. Intense competition means higher standards of accommodation and service, even in the lower-priced places. In particular, the difference between budget and mid-range hotels is becoming increasingly marginal, with the newer *hostales* now offering en suite bathrooms in most rooms. And, across all price brackets, staff are friendlier and keener to help than ever before. Fans of boutique hotels, meanwhile, will be pleased to hear that the minimalist concept has – finally – made it to Madrid.

STARS, PRICES AND DISCOUNTS

Star ratings should be taken as a guideline and not as a definitive rating system. The difference between a four- and five-star hotel in Madrid can sometimes be hard to spot, with little to choose between them. Mid-range accommodation is not the city's strong point,

but new three-star hotels are popping up in the centre thanks to chains such as **T3** and **High Tech Hotels**.

In this chapter we have arranged hotels and *hostales* by area and price category, according to the cost of a standard double room. Hotels charging over €300 are categorised as 'luxury'; those costing between €150 and €300 are classed as 'expensive'; 'mid-range' is between €60 and €150; 'budget' is less than €60. Breakfast is not included unless otherwise stated. In addition, in all but the cheapest hotels, plenty of cut-price offers are to be had at weekends and over the summer. In fact, nabbing a luxury hotel at a knock-down price is probably easier in Madrid than in most other European cities, especially if you book early. Check websites or call direct for details.

Note that *hostales*, also known as *pensiones*, is closer in meaning to 'guesthouse' than 'hostel'. Not all *hostales* have someone on the door 24 hours a day, so check how to get back in at night. These places, often full of dark corridors and 'interesting' decor, tend to be efficient family-run affairs, and while some owners speak English, any effort on your part to attempt a few words of Spanish will be well received.

It's also worth noting that many *hostales* and *pensiones* are located up several flights of stairs in old buildings with no lift. If this is likely to be a problem, check before you book.

BOOKING A ROOM

If you arrive in Madrid without accommodation and don't feel like pounding the pavements, try one of the following agencies:

Brújula

Estación de Atocha (91 539 11 73). Metro Atocha. **Open** 8am-10pm daily. **Map** p314 H10. *Estación de Chamartín (91 315 78 94). Metro Chamartín.* **Open** 7.15am-9.30pm daily.

A private agency (the name means 'compass') based in Atocha and Chamartín railway stations, Brújula can reserve rooms in any price category. You must leave a payment as a guarantee for the reservation and you will also be charged a €2.50 booking fee.

Viajes Aira

Terminals 1 & 2, Barajas Airport (91 305 42 24/ fax 91 305 84 19). **Open** 7am-midnight daily. Viajes Aira has two hotel reservation desks in the arrivals area of Barajas airport. It mainly deals with hotels of three stars and above, although it does have some *hostales* on its books. There is no booking fee.

Los Austrias & La Latina

See also p56 **Hostal Madrid**.

Expensive

Hotel Palacio San Martín

Plaza de San Martín 5, 28013 (91 701 50 00/fax 91 701 50 10/www.intur.com). Metro Sol. **Rates** €117- €143 single; €117-€219 double; €295 suite. **Credit** AmEx, DC, MC, V. **Map** p313 D7.

This hotel, housed in a 19th-century former palace, was converted into a hotel in 2001. Thankfully it has maintained much of its old glory, with period façade, stucco ceilings, wood panelling and an attractive central courtyard. A stunning rooftop terrace restaurant looks out over the surrounding area, while a huge presidential suite, on the rooftop, comes complete with jacuzzi – and more of those views. *Air-conditioning. Business services. Gym. Internet access. Parking (€15 per day). Restaurant. Room service. TV: pay movies.*

Mid-range

Hotel HH Campomanes

C/Campomanes 4, 28013 (91 548 85 48/www. hhcampomanes.com). Metro Ópera. **Rates** (incl breakfast) €83-€106 single; €94-€119 double; €119- €160 suite. **Credit** AmEx, DC, MC, V. **Map** p313 D7.

Especially popular among a design-appreciative public (for which, often, read 'gay'), the Campomanes oozes affordable chic, from the ergonomic white plastic chairs in the black-tiled lobby to the smart chequered grey and white bathrooms. The staff (black-shirted, naturally) are as welcoming and easy

The best Hotels

For pampering yourself

The **Gran Hotel Conde Duque** (*see p54*) and **Hotel Eurobuilding** (*see p54*) both have spas – perfect after all that schlepping around town.

For getting a feel of Old Madrid

Generations of travellers have turned to **Residencia Sud-Americana** (*see p49*) for its intimate, old-world atmosphere.

For taking a dip

Swim in style in the rooftop pool at the **Hotel Emperador** (*see p43*). The bar alongside will keep your liquid levels high.

For both business and pleasure

The **Hotel Eurobuilding** (*see p54*) and **Hotel Meliá Galgos** (*see p52*) are packed with business facilities, but also cater to leisure travellers.

For gay travellers

The **Hotel HH Campomanes** (*see left*), **Hotel París** (*see p45*) and **Hotel Mónaco** (*see p50*) are all notable for their gay-friendly ambience.

For making an entrance

The **Hotel Wellington** (*see p51*), with its elegant chandeliers and frescoes, will take your breath away.

For spotting a celeb

Try the **Hotel Eurobuilding** (*see p54*) for footballers, the **Ritz** (*see p50*) for anyone who's on a promotion tour, and the **Hotel Santo Mauro** (*see p53*) for stars searching for secrecy.

For feeling like a celeb

Hotel Hesperia Madrid (*see p53*) has the lot, not least a restaurant run by a Michelin-starred chef, a spa and its own helicopter pad.

For unusual decor

The **Hotel Villa Real** (*see p45*): let's face it, it doesn't get much better than a Roman mosaic in your bedroom.

on the eye as the spacious rooms, and the location on an elegant Ópera side street is unbeatable. In late 2004 the HH chain will become 'Room Mate', and this property will be renamed 'Room Mate Mario'.

Air-conditioning. Business services. Disabled: adapted room. Internet access. Telephone. TV: satellite.

Petit Palace Arenal

C/Arenal 16, 28013 (91 564 43 55/www.hthoteles. com). Metro Sol. **Rates** €85-€100 single/double. **Credit** AmEx, DC, MC, V. **Map** p313 D7.

Fans of chintz should steer well clear, but the new and excellent-value T3 chain of hotels is perfect for techno fiends on a budget. The Arenal's compact but sleekly designed rooms have flat-screen TVs and free ADSL connection, and more expensive rooms come equipped with a PC (also with free net access) and an exercise bike. Four of the superior rooms have showers fitted with solarium, sauna and radio. Guests are eligible for a discount at a nearby gym. The Hotel Tirol (*see p53*) in Argüelles is also a member of the T3 group.

Air-conditioning. Business services. Disabled rooms (2). Internet access. No-smoking floor. Parking (€14.45 per day). TV: cable.

Budget

Hostal Oriente

C/Arenal 23, 4 izq, 28013 (91 548 03 14/fax 91 547 84 53). Metro Ópera. **Rates** €35 single; €51 double; €70 triple. **Credit** DC, MC, V. **Map** p313 D7.

Right on the doorstep of the opera house, and just a short walk from Sol, the comfortable Oriente is in an excellent location. The 19 rooms all have compact bathrooms, TVs and air-conditioning, and the friendly staff are a further draw.

Air-conditioning. TV.

Hostal Riesco

C/Correo 2, 3°, 28012 (91 522 26 92). Metro Sol. **Rates** €35 single; €45 double. **No credit cards.** **Map** p313 E7.

This *hostal* feels more like a hotel, with its dark wood lobby, stucco ceilings and chintzy curtains. All rooms come with en suite bathrooms, and several have balconies bedecked with flowers. The location is hard to beat – it's rare to find such good-value accommodation so close to Sol and the Plaza Mayor.

Air-conditioning. TV room.

Sol & Gran Vía

Expensive

Hotel Arosa

C/Salud 21, 28013 (91 532 16 00/fax 91 531 31 27/ www.bestwestern.es/arosa.html). Metro Sol. **Rates** €100-€136 single; €142-€209 double. **Credit** AmEx, DC, MC, V. **Map** p313 E7.

This friendly, well-equipped and good-value 134-room hotel is situated right in the heart of the action. The spacious, air-conditioned rooms all come with clean, modern, wooden furnishings and bright

Hotel Lope de Vega. *See p45.*

marble bathrooms, and some of the more expensive doubles have a private seating area looking out on to the busy Gran Via. The public areas include a kitschy fake leopard-skin reception, and a restaurant and bar that Almodóvar would be proud of.
Air-conditioning. Airport transfer (€6 per person). Bar. Internet access. Parking (€15 per day). Room service. TV: pay movies, satellite.

Hotel Emperador

Gran Via 53, 28013 (91 547 28 00/fax 91 547 28 17/www.emperadorhotel.com). Metro Santo Domingo. **Rates** €189 single; €236 double; €364-€535 suite. **Credit** AmEx, DC, MC, V. **Map** p313 E6.
While the traffic speeds by on the Gran Via outside, the Emperador has to deal with its own constant flow of student groups and tourists. The hotel is well located for visiting the city's major sights and has a wonderful rooftop swimming pool (which is also open to non-residents for a fee). Rooms are conservatively decorated, and the bathrooms that have been renovated are a huge improvement on the old brown 1970s-style suites (some of which were still lurking at the time of writing).
Air-conditioning. Babysitting. Bar. Business services. Disabled: adapted rooms. Gym. Internet access. Parking (€22.47 per day). Room service. Swimming pool (outdoor). TV: cable.

Hotel Santo Domingo

Plaza de Santo Domingo 13, 28013 (91 547 98 00/ fax 91 547 59 95/www.hotelsantodomingo.com). Metro Santo Domingo. **Rates** €98-€137 single; €133-€202 double. **Credit** AmEx, DC, MC, V. **Map** p313 D6.
Courteous staff welcome guests to this well-located hotel. Rooms are individually decorated in elegant pastel colours and, despite the location, they're surprisingly quiet (especially those facing C/Isabel la Católica). Serious portraits stare down from their frames in the lobby and corridors, keeping the mix of tourist and business clientele company. Comfortable, central and just that little bit cheesy, it's a combination that works.
Air-conditioning. Babysitting. Bar. Disabled: adapted room. Internet access. Parking (€18 per day). Restaurant. Room service. TV: satellite.

Tryp Ambassador

Cuesta de Santo Domingo 5-7, 28013 (91 541 67 00/fax 91 559 10 40/www.trypambassador. solmelia.com). Metro Santo Domingo. **Rates** €154 single; €190 double; €230 suite. **Credit** AmEx, DC, MC, V. **Map** p313 D7.
Located in a former palace, the Ambassador manages to retain a vaguely baronial air despite being part of a chain. Suits of armour stand guard in the corridors, while plush upholstery adorns the public spaces and the large, light-filled atrium. The fact that the decent-sized rooms haven't been renovated recently only adds to the charm – think '70s-style bathroom suites and squeaky French windows. Breakfast is expensive (€19) but abundant and good.
Air-conditioning. Babysitting. Bar. Business services. Internet access. Parking (€20 per day). Restaurant. Room service. TV: satellite.

Mid-range

Hotel Carlos V

C/Maestro Vitoria 5, 28013 (91 531 41 00/fax 91 531 37 61/www.bestwestern.es/hotelcarlosv.html). Metro Sol. **Rates** (incl breakfast) €101 single; €133 double. **Credit** AmEx, DC, MC, V. **Map** p313 D/E7.
The corporate feel is avoided in this Best Western hotel with homely touches, from the motley but charming crew running reception and the *trompe l'oeil* lift door, to the tapestries in the corridors and the botanical prints in the colourful and elegant breakfast room. The rooms on the top floor are the nicest, and some have their own large, Astroturfed terraces (though you pay a bit extra for this).
Air-conditioning. Airport transfer (€6 per person). Bar. Internet access. Parking (€14 per day). Room service. TV: satellite.

Hotel París

C/Alcalá 2, 28014 (91 521 64 91/fax 91 531 01 88). Metro Sol. **Rates** (incl breakfast) €75 single; €96 double. **Credit** AmEx, DC, MC, V. **Map** p313 E7.
The mirrored entranceway sets the tone for this historic hotel and hints at its former days as one of Madrid's swankiest lodgings. That said, the building is a little dilapidated in parts, but the wooden-floored rooms are clean and spacious, their decor mixing 1980s colour schemes with Louis XIV style. The location is hard to beat, with balconies commanding views across the Puerta del Sol.
Restaurant. Room service. TV.

Budget

Hostal Andorra

Gran Via 33, 7°, 28013 (91 532 31 16/fax 91 521 79 31/www.arrakis.es/~andorra). Metro Gran Vía. **Rates** €39 single; €54 double. **Credit** AmEx, DC, MC, V. **Map** p313 F6.
Brightly painted rooms, floral bedspreads and comfortable leather recliners confirm the homely atmosphere of this centrally located *hostal*. While the roar of the Gran Via's traffic is unforgiving, the interior is calm, with cleanliness and facilities that belie the rates. Every room has satellite TV, and the bathrooms, while compact, are clean and modern.
TV: satellite.

Hostal Triana

C/Salud 13, 1°, 28013 (91 532 68 12/fax 91 522 97 29/www.hostaltriana.com). Metro Gran Vía. **Rates** €35 single; €45 double; €60 triple. **Credit** MC, V. **Map** p313 E7.
A popular and efficiently run business, this traditional 40-room *hostal* has been open for more than four decades. Located in the sometimes dodgy but always lively area between Gran Via and Sol, it welcomes guests of all ages and is good value. Rooms are sparklingly clean with modern en suite bathrooms. It's worth booking early.
Air-conditioning. Disabled: adapted room. Parking (€13 per day). TV.

Luxury

Hotel Villa Real

Plaza de las Cortes 10, 28014 (91 420 37 67/fax 91 420 25 47/www.derbyhotels.es). Metro Banco de España. **Rates** €322 single; €360 double; €469-€542 suite. **Credit** AmEx, DC, MC, V. **Map** p314 G8.
The Derby chain is owned by Catalan archaeologist Jordi Clos, and the entire hotel – as the name suggests – reflects his interest in Roman archaeology. The guest rooms are elegant, with marble bathrooms boasting large picture windows, and many have panels of Roman mosaics. Most double rooms have split-level sitting areas, some duplex suites come with a jacuzzi; luxury suites have private terraces.
Air-conditioning. Babysitting. Bar. Business services. Internet access. No-smoking rooms. Parking (€18 per day). Restaurant. Room service. TV: satellite.

Westin Palace

Plaza de las Cortes 7, 28014 (91 360 80 00/fax 91 360 81 00/www.palacemadrid.com). Metro Banco de España. **Rates** €470 single/double; €589-€3,799 suite. **Credit** AmEx, DC, MC, V. **Map** p314 G8.
One of the most famous hotels in Madrid, the Palace successfully combines old-world elegance with cutting-edge facilities. The lounge areas and stunning atrium have an air of sumptuousness, and the latter features opera performances once a month. The hotel's reasonably priced, comfortable bars and restaurants are popular with visiting celebs and politicians from the parliament buildings across the road, and, luckily for non-residents, they're open to all. The hotel is brought into the 21st century with a fully equipped fitness centre, sauna and solarium.
Air-conditioning. Airport transfer. Babysitting. Bar. Business services. Disabled: adapted rooms. Gym. Internet access. No-smoking floor/rooms. Parking (€25 per day). Restaurant. Room service. TV: satellite.

Expensive

Hotel Lope de Vega

C/Lope de Vega 40, 28014 (91 360 00 11/fax 91 429 28 29/www.hotelgreenlopedevega.com). Metro Antón Martín. **Rates** €135-€155 single; €170 double; €225 suite. **Credit** AmEx, DC, MC, V. **Map** p313 E8.
A stone's throw from the Prado, this anonymous-looking hotel is a shrine, of sorts, to one of Spain's most celebrated playwrights. The rooms are done up in standard-issue mid-range decor, but are a good size, comfortable and many have large balconies. Posted outside each one is information about Lope de Vega, and the corridors are lined with pictures of his productions. Other nice touches on the landings include books about the great man himself and other literary giants, along with bowls of fruit.
Air-conditioning. Bar. Internet access. Parking (€18 per day). Room service. TV: pay movies/satellite.

Hostal Alaska – big rooms at small prices. *See p47.*

Hotel Suecia

*C/Marqués de Casa Riera 4, 28014 (91 531 69 00/
fax 91 521 71 41/www.hotelsuecia.com). Metro
Banco de España.* **Rates** €123-€152 single; €190
double. **Credit** AmEx, DC, MC, V. **Map** p314 G7.
This smart-looking hotel, once a favourite of Ernest
Hemingway, is tucked behind the Círculo de Bellas
Artes. Originally opened as a Swedish-Spanish centre for cultural exchange, it still has a Scandinavian
air about it, with rooms decked out in understated,
modern decor but with warm colours. The sun terrace on the seventh floor is an added bonus, and perfect for dozing in the sun.
*Air-conditioning. Babysitting. Bar. Café. No-smoking
floor/rooms. Restaurant. Room service. TV: satellite.*

Mid-range

Hostal Persal

*Plaza del Ángel 12, 28012 (91 369 46 43/fax 91 369
19 52/www.hostalpersal.com). Metro Sol or Antón
Martín.* **Rates** (incl breakfast) €60 single; €75
double; €105 triple; €120 quad. **Credit** AmEx, MC,
V. **Map** p313 E8.
The Persal's rooms don't quite live up to the first
impressions given by the glass front and swish
lobby, but thankfully they're modern, spotlessly
clean and more than functional (it's well worth
paying the extra €10 for a nicer one on the upper
floors). If you're travelling as a family or a group,
ask about the quad rooms, which are a bargain when
split between four. The hard-working staff are especially welcoming and helpful.
Air-conditioning. Café. TV: satellite.

Hotel Asturias

*C/Sevilla 2, 28014 (91 429 66 76/fax 91 429 40 36/
www.hotel-asturias.com). Metro Sevilla.* **Rates** (incl
breakfast) €86 single; €107 double. **Credit** AmEx,
MC, V. **Map** p313 F7.
Within spitting distance of Sol, this bustling 19th-
century hotel is nothing to write home about from
the outside. Inside, though, the 170 rooms are bright
and spacious, decorated in simple whites and
creams, with carpets and furnishings that blend well
with the wooden floors and fittings. Some have
views over the gorgeous Teatro Reina Victoria, but
ask for an interior room if noise bothers you. At
lunchtime the restaurant buzzes with locals.
Bar. Restaurant. TV: satellite.

Hotel Mora

*Paseo del Prado 32, 28014 (91 420 05 64/fax 91
420 05 64). Metro Atocha.* **Rates** €57 single; €75
double. **Credit** AmEx, DC, MC, V. **Map** p314 G7.
If you like marble, you'll love the Mora's foyer, with
its caramel-coloured columns and chandeliers. The
rooms are functional but comfortable, and some
have views over the tree-lined Paseo del Prado. Not
surprisingly, given the location and price, it can be
hard to get a room, so try to book early. The hotel
restaurant serves a good-value *menú del día.*
*Air-conditioning. Bar. Parking (€17 per day).
Restaurant. TV (satellite).*

Hotel El Prado

*C/Prado 11, 28014 (91 369 02 34/fax 91 429 28
29/www.hotelgreenprado.com). Metro Antón Martín.*
Rates €79 single; €123 double. **Credit** AmEx, DC,
MC, V. **Map** p313 E8.

The sister hotel to the Lope de Vega (*see p45*), the Prado too has an anonymous look from the outside, but the rooms are prettily furnished, this time with a wine theme. Curtains and upholstery are adorned with vine patterns and the downstairs lounge is filled with books, videos and magazines about viti-culture. There are bowls of fruit to munch on in the public areas and free internet access in the lounge. *Air-conditioning. Bar. Business services. Internet access. TV: satellite.*

Hotel Santander

C/Echegaray 1, 28014 (91 429 95 51/fax 91 369 10 78). Metro Sevilla or Sol. **Rates** €64-€70 single; €70-€80 double. **Credit** MC, V. **Map** p313 F7.
The Santander's glamorous, gilded entranceway makes for a foyer with character, and if you can get over the rather offputting list of house rules (no vis-itors after midnight, no noise after 11pm, for exam-ple) you'll enjoy your stay. The rooms are elegant, kitted out with decent furniture and wooden floors. Some are more like suites, with small seating areas where you can have breakfast – room 105 is partic-ularly bright and spacious. *Air-conditioning. TV.*

Budget

Hostal Alaska

C/Espoz y Mina 7, 4°, 28012 (91 522 41 51/ www.hostalalaska.com). Metro Sol. **Rates** €30 single; €40 double; €50 triple. **Credit** MC, V. **Map** p313 E8.
Exceptionally large rooms, decorated with splashes of bright blue, give this comfortable, colourful *hostal* a bit of a beachside feel. The atmosphere is homely and laid-back, and guests have use of a fridge and

washing machine. The five doubles and one single all come with bathrooms, and many have balconies. A word of warning: there's no lift. The Alaska used to be known as the Hostal Valencia. *TV.*

Hostal Armesto

C/San Agustín 6, 1°, 28014 (91 429 90 31). Metro Antón Martín. **Rates** €45 single; €50 double. **Credit** MC, V. **Map** p314 G8.
This great-value six-room *hostal* in the centre of Huertas is run by a friendly husband and wife team. Rooms are spotless and all of them have their own small bathroom with shower; some boast views over the garden of the San Agustín palace next door. The Armesto is a particularly good choice for art lovers on a tight budget, being well situated for the famous art museum triumvirate. *TV.*

Hostal Astoria

Carrera de San Jerónimo 30-32, 5°, 28014 (91 429 11 88/fax 91 429 20 23/www.hostalastoria.com). Metro Sevilla or Sol. **Rates** €48 single; €59 double. **Credit** MC, V. **Map** p314 G7.
Managed by friendly staff, the Astoria is a good choice if you want to be centrally located, with basic facilities at a very good price. All 26 rooms are rel-atively spacious and have en suite bathrooms, but try to get the biggest available, and one preferably facing away from the street. *Air-conditioning. TV.*

Hostal Casanova

C/Lope de Vega 8, 1, 28014 (91 429 56 91). Metro Antón Martín. **Rates** €27 single; €37 double; €48 triple. **Credit** MC, V. **Map** p313 F8.

Location, location, location

Though Madrid is pretty small for a capital city, its accommodation is spread over a wide area, so it's a good to have an idea of what you want before you book.

Sol and **Gran Vía** are the best areas for mid-range accommodation right in the thick of things, and, though pretty touristy, are home to a clutch of decent bars and restaurants.

Heading north of here, **Malasaña** has a choice of good budget *hostales*, particularly along C/Palma. Bordering Malasaña to the east, **Chueca** is home to some great one-off properties like the Mónaco and the Ducal. Both areas, especially Malasaña, boast a real neighbourhood vibe, with nice shops and friendly faces.

South of Chueca, lively **Huertas** and **Santa Ana** are both great areas for cheap *pensiones* and *hostales*. On the edge of here, the Paseo

del Prado provides a variety of budget accommodation right on the doorstep of the Big Three art museums.

Other upmarket areas include **Retiro** and **Los Austrias**. Though located across town from each other (Retiro is between the Prado and the Retiro park in the east, Los Austrias is adjacent to the Royal Palace to the west), both are home to Madrid's old money, and both are peaceful – though bars and restaurants can be expensive.

Just north of the Parque del Retiro, around the chic shopping street Calle Serrano, is **Salamanca**. If you feel at home among the smart, wealthy set, you'll blend in well here. Business travellers should head for **Chamberí**, to the north of the centre, and, further north, to **Chamartín**, both of which are convenient for transport to the airport.

Run by a friendly family and in a quiet street just off bar-filled C/Huertas, this *hostal* is especially good value for those travelling in threes. Rooms are basic but bright, some with bathrooms, and all with air-conditioning.
Air-conditioning. Telephone.

Hostal Delvi
Plaza Santa Ana 15, 3˚ dcha, 28012 (91 522 59 98). *Metro Sevilla or Sol.* **Rates** €27 single; €30 double. **No credit cards. Map** p313 F8.
Located on lively Plaza Santa Ana and in a delight-fully eccentric building, the Casa de Guadalajara, the Delvi is ideal for backpackers. An entrance hall dec-orated with ceramics of winged cherubs leads you past the Guadalajara Club, then up to the third floor (there's no lift) where an elderly couple run this good-value *hostal*. Rooms are basic, but some have show-ers and a toilet, and others boast views of the square.

Hostal Horizonte
C/Atocha 28, 2º B, 28012 (91 369 09 96/www. *hostalhorizonte.com). Metro Antón Martín.* **Rates** €23-€36 single; €38-€72 double. **Credit** MC, V. **Map** p313 F8.
One of the oldest *pensiones* in Madrid, the Horizonte has stayed in the same friendly family throughout its 65-year history. The manager is the young and helpful Julio César, a font of knowledge about the city. Rooms are simply decorated, clean and comfy, and the welcoming atmosphere is unbeatable.

Hostal Martín
C/Atocha 43, 1˚ izq, 28012 (91 429 95 79/fax 91 429 09 64/www.hostalmartin.com). Metro Antón Martín. **Rates** €39 single; €60 triple. **Credit** AmEx, DC, MC, V. **Map** p314 G9.
This friendly, first-floor *hostal* has a pleasantly rough-and-tumble family feel about it. The 26 high-ceilinged air-conditioned rooms all come with an en suite bathroom and decent shower. The helpful cou-ple who run it speak English and German and can book you into other hotels if you're moving on to other parts of Spain. The hearty breakfast includes plenty of fresh fruit and very good coffee.
Air-conditioning. TV: satellite.

Hostal-Residencia La Coruña
Paseo del Prado 12, 3˚, 28014 (91 429 25 43). *Metro Banco de España.* Closed Aug. **Rates** €21 single; €35 double. **No credit cards. Map** p314 G7.
Well located for art lovers, this welcoming family-run *hostal* is basic but functional. The six bedrooms are clean, with high ceilings, chandeliers and plain furniture. All have washbasins, and two bathrooms are shared among guests.
TV.

Residencia Sud-Americana
Paseo del Prado 12, 6˚, 28014 (91 429 25 64). *Metro Banco de España.* **Rates** €18 single; €35 double. **No credit cards. Map** p314 G7.
This place has a real feel of Old Madrid, with mini Goya reproductions lining the creaky, wooden-

floored hallway. Whitewashed walls, high ceilings and dark wooden furniture give the rooms a cen-turies-old atmosphere and some have lovely views over the tree tops of the Paseo del Prado. One bath-room is shared between eight rooms, but all have their own washbasin. You'll find it very difficult to find this sort of old-world elegance elsewhere at such a cheap price, particularly if you're after a single room.

Hostal San Antonio
C/León 13, 2˚, 28014 (91 429 51 37). Metro Antón Martín. **Rates** €29 single; €45 double; €64 triple. **No credit cards. Map** p313 F8.
A clean, quiet and cool modern *hostal*, tranquil by day, buzzing on weekend nights. Rooms are com-fortable and generously sized for the price, and all come with air-conditioning and en suite toilet and shower room. Most look out on to a busy street, so it can get quite noisy at night.
Air-conditioning. TV.

Lavapiés

Budget

Hostal Apolo
C/Juanelo 24, 28012 (tel/fax 91 360 08 00). Metro Tirso de Molina. **Rates** (incl breakfast) €48 single/double. **Credit** MC, V. **Map** p313 E9.
This is the best of the few hotel options in the live-ly and multicultural Lavapiés area. The new owner is eager to please and proud of his establishment. Rooms are rather functional but clean and good value, and all have en suite bathrooms.
Air-conditioning. Bar/restaurant. TV.

Chueca

Expensive

Petit Palace Ducal
C/Hortaleza 3, 28004 (91 521 10 43/fax 91 521 50 64/www.hthoteles.com). Metro Gran Vía. **Rates** €155-€171 single; €187 double; €208 triple; €230 quadruple. **Credit** AmEx, DC, MC, V. **Map** p313 E6.
Part of the High Tech chain, the Petit Palace Ducal is one of the city's few boutique hotels. It only opened in 2003 but already manages to blend seam-lessly into its hyper-cool Chueca surroundings. Staff are young and friendly, and the striking red and black design eye-catching. All rooms have free high-speed internet access, and so-called High Tech rooms also come with flat-screen PCs, exercise bikes and sauna or hydromassage shower. The Ducal is also practical in its provision of family rooms, with bunk beds for those travelling *en familia*. Given all this, the prices are extremely reasonable, and it's even worth spending that little bit extra for a sixth-floor room with small terrace.
Air-conditioning. Bar. Business centre. Internet access. Telephone TV: satellite.

Mid-range

Hotel Mónaco

C/Barbieri 5, 28004 (91 522 46 30/fax 91 521 16 01). Metro Chueca or Gran Vía. **Rates** €55 single; €71-€128 double; €102 triple. **Credit** AmEx, DC, MC, V. **Map** p313 F6.

What some call its magic and others call its kitsch value has been maintained at the legendary Mónaco, with satin sheets, strategically placed mirrors, stuccoed ceilings and marble bathrooms… and a red-leather clad café. Once a gaudy upscale brothel, it entertained the likes of Mussolini's son-in-law and foreign minister Count Ciano, along with famous bullfighters. King Alfonso XIII would bring a whole string quartet to accompany the royal exertions from behind a curtain. When it became a hotel in 1959, much of the fabulous decor and louche atmosphere of the brothel were retained. Highlights include room 20, the king's room, with raised bath and the alcove where his quartet used to play; room 123, with a grand canopy and full-length mirror above the bed; and room 127 – a riot of shocking-pink plaster.
Air-conditioning. Bar. Parking (€16.50 per day). TV.

Budget

Hostal Benamar

C/San Mateo 20, 2 3D, 28004 (91 308 00 92/ benamar@benamar.es.telefonica.net). Metro Alonso Martínez or Tribunal. **Rates** €21 single; €34-€48 double; €60 triple. **Credit** MC, V. **Map** p310 G4.

Well situated between Chueca and Alonso Martínez, this *hostal* can be divided into two parts. The friendly owners promote the recently renovated section, with its marble floors, modern en suite bathrooms and computers in every room. The other section is older but clean, with shared bathrooms and cheaper rates.
Air-conditioning. Internet access. Parking (€12 per day). TV.

Hostal Residencia Santa Bárbara

Plaza de Santa Bárbara 4, 3°, 28004 (91 446 93 08/ fax 91 446 23 45). Metro Alonso Martínez. **Rates** €40 single; €56 double. **Credit** MC, V. **Map** p310 G4.

This well-connected *hostal* provides a friendly service in a secure building. Rooms are basic but clean, with walk-in shower facilities in each one. The friendly Italian owner and staff speak good English.
Air-conditioning. TV.

Malasaña & Conde Duque

Mid-range

Hostal Sil/Hostal Serranos

C/Fuencarral 95, 2°, 28004 (91 448 89 72/fax 91 447 48 29). Metro Bilbao. **Rates** €51 single; €63 double; €84 triple. **Credit** MC, V. **Map** p309 F3.

Clean and smartly decorated, these *hostales* are well located for night-time revelling – indeed, rooms looking out on to C/Fuencarral will bear witness to the

madrileño enthusiasm for partying well into the early hours. Although interior rooms are a little darker, the noise is minimal and the price slightly lower. All rooms have air-conditioning, small bathrooms and digital TV, and the properties are run by a fun couple and their English-speaking children.
Air-conditioning. Internet access. TV: satellite.

Hotel Alexandra

C/San Bernardo 29-31, 20015 (91 540 04 00/ fax 91 559 28 25/www.halexandra.com). Metro Noviciado. **Rates** (incl breakfast) €76 single; €107 double; €138 triple. **Credit** AmEx, DC, MC, V. **Map** p309 E4.

A few minutes' walk from the Gran Via and the metro, the Alexandra is well located for sightseeing. All rooms are clean and pretty quiet, but you can request an interior room to avoid the traffic noise from C/San Bernardo. Although the hotel is slightly anonymous in its style, the staff are friendly and the area and prices just that little bit less touristy than if you cross the Gran Via towards Sol.
Air-conditioning. Bar. TV: pay movies.

Salamanca & the Retiro

Luxury

Hotel Ritz

Plaza de la Lealtad 5, 28014 (91 701 67 67/fax 91 701 67 76/www.ritzmadrid.com). Metro Banco de España. **Rates** €514-€621 single/double; €1,017-€4,815 suite. **Credit** AmEx, DC, MC, V. **Map** p314 H7.

Petit Palace Ducal. *See p49.*

Madrid's Ritz was built in 1910, thanks to a personal intervention by King Alfonso XIII, who had been embarrassed at the time of his wedding to Princess Victoria four years earlier because his guests could not find a hotel that was up to scratch. When the hotel first opened, the handful of bathrooms, one telephone per floor and lift were considered the height of luxury, and it soon attracted politicians, royalty and writers. Today the 167 rooms maintain some of the original belle époque style, though the swirly carpets and occasionally shabby fittings are incongruous in such a setting. And, for the price, it has fairly minimal fitness facilities (and no pool). In terms of today's clientele, the Ritz has shaken off its slightly stuffy image and now welcomes celebs it once shunned; however, guests must still adhere to a strict dress code in the restaurant.
Air-conditioning. Babysitting. Bar. Business services. Disabled: adapted rooms. Garden. Gym. Internet access (wireless). No-smoking floor/rooms. Parking. Restaurant. Room service. TV (satellite).

Hotel Villa Magna

Paseo de la Castellana 22, 28046 (91 431 22 80/ fax 91 575 95 04/www.madrid.hyatt.com). Metro Rubén Darío. **Rates** €498 single; €556 double; €765-€3,745 suite. **Credit** AmEx, DC, MC, V. **Map** p310 I2.
Although it's a modern, rather nondescript building from the outside, the lavishly entitled Villa Magna, A Park Hyatt Hotel, more than lives up to its reputation – and tariffs – on the inside. The huge lobby, full of jewellery displays, international businessmen

and polite staff, leads to two excellent restaurants and a champagne bar, whose lunch menu is surprisingly reasonably priced. The 164 rooms and 18 suites, looking out over the busy Paseo de la Castellana or the exclusive C/Serrano, have good facilities and, like the rest of the hotel, are spacious and elegantly decorated. There's also a top-notch gym, if leisure is part of your agenda.
Air-conditioning. Babysitting. Bar. Business services. Disabled: adapted rooms. Garden. Gym. Internet access. No-smoking floor/rooms. Parking (€24.60 per day). Restaurants (2). Room service. TV (satellite).

Hotel Wellington

C/Velázquez 8, 28001 (91 575 44 00/fax 91 576 41 64/www.hotel-wellington.com). Metro Retiro. **Rates** €187-€257 single; €312 double; €428 suite. **Credit** AmEx, DC, MC, V. **Map** p311 J2.
More than half a century after it opened, the Wellington is still extremely graceful, with chandeliers, marble and murals, and groups of guests in formal eveningwear milling around the lobby. Polite staff are on hand to cater to guests' every need. The hotel is just a stone's throw from the city's most expensive shopping area, Salamanca, and has a summer pool with terrace – ideal for relaxing on after all that retail therapy. Rooms vary in size and are decorated in a conservative but classic style, and the hotel's main restaurant, Goizeko, serves Basque dishes in elegant surroundings.
Air-conditioning. Babysitting. Bar. Business services. Internet access. No-smoking rooms. Parking (€20 per day). Restaurant. Room service. Swimming pool (outdoor). TV (satellite).

Hostal Arco Iris.

Expensive

Hotel Alcalá

C/Alcalá 66, 28009 (91 435 10 60/fax 91 435 11 05/ www.nh-hoteles.com). Metro Príncipe de Vergara. **Rates** €183 single; €267 double. **Credit** AmEx, DC, MC, V. **Map** p314 I6.

Even though the chain status of this hotel gives it uniformity and a certain anonymity, the NH Alcalá offers modern accommodation with good facilities and professional staff. Not surprisingly, its location (right near the Retiro) and style (rooms with contemporary decor and good sound-proofing) make it a popular choice. The restaurant serves Basque food, while an early-riser breakfast caters to business travellers on a tight schedule.

Air-conditioning. Babysitting. Bar. Internet access. No-smoking floor/rooms. Parking (€18.90 per day). Restaurant. Room service. TV: pay movies, satellite.

Hotel Meliá Galgos

C/Claudio Coello 139, 28006 (91 562 6600/fax 91 562 76 62/www.solmelia.com). Metro Rubén Darío. **Rates** €120-€278 single/double; €374-€513 suite. **Credit** AmEx, DC, MC, V. **Map** p311 J1.

This large, glitzy and bustling hotel is part of the Sol Meliá group. It's located in the heart of the business district, so it comes as no surprise that there are 11 conference rooms – but is also popular with the well-heeled leisure set. The 'Servicio Real' floor offers a separate reception, a free bar, yet more mod cons in the rooms and secretaries for hire, and even the standard rooms are large and comfortable – if

somewhat dated in decor. The gym comes complete with sauna and whirlpools, while the breakfast spread is spectacular.

Air-conditioning. Bar. Business services. Gym. Internet access. Parking (€29 per day). Restaurant. Room service. TV: pay movies/satellite.

Mid-range

Hostal-Residencia Don Diego

C/Velázquez 45, 28001 (91 435 07 60/www.hostal dondiego.com). Metro Velázquez. **Rates** €63 single; €87 double; €117 triple. **Credit** AmEx, DC, MC, V. **Map** p311 J2.

The Don Diego lies above a row of upmarket private apartments on one of Madrid's most exclusive streets. Rooms are plain but clean and good value, and, because of the location, the *hostal* is popular with the business crowd and those attending trade shows at the IFEMA.

Air-conditioning. Internet access. TV: satellite.

Budget

Hostal Arco Iris

C/O'Donnell 27, 6 dcha, 28009 (91 575 50 15/ hostal-arcoiris@telefonica.net). Metro O'Donnell. **Rates** €35 single; €40 double. **Credit** AmEx, DC, MC, V. **Map** p311 K5.

Although it's a little more expensive than most *hostales*, the Rainbow's colour schemes make a refreshing change when compared with the dark corridors of the other budget accommodation in the

city centre. Rooms are modern and bright, with clean bathrooms, and the friendly staff are happy to add extra beds to make triples or twins. Stays of two nights or more receive a discount. Well worth a look.
Air-conditioning. Babysitting. Internet access. TV.

Argüelles

Expensive

Hotel Husa Princesa

C/Princesa 40, 28008 (91 542 21 00/fax 91 542 73 28/www.hotelhusaprincesa.com). Metro Ventura Rodríguez. **Rates** €187 single; €222 double; €534-€662 suite. **Credit** AmEx, DC, MC, V. **Map** p308 C4.
Beyond the Plaza de España and the hustle and bustle of Gran Vía lies the Husa Princesa, decorated with large reproductions of Goya and Velázquez classics in each room. Two floors are known as 'club class', providing extra amenities such as a pillow menu, butler service and mid-morning snacks. The hotel's gym and large sports complex are impressive, incorporating a temperature-controlled indoor pool, saunas, steam baths and 150 exercise machines, plus an aerobics and beauty treatment area. The hotel is a favourite of airline staff, who can often be seen sunning themselves on the outdoor terrace tapas bar and café. Offers include weekend breaks with flamenco show included and a flat rate on all rooms booked on the internet.
Air-conditioning. Bar. Business services. Gym. No-smoking floor/rooms. Parking (€25.30 per day). Restaurant. Room service. Swimming pool (indoor). TV: pay movies, satellite.

Mid-range

Hotel Tirol

C/Marqués de Urquijo 4, 28008 (91 548 19 00/fax 91 541 39 58/www.t3tirol.com). Metro Argüelles. **Rates** €105-€120 single; €115-€160 double; €140-€160 triple; €175 suite. **Credit** MC, V. **Map** p308 B/C3.
Situated within easy reach of the Parque del Oeste, the Tirol is well located for those wishing to discover the greener side of Madrid. The hotel recently became part of the T3 chain, and while some rooms have been renovated, with modern decor, others have yet to be revamped, a fact reflected in their price.
Air-conditioning. Business services. TV: satellite.

Chamberí

Luxury

Hotel Hesperia Madrid

Paseo de la Castellana 57, 28046 (91 210 88 00/fax 91 210 88 99/www.hesperia-madrid.com). Metro Gregorio Marañón. **Rates** €266-€305 single; €310-€340 double; €661-€3,606 suite. **Credit** AmEx, DC, MC, V.

Part of a Catalan chain, Hesperia Madrid is what you'd call 'contemporary luxury'. The dimly lit entrance gives way to white and cream surroundings, while plants lend a necessary splash of colour. In contrast, guest rooms feature dark wood and strong tones. Interior rooms have larger bathrooms, though guests wanting a jacuzzi and terrace will have to move up to the Executive and Presidential levels. The Catalan restaurant, Santceloni, directed by Michelin-starred chef Santi Santamaría, is among the best in the city. The hotel even has its own helicopter pad – perfect for real high flyers.
Air-conditioning. Babysitting. Bar. Business services. Garden. Internet access (wireless). No-smoking floor/rooms. Parking. Restaurant. Room service. TV: satellite.

Hotel Orfila

C/Orfila 6, 28010 (91 702 77 70/fax 91 702 77 72/ www.hotelorfila.com). Metro Alonso Martínez or Colón. **Rates** €297 single; €365 double; €409-€728 suite. **Credit** AmEx, DC, MC, V. **Map** p310 H4.
This small mansion in a tranquil residential area has been transformed into a quietly elegant five-star hotel. Built in the 1880s as a private home for an artistic family, the Orfila also contained a theatre and a literary salon during the 1920s. Thankfully, the hotel has held on to its 19th-century decor, not to mention its façade, carriage entrance and dramatic main stairway. The bedrooms are wonderfully quiet – once installed it's hard to believe you're in the middle of a bustling city – and one of the four suites is intimately tucked away in the attic. The elegant restaurant looks on to the lovely garden patio, and guests take tea in the lobby in the afternoon.
Air-conditioning. Babysitting. Bar. Garden. Internet access. Parking (€18 per day). Restaurant. Room service. TV.

Hotel Santo Mauro

C/Zurbano 36, 28010 (91 319 69 00/fax 91 308 54 77/www.achotelsantomauro.com). Metro Rubén Darío. **Rates** €273 single; €329 double; €500 suite. **Credit** AmEx, DC, MC, V. **Map** p310 H2.
Famous in recent times as David Beckham's first residence in Madrid, this exquisite hotel is discreetly hidden away in the embassy-lined streets that separate the Castellana from busy C/Santa Engracia. Out of sight behind tall walls and trees, the elegant and peaceful entrance prepares guests for the experience to come. The 51 rooms, housed in two parts of what was the residence of the Duke of Santo Mauro, are all individually and luxuriously decorated, and boast king-size beds and floor-to-ceiling picture windows hung with opulent silk drapes. The old palace library has been converted into a high-class restaurant and former ballrooms are now conference rooms opening on to an immaculately kept garden. An indoor swimming pool is a further draw.
Air-conditioning. Babysitting. Bar. Business services. Disabled: adapted room. Garden. Gym. Internet access (wireless). No-smoking floor/rooms. Parking (€16.05 per day). Restaurant. Room service. Swimming pool (indoor). TV (satellite).

InterContinental Castellana Madrid

Paseo de la Castellana 49, 28046 (91 700 73 00/
fax 91 319 58 53/www.madrid.intercontinental.com).
Metro Gregorio Marañón. **Rates** €450-€562 single/
double. **Credit** AmEx, DC, MC, V. **Map** p310 I2.

The InterContinental is a longstanding Madrid
favourite. The elegant decor in the lobby extends to
the rooms, most of which overlook the Paseo de la
Castellana. The hotel appeals to a wide-ranging
clientele, being well located for the business districts
but also offering special packages for fans visiting
the Bernabéu stadium. In terms of eating and drinking options, the modern Bar 49 is perfect for a cocktail or two before dinner, the El Jardin restaurant
serves French cuisine outdoors during the summer
months, and the new El Café serves light meals overlooking the lovely garden.

Air-conditioning. Airport transfer. Bar. Business
services. Gym. Internet access. Parking (€20.35 per
day). Restaurants. Room service. TV (satellite).

Expensive

Gran Hotel Conde Duque

Plaza Conde del Valle Suchil 5, 28015 (91 447 70 00/
fax 91 448 35 69/www.hotelcondeduque.es). Metro
San Bernardo. **Rates** €138-€270 single; €260-€339
double. **Credit** AmEx, DC, MC, V. **Map** p309 E3.

A quiet, out-of-the-way hotel with front rooms facing a leafy pretty plaza. Rooms are tastefully kitted
out with yellow and green upholstery, while the belle
époque salon downstairs serves afternoon tea. Beds
are king-size and one room, 315, has a waterbed.
Previous guests have included Celia Cruz and
Marcel Marceau, and Pedro Almodóvar has been
spotted in the bar. Guests can use the gym across
the road and there are plans to add a spa downstairs
by late 2004/early 2005. Special rates, inclusive of
breakfast, often apply at weekends.

Air-conditioning. Airport transfer. Babysitting. Bar.
Business services. Gym. Internet access. No-smoking
floor. Parking (€11.85 per day). Restaurant. Room
service. TV (satellite).

Hotel Zurbano

C/Zurbano 79-81, 28003 (91 441 45 00/fax 91
441 32 24/www.nh-hoteles.com). Metro Gregorio
Marañón. **Rates** €164 single; €199 double; €302
suite. **Credit** AmEx, DC, MC, V.

Part of the NH chain, the Zurbano is split between
two buildings. Rooms are immaculate (if a little
bland) and incredibly well soundproofed, given the
location right near the chaotic C/José Abascal and
its never-ending traffic jams. The size of the rooms
varies according to the building (the one furthest up
on the street tends to have the biggest bedrooms).
For travellers needing to be near the northern business district or within easy reach of Barajas airport,
the location couldn't be better.

Air-conditioning. Babysitting. Bar. Business services.
Café. Disabled: adapted rooms. Internet access
(wireless). No-smoking floor/rooms. Parking (€16.05
per day). Restaurant. Room service. TV (pay
movies/satellite).

Chamartín

Expensive

Hotel Eurobuilding

C/Padre Damián 23, 28036 (91 353 73 00/fax 91
345 45 76/www.nh-hoteles.com). Metro Cuzco. **Rates**
€161-€264 single/double; €417-€539 suite. **Credit**
AmEx, DC, MC, V.

The very name conjures up images of blandness, but
this hotel is set in an appealing residential area. Yes,
it's a twin-tower giant, with 469 rooms, but for
sports fans and business travellers the location is
hard to beat, right near the Palacio de Congresos and

Hot properties

Madrileños are romantic and passionate
people by nature, and this is reflected in their
city's accommodation, with classy hotels in
all price categories. If your nuptuals are
nearing, it's well worth considering Madrid
as a honeymoon destination.

If money is no object, aim for the top end
of the scale, namely the exclusive **Hotel
Hesperia Madrid** (*see p53*); the ultra-private
favourite of the Beckhams, the **Hotel Santo
Mauro** (*see p53*); or the elegant **Hotel Villa
Magna** (*see p51*). All of them are situated
on or near the Paseo de la Castellana, whose
bars have outside tables in summer, should
you wish to venture outside at some point.
When you're making booking enquiries at

these higher-end places, don't forget to ask
about special deals for honeymooners,
especially on suites.

If the purse strings won't stretch that far,
even mid-range and budget accommodation
can save money without compromising on
romance. If you can turn a blind eye to a bit of
cracked plaster, well-located mid-range hotels
such as the **Hotel París** (*see p45*) in Sol and
the **Hotel Mónaco** (*see p50*) in Chueca both
provide old-fashioned atmosphere and are
right in the centre of the action.

Meanwhile, the big colourful rooms of the
budget **Hostal Alaska** (*see p47*) may not be
the height of luxury, but at least you can blow
the rest of your budget on champagne in bed.

Kicking back at **La Residencia de El Viso**.

Real Madrid's Estadio Bernabéu. The hotel offers virtually every imaginable service and facility – including medical facilities and the luxury Spa Elysium – and has what are perhaps the city's best hotel pools, both indoor and outdoor (also open to non-residents for a tidy sum). Apartment-size suites are available for long stays. The friendly staff are extremely helpful.
Air-conditioning. Babysitting. Bar. Business services. Disabled: adapted rooms. Gym. Internet access (wireless). No-smoking rooms/two floors. Parking (€20 per day). Restaurant. Room service. Swimming pools (indoor/outdoor). TV (satellite).

Mid-range

Hotel Don Pío
Avda Pío XII 25, 28016 (91 353 07 80/fax 91 353 07 81/www.hoteldonpio.com). Metro Pío XII. **Rates** €77-€138 single; €110-€154 double. **Credit** AmEx, MC, V.
Quite a way from the centre but right opposite Pío XII metro and Chamartín railway station, and just 15 minutes from the airport, this hotel offers good facilities for the price. The lobby is decorated with dark wooden panelling and antique furniture, while the 41 spacious rooms, arranged round a glass-roofed atrium, are clean, bright and spacious. The marble bathrooms feature hydromassage baths – handy if you've walked back to the hotel after a day's sightseeing. Rates are even better at weekends.
Air-conditioning. Business services. Café. Internet access (wireless). Parking (€10 per day). Restaurant. Room service. TV: satellite.

La Residencia de El Viso
Calle Nervión 8, 28002 (91 564 03 70/fax 91 564 19 65/www.residenciadelviso.com). Metro República Argentina. **Rates** €82 single; €138 double. **Credit** AmEx, DC, MC, V.
El Viso is an exclusive, leafy suburb to the east of the Castellana, home of footballers and diplomats alike. As such, La Residencia is a far cry from the B&Bs found in the centre of town, with a lovely garden patio and a good restaurant. The staff are professional and the rooms (only two of which have a double bed) airy and clean. If it's an intimate couple of days in exclusive but reasonably priced surroundings you're after, then this is the place for you. And if you do find yourself pining for some action, the metro is within easy reach.
Air-conditioning. Babysitting. Bar. Garden. Internet access. Restaurant. TV: satellite.

Aparthotels

Aparthotels are generally made up of self-catering suites or small apartments, usually with kitchen facilities (sometimes basic), reception and maid service. They offer reduced weekly, monthly or longer-term rates, so are handy if you're staying in town for a while.

Aparto-hotel Rosales
C/Marqués de Urquijo 23, Argüelles, 28008 (91 542 03 51/fax 91 559 78 70/www.apartohotel-rosales. com). Metro Argüelles. **Rates** €123 single; €133 double; €166-€199 apartments. **Credit** AmEx, DC, MC, V. **Map** p308 B/C3.

Halfway between a conventional hotel and apart-hotel, the Rosales provides accommodation ranging from spacious and comfortably furnished bedsitters to suites. All boast kitchens and marble-clad bathrooms, and larger rooms also have a lounge. Other facilities include a coffee shop and a decent restaurant. Perfectly located for the Parque del Oeste. *Air-conditioning. Café. Parking (€13.90 per day). Restaurant. Room service. TV (satellite).*

Hostal Madrid

C/Esparteros 6, 2°, Los Austrias, 28012 (91 522 00 60/fax 91 532 35 10/www.hostal-madrid.com). Metro Sol. **Rates** €50-€58 single; €70 double; €100-€125 apartments. **Credit** MC, V. **Map** p313 E7.
The rooms at this centrally located *hostal* are basic, their white and yellow paintwork a little on the dilapidated side and the bathrooms somewhat cramped. The five spacious self-catering apartments are a better bet if there are more than two of you. Each has one or two bedrooms, a kitchen and washing facilities, and three have terraces with views over the city. Five smaller apartments have the same facilities but cost less. Note that discounts are available on stays of more than a week.
Air-conditioning. Internet access (wireless). TV.

NH Suites Prisma

C/Santa Engracia 120, Chamberí, 28003 (91 441 93 77/fax 91 442 58 51/www.nh-hoteles.com). Metro Ríos Rosas. **Rates** €85-€202 suite apartments. **Credit** AmEx, DC, MC, V.
Close to AZCA and the Castellana, this hybrid aparthotel consists of 103 huge suites that are perfect for long stays – especially if you need to work. All have an office area, sitting room, basic kitchenette and bathroom, and all are decorated in the NH chain standard of dark blue and wood. Close by is one of Madrid's most popular public pools, the Canal de Isabel II (*see p244*), which also has tennis courts.
Air-conditioning. Bar. Café. Internet access. Restaurant. Room service. TV: pay movies, satellite.

Youth hostels

Much of Madrid's youth hostel accommodation is situated outside the city centre, within easy reach of the mountains – great if you're into walking or skiing. A list of council-owned youth hostels in and around the city can be found on the website www.munimadrid.es (go to 'Tourist Information' then 'Find Accommodation', then 'Rural Lodgings'). Otherwise, the Albergue San Fermín is a good private hostel.

Albergue San Fermín

Avda de los Fueros 36, South of centre, 28041 (91 792 08 97/fax 91 500 51 34/www.san-fermin.org). Bus 23 from Plaza Mayor/123 from Metro Legazpi/85, 86 or 59 from Atocha. **Rates** (incl breakfast) €11.60 per person; €7.80 under-26s. *Locker* €1.35. *Towel* €1.35. **Credit** AmEx, DC, MC, V.

Part of a local regeneration project for the San Fermín area to the south of the centre, this hostel is great value. The modern building houses clean and bright dorms as well as computer facilities, a TV room and a hall for cultural events.

Barbieri International Hostel

C/Barbieri 15, Chueca, 28004 (91 531 02 58/fax 91 531 02 62/www.barbierihostel.com). Metro Chueca or Gran Vía. **Rates** (incl breakfast) €14.50-€16 per person. *Daytime use incl storage & facilities* €5. *Locker* €1. **Credit** MC, V. **Map** p313 F6.
Right in the middle of Chueca, this hotel is popular with budget travellers of all nationalities. The double rooms and dorms for four or eight people are basic but clean, and there are kitchen facilities, a TV room with DVD player and a book exchange service. Staff are very friendly and the atmosphere relaxed, and because the reception area is manned 24 hours a day there's no curfew.

Campsites

There's a fair sprinkling of campsites all around the Madrid region and towards the Guadarrama and Gredos mountains. Most are open year-round. A full list of local sites is available from tourist offices.

Camping El Escorial

Carretera de Guadarrama a El Escorial, km 3.5, 28280 (91 890 24 12/fax 91 896 10 62/www.campingelescorial.com). Bus 664 from Moncloa; by car N-VI, exit 47. **Rates** €5.10 per person, per car, per tent. *Electricity* €3.50. **Credit** MC, V.
This luxury campsite, located in the foothills of the Sierra de Guadarrama around 45 minutes from Madrid, is set in 40 hectares (99 acres) of grounds lined with oak trees. There are wooden chalets that accommodate five people and have heating for winter stays, as well as pitches for caravans, tents and motorhomes. Facilities are ample – in addition to four swimming pools and various sports courts (football, basketball, tennis and more), there are two discos, a restaurant, café-bar, launderette and supermarket, plus organised activities for children. Not far from the skiing resort of Navacerrada and a short drive from El Escorial, this is a good base for discovering the province.

Camping Osuna

Avda de Logroño s/n, Northern suburbs, 28042 (91 741 05 10/fax 91 320 63 65). Metro Canillejas. **Rates** €6.70 per person, tent or car; €6.15 under-10s; €4.80 bike; €9.80 caravan. *Electricity* €4.50. **No credit cards.**
This is the closest campsite to central Madrid, and the only one within reasonable distance of a metro station. There are rooms for two people as well as pitches for tents and caravans. Services include a supermarket, laundry facilities, a restaurant and a bar with a summer terrace that features live entertainment in the evenings.

Sightseeing

Features

Maps

Introduction

From *kilómetro cero* out to the 'burbs.

Seen from the air, or on a map, two of Madrid's main features immediately stand out. One is the immensely long **Paseo de la Castellana**, a north-south arterial avenue that slices Madrid in two and links the old city with its newer northern business districts. Either side of the Castellana the street layout is a rational, grid-iron pattern. The second unmissable feature is the cramped old city with its maze of narrow streets centred on the **Puerta del Sol**. This is literally the centre of the city, in that all street numbers in Madrid count outwards from Sol, and it contains *kilómetro cero* (marked by a plaque in the pavement), from which distances to the rest of Spain are measured. Much of old Madrid converges on this square. The Habsburg city (Los Austrias), including **Plaza Mayor**, the heart of Golden Age Madrid, lies just south-west along C/Mayor. **Plaza Santa Ana** and **Huertas** are to the south-east. Running east from Sol is C/Alcalá, which connects the square with the **Plaza de Cibeles**, the junction with the Castellana that leads to modern Madrid. Just north of Sol the historical but buzzing areas of **Malasaña** and **Chueca** border on the Gran Vía.

Don't miss Madrid

Have an art attack

Wear comfortable trainers and take plenty of energy bars to get around Madrid's three art palaces, the **Prado** (*see p63*), the **Thyssen** (*see p65*) and the **Reina Sofía** (*see p69*).

Have a row

Messing about in boats is easily done at the leafy, shaded **Retiro** (*see p99*), or the vast and verdant **Casa de Campo** (*see p105*).

Get high

A ride on the **Teléferico de Madrid** cable car (*see p107*) or a trip up the communications tower, the **Faro de Madrid** (*see p107*), gives spectacular views.

Purple haze

Pollution, ironically, makes for incredible magenta sunsets. Take them in either from a *terraza* at **Las Vistillas** (*see p72*) or the **Paseo del Pintor Rosales** (*see p107*).

Nun better

The **Real Monasterio de las Descalzas Reales** (*see p79*) has a collection of sumptuous art, the **Convento de la Encarnación** (*see p79*) an eerie display of saintly remains. But the biscuits from the **Convento de las Carboneras** (*see p72*) are simply divine.

Fair and square

With nippers in tow, check out the **Parque de Atracciones** funfair (*see p105*), and then let them loose in the playground in the stunning **Plaza de Oriente** (*see p75*) while you recover on the sidelines with a stiff drink.

The royal oui

Hello! readers can visit the otherwise unremarkable **cathedral** (*see p75*) to see where Felipe and Letizia said 'I do', and then the many-splendoured **Palacio Real** next door (*see p75*), where the wedding banquet was held.

name of its own, so different people may refer to the same area by different names. Residents often use the name of the nearest metro station for convenience and exactly what constitutes a *barrio*'s particular character is also something that can be elusive, involving myriad details that only locals fully appreciate. The area division we use throughout this guide simplifies Madrid's intricate geography, for convenience and comprehensibility.

TICKETS AND TIMES

Spanish national museums give discounts for students, and admission is free to everyone, Spanish or otherwise, under 18 or over 65 (ID is usually required). Many museums are free on Sundays (when they can get very crowded) or, for EU citizens, Wednesdays, and some smaller museums are still free at all times.

Most museums are shut on Mondays, with the exception of the Reina Sofía, which closes on a Tuesday. Many of the national museums offer volunteer guides free of charge, but they rarely speak English. To have a personal English-speaking guide you normally have to pay. Only the major museums have catalogues in English; similarly, most exhibits are labelled exclusively in Spanish, with a few exceptions, such as the Thyssen.

One of Madrid's greatest features is its compact, easily negotiable size. The **Prado**, the **Thyssen** and the **Reina Sofía** sit along the Paseo del Prado in what is known as the 'Golden Triangle' of art. Most other historic attractions are close by too, falling between Glorieta de Bilbao and the Puerta de Toledo and Atocha (from north to south), and between the Palacio Real and Plaza de Cibeles (from west to east). A car is a hindrance in old Madrid and, even though public transport is good, walking is often the easiest (and quickest) option. A map is useful but not indispensable: even visitors who like to wander with no specific destination in mind are easily orientated by the changing flavours of the neighbourhoods.

Though small, central Madrid does have several well-defined *barrios*. The borders are often easy-to-spot main arteries. There is a problem of nomenclature since, within any given *barrio*, locals may consider a cluster of streets to have a special feel and so give it a

Tours

Bus tours

See also p60 **Descubre Madrid**.

Madrid Vision

91 779 18 88/www.madridvision.es. **Tours** *21 Dec-20 Mar* 10am-7pm daily. *21 Mar-20 June* 10am-9pm daily. *21 June-20 Sept* 9.30am-midnight daily. *21 Sept-20 Dec* 10am-9pm daily. **Tickets** €10.60; €5.30 7-16s; free under-7s. **No credit cards**.
Three circular routes – Historical, Modern and Monumental Madrid – cover the major sights in the centre and parts of Salamanca and the Retiro. Good places to board include Sol, Gran Vía and the Plaza

de España, but the tickets, which you buy on board, enable you to get on and off as many times as you like in the same day. A reasonable commentary is available in various languages, via headphones.

Coach tours

The following two companies offer city tours featuring bullfights, flamenco and so on. More expensive tickets usually include dinner and a show. They also provide the same time-worn menu of tours of the towns around Madrid (Toledo, Segovia, El Escorial and so on), as well as trips to the Warnerbros Park in San Martín de la Vega. Phone for further details, including departure times and prices.

Companies

Juliá Travel *Gran Vía 68 (91 559 96 05). Metro Santo Domingo.* **Open** 8am-8pm Mon-Sat. **Credit** MC, V. **Map** p313 D6.
Trapsatur *C/San Bernardo 5, Malasaña (91 541 63 20/www.trapsatur.com). Metro Santo Domingo.* **Open** 8am-8pm daily. **Credit** MC, V. **Map** p309 E5.

Walking tours

Carpetania Madrid

C/Jesús del Valle 11, 4 dcha, Malasaña (91 531 40 18/www.carpetaniamadrid.com). Metro Noviciado. **Open** 9am-9pm daily. **Tours** €5-€7. **Credit** AmEx, DC, MC, V. **Map** p309 E4.

All the guides here are art history specialists. As well as some well-thought-out routes around the city – based on literary themes, parks and gardens etc – there are expert guided tours available for all exhibitions, temporary and permanent.

Descubre Madrid

C/Mayor 69, Los Austrias (91 588 29 06/7). Metro Sol. **Open** *Sept-June* 8.30am-2.30pm Mon, Tue, Thur, Fri; 8.30am-2.30pm, 4-6pm Wed. *July, Aug* 8.30am-2.30pm Mon-Fri. **Tickets** *On foot* €2.50-€7. *By bus* (Sept-May only) €6.10; €4.65 concessions. **Credit** AmEx, DC, MC, V. **Map** p313 D8.
With over 100 different itineraries (by bus and on foot), this service, run by the tourist board, offers the opportunity to get up close to all aspects of the city, focussing on architecture, literature, history and individual *barrios*. Some tours include sights that are otherwise hard to get into. Walking tours depart from the tourist office in the Plaza Mayor (*see p294*), though you're advised to book beforehand at the tourist board central office at the above address to guarantee a place. Let them know in advance if you want an English-speaking guide.

Descubremadrid.com

If you prefer to see the city independently, this website (not connected with Descubre Madrid; *see above*) has a large number of routes. By day, they cover literary, medieval and art themes; at night there are different ones. All come complete with maps, history and suggested refuelling stops; they are written in English and Spanish and can be printed out.

Madrid Card

Feeling energetic? Determined to squeeze the maximum out of your long weekend? Well, then, the new Madrid Card may be for you. Available for one, two or three days, the card offers admission to up to 40 of the city's main museums, unlimited use of public transport and the Madrid Vision tour bus (*see p59*), as well as discounts at many shops, restaurants, clubs, theatres and so on. Information about associated establishments comes in a detailed guide, with map. The hitch is that the card is quite expensive, and anyone planning on visiting the Prado, Thyssen and Reina Sofía will find that each takes up the best part of a day, and indeed all three can be visited in a more leisurely fashion with the Paseo del Arte voucher (*see p62*). In fact, it's only possible to get your money's worth out of the card with bags of energy and a resolve to visit smaller, further-flung attractions. The heat of a Madrid summer can preclude this, however, as can being in the city on a Monday, when most museums are closed. **Information** 91 713 04 44/www.madrid card.com. **Tickets** 1 day €28. 2 days €42; €38 if bought online. 3 days €55; €50 if bought online. Available from tourist offices (*see p294*), Atocha and Chamartín stations and in many travel agencies.

The Paseo del Arte

Art's holy trinity.

In the **Prado**, the **Thyssen** and the **Reina Sofía**, Madrid has three world-class art palaces, sitting along the Paseo del Prado, in what has increasingly, and slightly facetiously, come to be known as the 'Golden Triangle'. This formidable trio has made Madrid the world's capital of art for many people, and with the changes afoot at the time of writing, this label is only set to stick more firmly.

The big three are getting bigger. Starting in the mid-1990s, the Prado, Reina Sofía and Thyssen each conceived expansion plans that were then hatched and nurtured and are now finally beginning to take real shape. By the time they are all completed, the government will have spent, it is reckoned, around €150 million (and counting), the largest public investment in the history of the three museums. The initiative takes advantage of the proximity of the three art collections, barely ten minutes' walk from one another. Together they will form what is known as the 'Paseo del Arte', much in the manner of Berlin's 'Museum Island', London's 'Museum District' or Washington's 'Museums on the Mall'. The axis that unites them all, the Paseo del Prado, is also to be remodelled by a team of architects headed by the 2001 Wolf Prize winner Álvaro Siza, from Portugal. Currently the three museum projects are in different stages of completion. *See also p100* **Watch this space**.

First past the post was the Thyssen, which unveiled its new wing in June 2004. It comprises 16 new exhibition rooms, a new café-restaurant and offices in two buildings adjacent to the Palacio de Villahermosa, making the museum L-shaped. The project represents an expansion of 50 per cent on the museum's original space.

Second in the race is the Reina Sofía. French architect Jean Nouvel is in control of the project, which includes a three-building extension and gives the museum a second façade, facing south-west. As well as the massive amounts of additional space, the way the three

Botticelli's *The Story of Nastagio degli Onesti*, at the **Prado**. *See p64.*

Room 56-A

The 'A' could well stand for apocalypse, because in this room of the Prado are two of the greatest paintings ever done of the Last Judgement: Pieter Breughel the Elder's *The Triumph of Death*, painted in 1562, and *The Garden of Earthly Delights*, the triptych by Hieronymous Bosch (El Bosco to the Spanish), thought to have been completed around 1501. It is one of the greatest canvases of all times, a painting that spans centuries at a leap.

The Triumph of Death is no lightweight effort either, and even if Breughel had not also been Flemish and an unabashed admirer of Bosch's painting, it would still be a good choice to put near *Earthly Delights*. It is

constructions are to be laid out will also provide this crowded area of Madrid with a new public square. The new constructions, light and 'dematerialised', with glass playing a major role, are united under a massive zinc roof, which contrasts radically with the massive, opaque solidity of the Sabatini building. The building dedicated to temporary shows is already open and it is hoped that the others will be functioning by late 2004 or early 2005.

Last but not least is the Prado, whose plan is perhaps the most ambitious. It is certainly the most controversial and most subject to delays. With no large backyard and only one annexe (the Casón del Buen Retiro), the Prado can only expand by taking over nearby sites. Behind the museum is the San Jerónimo church, whose

adjoining cloisters, a national heritage site, were earmarked for the construction of a large building for temporary shows, with Rafael Moneo at the helm. His cube-shaped building, not to mention its location on the site of the cloisters, has caused a furore, as has the proposed takeover of the Palacio del Buen Retiro, currently housing the Military Museum. Realistic expectations are that the work will be completed towards the end of the first decade. Final budget? Nobody's even guessing.

TICKETS

An under-publicised joint ticket, the Paseo del Arte, gives entry to the Prado, the Reina Sofía and the Thyssen-Bornemisza for €7.66, an overall reduction of 25 per cent. It is available smaller, a single canvas, but imagined in an hallucinatory detail that is every bit a counterweight to the Bosch. In it, hundreds of skeletons herd the living into a huge rectangular box, a coffin big enough to hold all the quick in the world and turn them into dead. The humans are terrified, helpless, shoved, pushed and prodded along by skeletons. There is a huge bony horse and astride it is a skeletal general in death's army, huge scythe in one hand, reaping as he tramples through the waves of terrified human beings. A dog feeds on a dead woman's body. The horizon is high on the painting, the whole shocking scene in the foreground fades into dark spectral colours punctuated by pockets of leaping flames, gleaming brimstone in the crepuscular light.

On the facing wall is Bosch's triptych, two metres high, the centre panel twice the width of the wings, which fold in over it. Painted on the back of the wings, so that it forms another scene when they are covering the centre panel, is the third day of creation as described in the book of Genesis: the globe of Earth a wet twilight fog of greys and blues, spectral, quiet, uninhabited. Waiting, with the animal world yet to come. This is a part of the painting that is much less known than the main triptych, which depicts our peopled world in its implacable fullness and flesh. All the joys and sufferings of the human race are here, in amazingly modern detail.

The left panel shows the Garden of Eden in its innocence, but even here all is not peace and light, as beasts swallow other beasts, hinting at the savage brute world on which ours is built. In the centre panel is the antediluvian world of the senses – the world as we know it, a variety of human pleasure as modern as television or Hollywood's latest scandal. Sensual romps that we have no trouble recognising as our own. The pleasures of the flesh in trysts, threesomes, group gropes, everyone indulging. Beside it, in the last panel, hell itself, Judgement Day, when the former revellers are tied and tortured by ghouls and animals: miserable, dominated, impaled, ensnared and enslaved, their cities burning in the implacable darkness of the last days.

The Garden of Earthly Delights is full of the most modern of physical forms, from a round earth to airships. The power of its images is undimmed across the centuries, and its images resonate. It is easy to get lost in these panels.

from the ticket desks at all three museums; after visiting one you can visit the other two at any time within the same calendar year. Each museum also has its own 'friends' tickets, giving unlimited entry for one year, which are more expensive and more widely publicised. A better deal is the €36.06 annual museum ticket, available from any state-run museum, which gives unlimited entry to all the main museums, with the exception of the Thyssen.

The Prado

Housed in a gigantic neo-classical building begun by Juan de Villanueva for King Charles III in 1785, the Prado is Madrid's best-known attraction. Charles originally wanted to establish a museum of natural sciences, reflecting one of his chief interests, but by the time it opened, in 1819, this plan had changed: the Prado was a public art museum – one of the world's first – displaying the royal art collection. Spain's 'non-king', Joseph Bonaparte, had first proposed the idea and it was taken up by the restored King Fernando VII, who took on board the demands of the Real Academia de Bellas Artes and those of his second wife, María Isabel de Braganza, considered the museum's true founder.

The Prado is currently undergoing a highly ambitious expansion programme that involves several phases and that almost certainly has a few years left to run. The remodelling of the Casón del Buen Retiro, an annexe opposite the Retiro park, is due to be completed some time in 2005; this building will then house the 19th-century collections. Behind the main museum, on the site of the cloisters adjoining the San Jerónimo church, the new and highly controversial cube-shaped edifice designed by Rafael Moneo for temporary shows is nearing completion and should be unveiled in the spring of 2005. The eventual annexation and refurbishing of the nearby Palacio del Buen Retiro, which currently houses the Museo del Ejército, is expected to take somewhat longer.

As for the collection itself, the core is still the royal holdings, so it reflects royal tastes and political alliances from the 15th to the 17th centuries. Court painters Diego de Velázquez and Francisco de Goya, as might be expected, are well represented. Political ties with France, Italy and the southern, Catholic Netherlands also assure the presence of works by Titian, Rubens and Hieronymous Bosch, among others. The collection did have some gaps, mainly owing to Spain's hostilities with England, Holland and other Protestant states and the Spanish monarchs' unfamiliarity with artists pre-dating the High Renaissance, but recent acquisitions have evened things out somewhat.

Spanish monarchs had begun collecting long before, and by the 1500s Queen Isabella already had a substantial collection of works by Flemish artists. During the reigns of Emperor Charles V (1516-56) and Philip II (1556-98), Italian and Flemish works continued to dominate. Titian was a favourite of both kings, and the eclectic Philip II also purchased several works by Bosch, among them the enigmatic, slightly surreal triptych *Garden of Earthly Delights*, which he had hanging on his bedroom wall in El Escorial. The white face beneath a hat in the 'Hell' panel is widely believed to be the artist himself. *See also p62* **Room 56-A**.

Philip II (1621-65) is seen as the greatest of the Habsburg art collectors, and the leading connoisseur of his day. Flemish influence was still very strong, and the king was a major patron of Rubens. The latter was contemptuous of Spanish painters until he saw the work of the young Velázquez, who would serve Philip IV as court painter for nearly 40 years (1623-60). Velázquez also supervised the acquisition of other works for Philip IV, adding nearly 2,000 paintings by Renaissance and 17th-century masters.

Spain's first Bourbon King, Philip V (1700-46), brought with him one of the museum's most extraordinary possessions: the Tesoro del Delfín, or the 'Treasures of the Grand Dauphin'. The Dauphin, eldest son of Louis XIV of France and father of Philip V of Spain, accumulated a massive art collection, part of which was left to Philip. The 'Treasure' consists mostly of 16th- and 17th-century Italian *objets d'art*, such as rock-crystal vases studded with semi-precious stones and with gold and silver trimmings. Currently in the basement of the main museum, the collection is due to be relocated in the Palacio del Buen Retiro at the unspecified point in the future when the Museo del Ejército vacates the building.

The last monarch to add significantly to the royal collection was Charles IV (1788-1808), the employer of Goya, possibly the least respectful court painter

who ever lived (for Goya's portrait of Charles IV's family, *see p18* **In the frame**). Following Charles's death, the collection would be supplemented by later purchases and works seized from religious houses following their dissolution in the 1830s.

HIGHLIGHTS

With such a concentration of masterpieces, it is impossible to do the Prado justice in one visit. The free maps provided at the entrances, available in English, help orient the visitor. Recent remodelling of the entry points means that it is now possible to enter via the north end directly to either the first floor or ground floor. Alternatively, enter via the south end, opposite the Botanical Gardens.

The ground floor contains earlier painting and sculpture: stunning Spanish Romanesque murals and Gothic altarpieces; works from the Italian Renaissance (masterpieces by Botticelli, Rafael, Titian, Caravaggio and many others); 15th-century Flemish painting, with the world's greatest collection of Hieronymus Bosch; plus El Greco, and German paintings such as Dürer's extraordinary 1498 *Self-Portrait*. Also on this floor are classical and Renaissance sculpture, and the vault that currently houses the Tesoro del Delfín, until its eventual transfer to the Palacio del Buen Retiro.

Entering via the Puerta Alta de Goya, you reach the first, and what is considered the 'principal', floor. Here you encounter French and Italian 16th- and 17th-century painting, with works by Poussin, Claude Lorrain and Artemisia Gentileschi, among others, followed, on the left, by several rooms of Flemish works (Rubens, Breughel, van Dyck). Stretching ahead on the right is a long gallery with Spanish paintings of the same period, featuring Murillo and Ribera. This leads to one of the Prado's greatest attractions: the Velázquez Rooms.

In the great hall in the centre of this floor are Velázquez's massive state portraits of Philip IV and his court, with their air of melancholic grandeur, and his wonderful *Surrender of Breda* (known in Spanish as *Las Lanzas*), which are all due to move to the Palacio del Buen Retiro at some point. Pride of place, though, is taken by *Las Meninas*, often described as the greatest painting in the world, because of its complex interplay of perspectives and realities. Velázquez inserted himself at the left of the picture, supposedly painting a portrait of the king and queen, who appear bizarrely in a 'mirror' at the end of the room, but in whose place stands every viewer, watched forever by Velázquez, the little Infanta Margarita and other figures in the painting. Different but equally impressive are the artist's extraordinary *Los Borrachos* ('The Drunkards') and the portraits of the royal dwarves.

The rooms devoted to the other great Spanish painter most associated with the Prado, Goya, are at the south end of the first floor and on the floor above. Every stage of Goya's career is superbly represented in the Prado: his cynical portraits of the royal family and the aristocracy, and the renowned *Majas* (*see*

Museo Thyssen-Bornemisza.

p15 **In the frame**). An important recent addition to the Goya collection is his portrait of the *Marquesa de Chinchón*. There are also his tremendous images of war, such as the masterpiece *The Third of May* (*see p22* **In the frame**), depicting the executions carried out by French troops in Madrid in 1808. Still more fascinating are the *Pinturas Negras* or 'Black Paintings', the turbulent pictures executed in his final years. Witchcraft, violence and historical drama combine in an astonishing array of monstrous images, many originally painted on the walls of his home, the Quinta del Sordo, between 1819 and 1823. On the second floor there are his earlier, lighter, portraits and the carefree tapestry cartoons he designed for the royal palaces. Here too are European paintings from the 18th century. A couple of rooms also contain works by the German neo-classical master Mengs, the Italian Tiepolo and the French painter Watteau.

Museo del Prado

Paseo del Prado s/n, Retiro (91 330 28 00/91 330 29 00/www.museoprado.es). Metro Atocha or Banco de España. **Open** 9am-7pm Tue-Sun. **Admission** €3.01; €1.50 concessions; free under-18s, over-65s. Free to all Sun. *Paseo del Arte ticket €7.66.* **Credit** (shop only) AmEx, DC, MC, V. **Map** p314 H8.

The Thyssen

When the Thyssen-Bornemisza Museum opened in 1992, Madrid added the second point to its 'Golden Triangle'. The private collection of the late Baron Hans-Heinrich Thyssen-Bornemisza is widely considered the most important in the world. Consisting of 775 paintings, it first came to Madrid on loan, but in 1993 a purchase agreement was signed with the Spanish state. The Baron's decision to sell was doubtlessly influenced both by his wife, Carmen 'Tita' Cervera, a former Miss Spain, and by the offer to house the collection in the then-empty and available Palacio de Villahermosa, an early 19th-century edifice that was superbly reconverted by the architect Rafael Moneo at a fantastic cost. Thanks to this revamp, involving terracotta-pink walls, marble floors and skylights, it is possible to view the works with near-perfect illumination. In early June 2004, the museum unveiled its new wing, in which some 200 paintings and sculptures from Carmen Cervera's own collection are on display.

The collection was started by the Baron's father in the 1920s but was dispersed among his heirs after he died in 1947. The Baron bought back the paint-

ings from his relatives and then extended the collection, buying up first Old Masters and then more contemporary works during the 1960s. The Baron's own home in Lugano, Switzerland, only had space to exhibit around 300 works, leading him to look for a larger home for the collection, most of which may now be seen in Madrid, though some paintings are housed in the MNAC museum in Barcelona.

THE COLLECTION

Following the collection in chronological order gives you a lesson in Western art history. Beginning on the second floor, you'll find 13th-century works, notably by the early Italians, such as Duccio di Buoninsegna's *Christ and the Samaritan Woman*. You finish the tour on the ground floor, where Roy Lichtenstein's *Woman in Bath* is on show, or in the basement café, where Renato Guttuso's 1976 *Caffè Greco* hangs. On your way, you'll see examples of all the major schools. The collection partly complements the Prado and Reina Sofía's collections with substantial holdings of 17th-century Dutch painting, Impressionism, German Expressionism, Russian constructivism, geometric abstraction and Pop Art.

The Thyssen's detractors say the collection is a ragbag, catch-all collection of every kind of style, put together without discrimination or an eye for quality. However, one of its great attractions is that, while it is extraordinarily broad in scope, it is also recognisably a personal collection reflecting a distinctly individual taste, as seen in the wonderful room dedicated to early portraits, with works by

Antonello da Messina and Hans Memling. Equally quirky is the section on early North American painting, including a *Presumed Portrait of George Washington's Cook* by Gilbert Stuart and works by American artists who are rarely seen in Europe, among them Thomas Cole, Frederick Remington and Winslow Homer.

The Thyssen also has its share of real masterpieces. Among the Old Masters, the works of Duccio, van Eyck and Petrus Christus stand out. The museum's most famous painting, however, is the great Florentine master Domenico Ghirlandaio's idealised *Portrait of Giovanna Tornabuoni* (1488), in the Portrait Room. Two rooms further on is Vittore Carpaccio's allegorical *Young Knight in a Landscape* (1510), another gem. From among the masters of the Flemish School is the sublime *Annunciation* diptych by van Eyck, which is more like a three-dimensional sculptural relief than a painting. The Thyssen is particularly strong in the German Renaissance, with many works by Cranach the Elder, a remarkable series of portraits by different artists and Albrecht Dürer's *Jesus Among the Doctors*, which portrays an idealised, almost effeminate Christ pressed upon by diabolical doctors.

From the later 16th century and baroque there are superb paintings, such as Titian's *Saint Jerome in the Wilderness*, Mattia Preti's unsettling *A Concert* and Caravaggio's magnificent *Saint Catherine of Alexandria*. There are also representative works by El Greco, Rubens, Guercino, Tintoretto and Jusepe Ribera, and a Bernini marble, *Saint Sebastian*.

Kandinsky at the **Thyssen**.

The first floor, below, begins with several rooms of 17th-century Dutch pictures – arguably the least interesting section of the Thyssen – followed by the most varied part of the museum – with such pieces as a sombre *Easter Morning* by Caspar David Friedrich; a Goya portrait of his friend, *Asensio Juliá*; a great selection of Impressionists (Monet, Manet, Renoir, Cézanne, Degas dancers, two beautiful and little-known van Goghs); and even Constable's 1824 *The Lock* – although not jumbled together, but carefully ordered and arranged. The collection is generally strong in German art of all kinds, with several rooms of Expressionists and powerful works by Emil Nolde, Ernst Ludwig Kirchner, Otto Dix, Max Beckmann and Blue Rider group artists Franz Marc and Kandinsky (including the latter's *Church of St Ludwig in Munich, pictured p67*).

Also present, on the ground floor, are some more familiar modern masters – Braque, Mondrian, Klee, Max Ernst and Picasso (in the shape of his 1911 *Man with a Clarinet*), among others. The last few rooms focus on the USA, with a fabulous Georgia O'Keeffe, *New York with Moon*, plus *Hotel Room* by Edward Hopper and Robert Rauschenberg's 1963 *Express*. *Large Interior, Paddington* by Lucian Freud, an early David Hockney, *In Memoriam Cecchino Bracci*, and Ronald Kitaj's *The Greek from Smyrna* are also on display.

THE CARMEN THYSSEN-BORNEMISZA COLLECTION

This extension opened in June 2004 and incorporates two adjoining buildings: Nos.19 (the Palacio de Goyeneche) and 21 of the C/Marqués de Cubas. The new space exhibits some 220 works of the 300 belonging to the private collection of 'Tita' Cervera, which she has ceded to the Spanish state for an 11-year period (though three were already up and the collection's future remains uncertain). In addition there is a huge area for temporary shows and the library, restoration workshops and cafeteria have all been enlarged.

Access is from Room 18 on the second floor, which leads straight into rooms with early Italian and Flemish works by the likes of Luca Giordano, Jan Breughel and van Dyck, outstanding among which is the latter's *Christ on the Cross*. Moving on, you enter a well-illuminated gallery with views and landscapes by Canaletto, Constable, Corot, Guardi and van Gogh. In the next room are 18th-century French and Italian painting and beyond that is a selection of 19th-century North American painting, 'Naturalism and the Rural World'. Room H has the early Impressionists, among them Degas, Pisarro, Monet, Renoir and Sisley. Downstairs on the first floor are works by North American Impressionists and others from the late Impressionist period. Two rooms are given over to Gauguin, including his *Mata Mua* and *Coming and Going, Martinique (pictured below)*, and other post-Impressionists. From then on, you move into German Expressionists, Fauvists and the early 20th-century avant-garde movements. In addition, there is a Rodin Room, where one of the Baroness's four sculptures by the French artist is on show; the others are spread throughout the first floor.

Museo Thyssen-Bornemisza

Palacio de Villahermosa, Paseo del Prado 8, Huertas & Santa Ana (91 420 39 44/www.museothyssen.org). Metro Banco de España. **Open** *Sept-mid July* 10am-7pm Tue-Sun. *Mid July-Aug* 10am-11pm daily. **Admission** €6; €4 concessions; free under-12s. *Paseo del Arte ticket* €7.66. *Temporary exhibitions* varies. **Credit** AmEx, DC, MC, V. **Map** p314 G7.

Gauguin at the **Thyssen**.

Reina Sofía.

The Reina Sofía

Occupying an immense, slab-sided building, the Reina Sofía boasts an impressive façade with glass and steel lift-shafts, designed by British architect Ian Ritchie. Now, though, the museum has an equally impressive rear, in the form of three buildings, principally of glass and steel, arranged around a courtyard and all covered by a triangular, zinc-and-aluminium roof, the work of French architect Jean Nouvel. This ambitious extension project adds almost 30,000 sq m to the already vast art space in the patio to the south-west of the main edifice. It includes temporary exhibition spaces (now open), an auditorium and a library – both of which should be functioning by the end of 2004.

The Reina Sofía's great jewel is unquestionably *Guernica*, Picasso's impassioned denunciation of war and fascism commemorating the 1937 destruction of the Basque town of Guernica by German bombers supporting the Francoist forces in the Spanish Civil War. Some art historians, sometimes encouraged by Picasso himself, have seen it more in formal terms, as a reflection on the history of western painting using elements from the work of the Old Masters. Picasso refused to allow the painting to be exhibited in Spain under the Franco regime, and it was only in 1981 that it was finally brought to Spain from the Museum of Modern Art in New York. *Guernica* has been in the Reina Sofía since 1992, when it was transferred from the Casón del Buen Retiro amid great controversy. The artist had intended the painting to be housed in the Prado – of which the Casón is at least an annexe – and his family bitterly opposed the change of location. The acquisition of *Guernica* hugely boosted the prestige of the Reina Sofía, but the conflictive saga of the painting's final resting place has continued: Bilbao,

capital of the Basque province of Vizcaya, which contains the town of Guernica, has staked a claim on the picture for its Guggenheim Museum. However, since the painting belongs to the Spanish state, any such move is very unlikely.

The rest of the Reina Sofía's permanent collection, which came mainly from the old Museo Español de Arte Contemporáneo in Moncloa, has been much criticised. For many, the museum's claim to be an international centre for contemporary art is frankly fallacious. At best, it is pointed out, it is a reasonable collection of Spanish contemporary art, with some thin coverage of non-Spanish artists. It certainly contains works by practically all the major Spanish artists of the 20th century – Picasso, Dalí, Miró, Julio González, Tàpies, Alfonso Ponce de León and Antonio Saura are all present – but even here the representation of individual artists is often patchy, with few major works.

In response, an active acquisitions policy adopted in the early 1990s has sought to fill some gaps in the range of Spanish art and to add works by major foreign artists. Representative pieces by Donald Judd, Anish Kapoor, Bruce Nauman, Tony Cragg, Ellsworth Kelly and Julian Schnabel were all added, along with Picasso's 1928 *Figura*. However, the acquisitions budget has been very tight in recent years, especially in the context of the museum's expansion scheme and that of the Prado. José Guirao, director until June 2000, focused resources on the Spanish collection, with early pieces by Miró and Gris. Under his replacement, Juan Manuel Bonet, the museum acquired works by André Breton, Man Ray, Joaquín Torres García and others.

The new director, Ana Martínez de Aguilar, faces a very tough challenge, given the museum's new dimensions, and the art world will be watching her every move. The experts believe that the museum

Dalí at the **Reina Sofía**.

should bring 'grand' international temporary shows, practically non-existent over the last five years; review and improve the permanent collection; and define a clear acquisitions policy. The possibilities are immense, as are the chances of failure.

THE COLLECTION

The permanent collection is currently on the second and fourth floors of the Sabatini building and temporary exhibitions have until now been presented on the ground and third floors. However, the opening of the extension will mean changes in this layout in the near future. The third floor will provide additional space for exhibiting a wider selection of pieces from the permanent collection, some of which have only ever been on show temporarily, in rotation. The ground floor will continue to be used for temporary shows and now also features Espacio Uno, a space for cutting-edge installations and new multimedia work.

As things stand, the second floor begins with a selection of works that look at the origins of Modernism in Spanish art, haphazardly placing together artistic currents from different parts of Spain – Basque painters such as Zuloaga and Regoyos and Echevarría, Catalan Modernists such as Rusiñol, Nonell and Casas – even though they have relatively little in common. Next is the first Avant-Garde Room, with pieces by the Uruguayan Joaquín Torres García and other artists who worked in Spain, such as Picabia and the Delaunays, followed by a room dedicated to Juan Gris. Then comes the major draw for most visitors: the Picasso Rooms, divided into pre- and post-Civil War, with *Guernica* in the centre.

Miró, Julio González and Dalí have rooms of their own. Paintings by the latter include *The Great Masturbator* and *The Enigma of Hitler, pictured above*. Several of the works by Miró are from his later life, the 1970s. After a room on international Surrealism (Ernst, Magritte), there follows one on Luis Buñuel; the final displays on this floor look at Spanish art of the 1930s, taking you to the end of the Civil War (1939).

The fourth floor runs from Spain's post-war years up to the present day, starting with figurative art and the beginnings of abstraction in Spain, taking in Tàpies, Mompó, Oteiza, Palazuelo and Equipo 57. For international context, there are also works by Bacon, Henry Moore and Lucio Fontana, alongside Saura and Chillida. Later rooms feature Pop Art, figurative work by Arroyo, and Minimalism, with pieces by Ellsworth Kelly, Dan Flavin and Barnett Newman. Overall, though, the collection of non-Spanish art remains very limited.

The Reina Sofía serves as a venue for many other activities. It runs the Palacio de Cristal and Palacio de Velázquez exhibition halls (in the Retiro), which are used to present dynamic shows of sculpture and installations. It's also home to Madrid's principal contemporary music centre, the Centro para la Difusión de la Música Contemporánea (*see p219*). This is soon to move into the extension, where there will be a 450-seat auditorium and two smaller ones. The museum also has exceptional book, music, art and video libraries, and a superior book and souvenir shop.

Museo Nacional Centro de Arte Reina Sofía

C/Santa Isabel 52, Lavapiés (91 467 50 62/ http://museoreinasofia.mcu.es). Metro Atocha.
Open 10am-9pm Mon, Wed-Sat; 10am-2.30pm Sun.
Admission €3.01; €1.50 students; free under-18s, over-65s. Free to all 2.30-9pm Sat & all Sun. *MCARS annual ticket €24.04. Paseo del Arte ticket €7.66.*
Credit (shop only) AmEx, DC, MC, V. **Map** p314 G10.

The Old City

The beating heart of the metropolis.

South of Gran Vía

Los Austrias

The oldest part of the city, site of the Muslim town and of most of medieval Madrid, falls between **Plaza de la Cebada**, **Plaza Mayor** and the **Palacio Real**. Even though most of the streets still follow their original medieval lines, this may not be immediately apparent today. Like several other parts of the Old City, this area has been smartened up recently, and is now home to a slew of wine bars and expensive restaurants. Tucked away in side streets are the 12th-century **San Nicolás de los Servitas** (*see p76*) and the city's other Mudéjar tower, the 14th-century **San Pedro el Viejo** (*see p74*). If you continue down C/Segovia beneath the viaduct, you will pass a forlorn fragment of the ninth-century **Muralla Árabe** (Arab wall), the only substantial relic of Madrid's Muslim founders. The area around it, known as the **Parque Emir Mohammed I**, is occasionally used as a venue in summer arts festivals.

Back into town, along C/Mayor is the **Plaza de la Villa** (*see p74*), Madrid's oldest square and home to the city hall, the **Casa de la Villa**. In pre-Habsburg times the square was also the preferred place of residence for the elite; one such residence, the **Torre de los Lujanes**, is still there. Along with the third construction on the square, the **Casa de Cisneros**, these buildings make up a compendium of the history of Madrid from provincial town to imperial capital.

Despite its ancient beginnings, the area has come to be known as the 'Madrid de los Austrias', after the Habsburgs, although in truth Philip II and his dynasty can scarcely claim responsibility for very much of it. The greatest monument they *did* build, however, stands at the area's core: the **Plaza Mayor**, archetypal creation of Castilian baroque (a style also known as 'Herreran', after its key architect). On the south side of the plaza there is a **tourist office** (*see p294*) at the corner of C/Toledo, on which stand the twin baroque towers of **San Isidro** (*see p73*), perhaps Madrid's most important historic church. Continue down here to reach **La Latina** and the **Rastro** flea market.

Palacio Real. *See p75.*

Back in the plaza, the **Arco de los Cuchilleros** (Knifemakers' Arch) runs from the south-west corner via a spectacular bank of steps leading down through C/Cuchilleros to the **Plaza de la Puerta Cerrada**, decorated with some engaging 1970s murals. From here the **C/Cava Baja**, home to many of the most celebrated *mesones*, temples to Madrid's traditional cuisine, runs south.

To the south-east of the square, at the **Plaza de la Provincia**, is another major work in the Herreran style: the squatly proportioned **Palacio de Santa Cruz**, which was the work of several architects between 1629 and 1643. Despite its grand appearance, the palace was originally the court prison, with a dungeon so deep that prisoners had to rub their rags with lard and set them alight to stop themselves from going blind. These days the building has a somewhat more dignified role as the Foreign Ministry. In former times executions often took place in the Plaza de la Cebada, just a tumbril ride away.

For centuries C/Mayor was Madrid's main thoroughfare. The cross-streets between Mayor and Arenal offer an odd mixture of bookbinders and picture-framers, liturgical outfitters and Galician restaurants. The western end of C/Mayor, near the **Palacio Real**, has several old palaces and runs out west into C/Bailén, connected southwards to a splendid 1930s concrete **viaduct** that offers views of the sierra and the Casa de Campo. The viaduct's notoriety as a suicide point has led the city authorities to place giant glass panels all along it, giving it a very strange look and feel – without doing that much to deter the jumpers. At the southern end of the viaduct are the hill and park of **Las Vistillas**. The park has more great views and is often used for neighbourhood events, concerts and dances during fiestas and in summer. Beyond the park are the river and the elegant arches of the **Puente de Segovia**, a bridge commissioned by Philip II from Juan de Herrera and completed in 1584 to make it easier for the king to get to El Escorial.

Walk through Royal Madrid

Duration: 45mins
Walk marked in yellow on pp312-313.
The 16th-century exteriors that once fronted Madrid's interconnecting squares – Paja, Plaza de la Cruz Verde, Plaza de los Carros – were mostly replaced in the 1800s. Nevertheless, these intimate plazas and most of the winding streets of the district of Los Austrias still follow their original Arab and medieval courses, and with a little imagination a walk around these alleys can still be evocative of the atmosphere of the Habsburg city, and the medieval town before it.
Begin at Plaza Mayor, and walk down the steps under the Arco de Cuchilleros in the SW corner.
Walking down C/Cuchilleros, named after the knifemakers who long ago plied their trade here, look out for the 18th-century **El Sobrino de Botín** (more commonly known as Botín; *see p119*) on the left, allegedly the oldest restaurant in the world. Continue across the Puerta Cerrada into C/Cava Baja, and you will be walking along the line of the 12th-century wall, which is now lined with restaurants specialising in traditional *madrileño* cuisine.
Cut right up C/Almendro, and take the first right again down the narrow Pretíl de Santisteban.

At the end is the pretty C/Nuncio, which is now home to some of the many new wine bars that have sprung up in the area. Turn left, and on the Costanilla de San Pedro is the dusty 17th-century church of **San Pedro el Viejo**, with its 14th-century minaret-like Mudéjar tower.
Carry on past San Pedro, left down C/Príncipe de Anglona, veer left and enter Plaza de la Paja.
'Straw Square' was the grain and fodder market at the heart of medieval Madrid, and probably marked the southernmost point of the Arab wall. The only substantial buildings that survived 19th-century reconstruction are the church of **San Andrés** (*pictured*) and the **Capillas del Obispo** and **San Isidro**.
Walk up the Costanilla de San Andrés.
On the other side of San Andrés there is what appears to be one, albeit rambling, square. However, different sections of the square are traditionally known by different names. As well as the **Plaza de la Cebada** (Barley Square), once the site for public executions, and the **Plaza de San Andrés**, there is the **Plaza de la Puerta de Moros** (Moors' Gate) – site of the gateway to the Muslim quarter, or Morería, under Christian rule.
From there turn right down Carrera de San Francisco.

Iglesia-Catedral de San Isidro (La Colegiata)

C/Toledo 37 (91 369 20 37). Metro La Latina or Tirso de Molina. **Open** Sept-July 7.30am-1pm, 6.30-8.30pm Mon-Sat; 9am-2pm, 5.30-8.30pm Sun. Aug 7.30am-8.30pm Mon-Sat; 8.30am-1.30pm, 7.15-8.30pm Sun. **Map** p313 D8.

Still popularly known as La Colegiata, this massive church (which was built in 1622-33) once formed part of an important Jesuit college attended by many of the Golden Age playwrights. The high-baroque design was by Pedro Sánchez, who was inspired by the quintessential church of the Jesuits, the Gesù in Rome; the façade was completed by Francisco Bautista in 1664. In 1768, after Charles III expelled the Jesuits from Spain, the church was separated from the college, dedicated to San Isidro and altered by Ventura Rodríguez to house the remains of the saint and his wife, which had been brought here from the Capilla de San Isidro (see p74). La Colegiata was the city's provisional cathedral for nearly a century, between 1885 and 1993, when the Catedral de la Almudena (see p75) was finally finished and inaugurated.

Museo de San Isidro

Plaza de San Andrés 2 (91 366 74 15/ www.munimadrid.es/museosanisidro). Metro La Latina. **Open** Sept-July 9.30am-8pm Tue-Fri; 10am-2pm Sat, Sun. Aug 9.30am-3pm Tue-Fri; 10am-2pm Sat, Sun. **Admission** free. **Map** p312 C8.

Dedicated to the city's patron saint, the well-digger and labourer San Isidro, this museum sits on the spot where he supposedly lived and performed one of his most famous miracles: when his son, Illán, fell into a well, Isidro made the water rise and thus was able to rescue the unfortunate lad. The well – or a well, anyway – is preserved inside the house, as is the chapel built in 1663 on the spot where Isidro allegedly died. According to legend, he was originally buried here too. This is, then, a museum that deals in legends as much as in solid artefacts, and the current material on show is a little limited.

More interesting are the finds from local archaeological digs, formerly kept in the Museo Municipal and now in the basement here. They include items from lower-Palaeolithic settlements in the area, as well as artefacts from the Roman villas along the Manzanares, from the Muslim era.

The cavernous dome of **San Francisco el Grande** at the end is seen in several of Goya's skylines.

To the right of the church, continue along Travesía de las Vistillas to C/Morería, which winds back over C/Bailén down to Plaza de la Morería.

The knot of streets between here and **Plaza de la Paja** and **Puerta de Moros** formed the Morería, to which Madrid's community of Mudéjar Muslims were confined for four centuries. The little **Plaza de la Morería** (also called Plaza del Alamillo) was the site of the mosque and the Aljama, the Muslim community courts.

From there follow C/Alamillo to C/Segovia. Cross over it, and head up through C/Conde, left at C/Cordón to the Plaza de la Villa.

This little alley leads round into the **Plaza de la Villa**, with the city hall. It began life as the Arab souk, and so continued to be Madrid's main square until the creation of the Plaza Mayor. At night, especially in winter, it is just possible to imagine it as it must have been in the 17th century.

Turn right down C/Codo (Elbow Street) to Plaza Conde de Miranda.

Stop off at the 17th-century **Convento de las Carboneras**, a closed order of nuns who sell own-baked biscuits through a grill in the wall (see p178).

Plaza Mayor

Metro Sol. **Map** p313 D8.

The Plaza Mayor began life in the 15th century as a humble market square, then known as the Plaza del Arrabal ('Square outside the Walls'). In the 1560s, after Madrid was made capital of Spain by Philip II, architect Juan de Herrera drew up plans for it to be completely rebuilt, but the only part constructed immediately was the **Casa de la Panadería** ('the Bakery'). Dominating the square with two towers, it was finished under the direction of Diego Sillero in 1590 and is typical of the Herreran style, with grey slate roofs and spiky pinnacles. In the early 1990s, in a move that would not even be contemplated in most countries, this historic edifice was decorated with some colourful murals, verging on the psychedelic. The rest of the plaza was built by Juan Gómez de Mora for Philip III and completed in 1619. Large sections had to be rebuilt after a disastrous fire in 1790. Bullfights, carnivals and all the great festivals and ceremonies of imperial Madrid were held here. At its centre is a 1616 statue of Philip III on horseback by Giambologna and Pietro Tacca, which stood originally in the Casa de Campo and was moved here in the 19th century.

The square is still an important hub for the city, and most Madrid-wide celebrations, such as the Veranos de la Villa or San Isidro festivals, are centred here. For Christmas it houses a traditional fair with stalls. Best enjoyed on quiet weekday mornings, Plaza Mayor has plenty of pavement cafés from which to contemplate its graceful architecture. On Sunday mornings the plaza bustles with a stamp and coin market (*see p187*).

Plaza de la Villa

Metro Ópera or Sol. **Map** p313 D8.

Madrid's oldest square, home to the city's main market place in Muslim and early medieval times, contains three distinguished buildings, all in different styles. Dominating it is the **Casa de la Villa**, or City Hall, designed in Castilian-baroque style by Juan Gómez de Mora in 1630, although financial problems prevented it from being completed until 1695. The façade was also altered by Juan de Villanueva in the 1780s. It contrasts nicely with the **Casa de Cisneros**, which was built as a palace by a relative of the great Cardinal Cisneros in 1537. Restored in 1910, it now also houses municipal offices. Opposite the Casa de la Villa is the simple **Torre de los Lujanes**, from the 1460s, once the residence of one of Madrid's aristocratic families. It is believed that King Francis I of France was kept prisoner in the tower by Charles V after his capture at the Battle of Pavia in 1525.

San Andrés, Capilla del Obispo & Capilla de San Isidro

Plaza de San Andrés 1 (91 365 48 71). Metro La Latina. **Open** 8am-1pm, 6-8pm Mon-Thur, Sat; 6-8pm Fri. Open for services only Sun. **Map** p312 C8.

The large church of San Andrés, in the heart of Old Madrid, dates from the 16th century, but was badly damaged in the Civil War in 1936 and later rebuilt in a relatively simple style. Attached to it, though (but with separate entrances), are two of Madrid's most historic early church buildings. The **Capilla del Obispo** (Bishop's Chapel, 1520-35), with its entrance on Plaza de la Paja, is the best-preserved Gothic building in the city. It contains finely carved tombs and a 1550 altarpiece by Francisco Giralte, but it has been closed for restoration for some time, and no one is able to predict when it might open again. Further towards Plaza de los Carros is the **Capilla de San Isidro**, built in 1642-69 by Pedro de la Torre to house the remains of the saint, which were later transferred to the Iglesia-Catedral de San Isidro (*see p73*).

San Pedro el Viejo

Costanilla de San Pedro (91 365 12 84). Metro La Latina. **Open** 6-8pm daily (phone to check). **Map** p313 D8.

This Mudéjar brick tower dates from the 14th century, although the rest of the church dates from much later, having been rebuilt in the 17th century.

Ópera

The area between Plaza Mayor and the **Palacio Real** (*see p76*) is named after the **Teatro Real** opera house at its centre. As well as containing some of the city's most important buildings

Plaza de la Villa.

Taking it easy on the **Plaza de Oriente**.

On the esplanade between the cathedral and the palace, archaeological excavations are under way to unearth the remains of the original Muslim fortress and of the foundations of Philip II's Alcázar, covered over by the building of the later Palacio Real. Some of the masonry uncovered, including impressive Moorish arches, is open to public view. Behind the palace, the delightful **Campo del Moro** gardens run down towards the Manzanares and the Paseo de la Florida.

Campo del Moro

Paseo de la Virgen del Puerto (91 454 88 00).
Metro Príncipe Pío. **Open** *Oct-Mar* 10am-6pm daily.
Apr-Sept 10am-8pm daily. **Map** p312 B7.
This vast garden was named after a Muslim leader in the Middle Ages, Ali Ben Yusut, who attempted to capture the fortress that is now the Palacio Real. Unfortunately, access is only possible from the Paseo de la Virgen del Puerto side, and so to reach the entrance you have a fairly long walk down Cuesta de San Vicente or Cuesta de la Vega. As a reward, however, you will see two fine monumental fountains. Nearest the palace is *Los Tritones*, originally made in 1657 for the palace in Aranjuez (*see p269*); the other is *Las Conchas*, designed in the 18th century by Ventura Rodríguez. Both were moved here in the 1890s.

Catedral de la Almudena

C/Bailén 10 (91 542 22 00). Metro Ópera.
Open 10am-2pm, 5-9pm daily. **Map** p312 C7/8.
This is not Spain's most impressive cathedral, and it's something of a miracle that it exists at all. For centuries, Church and State could not agree on whether Madrid should have a cathedral; once they did, it took 110 years to complete it. In 1883 work began on a neo-Gothic design by the Marqués de Cubas, but this scheme went off course after only the crypt was completed. Another architect, Fernando Chueca Goitia, took over in 1944, and introduced a neo-classical style. Although the cathedral has failed to win much affection over the years, it was finally finished in 1993 and visited by the Pope. The site once contained the church of Santa María de la Almudena, formerly the main mosque of Muslim Madrid (the name comes from the Arabic *al mudin*, 'the mill') until it was knocked down by liberal reformers in 1870. One of its more interesting pieces is the 13th-century polychromatic funerary chest of San Isidro.

Palacio Real (Palacio de Oriente)

Plaza de Oriente, C/Bailén (91 454 88 00). Metro
Ópera. **Open** *Oct-Mar* 9.30am-5pm Mon-Sat; 9am-2pm Sun. *Apr-Sept* 9am-6pm Mon-Sat; 9am-3pm Sun. **Admission** €9 with guided tour; €8 without; €3.50 concessions. Free to EU citizens Wed. **Credit** AmEx, DC, MC, V. **Map** p312 C7.
Commissioned by Philip V after the earlier Alcázar was lost to a fire in 1734, the Royal Palace is rarely used by the royal family, and many of its 3,000

(the **cathedral** among them), this is one of the most elegant areas of Madrid. A tunnel whisks traffic under the stunning **Plaza de Oriente**, so named because it sits east of the palace, making it one of the most pleasant spots to linger over coffee. Curiously, Madrid owes this stately square, which seems to complement the Palacio Real ideally, not to the Bourbon monarchs but to Spain's 'non-king', Joseph Bonaparte, who initiated the clearing of the area during his brief reign (1808-13). After his departure it was left as a dusty space for many years before being laid out in formal style in 1844. During the dictatorship, devotees from all over the country stormed the square for a glimpse of Franco, who addressed his rallies from the palace balcony.

At the centre of the square is a fine equestrian statue of King Philip IV that once stood in the courtyard of the Palacio del Buen Retiro. It was made in the 1640s by the Italian sculptor Pietro Tacca, who – on the insistence of the Count-Duke of Olivares – was required to create the first-ever monumental bronze statue featuring a rearing horse, rather than one with four feet on the ground. This remarkable feat was achieved with engineering assistance from Galileo.

Sightseeing

rooms are open to view. The architects principally responsible for the final design, which reflects the taste of the Spanish Bourbons, were Italian – Giambattista Sacchetti and Francesco Sabatini – with contributions by the Spaniard Ventura Rodríguez. Filippo Juvarra, Philip V's first choice, had planned a palace four times as large, but after his death the project became a little less ambitious. Completed in 1764, the late-baroque palace is built almost entirely of granite and white Colmenar stone, and, surrounded as it is by majestic gardens, contributes greatly to the splendour of the city.

Inside you must keep to a fixed route, but are free to set your own pace rather than follow a tour. The entrance into the palace is awe-inspiring: you pass up a truly vast main staircase and then through the main state rooms, the Hall of Halbardiers and Hall of Columns, all with soaring ceilings and frescoes by Corrado Giaquinto and Giambattista Tiepolo. In the grand Throne Room there are some fine 17th-century sculptures commissioned by Velázquez, which were saved from the earlier Alcázar. Other highlights are the extravagantly ornate private apartments of the palace's first resident, Charles III, again decorated by Italians. Particularly striking are the Gasparini Room, the king's dressing room, covered in mosaics and rococo stuccoes by Mattia Gasparini; and the Porcelain Room, its walls covered entirely in porcelain reliefs. A later addition is another giant: the State Dining Room, redesigned for King Alfonso XII in 1880 and still used for official banquets. There are also imposing collections of tapestries, table porcelain, gold and silver plates and finally clocks, a particular passion of the little-admired King Charles IV.

One of the real highlights is the Real Armería (Royal Armoury), reached via a separate entrance off the palace courtyard, with a superb collection of ceremonial armour, much of it actually worn by Charles V and other Habsburgs. Look out too for the suits of armour worn by El Cid and his horse – impressively displayed on life-size statues. On the other side of the courtyard the Real Farmacia, the Royal Pharmacy, is also worth a visit. One of the oldest in Europe, it was wholly dedicated to attending to the many ailments of Spain's crowned heads over several centuries. In years to come, an opportunity to view the excavations of the older Alcázar and Muslim fortress beneath the palace will also form part of the visit. The palace is closed to the public when official receptions or ceremonies are due, so it's a good idea to check before visiting. On the first Wednesday of each month the Royal Guard stages a ceremonial Changing of the Guard in the courtyard, at noon.

There are tours of the Palace throughout the day, but frequency depends on the volume of visitors.

San Nicolás de los Servitas

Plaza San Nicolás (91 559 40 64). Metro Ópera. **Open** 8.30am-1.30pm Mon; 9-9.30am, 6.30-8.30pm Tue-Sat; 10am-2pm, 6.30-8.30pm Sun. **Map** p312 C7. The oldest surviving church in Madrid stands just a few minutes from Plaza de Oriente. Its 12th-century tower is one of two Mudéjar towers (*see also p74* San Pedro el Viejo), built by Muslim craftsmen living under Christian rule, in the city. Most of the rest of the church was rebuilt later, during the 15th and 16th centuries.

La Latina

La Latina, the area below Plaza de la Cebada, takes its name from the nickname of Beatriz Galindo, teacher of Latin and confidante to Queen Isabella. At the end of the 15th century she paid for a hospital to be built on the square

Catedral de la Almudena. *See p75.*

Casa de Correos

that bears her name. Its site is now occupied by the **Teatro La Latina**, a stronghold of traditional Spanish entertainment. The district is relatively quiet except during its grand fiestas, around the time of **La Paloma** in August (*see p194*).

Basílica de San Francisco el Grande

Plaza de San Francisco (91 365 38 00). Metro La Latina. **Open** *Oct-June* 11am-12.30pm, 4-6.30pm Mon-Fri. *July-Sept* 11am-12.30pm, 5-7.30pm Mon-Fri. Last admission half hr before closing. **Admission** (guided tour only) €3; €2 concessions. **Map** p312 C9. This huge, multi-tiered church between Puerta de Toledo and the Palacio Real is difficult to miss. A monastery on the site, reputedly founded by Saint Francis of Assisi, was knocked down in 1760; in its place, between 1761 and 1784 Francisco Cabezas and later Francesco Sabatini built this neo-classical church. Most challenging was the construction of the spectacular dome, with a diameter of 33m (108ft). The dome has recently been restored, but work on the rest of the basilica is expected to go on for several more years, so expect some parts to be covered with scaffolding. Inside there is an early Goya, *The Sermon of San Bernardino of Siena* (1781), and several frescoes by other artists.

Sol

The **Puerta del Sol** represents the very heart of Madrid, both because it contains kilómetro cero (the mark from which distances from the city are measured) and for its time-honoured role as chief meeting place. Famously, through the centuries people have come to Sol to find out what's going on. Until the 1830s the block between C/Correo and C/Esparteros was occupied by the monastery of San Felipe el Real, the steps and cloister of which were, in Habsburg Madrid, one of the recognised *mentideros* – literally 'pits of lies', or gossip-mills – where people came to pick up on the latest news, anecdotes or scurrilous rumours. In a city with no newspapers – but where who was in or out of favour was of primary importance – *mentideros* were a major social institution, and rare was the day when at least one of the great figures of Spanish literature, such as Cervantes, Lope or Quevedo, did not pass by here. The steps of San Felipe were also overlooked by one of the largest brothels of the era, another attraction for men about town. On a more respectable note, the Café Pombo, home to legendary *tertulias* (*see p160* **In the frame**), stood on the corner of C/Carretas. It is still Madrid's most popular meeting point, particularly the spot by the monument with the symbols of Madrid (a bear and a *madroño* or strawberry tree) at the junction with C/Carmen.

Under the Habsburgs the Puerta del Sol, the main, easternmost gate (*puerta*) of 15th-century Madrid, was surrounded by churches and monasteries. It was rebuilt in its present form in 1854-62. The square's most important building is the **Casa de Correos**, built in 1766 by Jaime Marquet as a post office for Charles III. Today it houses the regional government, the

Defining the indefinable

Few writers have been as central to the life and culture of Madrid as Ramón Gómez de la Serna, one of the most original and influential Spanish authors of the 20th century. Born in 1891 in the old Habsburg heart of Madrid, he trained initially as a lawyer, but never practised. When only 19, while standing on the balcony of his home at C/Puebla 11, he claimed to have had the inspiration for the near untranslatable literary form for which he would best be remembered: *greguerías*.

'Humour + metaphor = *greguerías*', was how Ramón himself defined these brief poetic statements in which words, ideas and objects are brought together in almost stream-of-consciousness fashion ('It is only in botanical gardens that trees carry visiting cards'). These 'attempts to define the indefinable, to capture the fugitive', as La Serna explained them on another occasion, had a significant influence on the Spanish surrealist movement, and on avant-garde literature generally, in Europe and Latin America.

La Serna's love of the absurd and the ephemeral, and his ability to uncover the poetical and the extraordinary in the outwardly unremarkable, made him the ideal commentator on Madrid, a city he described as 'the most difficult capital in the world to understand'. A great many of his more-than-100 books are dedicated to his native city, beginning in 1914 with his first mature work, *El Rastro*, a near 350-page study of Madrid's flea market, a place whose stunning diversity of objects echoes his prose style, with an occasionally indigestible medley of aphorisms and random observations.

As a writer on Madrid, La Serna was matched in his copiousness only by the early 19th-century scholar Ramón Mesonero Romanos; but the Madrid author with whom he felt the closest empathy was the latter's charismatic contemporary Mariano José de Larra, who likewise combined a passionate obsession with the city with a hatred of its middle-class conventions. An empty seat was always kept for the ghost of Larra in the celebrated Saturday night gatherings that La Serna began organizing at the Café Pombo (*see p160* **In the frame**). These attracted nearly all of Madrid's liberal intelligentsia, and led to Ramón's transformation from mere observer of the city into one of Madrid's most celebrated institutions. The book that would

come out of these meetings, *Pombo, biografía del celebre café y otros cafés famosos*, though it rambles on at inordinate length, is filled with dazzling passages, and leaves no aspect of café culture untouched, not even the marble tops of the tables.

Exiled to Buenos Aires at the start of the Civil War, La Serna lived there until his death in 1963, his writings making a profound impact on the Argentine author Jorge Luis Borges. Constantly he thought back on Madrid, but returned there only on one occasion, which left him bitterly disappointed. His corpse was later brought over to Madrid's Sacramental de San Justo, and his Buenos Aires study was reassembled recently in Madrid's **Museo Municipal** (*see p88*), alongside that of Mesonero Romanos. The uncluttered simplicity of the latter's study contrasts with the fantastical anarchy of La Serna's, which mesmerizes the visitor with such details as convex mirrors, a stuffed leopard, flying swans on the walls and revolving mirror balls worthy of any suburban disco.

EN ESTA CASA NACIO EN 1888
EL ESCRITOR
RAMON GOMEZ DE LA SERNA
EL AYUNTAMIENTO DE MADRID
LE DEDICA ESTA CONMEMORACION
EN 1949

Comunidad de Madrid, but in the Franco era it had much grimmer connotations, as the Interior Ministry and police headquarters. It was altered significantly in 1866, when the large clock tower was added; this is now the building's best-known feature, since it's the clock the whole country sees on New Year's Eve, when revellers crowd into the square to eat their lucky grapes, one for each stroke of midnight. In the 1990s the tower developed a precarious incline due to rot in its timbers, but it was rebuilt and unveiled once again in 1998. Sol is also where Napoleon's Egyptian cavalry, the Mamelukes, charged down on the *madrileño* crowd on 2 May 1808, as portrayed in one of Goya's most famous paintings.

Tucked in the middle of the area between Sol, Arenal, C/Alcalá and Gran Vía is the **Real Monasterio de las Descalzas Reales**, bursting with artworks and a deliciously unexpected oasis amid the traffic and bustle of Sol. At the west side of the area, just above the Plaza de Oriente, is the peaceful and little visited **Convento de la Encarnación**, also worth a look. Just north of that, occupying the site of another convent, is the old 19th-century **Palacio del Senado** (Senate), now made redundant by its back-to-back counterpart in granite and smoked glass by Santiago Goyarre.

Running almost alongside C/Preciados up to Gran Vía is shabby C/Montera, lined with cheap, dated shops and the main area for street prostitution in the city centre. At the top, parallel with Gran Vía, is C/Caballero de Gracia, with a 19th-century oratory that lays on special Masses for the working girls, many of them Latin American, who operate along the street. While seedy, this area is not generally dangerous, and is heavily policed. Care should be taken walking around late at night, however, especially if you're on your own.

Convento de la Encarnación

Plaza de la Encarnación 1 (91 547 05 10/ information 91 454 88 00). Metro Ópera or Santo Domingo. **Open** 10.30am-12.45pm, 4-5.45pm Tue-Thur, Sat; 10.30am-12.45pm Fri; 11am-1.45pm Sun. **Admission** €3.60; €2 concessions. Free to EU citizens Wed. **Map** p312 C6.

Before the Alcázar burned down, this understated convent was its treasury, connected by a concealed passageway. In 1611 it was inaugurated as a monastery by Philip III and his wife Margaret of Austria, and rebuilt to a design by Gómez de Mora. However, much of the original building, including the church, was damaged by fire in 1734 and rebuilt in a classical-baroque style in the 1760s by Ventura Rodríguez. It still contains a community of around 20 nuns, but most of the building is open to the public. Although not as lavishly endowed as the Descalzas Reales, it contains a great many pieces of

17th-century religious art, the most impressive of which is Jusepe Ribera's shimmering chiaroscuro portrait of John the Baptist. The Encarnación's most famous and memorable room, however, is the *reliquiario* (relics room). In its glass casements are displayed some 1,500 saintly remains, bone fragments and former possessions of saints and martyrs, in extravagantly bejewelled copper, bronze, glass, gold and silver reliquaries. Its prize possession is what purports to be the solidified blood of San Pantaleón, kept inside a glass orb. The blood reportedly liquefies each year from midnight on the eve of his feast day, 27 July (*see p83* **Sainted love**). Note that visits are by guided tour only, and tours leave 30 minutes after the first person signs up; so there's little point turning up as it opens.

Real Monasterio de las Descalzas Reales

Plaza de las Descalzas 3 (information 91 454 88 00). Metro Callao or Sol. **Open** 10.30am-12.45pm, 4-5.45pm Tue-Thur, Sat; 10.30am-12.45pm Fri; 11am-1.45pm Sun. **Admission** €4.81; €2.40 concessions. Free to EU citizens Wed. **Map** p313 D7.

The convent of the Descalzas Reales ('Royal Barefoot Nuns') is the most complete 16th-century building in Madrid and still houses a cloistered community. It was originally built as a palace for Alonso Gutiérrez, treasurer of Charles V, but was converted into a convent in 1556-64 by Antonio Sillero and Juan Bautista de Toledo after Philip II's widowed sister Joanna of Austria decided to become a nun. Founded with royal patronage, the Descalzas became the preferred destination of the many widows, younger daughters and other women of the royal family and high aristocracy of Spain who entered religious orders. Hence it also acquired an extraordinary collection of works of art – paintings, sculptures, tapestries and *objets d'art* – given as bequests by the novices' families. Equally lavish is the baroque decoration of the building itself, belying its sternly austere façade, with a grand painted staircase, frescoed ceilings and 32 chapels, only some of which can be visited.

The largest non-Spanish contingent in its art collection is Italian, with Titian, Bernardino Luini, Angelo Nardi and Sebastiano del Piombo, and Flemish, with Breughel (an *Adoration of the Magi*), Joos Van Cleve and Rubens. The Descalzas is also an exceptional showcase of Spanish baroque religious art, with works by Gaspar Becerra, Zurbarán, Claudio Coello and even a tiny painting attributed to Goya. In addition, as you walk around you can catch glimpses of the nuns' courtyard vegetable garden, which has remained virtually unchanged since the convent was built, and is closed to the public. The monastery was seen by very few until the 1980s, when it was restored and partially opened as a museum. It can be visited only with official tours, which leave every 20 minutes and last around 50 minutes. Frustratingly, the guides rarely speak English, there is no printed information about the

Walk through Literary Madrid

Duration: 30mins
Walk marked in green on pp313-314.

The cafés, theatres and churches around Plaza Santa Ana (*pictured*), in the Huertas neighbourhood, were the centre of literary life during Spain's 16th- and 17th-century Golden Age.

Begin at the junction of C/Atocha with Costanilla de los Desamparados.

At C/Atocha 87 you will see what used to be the printing press where the first edition of *Don Quixote* was published. This is now the **Museo Cervantino**. See the bronze bas-relief of a scene from the book and, above it, the head of Cervantes.

Walk up Desamparados and turn right down C/Moratín.

At the **Plazuela de San Juan**, look up (above the Jazz Bar) to see the plaque celebrating the poet and playwright Leandro Moratín, who was born here in 1760.

Turn left up C/Jesús and left again on C/Lope de Vega.

The church ahead of the junction, on the right, is the **Iglesia de Jesús de Medinaceli**, famously a 17th-century centre of rumour and gossip, especially when attended by the great actresses of the time. Up on C/Lope de Vega, on the left, is the **Convento de las Trinitarias**, where Cervantes was originally buried (his remains have since disappeared). Every year on the anniversary

of his death, a commemorative mass is held for him and the other great Spanish writers.

Turn right up C/Quevedo.

On the right-hand corner is a plaque marking the house where 17th-century rivals Francisco de Quevedo and Luis de Góngora lived. Quevedo, a satirical writer, made mincemeat of the hapless and terminally ill poet Góngora in an exchange of satirical verse. He also triumphed posthumously, when the council renamed the street after him, omitting to mention Góngora on the plaque. At the end of the street, on C/Cervantes 11, is the brick-fronted house, now the **Casa-Museo de Lope de Vega** (*see p85*), where Lope de Vega lived and died. No.2 on this street was built on the site of Cervantes' old house.

Turn left, and right down C/León to C/Prado.

At No.21 is the Ateneo library, with an impressive marble staircase and walls lined with portraits of Spain's greatest figures. Ask nicely and they will allow you to wander through its delightfully antiquated rooms. Back up C/Prado, you arrive at the Plaza Santa Ana, home to the **Teatro Español** (*see p247*) and many established bars, such as the **Cervecería Alemana** (*see p155*), where writers such as the playwright Ramón del Valle-Inclán and, later, Ernest Hemingway were regulars. The theatre itself sits on the site of one of the great open-air *corral* theatres of the Golden Age.

---

convent, and the paintings are not labelled. It is still an enjoyable place to visit, though, for the sheer sumptuousness of its artworks and fittings.

Gran Vía

The **Plaza de España**, at the western end of the Gran Vía, is dominated by Franco's bombastic architecture. It is flanked by two classic buildings of the type sponsored by the regime when out to impress: the '50s-modern **Torre Madrid** (1957) and the enormous **Edificio España** of 1948-53. The three statues in the middle – of Cervantes, Don Quixote and Sancho Panza – are by Teodoro Anasagasti and Mateo Inurria, from 1928. The square around them is big, noisy and not a particularly relaxing place to sit.

The Gran Vía itself was created in 1910 by slicing through the Old City so that traffic could easily reach Cibeles from C/Princesa. Intended to be a broad modern boulevard, it got grander still when World War I made neutral Madrid a

clearing house for international money. With the economy booming, developers and architects set out to embrace modernity as hard as they could to show that, if you wanted something impressive, they could provide it. In the following decades, each generation added its own stamp and the result is certainly eclectic.

Heading down the Gran Vía, the area north and east of Sol was originally the city's financial district, hence the number of grand edifices owned by banks and insurance companies. Its other great avenue is **C/Alcalá**, which follows the centuries-old main route into Madrid from the east. In the 18th century, when it was lined by aristocratic palaces, it was described as the grandest street in Europe. It is still pretty impressive today, with a wonderful variety of 19th- to early 20th-century buildings, from the dignified 1882 **Banesto** building (corner of C/Sevilla) to the cautiously modernist **Círculo de Bellas Artes** (*see p81*). There are also fine older constructions along the street, such as the austere neo-classical Finance

Facing the theatre, turn left up C/Príncipe.
This street was home to many of the favoured literary haunts of the day, but the only one that remains is **Las Cuevas de Sésamo** at No.7 (*see p231*), worth a visit for the quotes

painted on the walls and the little sheaf of photocopies they will give anyone who's interested in the history of the place.
At Plaza Canalejas turn sharp left down C/Cruz.
C/Victoria on the left has a plaque marking the site of the writers' and politicians' meeting point and subject of Benito Pérez Galdos' eponymous novel, **La Fontana de Oro**. The Irish theme bar built on the site shares the name but little else. Further up C/Cruz is a mural (*pictured*) depicting a reflection of the street behind, and asking 'Where has the theatre gone? Or is the street the theatre?' The theatre question is the **Corral de la Cruz**, another open-air theatre that stood on the site.
Turn left down C/Álvarez Gato, right through the square and continue down C/San Sebastián.
What is now a florist in the little yard on the corner with C/Huertas used to be the graveyard for the adjacent **Iglesia de San Sebastián**; the ancient olive tree remains as a symbol of all the literary luminaries buried there. Opposite the florist's is a plaque showing the site of the **Fonda de San Sebastián** – favoured hangout of the 18th-century writers. Further down, in the church itself, look out for the plaques celebrating all the writers baptised, married or buried here.

Ministry, built as the **Aduana**, or customs administration, by Francesco Sabatini in 1761-9, and, alongside it, the **Real Academia de Bellas Artes de San Fernando** (*see below*). At the point where Alcalá and Gran Vía meet, there is Pedro de Ribera's exuberantly baroque church of **San José** (1730-42), with a plaque inside to commemorate the fact that Simón Bolívar was married here in 1802.

Círculo de Bellas Artes

C/Alcalá 42 & C/Marqués de Casa Riera 2 (91 360 54 00). Metro Banco de España. **Open** *Café* 9am-midnight Mon-Thur; 9am-3am Fri, Sat. *Exhibitions* 11am-2pm, 5-9pm Tue-Sat; 11am-2pm Sun. **Admission** €1. Free 2-4pm Mon-Sat. **Map** p314 G7.
The Círculo de Bellas Artes occupies a superb building, designed by Antonio Palacios and completed in 1926. It is a key player in every aspect of the Madrid arts scene: as well as a beautifully airy main floor café, with a gracious pavement terrace, the Círculo offers a plethora of classes, exhibitions, lectures and concerts in its theatre and concert hall, plus an annual masked ball for carnival.

Museo de la Real Academia de Bellas Artes de San Fernando

C/Alcalá 13 (91 524 08 64/Calcografía Nacional 91 524 08 83). Metro Sevilla or Sol. **Open** 10am-2pm Mon, Sat, Sun; 9am-7pm Tue-Fri. *Calcografía Nacional* 9-2.30pm Mon-Fri. *Temporary exhibitions* 10am-2pm, 5-8pm Tue-Fri; 10am-2pm Sat, Sun. **Admission** €2.40; €1.20 students; free under-18s, over-65s. Free to all Wed. *Calcografía Nacional* free. **No credit cards. Map** p313 F7.
This undervisited museum is in fact one of Madrid's most important and oldest permanent artistic institutions (it was founded in 1794). The eclectic collection is partly made up of works of varying quality donated by aspiring members in order to gain admission to the academy. The museum's greatest possessions, though, are its 13 works by Goya, an important figure in the early years of the Academia. They include two major self-portraits; a portrait of his friend, the playwright Moratin; a portrait of Charles IV's hated minister Godoy; and the *Burial of the Sardine* (*see p192* **In the frame**), a carnival scene that foreshadows his later, darker works. Another of the academy's most prized possessions is the Italian

Real Academia de San Fernando.

This was once the haunt of Madrid's Golden Age literary set (*see p80* **Walk through**), which explains the district's fussy alternative name of Barrio de las Letras ('The District of Letters'). Here were the theatres that provided them with a living, along with whorehouses and low dives for entertainment. It is still the city's most distinctive theatre district. Close by, but not too close, lived the nobles who might have tossed a couple of ducats their way if they buttered them up in a sonnet. Otherwise there were feuds, libellous exchanges and duels to fall back on.

Lope de Vega's charming old house, the **Casa-Museo Lope de Vega** (*see p85*), with its tiny garden, is on the street named after his enemy, Miguel Cervantes, the author of *Don Quixote*. Cervantes lived around the corner on C/León, but was buried in the enclosed convent of the **Trinitarias Descalzas** (the 'Barefoot Trinitarians') on C/Lope de Vega, which seems deliberately confusing. Coming upon the massively plain, slab-like brick walls of the Trinitarias amid the Huertas bars is a great surprise, and gives a vivid impression of what old Madrid must have looked like before the great clear-out of religious houses in the 1830s, of which this is a rare survivor.

A reverential nod is in order to the wonderful **Ateneo** library on C/Prado, the literary and philosophical club that became a cultural institution and has been a major centre of discussion and thought at many times in its history, most notably in the years leading up to the Republic of 1931 (*see p287*). In the old days, Ateneo members could also find any number of cafés nearby with a suitably literary atmosphere. A few of them are still around, such as **El Salón del Prado** (*see p156*).

The **Carrera de San Jerónimo** borders the north of the district. Once part of the Ceremonial Route of the Habsburg and Bourbon monarchs, today it is one of the centres of official Madrid. On one side is the **Congreso de los Diputados**, Spain's parliament building, while opposite is the **Westin Palace** hotel (*see p45*), where politicians go to mingle and relax. Further up the hill is **Lhardy**, the classic Franco-Spanish restaurant founded in 1839 (*see p126*). North of San Jerónimo, behind the Congreso, is the grand 1856 **Teatro de la Zarzuela**, the city's most characterfully distinguished music theatre.

To the south of the Carrera de San Jerónimo several streets run back towards Huertas proper. On C/Echegaray is **Los Gabrieles** (*see p156*), a bar and venue sheathed in perhaps the world's most photographed wall-to-wall tiles. Another beautifully tiled bar, **Viva Madrid** (*see p156*), lies just around the corner on

mannerist Giuseppe Arcimboldo's *Spring (pictured above)*, a playful, surrealistic portrait of a man made up entirely of flowers. It was one of a series on the four seasons painted for Ferdinand I of Austria in 1563: *Summer* and *Winter* are still in Vienna, but the whereabouts of *Autumn* is unknown. There are also important portraits by Velázquez and Rubens, and several paintings by Zurbarán. Among the later works, the best known are some Picasso engravings and a Juan Gris; the most surprising are the colourful fantasies of Múñoz Degrain and the De Chiricoesque work of Julio Romero de Torres. Look out too for Leandro Bassano's superb *La Riva degli Schiavoni*.

The academy also has a valuable collection of plans and drawings, including those of Prado architect Juan de Villanueva, and rare books. In the same building is the Calcografía Nacional, a similarly priceless collection and archive of engraving and fine printing, which has many of the original plates for the great etching series of Goya.

Huertas & Santa Ana

Spain has the greatest number of bars and restaurants per capita of anywhere in the world, and you can get the impression that most of Madrid's are crowded into the wedge-shaped swathe of streets between Alcalá and C/Atocha. Oddly enough, this clearly defined area has an identity problem, for the authorities can never agree on a name; however, if anyone suggests a pub crawl down Huertas, or a jar in Santa Ana, it will always bring you – and several thousand others on any weekend – to the right place.

Sainted love

If you are female and single and happen to be in Madrid on 13 June, you might want to make a discreet pilgrimage to the Ermita de **San Antonio de la Florida** (Paseo de la Florida). This is the feast day of Anthony of Padua, a saint whose many attributes supposedly include the ability to rustle up boyfriends out of thin air – for Madrid girls at least. The tradition was perhaps started by young seamstresses, as the custom is to turn up at the church with a handful of pins. The girls queue up to drop the pins in the font, then stick their hand into the water. The test is whether the pins stick to their hand. If so, love is just around the corner. It's got to be worth a go.

Those of a romantic persuasion could also venture into the **Iglesia de San Antón** (pictured) on C/Hortaleza. If you feel your way through the gloom to the reliquary, you will be rewarded by the sight of what is claimed to be St Valentine's skull in a glass-fronted wooden box. For most people, the experience is spooky rather than sentimental, so perhaps not the best place for declarations of love.

This church is dedicated to Saint Anthony of Egypt, who, like Saint Francis, had quite a way with animals. On 17 January the people of Madrid commemorate this by bringing not only their pets, but also farm animals to the church to be blessed. This causes something of a livestock bottleneck in the narrow, busy C/Hortaleza, as dogs, cats, rabbits, goats, donkeys and pigs wait to enter the church. Not far away, at the **Iglesia de Santa Pascual** on the Paseo de Recoletos, you might catch sight of a famous face slinking in or out. The church contains a figure of Saint Clare, who in recent times has been appointed the patron saint of television. Actors, actresses and stars of reality TV pop in to ask her to help them get the role that will finally make them a household name.

On 27 July, expect to see a very long queue of people if you are in the vicinity of the **Convento de la Encarnación** (*see p79*). The reliquary of this 17th-century convent contains a phial of blood purportedly belonging to Pantaleón, the doctor saint. On his feast day, the dubious contents of the phial miraculously liquefy, which augurs great things for those who witness the event. Yet more expectant queuing goes on every Friday outside the **Iglesia de Jesús de Medinaceli** on Plaza de Jesús. Inside the church is a statue of Jesus of Nazareth that had fallen into the hands of the Moors and was retrieved against all odds by Trinitarian monks in the 17th century. Kissing the statue's foot is believed to be very auspicious. After announcing their engagement in 2003, one of the first things Prince Felipe and his wife-to-be Letizia did was turn up at the church to do just that.

They got married in the **Catedral de la Almudena**, named after a wooden figure now to be found in the crypt. When the Moors arrived in Madrid, they displaced the Visigoths, who, before fleeing, hid the statue in the wall of their fortress, along with two burning candles. A few centuries later, when the Christians regained power, the hiding place was discovered – and guess what? Those candles were still flickering away. This happy event has led to a public holiday on 9 November, something that has kept Almudena as everybody's favourite saint, with no further miracles required.

Walk through Working Madrid

Duration: 30mins
Walk marked in blue on pp313-314.

Tatty, atmospheric Lavapiés shows Madrid's past, present and future. Once the Jewish quarter, long the main working-class area and still home to a large gypsy community, Lavapiés is now the most racially mixed neighbourhood in the city. It has also acquired something of a (sometimes exaggeratedly) bad reputation, but it's generally safe by day.

Begin at Plaza Tirso de Molina.

At its eastern end is the **Teatro Nuevo Apolo**, with a quirky façade that mixes art deco and neo-Mudéjar. On the south side of the plaza is the present headquarters of the CNT anarchist workers' union, a reflection of Lavapiés' long-term association with left-wing politics.

Turn down C/Mesón de Paredes.

The street is named after the long-gone inn of Señor Paredes, inventor of the *emparedado*, a type of sandwich. For refreshment today, there is the historic **Taberna de Antonio Sánchez** at No.13 (*see p147*). Mesón de Paredes once boasted all manner of shops, but nowadays what most strikes the eye is the number of *venta al mayor* (wholesale) signs, indicating shops offering a wide range of bargain-basement jackets, T-shirts, jewellery and other accessories, and mostly Chinese-run.

Turn right down C/Abades and left on C/Embajadores.

'Ambassadors Street' was so named because all Madrid's foreign embassies were moved here during a 17th-century outbreak of the plague. Just by the corner of C/Oso, amid the urban disorder, there is the baroque church of **San Cayetano**, built by a variety of architects, including Ribera and Churriguera, between 1678 and 1761. Despite the many hands involved in its construction, its façade is one of the most finely worked in Madrid. Opposite, a plaque recalls that this was the house of the great architect Pedro de Ribera himself, during the 1730s.

Turn left at C/Sombrerete.

'Little Hat Street' was named after the hat in which a Portuguese monk, Miguel dos Santos, was paraded through the streets before being hanged in the 16th century. He had been accused of acting as accomplice to a pastry chef, Gabriel de Espinosa, who claimed to be the missing heir to the

Portuguese throne. After the hanging, the hat was left on a muck heap in this street. Where the street opens out to become the **Plaza Agustín Lara** are the ruins of the 18th-century church and school of the **Escuelas Pías de San Fernando**, destroyed in the Civil War, and now being built up into a library. Facing the ruins across from C/Mesón de Paredes is Madrid's most famous *corrala* tenement block (*see p86*).

Continue to Plaza de Lavapiés.

A former stamping ground for the *majos* and *majas* (*see p15* **In the frame**), and once the centre of the Jewish neighbourhood, the Plaza has a scruffy appeal. From here runs **C/Argumosa**, broad and tree-lined and lined with pavement cafés.

At the far end, turn left into C/Doctor Fourquet.

Home to several art galleries, especially the highly respected **Helga de Alvear**, this street also leads conveniently to C/Santa Isabel and the **Reina Sofía**.

C/Manuel Fernández y González, while the nearby **Villa Rosa** on C/Nuñez de Arce also has an impressive tiled exterior.

Last, but in no way least, there is the core of the district, **Plaza Santa Ana**. Like Plaza de Oriente, this popular square was bequeathed to Madrid by poor, unappreciated Joseph Bonaparte, who tore down yet another convent to do so. Somebody should thank him: lined by some of the city's most popular bars and pavement terraces, Santa Ana has long been one of Madrid's favourite places for hanging out for an entire afternoon or three. On the eastern side of the plaza is the distinguished **Teatro Español**, on a site that has been a theatre continuously since 1583, when the Corral del Príncipe opened its doors to the *mosqueteros*, a heckling mob whose reactions were so violent, they sometimes forced terrified playwrights to change plots mid-play.

Casa-Museo Lope de Vega

C/Cervantes 11 (91 429 92 16). Metro Antón Martín. **Open** 9.30am-2pm Tue-Fri; 10am-2pm Sat. Closed Aug. **Admission** €2; €1 students, over-65s. Free to all Sat. **No credit cards. Map** p314 G8.
Spain's most prolific playwright and poet, Félix Lope de Vega Carpio (1562-1635) spent the last 25 years of his life in this simple, tranquil three-storey house, oddly enough on a street now named after his rival Cervantes (who, confusingly, is buried in a convent on the nearby C/Lope de Vega). The house and charming garden – remarkable survivors from the Golden Age – are the most interesting things to see. The furniture and ornaments, obtained from a variety of sources, are approximations to Lope de Vega's household inventory rather than the originals. However, even the garden, where Lope would sit after a day's writing, contains the same fruit trees and plants he detailed in his journals. The house can be visited with guided tours. Some guides speak English; call in advance to check.

Colección Permanente del Instituto de Crédito Oficial (ICO)

C/Zorrilla 3 (91 420 12 42/www.ico.es). Metro Banco de España. **Open** 11am-2pm Tue-Sat; 10am-2pm Sun. **Admission** free. **Map** p314 G7.
This small museum is run by the ICO, a state credit bank. Its collection has three main parts: most important is Picasso's *Suite Vollard* series, a milestone in 20th-century prints, dating from 1927 to 1937. There is also a fine selection of modern Spanish sculpture and some international painting from the 1980s.

Congreso de los Diputados (Las Cortes)

Plaza de las Cortes (91 390 65 25/6). Metro Banco de España or Sevilla. **Open** *Guided tours* 10.30am-12.30pm Sat. Closed Aug. **Admission** free. **Map** p314 G7.

Spain's parliament, the Cortes, was built in 1843-50 by Narciso Pascual y Colomer on the site of a recently demolished monastery, which has led to no end of problems, as the plot is too cramped to accommodate the legislators' ancillary offices. A classical portico gives it a suitably dignified air, but the building is best distinguished by the handsome 1860 bronze lions that guard its entrance. Tourists are welcome on the popular free Saturday guided tours. Given demand, it's best to phone ahead; groups of more than 15 can also book to visit on weekdays.

Lavapiés

South of Sol and the Plaza Mayor is the area traditionally considered the home of Madrid's *castizos*. *Castizos* are something like London's East End cockneys: rough-diamond chirpy types straight out of a Spanish *My Fair Lady*. Many of them materialise round here in best bib and tucker – cloth caps for the men; long, frilly dresses for the ladies – for the city's summer festivals. Since the end of the '90s, however, Lavapiés has taken on a new characteristic: as a big recipient of non-Spanish immigration – from China, Pakistan, North and West Africa – it is becoming the city's most multicultural neighbourhood.

These districts have always been the kind of place where newcomers to the city could find a niche. Historically they were known as the *barrios bajos*, in the double sense of low-lying and full of low life – the closer to the river, the shabbier the surroundings. In imperial Madrid, most of the food brought to the city came in through the **Puerta de Toledo** (*see p87*), and many of the tasks that the upper classes wanted neither to see nor smell, such as slaughtering and tanning, were concentrated here. Consequently, these districts became home to Madrid's first native working class. In the 18th century the *majos* and *majas* from these streets were admired by the intelligentsia for their caustic wit (for Goya's portraits of them, *see p15* **In the frame**), perhaps sowing the seed for the *castizo* tradition.

On the eastern edge of La Latina is the **Rastro**, Madrid's time-honoured Sunday flea market. It runs all the way down Ribera de Curtidores to the Ronda de Toledo from **Plaza Cascorro**, with its monument honouring a young soldier raised in a nearby orphanage, who volunteered for a suicide mission in Cuba in the 1890s. A true cultural phenomenon, the Rastro is also a district with a strong identity, moulded by centuries of acting as an emporium for goods of all kinds. The market is a social experience more than a shopping destination, but look out for the pickpockets. For more on the Rastro, *see p181*.

Sightseeing

If, on the other hand, instead of trying to make your way down the Rastro, you head from Plaza Cascorro slightly eastwards down **C/Embajadores**, you will enter Lavapiés proper. Because of the rapid changes in the area, Lavapiés is sometimes portrayed, in local conversations and the press, as an urban crisis zone to be avoided. This is one of the areas with a high incidence of petty crime, commonly associated with gangs of North African boys living on the streets, who have especially bad relations with the local Chinese shopkeepers. However, these images have a tendency to get out of proportion: there are places in Lavapiés it's probably best to steer clear of (the small square halfway down Mesón de Paredes, by C/Cabestreros, is the most obvious example), but it would be a shame if this led anyone to avoid the whole neighbourhood, for this web of sloping, winding streets remains one of the most characterful parts of Old Madrid.

Plaza Tirso de Molina, with its statue of the Golden Age dramatist whose name it bears, is the main crossroads between these *barrios bajos* and the city centre proper. From here C/Mesón de Paredes, which is one of the two main arteries of historic Lavapiés (the other is C/Embajadores), winds off down the hill. Along Mesón de Paredes today there are still

A young martyr in **Plaza Cascorro**. *See p85.*

some of Madrid's most historic *tabernas*, but they stand next to shops selling tropical fruit, Moroccan tea houses, halal butchers, African fabric stores and any number of Chinese-owned wholesale stores selling discount jewellery and T-shirts.

Also on Mesón de Paredes, near the bottom by C/Sombrerete, is **La Corrala**, the city's best surviving example of an 1880s courtyard tenement, garnished – as tradition dictates – with freshly washed sheets and underwear billowing from the balconies. After the demolition of Madrid's monasteries in the mid 19th century, many streets in these districts were rebuilt with these distinctive, open-balconied tenements. *Corralas* always faced an inner patio, multiplying noise and lack of privacy, factors of urban life that luckily have rarely bothered Spaniards. The *corrala* has become a characteristic of neighbourhood life; this one, restored in the 1980s, is used in summer as a setting for a season of *zarzuela* comic operas. A later *corrala*, not easily visible from the street, is at C/Embajadores 60. At the bottom of this area is a dynamic new exhibition space and cultural centre, **La Casa Encendida** (*see p87*).

The **Plaza de Lavapiés** is believed to have been the centre of Madrid's medieval Jewish community, expelled, like all others in her dominions, by the very pious Queen Isabella in 1492. Today the recently renovated square has several good cafés and restaurants. The narrow, very steep streets between the plaza and C/Atocha are much more tranquil than those around Mesón de Paredes, and, with exuberant boxes of geraniums on virtually every balcony, often strikingly pretty. Despite all the changes in the area, these closely packed streets of old apartments, shops and small workshops still convey the essence of a very distinctive urban way of life. At the top of the area by C/Atocha is the **Filmoteca Española** film theatre, in the old Cine Doré (*see p202*).

Running away from the south-east corner of the Plaza de Lavapiés is **C/Argumosa**, known as the 'Costa Argumosa', with more shops plus restaurants and outdoor-terrace bars that make a popular summer alternative to more expensive and more hectic places further into town. Argumosa leads towards Atocha and the **Centro de Arte Reina Sofía**, the opening of which has led to the appearance nearby of attractive one-off shops and galleries. Close by, filling a big stretch of C/Santa Isabel, is the 17th-century **Convento de Santa Isabel**, sponsored, like the Encarnación, by Margaret of Austria, wife of Philip III, and one of the largest religious houses to escape the liberals' axe in the 1830s.

La Casa Encendida, home to performances throughout the year.

La Casa Encendida

Ronda de Valencia 2 (91 508 38 75/www.lacasa encendida.com). Metro Embajadores. **Open** 10am-10pm daily. **Admission** free. **Map** p313 E10.

This exciting new multidisciplinary centre in a large neo-Mudéjar building was conceived as a space for cultural interchange. Spread over four floors, the 'Burning House' is directed by José Guirao, former director of the Reina Sofía. It offers exhibitions principally by emerging artists working in all genres, but also features cutting-edge performance art and music (including short seasons of video artists) and activities for kids. The centre also includes a fairtrade shop, a library and classrooms for courses in, above all, IT and languages.

Puerta de Toledo

Glorieta de la Puerta de Toledo. Metro Puerta de Toledo. **Map** p312 C10.

Slightly swallowed up in the traffic at the meeting point of the Old City and the roads in from the southwest, this neo-classical gate was one of the monuments commissioned by Napoleon's brother Joseph in his brief span as King of Spain. After his departure it was rejigged to honour the delegates from the Cortes in Cádiz, and then King Fernando VII.

North of Gran Vía

Chueca

The neighbourhood of Chueca, bounded by the Gran Vía, C/Fuencarral and the Paseo de Recoletos, has been through several transformations. In the 18th century C/Hortaleza was the site of the Recogida, a refuge for 'public sinners', where women could be confined for soliciting on the street or merely on the say-so of a male family member. Release was only possible through marriage or a lifetime tour of duty in a convent. In the 19th century Chueca became a more respectable, affluent district, but by the 1970s and early '80s it had turned into a shabby, declining area. Since then, though, it has undergone a spectacular revival, due, above all, to it having become the gay centre of Madrid.

The epicentre of the scene is **Plaza de Chueca**; its terraces are packed with buzzing crowds on hot summer nights, and the only limitation on the scene could be whether the plaza can actually hold any more people. On the back of the gay scene, many more restaurants, trendy shops, cafés and clubs have opened up, and Fuencarral, the borderline between Chueca and Malasaña, is now the heart of Madrid's club-fashion scene. Many gay venues have acquired a fashionable crossover status among the hip non-gay crowd (to the extent that some gays now find some Chueca clubs too 'diluted'). Whatever, Chueca has established itself as a booming free zone for socialising of all kinds, gay and heterosexual.

The north side of the district, above C/Fernando VI, is not really Chueca proper and is often known as **Alonso Martínez**, after the metro station. It's not so much part of 'gay Chueca' either, although it too has many new restaurants and bars. Instead, it's one of the foremost preserves of Madrid's teen scene. Streets such as Fernando VI or C/Campamor and Plaza Santa Bárbara are lined with bars and clubs catering to a young crowd, and on weekend nights the roads are packed too, with noisy (but safe) crowds of kids. Just west of here are the city's history museum, the **Museo Municipal**, and the **Museo Romántico** (for both, *see p88*), closed until 2006.

Plaza de Chueca. *See p87.*

Towards Recoletos, Chueca also becomes more commercial and more upmarket by day. C/Barquillo is full of electrical shops, while C/Almirante and its cross-street C/Conde de Xiquena are important fashion shopping zones. Off Almirante in C/Tamayo y Baus is one of Madrid's most important theatres, the **Teatro María Guerrero**.

This area is also part of official Madrid, with the giant **Palacio de Justicia** on C/Bárbara de Braganza. It was formerly the Convento de las Salesas, built in 1750-58 under the patronage of Queen Bárbara, wife of Fernando VI. It has housed law courts since 1870. Its refined classical baroque contrasts nicely with the art nouveau of the **Palacio Longoria**, a few streets away. To the south of Chueca, towards C/Alcalá, there is an isolated relic of Philip II's Madrid, the **Plaza del Rey** and venerable 1580s **Casa de las Siete Chimeneas**, originally designed by Juan de Herrera, architect of El Escorial.

Museo Municipal

C/Fuencarral 78 (91 588 86 72/www.munimadrid. es/museomunicipal). Metro Tribunal. **Open** *Sept-July* 9.30am-8pm Tue-Fri; 10am-2pm Sat, Sun. *Aug* 9.30am-2.30pm Tue-Fri; 10am-2pm Sat, Sun. **Admission** free. **Map** p310 G4.
Until the end of 2006 at the earliest, only part of this museum is open, owing to thorough renovation

work. The building itself boasts an exuberantly ornate entrance by Pedro de Ribera, one of the finest examples of baroque architecture in Madrid, and worth seeing in itself. In the part that is open there is an exhibition, 'Madrid Ciudad', that comprises the best of the museum's collections of artefacts dating from Habsburg times through to the 19th century. For pre-Habsburg Madrid, visit the Museo de San Isidro (*see p73*).

Museo Romántico

C/San Mateo 13 (91 445 64 02/www.mec.es). Metro Tribunal. **Closed for renovation. Map** p310 G4.
Closed at least until mid or late 2006, the Romántico contains a charming collection of furniture, paintings, ornaments, early pianos and other pieces that evoke the Romantic period of 19th-century Spain. Phone the above number or check the website for details of when it will reopen.

Sociedad General de Autores (Palacio Longoria)

C/Fernando VI, 4 (91 349 95 50). Metro Alonso Martínez. **Map** p310 G4.
Given the extraordinary output of Catalan *modernista* architects such as Gaudí in Barcelona in the early 20th century, it is remarkable, to non-Spaniards at least, that there is not a single example of their work in Madrid. The only thing at all like it is this building in Chueca, designed by José Grasés Riera in 1902 as a residence for banker Javier González Longoria. The façade looks as if it was formed out of

wet sand, moulded by an expert in giant cake decoration – if a building could be considered voluptuous, this would be it. It was once thought that Catalan architecture influenced Grasés, but Héctor Guimard and French art nouveau seem to have been a more direct inspiration. It is now owned by the Spanish writers' and artists' association.

Malasaña & Conde Duque

By day, Malasaña, between C/Fuencarral and San Bernardo, still has a quiet neighbourhood feel, with grannies watering their geraniums on wrought-iron balconies and idiosyncratic corner shops. By night, though, this is long been an epicentre of Madrid's bar culture. It's nothing like as trendy or as adventurous as Chueca, though; rather, Malasaña is still associated with laid-back cafés, rock bars and cheap, grungy, student socialising.

On 2 May 1808 this area was the centre of resistance to the French. The name of the district comes from a 17-year-old seamstress heroine, Manuela Malasaña, shot by the invaders for carrying concealed weapons (her scissors) or ammunition to the Spanish troops – there are various versions of her exploits. The name of the main square, **Plaza Dos de Mayo**, also recalls that day. Where the square is today was then the Monteleón artillery barracks, from where the artillery captains Daoíz and Velarde galvanised the resistance of the people. The last remaining part of the barracks, a gate, stands in the square with a monument to the two men.

The area gained a tough reputation in the 1980s, when used needles and broken bottles used to litter the plaza in the mornings, but urban renovation schemes have been most successful. It is now one of the centres of the San Isidro festivals in May, hosting nightly concerts, fairs and outdoor parties.

The streets between Fuencarral and San Bernardo abound with great cafés, bars and restaurants. There are also indications – such as the broad-arched doorways for carriages – that the 19th-century well-to-do once lived here. One of the most rewarding streets is **C/San Vicente Ferrer**, with jewellery shops and a delightful 1920s tile display advertising the long-defunct pharmacy Laboratorios Juanse. Other old ceramic signs on the **C/San Andrés** feature a little boy signalling that his chamber pot is full, and a dramatic, reclining vamp. C/de la Palma and C/Divino Pastor, with craft and jewellery shops, are equally worth a stroll. To the north is Glorieta de Bilbao, site of one of Madrid's best traditional cafés, the **Café Comercial** (*see p163*).

The atmosphere gets more lively as you approach the streets near Fuencarral that lead down to the Gran Vía, such as **Corredera Baja de San Pablo**. This is an area of cheap restaurants, wholesale produce dealers in white aprons, shops selling nothing but light bulbs and working-class people who have known each

Plaza Dos de Mayo, where heroism has given way to heroin.

Sightseeing

other all their lives. Recent additions are club-style fashion shops, especially towards or on C/Fuencarral. At the corner of the Corredera Baja and C/Ballesta there is an unusual brick church, built by Philip III for his Portuguese subjects in Madrid. Later it was set aside for German Catholic émigrés, and is still known as **San Antonio de los Alemanes**. It is rarely open to visitors. Just a block away along C/Pez, often unnoticed amid the shops, bars and theatres that surround it, is the slab-walled convent of **San Plácido**, another of Madrid's surviving religious houses. Down where C/Fuencarral meets Gran Vía is the **Fundación Telefónica** exhibition space.

The area west of C/San Bernardo is most commonly known as **Conde Duque**, after its finest monument, the **Centro Cultural Conde Duque**, which occupies the giant barracks (*cuartel*) built in 1717-54 by Pedro de Ribera for King Philip V's royal guard. It was wonderfully renovated by the Tierno Galván city council in the 1980s as an arts centre (*see below*). Nearby is the **Museo Municipal de Arte Contemporáneo** (*see below*), and slightly hidden next to it is one of Madrid's least-seen treasures, the **Palacio de Liria**.

Centro Cultural Conde Duque

C/Conde Duque 11 (91 588 58 34/www.muni madrid.es). Metro Noviciado or Ventura Rodríguez. **Open** *Sept-June* 10am-2pm, 5.30-9pm Tue-Sat; 10.30am-2.30pm Sun. *July-Aug* 10am-9pm Tue-Sat; 11am-3pm Sun. **Admission** free. **Map** p309 D3.
Housed in a former barracks, built in the 18th century for Philip V's guard by Pedro de Ribera, the magnificently restored Conde Duque is a multipurpose cultural centre. Around a dozen shows, both artistic and historical, are held annually in the two exhibition spaces and the two vast patios. Open-air concerts in summer bring in a range of performers. Also housed here are the city's newspaper and video libraries, as well as the Museo Municipal de Arte Contemporáneo (*see below*), which opened in 2001.

Fundación Telefónica

C/Fuencarral 3 (91 531 29 70/www.fundacion. telefonica.com/arte_tecnologia). Metro Gran Vía. **Open** 10am-2pm, 5-8pm Tue-Fri; 10am-2pm Sat, Sun. Closed Aug. **Admission** free. **Map** p313 E6.
Run by Telefónica, the national telephone company, this foundation functions on several levels. The Museo de las Telecomunicaciones is a permanent exhibition illustrating the history of telecommunications. Another large space is used to display selections from its permanent collection of Spanish art, including various works by Eduardo Chillida, Luis Fernández, Miró, Picasso and Tàpies and it also has a permanent show based around post-Civil War Spanish artists of the so-called Madrid and Paris schools, the latter in exile. Temporary exhibitions feature both the arts and technology.

Museo Municipal de Arte Contemporáneo

C/Conde Duque 9 (91 588 58 61). Metro Noviciado. **Open** 10am-2pm, 5.30-9pm Tue-Sat; 10.30am-2.30pm Sun. **Admission** free. **Map** p309 D4.
Madrid city council's contemporary art collection has an emphasis on painting and graphic work, but with a significant presence of sculpture, photography and drawing too. The first floor is arranged so as to relate works and artists of different generations and media to show the plurality of Madrid's art scene. Some of the highlights include work by Eduardo Arroyo, Ouka Lele, Eduardo Úrculo, Jorge Oteiza and Eva Lootz.

Palacio de Liria

C/Princesa 20 (91 547 53 02/fax 91 541 03 77). Metro Ventura Rodríguez. **Open** *Guided tours* 10am, 11am, noon Fri. Booking essential. Closed July-Oct. **Admission** free. **Map** p309 D3.
This sober, neo-classical palace, completed in 1783 and refurbished in the 1910s by Edwin Lutyens, is still very much the private property of Spain's premier aristocrat, the Duchess of Alba. The extraordinary collection includes work by Rembrandt, Palma Vecchio, Titian and Rubens, and one of the most important Goyas in private hands: his portrait of an earlier Duchess of Alba in red and white. The problem is, the current duchess has no need to open her palace to public view. Space on the Friday guided tours has to be requested several weeks in advance.

Tiling in **Malasaña**.

Salamanca
& the Retiro

From Prada to Prado.

Palacio de Comunicaciones. *See 94*.

Salamanca is an area best known for its designer shopping and the futuristic architecture along its Paseo de la Castellana, but the area is also home to some of the city's most fascinating small museums. South of here the Retiro is a verdant oasis of entirely old-fashioned delights: a boating lake, puppet shows and old men playing dominoes under the plane trees. Linking the two areas are wide boulevards, adorned with handsome statues, inspiring fountains and three of the greatest museums in the world.

Salamanca

In the mid 19th century, as it became evident that Spanish cities needed to expand beyond their old walls, attempts were made to ensure that this happened in an orderly way. Madrid and Barcelona had plans approved for *ensanches* ('extensions'). Carlos María de Castro's 1860 plan for Madrid envisaged the expansion of the city north and east in a regular grid pattern, with restrictions on building height and public open spaces at regular intervals within each block to ensure a healthy, harmonious landscape. The problem, however, was that for a good while few members of Madrid's middle classes seemed to have the money or motivation to invest in such a scheme, and they preferred to stay within the cramped, noisy Old City. That Madrid's *ensanche* got off the ground at all was due to a banker, politician and speculator notorious for his dubious business practices, the Marqués de Salamanca.

The marquis had previously built his own vast residence, now the **Banco Hipotecario**, on Paseo de Recoletos in 1846-50. He spent one of the several fortunes he made and lost in his lifetime building a first line of rectangular blocks along C/Serrano, from C/Goya up to Ramón de la Cruz. However, his ambitions overstretched his resources, the apartments proved expensive for local buyers, and he went terminally bankrupt in 1867. Nevertheless, it is to the rogue Marqués, not the old Castilian university town, that Madrid's smartest *barrio* owes its name.

It was only after the Restoration of 1874 that Madrid's wealthier citizens really began to appreciate the benefits of wider streets and residences with more class than the musty old neighbourhoods could supply. Once the idea caught on, the exodus proceeded apace, and the core of Salamanca was built up by 1900. The wealthiest families of all built individual palaces along the lower stretch of Castellana, in a wild variety of styles – French imperial, Italian Renaissance, neo-Mudéjar. The block on C/Juan Bravo between Calles Lagasca and Velázquez contains a magnificent example:

the neo-baroque palace of the **Marqueses de Amboage**, now the Italian Embassy. From the C/Velázquez side it's possible to get a good view of the extraordinarily lush gardens. Other mansions are scattered around the district, tucked in between apartment blocks. Those who could not quite afford their own mansion moved into giant mansions in the streets behind. The area has been the centre of conservative, affluent Madrid ever since.

Salamanca is a busy area, with streets that often boom with traffic, and so the best time to explore it is Saturday morning, when the shops are open but traffic has slackened. Streets such as Calles Jorge Juan, Ortega y Gasset, Goya and Juan Bravo yield top designers, art galleries and dealers in French wines, English silver or superior leather goods. Salamanca also has its own social scene, based around C/Juan Bravo, with shiny, smart bars and discos. Towards the east end of C/Goya there is a slightly more affordable shopping area; on the very eastern flank of Salamanca is Madrid's temple of bullfighting, **Las Ventas**; and south of here is the little numismatic **Museo Casa de la Moneda** (*see below*).

Art buffs are advised to head for the marble tower with sculpture garden at C/Castelló 77, base for the **Fundación Juan March**'s first-rate collection of modern art, which also hosts great contemporary art shows and free classical concerts (*see below*). For private art galleries, C/Claudio Coello, parallel to C/Serrano, is the city's most elegant centre. At the north end of Serrano is the eclectic **Museo Lázaro Galdiano** (*see p93*).

The blocks of Serrano, Claudio Coello and Lagasca below C/Ortega y Gasset are the oldest part of Salamanca, the first section built up by the Marqués in the 1860s. Streets here are narrower, traffic less intense and shops closer together, making the area more amenable for strolling, browsing and snacking. There are charming buildings with intriguing details – such as the glass-galleried block on the corner of Claudio Coello and C/Ayala. The block between Claudio Coello and Lagasca on C/Ayala also contains the **Mercado de la Paz**, Salamanca's excellent market.

Fundación La Caixa

C/Serrano 60 (91 426 02 02). Metro Serrano. **Open** 11am-8pm Mon, Wed-Sat; 11am-2.30pm Sun. **Admission** free. **Map** p311 I3.
Run by La Caixa, a Catalan savings bank, this space has rightly won praise for the quality of its exhibitions. Over the last couple of years shows have featured art and artefacts of the Nubian people, the Greek artist Nikos Navridis and never-before-seen photographs by the Catalan intellectual and US resident Josep Alemany.

Fundación Juan March

C/Castelló 77 (91 435 42 40/www.march.es). Metro Núñez de Balboa. **Open** *Mid Sept-mid June* 11am-8pm Mon-Sat; 10am-2pm Sun. *Mid June-July, first 2wks Sept* 10am-2.30pm daily. Closed Aug. **Admission** free. **Map** p311 K2.
This cultural foundation, set up by the wealthy financier Juan March in 1955, is one of the most important in Europe. Every year, two or three major exhibitions are held here, and a selection of the foundation's own collection of 1,300 works of contemporary Spanish art is also on permanent display. 'Turner and the Sea', 'Kandinsky, the Origin of Abstraction' and the Louvre's Rothschild Collection have been the most recent shows. 'Figures of Modern France' will run until January 2005. Free concerts, held at midday, are also worth checking out.

Museo Arqueológico Nacional

C/Serrano 13 (91 577 79 12/www.man.es). Metro Serrano. **Open** 9.30am-8.30pm Tue-Sat; 9.30am-2.30pm Sun. **Admission** €3.01; €1.50 students; free under-18s, over-65s. Free to all 2.30-8.30pm Sat & all Sun. **No credit cards. Map** p310 I5.
One of Madrid's oldest museums, dating back to 1867, this shares the same building as the Biblioteca Nacional and Museo del Libro. It traces the evolution of human cultures, from prehistoric times up to the 15th century, and the collection of artefacts includes finds from the Iberian, Celtic, Greek, Egyptian, Punic, Roman, Paleochristian, Visigothic and Muslim cultures. Remarkably, the great majority of pieces came from excavations carried out within Spain, illustrating the extraordinary continuity and diversity of human settlement in the Iberian peninsula. To tour the whole museum in chronological order, begin in the basement, which holds palaeontological material such as skulls, tombs and a mammoth's tusks, still attached to its skull. Some of the most interesting relics are from the area around Madrid, such as the many 4,000-year-old neolithic bell-shaped pottery bowls. The first floor holds the museum's most famous possession, the *Dama de Elche*, the intricate stone bust of an Iberian priestess, believed to date from 500BC. Further up, the usual definition of archaeology is stretched somewhat to include interesting exhibitions on post-Roman Visigothic and Muslim Spain, with wonderful ceramics and fine metalwork from Moorish Andalucia. After that there is a whole series of rooms dedicated to pieces from the Middle Ages and later eras. In the garden, steps lead underground to a reproduction of the renowned Altamira prehistoric cave paintings in Cantabria.

Museo Casa de la Moneda

C/Dr Esquerdo 36 (91 566 65 44/www.fnmt.es/ museo). Metro O'Donnell. **Open** *Sept-July* 10am-2.30pm, 5-7.30pm Tue-Fri; 10am-2pm Sat, Sun. *Aug* 10am-2pm Mon-Fri. **Admission** free.
This museum for enthusiasts of philately and numismatics boasts a huge collection, dating from the 18th century, that is among the most important

Museo Lázaro Galdiano.

in the world. The history of coins is represented in chronological order, and complemented by various displays of seals, bank notes, engravings, rare books and medals, plus around 10,000 16th- to 18th-century sketches and drawings from Spain, Italy and Flanders. Recent acquisitions include the die in which the last peseta coins were cast and examples of the last print-run of 10,000 peseta notes. Temporary shows, such as the recent 'Coins of Islam', are often fascinating.

Museo Lázaro Galdiano

C/Serrano 122 (91 561 60 84/www.flg.es). Metro Gregorio Marañón. **Open** 10am-4pm Mon, Wed-Sun. **Admission** €4; €3 concessions. Free to all Wed. **No credit cards. Map** p311 J1.
This unjustifiably little-known museum holds the extraordinarily eclectic collection of 15,000 paintings and *objets d'art*, covering 24 centuries, that was accumulated over 70 years by the financier and bibliophile José Lázaro Galdiano (1862-1947). Its holdings include paintings by Goya and Bosch, an important collection of work from the Dutch and English schools, and some wonderful Renaissance ornamental metalwork. The four-storey mansion and its gardens are a sight in themselves.

Plaza de Toros de Las Ventas

C/Alcalá 237 (91 356 22 00/museum 91 725 18 57). Metro Ventas. **Open** (Museum) *Nov-Feb* 9.30am-2.30pm Mon-Fri. *Mar-Oct* 9.30am-2.30pm Tue-Fri; 10am-1pm Sun. **Admission** (Museum) free.
More than 22,000 spectators can catch a bullfight in this, Spain's largest arena, completed in 1929. Like most early 20th-century bullrings, it is in neo-Mudéjar style, with much use of ceramic tiles in a design that could almost be called playful. Around it there is ample open space to accommodate the crowds and food vendors, so it's easy to get a good look at the exterior. It's not necessary to go to a *corrida* to see the ring from within. When the bulls are

back on the ranch concerts are often held here, and alongside the ring there is the Museo Taurino. The museum holds sculptures and portraits of famous matadors, as well as *trajes de luces* (suits of lights), including the pink-and-gold outfit worn by the legendary Manolete on the afternoon of his death in the ring in 1947 (alongside the blood-transfusion equipment that was used in attempts to save him). Among the 18th-century paintings is a portrait of *torero* Joaquín Rodriguez Costillares, once thought to be by Goya but now labelled as anonymous.

Plaza de Cibeles

Midway between the Puerta del Sol and the Retiro park, this four-way intersection and its statue and fountain signify Madrid to Spaniards as much as the Eiffel Tower or the Empire State Building identify their particular cities. It is surrounded by some of the capital's most prominent buildings: the **Palacio de Comunicaciones** (*see p94*) or post office – housing the tiny **Museo Postal y Telegráfico**, the **Banco de España** (for both, *see below*), the **Palacio Buenavista** (now the Army headquarters) and the **Palacio de Linares**, which now houses the **Casa de América** (*see p95*). The Ventura Rodriguez statue in the middle is of Cybele, the Roman goddess of fertility and symbol of natural abundance, on a chariot drawn by lions. The goddess and the fountain around her have traditionally been the gathering point for victorious Real Madrid fans (Atlético supporters soak themselves in the fountain of Neptune, by the Thyssen museum) and the place where wins by the Spanish national football team have been celebrated.

Banco de España

Plaza de Cibeles. Metro Banco de España. **Map** p314 G7.
This grandiose pile was designed in 1882 by Eduardo Adaro and Severiano Saínz de la Lastra to house the Bank of Spain. The eclectic style was most influenced by French Second Empire designs, with a few Viennese touches. The decorative arched window and elaborate clock above the main entrance are best appreciated from a distance.

Museo Postal y Telegráfico

Palacio de Comunicaciones, C/Montalbán (91 396 20 00/www.correos.es). Metro Banco de España. **Open** 9am-2pm, 5-7pm Mon-Fri; 10am-1.30pm Sat. **Admission** free. **Map** p314 H7.
This small museum contains a huge wealth of stamps from all over the world. There are also exhibits on the history of the mail and telecommunications networks, including a mock-up of the Hispasat satellite, antique switchboards, Morse-code machines, postmen's uniforms, post horns, bicycles, seals, scales and 19th-century lion's-head letterboxes.

Sightseeing

Palacio de Comunicaciones

Plaza de Cibeles (91 521 65 00). Metro Banco de España. **Open** 8.30am-9.30pm Mon-Fri; 8.30am-2pm Sat. **Map** p314 H7.

Newcomers to Madrid find it hard to believe that this extraordinary construction, dwarfing the Plaza de Cibeles and regularly compared to a sandcastle or a wedding cake, could be just a post office (though this is set to change if the city council has its way). It was designed in 1904 by Antonio Palacios and Joaquín Otamendi. Completed in 1918, it is the best example of the extravagant style favoured by Madrid's elite at its most expensive. The design was influenced by Viennese art nouveau, but it also features many traditional Spanish touches, with a grand entrance (complete with oversized revolving door), a Hollywood film-set staircase, soaring ceilings, stunning columns and grand marble floors.

Paseo de Recoletos

While other cities have rivers cutting through them as navigational points of reference, Madrid has two great avenues: the Gran Vía and its continuation, C/Alcalá, running east–west, and the **Paseo de la Castellana** – which becomes the **Paseo de Recoletos** and the **Paseo del Prado** as it runs north–south. The leg that runs north of Cibeles, Paseo de Recoletos, was mostly added in the 1830s and '40s. The Palacio de Linares, now the **Casa de América** (*see p95*), is perhaps the best preserved of the palaces built by wealthy families after the Restoration. The curiously grand marble palace a little further north on the right, now the **Banco Hipotecario**, was once the residence of the Marqués de Salamanca, 19th-century Madrid's huckster-in-chief (*see p91*). It famously had the first flushing toilets in Madrid, an amenity the marquis later offered to residents in his new housing developments.

At the north end of Recoletos, on the right, stands the huge building housing the **Biblioteca Nacional** and, behind it, the **Museo Arqueológico Nacional** (*see p92*). The most ambitious project of the reign of Isabel II, the building was commissioned in 1865, but only completed in 1892. It overlooks

Architecture at a glance

Mudéjar

For centuries after their 'reconquest', Madrid continued to have large populations of Muslims living under Christian rule, the Mudéjares. The Castilian monarchs were greatly in thrall to their superior building skills, especially bricklaying and tiling, and throughout the Middle Ages many of the country's most important buildings incorporated their techniques. Hallmarks of the style are Moorish arches and intricate geometric patterns in brickwork, as seen on the 12th-century tower of Madrid's oldest surviving church, **San Nicolás de los Servitas**. Madrid's other Mudéjar tower, on **San Pedro el Viejo**, was built 200 years later. Other medieval buildings in Madrid, such as the 15th-century **Torre de los Lujanes** in Plaza de la Villa, were much plainer in style, reflecting the town's humble status before 1561.

Herreran or 'Court' style

As royal seat, the tastes of successive rulers were especially important for the city. Philip II's favourite architect, Juan de Herrera, was the first to leave a stamp on the city. His major constructions, such as the **Puente de Segovia** (1584) and the first stages of the **Plaza Mayor**, gave Madrid a shape that lasts to this day. **El Escorial** (*see p255*), designed

The art nouveau **Palacio Longoria**. *See p96.*

the **Plaza de Colón**, where, at Columbus's feet, a cascading wall of water, beautifully cooling in summer, conceals the entrance to the **Centro Cultural de la Villa** arts centre (*see below*). Controversial plans recently drawn up for the area include moving Columbus to the centre of the roundabout, losing the famous waterfall and instead enclosing the entrance to the Centro Cultural in an enormous glass 'egg'.

Casa de América

Palacio de Linares, Paseo de Recoletos 2 (91 595 48 00/www.casamerica.es). Metro Banco de España. **Open** 11am-2pm, 5-8pm Tue-Sat; 11am-2pm Sun. **Admission** free. **Map** p314 H6.

Housed in the 1872 Palacio de Linares, the Casa de América showcases Latin American art, both by established figures and emerging talents. It also has the important role of promoting cultural contacts between Spain and the Continent. As well as this, there are film seasons, music, theatre and talks given by leading writers, film directors, playwrights and political figures. There are also print and video libraries, a good bookshop and a terrace with arts events in summer.

Centro Cultural de la Villa

Jardines del Descubrimiento, Plaza de Colón (91 480 03 00/www.munimadrid.es). Metro Colón. **Open** 10am-9pm Tue-Sat; 10am-2pm Sun. **Admission** free. **Map** p310 I4.

Behind the deafening but refreshing water cascade in Plaza Colón, below the Columbus monument, is the city council's only purpose-built cultural centre. On offer is a mixed bag of theatre, puppets, opera and *zarzuelas* in the summer, as well as art exhibitions, usually featuring important Hispanic artists.

Museo del Libro (Book Museum)

Biblioteca Nacional, Paseo de Recoletos 20 (91 580 78 25/91 580 77 44). Metro Colón. **Open** 10am-8.45pm Tue-Sat; 10am-1.45pm Sun. **Admission** free. **Map** p310 I5.

With over three million volumes, Spain's national library has been called the 'Prado of paper'. Among the wealth of printed matter there is every work published in Spain since 1716, Greek papyri, Arab, Hebrew and Greek manuscripts, Nebrija's first Spanish grammar, bibles, and drawings by Goya, Velázquez, Rembrandt and many others. Given the precious and fragile nature of the texts, access was

by Herrera and Juan Bautista de Toledo, firmly established the style: austere, rigid and typically employing grey slate for rooftops and pointed turrets. It is also known as Castilian baroque, but few of its features are especially Castilian: the slate pinnacles came from Flanders, which appealed to Flemish-born Charles V and his son Philip.

Herrera's chief disciple, Juan Gómez de Mora, modified his master's legacy with a less monolithic, lighter style. He oversaw the completion of the Plaza Mayor in 1619 (his original plan is still recognisable in the slate spires, high-pitched roofs and dormer windows around the square) and the 1630 **Casa de la Villa** (the City Hall, Plaza de la Villa). He also worked on the **Palacio de Santa Cruz** (1629-43), near the Plaza Mayor, nowadays the Foreign Ministry. It shows Italian baroque influences, with a façade much more richly shaped than anything Herrera would have tried.

Baroque

Despite the Bourbon passion for things French and Italian, under Philip V a local architect, Pedro de Ribera, was commissioned for many projects. Among them were the 1722 hospice, now the **Museo Municipal** (*see p88*), the **Conde**

Duque barracks, now the Centro Cultural Conde Duque, the **Puente de Toledo** and many churches. Ribera's buildings, while still following the Herreran tradition, feature exuberant baroque façades centred on elaborately carved entrance porticoes, which lend a touch of fantasy absent from Habsburg Madrid. Many Ribera entrances survive on buildings that have since been rebuilt, as in the 1734 **Palacio de los Duques de Santoña** at C/Huertas 13, now occupied by the Chamber of Commerce. In churches, such as **San José** on C/Alcalá, Ribera gave Madrid's religious architecture a delicately ornate style. Ribera was greatly influenced by José de Churriguera, an important baroque architect of whose work little remains. He, too, was known for his extravagant portals, such as that on the **San Cayetano** church on C/Embajadores.

Neo-classicism

Charles III shared the ideals of the Enlightenment of the late 18th century, as is evident in his love of neo-classicism. His most trusted architect, Francesco Sabatini, was responsible for the **Puerta del Alcalá** and introduced ideas of neo-classicism in the planning and construction of the **Palacio Real**. One of his most important works was ▶

limited to scholars, but in 1996 the administration opened this museum to allow the public a glimpse of the library's riches. The displays are conceived as interactive, steering visitors through bibliographical history via multimedia applications including laser shows, videos and holographs.

Paseo de Castellana

Sights along the Castellana are listed here from bottom to top, south to north. The metro system partly avoids the avenue, but the 27 bus runs up and down the whole stretch, covering the Paseo del Prado, Recoletos and the Castellana.

In 1860, when he designed Madrid's 'extension', Carlos María de Castro took the significant decision, since the Paseo del Prado and Recoletos were already there, to continue along the same route with the main avenue of the new district. Thus the Castellana was born. Until the Republic of 1931 demolished Madrid's old racetrack, the avenue reached only as far as C/Joaquín Costa. Today it snakes away freely northwards, through thickets of office blocks. It

also contains, near the junction with C/Juan Bravo (location of the **Museo de Esculturas al Aire Libre**, *see p98),* Madrid's 'beach' of upmarket terrace bars, at the height of fashion in the mid 1990s and still thronged with *pijos* (something like Sloanes). To the east is the Salamanca district, the heart of affluent Madrid, and the city's most upscale shopping area.

In the 1970s and '80s banks and insurance companies vied with each other to commission in-vogue architects to create corporate showcases along the upper Castellana; see the **Bankinter** building at No.29 and **Bankunión** at No.46. Beyond the latter, the **Museo de Ciencias Naturales** (*see p97)* is set back from the road on a grassy hill; further still, on the left, is the Kafkaesque grey bulk of the enormous **Nuevos Ministerios** government buildings. Begun in 1932, this complex contains many government ministries, and is one of the largest projects bequeathed by the Spanish Republic to Madrid. It was designed by a team led by Secundino Zuazo, chief architect of the Gran Madrid plan (*see p22),* in a monolithic

▶ ## Architecture at a glance (continued)

the **Casa de la Aduana** (now the Ministry of Finance) at C/Alcalá 5-11. The great exponents of the sober, 'pure' neo-classicism of the later years of Charles III's reign, however, were Spaniards: Ventura Rodríguez, who had also worked on the Palacio Real, and Juan de Villanueva, architect of the **Museo del Prado** and the **Observatorio**.

Neo-Mudéjar

This style, initiated by architects Ricardo Rodríguez Ayuso and Lorenzo Álvarez Capra around 1870, and still popular decades later, incorporated Moorish arches, arabesque tiling and interlaced brickwork with modern use of glass and iron, most notably in the **Las Ventas bullring**, completed in 1934. One outstanding example is the **Escuelas Aguirre**, complete with minaret tower and glass-and-iron lookout gallery, at the intersection of C/Alcalá and C/O'Donnell. Also worth a look are the 1911 **Iglesia de la Paloma** (C/Paloma) in La Latina and the block of flats at **C/Barquillo 21**, in Chueca. In contrast, one of the most extraordinary constructions of the time, Ricardo Velázquez's **Ministerio de Agricultura** in Atocha, is a remarkable combination of Castilian brickwork and extravagant, French Beaux Arts-style sculpted decoration.

Art nouveau to art deco

Art nouveau (confusingly called *modernismo* in Spain), so characteristic of Barcelona, aroused little interest in Madrid, but there are some examples. The ornate **Palacio Longoria** (1902), by Jose Grasés Riera, is the best known, but the **Casa Pérez Villamil** at Plaza Matute 6 is also superb.

The most important architect of the early 20th century was Antonio Palacios, whose neo-baroque **Palacio de las Comunicaciones**, housing the main post office, is so extraordinary that it was quickly dubbed 'Our Lady of Communications'. His later, and possibly more important work, was the **Círculo de Bellas Artes**; less baroque and having more in common with art deco. This was a trait common to blocks like the **Capitol** building on Gran Vía or the curious model housing district of **El Viso**.

Franquista kitsch

Francoist architectural thinking was dominated by nostalgia for a glorious past, and so Madrid acquired monster constructions combined with ideas from German and Italian Fascist architecture. The results were often grandiose, bombastic and unwittingly kitsch. The foremost example is the **Ministerio del Aire**, at the top of

'30s rationalist style; then, after the victory of General Franco, the same architect added to the still-unfinished building some curving, traditionalist details more to the taste of the new regime. Inside it has a park-like garden, open to the public.

Beyond that, a huge branch of the Corte Inglés signals your arrival at the **AZCA** complex. The Asociación Zona Comercial A, known to some as 'Little Manhattan', is a glitzy skyscraper development first projected during the Franco regime's industrial heyday in the '60s, but it gained extra vigour in democratic Spain's 1980s boom to become a symbol of Madrid yuppiedom. At its centre is the **Plaza Picasso** – a small park, and amid the office blocks are a chic shopping mall, restaurants and other facilities to make it a self-contained 'workers' city'. At its north end is the **Torre Picasso**, designed by Japanese architect Minoru Yamasaki (also responsible for New York's World Trade Center) in 1988 and, at 157m (515ft), Madrid's tallest building. Beyond it is the circular **Torre Europa**.

A little further up again, opposite each other, are the Real Madrid stadium, **Estadio Bernabéu** (*see p240*) and the **Palacio de Congresos** conference centre. By this time, the view up the Paseo de la Castellana is dominated by the two leaning towers officially known as the **Puerta de Europa** at Plaza Castilla. These remarkable smoked-glass blocks, leaning in at 15º off the perpendicular, are perhaps the greatest monument to Spain's 1980s boom. They were begun with finance from the Kuwait Investment Office (so that the towers are more often called the **Torres KIO**) and left unfinished for years after a financial scandal in 1992. With their rather phallic fountain in the middle, they have now joined the landmarks of modern Madrid.

Museo de Ciencias Naturales

C/José Gutiérrez Abascal 2 (91 411 13 28/www. mncn.csic.es). Metro Gregorio Marañón. **Open** *Sept-June* 10am-6pm Tue-Fri; 10am-8pm Sat; 10am-2.30pm Sun. *July, Aug* 10am-6pm Tue-Fri; 10am-3pm Sat; 10am-2.30pm Sun. **Admission** €3; €2.40 concessions. **No credit cards**.

C/Princesa. In Plaza de España is the **Edificio España** skyscraper (*pictured*), the work of brothers Joaquín and José María Otamendi, completed in 1953. Salamanca also contains a good many retro constructions from the era, above all huge churches.

Modern times

With the rebirth of democracy, Spanish society had little time for nostalgia, and favoured forward-thinking architects such as Rafael Moneo for daringly imaginative 'grand revamps' of long-decrepit historic buildings. One outstanding example is the **Estación de Atocha**, a run-down, filthy 1880s cast-iron railway terminal that Moneo transformed into a spectacular multipurpose space. The **Thyssen** museum was similarly rebuilt by Moneo and the **Centro Cultural Conde Duque** was created out of Ribera's 1720s barracks, even making use of cracks in the old façade.

Outside the public domain, the most vigorous contributions to Madrid in recent memory have been the skyscrapers that line the upper Paseo de la Castellana, by the **AZCA** area, such as the **Catalana Occidente** insurance company building (No.50), the superb white 1988 **Torre Picasso** by Minoru Yamasaki, and the spectacular leaning towers of the **Puerta de Europa** at Plaza Castilla.

Sightseeing

A taste of the eighties at the **AZCA complex**. *See p97.*

The Natural Science Museum occupies two spaces in a huge building overlooking a sloping garden on the Castellana. Much of the north wing is given over to temporary exhibitions: generally a couple of small-scale ones are held annually and a larger, more ambitious one, lasting about a year, is organised every 18 months. They tend to be hands-on, inter-active and fun for kids. Permanently in this wing is 'Mediterranean Nature and Civilisation', a large exhibition of Mediterranean flora and fauna, illus-trating the region's biodiversity. The smaller space to the south contains a simpler, more old-fashioned presentation of fossils, dinosaurs and geological exhibits. A replica of a diplodocus dominates the two-floor space, surrounded by real skeletons of a glyptodont (giant armadillo) and other extinct ani-mals. The most distinguished skeleton here, though, is that of the Megatherium americanum, a bear-like creature from the pleistocene period unearthed in Luján, Argentina, in 1788. Don't confuse the street with the larger C/José Abascal, across the Castellana.

Museo de Esculturas al Aire Libre

Paseo de la Castellana 41. Metro Rubén Darío.
Map p311 I2.
An unconventional museum, this '70s space at the junction of the Castellana with C/Juan Bravo was the brainchild of engineers José Antonio Fernández Ordóñez and Julio Martínez Calzón. Designing a bridge across the avenue, they thought the space underneath would be a good art venue, and sculp-tor Eusebio Sempere convinced fellow artists to donate their work. All the major names in late 20th-century Spanish sculpture are represented – includ-ing Pablo Serrano, Miró, Chillida – and much of their work is spectacular, especially the dynamic stain-less-steel *Mon per a infants* ('A world for children') by Andreu Alfaro and the spectacular cascade by Sempere that forms a centrepiece.

The Retiro & around

The most attractive section of Madrid's north–south avenue, and the one that most new arrivals in Madrid first become familiar with, is the oldest: the **Paseo del Prado**, from Atocha up to Plaza de Cibeles. Once an open space between the city wall and the Retiro (*prado* means 'meadow'), it was given its present form in 1775-82, from a design chiefly by José de Hermosilla; it was the most important of Charles III's attempts to give his shabby capital the kind of urbane dignity he had seen in Paris and Italy. The king intended it to be a grand avenue lined by centres of learning and science. Originally called Salón del Prado, the form of the main section, from Cibeles to Plaza Cánovas del Castillo, was modelled on Piazza Navona in Rome, with three fountains by Ventura Rodríguez: **Cibeles** at the most northerly point, **Neptune** to the south and a smaller figure of **Apollo** in the middle. The southern stretch of the Paseo, tapering down to Atocha, has another statue, the *Four Seasons*, in front of the Museo del Prado. In the 19th century the Paseo del Prado was the great promenade of Madrid. Virtually the entire population, rich and poor, took a turn along it each evening, to see and be seen, pick up on the latest city gossip, make assignations and show off new clothes.

Despite the traffic, the tree-lined boulevard still has many attractions today, most notably Madrid's 'big three' great art museums (*see also pp61-70*, **Paseo del Arte**). As well as Charles III's creations, such as the **Jardín Botánico** (*see p103*) and the **Museo del Prado** itself, there are, at the very bottom, the **Centro de Arte Reina Sofía** and **Atocha** station (*see p101*). On the south side of the Botanical Gardens there are the rows of second-hand bookstalls of the **Cuesta de Moyano**. Further up, by the statue of Neptune, there is the **Museo Thyssen**, almost opposite such important elements in local life as the **Bolsa** and the **Hotel Ritz**. To the left, looking up, streets lead off into Huertas and the Old City, while to the right is the tranquil district of the Retiro.

When Philip II ruled Madrid, this whole area was just open country, apart from the church of **San Jerónimo** (*see p104*) and a few other royal properties. In the 1630s it was made into gardens – unprecedented in size for the era, at nearly 122 hectares (300 acres) – that became part of the **Palacio del Buen Retiro**, built by the Conde Duque de Olivares for Philip IV to impress the world. Gardeners were brought in from across Europe to create the park and its lake, and to ensure that it would feature shade and flowers throughout a Madrid summer. Charles III first opened sections of the park to the public in 1767, but it was only after the fall of Isabel II in 1868 that the gardens became entirely free to the citizens of Madrid. After it became a park, the Retiro acquired most of its many statues, particularly the giant 1902 monument to King Alfonso XII that presides over the lake.

Since it was made open to all, the Retiro has found a very special place in the hearts and habits of the people of Madrid. On a Sunday morning stroll, especially before lunch, you will see multigenerational families watching puppet shows, dog-owners and their hounds, children playing on climbing frames, vendors hawking everything from *barquillos* (traditional wafers) to etchings, palm and tarot readers, buskers from around the world, couples on the lake in hired boats, kids playing football, elderly men in leisurely games of *petanca* (boules), cyclists, runners, and a good many bench-sitters who want nothing more than to read the paper. During the week it's much emptier, and it's easier to take a look at some of the 15,000 trees, the rose garden and the park's fine exhibition spaces: the **Palacio de Cristal** (*see p104*), the **Palacio de Velázquez** (*see p104*) and the **Casa de Vacas** (*see p100*). Built in the 19th century, they were extensively renovated during the 1980s.

At the southern end of the park is the **Observatorio Astronómico** (*see p104*), a fine neo-classical building. However, the greatest curiosity of the park is Madrid's monument to Lucifer, in the moment of his fall from heaven. Known as the **Angel Caído** (Fallen Angel), this bizarrely unique statue on the avenue south of the Palacio de Cristal is thought to be the only monument to the devil in the world.

After the death of Philip IV in 1665, relatively little use was made of the Retiro, although the palace gained a new lease of life when the Alcázar burned down in 1734, as it became the primary royal residence in Madrid until the Palacio Real was completed in 1764. However, in 1808 Napoleon's troops made it into a barracks, and when the British army arrived in 1812 to fight over Madrid, much of it was destroyed.

On the north side of the park, forming a bridge between it and Salamanca, is the grand **Puerta de Alcalá** (*see p104*), still imposing despite being surrounded by the hectic traffic of the Plaza de la Independencia. The districts around and south of the Retiro are in some ways similar to Salamanca, but less emphatically affluent and more mixed. The knot of elegant streets between the park and the Paseo del Prado make up Madrid's most concentrated museum district, with, as well as the **Museo del Prado** itself, the **Museo del Ejército** (*see p103*), the **Museo Naval** (*see p103*), the **Bolsa de Comercio de Madrid** (*see below*) and the **Museo Nacional de Artes Decorativas** (*see p103*).

Just southwest of the park, right on Glorieta de Atocha, is one of the area's biggest but least-known sights: the magnificently grandiose 1880s **Ministry of Agriculture**, by Ricardo Velázquez, the same architect who designed the delicate exhibition halls inside the Retiro itself. A few blocks east from here along the (traffic-ridden) Paseo Reina Cristina, a turn right down C/Julián Gayarre leads to the **Real Fábrica de Tapices**. On Julián Gayarre there is also the much rebuilt **Basilica de Atocha** and the odd, often deserted, **Panteón de Hombres Ilustres**, containing the elaborate tombs of once-celebrated Spanish politicians of the 19th century.

Bolsa de Comercio de Madrid

Plaza de la Lealtad 1 (91 589 22 64). Metro Banco de España. **Open** *Exhibition space* noon Mon-Fri. **Admission** free. **Map** p314 H7.
In the same plaza as the Hotel Ritz, Madrid's stock exchange is a landmark as well as a business centre. Enrique María Repullés won the competition to design the building in 1884, with a neo-classical style chosen to reflect that of the nearby Prado. The build-

ing has two distinct areas: one is the trading area; the other, open to the public, houses an exhibition on the market's history. Visitors are admitted at noon only; phone to arrange a visit.

Centro Cultural Casa de Vacas
Parque del Retiro (91 409 58 19). Metro Retiro. **Open** 11am-2pm, 5-9pm Mon-Fri; 11am-9pm Sat. Times may vary. **Admission** free. **Map** p315 I7.

This exhibition space in the Retiro, close to the boating lake, is run by the local council and offers shows on a variety of subjects, ranging from children's books to wildlife photography and even footwear through the ages.

Estación de Atocha
Glorieta del Emperador Carlos V. Metro Atocha. **Map** p314 H10.

Watch this space

Thanks to Charles III's untiring efforts in the 18th century, the Paseo del Prado was to become the social heart of the city. Charles's idea was for this to become a centre of learning, with the main research institutions for arts and sciences, all open to the public, based here. He had it adorned with statues and fountains, and the whole area became known as the Salón del Prado. Early photos reveal women in parasols strolling while men in black bowlers hold ardent discussions and children frolic. The 19th-century writer Richard Ford effused: 'The Prado, a truly Spanish thing and scene, is unique; and as there is nothing like it in Europe, and oh, wonder! no English on it, fascinates all who passes the Pyrenees.'

Oh, wonder! In time, however, thanks to the invention of the combustion engine, the Paseo del Prado was to become less of a promenade and more of a motorway, with cars speeding through red lights and tour buses blocking the view of the famous fountains. The current mayor's Plan Especial Prado-Recoletos, however, seeks to remedy this. The team behind the project, headed by award-winning Portuguese architect Álvaro Siza, intends to reclaim the Paseo for pedestrians. By the time it is finished, in approximately 2012, a broad expanse of walkable promenade will link the big three museums to Atocha train station with minimal interference from passing traffic.

Madrid's classic wrought-iron and glass main rail station was built in 1888-92, to a design by Alberto del Palacio. It remained much the same, gathering a coating of soot, until the 1980s, when Rafael Moneo – he of the Museo Thyssen – gave it a complete renovation in preparation for Spain's golden year of 1992. Entirely new sections were added for the AVE high-speed train to Andalucia and the *cercanías* local rail network, and an indoor tropical garden was installed, in an imaginative blend of old and new.

Jardín Botánico

Plaza de Murillo 2 (91 420 30 17). Metro Atocha. **Open** *Oct-Feb* 10am-6pm daily. *Mar* 10am-7pm. *Apr, Sept* 10am-8pm daily. *May-Aug* 10am-9pm daily. **Admission** €2. Free under-6s. **No credit cards.** **Map** p314 H9.

Paseo del Prado.

The Plan Especial will restore other elements of the Prado and Recoletos area to their mid 19th-century glory. The towering statue of Christopher Columbus in the Plaza de Colón will be transferred back to its original spot in the centre of the adjacent roundabout. (The story goes that the pointing finger of the Columbus statue was intended to point towards the Dominican Republic, his first settlement, but an error in calculations means that he is currently pointing towards Greenland. Here's another chance to get it right.) The team will remove the modernist fountain façade of the Centro Cultural de la Villa, expand and rejuvenate areas of the Retiro park and the Botanical Gardens, and build a 'hill of sciences' on the south side of the Retiro to house new museums, a science centre and an 18th-century observatory.

Pedestrianisation is the most contentious and potentially disruptive element of the Plan: 12 lanes of traffic will be cut to six, four of which will be reserved for public transport.

Madrid's car-crazy populace will have to adjust their driving habits, using parallel streets and the M-30 loop. Carlos De Riaño, one of the head architects behind the Plan, explains matter-of-factly: 'It must be this way. Pedestrianisation is happening throughout Europe; people cannot drive so much in historical centres.'

The timing could not be better. At the time of its completion, all three of Madrid's star museums – the Prado, the Reina Sofía, and the Thyssen-Bornemisza – will have finished their high-profile expansions. The banking empire La Caixa will have installed a modern new community arts building just north of the Reina Sofía, masterminded by the famous architecture duo Herzog and De Meuron. In the not-too-distant future, strollers will be able to amble freely between Madrid's best museums, fountains and extraordinary new architecture, and the Prado 'salon' will be returned to its 19th-century self – Madrid's best place to see and be seen.

Madrid's luscious botanical gardens were created for Charles III by Juan de Villanueva and the botanist Gómez Ortega in 1781. They are right alongside the Paseo del Prado, just south of the Prado museum, but inside this deep-green glade, with over 30,000 plants from around the world, it's easy to feel that city life has been put on hold. A sign at the entrance asks that you treat the gardens as if they were a museum, but don't feel bad about getting comfortable with a book for a while; it is one of the best spots in Madrid to do so.

Museo de Antropología y Etnología

C/Alfonso XII 68 (91 539 59 95). Metro Atocha. **Open** 10am-7.30pm Tue-Sat; 10am-2pm Sun. **Admission** €2.40; €1.20 students; free under-18s, over-65s. Free to all 2.30-7.30pm Sat & all Sun. **No credit cards**. **Map** p314 H10.

This three-storey building between the Retiro and Atocha station houses several levels, each devoted to a specific region or country. The first level has an extensive collection from the Philippines (a former Spanish colony), dominated by a 6m (20ft) dugout canoe. Among the bizarre highlights are a 19th-century Philippine helmet made from a spiky blowfish, shrunken human heads from Peru and the skeleton of Don Agustín Luengo y Capilla, an Extremaduran who was 2.25m (7ft 4in) tall. Even more enticing is a shrivelled tobacco leaf-skinned mummy, said to have once been in Charles III's royal library. Both are in the annexe to the first level.

Museo del Ejército (Military Museum)

C/Méndez Núñez 1 (91 522 89 77). Metro Banco de España. **Open** 10am-2pm Tue-Sun. **Admission** €1; 50¢ students, under-18s, over-65s. Free to all Sat. **No credit cards**. **Map** p314 H8.

Due to move to Toledo, probably in 2005, the Military Museum currently occupies part of the Palacio del Buen Retiro. It holds a truly massive and often surprisingly sumptuous collection of military memorabilia, which includes some very rare treasures. Spain had a professional army earlier than most European countries, and the museum, accordingly, goes back further than the norm.

Its more remarkable treasures include La Tizona, said to be the sword of the legendary El Cid, and which, the story goes, he won in battle by slaying its owner King Bucar of Morocco; another sword used by the last Muslim king of Granada; a fragment of the cross planted by Columbus on his arrival in the New World, and a quite spectacular Arab tent used by the Emperor Charles V on military campaigns in the 1530s. Toy soldier enthusiasts can see a whole room devoted to miniatures, while the Rifle Room contains enough weaponry to make any gun-freak drool. Even more curious is a small room dedicated to a handful of Spanish heroines, with romanticised paintings of women such as seamstress Manuela Malasaña, killed by French soldiers in 1808 when she tried to defend herself with a pair of scissors, along with others who enlisted in wars

disguised as men. From that time there is another interesting relic: Napoleon's death mask, one of few in existence and made of ten kilos of solid bronze. There are rooms and rooms dedicated to the Spanish army in the 19th century, while the 20th-century sections give a strong impression that the museum remains as a refuge for the more intransigent and elderly members of the Spanish military. The rooms on Franco and the Civil War are completely celebratory, and this must surely be one of the only museums in the world today that unabashedly commemorates the Nazis' fight against Bolshevism, with a gung-ho room on the División Azul, the 'Blue Division' of Spanish fascist volunteers who fought with the German Army in Russia in World War II. A strange place.

Museo Nacional de Artes Decorativas

C/Montalbán 12 (91 532 64 99/www.mec.es). Metro Banco de España. **Open** 9.30am-3pm Tue-Sat; 10am-3pm Sun. **Admission** €2.40; €1.20 students; free under-18s, over-65s. Free to all Sun. **No credit cards**. **Map** p314 H7.

The Decorative Arts Museum houses more than 15,000 *objets d'art*, furniture and tapestries from all over Spain, plus many from China. One of the most prized rooms is the fifth-floor tiled kitchen, painstakingly transferred from an 18th-century Valencian palace, whose 1,604 painted tiles depict a domestic scene, with a huddle of servants making hot chocolate. Also of great interest is the second floor, where the Spanish baroque pieces are concentrated, among them ceramics from Talavera and Teruel, textiles, gold and silver work and jewellery cases from the Tesoro del Delfín (Treasure of the Grand Dauphin), the rest of which is in the Prado. Elsewhere are 19th-century dolls' houses, antique fans, an ornate 16th-century four-poster bedstead and a Sèvres jug given to Queen Isabel II by Napoleon III.

Museo Naval

Paseo del Prado 5 (91 379 52 99/www.museonavalmadrid.com). Metro Banco de España. **Open** 10am-2pm Tue-Sun. Closed Aug. **Admission** free. **Map** p314 H7.

Madrid's naval museum contains examples of the booty accumulated by Columbus and other early mariners during Spain's period of maritime expansion and an array of navigational instruments, muskets, guns and naval war paintings. Glass displays enclose primitive weapons, some of which, like the swords lined with sharks' teeth from the Gilbert Islands, promise greater damage than their Western counterparts. The most impressive room is dominated by a huge mural-map that traces the routes taken by Spain's intrepid explorers; in front of it are two equally impressive 17th-century giant globes. This same room also holds the museum's most valuable possession: the first known map of the Americas by a European – a parchment paper drawing by royal cartographer Juan de la Cosa believed to have been made for Ferdinand and Isabella in

1500. Worth a look also is the room occupied by items salvaged in 1991-3 from the *Nao San Diego*, which sank in the China Seas in 1600.

Observatorio Astronómico

C/Alfonso XII 3 (91 527 0107). Metro Atocha. **Open** 9am-2pm Mon-Thur. *Guided tours* 11am Fri. **Admission** free. **Map** p314 I7.

One of Charles III's scientific institutions, completed after his death in 1790. Beautifully proportioned, it is the finest neo-classical building in Madrid, designed by Juan de Villanueva. It still contains a working telescope, which can only be seen by prior request. One room is also open to the public.

Palacio de Cristal

Parque del Retiro (91 574 66 14). Metro Retiro. **Open** *Oct-Apr* 10am-6pm Mon, Wed-Sat; 10am-4pm Sun. *May-Sept* 11am-8pm Mon, Wed-Sat; 11am-6pm Sun. **Admission** free. **Map** p315 J8.

This 1880s glass and wrought-iron construction, an outpost of the Reina Sofía, is a lovely, luminous space for viewing art. Shows here often involve large-scale installations, sculpture or pieces conceived specifically for the space, such as Olafur Eliasson's recent 'Silent Functioning', a kind of 'garden' using ice, air, moss, lava and water combined with photography.

Palacio de Velázquez

Parque del Retiro (91 573 62 45). Metro Retiro. **Open** *Oct-Apr* 10am-6pm Mon, Wed-Sat; 10am-4pm Sun. *May-Sept* 11am-8pm Mon, Wed-Sat; 11am-6pm Sun. **Admission** free. **Map** p315 J8.

Built by Ricardo Velázquez for a mining exhibition in 1883, this pretty brick and tile building amid the trees of the Retiro is topped by large iron and glass vaults. Another Reina Sofía annexe, its galleries are wonderfully airy, and host very good temporary shows, including a recent one by Julian Schnabel. Contemporary dance has also featured recently.

Puerta de Alcalá

Plaza de la Independencia. Metro Retiro. **Map** p314 H/I6.

A short distance along C/Alcalá from Cibeles, in the middle of another traffic junction, stands one of the most impressive monuments built for King Charles III, a massive neo-classical gate designed by his favourite Italian architect Francesco Sabatini to provide a grand entrance to the city. It was built between 1769 and 1778, using granite and stone from Colmenar. Possible to miss in daytime traffic, it is unavoidably impressive at night.

Real Fábrica de Tapices

C/Fuenterrabía 2 (91 434 05 50). Metro Menéndez Pelayo. **Open** *Guided tours only* 10am-2pm Mon-Fri (last tour approx 1pm). Closed Aug. **Admission** €2.50. **No credit cards. Map** p315 J10.

Goya created some of his freshest images as designs for Madrid's royal tapestry factory, founded in 1721. In his day the factory was in Plaza Santa Bárbara in Chueca, but it has been at this location since 1889.

The hand-working skills and techniques used, though, have not changed at all, and on the tour one gets a clear idea of the intricate, painstaking work carried out in its two sections – the carpet room and the tapestry room. Goya designs are a mainstay of the work that's done here today (the factory also maintains carpets for royal palaces and the Ritz as well as undertaking work for private clients – for a pretty high price, though). Although the guided tours are normally in Spanish, if you phone or call in advance an English-speaking guide can usually be arranged for you.

San Jerónimo el Real

C/Moreto 4 (91 420 30 78). Metro Atocha or Banco de España. **Open** *Oct-June* 10am-1.30pm, 5-8.30pm daily. *July-Sept* 10am-1pm, 6-8.30pm daily. **Map** p314 H8.

Founded in 1464 and rebuilt for Queen Isabella in 1503, this church near the Retiro was particularly favoured by the Spanish monarchs, and used for state ceremonies. Most of the original building was destroyed during the Napoleonic Wars, and the present church is largely a reconstruction that was undertaken between 1848 and 1883. Controversially, the cloisters at the side of the church have been earmarked to be taken over for use as galleries by the Prado (*see p63*).

Museo del Prado. *See p63.*

Other Districts

The capital's suburbs are home to several brilliant museums, a popular
amusement park, an exhilarating cable car ride… and an Egyptian temple.

City walls and building restrictions over
the centuries have meant that even Madrid's
furthest-flung attractions are in a concentrated
area, within easy reach of the city centre.

North & west

Casa de Campo

Once a royal hunting estate, the verdant,
sprawling parkland of the **Casa de Campo**,
to the west of the city, was only opened to the
public under the Republic in 1931. Five years
later it became a key site for Franco's forces in
the Civil War battle for Madrid, its high ground
being used to shell the city centre and the
university. Remains of trenches still exist.

Today the Casa is home to the **Parque de
Atracciones** funfair and the **Zoo** (for both, *see
p197*), as well as, near Lago metro, **swimming
pools** (*see p243*) and **tennis courts** (*see p244*),
and a large boating lake. The cafés that ring
the lake make a fine place for an outdoor lunch,
and cyclists should note that most of the park's
roads are closed to cars on Sunday mornings.

Once you stray away from the criss-crossing
roads much of the park is surprisingly wild, and
it's possible to have a real country walk through
its woods and gullies. A favourite way to visit is
via the **Teleférico** cable car from the **Parque
del Oeste** (for both, *see p107*), which runs over
the trees almost to the middle of the Casa, where
there are viewpoints, an (undistinguished) bar-
restaurant and picnic spots.

Couples seeking seclusion favour the Casa
de Campo, both by day and night, and the area
by the Teleférico has been a gay cruising spot,
although police have been cracking down on
this. In contrast, one new feature of the modern
Casa is that Madrid's city authorities seem
near set on turning the roads from Lago metro
to the Zoo into a semi-official prostitution
zone, with the aim of moving prostitution from
the city centre. Consequently, by night, and
often by day, there are female and transvestite
prostitutes along these roads, displaying
their assets pretty outrageously to cruising
drivers. One very Spanish aspect of this is
that many of the other users of the park, by day
at least, don't let this bother them, but carry
on lunching, cycling or whatever, regardless.

Taking a break at the **Parque del Oeste**.

No peace for the gifted

The Spanish philosopher Miguel de Unamuno famously wrote that the dead in Spain were never allowed to rest. The truth of this observation will become apparent to anyone who wonders what has happened to the tombs of famous Spaniards who have died in Madrid. Remarkably, the remains of none of the city's outstanding Golden Age figures, including Cervantes, Lope de Vega and Calderón de la Barca, have survived, though there was a brief moment of excitement in 1999 following the discovery of bones wrongly believed to be those of Velázquez and his wife.

Even those Spaniards wealthy enough in the past to have paid for *sepultura perpetua* (others still have their bodies automatically removed from their tombs after ten years) have not been guaranteed a tranquil posthumous life. The expansion or destruction of churches have led to constant transferences of corpses, during the course of which a high proportion of these have been mislaid or misidentified.

In view of this unfortunate situation a decision was finally taken in 1869 to create what Spain so obviously lacked – a national pantheon for its heroes. The domed late 18th-century Basílica de San Francisco was set aside for this purpose, and on 19 June, the remains of Calderón and other famous

Spaniards were taken to the church in a triumphant procession involving cannon-fire and horse squadrons. But barely had the corpses had time to recover from their journey than the parishes from where they had come began to reclaim them. In the case of Calderón, the body would be moved several more times before disappearing altogether.

The fiasco of San Francisco did not put an end to the idea of a Spanish pantheon. In the 1890s, next to the then ruined 16th-century Basilica and Monastery of Atocha, the Panteón de Hombres Ilustres was built (*see* p99). However, this too proved a failure, and most of the illustrious corpses for whom it was intended were also taken away, leaving just the remains of largely forgotten politicians. Today it's one of Madrid's least visited sites, but nonetheless worth a look for its inappropriately Italianate architecture, and its splendidly elaborate tombs by Benlliure and other fashionable Spanish sculptors of the period.

While the Panteón de Hombres Ilustres is centrally located, visitors with a love of cemeteries in general will find themselves travelling to some of the city's poorest outlying districts. By far the largest of the city's cemeteries is that of the Almudena, out to the east (metro García Noblejas), the terrifying scale of which, not to mention the dusty grimness of the surroundings, gives it a compelling morbid appeal. Across the road is the comparatively intimate Civic Cemetery. Tidied up in the early 1990s following the burial here of the Communist leader Dolores Ibarruri ('La Pasionaria'), this contains the tombs of hundreds of opponents to Franco and the Catholic Church. At the end of the Civil War numerous Republican prisoners were shot here and thrown into a mass grave.

But the most absorbing of Madrid's cemeteries is the Sacramental de San Justo (*pictured*), attached to the cemetery of the Hermitage of San Isidro (bus 17) out west. In a state of poignant neglect, this overgrown, cypress-shaded wasteland is the resting place of some of the more distinguished writers of 19th- and 20th-century Spain, from the romantic Madrid poet Mariano José de Larra to prolific writer and man-about-town Ramón Gómez de la Serna. Luis Buñuel was greatly drawn to this cemetery; his memory of coming across the hair of a woman protruding from a cracked grave here was used by him in his film *The Phantom of Liberty*.

Teleférico de Madrid

Paseo del Pintor Rosales (91 541 74 50). Metro Argüelles. **Open** *Apr-Sept* noon-8.30pm Mon-Fri; noon-9pm Sat, Sun. *Oct-Mar* noon-7pm Mon-Fri; noon-7.30pm Sat, Sun. **Tickets** (return) €4.20; €3.30 concessions. Free under-3s. **Map** p308 B3.
An extraordinary 2.5km (1.5-mile) trip over the Casa de Campo and Parque del Oeste in a cable car. The views of the Palacio Real, the Río Manzanares, the city skyline and the park are breathtaking. There are also some interesting close-ups of the park's seedier goings-on.

Argüelles & Moncloa

West of Conde Duque lie the districts known as Argüelles and Moncloa. **Argüelles**, properly speaking, is the grid of streets between Plaza de España, C/Princesa, Plaza de Moncloa and Paseo del Pintor Rosales. The Paseo is known for its pleasant *terrazas* – open-air bars that are ideal for taking the air on summer evenings. The Paseo sits above the **Parque del Oeste**, which was designed by Cecilio Rodríguez in the 1900s and is now one of Madrid's most attractive spaces. Particularly beautiful in spring is **La Rosaleda**, the rose garden. The park formed part of the front line in the Civil War and was virtually destroyed, but has since been completely relaid. The Montaña del Príncipe Pío, at its southern end, is one of the highest points in Madrid, with great views of the Palacio Real and Casa de Campo, and the peculiarly incongruous **Templo de Debod** (*see p111*), an Egyptian temple that was presented to Spain in 1968. This was the site of the Montaña barracks, the Nationalists' main stronghold at the start of the Civil War, before it was demolished and the hill incorporated into the park. Below the Teleférico stop a path leads to the **Ermita de San Antonio de la Florida**, with its Goya frescoes (*see below*), and beyond that, the river. The fountain below the Teleférico used to preside over the roundabout at Príncipe Pío station, but was moved to the park in 1994. In its place by the station there is now the **Puerta de San Vicente** – an entirely new, quite convincing reconstruction of the 18th-century gate that once stood on this side of the city. On Sundays Madrid's Andean community takes over the Parque del Oeste, organising volleyball tournaments and picnics; after dark, the park roads around the fountain have, like the Casa de Campo, become a prostitution zone, particularly at weekends.

In the southern corner of the district, just off Plaza de España, is the **Museo Cerralbo** (*see p110*). In the opposite, northern corner, unmissable at the end of C/Princesa, stands one of the biggest, most significant creations of the Franco regime, the **Ministerio del Aire** or Air Ministry, built in the 1950s, in kitsch-Castilian baroque style and popularly known as the 'Monasterio del Aire'.

Alongside the Ministry is the Plaza de Moncloa, with Moncloa metro station and the departure points for many bus services to towns north and west of Madrid. There is also the fake-Roman triumphal arch that Franco had built to commemorate victory in the Civil War. To the north of the plaza, the **Moncloa** district is occupied mostly by the sprawling campus of the Universidad Complutense, the **Ciudad Universitaria**. Consequently, the streets just south and east have plenty of studenty bars. Within the university are specific attractions, too, notably the **Museo de América** (*see below*) and the **Faro de Madrid** observation tower, and beyond that the new **Museo del Traje** (*see p110*).

Ermita de San Antonio de la Florida

Glorieta de San Antonio de la Florida 5 (91 542 07 22). Metro Príncipe Pío. **Open** 10am-2pm, 4-8pm Tue-Fri; 10am-2pm Sat, Sun. **Admission** free. **Map** p308 A4.
This plain neo-classical chapel was completed by Felipe Fontana for Charles IV in 1798. Quite out of the way, north of Príncipe Pío station on the Paseo de la Florida, it is famous as the burial place of Goya, and for the unique, and recently restored, frescoes of the miracles of St Anthony, incorporating scenes of Madrid life, which he painted here in 1798. In contrast to the rather staid exterior, the colour and use of light in Goya's images are stunning. Featuring a rare mix of elements, including his unique, simultaneously ethereal and sensual 'angels', they are among his best and most complex works. On the other side of the road into the park is a near-identical second chapel, built in the 1920s to allow the original building to be left as a museum. There are free guided tours of the Ermita, in Spanish and English, at 11am and noon on Saturdays.

Faro de Madrid

Avda de los Reyes Católicos (91 544 81 04). Metro Moncloa. **Open** 10am-1.45pm, 5-8.45pm Tue-Sun. **Admission** €1; 50¢ concessions. **Map** p308 B1.
This radio and communications tower, at 92m (302ft), provides one of the best views of the whole of the city and the sierras in the distance. Diagrams along the floor point out highlights of the city, though with age they're becoming increasingly difficult to decipher. The best bit, though, is the stomach-lurching ride up in the glass lift.

Museo de América

Avda de los Reyes Católicos 6 (91 543 94 37/ http://museodeamerica.mcu.es). Metro Moncloa. **Open** 9.30am-3pm Tue-Sat; 10am-3pm Sun. **Admission** €3.01; €1.50 concessions. Free to all Sun. **No credit cards.**

Sightseeing

The garden of unearthly delights

Just to the north of the A-2 motorway, now surrounded by Madrid's eastern sprawl, there is a jewel of a romantic fantasy garden, a remarkably preserved monument to 18th-century taste, the **Capricho de la Alameda de Osuna**. Within its 14 hectares is an artificial river leading between lakes, woods, rose gardens, mock temples and a whole range of cool, surprising corners. The gardens were begun in the 1780s for the Duke and Duchess of Osuna, the most cultivated couple among the Spanish aristocracy of their day, enthusiastic promoters of the ideas and enquiring spirit of the Enlightenment and great patrons of artists, writers and musicians. The Capricho was their country estate, and under the direction of the Duchess became a special combination of salon and pleasure garden. In the 1790s an invitation to spend a day there was the hottest ticket in Madrid, for both the aristocracy and the intelligentsia.

The Capricho has been called 'the essence of a feminine garden', and its design closely reflected the Duchess's tastes. Her main architect was Jean-Baptiste Mulot, a French gardener who had previously worked for Marie-Antoinette, although much of the Capricho is in the English style, with simulated natural landscapes between smaller formal gardens. An Italian theatre designer, Angelo Maria Borghini, was responsible for many of the Capricho's fanciful buildings. Wandering visitors were to be surprised and delighted by a succession of different ambiences: secluded alcoves gave way to broad vistas, or they could glide on boats through the lakes and out to tiny artificial islands, sample the simple life at the Casa de la Vieja, a mock peasants' cottage, or discover mock Greek and Egyptian temples, a ballroom, an open-air theatre and the Abejero, a beehive in the shape of a classical temple. Within the Capricho the Osunas' aristocratic friends, men and women, could mingle with artists and intellectuals and talk freely, whether of gossip or great ideas, in an atmosphere very different from the paralysing etiquette of the royal court. New poems were read, and operas and music performed: Haydn was a favourite composer. This liberal informality encouraged by the Duchess – already deeply suspect for her 'French' ideas – also soon led to unstoppable rumours that there were far more illicit activities going on among the Capricho's intimate arbours than just chat.

The Duke and Duchess of Osuna were also among the first important patrons of Goya, and their support played a major part in winning him acceptance among high society. Among the several paintings that Goya produced for the Osunas' house at El Capricho were two oddities, the *Aquelarre* ('Witches' Sabbath') and *Escena de Brujas* ('Witchcraft Scene') – both now in the Museo Lázaro Galdiano – precursors of his later macabre, sensual paintings, which could indicate a more decadent taste in the Duke and Duchess alongside their more celebrated Enlightenment rationalism. The Capricho is also famous as the place where Goya, then aged 40, met the 23-year-old Duchess of Alba, in 1786, and so where his obsession with her began. Scandalous and impulsive, known for breaking whichever social

conventions suited her, dressing as a Madrid *maja* or street girl and having a string of male escorts from aristocrats to bullfighters, the Duchess of Alba was nevertheless a good friend of the high-minded Duchess of Osuna, and a frequent visitor to El Capricho.

The gardens were badly knocked about by Napoleon's troops – who also shot the head gardener, the French émigré Pierre Prévost – but were later reclaimed by the Duchess of Osuna, who lived on there until her death, aged 82, in 1834. El Capricho then suffered decades of decay and occasional destruction – especially during the Civil War – before it became the property of the city of Madrid, in the 1970s. A very impressive restoration programme is all but completed, but note that the gardens are still only open at weekends.

Capricho de la Alameda de Osuna

Paseo de la Alameda de Osuna (information 010). Metro Canillejas or bus 105. **Open** *Oct-Mar* 9am-5pm Sat, Sun. *Apr-Sept* 9am-9pm Sat, Sun.

This museum comprises the finest collection of pre-Columbian American art and artefacts in Europe, a combination of articles brought back at the time of the Conquest and during the centuries of Spanish rule over Central and South America, plus later acquisitions generally donated by Latin American governments. The collection includes near-matchless treasures: there is the *Madrid Codex*, one of only four surviving Mayan illustrated glyph manuscripts in the world; the *Tudela Codex* and illustrated manuscripts from central Mexico, which depict the Spanish Conquest; superb carvings from the Mayan city of Palenque, sent back to Charles III by the first-ever modern survey expedition to a pre-Hispanic American ruin in 1787; and the Gold of the Quimbayas, a series of exquisite gold figures from the Quimbaya culture of Colombia, which were presented to Spain by the Colombian government. All the main pre-Columbian cultures are represented – further highlights include Aztec obsidian masks from Mexico, Inca stone sculptures and funeral offerings from Peru, and finely modelled, comical and sometimes highly sexual figurines from the Chibcha culture of Colombia. There are also exhibits from the Spanish colonial period, such as the *Entry of the Viceroy Morcillo into Potosí* (1716) by the early Bolivian painter Melchor Pérez Holguín, a series of paintings showing in obsessive detail the range of racial mixes possible in colonial Mexico, and a collection of gold and other objects from the galleons *Atocha* and *Margarita*, sunk off Florida in the 18th century and only recovered in 1988.

The collection is arranged not by countries and cultures, but thematically, so that rooms are dedicated to topics such as 'the family', 'communication' and so on, with artefacts from every period and country alongside each other. Without some knowledge of the many pre-Columbian cultures this can be confusing and uninformative. Frustrating, then, but it's still a superb, intriguing collection, and temporary shows are usually interesting.

Museo Cerralbo

C/Ventura Rodríguez 17, Argüelles (91 547 36 46). *Metro Plaza de España.* **Open** 9.30am-3pm Tue-Sat; 10am-3pm Sun. **Admission** €2.40; €1.20 concessions. Free to all Wed & Sun. **No credit cards. Map** p308 C5.

Laid out in a sumptuous late 19th-century mansion in Argüelles is the incredible private collection of artworks and artefacts assembled by Enrique de Aguilera y Gamboa, the 17th Marqués de Cerralbo. A man of letters, reactionary politician and traveller who fanatically collected pieces everywhere he went, he bequeathed his collection to the state with the stipulation that it should be displayed exactly how he had arranged it himself. Thus the contents are laid out in a crowded manner, with paintings in three levels up the walls, and few items labelled. Among the many paintings, though, there are El Greco's *The Ecstasy of St Francis of Assisi* – the real highlight – and works by Zurbarán, Alonso Cano and other Spanish masters. The upstairs area contains an astonishing collection of European and Japanese armour, weapons, watches, pipes, leather-bound books, clocks and other curiosities. The mansion itself is of interest; virtually intact, it gives a good idea of how the aristocracy lived in the Restoration period – look out especially for the lavish ballroom.

Museo del Traje (Museum of Clothing)

Avda Juan de Herrera 2 (91 549 7150/www.museo deltraje.mcu.es). *Metro Moncloa.* **Open** 9.30am-7pm Tue-Sat; 10am-3pm Sun. **Admission** €3; €1.50 concessions. Free to all 2.30-7pm Sat & all Sun. **No credit cards. Map** p308 A1.

Opened in April 2004, this museum is a must for anyone interested in clothing in all its aspects. The collections comprise over 160,000 garments covering six centuries of Spanish fashion, though there are some items from much further back, among them fragments of Coptic cloth and Hispano-Muslim pieces. The permanent exhibition shows up to 600

Templo de Debod. *See p111.*

items at any one time, rotating them frequently both to protect them and to allow returning visitors to appreciate the breadth and diversity of the collections. It is arranged chronologically, in 14 spaces, among which are two outstanding monographic rooms, one covering regional costume, the other containing pieces by Mariano Fortuny y Madrazo, son of the painter, whose creations were worn by the likes of Isadora Duncan. Either side of these, some of the periods covered are the Enlightenment and the *castizo* (Madrid's working classes); early 19th-century French influences; Romanticism; *belle époque*, the avant-garde, post-Civil War fashion and the modern era. There is also a room dedicated to the great couturier Balenciaga and another to Spanish haute couture. As well as the exhibition there are 'didactic areas' where visitors can learn about why we wear clothes, how they are made and the forms they take. As well as all this, there is an area with internet access, a reading room, bookshop, café-restaurant and space for temporary shows, the first of which showed 100 years of photography from *Vogue*.

Templo de Debod

Montaña del Príncipe Pío (91 366 74 15). Metro Plaza de España or Ventura Rodríguez. **Open** *Apr-Sept* 10am-2pm, 6-8pm Tue-Fri; 10am-2pm Sat, Sun. *Oct-Mar* 9.45am-1.45pm, 4.15-6.15pm Tue-Fri; 10am-2pm Sat, Sun. **Admission** free.
This Egyptian structure, which sits on the outskirts of the Parque del Oeste, dates back 2,200 years and is dedicated to the gods Amun and Isis. It was sent, block by block, by the Egyptian government in 1968 in thanks for Spain's help in preserving monuments threatened by the Aswan Dam.

Chamberí

Directly north of Malasaña is the *barrio* of Chamberí, one of the first working-class districts outside the walls to be built up in the second half of the 19th century. Consequently central Chamberí became one of the few areas outside the old city considered to have genuine *castizo* character. A pleasant place to while away an evening is the circular **Plaza de Olavide**, ringed with pavement cafés. Just to the east of here is the charming **Museo Sorolla**. On the north side of Chamberí is Madrid's main water supply, the Canal de Isabel II. On C/Santa Engracia, a neo-Mudéjar water tower has been converted into a unique photography gallery, the **Sala del Canal de Isabel II** (*see below*).

Museo Sorolla

Paseo del General Martínez Campos 37 (91 310 15 84/www.emcu.es/nmuseos/sorolla). Metro Gregorio Marañón or Iglesia. **Open** 9.30am-3pm Tue-Sat; 10am-3pm Sun. **Admission** €2.40; €1.20 concessions. Free to all Sun. **No credit cards**. **Map** p310 H1.

Often considered a neo-Impressionist, Valencia-born Joaquín Sorolla was really an exponent of 'luminism', the celebration of light. He was renowned for his iridescent, sun-drenched paintings, including portraits and family scenes at the beach and in gardens. It's easy to dismiss Sorolla for his leisured themes, and for painting pictures that are incorrigibly reminiscent of greetings cards (and indeed they are often used as such), but most find his world a little seductive, or at least admire his spectacular use of light. This delightful little museum, which is housed in the mansion built for him in 1910, and where he spent his later years, was recently restored and is now more as it was when Sorolla occupied it. Visitors may now enjoy 250 works, among them sketches, watercolours and paintings; a solid selection of the holdings. The works are exhibited on the main floor, in his former studio areas. The salon, dining room and breakfast room have been returned to their original state and many of the artist's furnishings and eclectic decorative elements are distributed throughout. The garden, Moorish-inspired but with an Italianate pergola, is a delightful, peaceful oasis of calm, seemingly miles away from the roaring traffic outside.

Sala del Canal de Isabel II

C/Santa Engracia 125 (91 545 10 00). Metro Ríos Rosas. **Open** 11am-2pm, 5-8.30pm Tue-Sat; 11am-2pm Sun. **Admission** free.
Considered one of the finest examples of industrial architecture in Madrid, this water tower, built in elaborate neo-Mudéjar style in 1907-11, is nowadays an attractive exhibition space that specialises in photography. Several shows are held every year, ranging from good to world-class.

Tetuán & Chamartín

North of Chamberí is **Tetuán**, a modern, working area centred on C/Bravo Murillo, and, to the east, **Chamartín**, which contains the major business area of modern Madrid. For the visitor the main point of interest is the local market, the **Mercado de Maravillas**, at C/Bravo Murillo 122, just north of Cuatro Caminos – it's the largest market in the city. On Sunday mornings, too, a 'Rastro' gets going on C/Marqués de Viana. Blind or partially sighted visitors should check out the **Museo Tiflológico**, just north of here.

Across the Castellana, north-east of Nuevos Ministerios, is **El Viso**, an anomaly in high-rise Madrid. It was developed in the 1920s as a model community on garden-city lines, on the fringes of the city at that time, and some of its individual houses are museum-worthy examples of art deco. The district has retained its desirable (and expensive) status. At the southern tip of this area is the incongruously political cultural centre, the **Residencia de Estudiantes**.

Sightseeing

Further east again is **La Prosperidad**, also once a model housing development, although most of its early buildings have been replaced by modern blocks. Within it is the **Auditorio Nacional de Música** (*see p215*).

Museo Tiflológico

C/La Coruña 18 (91 589 42 00/www.museo.once.es). Metro Estrecho. **Open** 10am-2pm, 5-8pm Tue-Fri; 10am-2pm Sat. Closed Aug. **Admission** free.
Owned and run by ONCE, the organisation for blind and partially sighted people, this special museum presents exhibitions of work by visually-impaired artists (the name comes from the Greek *tiflos*, sightless). Work here is intended to be touched, and is generally sculptural, three-dimensional, rich in texture and highly tactile. As well as temporary shows the museum has a large permanent collection of instruments devised to help the blind over the years, and a series of scale models of monuments from Spain and around the world.

La Residencia de Estudiantes

C/Pinar 21-23 (91 563 64 11/www.residencia. csic.es). Metro Gregorio Marañón. **Open** (during exhibitions, phone to check) 11am-3pm daily. **Admission** free.
The Residencia de Estudiantes was, from its foundation in 1910 until 1936, the most vibrant cultural centre in Madrid, and a powerful innovative force in the whole country. Though it was a students' residence – García Lorca, Buñuel and Dalí all stayed there in the early days – 'La Resi' also organised visits to Madrid by leading artists and scientists of the day and was active in the propagation of avant-garde ideas from outside Spain. The Civil War and the regime that came afterwards severely stifled intellectual freedom and the Residencia languished until the late '80s, when it was resurrected as a private foundation sponsored by Spain's official scientific research council. Once again a centre of excellence, it hosts talks by major international literary, scientific and artistic figures, plus conferences and exhibitions, poetry recitals, films and concerts.

The northern suburbs

The northern and western *extrarradio* offers a radical contrast to the south. The thing to do for those with the necessary cash in Madrid in the past 20 years or so has been to adopt the Anglo-Saxon way of life and move out of city flats to house-and-garden developments like **Puerta de Hierro**, north of the Casa de Campo, named after the 1753 iron gate to the royal hunting reserve of El Pardo. Its posh residences, though, are no match for **La Moraleja**, off the Burgos road, an enclave for executives and diplomats.

The growing districts to the east are not nearly so lush. The area along the A-2 motorway towards the airport is intended to be Madrid's major commercial development zone, with the Feria de Madrid trade fair complex and the **Parque Juan Carlos I**, which lies between the airport and the Feria de Madrid centre. Oddly enough, the area already contains, swallowed up in the urban spread, one of Spain's most

Museo del Traje – suit yourself.
See p110.

appealing and neglected 18th-century gardens, the **Capricho de la Alameda de Osuna** (*see p108*, **The garden of unearthly delights**).

Parque Juan Carlos I

Avda de Logroño & Avda de los Andes. Metro Campo de las Naciones.

This huge park, Madrid's newest green (and brown) space, lies between the airport and the Feria de Madrid trade fair centre. With time it should become one of the city's more attractive spaces, but it has taken a while for the trees to grow to provide shade. That said, the park's current draws include a series of different gardens within a circle of olive trees, an artificial river and other water features.

El Pardo

Around ten miles (15 kilometres) to the north-west of the city lies a vast expanse of parkland. Here is the main residence of the Spanish royal family, the **Palacio de la Zarzuela**, but the reason most people will venture up here is for the peculiar sensation of nosing around in the house where General Franco lived and worked for the 35 years up to his death in 1975, the **Real Palacio de El Pardo**, situated in the peaceful 18th-century town of El Pardo. Today the place serves mainly to host foreign dignitaries and heads of state, most notably in recent years during the 2004 wedding of the heir to the throne, Prince Felipe.

The hills and woodlands are also worth a visit, however, being remarkably unspoilt thanks to those long protected years of dictatorial and regal status, and they contain an amazingly rich wildlife. Not surprisingly, game features on many restaurant menus in the town.

Real Palacio de El Pardo

C/Manuel Alonso (91 376 15 00). Bus 601 from Moncloa. **Open** *Apr-Sept* 10.30am-5.45pm Mon-Sat; 9.30am-1.30pm Sun. *Oct-Mar* 10.30am-4.45pm Mon-Sat; 10am-1.30pm Sat. **Admission** €5; €2.50 concessions. Wed free to EU citizens. **No credit cards.**

In 1405 Henry III constructed a hunting lodge here, but the first monarch to take a really serious interest in El Pardo's excellent deer and game hunting estate was Charles I of Spain (Charles V of the Holy Roman Empire), who built a sizeable palace here. His successor, Philip II, added many important works of art but most of these were lost in a fire in 1604, and after various architectural changes the building was finally reconstructed on Charles III's orders by 18th-century architect Francesco Sabatini; superb murals by Bayeu and Maella were added at this time. The current furnishings, paintings and tapestries were added during the 19th and 20th centuries.

In addition to its main role today as a diplomatic rendezvous, the palace is partially open to the public and there are tours of its ornate and gaudy interior with its ornamental frescoes, gilt mouldings and some fine tapestries, many of which were woven in the Real Fábrica de Tapices to Goya designs. There's an ornate theatre, built for Charles IV's Italian wife Maria Luisa of Parma, where censorious film fan Franco used to view films with his cronies before deciding on their suitability for the great unwashed, but in truth the only rooms of real fascination are the Generalísimo's bedroom, dressing room and '70s bathroom – decorated to his own specifications.

Outside you can wander in the palace's attractive gardens or explore or picnic in at least part of the magnificent surrounding parkland known as Monte de Pardo – even though much of this is still closed to the public. Other nearby highlights include the Convento de los Capuchinos (Ctra del Cristo, 91 376 08 00, open 9am-1pm, 4.30-8pm daily), famed for Gregorio Fernández's wooden baroque sculpture of Christ; the Quinta del Pardo, a small 18th-century summer house, and the single-storey Casita del Príncipe, built in 1785 by Juan de Villanueva and noted for its lavish lounges, though both have been closed to the public for some years.

South

South of centre

The barrios of southern **Embajadores**, **Delicias**, **Arganzuela** and **Legazpi** occupy a triangular chunk of land just south of the old city, bordered by the Manzanares river, the M-30 motorway and the rail lines from Atocha. Low rents attract a fair number of resident foreigners. Conventional attractions are few – the **Museo del Ferrocarril** (*see below*) and the **Parque Tierno Galván**, with the **IMAX Madrid** and **Planetario de Madrid** (for both, *see p197*) – but the area contains the **Estación Sur** bus station, and two symbols of Madrid, the **Atlético Madrid** stadium and, alongside it, the Mahou brewery. Beyond that is the river, and the **Puente de Toledo**, which was built by Pedro de Ribera for Philip V in 1718-32.

Just south of the river is the **Parque de San Isidro**, containing a charming 18th-century hermitage dedicated to the city's patron saint. The hermitage is the traditional focus of the Romería (Procession) de San Isidro. The park still fills with life and crowds during the **San Isidro** fiestas every May (*see p193*). At other times it's very tranquil; the view from the hill of San Isidro is familiar as one painted many times by Goya, and is still quite recognisable, despite the tower blocks.

Museo del Ferrocarril

Paseo de las Delicias 61 (91 506 83 33/www.museo delferrocarril.org). Metro Delicias. **Open** 10am-3pm Tue-Sun. Closed Aug. **Admission** €3.50; €2 concessions. Free to all Sat. **No credit cards.**

Let there be light at the **Museo Sorolla**. *See p111*.

Housed in the elegant but disused Delicias station, with ironwork by Gustave Eiffel, is Madrid's railway museum, with an evocative collection of old locomotives, models, railway equipment and memorabilia. There is also a room dedicated to clocks, including the one that marked time when Spain's first ever train chugged from Barcelona to Mataró. You can climb on the trains, have a drink in an old restaurant car or watch film footage of Spanish railways. This great museum for kids offers occasional theatre performances, a bring-and-buy market for model train enthusiasts, and more. It is located about 100 yards off the main road, behind the national railway offices.

Vallecas

Vallecas, beyond the M-30 south-east of the city, was already an industrial suburb in the 1930s, and manages to remain one of the areas of Madrid with a firm sense of its own identity. It doesn't lay much claim to being traditionally *castizo*, however, even though many of its residents originally came here as overspill from the city centre. Rather, the name 'Vallecas' in Madrid immediately brings to mind the post-Civil War, post-1950s working class.

Vallecas is known for a strong sense of neighbourly solidarity. The area has its own football team, **Rayo Vallecano**, which is forever struggling to keep up with its money-laden neighbours. Car stickers proclaim 'Independence for Vallecas' (spelt 'Vallekas' by hipper natives, who have their own punky sense of cool). It also has a pleasant tree-lined main drag, more than enough to mark it out from the other areas around it. There have been problem districts nearby, such as **Entrevías**, home to some of Madrid's largest Gypsy communities.

Outer limits

Southern suburbs

Carabanchel, **Leganés**, **Getafe**, **Móstoles** and **Alcorcón** form Madrid's southern industrial belt, virtually all of it built up since the 1960s. Areas still within the city, such as **Orcasitas**, blend into the towns of the *extrarradio*, the outskirts, and concrete flyovers and tower blocks make up the urban landscape.

These areas are now better connected thanks to the extension of the metro system, and central city dwellers occasionally come down here for entertainment: **Alcorcón** holds a flamenco festival, and **Fuenlabrada** has a clutch of teen-macro-discos. The popularity of hard rock in these suburbs is also attested by Calle AC/DC in Leganés, inaugurated by the rock legends themselves in 2000. On the street is a converted bullring that has become one of the most important music venues in Madrid, **La Cubierta de Leganés** (*see p222*).

Eat, Drink, Shop

Features

Restaurants

For all the pakoras and baba ganoush, the *cocido* is most definitely here to stay.

Casa Ciriaco – no modern dishes here, just good old Castilian tucker. *See p118.*

Not so long ago, it used to be that even dishes from Asturias were thought exotic here in the capital. However, the times they are a changin' and now *madrileños* have become Spain's unlikely flag-bearers for culinary globalisation. Mexican, of course, has always been around, and Asian, particularly, has become de rigueur. But add to this list the overwhelming popularity of Italian, French, Cuban, Middle Eastern, Thai and Japanese restaurants in town and wonder at the future of the paella.

Among the many pluses of these international newcomers, three advantages stick out: style, spice and vegetables. Where the dining scene used to be all red-checked tablecloths or old-style elegance, now those who fancy the chic and minimal have a place to go and look glam. And if your taste buds are inclined to more nuances of spice, the hottest of chilli peppers or eye-watering wasabi, you can rest easy. Then, the good news for vegetarians is that the options are no longer limited to tortilla, or green beans with the ham picked out. The multitude of new Asian restaurants always has vegetarian options, as do, increasingly, the

Italian, Middle Eastern and other foreign eateries. So rejoice in the glories of diversification and eat your veggie fill.

That said, this city remains a bastion of unreconstructed Spanish cuisine. The famous *cocido madrileño* – a stew of various bits of meat, offal and vegetables served up in three courses – is still eaten religiously, particularly at weekends. The down-home *casas de comida* (eating houses) are packed daily with regulars who are perfectly happy with a plain *ensalada mixta* followed by a greasy pork chop and the ubiquitous *flan* for dessert. Even the young and cool are faithful to the less expensive classic *mesones* (old-style taverns), while the most upscale traditional places still require you to join a waiting list.

For *lo más típico*, head for the area around Los Austrias and La Latina, particularly along C/Cava Baja, leading south from the Plaza Mayor – a veritable pilgrim's way to the most traditional *madrileño* cuisine. If you're not up for lentils and roast lamb, head over to Chueca, where you'll find hipper, stylish restaurants (many of which offer great value at lunchtime) and a plethora of international eateries. Round these parts, one restaurant closes as another opens, but many have stood the test of time. The most upmarket restaurants, on the other hand, can be found in the Salamanca area, and particularly in hotels around the Paseo de la Castellana.

TIMING

Rule number one for visitors to Madrid: don't go out too early. *Madrileños* rarely eat lunch before 2pm, but go after 4pm and you may find people sweeping up around you. Probably due to a combination of substantial lunches and the heat, dinner is usually eaten late as well – around 10pm, and even later in the summer. It's advisable to book a table in most places for Friday and Saturday night, and at other times if you're in a big group. Many restaurants close on Sunday evening and all of Monday. August is livelier than it used to be, but most restaurants still close for at least two weeks. Where possible, we've indicated this, but it's best to ring and check.

By law, restaurants are obliged to declare on the menu if VAT (IVA) is included and if there's a cover charge. In practice, however, they almost never do, and there almost always is. There's no set rule for tipping, but leaving a euro or so is the norm for good service.

MENU DEL DIA

Opinions differ over whether the *menú del día* was introduced to attract tourists or to feed hungry workers who can't get home at lunchtime. Either way, it can be a great way to eat cheaply and well, and all but the swankiest restaurants are obliged to offer one. It usually consists of a starter, main course and dessert, bread and some occasionally dubious wine. Dishes cost much less than they would do à la carte (although portions tend to be smaller) and the *menú del día* also provides a chance to sample some of the more upmarket establishments on a budget. Standard Spanish restaurants offer typical *comida casera* (home cooking), and many international restaurants will follow suit, rather than offer anything that would be available à la carte.

Los Austrias & La Latina

La Botillería de Maxi

C/Cava Alta 4 (91 365 12 49). Metro La Latina. **Open** 1-4pm, 8.30pm-midnight Tue-Sat; 12.30-6pm Sun. Closed last 2wks Aug. **Main courses** €7-€10. **Set lunch** €8 Tue-Fri. **No credit cards.** **Map** p313 D8.
Fashionably scruffy young waiting staff and blaring flamenco in a no-frills classic setting make for an unpretentious blend of old and new. This is the

place for an offal first-timer – the *callos a la madrileña* (tripe in a spicy sauce) are acknowledged as the best in town. For less accustomed stomachs, there are enticing options too: *mojama* (wind-dried tuna), *merluza* (hake) 'meatballs' and all manner of inventive things made with manchego cheese.

La Camarilla

C/Cava Baja 21 (91 354 02 07). Metro La Latina. **Open** 1-4pm, 9pm-midnight Mon-Thur; 1-4pm, 9-12.30pm Fri, Sat; 1-4.30pm, 9pm-midnight Sun. **Main courses** €17-€19.50. **Set menu** €10.90 Mon-Thur, Sun; €15 Fri, Sat. **Credit** AmEx, DC, MC, V. **Map** p313 D8.
Of the many traditional restaurants on this stretch of road, La Camarilla offers the most innovative versions of Spanish home cooking: gazpacho with mango, *revuelto* (scrambled egg) with mushrooms

The best Restaurants

For paella
Don Paco (*see p121*); **La Paella de la Reina** (*see p133*).

To spend it like Beckham
El Bogavante del Almirante (*see p130*); **La Broche** (*see p140*).

For dinner and a show
La Favorita (*see p139*); **Gula Gula** (*see p125*).

For dinner à deux
La Sinfonia Italiana (*see p135*); **Come Prima** (*see p126*).

For no-frills Asian
Siam (*see p137*); **Kawara** (*see p125*); **Adrish** (*see p137*).

For blood 'n' guts
La Botillería de Maxi (*see left*); **Freiduría de Gallinejas** (*see p129*).

For minimalist chic
La Broche (*see p140*); **Nodo** (*see p139*).

For the catch of the day
Ribeira Do Miño (*see p133*); **Xentes** (*see p121*).

After the match of the day
Summa (*see p140*); **Asador Donostiarra** (*see p139*).

For carnivores with veggie mates
La Isla del Tesoro (*see p138*); **Siam** (*see p137*); **Indochine** (*see p133*).

Eat, Drink, Shop

and parmesan, and various tasty cod dishes. The setting is reminiscent of a genteel 1930s hotel and the staff incredibly friendly. Creative tapas and a hearty *menú del día* are served in a relaxed front room and luxurious gourmet meals in an adjoining formal dining room.

Casa Ciriaco

C/Mayor 84 (91 548 06 20). Metro Ópera or Sol. **Open** 1-4pm, 8.30pm-midnight Mon, Tue, Thur-Sun. Closed Aug. **Main courses** €10-€15. **Set menu** €17. **Credit** DC, MC, V. **Map** p312 C8.
Pick your way down the side of the open kitchen to a deep dining room hung with pictures of visiting royals, grateful celebrities and photos of the 1906 bombing of Alfonso XIII's wedding procession – which happened right outside the door. Undamaged, and still going strong, Casa Ciriaco was a meeting place for the intelligentsia in pre-Civil War days, and although it no longer attracts too many thinkers, the Castilian fare is a taste of days gone by. *Cochinillo* (suckling pig) is the speciality, along with partridge and butter beans, when in season.

Casa Lucio

C/Cava Baja 35 (91 365 32 52). Metro La Latina. **Open** 1-4pm, 9pm-midnight Mon-Fri, Sun; 9pm-midnight Sat. Closed Aug. **Main courses** €10-€18. **Set lunch** €35. **Credit** AmEx, DC, MC, V. **Map** p313 D8.
A restaurant unsurpassed by any other in Madrid for its famous patrons: King Juan Carlos, Bill Clinton and Penélope Cruz among them. This is the place of historical rendezvous, where Aznar and Bush's wives did lunch back when alliances were in the making. It also knows how to cook up one cracking *solomillo* (beef). The key to Lucio's glory is the use of a coal-fired oven and the best olive oil. Another star dish is a starter of lightly fried eggs laid on top of a bed of crisp, thinly cut chips. Be sure to ask for a table on the first floor.

Casa Marta

C/Santa Clara 10 (91 548 28 25). Metro Ópera. **Open** 1.30-4pm, 9pm-midnight Mon-Sat. Closed Aug. **Main courses** €7.15-€11.10. **Set menu** €8.10. **Credit** AmEx, DC, MC, V. **Map** p312 C7.
Every Saturday, according to the novel, Don Quixote ate *duelos y quebrantes* – scrambled eggs, ham, bacon, chorizo and brains – and you can still try them at Casa Marta – although they usually leave out the brains these days. A quaint old place, it's been a favourite since the beginning of the 20th century, when opera-goers and singers would stop in for a tipple after performances. The satisfying *platos de cuchara* ('spoon food') – warming bowls of *cocido*, beans and lentils – are another star turn that always pulls in the crowds.

Julián de Tolosa

C/Cava Baja 18 (91 365 82 10). Metro La Latina. **Open** 1.30-4pm, 9pm-midnight Mon-Sat; 1.30-4pm Sun. **Main courses** €20-€30. **Credit** AmEx, DC, MC, V. **Map** p313 D8.

La Viuda Blanca. *See p121.*

Probably the most modern in the *barrio*, this upscale Basque restaurant is all smooth wood, glass and brick, housed in a 19th-century building. With a very limited, simple menu, the main attraction here is the grilled steak (*chuletón de buey*), a contender for the city's best. Try the idiazábal cheese, a speciality from the little Basque town of the same name. The maître d' will steer you through an excellent selection of more than 100 wines.

Maldeamores

C/Don Pedro 6 (91 366 55 00). Metro La Latina. **Open** *Mid Aug-June* 9pm-12.30am Mon; 1.30-4.30pm, 9pm-12.30am Tue-Sun. *July* 9.30pm-12.30am daily. Closed 1st 2wks Aug. **Main courses** €17-€28. **Credit** MC, V. **Map** p312 C9.
Pretty food, pretty people, pretty delicious. With smart urban design and jazz music lilting in the background, tuck into plates like grouper marinated in orange and ginger, served with lychees and wrapped in spinach, or profiteroles of brie, shiitake mushrooms and pears. Deliciously different – even the wine list deviates from the norm, offering a wide selection of New World wines.

Palacio de Anglona

C/Segovia 13 (91 366 37 53). Metro La Latina. **Open** 8.30pm-2.30am Mon-Fri; 1.30-5pm, 8.30pm-3am Sat, Sun. **Main courses** €9.20-€13. **Credit** AmEx, DC, MC, V. **Map** p313 D8.
Palaces aren't always for princes – this one, for example, caters to a younger alternative crowd who come for the good pizzas and other reasonably priced dishes. The menu is a Mediterranean mix with an emphasis on Italian, with good salads and carpaccios and an imaginative use of ingredients.

Decor is modern yet comfortable and the friendly staff sport an appropriate number of piercings and carefully sculpted facial hair. Try the pasta with *buey de mar* (crab), a house speciality, and leave room for the excellent desserts.

El Sobrino de Botín

C/Cuchilleros 17 (91 366 42 17/91 366 30 26). Metro Sol. **Open** 1-4pm, 8pm-midnight daily. **Main courses** €7.40-€17.95. **Set menu** €30-€35. **Credit** AmEx, DC, MC, V. **Map** p313 D8.
The world's oldest restaurant (with a signed Norris McWhirter certificate to prove it) is still coming up with the goods after nearly 300 years. For all its popularity as a tourist destination, its nooks and crannies add up to an atmospheric – if cramped – dining spot. El Sobrino turns out great roasts, including that old Spanish favourite: *cochinillo* (suckling pig). The *cordero* (lamb) is also superb, as are the *almejas* (clams) *Botín*. And, yes, seeing as you asked, Hemingway did come here.

La Taberna del Alabardero

C/Felipe V 6 (91 541 51 92). Metro Ópera. **Open** 1-4pm, 9pm-midnight daily. **Main courses** €15-€20. **Gourmet menu** €23.40. **Credit** AmEx, DC, MC, V. **Map** p312 C7.
Father Lezama first started up his traditional tavern in 1974, when he put underprivileged boys to work as waiters in this converted 16th-century townhouse. With a lovely *terraza* that abuts the Teatro Real, it is still one of the most popular post-theatre dining spots, serving traditional tapas at the bar and Basque cuisine in the restaurant in the back. Lezama is no longer a priest but a very prosperous

restaurateur – he has opened six more restaurants throughout Spain and one in Washington, DC. Some of those original boys are now shareholders in the Alabardero Company.

Taberna Salamanca

C/Cava Baja 31 (91 366 31 10). Metro La Latina. **Open** 1-4pm, 8.30pm-midnight Tue-Thur; 1-4pm, 8.30pm-1am Fri, Sat; 1-4.30pm Sun. Closed mid Aug-mid Sept. **Main courses** €9-€15. **Set lunches** €7.50-€8.50 Tue-Fri. **No credit cards. Map** p313 D8.
On a street crammed with high-priced eateries, this is where the cool, young, and more frugal set comes to eat. There are three lunch *menús* to choose from, offering the usual Spanish pickings – the *croquetas*, courgette tortilla and endives with roquefort cheese are all pretty dependable. The staff are friendly and young, with a tendency to whack up the stereo.

El Viajero

Plaza de la Cebada 11 (91 366 90 64). Metro La Latina. **Open** 2-4.30pm, 9pm-12.30am Tue-Sat; 2-4.30pm Sun. Closed last 3wks Aug. **Main courses** €9-€12. **Set lunch** €10 Tue-Fri. **Credit** AmEx, DC, MC, V. **Map** p313 D9.
La Latina scenesters in sideburns and retro couture still flock to this three-storey bar/restaurant famous for its rooftop *terraza*. The food, a mixed array of Mediterranean dishes and barbecued meats, is delicious, if a little overpriced. The carpaccios are melt-in-the-mouth and the pastas, particularly the *taglioni marinera*, drip with flavour. Discriminating carnivores love El Viajero for the high-quality, hormone-free Argentine meat, while sweet-tooths rejoice over their tiramisu, one of the best in Madrid.

PLANET
HOLLYWOOD

PRODUCTION BEST AMERICAN FOOD

ADDRESS PLAZA DE LAS CORTES S/N

CAMERA 8

DATE	SCENE	TAKE
EVERY DAY FROM 9:30 AM TO 01:00 AM	MADRID	AWAY FOOD TOO

La Viuda Blanca

C/Campomanes 6 (91 548 75 29). Metro Ópera.
Open 1.30-4.30pm, 9.30pm-midnight Mon-Sat.
Closed 2wks Aug. **Main courses** €14-€18. **Set
lunch** €10. **Credit** AmEx, DC, MC, V. **Map** p313 D7.
Once you're past the hulking goon on the door and
your eyes have adjusted to the dazzling glamour,
this trendoid club-restaurant is surprisingly welcoming. The divine waiters are disarmingly friendly
and the food, particularly the set lunch, is great
value. Lamb stew with cardamom and mashed new
potatoes merits a special mention, as does turbot
chop suey with lemon butter. At night a DJ takes to
the decks, while the daytime charms include a
sunny, plant-filled atrium.

Viuda de Vacas

C/Cava Alta 23 (91 366 58 47). Metro La Latina.
Open 1.30-4.30pm, 9pm-midnight Mon-Wed, Fri,
Sat; 1.30-4.30pm Sun. Closed 1st 2wks Sept. **Main
courses** €9-€16. **Credit** MC, V. **Map** p313 D8.
Walking through the old red linen curtains that
frame the entrance of Viuda de Vacas is rather like
entering a Spanish movie set. Which is exactly as it
should be. Pedro Almodóvar has filmed here on several occasions, and just admiring the chipped-tile-
and-refectory-table interior, you can see why. This
classic in good Castilian home cooking has been in
the Canova family for three generations; it was
established long ago by the feisty grandmother (the
widow of Señor Vacas, hence the restaurant's odd
bovine name). Favourite dishes include the stuffed
courgettes and the baked hake or sea bream.

Xentes

C/Humilladero 13 (91 366 42 66). Metro La Latina.
Open 12.30pm-midnight Tue-Sun. Closed Aug.
Main courses €7-€23. **Credit** AmEx, DC, MC, V.
Map p313 D9.
With the TV blaring and some half-hearted nautical
decor, this is a rather strange setting for some of the
best seafood in Madrid. But the Galician patrons
at the bar happily scarf oysters and beer, and the
diners in the back are just as delighted with their
pulpo a gallega (octopus with paprika) and *arroz
con bogavantes* (lobster paella). Sample the Galician
tetilla cheese and wash it down with the lovely light
Albariño house wine.

International

Emma y Júlia

C/Cava Baja 19 (91 366 10 23). Metro La Latina.
Open 9pm-midnight Mon; 2-4pm, 9pm-midnight
Wed-Thur; 2-4pm, 9pm-1am Fri, Sat. Closed last
2wks July. **Main courses** €8-€12. **Credit** AmEx,
DC, MC, V. **Map** p313 D8.
Smack in the middle of a street known as the epicentre of stout *cocido*-type cuisine is this popular
Italian eaterie – a sound alternative when a big salad
and pizza are in order. The staff are friendly, the
environment laid-back, and the food solid. The
breaded artichokes are divine and the house red is

good and cheap. It's often wise to call in advance.
Francisco, the deadpan but witty Galician waiter,
will want to practise his English with you.

Marechiaro

C/Conde de Lemos 3 (91 547 00 42). Metro Ópera.
Open *Sept-July* 2-4pm, 9pm-midnight Mon-Fri; 9pm-
1am Sat. *Aug* 9pm-midnight Mon-Fri; 9pm-1am Sat.
Main courses €7-€11. **Credit** AmEx, DC, MC, V.
Map p313 D7.
You know a pizzeria is worth its salt when it attracts
this many Italians. Two Neapolitans are behind this
modest little place that offers some of the best pizzas in the city. Cooked in wood-fired ovens, they
have thin, flavourful crusts and fresh ingredients.
Pastas are good too, but definitely play second
fiddle. Decor is pungent-orange walls sporting an
odd mix of Venetian masks… and black-and-white
photos of Diego Maradona.

Vegetarian

El Estragón

*Costanilla de San Andrés 10 (91 365 89 82). Metro
La Latina.* **Open** 1.30-4pm, 8.30-11.30pm daily.
Main courses €11-€13.50. **Set lunch** €9.50. **Set
dinner** €25. **Credit** AmEx, DC, MC, V. **Map** p312 C8.
El Estragón's underlying concept appears to be 'vegetarian food for meat-eaters', and thus there is no
shortage of soya 'meatballs', 'hamburgers' and so
on. Where this place really excels, however, is in its
straightforward vegetarian dishes, such as a fabulous towering heap of *risotto verde* containing every
green vegetable you can think of, topped with
stringy emmental. It is also a delightful place to sit
and dream, with its terracotta tiles, perky blue-and-
white gingham and view over Plaza de la Paja.
Should contemplation pale, there is free net access.

Sol & Gran Vía

La Bola Taberna

*C/Bola 5 (91 547 69 30). Metro Ópera or Santo
Domingo.* **Open** 1-4pm Mon, Sun; 1-4pm, 8.30-
11.30pm Tue-Sat. Closed Aug. **Main courses** €12-
€13. **Set lunch** €11. **Credit** MC, V. **Map** p313 D6.
Holding court on a quiet backstreet, this dignified,
classic Madrid restaurant is considered by many
to be the home of *cocido*, the huge and hearty stew
beloved of *madrileños* and a test for the biggest
of appetites. La Bola is still run by the same family
that founded it in the 19th century, and the *cocido*
(which is only served at lunchtime) is still cooked
traditionally in earthenware pots on a wood fire.
Unfortunately, this impressive pedigree has led to a
certain complacency, verging on the arrogant, in
some of the waiting staff.

Don Paco

*C/Caballero de Gracia 36 (91 531 44 80). Metro
Gran Vía.* **Open** 1.30-4.30pm, 8.30-11.30pm Mon-Fri;
1.30-4.30pm Sat. Closed Aug. **Main courses** €9-€12.
Set dinner €25. **Credit** MC, V. **Map** p313 F7.

Eat, Drink, Shop

Menu glossary

See also p144 for tapas.

Eat, Drink, Shop

Basics

Primer plato (entrante) first course; **segundo plato** second or main course; **postre** dessert; **plato combinado** quick, one-course meal, with several ingredients served on the same plate; **aceite y vinagre** oil and vinegar; **agua** water; **con gas/sin gas** fizzy/still; **pan** bread; **vino** wine (**tinto** red, **blanco** white, **rosado** rosé); **cerveza** beer; **la cuenta** the bill; **servicio incluído** service included; **propina** tip.

Cooking styles & techniques

Adobado marinated; **al ajillo** with olive oil and garlic; **al chilindrón** (usually chicken or lamb) cooked in a spicy tomato, pepper, ham, onion and garlic sauce; **a la marinera** (fish or shellfish) cooked with garlic, onions and white wine; **a la parilla** charcoal-grilled; **al pil-pil** (Basque) flash-fried in sizzling oil and garlic; **a la plancha** grilled directly on a hot metal plate; **al vapor** steamed; **asado** (**al horno de leña**) roast (in a wood oven); **crudo** raw; **en salsa** in a sauce or gravy; **escabechado**, **en escabeche** marinated in vinegar with bay leaves and garlic; **estofado** braised; **frito** fried; **guisado** stewed; **hervido** boiled; **(en) pepitoria** casserole dish, usually of chicken or game, with egg, wine and almonds; **relleno** stuffed.

Huevos (eggs)

Huevos fritos fried eggs (sometimes served with chorizo); **revuelto** scrambled eggs; **tortilla asturiana** omelette with tomato, tuna and onion; **tortilla francesa** plain omelette; **tortilla de patatas** Spanish potato omelette.

Sopas y potajes (soups & stews)

Caldo (gallego) broth of pork and greens; **fabada** rich Asturian stew of beans, chorizo and *morcilla* (black blood sausage); **gazpacho** cold soup, usually of tomatoes, red pepper and cucumber; **purrusalda** (Basque) soup of salt cod, leeks and potatoes; **sopa de ajo** garlic soup; **sopa castellana** garlic soup with poached egg and chickpeas; **sopa de fideos** noodle soup.

Pescado y mariscos (fish & shellfish)

Almejas clams; **atún, bonito** tuna; **bacalao** salt cod; **besugo** sea bream; **bogavante** lobster; **caballa** mackerel; **calamares** squid; **camarones** small shrimps; **cangrejo, buey de mar** crab; **cangrejo de río** freshwater crayfish; **dorada** gilthead bream; **gambas** prawns; **kokotxas** (Basque) hake cheeks; **langosta** spiny lobster; **langostinos** langoustines; **lubina** sea bass; **mejillones** mussels; **mero** grouper; **merluza** hake; **ostras** oysters; **pescadilla** whiting; **pescaditos** whitebait; **pulpo** octopus; **rape** monkfish; **rodaballo** turbot; **salmonete** red mullet; **sardinas** sardines; **sepia** cuttlefish; **trucha** trout; **ventresca de bonito** tuna fillet; **vieiras** scallops.

Carne, aves, caza y embutidos (meat, poultry, game & charcuterie)

Bistec steak; **buey, vacuno** (cuts **solomillo, entrecot**) beef; **butifarra** Catalan sausage; **callos** tripe; **capón** capon; **cerdo** pork, pig; **chorizo** spicy sausage, served cooked or cold; **choto** kid; **chuletas, chuletones, chuletillas** chops; **cochinillo** roast suckling pig; **cocido** traditional stew of Madrid; **codillo** knuckle (normally ham); **codornices** quails; **conejo** rabbit; **cordero** lamb; **costillas** ribs; **estofado de ternera** veal stew; **faisán** pheasant; **gallina** chicken; **hígado** liver; **jabalí** wild boar; **jamón ibérico** cured ham from Iberian pigs; **jamón serrano** cured ham; **jamón york** cooked ham; **lacón** gammon ham; **lechazo, cordero lechal** milk-fed baby lamb; **liebre** hare; **lomo (de cerdo)** loin of pork; **morcilla** black blood sausage; **pato** duck; **pavo** turkey; **perdiz** partridge; **pollo** chicken; **riñones** kidneys; **salchichas** frying sausages; **sesos** brains; **ternera** veal (in Spain it is slaughtered later than most veal, so is closer to beef).

Arroz y legumbres (rice & pulses)

Alubias, judías white beans; **arroz a banda** rice cooked in shellfish stock; **arroz negro** black rice cooked in squid ink; **fideuà** seafood dish similar to a paella, but made with noodles instead of rice; **frijoles** red kidney beans; **garbanzos** chickpeas; **judiones** large haricot beans; **lentejas** lentils; **paella de mariscos** shellfish paella; **pochas (caparrones)** new-season kidney beans.

Verduras (vegetables)

Acelgas Swiss chard; **alcachofas** artichokes; **berenjena** aubergine/eggplant; **calabacines** courgettes/zucchini; **cebolla** onion; **champiñones** mushrooms; **col** cabbage; **ensalada mixta** basic salad of lettuce, tomato and onion; **ensalada verde** green salad, without tomato; **espárragos** asparagus; **espinacas** spinach; **grelos** turnip leaves; **guisantes** peas; **habas** broad beans; **judías verdes** green beans; **lechuga** lettuce; **menestra** braised mixed vegetables; **patatas fritas** chips; **pepino** cucumber; **pimientos** sweet peppers; **pimientos de piquillo** slightly hot red peppers; **pisto** mixture of cooked vegetables, similar to ratatouille; **setas** forest mushrooms; **tomate** tomato; **zanahoria** carrot.

Fruta (fruit)

Arándanos bilberries; **cerezas** cherries; **ciruelas** plums; **fresas** strawberries; **higos** figs; **macedonia** fruit salad; **manzana** apple; **melocotón** peach; **melón** melon; **moras** blackcurrants; **naranja** orange; **pera** pear; **piña** pineapple; **plátano** banana; **sandía** watermelon; **uvas** grapes.

Postres (desserts)

Arroz con leche rice pudding; **bizcocho** sponge cake; **brazo de gitano** ice-cream or custard swiss roll; **cuajada** junket (served with honey); **flan** crème caramel; **helado** ice-cream; **leche frita** custard fried in breadcrumbs; **membrillo** quince jelly (often served with cheese); **tarta** cake; **tarta de Santiago** sponge-like almond cake; **torrijas** sweet bread fritters.

Quesos (cheeses)

Burgos, villalón, requesón white, cottage-like cheeses, often eaten as dessert; **cabrales** strong blue Asturian goat's cheese; **idiazábal** Basque sheep's milk cheese; **mahón** usually mild, creamy cow's milk cheese from Menorca; **manchego (tierno, añejo, semi, seco)** hard sheep's-milk cheese (young, mature, semi-soft, dry); **tetilla** soft cow's milk cheese; **torta del casar** tangy sheep's milk cheese from Extremadura.

Eat, Drink, Shop

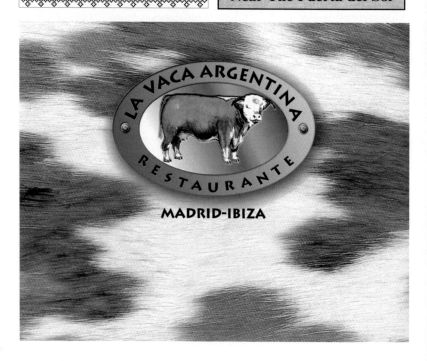

Don Paco, now in his 80s, is a former bullfighter from Jérez, and the Andalucian matador in him is charmingly apparent in his 40-year-old restaurant. With photos of famous visitors (the King and his parents were regulars, and Bob Hope ate here too) and Andalucian memorabilia covering the walls, Don Paco oozes southern style. *Tinto de verano* ('summer wine' cut with lemonade) on tap, ample sherry options… who needs Seville? The shrimp with mushrooms in aïoli is a must, followed by the stellar *arroz rociero*, an Andalucian paella with eight types of fish. Most lively for lunch.

Gula Gula

Gran Vía 1 (91 522 87 64/www.gulagula.net).
Metro Banco de España or Sevilla. **Open** 1-4.30pm, 9.30-11.30pm Mon-Wed, Sun; 1-4.30pm, 9.30pm-2.30am Thur-Sat. **Lunch buffet** €7-€10.50. **Dinner buffet** €17.50-€23.40. **Credit** AmEx, DC, MC, V. **Map** p314 G7.
Prepare yourself for muscled waiters in scant clothing, singing drag queens, and bawdy humour – this is Gula Gula (Greedy Greedy). It's all about the show, darling, less about the food, but even that isn't half-bad. Most people skip the hot dishes (though they have shown some moments of inspiration lately) and stick to the all-you-can-eat salad buffet, which is fair to middling. But what's truly inspiring here are the tiny leather shorts worn by the waiters.
Other locations: C/Infante 5, Santa Ana (91 420 29 19).

Suite

C/Virgen de los Peligros 4 (91 521 40 31). Metro Sevilla. **Open** 1.30-5pm, 9.30pm-3.30am Mon-Fri; 9.30pm-4.30am Sat. **Main courses** €10-€15. **Set lunch** €11.70. **Credit cards** AmEx, DC, MC, V. **Map** p313 F7.
With a bar-lounge-restaurant downstairs and a housey dancefloor upstairs, Suite is the 'eat, drink and dance' hybrid for nights when you feel like staying in one place. Located in an anonymous office building near Puerta del Sol, this is sleek 1970s retro: Austin Powers meets Ibiza (back when it was good). The food is as stylish as the cool young *madrileños* who eat here – opt for the salmon marinated in coffee or the grilled duck magret.

International

Caripén

Plaza de la Marina Española 4 (91 541 11 77).
Metro Santo Domingo. **Open** 9pm-3am Mon-Sat.
Closed Aug. **Main courses** €12-€35. **Credit** DC, MC, V. **Map** p312 C6.
At first glance, this French bistro seems a wee bit run down, but nonetheless it's all class – in a campy, Broadway kind of way. Behind the dangling blue Christmas-tree lights are tables occupied by singing, dancing, canoodling patrons having a very good time, oblivious to the excellent skate in black butter or crêpe with salmon and caviar. The merry atmosphere owes a lot to the staff, particularly Juanjo, who

floats through the restaurant spreading his charm like a host(ess) well versed in the art of entertainment. The late opening hours are another bonus.

Delfos

Cuesta de Santo Domingo 14 (91 548 37 64). Metro Santo Domingo. **Open** 1.30-4.30pm, 8pm-12.30am Tue-Sat; 1.30-4.30pm Sun. **Main courses** €10-€18. **Set lunch** €9.95 Tue-Fri. **Credit** AmEx, DC, MC, V. **Map** p313 D7.
Delfos is here to prove that Greek food is not all kebabs and salads. In taverna-style surroundings, with just-the-right-side-of-tack Greek details – statues and strings of blue-and-white flags – friendly waiters serve up an unexpected variety of dishes. A good start is the *pikilia megali*, a platter of garlicky Greek olives, rich fried feta cheese, refreshing tsatsiki, lemony taramasalata, stuffed vine leaves and more. The moussaka and lamb with nut and honey are also scrumptious. If you dare, try the retsina.

Kawara

C/Aduana 23 (91 532 89 03). Metro Sol. **Open** 1.30-4pm, 8.30-11.30pm Mon-Sat. **Main courses** €7-€14. **Set lunch** €11.50. **Credit** MC, V. **Map** p313 E7.
If you prefer your Japanese food without all the designer minimalist trimmings, this is your place. Hidden on a backstreet behind Sol, Kawara is a sashimi in the rough. Trust the tell-tale sign of authenticity (the patrons silently reading Japanese newspapers over their soup) and order the reasonably priced sushi tray: it comes with miso, followed by eight pieces of sushi and a large maki roll. Apart from that, there is a wide range of sashimi, noodle and meat dishes. Ask for tea, which will be replenished throughout your meal by Akiko, the sweet lady who runs the place.

Pasta Nostra Pizza Nostra

Carrera de San Jerónimo 32 (91 360 08 27).
Metro Sevilla. **Open** 1.30-4.30pm, 8.30pm-midnight Mon-Thur, Sun; 1.30-4.30pm, 8.30pm-1am Fri, Sat. **Main courses** €7.50-€9.60. **Credit** AmEx, MC, V. **Map** p313 F7.
Who said you couldn't get great 'za in Madrid? Pizzas at this unassuming Italian ristorante could convince even the most discriminating of patrons. Try the special of the house: the eponymous Pizza Nostra, an insanely tasty mix of bresaola, rocket, mozzarella and corn that keeps the locals coming back weekly. The crust is light and the cheese not too heavy, so even though the pizzas are the size of tractor tyres, they can be gobbled easily by one person. There are also ample pasta and salad choices.
Other locations: C/Jovellanos 5, Huertas & Santa Ana (91 532 11 00); C/Fuencarral, 116, Chamberí (91 593 0113).

Taj

C/Marqués de Cubas 6 (91 531 50 59). Metro Banco de España. **Open** 1-4pm, 8.30-11.30pm Mon-Thur; 1-4pm, 8.30pm-midnight Fri-Sun. **Main courses** €7.50-€13.75. **Set lunch** €10.95 Mon-Fri. **Credit** AmEx, DC, MC, V. **Map** p314 H6.

Eat, Drink, Shop

Everything about Taj promises serious curry – from the jingly-jangly muzak, to the fanned linen napkins and plastic flowers. The menu includes all the usuals, but the *degustación* of samosa, pakora, tandoori chicken, lamb curry, pilau and naan is a good bet. Try to get the curries *picante* (hot), though the waiters may decide that that can't be what you really mean and give you *medio* anyway. Desserts are a bit limited and the decor slightly naff, which is curiously reassuring.

Huertas & Santa Ana

El Cenador del Prado

C/Prado 4 (91 429 15 61). Metro Antón Martín. **Open** 1.30-4pm, 9pm-midnight Mon-Fri; 9pm-midnight Sat; 1.30-4pm Sun. **Main courses** €12.50-€17.75. **Set menu** €19.05. **Credit** AmEx, DC, MC, V. **Map** p313 F8.

Don't let the design extravagance – fuschia walls, explosive murals of fruit and gilt mirrors – distract you from the Herranz brothers' culinary talents: tasty Spanish cuisine with highly imaginative twists. Several decadent *menús de degustación*, one just for vegetarians, offer good value. The *patatas a la importancia* (fried in a garlic, parsley and clam sauce) are superlative, and the wine list is good and well priced. Skipping dessert here is an absolute no-no; try the pear with wine sauce and blue-cheese ice-cream. Dishes are artistically prepared and some are veritable sculptures.

Champagneria Gala

C/Moratín 22 (91 429 25 62). Metro Antón Martín. **Open** 1-3.30pm, 9-11.30pm Mon-Thur; 1.30-4pm, 9pm-midnight Fri-Sun. **Set menus** €13, €18. **No credit cards. Map** p314 G8.

This garden atrium, dripping in ivy and gaudy chandeliers, is a festive place to stick your fork in one of 22 varieties of paella. But it's the *porrón* – a long-spouted jug from which you pour a stream of wine down your throat – that makes this really fun: everyone must try their turn at this subtle art. The quality of the food, however, has diminished in recent years as the number of tourists has grown, and there have been numerous tales of over-salty paella and under-friendly service.

La Cueva de Gata

C/Moratín 19 (91 360 09 43). Metro Antón Martín. **Open** 11.30am-4.30pm, 7.30pm-midnight Mon-Sat. Closed 1st 2wks Aug. **Main courses** €10-€20. **Set lunch** €10. **Credit** AmEx, DC, MC, V. **Map** p314 G8.

Buttercup-yellow walls and tablecloths set off a constantly changing selection of bright oil paintings (all for sale), while downstairs there is a cave-like basement with a handful of tables that might be better for groups. Eating à la carte is still good value, but the set lunch has gone up a notch in quality and might include celery and apple soup to start, chicken with capers and cherry tomatoes, and a baked apple to finish. Other nice touches include the jug of iced water automatically placed on the table, soft Brazilian jazz and great lighting.

Lhardy

Carrera de San Jerónimo 8 (91 521 33 85/ www.lhardy.com). Metro Sol. **Open** 1-3.30pm, 8.30-11pm Mon-Sat; 1-3.30pm Sun. Closed Aug. **Main courses** €24-€40. **Credit** AmEx, DC, MC, V. **Map** p313 E7.

This landmark restaurant, which opened in 1839, is credited with having introduced French haute cuisine into the culinary wilderness of Madrid. Founder Emile Lhardy is said to have been enticed to the city by none other than *Carmen* author Prosper Mérimée, who told him there was no decent restaurant in the Spanish capital. These days it's rated as much for its history and *belle époque* decor as for the (expensive) food. The menu is as Frenchified as ever, although there's also a very refined *cocido*, good game and *callos* (tripe), in addition to an excellent, if pricey, wine list.

La Vaca Verónica

C/Moratín 38 (91 429 78 27). Metro Antón Martín. **Open** 2-4pm, 9pm-midnight Mon-Fri, Sun; 9pm-midnight Sat. **Main courses** €12-€14.50. **Set menu** €13.50. **Credit** AmEx, DC, MC, V. **Map** p314 G8.

With canary-yellow walls, puffed-up banquettes, bright paintings and a certain Gallic charm, Veronica the Cow is a whimsical reprieve from the bustling streets of Huertas. Attracting business types and hipsters alike, it's a fine choice for a quality *menú del día*. Pesto pasta, the abundant 'cow's tray' of chorizo, *morcilla* (black blood sausage) and other meats, and various salads are just some of the tasty options.

International

Come Prima

C/Echegaray 27 (91 420 30 42). Metro Antón Martín. **Open** 9pm-midnight Mon; 1.30-4pm, 9pm-midnight Tue-Sat. Closed 2wks Aug. **Main courses** €12-€17. **Set lunch** €12 Tue-Fri. **Credit** AmEx, DC, MC, V. **Map** p313 F8.

The toothsome risottos and home-made pastas here are a godsend for Italian gastronomes. Don't miss the risotto with mushrooms, parmesan and white-truffle oil, or the perfectly executed pasta with lobster. Since it opened a few years ago, Come Prima has brought in a classy crew of Spaniards (including, rumour has it, Prince Felipe), who pack the place out every night, even on a Monday. With white curtains and tablecloths, green wood-panelled walls and Italian opera posters, you could almost be in the Tuscan countryside.

Pizzeria Cervantes

C/León 8 (91 420 12 98). Metro Antón Martín. **Open** 1.30-4.30pm, 8.30-12.30pm Mon-Thur, Sun; 1.30-4.30pm, 8.30pm-1.30am Fri, Sat. Closed 2wks Aug. **Main courses** €7-€9. **Set lunch** €8.50. **Credit** AmEx, DC, MC, V. **Map** p313 F8.

This unassuming little hideaway doesn't shut down the kitchen during the day, so when most restaurants are sweeping the floors, you can take refuge in its tasty pizzas and pastas (the Chicana pizza with

Speed sating

It's a phenomenon often noted by visitors that Madrid lacks the sandwich bars found on every corner of most other European capitals. The Spanish have always been appalled by the idea of lunch as refuelling, let alone – horror of horrors – eating at one's desk. No, lunch here has always been a leisurely affair, and it can be hard to contact anyone between the hours of 1.30 and 4.30pm. With all this in mind, the recent appetite for the innovative and the fast has taken everyone by surprise.

Stand on the corner of C/Libertad and C/San Marcos in Chueca to get the picture. On one corner is **Diurno**, the café/takeaway/video rental hotspot (see p208), a wild success in the neighbourhood. On the opposite corner is the **Dosa Grill** (C/Libertad 17, 91 360 47 50), an airy little café to grab a quick and delicious dosa, also getting rave reviews. Two doors up sits **Deli Deluxe** (C/San Marcos 35, 91 522 42 04), a gourmet takeaway deli, and just next door, **The Wok** (C/San Marcos 31-33, 91 531 69 79) where queues of *madrileños* in need of a quick-fix plate of noodles spill out the door. Could it be that Madrid is speeding up?

No place better typifies the phenomenon than famed Catalan chef Ferran Adrià's venture into quality fast food, the abominably named **Fast Good** (see p140; pictured). The idea is to make fast food good food, and the rules of thumb are simple: use fresh, high-quality ingredients, aim for a few easy hot options like *panini* and burgers (all prepared with a gourmet flourish), ditch the animal fat in favour of olive oil, and chuck in a handful of extravagances like lychee and red peach juice for good measure. Make it fast and easy, create a colourful modern atmosphere amid Madrid's ever-busy office nexus, and wait and see what happens.

So far, so fast. Fast Good's rapid success is undeniable, and it's packed with eager diners virtually every night of the week. But this is far from the cheapo American franchises peddling mystery meat across the globe. This is a Spanish-originated endeavour providing swift good meals that fall somewhere between fast food and the *menú del día*. Plus, it's been branded with the Adrià stamp, an almost guaranteed seal of success (although we could live without the plastic cups and cutlery).

So does Madrid's current love affair with the speedy suggest that the days of the long Spanish lunch are numbered? Not in a million *menús del día*.

jalapeños is especially loved by fans of spicy hot food). Despite the name, this place exceeds the definition of pizzeria, with a long list of salads, crêpes, risottos and standard fare such as roast beef and *solomillo*. The neighbourhood regulars are fans of the cheap breakfast deal and love to linger over *café con leche* and the papers.

Vegetarian

Artemisa

C/Ventura de la Vega 4 (91 429 50 92). Metro Sevilla. **Open** 1.30-4pm, 9pm-midnight daily. **Main courses** €6-€20. **Set menu** €9.50. **Credit** AmEx, DC, MC, V. **Map** p313 F7.

With the nondescript decor so typical of Madrid's vegetarian restaurants, Artemisa might seem no different from the rest. But the salads are bigger and more creative, and the soy burgers have more flavour. The satisfying *menú de degustación* lets you try it all: veggie paella, *croquetas*, aubergine salad and more. They also have a few options for non-veggies: try the chicken Armagnac made with organic free-range chicken – absolutely scrumptious. **Other locations:** C/Tres Cruces 4, Sol & Gran Via (91 521 87 21).

Lavapiés

Casa Lastra Sidrería

C/Olivar 3 (91 369 08 37). Metro Antón Martín. **Open** 1.30-4pm, 8pm-midnight Mon, Tue, Thur-Sun. Closed July. **Main courses** €10-€15.50. **Set lunch** €12.30 Mon-Fri. **Credit** AmEx, DC, MC, V. **Map** p313 E9.

Asturian food is now gaining international acclaim, but the regulars at Casa Lastra have known how good it is for a long time. Always packed with happy locals munching cabrales (a strong Asturian blue cheese) and *pote asturiano* (stew with cabbage, haricot beans, black pudding, chorizo and potato) at the bar, or dining on *perdiz* (partridge) and *merluza a la sidra* (hake in cider) at the back, this is the place to come to sample good home cooking – and, of course, wash it down with a glass of traditional still cider.

Freiduría de Gallinejas

C/Embajadores 84 (91 517 59 33). Metro Embajadores. **Open** 11am-11pm Mon-Sat. Closed 3wks Aug. **Main courses** €6-€7. **No credit cards**.

Still going strong after a century, this is the best place in the city for deep-fried lamb intestines and other tasty titbits. Not for faint stomachs, this offal institution offers superbly prepared testicles, glands and stomach linings, all accompanied by strong red wine. Worth checking out just for the lively scene and for a taste of Old Madrid's innard circle.

Restaurante Soidemersol

C/Argumosa 9 (91 539 73 71). Metro Atocha or Lavapiés. **Open** 1-5pm, 8pm-midnight Tue-Sun. **Main courses** €5-€10. **Set lunch** €8 Mon-Thur, €10 Fri-Sun. **Credit** AmEx, DC, MC, V. **Map** p313 F10.

Also confusingly known as El Económico and Los Remedios (turn it backwards to see why), the Soidemersol is something of an institution. In recent years, the premises have had a bit of a facelift, but it retains a friendly neighbourhood feel, along with the wooden furniture and original tiling. Try the seafood risotto, calf's liver and onions, or beef ragoût with vegetables. There are tables outside in summer.

Tutti-Plen

C/Buenavista 18 (91 467 46 90). Metro Antón Martín. **Open** 1.30-4pm, 8.30pm-midnight Tue-Sat; 1.30-4.30pm Sun. **Main courses** €5.50-€8. **Set menu** €7. **Credit** AmEx, DC, MC, V. **Map** p313 F9.

Tutti-Plen's menu says: 'This isn't fast food; take your time and enjoy the atmosphere.' And it's best to heed this comment – dishes can take a while to arrive. When this funky restaurant opened a few years back, its 'so-laid-back-we're-horizontal' approach promised to make it a short-term venture, but it has proved a hit with the arty Lavapiés crowd. The very reasonably priced menu includes several vast salads and excellent crêpes, as well as the more upmarket salmon tartare and *lomo de buey* (steak), followed by wicked puddings.

International

Shapla

C/Lavapiés 42 (91 528 15 99). Metro Lavapiés. **Open** 10am-1.30am daily. Closed Sept. **Main courses** €5-€7. **Set menu** €7.25. **Credit** MC, V. **Map** p313 E9.

The restaurant formerly known as Casa Juanito decided to change its name. Pity – the contrast of bog-standard Spanish caff on the outside and the almost exclusively male clientele from India and Pakistan somehow added to its charm. And even though they've attempted to upscale (witness the arrival of the ubiquitous pink tablecloth), this is still the greasy spoon of Indian eating in Madrid. Expect the usual suspects, many of them veggie – at really low prices.

Chueca

El 26 de Libertad

C/Libertad 26 (91 522 25 22). Metro Chueca. **Open** *Sept-June* 1-4pm, 8pm-midnight Mon-Thur; 1-4pm, 8pm-1am Fri, Sat; 1-4pm Sun. *July, Aug* 1-4pm, 8pm-midnight Mon-Thur; 1-4pm, 8pm-1am Fri, Sat. **Main courses** €8.40-€16.80. **Set lunch** €9.50. **Credit** MC, V. **Map** p310 G5.

With its deep colours and lavishly set tables, El 26 de Libertad is over-the-top elegance bordering on the camp. But not too fine to be fun, and a favourite in the *barrio* – the bar is often brimming with *caña* drinkers. The food is Spanish, but with a creative edge in the *morcilla* (black blood sausage), cannelloni and anchovies filled with spinach and pine nuts, for example, and food presentation is as lavish as the decor. At lunchtime only a simple *menú* is available, so book for dinner to put them through their paces.

Eat, Drink, Shop

El Armario

C/San Bartolomé 7 (91 532 83 77). Metro Chueca.
Open 1.30-4pm, 9pm-1am Mon-Thur; 1.30-4pm,
8.30pm-1am Fri, Sat; 2-4pm, 8.30pm-2.30am Sun.
Closed 3wks July. **Set lunch** €8.50 Mon-Sat; €9
Sun. **Set dinner** €20. **Credit** AmEx, DC, MC, V.
Map p313 F6.

Aptly named 'The Closet', this restaurant in the
heart of Chueca makes up for its diminutive size
with generous portions. This is Mediterranean food
with an edge; soups and salads are above the norm.
The *menú del día* is a find, and might include cream
of spinach soup to start, followed by oriental chick-
en and a pud. It's always packed, so get there before
the crowds, especially for lunch. Friendly, charming
service is a real plus when eating at close quarters.
Other locations: La Coqueta C/Libertad 3,
Chueca (91 523 06 47).

Azul Profundo

*Plaza de Chueca 8 (91 532 25 64). Metro
Chueca.* **Open** 2-3.30pm, 9pm-midnight Tue-Sat.
Closed Aug. **Main courses** €16-€18. **Credit** MC,
V. **Map** p310 G5.

Improbable and airy ingredients matched in startling but successful combinations and served in a
series of tapas-sized portions: this must be the
Spanish *nueva cocina* that has international gastronomes slavering with pleasure. Azul Profundo is
one affordable place to get an idea of what this food
trend is all about. Young chef Andrés Madrigal is a
talent to look out for, but hopelessly let down by his
sour-faced waiting staff. Arrive late for one of the
two dinner settings (at 9 and 11pm) at your peril.

Bazaar

C/Libertad 21 (91 523 39 05). Metro Chueca.
Open 1-4pm, 8.30-11.45pm daily. **Main courses**
€6-€7.50. **Set lunch** €8.30. **Credit** AmEx, MC, V.
Map p310 G5.

The philosophy behind this wildly popular chain of
restaurants involves swish, elegant surroundings, a
sophisticated menu and dirt-cheap pricing. And yes,
it's all that. What are less palatable are the dour,
inexperienced waitresses and the production-line
cooking. This doesn't matter so much with starters
like rocket and feta salad, or puddings like fruit
carpaccio with soured yoghurt, and strawberry
tiramisu with cocoa ice-cream, but it does begin to
grate when your steak (wine reduction, wild mushrooms) has been spot-cooked in a microwave.
Other locations: La Gloria de Montero
C/Caballero de Gracia 10, Sol & Gran Via (91 523 44
07); **La Finca de Susana** C/Arlaban 4, Huertas &
Santa Ana (91 369 35 57).

El Bierzo

C/Barbieri 16 (91 531 91 10). Metro Chueca. **Open**
1-4pm, 8-11.30pm Mon-Sat. **Main courses** €6-€9.50.
Set menu €8. **Credit** MC, V. **Map** p313 F6.

El Bierzo is one of the best of Madrid's long-established *casas de comida* – honest, dependable neighbourhood joints where you can get a good *menú del
día* at a reasonable price. It buzzes, particularly dur-

ing lunch, with a loyal crowd feasting on simple
dishes: roast chicken, seven types of tortilla and
excellent *setas al ajillo* (wild mushrooms fried in garlic). Just a chat with the friendly owner, Miguel, is
worth coming here for.

El Bogavante del Almirante

*C/Almirante 11 (91 532 18 50). Metro Banco de
España or Chueca.* **Open** 2-4pm, 9pm-midnight Mon-
Sat; 2-4pm Sun. Closed 2wks Aug. **Main course**
€18-€20. **Credit** AmEx, DC, MC, V. **Map** p310 H5.

Almirante wins the award for most fanciful set
design. Nestled in a cave-like basement, a ponder-
ous lobster claw hangs from the ceiling, while black
outlines of sea creatures swirl across shrimp-pink
walls. The staff, clad in black, add to the scene,
which feels more Manhattan than Madrid. Seafood
is their forte. The fish specials are always excellent,
but the *arroz con bogavante* (lobster paella) takes the
prize. Almirante and its lobster have been attracting an international set since opening in 2000.

Café Oliver

C/Almirante 12 (91 521 73 79). Metro Colón. **Open**
1.30-4pm Mon; 1.30-4pm, 9pm-midnight Tue-Thur;
1.30-4pm, 9pm-1am Fri, Sat; 11.15am-4pm Sun. **Main
courses** €12-€15. **Set lunch** €12.50. **Credit** AmEx,
DC, MC, V. **Map** p310 H5.

Still an 'in' spot for the international crowd, Café
Oliver runs the gamut of French, Spanish, Italian
and Moroccan without falling into the dreaded
(con)fusion trap. Highlights include the couscous
with *salmonete* (red mullet), fettuccine with lobster
and *bomba de chocolate*, definitely a candidate for
top all-time pudding. The plush red velvet banquettes and large windows looking out on the street
make Café Oliver an ideal place for Chueca people-
watching. Ideal on a Sunday for American brunch:
pancakes, eggs benedict, waffles, coffee and newspapers. The downstairs cocktail bar is cool and
loungy, with DJs playing soul, R&B and house.

Casa Manolo

*C/Orellana 17 (91 308 73 78). Metro Alonso
Martínez.* **Open** 10am-4pm Mon-Thur;
10am-4pm, 9pm-midnight Fri, Sat. Closed
Aug. **Main courses** €10-€17. **Set lunch**
€12. **Credit** MC, V. **Map** p310 H4.

One of the best sources of *cocina casera*, or home
cooking, in Madrid, Casa Manolo has an endearing,
homely atmosphere, enhanced by the black-and-
white photo of the owner's grandmother and aunt
presiding over the restaurant. But even though it's
all about tradition, this place prepares creative
mouthwatering salads that put the usual *ensalada
mixta* to shame – the aubergine with tomato and
goat's cheese, for example, must be one of the best
in the city. And then there's lentil soup, *cocido* and
other hearty stews, all supremely prepared.

Extremadura

C/Libertad 13 (91 531 82 22). Metro Chueca. **Open**
1-4pm Mon; 1-4pm, 9pm-midnight Tue-Sat. **Main
courses** €12-€14. **Credit** DC, MC, V. **Map** p314 G6.

El Puchero. *See p183.*

With festive live piano accompaniment, this is the spot to try out specialities from one of Spain's least-known regions, Extremadura. It's both classy and country – beautifully set tables with enormous glasses (for the excellent wines) combine with painting and pottery from the region. The food is marked by Extremadura's former days of austerity, with game that could be hunted on the dry plains. The trademark dish, *migas*, is a mix of breadcrumbs, chorizo and peppers that shepherds concocted to make use of old bread. Try the *torta del casar*, a soft, pungent regional cheese.

Los Jiménez

C/Barbieri 14 (91 521 11 86). Metro Chueca. **Open** 12.30-4pm Mon; 12.30-4pm, 9pm-midnight Tue-Sat. Closed Aug. **Main courses** €9-€12. **Set lunch** €8. **Credit** MC, V. **Map** p313 F6.
Refreshingly unpretentious, Los Jiménez was serving no-frills food long before Chueca became the gay capital of Spain. Ghastly fluorescent lights, the smell of frying and a menu board that spans the wall behind the bar – basically, it's a good old-fashioned greasy spoon. Popular with old-time locals, new kids and anyone with an appreciation for good value, who come here for all the Spanish solids: oxtail stew, tripe, *cocido* and generous, if basic, salads.

Madrilia

C/Clavel 6 (91 523 92 57). Metro Gran Vía. **Open** noon-4pm, 9pm-midnight Mon-Thur, Sun; noon-4pm, 9pm-1am Fri, Sat. **Set lunch** €16. **Credit** AmEx, DC, MC, V. **Map** p313 F6.
Swanky, stylish, but not ridiculously expensive, this is an enclave for business-lunch types and the gay community. Madrilia cooks up fresh and fashion-

able food – vegetable lasagne with truffle sauce, breaded aubergine with honey, for example – in a very pretty way. If you hanker for some greens, here you will find vegetables creatively and amply present on the menu. Some waiters appear to have been chosen for cheekbones rather than experience, however, so you may find yourself occasionally ignored.

Momo

C/Augusto Figueroa 41 (91 532 71 62). Metro Chueca. **Open** 1-4pm, 9pm-midnight daily. **Main courses** €9-€14.50. **Set lunch** €8.50. **Set dinner** €12. **Credit** AmEx, DC, MC, V. **Map** p310 G5.
Momo claims to offer *cocina creativa* – an apt description, considering that their most popular dishes are fried manchego cheese and *mocos de chocolate* (literally, 'chocolate bogies'). The orange-walled decor is *creativo*, too, although it borders on arty hotchpotch. The reasonable menu at both lunch and dinner brings in a steady flow of fans, generally young and casual, but it can be a bit hit-or-miss – the battered fish is best avoided, but stuffed aubergines are better, and puddings generally reliable.

La Mordida

C/Belén 13 (91 308 20 89). Metro Chueca. **Open** 1.30-5pm, 8.30pm-1am daily. **Main courses** €9. **Credit** AmEx, DC, MC, V. **Map** p310 G4.
Joaquín Sabina, the gravelly voiced Madrid musician and legend, does restaurants, too, but who'd have expected it to be Mexican food? And such good authentic Mexican food too, straight from the heart of Tenochtitlan. Usually bursting with high-spirited tequila drinkers, this is the place to embrace *mole*, the Mexican chocolate sauce that often scares the uninitiated away. The *pavo* (turkey) *con mole* melts

in your mouth and the *cochinita pibil* (pork tacos with spicy chilli sauce) is equally exquisite. See which local celebs or Sabina song references you can identify on the wall's wildly painted murals.
Other locations: C/Fuentes 3, Los Austrias (91 559 11 36); Trva del Conde 4, Los Austrias (91 547 30 03).

La Paella de la Reina

C/Reina 39 (91 531 18 85). Metro Chueca. **Open** 12.30-4.30pm, 8-11.30pm daily. **Main courses** €12.25-€23.50. **Set lunch** €18. **Credit** AmEx, DC, MC, V. **Map** p313 F6.

It's all about paella. Not a tourist attraction, this is where *valencianos*, the real paella experts, come for their beloved rice. In this clean, well-run, simple restaurant that makes few concessions to interior design, the only noteworthy visual is the sheer beauty of the dishes. Aside from standards such as seafood paella or the traditional Valencian version with rabbit and chicken, you can also dig into an *arroz negro* (rice cooked in squid ink) or *arroz a la banda* (paella with the seafood on the side).

El Puchero

C/Larra 13 (91 445 05 77). Metro Bilbao or Tribunal. **Open** 2-4pm, 9pm-midnight Mon-Sat. Closed end July-early Sept. **Main courses** €12-€19. **Credit** AmEx, DC, MC, V. **Map** p309 F3.

Excitingly for El Puchero, red gingham is making a comeback after 30 years in the cold. Here it had never gone away – in tablecloths, cushions, lampshades and curtains. Almost unchanged too is the range of tasty country classics – from *civet de liebre* (hare stew) to *criadillas* (don't ask) – and some excellent seafood. It's a good idea to reserve at lunchtime, when the matronly waitresses are rushed off their feet with the demands of local office workers.
Other locations: C/Padre Damián 37, Chamberí (91 345 62 98).

Ribeira Do Miño

C/Santa Brígida 1 (91 521 98 54). Metro Tribunal. **Open** 1-4pm, 8-11.30pm Tue-Sun. Closed Aug. **Main courses** €11-€17.50. **No credit cards.** **Map** p310 G4.

Galician in origin, this one's for seafood lovers. Heaped platters of prawns, crab, goose-necked barnacles, lobster and other sea creatures make it the ideal place to roll up your sleeves and get cracking shells. Other typical *gallego* dishes that add a little heat to the fun are pancakes doused in *orujo* (a fiery spirit made from grapes) and set aflame, and the *queimada* – a bowl of *orujo* set on fire and then cooled with black coffee. No reservations are allowed, so grab a ticket and wait.

Salvador

C/Barbieri 12 (91 521 45 24). Metro Chueca. **Open** 1.30-4pm, 9-11.30pm Mon-Sat. Closed Aug. **Main courses** €15-€18. **Set lunch** €25. **Credit** AmEx, DC, MC, V. **Map** p313 F6.

Every inch of this old classic is crammed with bullfighting memorabilia. You'll find good traditional fare – lentil soup, *revueltos* (concoctions with scrambled egg, often with seafood or asparagus), *solomillo* (beef) with french fries – but the real treat is the atmosphere. The formal but friendly waiters will patiently answer questions about the decor, and some of the patrons look like they may have been bullfighters themselves… many, many years ago.

Tienda de Vinos (El Comunista)

C/Augusto Figueroa 35 (91 521 70 12). Metro Chueca. **Open** 1-4.30pm, 9pm-midnight Mon-Sat. Closed mid Aug-mid Sept. **Main courses** €4-€7.25. **No credit cards.** **Map** p310 H5.

This restaurant's popular name comes from its role as a lefty meeting point years ago, under Franco (but Tienda de Vinos is all you'll see above the door). It's one of the city's real classics and a visit is essential, and no one makes any grand claims about its unchanging and unchallenging menu. To start, there are soups: gazpacho, lentil or home-made broth, followed by liver and onions, lamb cutlets, kidneys in sherry and plenty of fish. Service is known for being deadpan, but if you're lucky, you'll get one of the two charming great-grandsons of the original owner.

International

Al-Jayma

C/Barbieri 1 (91 523 11 42). Metro Chueca or Gran Vía. **Open** 1.30-4pm, 9pm-midnight Mon-Fri; 1.30-4.30pm, 9pm-12.30am Sat, Sun. **Main courses** €3.90-€7.80. **Credit** AmEx, DC, MC, V. **Map** p313 F6.

With its Berber rugs and intricate tiling, Al-Jayma is a microcosm of Morocco within Madrid. Sit back on the floor cushions to nibble on houmous and falafel, share one of their sumptuous tagines (try the lamb with dates), dig into a mountain of couscous or feast on the vegetarian options. There are also tables, of course, for longer-limbed folk. Carafes of the house wine are cheap but good, and the mint teas are typically sweet. The shock comes with the bill and how little you pay for so much good food and atmosphere.

La Dame Noire

C/Pérez Galdós 3 (91 531 04 76). Metro Chueca or Tribunal. **Open** 9pm-midnight Mon-Thur, Sun; 9pm-2am Fri, Sat. **Set dinner** €18. **Credit** AmEx, DC, MC, V. **Map** p310 G5.

Welcome to Moulin Rouge, a culinary brothel of baroque kitsch. With a colour scheme of shocking reds, blues and golds, and a fine collection of crystal and china, candles and cherubs, this restaurant is divinely ornate. Amid the decadence, you pay reasonable prices for sumptuous French classics: fried camembert, a green salad with warm goat's cheese, pork tenderloin or veal brochette. If you're lucky, Jean-Luc, one of the owners, may wear his trousers that match the embossed wallpaper. Which is nice.

Indochine

C/Barquillo 10 (91 524 03 17). Metro Banco de España. **Open** 1.30-4pm, 9pm-midnight daily. **Main courses** €9.75-€13. **Set lunch** €11. **Credit** AmEx, DC, MC, V. **Map** p314 G6.

Eat, Drink, Shop

Yet another of the new pan-Asian restaurants to hit Madrid. Yes, it's Asian fusion with modern design, but Indochine is more relaxed and less style-conscious than the rest. It's best for a lunchtime *menú del día*: enjoy piquant sweet and sour soup followed by some decent pad thai and then – the most interesting part – green-tea ice-cream with caramelised walnuts on top (trust us, it's good). If you're going à la carte, the Peking duck is a safe bet. Make sure you ask for a table in the front, near the tall windows looking out on C/Hortaleza; the back rooms are a bit on the dreary side.

Lia

C/Reina 25 (91 522 34 83). Metro Gran Vía. **Open** 1.30-4.30pm, 9-11.30pm Mon-Thur; 1.30-4.30pm, 9pm-midnight Fri; 9pm-midnight Sat. Closed Aug. **Main courses** €10-€13. **Set lunch** €10. **Credit** AmEx, DC, MC, V. **Map** p313 F6.

An attractive mix of laid-back Santo Domingo and cool New York, this Dominican oasis is a friendly place to wash down solid Caribbean fare with cold Presidentes (the national beer of the Dominican Republic). Tour the island with the *menú de degustación*; or, if you want to keep the tab low, order

The nuevo nouvelle

When Jake and Brett are about to part ways in Madrid, at the end of Hemingway's *The Sun Also Rises*, what do they do? Go eat suckling pig and drink three bottles of Rioja at the world's oldest restaurant, **El Sobrino de Botín** (*see p119*), more commonly known as Botín. Back in the late 19th century, when King Alfonso XII's sister needed a break from the palace, she would wander over to **La Bola Taberna** (*see p121*) to get a bowl full of her favourite dish – a gutsy *cocido madrileño*. Every Saturday Don Quixote would tuck into a plate of *duelos y quebrantes* – a mess of scrambled eggs, ham, chorizo, brains and tripe – at **Casa Marta** (*see p118*).

Cocido, suckling pig and offal. This is Madrid's culinary history and, happily, her culinary present. The pig and Rioja at Botín are still great, despite the crowds of tourists and the demise of Lady Brett and Jake. The *cocido* is still eaten regularly at La Bola, though the Infanta has long gone. And Antonio Roiloa, the owner of Casa Marta, is still proud to serve Quixote's Saturday dish, though he often takes the brains out to appease more delicate tastebuds. These heavy dishes are as much Madrid as the Prado and Plaza Mayor.

So what does Madrid's ardent traditionalism mean for *nueva cocina*, the new wave of experimental cooking blowing over this way from the Catalan coast? Spearheaded by Catalan culinary legend Ferran Adrià, *nueva cocina* is renowned for its fantastical repertoire of edible foams, air and hot jellies, improbable pairings of flavour, and twists of texture and temperature. Can this surrealist revolution of food as we know it make any sense in a city in which the hearty stew reigns supreme?

Paco Roncero, a *madrileño* and one of Spain's up-and-coming chefs, thinks so.

Roncero, the man behind the Michelin-starred **La Terraza del Casino** (C/Alcalá 15, 91 521 87 00), finds himself in the challenging position of ambassador for *nueva cocina* in the capital. Adrià actually oversees the restaurant, with himself and Roncero working in tandem to concoct whimsical creations like a 'lollipop' of parmesan millefeuille, and barnacles in aspic with tea.

Things were slow to take off and Madrid was reluctant to embrace these Catalan culinary imports. But Roncero claims he is seeing an attitude shift: *madrileños* are showing curiosity, he says, and they come to the restaurant already knowing about the infamous foams and strange textures and wanting to journey through the *menú de degustación* – a wild array of the team's best inventions.

One of Roncero's specialities is reinventing the traditional dishes. Take his **Tortilla del Siglo 21** ('21st-century tortilla'). It is deconstructed tortilla, broken down into all of its main components, put back together as liquids and served in a cocktail glass with a spoon. *Madrileños* love it. It's not quite their beloved tortilla, but the essence of it, in much the same way that Miró isn't exactly painting a bird, but its essence. The *cocido*, however, remains untouched: Roncero explains, speaking with quiet reverence, that it is one dish he is not quite ready to take on. 'That one is still too difficult,' he says, 'but maybe in the future. I am starting to work on other traditional Madrid tapas – *croquetas, patatas bravas* – it's a work in progress.'

'We must always respect our traditional cooking,' Roncero insists. 'Leaving it behind is like leaving behind a part of who we are. But that doesn't mean we can't have fun with new things.'

from the menu and drink domestic beers. Try the yucca appetiser followed by *pollo guisado* – totally toothsome. Lia, the restaurant's namesake, owner and an actress from New York, is as gracious as her restaurant. Frequented by a smart, arty crowd.

La Panza es Primero

C/Libertad 33 (91 521 76 40). **Open** 1.30pm-1am daily. **Main courses** €7.50-€9.50. **Set lunch** €7.70. **Credit** AmEx, DC, MC, V. **Map** p310 G5.

Aflame with colour and funky Mexicana (indigenous art, skeletons and so on), The Belly Comes First is a Mexican *cantina* that has conquered Madrid with its nachos con guacamole. The most original item on the menu is the *pollo cabreado*, a chicken dish made with cabrales cheese from Asturias (hence the name) and *chipotle* sauce with smoked jalapeño peppers. There's no skimping on the spices, either – the chilli pepper symbols next to certain dishes on the menu indicate the heat factor.

Other locations: C/Campoamor 2, Chueca (91 319 82 15); C/Libertad 33, Chueca (91 521 76 40); C/Segovia 17, Los Austrias (91 364 12 28).

El Rey del Barrio

C/Hernán Cortés 19 (91 532 97 01). *Metro Chueca*. **Open** 1.30-4pm, 8pm-2am Tue-Fri; 1-6pm Sat, 2-6pm Sun. **Main courses** €8-€9. **Set lunch** €8. **Brunch** €9 Sat, Sun. **Credit** MC, V. **Map** p310 G5.

Mexican Rolando Echevarria has travelled the world, made documentaries, studied Mexico's indigenous populations and now, happily for Mexican food lovers, he has opened a restaurant. Decorated with Mexican film posters from the 1950s and '60s and painted by his father, this is an authentic piece of Mexico that should make all Tex-Mex impostors cringe with shame. With a good selection of tequilas, spicy sauces, moreish *mole*, and even mariachis to serenade the diners at weekends, coming here is like being invited to a Mexican fiesta.

La Sinfonia Italiana

C/Fernando el Santo 25 (91 308 12 96). *Metro Alonso Martínez*. **Open** 2-4pm, 9.30pm-midnight Mon-Sat. **Main courses** €12-€22. **Credit** MC, V. **Map** p310 H3.

With only eight tables, this little gem is *prima terra* for Italian food in Madrid. Exceptionally cosy and romantic, no detail is neglected, from the pre-meal prosecco, through the home-made pastas, to the heavenly tiramisu. The staff are consummately Italian – sincere, engaging, attractive and experts in the very serious matter of eating and drinking (the Italian wine list is fab). Ideal for an intimate evening.

WokCafé

C/Infantas 44 (91 522 90 69). *Metro Gran Vía*. **Open** 2-5pm, 9pm-2am Mon-Sat. **Main courses** €10-€15.50. **Set lunch** €9. **Credit** AmEx, DC, MC, V. **Map** p314 G6.

A mod Asian haven of mirrors, beaded curtains and rich red hues, this is still the cool place to flick your chopsticks. The swanky decor and location in the heart of Chueca pull in local personalities (it's said to

Friendly, eclectic **Bluefish**. *See p137.*

be a favourite of flamenco star Rafael Amargo and sassy French photographer Christine Spengler). The food – tempura, sushi, veggie stir-fries and lots of noodles – is fairly average, however, and portions are small (though there are occasional all-you-can-eat nights for a good price).

Zara

C/Infantas 5 (91 532 20 74). *Metro Chueca or Gran Vía*. **Open** 1-4pm, 8-11.30pm Mon-Fri. Closed Aug. **Main courses** €9-€12. **Set menus** €20-€25. **Credit** AmEx, DC, MC, V. **Map** p313 F6.

It's easy to walk right past these wooden doors and miss the little Havana with red-chequered tablecloths that lies within. Inés, the owner, left her home city over 30 years ago, but brought the best Cuban recipes with her – try the 'Typically Tropical' dishes like *ropa vieja* (literally, 'old clothes', but actually shredded beef), black beans and rice with pork, and minced beef with fried bananas. Daiquiris are the drink of the house: lime, banana, strawberry… whatever fruit is in season. Good Cuban food, low prices: you may have to wait in line.

Malasaña & Conde Duque

La Alacena de Paula

C/Palma 63 (91 532 54 41/reservations mobile 619 21 91 80). *Metro Noviciado*. **Open** 1-5pm, 9pm-midnight Mon-Sat. **Main courses** €9-€12. **Set lunch** €9.50. **Credit** DC, MC, V. **Map** p309 E4.

Soothingly lit, with yellow walls and plenty of candles, this tiny restaurant is a quiet haven on this busy stretch. The women who run it turn out some wonderfully creative dishes: wild duck with honey mustard, pine-nut praline and couscous; grilled entrecôte with asparagus and a wild mushroom ragoût; brie tempura with redcurrant sauce, and so on. A well-priced *menú del día* is the latest addition to the repertoire. Well worth a try.

La Musa

C/Manuela Malasaña 18 (91 448 75 58). Metro Bilbao. **Open** 1.30-4.30pm, 8.30pm-midnight daily. **Main courses** €7-€10. **Set lunch** €9. **Credit** AmEx, DC, MC, V. **Map** p309 E3.

The fried green tomatoes with goat's cheese are sensational, as is the ever-popular *bomba* – a baked potato stuffed with meat or vegetables. And if *carne*'s your thang, you'll be more than happy: choose between a generous plate of grilled meats, the glazed wild boar or the enormous skewer of pork with courgettes, red peppers and corn. For the indecisive there are *degustaciones* (tasting menus), which change regularly but are always interesting. The newer, slicker branch in La Latina has become the chic spot for post-Rastro Sunday drinkers. Be prepared to queue.

Other locations: La Musa Latina Costanilla de San Andrés 12, La Latina (91 354 02 55).

El Placer es Comer

C/Espíritu Santo 3 (91 360 45 16). Metro Tribunal. **Open** 1.30-4pm, 9pm-midnight Mon-Fri; 9pm-midnight Sat. Closed 3wks Aug. **Main courses** €8-€18. **Set lunch** €10.50. **Credit** AmEx, DC, MC, V. **Map** p309 E4.

This wildly colourful little bistro packs a heady dose of modern design: bright-red walls, minimalist tables and sleek lamps that hang down like stalactites. The gourmet menu is short but very sweet, offering such exotica as tuna tacos in yoghurt sauce, foie with mango, and watermelon soup with cactus ice-cream. This trendy spot leans to the high end, but the wine list – with some of Spain's best offerings – is reasonably priced.

International

Adrish

C/San Bernardino 1 (91 542 94 98). Metro Noviciado or Plaza de España. **Open** 1-4pm, 8.30pm-midnight Mon-Thur, Sun; 1-4pm, 8.30pm-1am Fri, Sat. **Main courses** €7-€11. **Set menus** €10.25. **Credit** MC, V. **Map** p309 D4.

The looks of the place may be a tad dreary, but you'll forget all about the mauve tablecloths once you taste the tandoori chicken with almonds (aka chicken chap). Adrish was one of the first restaurants to appear on the global restaurant street that is C/San Bernardino, and although it rarely seems full, it has survived with dignity. The large tandoori oven and charcoal grill produce some tasty dishes and a variety of naan breads, even if the spiciness has dropped

to a level acceptable to local palates. Vegetarians will no doubt be happy to see the thali of assorted curries with roti and rice.

Bluefish

C/San Andrés 26 (91 448 67 65). Metro Bilbao or Tribunal. **Open** 8pm-1am Tue-Sat; 1-6pm Sun. Closed last 2wks Aug. **Main courses** €6-€9. **No credit cards. Map** p309 F4.

Two Americans run this fabulously friendly little corner of New York on the Plaza Dos de Mayo. Stylish and colourful, with funky music and Italian film posters, Bluefish turns out satay chicken, Chinese dumplings and a spread of houmous, tabouleh, feta, olives and pitta bread with equal aplomb. Try the roast new potatoes with three different toppings: goat's cheese, spinach, roquefort and walnuts; smoked salmon with cream cheese; and cheddar with bacon. On Sundays, there's a hangover-busting brunch of pancakes, bagels, french toast, bacon and eggs and Bloody Marys.

Gumbo

C/Pez 15 (91 532 63 61). Metro Noviciado. **Open** 2-4pm, 9pm-midnight Tue-Sat; 2-4pm Sun. Closed 2wks Aug. **Main courses** €9.50-€12. **Set lunch** €8.50. **Credit** MC, V. **Map** p309 E4.

Bona fide N'Awlins chef Matthew Scott has some good Creole spices simmering in his gumbo pot. In a simple locale tastefully decorated (nice poster of *Gone With the Wind*), you can sample scrumptious New Orleans classics: fried green tomatoes, seafood gumbo, black steak. For festive group dinners, ask Matthew to bring out a parade of tapas-like dishes to share. And only a fool would resist the desserts: the pecan and the peanut butter pie are unforgettable. The *menú del día* is pretty well handled too.

Siam

C/San Bernardino 6 (91 559 83 15). Metro Noviciado or Plaza de España. **Open** 1-4pm, 8pm-midnight daily. **Main courses** €9.90-€11.50. **Set lunch** €8.90. **Credit** AmEx, DC, MC, V. **Map** p309 D4.

Texan David Haynes has poured his heart and the experience of years spent in Thailand into this restaurant, and the investment has paid off with a loyal and enthusiastic clientele. Authenticity is his thing (please don't ask for bread) and he imports vegetables and spices that he can't get hold of in the city. Try the spicy Thai green curry, or just ask him to recommend a menu. There is also a fabulous range of cocktails and special teas. While you eat, listen to David switch between French, Spanish, Texan and Thai as he serves.

Other locations: Bangkok C/Arenal 15, Sol & Gran Vía (91 559 16 96); Mai Thai Plaza Vázquez de Mella 10, Chueca (91 360 42 44).

Toma

C/Conde Duque 14 (91 547 49 96). Metro Noviciado or Plaza de España. **Open** 9pm-12.30am Tue-Sat. **Main courses** €10-€18. **Credit** MC, V. **Map** p309 D4.

La Brasserie de Lista.

A tiny restaurant with cherry-red walls and an informal feel, Toma has quickly become a real favourite of the *barrio*. Its homely, laid-back atmosphere can make the prices seem rather high, especially if you end up having to sit at the bar, but the food is commensurately good. From duck magret with pak choi to tuna tartare with lemon and soy, or rack of lamb with honey and mustard, the preparation is equally assured, and the results often divine. If it's available, finish with the creamy cappuccino cheesecake.

Vegetarian

La Isla del Tesoro

C/Manuela Malasaña 3 (91 593 14 40). Metro Bilbao or San Bernardo. **Open** 1.30-5pm, 9pm-1am daily. **Main courses** €8.80-€10.50. **Set lunch** €8.90. **Credit** AmEx, DC, MC, V. **Map** p309 E3.
One of Madrid's few vegetarian eateries not stuck in a circa-1978 gastronomic time warp, La Isla del Tesoro (Treasure Island) is often declared hands-down the best veggie restaurant in Madrid. Matching the international collectibles decor, dishes come from across the globe: try the famous couscous seitan or the *buen rollito* (fresh pasta stuffed with spinach, apple, leek, cheese and nuts). The *menú del día* features dishes from a different nation – from Pakistan to Mexico – each day.

Salamanca & the Retiro

La Brasserie de Lista

C/Serrano 110 (91 411 08 67). Metro Núñez de Balboa. **Open** 1-4pm, 9pm-midnight Mon-Thur; 1-4pm, 9pm-12.30am Fri, Sat; 1.30-4.30pm, 9pm-midnight Sun. **Main courses** €10-€17. **Set meal** €24.50. **Credit** AmEx, DC, MC, V. **Map** p311 J1.

A throwback from the obsession with French cuisine that gripped Spain after the dictatorship, this brasserie could be one of hundreds in Paris, all wood panelling and parlour palms. On the menu: Caesar salad, onion soup with emmental, sirloin steak with pepper sauce and hamburgers. Other, less predictable, dishes include a succulent duck magret with lime and *membrillo* (quince jelly) purée. The set menu is excellent, or there is a bar at the front where you can just enjoy some tapas.

Casa Portal

C/Doctor Castelo 26 (91 574 20 26). Metro Goya. **Open** 1.30-4.30pm, 8.30-11pm Tue-Sat; 1.30-4.30pm Sun. Closed Aug. **Main courses** €16.50-€19.90. **Credit** AmEx, MC, V. **Map** p315 K6.
Casa Portal specialises in all things traditional from Asturias, hence the mountain of cheeses in the window and the cider being poured from a great height. Apart from cider, this spot has been serving *fabada* (an Asturian bean stew with chorizo), tortilla, fish and shellfish for more than 50 years. Choose between the sawdust-strewn bar at the front and the dining room behind.

Paradis RF

Paseo de Recoletos 2 (91 575 45 40). Metro Banco de España. **Open** 1.30-4.30pm, 9pm-1am Mon-Fri; 9pm-1am Sat. **Main courses** €16. **Credit** AmEx, DC, MC, V. **Map** p314 H6.
Formerly the Paradis Casa de América, this has recently been taken over by celebrated Catalan chef Ramon Freixa. The new-look dining room is an unforgiving monochrome, but, set in a 19th-century mansion, the restaurant also boasts a pretty garden terrace. The menu concept is a curious one – you create your own brochette, choosing from a long list of imaginatively prepared meat and fish (such as tuna

with dates and pancetta), then you choose your vegetables (pears in wine and anis, say), and then pick a sauce (satay, perhaps, or a carrot reduction).
Other locations: **Paradis Madrid** C/Marqués de Cubas 14, Huertas & Santa Ana (91 429 73 03).

International

Mekong

C/Velázquez 87 (91 576 60 06). Metro Núñez de Balboa. **Open** 1-4pm, 8.30pm-midnight daily. Closed 2wks Aug. **Main courses** €12-€13.75. **Set lunch** €11.90. **Credit** AmEx, DC, MC, V. **Map** p311 J1.
Mekong's Chinese chef Chen Yu Yeh is an expert in oriental cuisine. Like the Mekong River, he crosses the borders of Burma, Laos, Thailand, Cambodia, China and Vietnam, extracting the tastiest ingredients and techniques from each, fusing without confusing. The pad thai is superb and the duck mouthwatering. The setting is chic and comfortable, the clientele a tad *pijo* and the service flawless.

Nodo

C/Velázquez 150 (91 564 40 44). Metro República Argentina. **Open** 1-4pm, 9pm-midnight daily. **Main courses** €11-€15. **Credit** AmEx, MC, V.
With minimalist decor and food to match, Nodo keeps the famous and the fashionable coming back for more. Style aside, some say it's the best sushi in town. Chef Albert Chicote's beef carpaccio with foie gras and coriander coulis typifies the menu, a successful blend of Japanese and Mediterranean. The sashimi and the tuna tataki with garlic get high marks; the service scores lower, but that might be a part of the minimalist serving ethic.

Other districts

A Casiña

Avda del Ángel, Casa de Campo (91 526 34 25). Metro Lago. **Open** 10am-midnight Mon-Sat; 10am-4pm Sun. **Open** 1.30-4pm, 8.30-11.30pm Mon-Sat; 1.30-4.30pm Sun. **Main courses** €12-€22. **Credit** AmEx, DC, MC, V.
A Casiña is one of several restaurants specialising in regional cuisine – in this case Galician – in the Casa de Campo. The restaurant is a reconstruction of a *pazo*, a Galician manor house, and really comes into its own in summer, with tables outside in the garden. Expensive but top-quality fish, shellfish and beef are the highlights, along with favourites from the region, such as *caldo gallego*, a broth made with pork, potatoes and cabbage. There is also a tapas bar, for a cheaper seafood experience.

Asador Donostiarra

C/Infanta Mercedes 79, Tetuán (91 679 62 64). Metro Tetuán. **Open** 1-4pm, 9pm-midnight Mon-Sat; 1-4pm Sun. **Main courses** €23.50-€31.75. **Credit** AmEx, DC, MC, V.
If you love meat and you love Real Madrid, you may want to splurge on a night out at the preferred *asador* (steakhouse) of David Beckham and the rest

of the team, located near the Bernabéu stadium. The celeb crowd is as legendary as the *solomillo*, and they often give away signed photos and other goodies from the team. Dissenting voices say that all the press has had an adverse effect, and the run-of-the-mill salad, steak and potato offerings are not commensurate with the hefty prices; others still claim it's the best *asador* in Madrid, with or without Becks, Figo and Zidane.

Casa Mingo

Paseo de la Florida 34, Casa de Campo (91 547 79 18). Metro Príncipe Pío. **Open** 11am-midnight daily. **Main course** €4-€6. **No credit cards.** **Map** p308 A4.
A vast and noisy Asturian cider house, open since 1888. This is a great opportunity to rub elbows with *madrileños* really enjoying themselves at one of the long wooden tables. The restaurant does only three things: roast chicken, salad and cider. Turn up before the city gets hungry (around 1.30pm) if you want a terrace seat, or take out a chicken and a bottle of cider and head for the River Manzanares for a picnic. At other times, expect to queue.

La Favorita

C/Covarrubias 25, Chamberí (91 448 38 10). Metro Alonso Martínez or Bilbao. **Open** 2-4pm, 9pm-midnight Mon-Fri; 9pm-midnight Sat. **Main courses** €18-€21. **Set lunch** €15. **Set dinner** €25. **Credit** AmEx, DC, MC, V. **Map** p310 G3.

Tatana, a taste of Argentina. See p140.

Eat, Drink, Shop

Opera fanatic Javier Otero converted this charming 1920s mansion into a restaurant and filled it with singing waiters – conservatoire students or artists just starting out on their careers. It's a surprisingly fun way to eat delicious Navarran food: the soprano hits a high note, you savour the *solomillo* with thistles and artichokes, and the whole experience elicits goose bumps. Javier's troupe is so good, in fact, that it is regularly invited to perform at festivals. And the food, made using fresh ingredients from Navarra, hits another high note. Booking is a must.

El Olivo

C/General Gallegos 1, Chamartín (91 359 15 35/ 359 03 52). Metro Cuzco. **Open** 1-4pm, 9pm-midnight Tue-Sat. Closed last 2wks Aug. **Main courses** €27-€31. **Credit** AmEx, DC, MC, V.

Frequented by an over-50 crowd, with a sombre olive-green interior, this old-school Mediterranean restaurant still ranks high with the city's more discriminating gastronomes. Olive oil is the keystone here: the kindly, very formal waiters wheel a cart of bottles over to the table for you to sample with bread; only the best is used for cooking, and there is even olive oil ice-cream (surprisingly good, since you ask). Specialities include the lobster and herb salad, the *solomillo* with foie, and a fine tarte tatin.

Santceloni

Hotel Hesperia Madrid, Paseo de la Castellana 57 (91 210 88 41/www.RestauranteSantceloni.com). Metro Gregorio Marañón. **Open** 2-4pm, 9-11pm Mon-Fri; 9-11pm Sat. Closed Aug. **Main courses** €36.50-€48. **Credit** AmEx, DC, MC, V.

Named after the village where the famed Barcelona restaurateur Santi Santamaria was born, and run by his protégé Oscar Velasco, the Santceloni was anointed with its first Michelin star after less than a year. Santamaria's success derives from using only the best of local ingredients. Try the poached egg with caviar and cauliflower, or one of Santamaria's trademark dishes: ravioli of sliced raw prawn with a filling of ceps. The tasting menu changes daily depending on available ingredients and will set you back a pretty penny, but it's a chance to relish the talents of one of Spain's celebrity chefs. For the Hotel Hesperia Madrid, *see p53*.

Tatana

C/Galileo 12, Chamberí (91 447 86 69). Metro San Bernardo. **Open** 1-5pm, 9pm-1am daily. **Main courses** €12-€22. **Set lunch** €10. **Credit** MC, V. **Map** p309 D1.

Descend down some steps to this great little Argentine-run restaurant where loungy sounds wash over a jumble of wooden tables, deep colours and smiling waiters. The home country is very evident on the menu, with lots of pasta (you select your type, then choose a sauce from a separate list) and untranslatable Argentine cuts of beef (*entraña, bife de lomo*). The lunchtime menu is a good one – decent salads to start, then roast chicken, perhaps, or stir-fried vegetables with prawns.

International

La Broche

Hotel Miguel Ángel, C/Miguel Ángel 29, Chamberí (91 339 34 37/www.labroche.com). Metro Rubén Darío. **Open** 2-4.30pm, 9-11.30pm Mon-Fri. Closed Easter & Aug. **Main courses** €30-€35. **Credit** AmEx, DC, MC, V. **Map** p310 I1.

Gleaming white on white and with hostesses wearing headsets, this is still one of Madrid's most modern restaurants, even after five years. Ferran Adrià's disciple Sergi Arola works with a *nueva cocina* vocabulary of edible foams and gels and unlikely combinations such as scallop carpaccio with green-apple purée. For all the quirkiness, it tastes pretty sublime too – good enough, in fact, to earn La Broche two Michelin stars. Don't be thrown off by its location in the staid Hotel Miguel Ángel – once inside, you are on another culinary planet.

El Comité

Plaza de San Amaro 8, Chamartín (91 571 87 11). Metro Santiago Bernabéu. **Open** 1.30-4pm, 9pm-midnight Mon-Fri; 9pm-midnight Sat. **Main courses** €14-€24. **Credit** AmEx, DC, MC, V.

A classic. Yes, it's out of the way and has the feel of an elite club, but this somehow enhances the appeal. A French restaurant offering exceptionally good food at a price, El Comité also offers the chance to see Madrid's discreetly elegant top people at play. Great starters include Harry's Bar carpaccio and a tempura of langoustines; a main-course highlight is the steak tartare.

Fast Good

C/Padre Damián 23, Chamartín (91 343 06 55). Metro Cuzco. **Open** noon-midnight daily. **Main courses** €5-€8.50. **Credit** AmEx, DC, MC, V.

This is the first installation in what is bound to be a trend – it's fast food à la Ferran Adrià, still the hottest chef in Spain and originator of the *nueva cocina* movement. In a colour-crazy, super-designed deli you can pick out innovative salads like the foie with green beans or panini with brie and spinach. The crowning glory, however, is the Fast Good hamburger – a superlative specimen. Everything is made fresh and light – even the fries are cooked in olive oil. So far a big success, despite the clunky name.

Summa

C/Profesor Waksman 5, Chamartín (91 457 32 27). Metro Cuzco. **Open** 2-4pm, 9pm-midnight Mon-Fri; 9pm-midnight Sat. **Main courses** €11.50-€13.40. **Set lunch** €15.60. **Credit** AmEx, MC, V.

Giant photos of a birch forest cover the windows and one wall, and in the middle is a traditional sushi bar with little boats floating round a stream from which you can pluck whatever you fancy. The menu incorporates the house Summa roll of salmon, avocado and crab and a great matzuzaki roll of tuna, plaice, squid, salmon, avocado and cheese in nori seaweed, and is fused with things Mediterranean. The all-you-can-eat lunch buffet takes some beating.

Tapas

Suitably sized nibbles for the city that sees life as one long party.

Casa Labra. See p143.

In their more fanciful moments, Spaniards will describe them as 'the world on a plate'. They will tell you that the eating of tapas is proof of the country's gregarious nature, its need to share and the importance it places on spending time in good company. Thanks to the tapa, it is possible to spend the whole night in a bar without requiring help to get home. This is the point so often missed by those outside the country, those who reproduce them for dinner parties or nibble them in expensive restaurants in London. For the Spanish, it's not about what you eat, it's about *how* you eat.

An accidental invention, tapas originated in Andalucía and were originally pieces of ham or chorizo that were placed on top of the plate, or slice of bread, used to cover a glass of wine and keep out the dust and flies. The word *tapa*, in fact, means 'lid'. The idea became widely established during the 19th century, with the principal objective of making the customer thirsty in order to sell more drinks. The tapas boom really occurred, however, in the 1940s after the Civil War, when many of Madrid's existing bars first appeared.

Tapas vary from region to region, and examples of most are available in Madrid. Galician bars highlight octopus, prawns and seafood, traditionally with white Ribeiro wine, served in little ceramic bowls. In Extremaduran bars you will always find *migas* (crumbs), fried and mixed with chorizo. Asturian bars specialise in cider (*sidra*), theatrically poured from above the head to separate out sediment, accompanied by blood sausage, *morcilla*, or blue *cabrales* cheese. Andalucían bars offer cold dry fino sherry with *mojama* (dry-cured tuna) or sardines. Madrid's own specialities are *patatas bravas*, offal (particularly *callos*, tripe), and snails in a hot sauce.

Recently, tapas have become more sophisticated and thus more expensive, and an evening's *tapeo* can cost more than a full meal in a restaurant. Don't be afraid to dispose of the debris (olive stones, prawn shells and screwed-up paper napkins) by dropping them on the floor, except in the more upmarket places where you should copy what the locals are doing; and remember that a lot of tapas are designed to be eaten with the fingers.

Casa Alberto. *See p144.*

Los Austrias & La Latina

El Almendro 13

C/Almendro 13 (91 365 42 52). Metro La Latina.
Open 1-4pm, 8pm-1am Mon-Fri; 1-5pm, 8pm-1am
Sat, Sun. **No credit cards. Map** p313 D8.
A sleepy, traditional bar during the week, which
hots up at weekends, and the drinkers often drift out
on the pavements. A peculiar speciality is the *rosca*,
akin to a oversized bagel, with various fillings.
These are invariably accompanied by a glass of the
house *manzanilla*, a dry sherry.

As de los Vinos
– La Casa de las Torrijas

C/Paz 4 (91 532 14 73). Metro Sol. **Open** 10am-
4pm, 6-11.30pm Mon-Thur; 9.30am-4pm, 6pm-
midnight Fri, Sat. Closed Aug. **No credit
cards. Map** p313 E8.
A charmingly old unkempt bar, tiled and mirrored,
with table-tops constructed from old enamel adverts.
Since 1907, it has served little more than *torrijas* –
bread soaked in wine and spices, coated in sugar and
deep-fried – and house wine. There is a handful of
other, simple, tapas, however, and a basic set lunch.

Bodegas Ricla

C/Cuchilleros 6 (91 366 2069). Metro Ópera. **Open**
7pm-midnight Mon; 11.30am-3.30pm, 7pm-midnight
Tue-Thur; 11.30am-3.30pm, 7pm-1.30am Fri; 12.30-
4pm, 7pm-1.30am Sat; 12.30-4pm Sun. **No credit
cards. Map** p313 D8.
A tiny, bright and friendly mother-and-son operation, Bodegas Ricla does a great line in garlicky
boquerones and an incongruous one in soft rock.

Cheap but good wine and sherry are available by the
litre, poured from tall clay urns, or there is vermouth
on tap. Also worth trying are the *cecina* (thin slices
of cured venison) and cabrales cheese in cider.

Casa Antonio

C/Latoneros 10 (91 366 63 36). Metro La Latina.
Open 12.30-3.30pm, 8pm-midnight Mon-Thur, Sun;
noon-3.30pm, 8.30pm-12.30am Fri, Sat. **No credit
cards. Map** p313 D8.
With great wines from around Spain by the glass,
and some Italian-influenced tapas, the only way to
go wrong here is to order Coca-Cola – a rather stern
sign warns that it is not stocked. A traditional and
much loved *taberna*, Casa Antonio is always packed.

Juana la Loca

*Plaza Puerta de Moros 4 (91 364 05 25). Metro
La Latina.* **Open** noon-1.30am Tue-Sun. **No
credit cards. Map** p312 C9.
Where the hip go to *tapear*, Juana la Loca is kind
of pricey, but offers some undeniably creative cooking; a miniature portion of ostrich, plum and crispy
bacon, for example, or foie gras with caramelised
apple. Salmon with dill, avocado and fresh cheese
is also tasty, along with a giant prawn and wild
mushroom vol-au-vent.

Matritum

C/Cava Alta 17 (91 365 82 37). Metro La Latina.
Open 8.30pm-12.30am Tue; 1-4.30pm, 8.30pm-
12.30am Wed-Sun. **Credit** DC, MC, V. **Map** p313 D8.
It takes its name from the Latin for Madrid, but
Matritum has a great selection of tapas and wine
from other regions of Spain, most notably Catalonia.

Try *gambas all cremat* (prawns with burnt garlic) or fabulous canapés such as *cabrales* cheese with apple compôte or *sobrassada* – a spicy, spreadable sausage from Mallorca. The wine list, too, is dominated by Catalan labels, with many notably good bottles from the Penedes.

La Taberna de Cien Vinos

C/Nuncio 17 (91 365 47 04). Metro La Latina.
Open 1-3.45pm, 8-11.45pm Tue-Sun. **No credit cards. Map** p313 D8.
The 'Taberna' is a bit misleading, as there's nothing particularly old-fashioned here, but the 'Cien Vinos' ('100 wines') is spot on. Mainly Spanish, there are also a good few from France and a handful from the rest of the world. There are upmarket tapas (try boletus with scamorza) to go with them.

Taberna Según Emma

C/Conde de Miranda 4 (91 559 08 97). Metro Ópera.
Open 4pm, 8pm-1am Tue, Thur-Sun; 1-4pm Wed.
Credit V. **Map** p313 D8
Step down into a small, lively space with lime-green walls and wooden tables – run by thirtysomethings, for thirtysomethings. This used to be an Asturian bar and cheeses from the region and favourites such as clams with haricot beans remain, alongside newer tapas such as rocket with parmesan or tuna salad.

La Taberna del Zapatero

C/Almendro 27 (91 364 07 21). Metro La Latina.
Open 8.30pm-midnight Mon, Tue; 1.30-4.30pm, 8.30pm-midnight Wed-Sat; 1.30pm-midnight Sun. **No credit cards. Map** p313 D8.
Occupying the shop of an old shoemaker (*zapatero*), this is now a boisterous tapas bar. Old cobblers' tools are dotted about the place in tribute, and the excellent canapés are known as *suelas*, 'soles'. Fill your boots with asparagus with brie, cod brandade or stuffed tomatoes.

El Tempranillo

C/Cava Baja 38 (91 364 15 32). Metro La Latina.
Open 1-4pm, 8pm-midnight daily. Closed 2wks Aug.
Credit V. **Map** p313 D8.
Never less than rowdy, decorated in bullring ochre and bare brick, with flamenco on the sound system, El Tempranillo offers an impressive range of labels from nearly every wine-producing region in Spain. The tapas are addictive too: try the wild mushrooms in scrambled egg, the sweetbreads, or any of the variety of cured meats.

La Torre del Oro

Plaza Mayor 26 (91 366 50 16). Metro Sol. **Open** 11am-2am daily. **Credit** AmEx, DC, MC, V. **Map** p313 D8.
It's smack on the Plaza Mayor, so don't expect any bargains, especially if you sit out in the square, but this Andalucían bar is the real deal, with bullfighting memorabilia and incomprehensible waiters. If you can understand and make yourself understood, ask for prawns or whitebait (*pescaítos*), and accompany them with a cold, dry fino.

Sol & Gran Vía

Las Bravas

Pasaje Matheu 5, off C/Victoria (91 521 51 41).
Metro Sol. **Open** 12.30-4pm, 7.30pm-midnight Sun-Thur; 12.30-4pm, 8pm-1am Fri, Sat. **No credit cards. Map** p313 E7.
Decorated in the luminous orange that characterises its mass-produced sauce, Las Bravas still merits a mention for having, allegedly, invented the *patata brava*. These days, you'll do better elsewhere, unless you're attracted to supermarket lighting.
Other locations: throughout the Sol area.

Casa Labra

C/Tetuán 12 (91 531 00 81). Metro Sol. **Open** 9.30am-3.30pm, 6-11pm daily. **No credit cards. Map** p313 E7.
Famously the birthplace of the Spanish Socialist Party back in 1879, this legendary bar, with its brown 1950s paintwork and luggage racks, is worth a visit for its history alone. The speciality of the house is the cod *croquetas* served up by dour white-jacketed waiters.

El Escarpín

C/Hileras 17 (91 559 99 57). Metro Ópera or Sol.
Open 10am-midnight daily. **Credit** AmEx, DC, MC, V. **Map** p313 D7.
So vast that you'll always find a seat, this Asturian cider bar has the look – bare bricks and long wooden tables – to go with the regional tapas. Natural cider (*sidra*) should be your first request, followed by *lacón* (gammon), *fabada asturiana* (a stew of beans and pork) or chorizo. In cider, naturally.

Matritum. *See p142.*

Tapas glossary

There are three basic sizes of tapa portion: a *pincho* (more or less a mouthful), a *tapa* (a saucerful or so) and a *ración* (a small plateful). Some bars offer *media raciones* (a half-*ración*). If there's something you like the look of that isn't identifiable on the menu or the list behind the bar, just point to it. Bread (*pan*) normally comes automatically, but if not, just ask. Normally, you let a tapas bill mount up and pay when you've finished, not when you order; it's usually about 25 per cent more expensive if you sit at a table rather than eat at the bar.
    For more food terminology, *see p122*.

Basics

Bocadillo sandwich in a roll or part of a French loaf; **cazuelita** small hot casserole; **montados** canapé-style mixed tapas, often a slice of bread with a topping; **pincho/pinchito** small titbit on a toothpick, or mouthful-sized *tapa*; **pulga/pulguita** small filled roll; **ración** a portion (small plateful); **tabla** platter (of cheeses, cold meats); **tosta** slice of toast with topping; **una de gambas, chorizo...** one portion of prawns, chorizo...; **por unidad** per item.

Carne, aves y embutidos (meat, poultry & charcuterie)

Albóndigas meat balls; **alitas de pollo** chicken wings; **callos** tripe; **cecina** dry-cured beef; **chistorra** Navarrese sausage with paprika; **chorizo** spicy sausage, eaten cooked or cold; **criadillas** bulls' testicles; **flamenquines** ham and pork rolls in breadcrumbs; **longaniza, fuet** mild but chewy, often herby, salami-type sausages; **mollejas** sweetbreads; **morcilla** a black, blood sausage; **oreja (de cerdo)** pig's ear; **pincho moruno** grilled meat brochette; **riñones al Jerez** kidneys cooked in sherry; **salchichón** a large, fatty, soft, salami-type sausage; **San Jacobo** fried ham and cheese escalope; **sobrassada** soft Mallorcan paprika sausage; **torrezno** grilled pork crackling; **zarajo** grilled sheep's intestine on a stick.

Pescado y mariscos (fish & shellfish)

Ahumados smoked fish; **almejas** clams; **anchoas** salted conserved anchovies; **anguilas** eels; **angulas** elvers; **berberechos** cockles; **bienmesabe** marinated fried fish; **boquerones en vinagre/fritos** pickled fresh anchovies; **calamares a la romana** squid rings fried in batter; **calamares en su tinta** squid cooked in their ink; **carabineiros** large red ocean prawns; **centollo** spider crab; **chanquetes** tiny fish, served deep fried; **chipirones en su tinta** small Atlantic squid in their ink; **chopito** small cuttlefish; **cigalas** crayfish; **croqueta de bacalao** salt cod croquette; **fritura de pescado** flash-fried fish; **gambas al ajillo** prawns fried with garlic; **gambas en gabardina** prawns deep-fried in

Huertas & Santa Ana

Alhambra

C/Victoria 9 (91 521 07 08). Metro Sol. **Open** 10am-12.30am Mon-Thur, Sun; 10am-2.30am Fri, Sat. **No credit cards. Map** p313 E7.
Named after Granada's magical palace and done up in suitably Andaluz-Moorish style, this is a pretty and peaceful spot during the day, serving basic tapas along with oxtail stew and gazpacho, and a simple set lunch. It's a different proposition at night, however; awash with Spanish pop, techno and hormones. *See also p229.*

Casa Alberto

C/Huertas 18 (91 429 93 56). Metro Antón Martín. **Open** *Sept-June* noon-12.30am Tue-Sat; noon-4pm Sun. *July, Aug* noon-5.30pm, 8pm-1.30am Mon-Sat. **Credit** AmEx, DC, MC, V. **Map** p313 F8.
One of the city's most evocative old *tabernas*, hung with oil paintings and presided over by a septuagenarian. It still has its old zinc bar complete with running water trough to keep the wine cool and a draught beer head with five founts. Try lambs' trotters, garlicky prawns, chorizo in cider or oxtail stew as tapas, or as more substantial dishes in the restaurant at the back.

batter; **huevas** fish roe; **mojama** dried and salted tuna fish; **navajas** razor clams; **nécora** swimming crab; **percebes** gooseneck barnacles; **pulpo a feira/a la gallega** octopus with paprika and olive oil; **quisquillas** shrimps; **salpicón** cold chopped salad, often with some shellfish; **sepia** large squid; **soldaditos de pavía** strips of salt cod, fried in light batter; **tigres** mussels cooked with a spicy tomato and béchamel sauce; **zamburiñas** small scallops.

Vegetales (vegetable tapas)

Aceitunas, olivas (adobados, rellenos) olives (pickled, stuffed); **almendras saladas** salted almonds; **pan con tomate** bread rubbed with fresh tomato and olive oil; **patatas bravas** deep-fried potatoes with hot pepper sauce; **perdiz de huerta** lettuce hearts; **pimientos de Padrón** fried, and occasionally hot small green peppers; **queso en aceite** cheese marinated in olive oil; **setas** wild mushrooms.

Other tapas

Caracoles snails; **croquetas** potato croquettes (which may be made with chicken, ham, tuna, and so on); **empanada** flat pies, usually made with a tuna filling; **empanadilla** small fried pasties, usually with a tomato and tuna filling; **ensaladilla rusa** potato salad with onions, red peppers, usually tuna and other ingredients in mayonnaise, now a completely Spanish dish, but still called a Russian salad; **huevos rellenos** stuffed cold hard-boiled eggs; **migas (con huevo frito)** fried breadcrumbs (with fried egg); **pisto manchego** ratatouille with meat (usually ham) and egg; **revuelto** scrambled eggs.

Cervecería la Moderna

Plaza Santa Ana 12 (91 420 15 82). Metro Sol. **Open** 11.30-2.30am daily. **No credit cards. Map** p313 F8.
A large bar-restaurant, mercifully untouristed given its location on the Plaza Santa Ana. A varied but consistently good range of tapas includes hare pâté with whisky; Mexican tacos with beef, cheese and mustard sauce; swordfish and smoked tuna.

La Dolores

Plaza de Jesús 4 (91 429 22 43). Metro Antón Martín. **Open** 11am-1am Mon-Thur, Sun; 11am-2am Fri, Sat. **No credit cards. Map** p314 G8.

Another Madrid classic, with wonderful tiling outside, and rows of dusty beer steins inside, La Dolores has been serving ice-cold frothy beer since the 1920s. There is also a short list of tapas, which are good if a teensy bit overpriced. Specialities are anchovies, and smoked fish, such as *mojama*; wind-dried tuna.

La Fábrica

C/Jesús 2 (91 369 06 71). Metro Antón Martín. **Open** 11am-1am Mon-Thur, Sun; 11am-2am Fri, Sat. **No credit cards. Map** p314 G8.
There are long, long lists of the canapés on offer, but most are on display. Try the *matrimonio* (anchovies preserved and fresh, the perfect combination); the theme continues with *divorcio* (anchovies and mussels; no kind of match); or the *orgía* (all three). Ahem.

Los Gatos

C/Jesús 2 (91 429 30 67). Metro Antón Martín or Sevilla. **Open** noon-1am Mon-Thur, Sun; noon-2am Fri, Sat. **No credit cards. Map** p312 G8.
With their reputation for staying out all night, *madrileños* are popularly known as '*los gatos*' (the cats) and there's nowhere better than here to begin a night prowling the tiles. The bar is hung with all manner of paraphernalia from gramophones to choirboy mannequins – here you can get a selection of tasty canapés, and a good frothy beer.

Lhardy

Carrera de San Jerónimo 8 (91 522 22 07). Metro Sol. **Open** 9.30am-3pm, 5-9.30pm Mon-Sat; 9.30am-3pm Sun. **Credit** AmEx, DC, MC, V. **Map** p313 E7.
A quiet and refined place, famous for its anchovy or chorizo vol-au-vents, its superb and dainty cakes, and, above all, its two silver samovars from which you help yourself to consommé or water. There are also ham or chicken croquettes, and barquetas de riñones – pastry boats with kidneys.

La Platería

C/Moratín 49 (91 429 17 22). Metro Antón Martín. **Open** 7.30am-1am Mon-Fri; 9.30am-1am Sat, Sun. **Credit** MC, V. **Map** p314 G8.
Everything from the the smoked salmon and red peppers to *caldo gallego*, grilled asparagus or baked potatoes with eggs and garlic, is available in half portions, so this is a perfect place for a quick snack 'twixt two of the big three museums. The bar is rather cramped, but there are tables outside.

Taberna de Conspiradores

C/Moratín 33 (91 369 4741). Metro Antón Martín. **Open** 7.30pm-1am Tue-Thur; 7.30pm-2.30am Fri; 1-4pm, 7.30pm-1am Sat, Sun. **Credit** AmEx, MC, V. **Map** p314 G8.
The food, wine and liqueurs on offer here are all from from Extremadura, unusually. The speciality of the house is *migas* – fried breadcrumbs baked with sausage, garlic and pancetta – and a dense, rich venison stew. The small space is lined with black and white photographs from the Magnum greats, and occasionally sees live performances of world music or flamenco.

Eat, Drink, Shop

Eat and drink your way around the world

La Tapería

Plaza Platería de Martínez 1 (91 429 4094). Metro Antón Martín. **Open** 9am-1am Mon-Thur, Sun; 9am-1.30am Fri, Sat. **Credit** AmEx, DC, MC, V. **Map** p314 G8.

The decor has a bit of a modern, corporate look, but it's nice enough, and the tapas are occasionally excellent. Look out for duck liver with apple, sherry and goat's cheese, brie millefeuille with Iberian ham and the mushroom tartlet. The baked new potatoes dipped in a spicy sauce are good to share.

Vinoteca Barbechera

C/Príncipe 27 (91 555 07 54/www.vinoteca barbechera.com). Metro Antón Martín or Sevilla. **Open** 11am-midnight Mon-Thur, Sun; 11am-1-30am Fri, Sat. **Credit** AmEx, MC, V. **Map** p313 F8.

It looks a lot grander than it is, which is not to say that the tapas aren't good, just that the bill is a pleasant surprise in these rather lofty surroundings. *Pinchos* include smoked salmon with cream cheese, cabrales with quince jelly and goose liver with apple.

Rastro & Lavapiés

Café Melo's

C/Ave María 44 (91 527 50 54). Metro Lavapiés. **Open** 9am-2am Tue-Sat. Closed Aug. **No credit cards.** **Map** p313 E9.

It's got all the aesthetic charm of a kebab shop, but this bright little bar is something of a classic. It's famous for its *zapatillas* – huge, open sandwiches (the word, like ciabatta, means 'slipper') with various toppings. A big favourite for late-night munchies with the bohemian element of the *barrio*.

Los Caracoles

Plaza de Cascorro 18 (91 365 94 39). Metro La Latina. **Open** 10.30am-3.30pm, 7-10.30pm Tue-Sat; 10.30am-4pm Sun. **No credit cards.** **Map** p313 D9.

Again, this is no looker, but it's a popular post-Rastro stop. Its specialities include the eponymous snails in spicy sauce, knuckle of ham, and *zarajo*, the lamb's intestines wrapped round sticks without which your Madrid trip would not be complete.

La Casa de las Tostas

C/Argumosa 29 (91 527 08 42). Metro Lavapiés. **Open** 12.30-4pm, 7pm-1am Mon-Thur, Sun; 7pm-2am Fri, Sat. **No credit cards.** **Map** p313 F10.

Welcome to the House of Toast. Toast with scrambled eggs, prawns and wild mushrooms; toast with gammon and melted cheese; toast with salmon in white vermouth; toast with anchovies and roquefort; toast with cod pâté. And most importantly, toast with wine, many of them available by the glass.

Los Hermanos

C/Rodas 28 (91 468 33 13). Metro Tirso de Molina. **Open** 7am-11pm Mon-Fri; 7am-5pm Sat, Sun. Closed Aug. **No credit cards.** **Map** p313 D10.

Just off the main drag of the Rastro is this bar with a strong neighbourhood feel, generous complimentary tapas, a huge range of *raciones* or a great range

of *bocadillos*, including a hangover-busting bacon and egg. On Sundays there's a €10 *menú del día* for the market crowd, available in a quieter side room.

El Sur

C/Torrecilla del Leal 12 (91 527 83 40). Metro Antón Martín. **Open** 8pm-midnight Tue-Thur; 1-5pm, 8pm-1am Fri-Sun. **Credit** MC, V. **Map** p313 F9.

Named for Victor Erice's seminal film, decorated with cinematic posters and popular with long-haired soulful types coming back from the nearby Filmoteca. Juan, the friendly and efficient owner, offers an interesting selection of *raciones*: try *ropa vieja* (shredded beef, Cuban style) with thinly sliced, fried potatoes; the towering house salad with endive, walnuts and cheese, or 'Arabian' lentils.

La Taberna de Antonio Sánchez

C/Mesón de Paredes 13 (91 539 78 26). Metro Tirso de Molina. **Open** noon-5pm, 8pm-midnight Mon-Sat; noon-4pm Sun. **Credit** MC, V. **Map** p313 E9.

Little has changed in this historic bar over the years, from the zinc bar to the bull's head on the wall. Its various owners have all been involved in bullfighting, and *tertulias* between critics, *toreros* and aficionados are still held here. It's a local, friendly place, with superior tapas, best of which is actually the scrumptious salad you get free with a drink.

El Tío Vinagre

C/San Carlos 6 (mobile 620 380 410). Metro Lavapiés or Tirso de Molina. **Open** 7pm-1.30am Mon-Thur; 7pm-2.30am Fri, Sat; 1pm-1.30am Sun. **No credit cards.** **Map** p313 E9.

Under new ownership, and a notch hipper, 'Uncle Vinegar' has wines from around the country, board games and a few tapas: *empanadas*, gazpacho, goat's cheese salad and cured venison. The wooden panelling and marble bar have been enhanced with modern touches, Mojitos foremost among them.

Chueca

La Bardemcilla

C/Augusto Figueroa 47 (91 521 42 56). Metro Chueca. **Open** noon-4.30pm, 8pm-2.30am Mon-Thur; 8pm-2am Fri, Sat. **Credit** AmEx, MC, V. **Map** p310 G5.

A fun, mellow place, owned by the royal family of Spanish cinema, the Bardems, with filmic references everywhere, from the doll's house set from *Before Night Falls* to the names of the tapas. *Jamón, Jamón* is *croquetas* (geddit?); *Victor o Victória* is *gazpacho* or consommé, depending on the season, and so on.

El Bocaíto

C/Libertad 6 (91 532 12 19). Metro Chueca. **Open** 1-4pm, 8-30pm-midnight Mon-Fri; 8.30pm-midnight Sat. Closed Aug. **Credit** DC, MC, V. **Map** p310 G5.

Film-set traditional, from the bullfighting posters and riot of Andalucían ceramics to the old-school tapas and unsmiling, white-jacketed waiters. If you're famous, however, they will grin for the camera, just as they did with Pedro, Penélope, Hugh and, goddammit, Mark Knopfler.

Doing vermouth

It's Sunday... ¿me pones un vermut?

Madrid is a city where Sunday feels like a Friday. Preparing for Monday – laundry, homework, doing the bills – is not given much thought; such tasks can wait until a schoolnight. *Madrileños* like to squeeze the most out of their weekends, hence the Sunday post-Rastro drinking tradition in the *barrio* of La Latina, local merrymaking at its best. On sunny days, the squares and terrazas of La Latina (Plaza de la Paja, Plaza de San Andrés, Plaza del Humilladero) brim with hedonism. Sassy girls in summer dresses lounge on church steps; hipsters with hefty sideburns loll in cafés, caña in hand; blue-rinsed matriarchs sit on park benches chatting and feeding the pigeons. On rainy days, the best bars in the area burst with smoking, drinking, talking madrileños. This giddy atmosphere has a distinctly bohemian feel; neighbourhood drunks, artists, actors, *politicos*, grandmothers, the occasional juggler and an impressive number of dogs all turn out to take part.

The essence of the Sunday tradition is vermouth, and the whole ritual, tapas and all, is occasionally known as '*haciendo el vermut*' – 'doing vermouth'. Served with ice and a slice of lemon or orange, it's more refreshing with a spritz of seltzer water – ask for it '*con sifón*'. It's not the dry vermouth most familiar to Martini-lovers, but a sweet red vermouth, often best when served from the tap (*grifo*), though there are exceptions. The popular bar **El Bonano** (Plaza de Humilladero 4, 91 366 68 86) serves a delicious bottled variety called Vermut del Pueblo from Catalonia. Ironically, the best vermouths are from around Barcelona, but the Catalans have never shared *madrileños'* affection for the drink. La Latina drinkers claim that the prime vermouth hour is 1pm, and as one bartender explained, 'I don't know why, but for *madrileños*, it's a religion.'

Vermouth is made from a basic dry white wine blended with an infusion of herbs, flowers, fruit peels, seeds and plants. It's

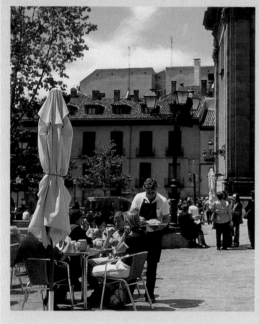

quite sweet and fortified with brandy, giving it a high alcohol content and making it quick to elevate the spirits (essential after a late Saturday night). In Madrid restaurants, vermouth is often the aperitif of choice before the big Sunday lunch.

Originally founded in 1870, the much-loved **Casa Antonio** (*see p142*), which faces out on to the Plaza de la Puerta Cerrada, is one of the oldest *vermut* bars in Madrid. Hipper places to try it are **La Carpanta** (C/Almendro 22, 91 366 57 83) and the nearby **La Corolla** (C/Almendro 10, 91 364 52 32). Often frequented by three golden labradors, the best pavement tables for a Sunday vermouth are at **Café del Nuncio** (C/Nuncio 12, 91 366 08 53).

Tip: when asking for *un vermut* in Spanish, don't pronounce the 't'.

Santander

C/Augusto Figueroa 25 (91 522 49 10). Metro Chueca. **Open** *Nov-June* 10.45am-4pm, 7.30-11pm Mon-Sat. *July, Sept, Oct* 10.45am-4pm, 7.30-11pm Mon-Fri; 10.45am-4pm Sat. Closed Aug. **No credit cards. Map** p310 G5.

Cramped, bright and shabby-genteel, Santander turns out a vast range of tapas, including some deceptively delicate bites. Try the choux de langoustines, the cod brandade vol-au-vent or the miniature beef crêpe and marvel at the price. A gem.

Malasaña & Conde Duque

Albur

C/Manuela Malasaña 15 (91 594 27 33). Metro Bilbao. **Open** noon-midnight Mon-Thur; noon-midnight Fri, Sat. **Credit** MC, V. **Map** p309 F3.

The speciality is *revueltos* (scrambled egg) with prawns, wild mushrooms and so on, but there's also good ham, chorizo, black pudding, and a variety of wines to accompany them. Generally a quiet place, with soothing buttercup-yellow walls, it gets quite lively later on with a young Malasaña crowd.

Casa do Compañeiro

C/San Vicente Ferrer 44 (91 521 57 02). Metro Noviciado. **Open** 1.30pm-2am daily. **No credit cards. Map** p309 E4.

A tiny jewel among tapas bars, with wonderful tiling inside and out. The tapas are mainly Galician, with lots of octopus, gammon, pig's ear and, of course, *caldo gallego*, the typical broth with cabbage and pork. A crisp, dry *fino* is the perfect accompaniment.

La Casta

C/Cristo 1 (91 547 77 40). Metro Noviciado. **Open** 1-3.30pm, 7pm-1.30am daily. **No credit cards. Map** p309 D4.

A cool and relaxing tapas bar with gently revolving ceiling fans and terracotta floors. Tapas include smoked cod, trout and salmon, or there are wooden *tablas* spread with cheese or ham. More unusually, there is Leffe and Guinness on tap. C/Cristo is pedestrianised and there are tables outside, but expect to be assailed by a mixed bag of buskers.

Conache

Plaza de San Ildefonso (91 522 9500). Metro Tribunal. **Open** 10am-1am Mon-Sat. **Credit** AmEx, MC, V. **Map** p309 F4.

The Conache look is casually hip, but the bright lighting and fruit machines keep the scenesters away. The food, however, is where it's at. Try stir-fried veg with prawns, little rolls of venison and apple, or spinach and brie with figs, and finish with a sublime cheese mousse with fruits of the forest.

La Fortuna

Plaza de los Mostenses 3 (91 547 30 98). Metro Plaza de España. **Open** 11.30am-midnight Mon-Thur; 11.30am-1am Fri, Sat. Closed 3wks Aug. **Credit** MC, V. **Map** p309 D5.

It's been around, off and on, since 1800, though renovations have erased all the evidence but a very early photograph. A local favourite is the breakfast of fried egg, bacon and chips, but a decent range of tapas is available all day. Other specialities are *migas*, clams in sherry, and *salmorejo* (a thicker gazpacho).

El Maño

C/Palma 64 (91 521 50 57). Metro Noviciado. **Open** 7.30pm-12.30am Mon-Thur; 12.30-3.30pm, 7.30pm-12.30am Fri-Sun. **No credit cards. Map** p309 E4.

A relaxed place, with french windows opening on to the street in summer, marble-topped tables, faded yellow paintwork and art deco touches. A good selection of wine is chalked up on the walls, some of it poured from ancient barrels, and there are tortillas served with *pisto*, ragu or squid, brochettes of chicken and lamb and a small selection of canapés.

La Taberna de la Copla

C/Jesús de la Valle 1 (91 522 44 22). Metro Tribunal. **Open** 1-4pm, 8pm-1.30am Tue-Sat, 1-4pm Sun. **No credit cards. Map** p309 E4.

Copla is a form of Spanish ballad, as sung by those depicted here in the dozens of crumbling photos. Tapas are named for famous *coplas* – Juanita Reina is ham with tomato; Principe Gitano is tuna with peppers, and a range of tortillas includes La Zarzamora (plain); Ojos Verdes (with ham), and Cinco Farolas (with tuna).

La Taberna de Corps

Plaza Guardia de Corps 1 (91 547 53 27). Metro Ventura Rodriguez. **Open** 1.30pm-1am Mon-Sat; 1.30-5pm Sun. **No credit cards. Map** p309 D4.

The *surtido* (mixed plate) of canapés and excellent selection of wines aside, the main attraction here (and it sure isn't the dour staff) is the location on a quiet leafy *plaza*. Grab a Rioja or a draught *vermut* and settle down with the papers.

Taberna 9

C/San Andrés 9 (no phone). Metro Tribunal. **Open** *Sept-June* 7.30pm-1am Tue-Thur, Sun; 7.30pm-2.30am Fri, Sat. *July, Aug* 8.30pm-2am Tue-Thur, Sun, 8pm-2.30am Fri, Sat. **No credit cards. Map** p309 F4.

Fun, funky and very much of its neighbourhood, with a young crowd. Taberna 9 has a straightforward list of canapés, including a good scrambled egg with chorizo, and serves house wine by the very cheap *chato* – a small glass.

La Tabernilla del Gato Amadeus

C/Cristo 2 (91 541 41 12). Metro Noviciado. **Open** 1pm-1am daily. **No credit cards. Map** p309 D4.

Named after a late, great, Persian cat, this is a tiny, welcoming bar, whose *croquetas* are legendary. The other favourite is the *patatas con mojo picón* (baked new potatoes with a spicy sauce). Although there's not much seating inside (the sister bar nearby is bigger), in summer there are tables outside.

Other locations: C/Limón 32, Malasaña & Conde Duque (91 542 54 23).

Eat, Drink, Shop

Probably one of the most famous tapas bars in Madrid, and name-checked in a song by the Catalan folk singer Serrat, the food is little changed since the '50s and of a high standard. If your appetite is up to it, try the *brascada* (sirloin with ham and onions); otherwise there are delicate little canapés of smoked salmon tartare, melted brie and similar treats.

North & west

Argüelles

Alhuzena

C/Martín de los Heros 72 (91 544 30 18). Metro Argüelles. **Open** *Sept-June* 8pm-3am daily. *July* 8pm-3am Mon-Sat. Closed Aug. **Credit** DC, MC, V. **Map** p308 B3.
A quirky basement bar, kicking to the strains of flamenco and best described as rustic technicolour, with its wooden painted furniture and Gaudiesque mosaic bar. Wine is served in little *chatos*, and the tapas are outstanding: artichokes filled with jamón ibérico, mozzarella with tomato and pesto and crêpes with spinach and ricotta among them.

Chamberí

Another area with a tapas round of its own – Calles Cardenal Cisneros and Hartzenbush are lined with cheapish bars.

Bodegas la Ardosa

C/Santa Engracia 70 (91 446 58 94). Metro Iglesia. **Open** 9.30am-3.30pm, 6-11pm daily. Closed mid July to end Aug. **No credit cards**. **Map** p310 G2.
A tiny local bar with a lovely old tiled exterior (confusingly marked No.58) and walls lined with bottles of wine. There are especially good *patatas bravas* and fried pigs' ears, as well as sardines, an array of wonderful shellfish and good beer.

La Nueva

C/Arapiles 7 (91 447 95 92). Metro Quevedo. **Open** 11am-midnight Mon-Sat. Closed Aug. **Credit** DC, MC, V. **Map** p309 E2.
A gorgeous old bar, La Nueva was recently taken over and scrubbed up, losing a little of its character along the way. The new Russian ownership has added oysters, champagne, and a vodka and Beluga caviar tasting for €195.50 a head. Meanwhile, back on Planet Earth, there are prawns, or tripe with chickpeas.

Taberna los Madriles

C/José Abascal 26 (91 593 06 26). Metro Alonso Cano. **Open** 11am-12.30am Mon-Fri; 11am-4pm, 7pm-12.30am Sat. **No credit cards**.
The speciality of this diminutive bar is the *pincho Los Madriles*, with red pepper and anchovies. Also worth trying are the tuna and prawn *pinchos*, the fried potatoes and the *callos*. Decorated with hundreds of black and white photos of its regulars as kids, this old-style bar can get a bit cramped, but has tables outside in summer.

Bodegas la Ardosa.

Salamanca & the Retiro

Cervecería Santa Bárbara

C/Goya 70 (91 575 00 52). Metro Goya. **Open** 8am-midnight daily. **Credit** MC, V. **Map** p311 L4.
The prawns are the thing here, consumed in rosy platefuls by the uptown shoppers crowded round the horseshoe-shaped bar. Always full, with a loyal clientele, it is one of the city's meeting places, with a good selection of beers, and tables outside.

Estay

C/Hermosilla 46 (91 578 04 70). Metro Velázquez. **Open** 8am-1am Mon-Sat. **Credit** AmEx, DC, MC, V. **Map** p311 J4.
Estay's bright, air-conditioned interior filled with baying young mothers laden with shopping bags does not immediately suggest gastronomic promise. Stick with it, however, for scrumptious and sophisticated tapas and cheap wines by the glass.

Hevia

C/Serrano 118 (91 562 30 75). Metro Gregorio Marañón. **Open** 9am-1am Mon-Sat. Closed Aug. **Credit** AmEx, DC, MC, V. **Map** p311 J1.
A quiet, well-heeled crowd frequents this smart bar. Tapas are correspondingly sophisticated – foie gras, caviar, crab and duck liver pâté – and correspondingly pricey. In summer there are tables outside.

José Luis

C/Serrano 89-91 (91 563 09 58). Metro Núñez de Balboa. **Open** 9am-1am Mon-Sat; noon-1am Sun. **Credit** AmEx, DC, MC, V. **Map** p311 J2.

Cafés & Bars

A beginner's guide to the drinking capital of Europe.

The outrageous claims abound: Madrid has over 100,000 bars (around one per 100 residents); the Calle Alcalá has more bars than Belgium; the city has more bars per square metre than anywhere else in Europe. The really extraordinary thing is that they're probably all true. *Madrileños*, even by normal Spanish standards, are a sociable bunch who place a lot of importance on eating and drinking in company. Consequently the first coffee of the day tends to be drunk in a bar on the way to work, and the second will happen around 10.30 or so when groups of office workers head out for breakfast.

In bars in Spain it is customary to pay at the end, although different rules apply in touristy places or on outdoor terraces. To get a waiter's attention try a firm, but questioning, '*oiga*' (literally, 'hear me', a perfectly polite way of attracting someone's attention). Once you've got him/her, ask '*¿Me pones un…?*' ('Could you bring me a…?'). Tipping is discretionary. Change is usually returned in a small dish, and people generally leave just a few coins, regardless of the amount spent. In most bars, you can throw olive stones on the floor, along with toothpicks, paper napkins and so on, but watch what the locals are doing.

COFFEE AND TEA

A *café con leche* is a largish, milky coffee, which can be also served in a glass (*vaso*); ask for a *taza grande* if you want it even bigger. An espresso is a *café solo*; the same with a dash of milk is *un cortado*, while *un americano* is diluted with twice the normal amount of water. With a shot of alcohol, a *solo* becomes a *carajillo*. A true *carajillo* is made with coffee, sugar, some coffee beans and brandy, which is then set alight on top so that the mixture gets mulled a little; a *carajillo* can also be just a *solo* with a shot of *coñac*, and you can equally ask for a *carajillo de whisky, de ron* (rum), *de Bailey's* (pronounced 'bye-lees'), *de anís* or anything else you fancy. Decaffeinated coffee is *descafeinado*, and you will normally be asked if you want it from a sachet (*de sobre*), or the machine (*de máquina*). In summer a great alternative is *café con hielo* – black coffee with ice.

Tea in bars is usually awful, and unless you specifically request otherwise will often come as a glass of hot milk with a teabag on the side. Very popular, however, are herb teas, *infusiones*, such as *menta* (mint) or *manzanilla* (camomile) and nowadays there are a few more cafés around that have at least a little awareness of what decent tea might be.

Los Gabrieles. *See p156.*

Anticafé.

BEER

Draught beer (*de barril*) is served in *cañas*, a small measure that varies but is less than half a pint, *tubos* in a tall thin glass, or as *dobles* (a little bigger). Some places even serve *pintas* (pints), often in a *jarra*, a large heavy glass with a handle. Bottled beer usually comes in *tercios*, a third of a litre, or in *botellines*, a quarter of a litre. Spain produces some good-quality beers. In Madrid, the favourite is the local Mahou, with two basic varieties – green label Mahou Clásica and the stronger red label Cinco Estrellas. San Miguel is less common, while Andalucían favourite Cruzcampo is growing in popularity. A darker Mahou beer (*negra*) is also available. Shandy is *clara*, and is made with bitter lemon). Imported beers are now common, too, but nearly always cost more.

WINES, SPIRITS AND OTHER DRINKS

All bars have a sturdy cheap red (*tinto*) on offer, and usually a white (*blanco*) and a rosé (*rosado*). Madrid's traditional summer drink is *tinto de verano* (red in a tall glass over ice, with a slice of lemon and topped up with lemonade). Most bars listed here will have at least one decent Rioja and probably a cava, but truly good wines are normally only found in the new-style *tabernas* that take pride in their lists.

Sherry is *jerez*. The type virtually always drunk in Spain is dry *fino*, served very cold. A good fuller-bodied variety is *palo cortado*. Sweet sherries have traditionally been only for export. Red vermouth (*vermut*) with soda is another Madrid tradition, usually as an aperitif, and has recently come back into fashion a little. For a powerful after-dinner drink, try Galician *orujo*, a fiery spirit similar to grappa, which comes plain (*blanco*) or *con hierbas*, in a

luminous green colour. Other *digestivos* include *patxarán*, a fruity aniseed-flavoured liqueur from Navarra, and the more Castilian *anis*, the best of which hails from Chinchón and is available dry (*seco*) or sweet (*dulce*).

NON-ALCOHOLIC DRINKS

Low- and alcohol-free beers (Laiker, Buckler, Kaliber) have an important niche in the market; other favourites for non-alcohol drinkers are the Campari-like but booze-free Bitter Kas, and plain tonic (*una tónica*) with ice and lemon. Fresh orange juice, *zumo de naranja*, is often available. Trinaranjus is the best-known bottled juice brand; favourite flavours are orange, pineapple (*piña*) and peach (*melocotón*). *Mosto* is grape juice, served in small glasses, sometimes with ice and a slice. A great and unappreciated Spanish speciality, though, are its traditional summer refreshers: most unusual is *horchata*, a milky drink made with tiger nuts. It has to be drunk fresh, from a specialised shop, as it curdles once made. The same places also offer *granizados* – crushed ice with fresh lemon, orange or coffee. Mineral water (*agua mineral*) can be ordered anywhere, either sparkling (*con gas*) or still (*sin gas*).

Many entries in the **Nightlife** and **Tapas** chapters are also good all-rounders, acting as cafés or bars for at least part of the day.

Los Austrias & La Latina

Anticafé

C/Unión 2 (91 559 41 63/www.anticafe.net).
Metro Ópera. **Open** *Sept-June* 7pm-3am daily.
July, Aug 4pm-3am daily. **Admission** free.
Credit AmEx, DC, MC, V. **Map** p313 D7.
It sounds like a fair-trade movement, but is in fact a hotbed for a diverse range of creativity. The tiny stage downstairs regularly accommodates a varied programme of anything from Latin jazz and flamenco to a good old-fashioned jam, all by local artists. Occasional DJ sessions also take place, as do film screenings, dance classes and poetry readings.

Café del Nuncio

C/Nuncio 12 & C/Segovia 9 (91 366 08 53). Metro La Latina. **Open** noon-2am Mon-Thur; noon-3am Fri, Sat; 2pm-2am Sun. **No credit cards. Map** p313 D8.
Split into two halves at either end of the narrow Escalinata del Nuncio, the Café del Nuncio has lovely cool, dark interiors with gently rotating ceiling fans and soft classical music. The real charm, however, lies in the terrace outside on the stepped slope dividing the two spaces; this is one of the most picturesque streets in the old city.

Café de Oriente

Plaza de Oriente 2 (91 541 39 74). Metro Ópera.
Open 8.30am-1.30am Mon-Thur, Sun; 8.30am-2.30am Fri, Sat. **Credit** AmEx, DC, MC, V. **Map** p312 C7.

Eat, Drink, Shop

The *belle époque* interior is entirely fake yet entirely convincing, making this one of the most peaceful and elegant spots to flick through the newspapers or recover from the exertions of the Palacio Real opposite. Despite its location, with tables outside on the stunning Plaza de Oriente, the café seems to be as popular with locals as tourists, who are perhaps put off by its air of grandeur.

Café del Real
Plaza de Isabel II (91 547 21 24). Metro Ópera. **Open** 9am-1am Mon-Thur, Sun; 10am-2.30am Fri, Sat. **No credit cards. Map** p313 D7.
This likeable, slightly cramped café with a lovely façade is good for a restorative coffee or slice of cake (chocolate or carrot), though prices are a tad high. Head upstairs to a low-beamed room with red leather chairs and old opera posters, overlooking the *plaza*. The café was a particular haunt of intellectuals, artists and actors in the '80s, but it's a popular stop-off for a wider crowd these days.

Chocolatería San Ginés
Pasadizo de San Ginés 5 (91 365 65 46). Metro Ópera or Sol. **Open** 6pm-7am Mon, Tue; 10am-7am Wed-Sun. **No credit cards. Map** p313 D7.
Serving chocolate and *churros* (deep-fried batter sticks) to the city night and day since 1894, this veritable institution has had to introduce a ticketing system – pay before you order – to deal with the 5am queues of exhausted clubbers and chipper old ladies. The lighting is a bit much if you fall into the former category, but there are at least tables outside.

De 1911
Plazuela de San Ginés 5, corner C/Coloreros (91 366 35 19). Metro Ópera or Sol. **Open** 6pm-1.30am Mon-Thur; 6pm-3am Fri, Sat. **No credit cards. Map** p313 D7.
Despite the address, De 1911 actually sits on the the tiny pedestrian street C/Coloreros, on which it has tables. It is indeed from 1911, but is a curious mix of *belle époque* and neon; Greek statuary and Coca-Cola signs. There's Guinness on tap, strong cocktails and some good tapas: try chorizo in cider or a ham, cheese and tomato brochette.

Delic
Costanilla de San Andrés 14 (91 364 54 50). Metro La Latina. **Open** 11am-2am Mon-Thur; 11am-2am Fri, Sat; 11am-midnight Sun. Closed last 2wks Aug. **No credit cards. Map** p312 C8.
A perennial favourite with seemingly everybody; from those looking for a peaceful morning coffee on the leafy Plaza de la Paja to those meeting up for a few bolstering cocktails before a big night out. A globe-trotting menu includes tabouleh, Japanese dumplings and filled ciabatta, and the Chilean chocolate cake is utterly irresistible.

La Fontanilla
Plaza Puerta Cerrada 13 (91 366 27 49). Metro La Latina. **Open** 11am-2am daily. **Credit** MC, V. **Map** p313 D8.

La Fontanilla claims to be not the biggest or the best or the oldest, but the smallest Irish pub in Madrid. There's no disputing this singular claim, but it does manage to cram in a couple of wooden tables alongside wide hatches opening on to the street. The myriad beers racked up the walls are sadly not for sale, but there is Murphy's and Guinness, at least, along with some incongruous canapés to nibble at.

Rey de los Vinos
C/Bailén 19 (91 559 53 32). Metro Ópera. **Open** 10am-3pm, 6-11pm Mon, Tue, Thur-Sun. Closed Aug. **No credit cards. Map** p312 C8.
Kept much as it has been for the last century – very simple, but spacious and light inside with a wide counter and mirrored walls – the King of Wines serves good canapés, and is a great place for a drink after visiting the cathedral. Prices are quite high, especially if you sit outdoors.

Taberna Gerardo
C/Calatrava 21 (91 221 96 60). Metro Puerta de Toledo. **Open** *Sept-June* noon-4pm, 8pm-midnight Mon-Sat; noon-5pm Sun. *July, Aug* noon-4pm, 8pm-1am Mon-Sat; noon-5pm Sun. **No credit cards. Map** p312 C9.
A lively and unpretentious wine bar, Taberna Gerardo is an essential part of the neighbourhood, offering excellent sausage, ham and seafood tapas, as well as a particularly good selection of cheeses.

El Ventorrillo
C/Bailén 14 (91 366 35 78). Metro Ópera. **Open** 10am-2am daily. **No credit cards. Map** p312 C8.
Just down from the Palacio Real, this terraza offers the finest sunsets in Madrid, with a magnificent location looking out over the Casa del Campo and all the way to the Guadarrama. Not cheap, however.

Sol & Gran Vía

Café del Círculo de Bellas Artes
C/Alcalá 42 (91 521 69 42). Metro Banco de España. **Open** 9am-1am Mon-Thur, Sun; 9am-3am Fri, Sat. **Admission** €1; free 2-4pm. **Credit** DC, MC, V. **Map** p314 G7.
A quintessential point of reference in the city's café society, the Bellas Artes is utterly elegant. Under new ownership, it is now free to enter at lunchtime for the *menú del día*. Otherwise take a seat amid the columns and female nudes and frown over *El País* with coffee and a croissant to fit right in.

La Mallorquina
Puerta del Sol 8 (91 521 12 01). Metro Sol. **Open** 9am-9.15pm daily. Closed mid July-Aug. **No credit cards. Map** p313 E7.
While the bakery downstairs supplies box after ribbon-tied box of flaky *ensaïmada* pastries, croissants and *napolitanas* to what seems like half of Madrid, the upstairs *salón* crackles with the animated chat of *madrileña* blue-rinses and savvier tourists. Windows overlooking the Puerta del Sol make this an unbeatable central spot for breakfast.

Eat, Drink, Shop

Museo Chicote

Gran Vía 12 (91 532 67 37). Metro Gran Vía.
Open 8am-3am Mon-Sat. **Credit** AmEx, DC, MC,
V. **Map** p313 F6.

Its art deco interior is starting to look slightly shabby
around the edges, but Chicote is still the doyen of
Madrid cocktail bars. This was famously where
Hemingway and other international press hacks
would spend their days sheltering from the artillery
shells flying down the Gran Vía during the Civil
War. Grace Kelly and Ava Gardner, along with just
about every Spanish writer, actor or artist of the last
60 years have passed through too.

Huertas & Santa Ana

Café del Español

*C/Príncipe 25 (91 420 43 05). Metro Antón Martín
or Sol.* **Open** noon-1am Mon-Wed, Sun; noon-2am
Thur; noon-3am Fri, Sat. **Credit** V. **Map** p313 F8.
Terribly elegant, with columns, green-glass chandeliers and red-velvet banquettes, this quiet café is
modelled on its neighbour, the Teatro Español. It's
popular for an slice of tarte tatin or a *bocatín* (little
sandwich), though is let down by its coffee.

Casa Pueblo

C/León 3 (91 429 05 15). Metro Antón Martín.
Open 5pm-2.30am daily. **Credit** AmEx, MC, V.
Map p313 F8.
A handsome, old-fashioned jazz bar hung with
antique clocks and black and white photos, Casa
Pueblo is popular with a slightly older crowd that
knows its whisky. Occasional live music includes
jazz and tango (on a Wednesday).

Cervecería Alemana

Plaza Santa Ana 6 (91 429 70 33). Metro Sol. **Open**
11.30am-12.30am Mon, Wed, Thur, Sun; 11.30am-
2am Fri, Sat. **No credit cards**. **Map** p313 F8.

Famous for being Hemingway's daily haunt (his
table, should you be wondering, is in the near right-
hand corner). The decor is turn-of-the-century
German bierkeller, with dusty old paintings and
dark wood. The tapas are uninspired and the waiters gruff, but for many this will be an essential stop.

Cervecería Santa Ana

*Plaza Santa Ana 10 (91 429 43 56). Metro
Antón Martín or Sol.* **Open** 10am-midnight
daily. **No credit cards**. **Map** p313 F8.
Another on this strip of beerhouses (the most exotic
brew on offer here is Guinness), this one was never
frequented by Hemingway and is consequently
cheaper. Two entrances lead into two different
spaces; one with seating and one without, and there
are tables outside. Good for a light lunch, with
decent salads and a range of *pulgas* (small rolls).

Dos Gardenias

*C/Santa María 13 (91 429 29 69). Metro Antón
Martín.* **Open** *Sept-May* 8pm-3am Tue-Sun. *June-
Aug* 10pm-3am Tue-Sun. **No credit cards**.
Map p313 F8.
There's no sign on the door – just look out for this
mellow little space painted in warm yellow, orange
and blue and the emanating chilled-out vibes, soft
flamenco and Brazilian jazz. Kick back on a velvet
sofa with the house speciality: a Mojito made with
brown sugar and Angostura bitters.

Fookar

C/Fúcar 1 (91 420 04 64). Metro Antón Martín.
Open 9.30am-4pm, 7.30pm-2am Mon-Thur; 9.30am-
4pm, 7.30pm-3am Fri, Sat. **No credit cards**.
Map p314 G9.
A new and gleefully eccentric little café, with whitewashed brick walls enlivened with splashes of colour
– collaged mannequins, installations with plastic
fruit and net tutus as lightshades – and where even

Cafe del Nuncio. *See p152.*

Cervecería Santa Ana. *See p155.*

the loos are kooky. Downtempo and bossa nova set the daytime tone, when regulars drop in to use the free internet access, but things liven up at night.

Los Gabrieles

C/Echegaray 17 (91 429 62 61). Metro Sevilla or Sol. **Open** 1pm-2.30am Mon-Thur, Sun; 1pm-3.30am Fri, Sat. **No credit cards. Map** p313 F8.

When it was announced in early 2004 that the famous 'Bull Bar' was to be the next victim of local property speculation, the outcry spread to international media. The government stepped in and afforded this most impressive of all the tiled bars in Madrid museum status, guaranteeing at least a decade's protection. Until the '70s Los Gabrieles was a brothel, run by Gypsies. It then became a bar, and in the Movida years attracted all the city's beautiful and famous. These days it attracts moneyed youth and tourists, but it's still worth seeing while you can.

Manhattan Martini Bar

C/Moratín 5 (no phone). Metro Antón Martín. **Open** 9pm-2am Tue-Thur; 9pm-2.30am Fri, Sat. **No credit cards. Map** p314 G8.

This imported chunk of New York nightlife has a slightly quirky home, but a clear mission – to supply the best cocktails in town. American-owned and adorned with the requisite black and white shots of Manhattan, this is *the* place to get a Cosmopolitan or a Manhattan Blast. It's frequented by a mix of American residents, students and Spaniards.

Naturbier

Plaza Santa Ana 9 (91 429 39 18). Metro Antón Martín or Sol. **Open** 11am-1am Mon-Thur, Sun; 11am-2am Fri, Sat. **Credit** MC, V. **Map** p313 F8.

The least exciting-looking of all the beer cellars lining this side of the Plaza Santa Ana, Naturbier's big draw is its home-made organic beer – in fact it's the only place in Madrid to brew its own. The tapas are also worth checking out, despite the pricing, which is somewhat creative.

Reporter

C/Fúcar 6 (91 429 39 22). Metro Antón Martín. **Open** noon-1am Tue-Fri; 7pm-2am Sat; midnight-6pm Sun. **No credit cards. Map** p314 G9.

The *piña coladas* here are said to be the best in town, but otherwise there are good fruit juices and (during the day, at least) a little garden in this stylish Huertas cocktail-café, with low-volume jazz and occasional photo shows. It also serves tapas and light meals in the afternoon.

El Salón del Prado

C/Prado 4 (91 429 33 61). Metro Antón Martín. **Open** 2pm-2am Mon-Thur; 2pm-2.30am Fri, Sat; 2pm-1am Sun. Closed 2wks mid Aug. **No credit cards. Map** p313 F8.

With its air of hauteur, El Salón del Prado emulates, with no little success, one of the grand cafés of the Habsburg empire. It was actually created in the 1980s, but its velvet drapes and marble-topped tables are already looking suitably worn. In summer, try its *horchata* (tiger nut milk) and *granizados*.

Salón de Té Sherazade

C/Santa María 16 (91 369 24 74). Metro Antón Martín. **Open** 5pm-3am Mon-Thur, Sun; 5pm-4am Fri, Sat. **No credit cards. Map** p313 F8.

Filled with kilims, hookah pipes, cushions and bronze lanterns, this Moroccan seraglio calls itself a tea room, but effectively functions as one of the most atmospheric chillout bars of the city. The small room downstairs, particularly, is strewn with supine twentysomethings finding inner peace.

La Venencia

C/Echegaray 7 (91 429 73 13). Metro Sevilla or Sol. **Open** 1-3pm, 7.30pm-1.30am daily. **No credit cards. Map** p313 F8.

Totally unreconstructed, La Venencia is gloriously shabby, with old, peeling sherry posters, barrels behind the bar and walls burnished gold by decades of tobacco smoke. It serves only sherry, along with manchego cheese and chorizo by way of tapas. Orders are still chalked up on the bar, and an enamel sign asks customers not to spit on the floor.

Viva Madrid

C/Manuel Fernández y González 7 (91 429 36 40). Metro Sevilla or Sol. **Open** 1pm-2am Mon-Thur, Sun; 1pm-3am Fri, Sat. **No credit cards. Map** p313 F8.

Like Los Gabrieles, this tiled bar has become a tourist destination in its own right. It is beautiful, with vaulted ceilings and evocative decor, but tends to get rammed with young foreigners looking to pull, or at least get plastered – you either love it or loathe it. Best appreciated in the afternoon by anyone over 21.

A vine romance

Madrid is an oenophile's playground, with none of the solemnity and hefty price-tags attached to wine-drinking elsewhere. Everyone drinks it, from builders to nuns. It so pervades daily life that the Spanish Ministry of Agriculture categorises wine as *alimentación* (food) rather than an alcoholic beverage.

Wine-lovers around the globe have now caught on to the fact that Spanish labels are the best value for your euro. *Wine Spectator* claims it is one of the hottest regions in Europe, while American wine tsar Robert Parker is handing out top marks to Riojas and Priorats. The sad fact remains, however, that a lot of bars are happy to serve plonk. To taste the good stuff, get thee to a wine bar. Madrid has a number of cosy little *enotecas* where you can settle in at the bar and try different tasty wines by the glass. **La Cruzada** (C/Amnistía 8, 91 548 01 31), for example, offers a delectable selection of reasonably priced *vinos*. King Alfonso XII reportedly used to frequent this bar when he needed to escape the nearby royal palace for a clandestine tipple. Check out the lovely carvings of bare-breasted women on the wooden bar, which date back to the time of its opening in 1827.

La Otra (C/Cuchilleros 14, mobile 659 48 90 25), a small wine and tapas bar near the Plaza Mayor, is a good way to learn what's hot in the Spanish wine world. In autumn when new wines are coming out, La Otra hosts fun casual tastings (dates are not fixed, you just stop by). Other reliable spots for quality wines include **La Taberna de los Cien Vinos** (*see p143*), **González** (*see p178*), **Entrevinos** (C/Ferraz 36, 91 548 31 14), **Vinoteca Barbechera** (*see p147*), and **Vinitis** (C/Ventura de la Vega, 15, 91 420 40 90, www.vinitis.com).

An entertaining way to dive into Spanish wine is to attend one of Madrid's many wine-tasting classes, known as *cursos de cata*. Simply Spain Tours (91 474 32 93 or mobile 652 66 58 65, www.simplyspaintours madrid.com) arranges casual wine and tapas tours of Madrid, or a three-hour course taught by a professional sommelier (followed by gourmet tapas) gets you happily swirling, sniffing and sipping good wine. Call in advance. **AtSpain** (91 547 50 91, www.atspain.com), an online shop for Spanish gifts and gourmet products, also arranges fun English wine and tapas classes with sommeliers from Madrid's best wine stores. You might also pay a visit to the Torres Bodega's newly opened **Centro Cultural del Vino** (C/Martires Concepcionista 19, 91 401 77 62), which offers very professional classes covering everything from soil types to food pairing, over the course of two nights. The city's best wine shops, **Reserva y Cata**, **Lavinia** and **Bodega Santa Cecilia** (for all, *see p182*) also give regular *cursos de cata* in Spanish.

González.

Eat, Drink, Shop

TimeOut
Online

vw.timeout.cc

ver 50 of the world
greatest cities.
On one great site.

Yesterday

C/Huertas 10 (no phone). Metro Sevilla or Sol.
Open 8.30pm-2.30am Mon, Wed, Thur, Sun; 9pm-3.30am Fri, Sat. **No credit cards. Map** p313 E8.
Back in the '70s this was one of the first bars to open in an area that's now awash with them. On a heaving Saturday it's an oasis; lively but not rammed, with no pretensions, no DJs and no cocktails – just a cosy, antique-filled bar with good music and friendly Spanish-American owners.

Rastro & Lavapiés

El Eucalipto

C/Argumosa 4 (mobile 629 334 998). Metro Lavapiés. **Open** 5pm-2am Mon-Sat; 1pm-2am Sun. **No credit cards. Map** p313 F10.
Totally tropical, with a beach bar look and pictures of Cuban singers around the walls, El Eucalipto is all about fruit. There are long lists of juices; *batidos* (milkshakes and smoothies); lime, strawberry, mango, raspberry and banana daiquiris; caipirinhas, piña coladas and more.

La Heladería

C/Argumosa 7 (91 528 80 09). Metro Lavapiés. **Open** 10am-midnight Mon-Thur, Sun; 10am-1am Fri, Sat. Closed Nov-Mar. **No credit cards. Map** p313 F10.
Peruvian owner Yoli is unfailingly charming, and happy to let you try her excellent ice-creams before you buy – blackberry (*mora*) and lemon come recommended. Try the *blanco y negro*, a delicious café frappé with ice-cream, or one of her milkshakes.

Montes

C/Lavapiés 40 (91 527 00 64). Metro Lavapiés. **Open** noon-3.30pm, 8pm-midnight Tue-Thur; noon-3.30pm, 8pm-1.30am Fri, Sat; noon-5pm Sun. Closed Aug. **No credit cards. Map** p313 E9.
Ignore the inauspicious exterior and raucous crowd spilling on to the street, and inside you'll find a wide variety of excellent wines, backed up by top-notch tapas. The bar is owned by genial Don César, who is something of a gourmet. Bottles of wines are stacked up above the bar with his handwritten comments attached to each one.

Nuevo Café Barbieri

C/Ave María 45 (91 527 36 58). Metro Lavapiés. **Open** 3pm-2am Mon-Thur, Sun; 3pm-3am Fri, Sat. **No credit cards. Map** p313 F9.
An airy and peaceful space with high ceilings and a dusty elegance, its marble-topped tables slightly chipped and its red-velvet banquettes a little worn. A favourite haunt of journos and wannabe travel writers, Barbieri has plenty of newspapers and magazines, but its ordinary coffee comes at a premium.

Oliveros

C/San Millán 4 (91 354 62 52). Metro La Latina. **Open** 1-5pm, 8pm-12.30am Tue-Sat; noon-6pm Sun. Closed mid Aug-mid Sept. **Credit** MC, V. **Map** p313 D9.

Oliveros is the genuine article, and although it was closed for years, it has been miraculously preserved in its original mid 19th-century state, complete with tiles and zinc bar. Opening hours can be somewhat erratic, however.

Taberna de Tirso de Molina

Plaza de Tirso de Molina 9 (91 429 17 56). Metro Tirso de Molina. **Open** 8am-2am daily. **Credit** MC, V. **Map** p313 E8.
It has a good stab at looking traditional with tiles, nautically uniformed waiters and exposed brickwork, but this *taberna* is in fact quite new. There are plenty of tables where you can eat a decent breakfast on the way to the Rastro, or a very generous set lunch for €6.90. Tapas are available all day, along with heftier dishes such as the towering *parellada de marisco* (seafood platter).

Vinícola Mentridana

C/San Eugenio 9 (91 527 87 60). Metro Antón Martín. **Open** 1pm-1am Mon-Thur, Sun; 1pm-2am Fri, Sat. **No credit cards. Map** p314 G9.
Frequented by the bohemian hip element of the Lavapiés, this cool wine bar, with tall windows open on to the street, is gently evocative of the old *bodega* it used to be. An impressive list of well-priced wines by the glass is complemented by tasty canapés, along with mulled wine and *caldo* (broth) in winter, or gazpacho and *granizado* in summer.

Chueca

Ángel Sierra

C/Gravina 11 (91 531 01 26). Metro Chueca. **Open** 12.30pm-12.30am Mon-Thur, Sun; 12.30pm-2.30am Fri, Sat. **No credit cards. Map** p310 G5.
This battered old bar with its tiled walls, zinc bar top, overflowing sink and glasses stacked on wooden slats has become the Chueca meeting-place *par excellence*, thanks to its position overlooking the main square. A newer room to the back of the bar, however, has a faux pub look enhanced with amplified MOR radio and a rule that only doubles and pints are served after midnight.

El Bandido Doblemente Armado

C/Apodaca 3 (91 522 10 51). Metro Bilbao. **Open** 4pm-midnight Mon-Thur; 4.30pm-2am Fri; 6pm-2am Sat. Closed 1wk mid Aug. **Credit** AmEx, DC, MC, V. **Map** p310 G4.
An assured and attractively designed café-bookshop, equally at ease providing afternoon sandwiches, evening poetry readings or late-night cocktails. It's spaciously laid out, and also has friendly staff who are knowledgeable on the latest literary trends in Spain.

Bar Cock

C/Reina 16 (91 532 28 26). Metro Gran Vía. **Open** *Sept-June* 7pm-3am daily. *July, Aug* 9pm-4am Mon-Sat. **Credit** AmEx, DC, MC, V. **Map** p313 F6.
A former brothel, Bar Cock is still linked to the Museo Chicote cocktail bar on Gran Vía (*see p155*)

by a tunnel. Very stagey, furnished in the style of what Spaniards think of as 'English pub' – red-velvet curtains, embossed leather armchairs and a fake half-timbered effect, it still continues to attract those who like to think of themselves as in the know. As a result it can get very crowded, especially at weekends.

Del Diego

C/Reina 12 (91 523 31 06). Metro Gran Via. **Open** *Sept-July* 7pm-3am Mon-Thur; 7pm-3.30am Fri, Sat. Closed Aug. **Credit** AmEx, MC, V. **Map** p313 F6.

Not to all tastes, with an unchanging, late '80s, steel-and-blonde-wood *Wall Street* vibe, Del Diego is nevertheless deservedly renowned for its consummately smooth barmen and superb cocktails. Pull up a stool and try a zingy mint julep del Diego to kickstart a night's wheeling and dealing.

Finnegan's

Plaza de las Salesas 9 (91 310 05 21). Metro Alonso Martínez. **Open** 11am-2am Mon-Fri; 1pm-2am Sat, Sun. **Credit** DC, MC, V. **Map** p310 H4.

One for rugby fans, Finnegan's has its own team, the Madrid Lions, and a talent for sniffing out every conceivable match to show on its large screens. In

lean sporting times the void is filled with pub quizzes and DJs (mostly rock) at weekends. Pints of Beamish, Newky Brown and John Smith's complement burgers and other pub grub.

Olivera

C/Santo Tomé 8 (no phone). Metro Chueca. **Open** 9pm-2.30am daily. **No credit cards. Map** p310 H5.

A relaxed lounge bar, presided over by a portrait of Yugoslav film star Olivera Markovic, who happens to be the owner's mother. The musical mood is nu jazz and funk, and the mismatched armchairs and sofas make it an easy place to end up staying all night. Increasingly, though, it's become a stop-off on the pre-club round.

Stop Madrid

C/Hortaleza 11 (91 521 88 87). Metro Chueca or Gran Via. **Open** noon-3am daily. **Credit** MC, V. **Map** p310 H4.

When it opened in 1929, this was the first ham and charcuterie shop in Madrid. It's undergone a few changes since then, but many of the original fittings have been retained, and great pride is taken in sourcing the best ingredients for tapas. Of the 50-strong wine list, all are available by the glass.

In the frame Tertulias

The intellectual life of Spain once revolved around the ephemeral institution known as the *tertulia*. Originating in the humanist salons of 16th-century Seville, the *tertulia* is a gathering of people united by a common interest, which can be anything from mathematics to gastronomy, but has traditionally been literature. And Spain being a country where people tend to go out together rather than meet up in each other's houses, these gatherings have invariably been held in bars, restaurants, and, above all, cafés.

The rise of the *tertulia* in Madrid, as depicted in many paintings of the time, coincided with the city's emergence in the early 19th century as the centre of a café life rivalling that of Paris and Vienna. Café life has always flourished at times of great political repression, the café being a place whose proverbial smoky gloom has provided a suitably furtive retreat for dissidents. During the grey, autocratic rule of Spain's Ferdinand VII, the *tertulia* became an expression of political and cultural freedom.

Tertulias took place in many of the cafés that by the 1830s had almost entirely encircled the Puerta del Sol, hub of *madrileño* life. But the most influential of

these gatherings was the one associated with a tiny, rat-infested basement café next to the neo-classical Teatro Español (the present bland reconstruction bears little resemblance to the original establishment) The place was officially called the Café del Príncipe, but everyone came to know it as the 'Parnasillo' or 'Little Parnassus', on account of its attracting all the fashionable writers of the day. Among these was the much revered satirical essayist Mariano José de Larra and the writer Ramón de Mesonero Romanos, who famously wrote of the Parnasillo that 'this miserable little room' succeeded in shaking the very foundations of Spanish life and culture.

With the evolution towards the end of the 19th century of Madrid's idiosyncratically late eating and drinking hours, *tertulias* proliferated as never before, reaching their apogee in the 1920s, under the guidance of a *madrileñista* writer sometimes referred to as 'the second of the Ramones', Ramón Gómez de la Serna (*see p78* **Defining the indefinable**). Every Saturday night, from around ten o'clock until dawn, a *tertulia*, presided over by Gómez de la Serna, was held in what was soon dubbed 'The Sacred Crypt of the Pombo', a now vanished café off

Stromboli Café

C/Hortaleza 96 (91 319 46 28). Metro Alonso Martínez or Chueca. **Open** 6.30pm-3am Mon-Thur, Sun; 6.30pm-3.30am Fri, Sat. **Credit** MC, V. **Map** p310 G4.

Slick design (zebra-print stools and glitter balls) and piles of free style mags cater to a young and cooler-than-thou crowd. With downtempo and chillout hotting up with the arrival of the DJ at midnight, Stromboli functions principally as an opportunity for some low-key strutting and a warm-up for the night ahead.

Zanzíbar

C/Regueros 9 (91 319 90 64). Metro Alonso Martínez. **Open** *Sept-July* 8pm-2am Tue-Thur, Sun; 8pm-3.30am Fri, Sat. *Aug* 8pm-2am Thur; 8pm-3.30am Fri, Sat. **No credit cards.** **Map** p310 H4.

Good causes and ethnic chic combine to create a cute and colourful hangout for right-on revellers. On a small stage at the back there are frequent appearances by bossa nova bands, singer-songwriters and storytellers (though the view is largely blocked by a giant papier-mâché tree); at other times reggae and soft flamenco tickle the speakers. A few bar snacks are available, along with fair-trade coffee.

Malasaña & Conde Duque

La Ardosa

C/Colón 13 (91 521 49 79). Metro Tribunal. **Open** 11.30am-1.30am Mon-Thur, Sun; 11.30am-2.30am Fri, Sat. **No credit cards.** **Map** p309 F5.

Having an affair? Duck under the counter to the most intimate bar-room you could wish for. Out front, meanwhile, this is a lovely old tiled *taberna* lined with dusty bottles, old black and white lithographs and beer posters. A range of canapés has just been added, and the speciality of the house is its draught beer – Bombardier, Budvar and Guinness.

Bar El 2 De

C/Velarde 24 (91 445 88 39). Metro Tribunal. **Open** *Sept-June* 1pm-2am Mon-Wed, Sun; 1pm-3am Thur-Sat. *July, Aug* 6pm-2am Mon-Wed, Sat; 1pm-3am Thur, Fri. **No credit cards.** **Map** p309 F4.

This is the emblematic Malasaña bar, packed at weekends and drowsily mellow in the afternoons, with a tiled bar and engraved mirrors, nicotine-stained walls and ceiling fans. To drink there's vermouth, lager and Beamish on tap, plus plenty of bottled beers and a small range of wines, served (if you dare) in *porrones*, long-spouted drinking jars.

Eat, Drink, Shop

the Puerta del Sol. The solemnity of these celebrated meetings was captured in a sombre painting by the Madrid painter José Gutiérrez Solana (*pictured*). La Serna is pictured standing, in the centre. These gatherings were also slightly ridiculed by the young film-maker Luis Buñuel, who later described how 'we used to arrive, greet each other, and order a drink – usually coffee, and a lot of water – until a meandering conversation began about the latest literary publications or political upheavals.'

The many liberal and avant-garde associates of the Pombo nearly all went into exile after the Spanish Civil War, thus radically diminishing the cultural life of the capital.

Subsequently many of the cafés in the centre of Madrid were succeeded by the headquarters of large banks; and many more suffered the humiliation of being transformed into formica-lined, American-style cafeterias. **La Tertulia del Café Pombo**, *by José Gutiérrez Solana, is found at the Reina Sofía (see p65).*

These books are
made for walking

Café Isadora.

Café Comercial

Glorieta de Bilbao 7 (91 521 56 55). Metro Bilbao. **Open** 7.30am-1am Mon-Thur; 7.30am-2am Fri; 8.30am-2am Sat; 10am-1am Sun. **No credit cards. Map** p309 F3.

Still the classic Madrid bar, with its original battered brown leather seats, revolving doors and marbled walls. A nod to the modern age comes in the shape of the internet terminals upstairs, where American gap-year students write home about the old men playing chess alongside them.

Café Isadora

C/Divino Pastor 14 (91 445 71 54). Metro Bilbao. **Open** 4pm-2am Mon-Thur, Sun; 4pm-2.30am Fri, Sat. **No credit cards. Map** p309 F4.

An elegant shrine to Isadora Duncan, with a chequered floor, marble-topped tables and an eerie collection of prints of 'that scarf', alongside frequently changing exhibitions. Along with a range of *patxaráns*, many of them home-made, is a list of 'aguas'; cocktails made with cava. *Agua de Valencia* is the original and best, featuring orange juice, gin, Cointreau and vodka.

Café Manuela

C/San Vicente Ferrer 29 (91 531 70 37). Metro Tribunal. **Open** *Oct-May* 4pm-2am daily. *June-Sept* 6pm-2.30am. **Credit** MC, V. **Map** p309 F4.

Stacked to the rafters with board games, Café Manuela has been a hive of activity since the Movida days. Its handsome art nouveau decor and conveniently nicotine-coloured walls are still the backdrop to occasional live music and other performances, but otherwise it's a great place to reacquaint yourself with Cluedo and Mastermind.

Café El Moderno

Plaza de las Comendadoras 1 (91 531 62 77). Metro Noviciado. **Open** *Sept-July* 3pm-1.30am Mon-Thur, Sun; 3pm-2.30am Fri, Sat. *Aug* 5.30pm-1.30am Mon-Thur, Sun; 5.30pm-2.30am Fri, Sat. **No credit cards. Map** p309 D/E4.

El Moderno's art deco look is entirely fake, but none the worse for it, and, along with its large terrace, attracts a mixed crowd of local characters and curious tourists. The specialities are teas, milkshakes

and hot chocolates, with an impressive 30 varieties of each. Fans of *Sex and Lucia* will recognise the building as Lorenzo's apartment block.

Café de Ruiz

C/Ruiz 11 (91 446 12 32). Metro Bilbao. **Open** 2pm-2am daily. **Credit** MC, V. **No credit cards. Map** p309 F3.

Recently smartened up, with prices buffed up to match, Café de Ruiz is as elegant as ever, with comfortable sofas and dramatic flower arrangements. A big draw is its homemade ice-cream and other tempting sweet treats, such as hot chocolate with *churros*, milkshakes, lemon tart and cheesecake.

Cafeina

C/Pez 18 (no phone). Metro Noviciado. **Open** 3pm-2am Mon-Thur; 3pm-3am Fri, Sat. **Credit** MC, V. **Map** p309 E5.

By day dogs chase kids through table legs while their parents chat over mugs of herbal tea. By night the hip hop and jazz DJs attract a different crowd, young and animated, which mill around the bar clutching killer G&Ts, or smooch on the sofas in the cosy bare-bricked basement. The big night here is Wednesday, for DJ'd flamenco.

Casa Camacho

C/San Andrés 4 (91 531 35 98). Metro Tribunal. **Open** noon-2.30am daily. Closed mid Aug-mid Sept. **No credit cards. Map** p309 F4.

A rough diamond, the diminutive Casa Camacho has changed little since it opened in 1928, except for the addition of a fruit machine and a TV – both in constant use. Pre-war dust coats the bottles and plastic flowers on display and the floor is a sea of toothpicks and cigarette ends, but for a slice of real neighbourhood life it can't be beat.

La Coctelería

C/Minas 1 (no phone) Metro Noviciado. **Open** 6pm-2am daily. **No credit cards. Map** p309 E4.

A shabby chic lounge bar, serving tisanes and milkshakes by day (when the stylish bar staff outnumber the customers) and cocktails by night. A cavernous basement is cool in every sense, its dimly lit hidden corners furnished with junk shop armchairs and glass-topped coffee tables covered in style mags. Prices are a little higher than the surroundings would suggest.

La Granja de Said

C/San Andrés 11 (91 532 87 93). Metro Tribunal. **Open** 10am-1am daily. **Credit** AmEx, DC, MC, V. **Map** p309 E4.

An inviting Moroccan tea house with all the trimmings: copper lanterns, wall-hangings, Moorish tiling and atmospheric lighting. It's popular with a young, studenty crowd, who linger long over speciality teas – try Taj Mahal (with cinnamon, orange and rose petals) or Oriente Express (green tea with apple, cloves and orange) – plus couscous, salads and tajines.

La Ida

C/Colón 11 (91 522 91 07). Metro Tribunal. **Open** 10am-2am daily. Closed Aug. **No credit cards. Map** p309 F5.

La Movida meets *Friends* in this cramped but jolly little café, where everybody appears to know everybody else. This is where the painfully cool neo-punks from the nearby Mercado Fuencarral come to let their guard down, tucking into courgette tart and canapés at the scrubbed pine tables amid perky green walls. Sundays are especially mellow: the perfect set for The One Where They All Got Tattoos.

Lola Loba

C/Palma 38 (91 522 71 66/www.lolaloba.com). Metro Noviciado. **Open** Sept-June 10am-2am Mon-Fri; 5pm-2.30am Sat, 5pm-1am Sun. July 5pm-1am daily. Closed Aug. **No credit cards. Map** p309 E4.

Named after a *copla* singer who ran away from her abusive American millionaire husband and opened this bar. In 1872 he found her and murdered her, and 'tis said her ghost still prowls within the redbrick walls. What is not known is whether she approves of the jazz, funk and house, or the fab *tostas*, slathered in mozzarella, tomato and basil; caramelised onion with brie, or smoked salmon with camembert.

Mendocino Café

C/Limón 11 (91 542 91 30). Metro Noviciado. **Open** Sept-July 10am-midnight Mon-Thur; noon-2.30am Fri, Sat; noon-midnight Sun. Aug 5pm-midnight Thur-Sun. **No credit cards. Map** p309 D4.

Now under Brazilian ownership, this is one of the most relaxing cafés in a neighbourhood full of them. It's kept its West Coast name and ambience, with sea-blue walls and fresh flowers, downtempo and lounge on the stereo and a plethora of board games. Sandwiches and salads are served throughout the week, with pancakes for Sunday brunch.

La Palmera

C/Palma 67 (630 884 470). Metro Noviciado. **Open** 8pm-2am daily. **No credit cards. Map** p309 E4.

The tiles in this tiny, crowded bar date back to its opening at the beginning of the last century, and have featured in various magazines. For years it lay

El Parnasillo.

in terminal decline, until it was bought in the late 1990s by a long-term regular. It almost exclusively serves vermouth and beer to a crowd that, for some reason, includes a loyal German following.

El Parnasillo

C/San Andrés 33 (91 447 00 79). Metro Bilbao. **Open** 2.30pm-3am Mon-Thur, Sun; 2.30pm-3.30am Fri, Sat. **No credit cards. Map** p309 F3.

Long frequented by writers, artists, journalists and intellectuals, the art nouveau El Parnasillo was very much at the centre of Madrid's cultural renewal in the '70s and '80s, to the extent that it was bombed by a far-right group. It's unlikely to excite the same emotion these days, but is still an evocative place for a cocktail, sarnie or *pa tumaca* (bread rubbed with tomato) topped with cheese, ham or smoked salmon.

Pepe Botella

C/San Andrés 12 (91 522 43 09). Metro Tribunal. **Open** Sept-July 11am-2am Mon-Thur, Sun; 11am-3am Fri, Sat. Aug 3pm-2am Mon-Thur, Sun; 3pm-3am Fri, Sat. **No credit cards. Map** p309 F4.

A cineaste's delight, the colourful Pepe Botella is decked out with film posters and frequented by the likes of director Alejandro Amenábar and actor Eduardo Noriega. For all that, it's wonderfully unpretentious, and attracts an intelligent bunch of mainly thirty- and fortysomethings, who engage in lively debate while smoking for Spain.

El Pez Gordo

C/Pez 6 (91 522 32 08). Metro Callao or Noviciado. **Open** 8pm-2am Mon-Sat. **No credit cards. Map** p309 E5.

Popular with audiences and actors from the nearby Teatro Alfil, the Fat Fish buzzes at night and is fabulously mellow during the day. The main attraction (aside from the photos of the owner's hideous bulldog) comes in the shape of the creative tapas. Try

Eat, Drink, Shop

fried plantain with guacamole, goose confit with red fruit compôte, or the *patatas Pez Gordo* with alioli, anchovies and hot peppers.

Subiendo al Sur

C/Ponciano 5 (91 548 11 47). Metro Noviciado or Plaza de España. **Open** *Sept-July* 11.30am-5pm, 8pm-2am Tue-Sat; 11.30am-5pm Mon, Sun. *Aug* 8pm-2am Tue-Sat. **No credit cards. Map** p309 D4.
Easily missed, this cooperative-run fair trade café and shop is an absolute gem. All profits go to good causes, with products such as Mecca Cola (20% to Palestinian kids) given top billing. The charming co-owners take turns in the kitchen, each lending ideas from their home country to the daily-changing menu, so chicken in peanut sauce from Equatorial Guinea sits alongside Senegalese *bobotie* and Mexican chicken *mole*. Highly recommended.

Salamanca & the Retiro

Balmoral

C/Hermosilla 10 (91 431 41 33). Metro Serrano. **Open** 12.30-3pm, 7pm-2am Mon-Thur; 12.30-3pm, 7pm-2.30am Fri, Sat. **Credit** AmEx, DC, MC, V. **Map** p311 I4.
A very surreal place, probably unique in Spain as drinking experiences go. If Balmoral Castle had a cocktail bar, it would look something like this, with stags' heads and skulls, stuffed grouse, leather banquettes and oil paintings, and deep armchairs gathered round a fireplace. Along with the cocktails, there is a small but decent selection of whiskies.

El Botánico

C/Ruiz de Alarcón 27 (91 420 23 42). Metro Banco de España. **Open** 8.30am-midnight daily. **Credit** AmEx, DC, MC, V. **Map** p314 H8.
Confusingly, this quiet bar-restaurant actually sits on C/Espalter, just around the corner, and overlooking the botanical gardens. Tucked away from the tourist drag, it's very quiet considering its proximity to the Prado, and has a peaceful, shaded terrace. It's a good spot for breakfast, and there are tapas later in the day.

Café Gijón

Paseo de Recoletos 21 (91 521 54 25). Metro Banco de España. **Open** 7.30am-1.30am daily. **Credit** AmEx, DC, MC, V. **Map** p314 H6.
Still charming after all these years, this is Madrid's definitive literary café, open since 1888. It still holds poetry *tertulias* on Monday nights, and publishes a magazine filled with doodles and thoughts from visiting writers. A pianist tinkles the ivories to a packed terrace in summer, while in winter it's heaving inside. Look out for the aged Alfonso, who has been selling cigarettes, matches and lottery tickets, just inside the entrance, for nearly 30 years.

Gelati e Frullati

Avda Felipe II 8 (91 577 09 52). Metro Goya. **Open** *Oct-May* 8am-11.30pm daily. *June-Sept* 7.30am-2am daily. **No credit cards.**

Under new, Italian, ownership, this fabulous *gelateria* serves the best ice-cream in the city and probably the whole of Spain. Twelve flavours (which rotate daily) are created in a back room, as are fresh panini, focaccia and sublime tiramisu, along with excellent Italian coffee. Enthusiastic staff will guide you through, insisting that you try the ambrosial vanilla, the zingy *zabaglione*, and in winter the *helado de panettone*.

Jazzanova

Paseo de la Castellana 8 (91 578 34 87/www. jazzanovabar.com). Metro Colón. **Open** noon-2.30am Mon-Sat; 1.30-7.30pm Sun. **Credit** AmEx, MC, V. **Map** p310 I4.
Jazzanova is a supremely smooth bar-restaurant-club, its black walls softened by clever uplighting, orange velvet cushions and a mellow soundtrack of jazz and blues. Brunch on Sundays is dished up with cocktails and live music, though not, sadly, on the terrace outside, which is limited to drinking only. The upmarket location and older clientele mean predictably higher prices.

Kitty O'Shea's

C/Alcalá 59 (91 575 49 01). Metro Banco de España. **Open** 11am-2am Mon-Thur; 11am-3am Fri, Sat. **No credit cards. Map** p314 G7.
The Madrid outpost of what is now a global chain of Oirish theme pubs. With Guinness, Murphy's, pub grub, chatty staff and plenty of rugby and Premier League matches on two big screens and three TVs, it's all much as you'd expect. Of more interest, perhaps, is that it sits on the site of the historic Café Lion, a haunt of post-Civil War literati.

El Pavellón del Espejo

Paseo de Recoletos 31 (91 319 11 22). Metro Colón. **Open** 8am-1am Mon-Thur; 8am-3am Fri; 10.30am-3am Sat, Sun. **Credit** AmEx, DC, MC, V. **Map** p314 H6.
Not nearly as historic as the Gijón, although it may look it: when it opened in 1978, 'The Mirror' set out to be the art nouveau bar Madrid never had, with positively Parisian 1900s decor. Its terrace bar on the Paseo occupies a splendid glass pavilion reminiscent of a giant Tiffany lamp. Fashionable and comfortable, it has excellent tapas at reasonable prices, unlike its better-known neighbour.

Argüelles

Bruin

Paseo del Pintor Rosales 48 (91 541 59 21). Metro Argüelles. **Open** 7.30am-10.30pm Mon-Fri; 12.30pm-2am Sat; 12.30pm-10.30pm Sun. **No credit cards. Map** p308 B3.
A wonderfully old-fashioned ice-cream parlour, with a terrace overlooking the Parque del Oeste. In contrast to its '50s feel, some of its 40 home-made flavours are decidedly modern: try olive oil, tomato, idiazábal cheese, tomato or sherry. Diabetics get a look-in, too, with the sugar-free varieties.

Shops & Services

Capital investment opportunities.

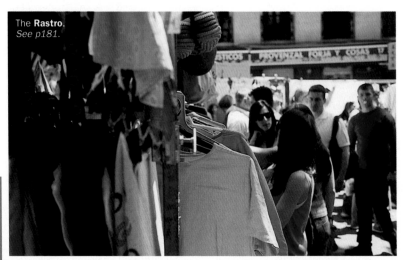

The **Rastro**.
See p181.

See p181.

As the tentacles of globalisation creep further into our everyday lives, high streets and cityscapes begin to look more and more alike, not just on a national level but internationally too. While this is of course in evidence in Madrid, what strikes you as you wander its shopping avenues is the curious mix of the traditional and the new. High-street chains and international franchises rub shoulders with museum-piece, family-run businesses. Department stores where you can find just about anything jostle for space with ancient shops normally dedicated to just one product, espadrilles maybe, or Spanish ceramics.

Madrid is not a large city, and its main shopping areas break down into several distinctive zones, all conveniently within walking distance – or a short metro ride – of each other. Between Sol and Gran Vía are **C/Preciados** and **C/Carmen**, always bustling with shoppers, and boasting a mix of chains and smaller stores selling cheap and mid-price clothes, shoes and accessories. Several branches of El Corte Inglés are to be found in this area. **Gran Vía** itself is given over to the flagship stores of many a household name – H&M, Zara and the Nike Store, to name but three. After battling through the crowds of dawdling shoppers, the tranquil area of **Los Austrias**

come as a welcome respite, given over to musical instrument stores, bohemian gift shops and treasure troves of decorative items. If you're all about labels, then **Salamanca** is the place to be, in particular C/Serrano, where on the same block you will find Loewe, Yves St Laurent and La Perla, as well as smaller designer boutiques throughout the area. Finally, **Chueca** is undoubtedly the hippest area in town, in particular C/Fuencarral. Thanks to that epicentre of cool, the shopping mall El Mercado de Fuencarral, the neighbourhood is becoming Madrid's Soho, with names such as Levi's, Puma and Diesel coexisting with the one-off shops that have helped make the street such a hotbed for Madrid's fashion-conscious youth.

The city's flea market, the Rastro, is an obligatory visit, but more for the atmosphere than the goods – you will almost definitely walk away empty-handed. At the time of going to press, in another massively unpopular move, the city's mayor is threatening to bring tighter restrictions to the Rastro, reducing the number of stalls and even relocating the market to several out-of-town locations. Judging by the opposition to the proposal – nearly 50,000 signatures have already been collected in protest – Madrid's most famous Sunday morning destination looks set to remain intact.

OPENING HOURS

Opening times are changing, as is the traditional August break. While smaller stores will still close for two or three hours at lunch and stay shut on Saturday afternoons, some mid-size and nearly all large outlets will remain open all day. If you are yet to get used to a two o'clock lunch and can face the heat in the summer, head to the bigger stores in the afternoon and you will miss the crowds. Pressure from large retailers brought about a relaxation of the laws on Sunday opening too, all amid much grumbling from small businesses, who find it very hard to compete with such timetables. As a result, large retailers can – and do – open every first Sunday of the month. A further bonus on these Sundays is the closure of Gran Vía to private transport, plus a free concert in Plaza Callao courtesy of Radio 3. As revenue from tourists becomes more vital to the shopkeepers of Madrid, August is no longer a month where the city closes down.

SALES AND TAX REFUNDS

Sales are usually on through January and February and then July and August. The rate of IVA, or VAT, is 16%. For non-EU residents, you can claim refund cheques for purchases over the value of €90.15. You can then reclaim the VAT at the Global Refund Office in Barajas airport. Look out for the Tax Free sticker in the window of participating outlets.

One-stop shops

El Corte Inglés

C/Preciados 1-4, Sol & Gran Vía (all branches 91 418 88 00/Tel-entradas ticket phoneline 902 40 02 22/www.elcorteingles.com). Metro Sol. **Open** 10am-9.30pm Mon-Sat; 11am-9pm 1st Sun of mth except Aug. **Credit** AmEx, DC, MC, V. **Map** p313 E7.

Spain's biggest retail concern has blown all competition out of the water. El Corte Inglés is the solution when all else fails for some, but the first choice for many. You can get practically everything you need, be it clothes, household goods, books or multimedia products, and there is also a range of services from key-cutting to ticket booking. Most outlets also have well-stocked, if expensive, supermarkets. Information points staffed by multilingual employees are a plus as is the post-sale, money-back guarantee. This branch specialises in music and computers, the branch opposite in books, the one on the Paseo de la Castellana has large sports, computer and toy departments and C/Serrano is mostly given over to fashion, jewellery and cosmetics.
Other locations: throughout the city.

Fnac

C/Preciados 28, Sol & Gran Vía (91 595 61 00/ www.fnac.es). Metro Callao. **Open** 10am-9.30pm Mon-Sat; noon-9.30pm Sun, public hols. **Credit** AmEx, MC, V. **Map** p313 E7.

The French giant offers a huge range of CDs, DVDs, videos and books plus computer hardware and software, all at competitive prices and under one roof. Among the CDs there are good world music and flamenco sections, and the helpful staff can look up titles on the database. The top floor holds a reasonabe English-language book section, with recent paperbacks as well as classics. On the second floor is a room to sit and read while listening to music. Downstairs there's a ticket booking service, a café and paper shop with a good range of foreign press and magazines, and the Fnac Forum, which hosts readings and film and record launches.

Top ten Shops

Anthurium
The trendiest, most stylish florist's in town. *See p178.*

El Apartamento
Retro furniture, fittings and homewares from this little locale in Malasaña. *See p168.*

The Deli Room
Choice cuts by Spanish designers served up in supermarket-chic surroundings. *See p173.*

Desigual
Quality clubwear for both sexes from this shop that pulsates with house music. *See p175.*

La Duquesita
The loveliest little period-piece cake shop you'll find anywhere. The cakes are good too. *See p178.*

Fotocasión
A treasure trove of new and second-hand cameras and accessories. *See p186.*

Joaquín Berao
Solid silver jewellery in chunky, flowing designs. Pricey but not overly so. *See p177.*

Lavinia
A new approach to wine shops: big and bright and bursting with bottles. *See p182.*

Mamblona
Hand-made textiles from Spain and abroad – excellent for gift ideas. *See p173.*

Up Beat Discos
Soul, jazz and reggae discs are the reason for visiting this '60s-feel shop. *See p185.*

Eat, Drink, Shop

After-hours

Three names dominate after-hours shopping in Madrid. The most ubiquitous, and open 24 hours a day, is **Sprint** (7/11 re-branded), which sells prepared food, hot and cold drinks, plus press and magazines. **OpenCor** and **Vip's** have shorter hours (8am-2am and 9am-3am respectively), but have a greater selection of goods, including supermarket products, fresh food, CDs, DVDs, books and gifts. In Vip's, Spanish and English-language press is sold, the book section has coffee-table art, often at bargain prices, and you can get films processed. Attached to most Vip's is a Gino's pizzeria.

After-hours shops are not allowed to sell alcohol after 10pm (9pm on Sundays). All have branches throughout town, but below are the most central.

OpenCor

C/Fuencarral 118, Chamberí (91 591 38 96) Metro Bilbao. **Open** 8am-2am daily. **Credit** AmEx, DC, MC, V. **Map** p309 F3.

Sprint

C/Arenal 28, Los Austrias (no phone). Metro Ópera. **Open** 24hrs daily. **No credit cards**. **Map** p313 D7.

Vip's

Gran Vía 43 (91 559 66 21). Metro Callao or Santo Domingo. **Open** 9am-3am daily. **Credit** AmEx, DC, MC, V. **Map** p313 D6.

Shopping centres

ABC Serrano

C/Serrano 61 & Paseo de la Castellana 64, Salamanca (91 577 50 31/www.abcserrano.com). Metro Rubén Darío. **Open** 10am-9.30pm Mon-Sat. **Map** p311 J2.

Occupying the building that once housed the ABC newspaper (hence the name), this upmarket and conveniently located shopping mall has eight floors. Four of them are dedicated to fashion, both designer and high street, sportswear, jewellery, crafts and hi-fi. There are three restaurants on the upper floors, a café on the ground floor and a lively summer *terraza* on the fourth, as well as a gym at the top.

Centro Comercial La Vaguada (Madrid 2)

Avda Monforte de Lemos 36, Barrio del Pilar (information 91 730 10 00/www.lavaguada.com). Metro Barrio del Pilar. **Open** 10am-10pm Mon-Sat; 11.30am-10pm Sun. Leisure area only 10am-2.30am Mon-Sat.

Madrid's first giant mall, and still the largest within the city itself, La Vaguada has around 350 outlets selling just about everything. Predictably, there's also a branch of the ubiquitous El Corte Inglés (see p167). The upper floor is given over to leisure, with cinemas and a bowling alley. It's a bit of a trek, but the metro line is fast.

El Jardín de Serrano

C/Goya 6-8, Salamanca (91 577 00 12/www.jardin serrano.es). Metro Serrano. **Open** 10am-9pm Mon-Sat. **Map** p311 J4.

This mall may be small but it's a gem, with designer boutiques, expensive shoe shops and a classy café.

Serrano 88

C/Serrano 88, Salamanca & Retiro (91 575 53 31). Metro Rubén Darío. **Open** 10.30am-2.30pm, 5-8.30pm Mon-Sat (shops may vary). **Map** p311 I2.

Another small shopping mall, dominated by shops selling upmarket designer fashion, party clothes and accessories, mainly for women.

Antiques

If you want antiques, head to the **Rastro** (see p181). On the main drag, C/Ribera de Curtidores, are several arcades where you'll find everything from old junk to authentic antiques. The adjoining streets, such as C/Mira el Río Alta and C/Carnero, are more downmarket and can yield real bargains. Elsewhere, there are a handful of antique shops in the C/Prado area, over in Salamanca, on and around C/Claudio Coello, are lots of upmarket, specialist dealers.

El Apartamento

C/Ruiz 11, Malasaña (91 445 77 68/www.elapartamento.biz). Metro Bilbao. **Open** 11am-2pm, 5-8.30pm Tue-Sat. **Credit** MC, V. **Map** p309 E3.

Named after the Billy Wilder movie, this shop specialises in furniture and household items from the '50s, '60s and '70s. Expect lovely tumblers, Formica coffee tables, rolls of wallpaper and plenty more.

Fábrica de Trallas

C/Carnero 21, La Latina (no phone). Metro La Latina. **Open** 10am-2pm, 5-8pm Mon-Fri; 10am-2pm Sat. Closed last 2wks Aug. **No credit cards**. **Map** p313 D10.

Old radios, gramophones and phones, many in Bakelite, are sold at this shop, where serious collectors may find that long sought-after piece.

Galerías Piquer

C/Ribera de Curtidores 29, Rastro (no phone/www.dai.es/piquer). Metro Puerta de Toledo. **Open** 10.30am-2pm, 5-8pm Mon-Fri; 10.30am-2pm Sat, Sun. **Credit** varies. **Map** p313 D9.

The antique shops in this Rastro arcade stock pieces for punters who don't want to have to brush the dust off their purchases. Opening times may vary.

Tiempos Modernos

C/Arrieta 17, Los Austrias & La Latina (91 542 85 94). Metro Ópera. **Open** 11am-2pm, 5-8.30pm Mon-Fri; 11am-2pm Sat. Closed mid Aug. **Credit** AmEx, DC, MC, V. **Map** p313 D7.

This place deals in modern Spanish painting and hosts temporary shows of exhibitions of photography and artwork. The main line of business, though, is the great range of '40s, '50s and '60s furniture.

Petra's international Bookshop.
See p170.

El Transformista

*C/Mirá el Río Baja 18, Rastro & Lavapiés (91 539
88 33). Metro Puerta de Toledo.* **Open** 11am-2pm
Tue-Sun. **No credit cards. Map** p313 D10.
Original '50s and '60s furniture and collectibles are
up for grabs at this shop. Almodóvar is rumoured
to source items for his movies here.

Books

Fnac (*see p167*) has an excellent general
selection. A traditional centre of the book trade
is **Calle de los Libreros** ('Booksellers' Street')
off Gran Vía, with many specialist bookshops.

La Casa del Libro

*Gran Vía 29 (91 521 21 13/www.casadellibro.com).
Metro Gran Vía.* **Open** 9.30am-9.30pm Mon-Sat;
11am-9pm Sun. **Credit** AmEx, DC, MC, V. **Map**
p313 E6.
Madrid's most comprehensive bookshop by far, La
Casa del Libro covers just about every subject imaginable in Spanish, but also has good sections of literature, reference and teaching material in English
and other languages.

Librería de Mujeres

*C/San Cristóbal 17, Los Austrias (91 521 70 43).
Metro Sol.* **Open** *Oct-June* 10am-2pm, 5-8pm Mon-
Fri; 10am-2pm Sat. *July-Sept* 10am-2pm, 5-8pm
Mon-Fri. **Credit** MC, V. **Map** p313 D7.
Madrid's best women's bookshop goes by the motto
'*Los libros no muerden, tampoco el feminismo*' –
'Books don't bite, neither does feminism'.

La Tienda de Madrid

*Mercado Puerta de Toledo, 5th floor, Ronda de
Toledo 1, Lavapiés (91 364 16 82). Metro Puerta de
Toledo.* **Open** 10.30am-9pm Tue-Sat; 10.30am-
2.30pm Sun. **No credit cards. Map** p313 D10.

Temporarily rehoused in the Mercado de Toledo
market, the Museo Municipal's bookshop offers a
wealth of written materials, mainly in Spanish, covering all aspects of the city's history and culture,
some of them beautiful coffee-table editions.

Children

Mar de Letras

*C/Santiago 18, Los Austrias (91 541 71 09). Metro
Ópera.* **Open** 10.30am-2pm, 5-8.30pm Mon-Fri;
10.30am-2.30pm Sat. Closed 1wk Aug. **Credit** DC,
MC, V. **Map** p313 D7.
A well-stocked bookshop specialising in kids' edi-
tions. Look out too for the English titles, regular
English storytelling evenings and educational toys.

English-language books

Booksellers

*C/José Abascal 48, Chamberí (91 442 79 59).
Metro Gregorio Marañón.* **Open** 9.30am-2pm, 5-8pm
Mon-Fri; 10am-2pm Sat. **Credit** AmEx, DC, MC, V.
Madrid's best English-language bookshop sells a
wide selection of literature, children's books, videos
and DVDs, as well as materials for TEFLers.
Other locations: C/Fernández de la Hoz 40,
Chamberí (91 702 79 44).

J&J Books & Coffee

*C/Espíritu Santo 47, Malasaña (91 521 85
76/www.jandjbooksandcoffee.net). Metro Noviciado.*
Open 10am-10pm Mon-Thur; 10am-midnight Fri,
Sat; 2-8pm Sun. **No credit cards. Map** p309 E4.
Spread over two floors, J&J is at once a relaxing little
café (at ground-floor level) and a well-stocked second-
hand bookshop (in the large basement). Activities
held here include open-mic sessions, quizzes and so
on, and staff can source books that aren't in stock.

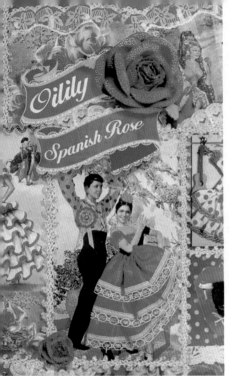

Pasajes

C/Génova 3, Chueca (91 310 12 45). Metro Alonso Martínez. **Open** 10am-2pm, 5-8pm Mon-Fri; 10am-2pm Sat. **Credit** MC, V. **Map** p310 H4.

This linguists' treasure trove sells a great range of fiction and non-fiction, language-learning materials, maps, audio books and videos. Most things are in English, French, German and Spanish.

Petra's International Bookshop

C/Campomanes 13, Sol & Gran Vía (91 541 72 91). Metro Ópera or Santo Domingo. **Open** *Sept-June* 11am-9pm Mon-Sat. *July, Aug* 11am-10pm Mon-Sat. **No credit cards**. **Map** p313 D7.

A great range of second-hand books in English and other languages is on offer in this laid-back little shop. Here you can offload excess books or trade them for others. Sadly, Petra the cat, who gave the shop its name, has now passed on.

Second-hand & rare

Most bookshops dealing in rare and antique books are around the **C/Huertas** area. A great place for cheap second-hand books is the **Cuesta de Moyano**, on C/Claudio Moyano, by the Jardín Botánico (Map p314 H9). It has a line of kiosks selling second-hand books, from rare editions to remainders. Some are open all week, but Sunday mornings are busiest.

Librería San Ginés

Pasadizo de San Ginés, Sol (91 366 46 86). Metro Sol. **Open** 11am-8pm Mon-Fri; 11am-2.30pm Sat. **No credit cards**. **Map** p313 D7.

This Old Curiosity Shop-type place, in an atmospheric passageway, sells everything from scruffy English paperbacks to antique editions.

Travel & maps

Desnivel

Plaza Matute 6, Huertas & Santa Ana (91 429 97 40/www.libreriadesnivel.com). Metro Antón Martín. **Open** *Sept-July* 10am-2pm, 4.30-8pm Mon-Fri; 10am-2pm Sat. *Aug* 10am-2pm, 4.30-8pm Mon-Fri. **Credit** MC, V. **Map** p313 F8.

This excellent travel and adventure bookshop sells a wide range of maps and books covering Spain and other countries. Desnivel's own publications include walking and climbing guides, and the shop also has information on organised walks, hikes and so on.

La Tienda Verde

C/Maudes 23 & 38, Chamberí (91 534 32 57/ www.tiendaverde.org). Metro Cuatro Caminos. **Open** 9.30am-2pm, 5-8.30pm Mon-Sat. **Credit** AmEx, DC, MC, V.

Madrid's original and best shop for travel books and maps, the 'Green Shop' now occupies two premises on the same street. At No.23 you will find tourist and nature guides, while No.38 sells maps and specialised mountaineering books.

Togs for sprogs at **Oilily**. *See p171*.

Children

Clothes

As well as smaller boutiques, larger chains also do affordable, cool clothes for kids, among them **Zara** (*see p175*) and **H&M** (*see p175*).

Max Kinder

C/Carretas 19, Los Austrias (91 522 80 50). Metro Sol. **Open** 10am-8.30pm Mon-Sat. **Credit** MC, V. **Map** p313 E8.
This shop is the junior version of Max Moda, across the street, and does a reasonable range of basic clothes for children from three months to 16 years.

Oilily

C/Hermosilla 16, Salamanca (91 577 56 39/ www.oilily-world.com). Metro Serrano. **Open** *Sept-mid July* 10am-8pm Mon-Sat. *Mid July, Aug* 10am-2pm, 5-8.30pm Mon-Fri; 10am-2pm Sat. **Credit** AmEx, DC, MC, V. **Map** p311 I4.
The to-die-for togs from this French firm will guarantee that your offspring stand out from the crowd. It's just a shame it's only for the little people. About as far from traditional Spanish childrenswear as it's possible to imagine.

Step

C/Almirante 28, Chueca (91 522 69 21). Metro Chueca. **Open** 11am-8.30pm Mon-Sat. **Credit** AmEx, DC, MC, V. **Map** p310 H5.
Drop-dead designer shoes by names like Moschino and Kenzo for mini fashpack members.

Toys

Bazar Mila

Gran Vía 33 (91 531 87 28). Metro Callao. **Open** 9.30am-8.30pm Mon-Sat. **Credit** AmEx, DC, MC, V. **Map** p313 E6.
Large and conveniently located, this shop stocks a decent range of toys, including Barbies, Action Man and Scalextric, plus some collectable toy cars.

Don Juego

C/Alcalá 113, Salamanca (91 435 37 24). Metro Príncipe de Vergara. **Open** *Sept-July* 10am-2pm, 5-8.30pm Mon-Sat. *1st 2wks Aug* 10am-2pm Mon-Sat. Closed last 2wks Aug. **Credit** MC, V. **Map** p311 K5.
This shop specialises in board games, for both kids and adults – as well as mah-jong, solitaire, Chinese chequers and chess, it specialises in Go.

Imaginarium

C/Núñez de Balboa 52, Salamanca (91 577 33 55). Metro Núñez de Balboa or Velázquez. **Open** 10am-9pm Mon-Sat. **Credit** AmEx, DC, MC, V. **Map** p311 J3.
Imaginarium is a standard solution when looking for challenging toys with imagination. Expect to find puppet theatres, modelling materials and shape-recognition, number and alphabet-learning games. **Other locations**: throughout the city.

Sanatorio de Muñecos

C/Preciados 21, Sol (91 521 04 47). Metro Sol. **Open** 10am-8pm Mon-Sat. **Credit** AmEx, DC, MC, V. **Map** p313 E7.
The 'dolls' hospital' does indeed mend dolls, but also functions as the oldest toy shop in Madrid, full of parents gazing nostalgically at the old-school model cars, teddy bears and so on.

Cleaning & laundry

Self-service *lavanderías* (launderettes) are thin on the ground in Madrid: in most there will be an attendant.

Lavandería Automática

C/Don Felipe 4, Malasaña (91 523 32 45). Metro Tribunal. **Open** 10am-9pm daily. **No credit cards.** **Map** p309 F4.

Lavandería Donoso Cortés

C/Donoso Cortés 17, Chamberí (91 446 9690). Metro Quevedo or Canal. **Open** *Sept-July* 9am-2pm, 3.30-8pm Mon-Sat. *Aug* 9am-2.30pm Mon-Sat. **No credit cards.** **Map** p305 E1.

OndaBlu

C/León 3, Huertas (91 369 50 71). Metro Antón Martín. **Open** 9am-10.30pm daily. **No credit cards.** **Map** p313 F8.
Also has internet connection.

Crafts & gifts

Antigua Casa Talavera

C/Isabel la Católica 2, Sol & Gran Vía (91 547 34 17). Metro Santo Domingo. **Open** 10am-1.30pm, 5-8pm Mon-Fri; 10am-1.30pm Sat. **Credit** AmEx, MC, V. **Map** p313 D6.
This long-standing family business specialises in traditional blue and white Spanish ceramics. Every available space is crammed with hand-painted designs all sourced from small Spanish producers. The charming owner speaks good English.

Piedra de Luna

Plaza General Vara del Rey 11, La Latina (91 365 01 34). Metro La Latina. **Open** *Sept-June* 10.30am-2pm, 5-8.30pm Mon-Fri; 10.30am-2pm Sat; 10am-3pm Sun. *July, Aug* 5.30-9pm Mon-Fri; 10am-3pm Sun. **Credit** AmEx, DC, MC, V. **Map** p313 D9.
If you dig the hippy look, don't miss this treasure trove of craftwork from around the world. Tuareg kilims, Moroccan ceramics and Indian silver jewellery and textiles all feature.

Popland

C/Manuela Malasaña 7, Malasaña (91 446 38 95/ www.popland.es). Metro Bilbao. **Open** 11am-9pm Mon-Sat. **Credit** DC, MC, V. **Map** p309 F3.
For times when only a Jesus action figure will do, Popland saves the day. The shop is packed with all things pop-culture and plastic, but also film posters, shower curtains and T-shirts. There's also a good range of greetings cards – quite a rarity in Madrid.

Eat, Drink, Shop

Design & household

BD Madrid

C/Villanueva 5, Salamanca (91 435 06 27). Metro Serrano. **Open** 9.30am-1.30pm, 4.30-8pm Mon-Fri; 10am-1.30pm Sat. Closed Aug. **Credit** AmEx, DC, MC, V. **Map** p311 J5.

BD carries a stunning selection of contemporary furniture designs from Spanish and international names, many with a retro feel. The company is now producing its own pieces, including a kitchen range. Hefty price tags, but worth a visit if only to peruse.

Expresión Negra

C/Piamonte 15, Chueca (91 319 95 27). Metro Chueca. **Open** 11am-2.30pm, 5-8.30pm Mon-Sat. **Credit** AmEx, DC, MC, V. **Map** p310 H5.

Expresión Negra is a great place to indulge in a spot of retail therapy and help the environment at the same time. As well as breathing new life into

Fashion tribes

Heavies

Pronounced with a guttural, Scottish 'ch' at the beginning, these are the rockers that time forgot. Look for leather and studs, heavy metal T-shirts, big boots and long jackets.
Where to find them: In your nearest park engaging in a botellón (see p225), and in the suburbs.
Essential accessories: Bottle of Mahou beer, plenty of cigarettes and unruly facial hair.
Seen at: the **Rastro** (see p181) for Metallica T-shirts, **Sprint** (see p168) for beer and baccy and **Up Beat** (see p185) for Dr Marten's.

Muscu-locos

The Muscle-Boys. A play on words meaning a mix of 'muscular' and 'crazy about muscles'. Tight tops and vests for this lot, and not just in the summer – biceps as big as your head warrant showing off. These boys are mad about their image and cultivate it in the gym and in the high-fashion boutiques.
Where to find them: The gay quarter of Chueca is the place to marvel at their chiselled features and sculpted torsos. Here they shop, bar-hop and admire each other from afar... and sometimes not so afar.
Essential accessories: Very short shorts, Speedos for the pool, and a roving eye.
Seen at: **Amantis** (see p211) for toys, **Berkana** (see p211) for books and **SR** (see p213) for leather goods.

Fiesteros

The party people. Pierced and tattooed to the hilt, this polysexual crew are the hippest of the hip kids. The requisite uniform is a mixture of purpose-made and improvised clubwear that flaunts the midriffs of the girls and the biceps of the boys. This tribe lives to party and to be gorgeous.
Where to find them: Their natural habitat is Malasaña and the Mercado Fuencarral where they shop, chat and get even more piercings.

Essential accessories: VIP passes for the next big party, fashionable mullet haircuts from Juan, ¡por Diós! and big Dior sunglasses.
Seen at: **Miss Sixty** (see p176) for clubwear, **Lanikoi** (see p176) for skatewear and **Desigual** (see p175) for... well, more clubwear.

Pijos & pijas

The posh kids. Big, floppy '80s-style haircuts – and that's just the boys. Lacoste polo shirts, a jumper tied around the shoulders and white jeans top off the look. For the girls it's canvas shoes, pink and white striped rugby shirts and immaculately styled barnets.
Where to find them: Branches of El Corte Inglés in the designer sections, Calle Serrano and any bar or club that was cool with the fiesteros two months previously.
Essential accessories: Daddy's credit card, a Smart car and a comb to keep that floppy hair in check.
Seen at: **ABC Serrano** (see p168) shopping centre to hang with the in crowd, **Adolfo Domínguez** (see p173) for sporty sweaters and **Sana Sana** (see p183) for a massage when all that shopping gets too much.

Señores y señoras

The mature couple. For él the distinguished grey hair will be slicked back and the obligatory moustache neatly trimmed. For ella an immaculately coiffed 'do is a must, with the make up erring on the heavy side. A camel hair jacket for him, a fur coat for the lady. Cigars and cigarettes respectively.
Where to find them: Salamanca, where they'll double park for an hour while la señora gets a new bag.
Essential accessories: A small yappy dog, a Mercedes and plenty of bling.
Seen at: **Purificación García** (see p175) for something smart, **Mantequerías Bravo** (see p181) for some posh nosh and **Loewe** (see p177) for indulgent leather accessories.

recycled objects – briefcases, lamps and other objects made out of used Coke cans, sardine tins and so on – the shop also puts a different spin on African handicrafts, with brightly coloured throws, textiles and some unusual metalwork.

Mamblona
C/Regueros 2, Chueca (91 310 41 95). Metro Chueca. **Open** 11am-2pm, 5-8.30pm Tue-Sat. Closed Aug. **Credit** AmEx, MC, V. **Map** p310 G4.
A charming shop that carries a range of mostly hand-made textiles – cushions, homeware and fashion accessories. Products are sourced from India, the UK and Finland; a few are Spanish-made.

PlazAarte
Costanilla de los Capuchinos 5, Chueca (91 522 85 93). Metro Chueca. **Open** Sept-June 11.30am-3pm, 5.30-9pm Mon-Sat. *July* 6-9.30pm Mon-Fri; 11.30am-2.30pm, 6-9.30pm Sat. *Aug* 6-9.30pm Mon-Sat. **Credit** AmEx, DC, MC, V. **Map** p313 F6.
A trendy, Swedish-owned shop/gallery specialising in contemporary items for the home by up-and-coming national and international designers.

Víctimas de Celuloide
C/Santiago 4, Los Austrias (91 547 61 35/ www.victimasdeceluloide.com). Metro Ópera. **Open** 10.30am-2pm, 5.30pm-9.30pm Mon-Sat. **Credit** AmEx, DC, MC, V. **Map** p313 D7.
'Because we are all victims of celluloid,' says the proprietor of this shop selling interior design pieces with a twist, mainly from Nordic suppliers. A pop art influence is noticeable in the selection.

Vinçon
C/Castelló 18, Salamanca (91 578 05 20/ www.vincon.com). Metro Velázquez. **Open** 10am-2pm, 5-8.30pm Mon-Fri; 10am-8.30pm Sat. **Credit** AmEx, MC, V. **Map** p311 K4.
The Madrid outpost of the classic Barcelona design store occupies a former 1920s silver factory. It has everything for the cred-seeking homeowner – furniture, home and garden accessories and attractive gift ideas, often at surprisingly low prices.

Fashion

Boutiques

The Deli Room
C/Santa Bárbara 4, Malasaña (91 521 19 83/ www.thedeliroom.com). Metro Tribunal or Gran Vía. **Open** 11am-2pm, 5-8.30pm Mon-Fri; 11am-2pm, 5-8.30pm Sat. **Credit** MC, V. **Map** p309 F4.
The Deli Room serves up choice cuts from Spanish designers, all presented in stainless-steel deli counters replete with weighing scales and supermarket lighting. It may sound weird but it works.

Exotic-Delitto e Castigo
C/Villanueva 20, Salamanca (91 431 89 33). Metro Retiro or Serrano. **Open** 11am-2.30pm, 5-9pm Mon-Sat. **Credit** AmEx, DC, MC, V. **Map** p311 I5.

Víctimas de Celuloide.

This chic establishment is one of the trendiest in Madrid, carrying smart-casual eveningwear from D&G, Lacroix, Gaultier and Valentino. The C/Villanueva branch holds more sporty/casual lines.

HAND
C/Hortaleza 26, Chueca (91 521 51 52). Metro Chueca. **Open** 11am-2pm, 5-9pm Mon-Sat. Closed 2wks Aug. **Credit** AmEx, DC, MC, V. **Map** p313 F6.
HAND stands for for Have a Nice Day, and is run by two discerning Frenchmen. An interesting boutique, it mixes French labels with bits and pieces brought back from their travels in India.

Lotta
C/Hernán Cortés 9, Chueca (91 523 25 05). Metro Chueca or Tribunal. **Open** June-Sept 11am-2pm, 5-9pm Mon-Sat. *Aug* 6-10pm Mon-Sat. **Map** p310 G5.
The Swedish proprietor of Lotta set up her first vintage clothing store in the Rastro in 1992. Now this shop carries vintage clothing from the '50s to the '80s and also stocks colourful dresses designed by the owner herself, using materials from Scandinavia.

Designers

For Spanish leather specialist **Loewe**, *see p177.*

Adolfo Domínguez
C/Ortega y Gasset 4, Salamanca (91 576 00 84/www.adolfodominguez.com). Metro Núñez de Balboa. **Open** 10.15am-2pm, 5-8.30pm Mon-Sat. **Credit** AmEx, DC, MC, V. **Map** p311 J3.
Simple, classical clothing from the well-known Galician designer. Suits are well cut and long-lasting, while accessories and shoes are also big draws.

TIMELESS FASHION JEWELR

CARRERA y CARRERA

MADRID 1885

Agatha Ruiz de la Prada
C/Marqués de Riscal 8, Chamberí (91 319 05 01/
www.agatharuizdelaprada.com). Metro Rubén Darío.
Open *Sept-June* 10am-2pm, 5-8pm Mon-Fri. *Aug*
10am-2pm, 5-8pm Mon-Sat. **Credit** AmEx, MC, V.
Map p310 I3.
Loud and colourful designs distinguish this designer's work, many emblazoned with her trademark hearts and flowers. The childrenswear range is hugely popular, as is the homeware.

Amaya Arzuaga
C/Lagasca 50, Salamanca (91 426 28
15/www.amayaarzuaga.com). Metro Serrano. **Open**
10.30am-9pm Mon-Sat. **Credit** AmEx, DC, MC, V.
Map p311 J4.
One of the few Spanish designers with an international presence. The designs are not for everyday wear, but there are some great outfits to be discovered, with a hard-edged punky look. The knitwear is also excellent.

Custo
C/Fuencarral 29, Chueca (91 360 46 36/www.custo-
barcelona.com). Metro Gran Vía or Chueca. **Open**
10am-9pm Mon-Sat. **Credit** AmEx, DC, MC, V.
Map p310 G5.
This Catalan designer is famous for his funky patterned T-shirts, but has expanded the range to include creative and flattering dresses, skirts and coats. Custo sells in boutiques around the world, but is also rapidly expanding its own network of shops, with another branch due to open on C/Mayor.

Purificación García
C/Serrano 28, Salamanca (91 435 80 13/
www.purificaciongarcia.es). Metro Serrano. **Open**
10am-8.30pm Mon-Sat. **Credit** AmEx, DC, MC, V.
Map p311 J4.
This is where Madrid's older but elegant woman heads when she wants something smart for the office. Well cut and using natural materials, the clothes are very well priced for the quality.

Sybilla
Callejón de Jorge Juan 14, Salamanca (91 578 13
22). Metro Retiro or Serrano. **Open** 10.30am-8.30pm
Mon-Sat. Closed 2wks Aug. **Credit** AmEx, DC, MC,
V. **Map** p311 J5.
As well as her usual eye-catching outfits for actresses attending the Goyas (the Spanish equivalent of the Oscars), Sybilla now stocks a new range, Jocomomola, aimed at the younger crowd.

High-street fashion

H&M
C/Gran Vía 32 (901 120 084/www.hm.com). Metro
Gran Vía. **Open** 10am-9pm Mon-Sat. **Credit** AmEx,
DC, MC, V. **Map** p313 E6.
The flagship Madrid branch of the Swedish chain. While the clothes may lack quality, the rock-bottom prices compensate. Don't miss the massive underwear floor and bargain beauty and hair accessories.

Mango
C/Fuencarral 70, Chueca (91 523 04
12/www.mango.es). Metro Bilbao. **Open** 10am-9pm
Mon-Sat. **Credit** AmEx, MC, V. **Map** p308 C2.
This Barcelona-based chain can claim responsibility for dressing the majority of young women in Spain. Like Zara, Mango focuses on fresh designs aimed squarely at fashion-conscious teens and working women. This branch has an outlet on the second floor with last season's collection at bargain prices.
Other locations: throughout the city.

Top Shop
Puerta del Sol 6, Sol (91 532 12 26/
www.topshop.co.uk). Metro Sol. **Open** 10am-9pm
Mon-Sat. **Credit** AmEx, DC, MC, V. **Map** p313 E7.
A three-floor store of the British chain slap-bang in the middle of Sol, plying its trademark mix of high fashion and good-value basics. Beware, though, the stock is a lot more limited than in the UK.

Zara
C/Princesa 45, Malasaña & Conde Duque (91 541
09 02/www.zara.es). Metro Argüelles. **Open** 10am-
8.30pm Mon-Sat. **Credit** AmEx, DC, MC, V. **Map**
p308 C3.
The Galician giant of the fashion continues to dominate both the domestic and international markets. The key to its popularity lies in its ability (and speed) in taking the latest catwalk looks from the major designers and churning out reasonable quality near-replicas at popular prices.
Other locations: throughout the city.

Street & clubwear

Desigual
C/Fuencarral 36, Chueca (91 360 45 24/
www.desigual.com). Metro Tribunal or Gran Vía.
Open *Sept-June* 10.30am-9.30pm Mon-Sat; 12.30-
8.30pm Sun. *Aug* 10.30am-2.30pm, 5.30-9.30pm Mon-
Sat. **Credit** AmEx, MC, V. **Map** p310 G5.
Desigual has become a real hit with the club-kids , and it's easy to see why: gorgeous shop assistants, pumping house music and affordable, quality club and streetwear for men and women.

Flip
C/Mayor 19, Los Austrias (91 366 44 72). Metro
Sol. **Open** 10.30am-9pm Mon-Sat. **Credit** AmEx,
MC, V. **Map** p313 D7.
Well-chosen stock from the likes of g-sus, Miss Sixty, Kangol and Black Flys, all presided over by über-hip and highly pierced, highly tattooed staff.

Gas
C/Fuencarral 16, Malasaña (91 701 05 01/
www.gasjeans.com). Metro Gran Vía. **Open**
10am-9pm Mon-Fri; 10am-10pm Sat. **Credit** MC, V.
Map p310 G5.
'Keep it simple' is the Gas motto and it certainly does, with collections of crisp cotton and linen separates, but mainly denim.

Eat, Drink, Shop

Grand designs at **Sybilla**. See p175.

Lanikoi

C/Alberto Aguilera 1, Malasaña (91 591 34 13).
Metro San Bernardo. **Open** *Sept-July* 10.30am-9pm
Mon-Sat. *Aug* 10.30am-2.30pm. **Credit** AmEx, MC,
V. **Map** p309 E3.
This three-storey emporium has all the essentials for
the keen snowboarder, surfer and skateboarder, or
anyone looking for streetwear by the likes of Etnies,
Carhartt, Diesel and Stylelab.

Miss Sixty

C/Mesonero Romanos 2, Sol (91 531 89 73). Metro
Callao. **Open** 10am-8pm Mon-Sat. **Credit** AmEx,
DC, MC, V. **Map** p313 E6.
An oasis of cool in Madrid's most crowded shopping
area, the French denim designer's sleek three-storey
outlet furnishes its clientele with everything a (skin-
ny) girl could want.

Pepita is Dead

C/Doctor Fourquet 10, Lavapiés (91 528 87 88/
www.pepitasdead.com). Metro Atocha. **Open** 11am-
2pm, 5-8.30pm Mon-Sat. Closed 3wks Aug. **Credit**
AmEx, DC, MC, V. **Map** p310 G9.
Along with Lotta, Pepita is Dead is the only shop in
Madrid to specialise in vintage clothing. These items
– mens-, womens- and childrenswear, plus accessories – are all unworn originals, carefully chosen
from the '60s to the '80s.

San Francisco Skate Farm

C/Argensola 3, Chueca (91 308 69 75). Metro
Alonso Martínez. **Open** 10.30am-2pm, 5-8.30pm
Mon-Fri; 10.30am-2pm, 5-8pm Sat. **Credit** MC, V.
Map p310 H4.
For the discerning boarder, the San Francisco Skate
Farm can kit you out with trucks, decks, tools, volu-
minous combat trousers, trainers and hoodies – plus
DVDs and videos of the pros in action.

Snapo

C/Espíritu Santo 5, Malasaña (91 532 12 23) Metro
Noviciado or Tribunal. **Open** 11am-2.30pm, 5-8.30pm
Mon-Sat. **Credit** AmEx, DC, MC, V. **Map** p309 E4.

Snapo stocks streetwear with attitude, most of it
from its own label, Fucking Bastardz Inc. Designs
are funny and cheeky, with mainly T-shirts, plus
bags, caps and a limited range of womenswear.

Sportivo

C/Conde Duque 20, Malasaña (91 542 56 61). Metro
San Bernardo. **Open** 10am-9pm Mon-Sat. **Credit**
AmEx, MC, V. **Map** p309 D4.
With a great range of menswear labels, including
Cantskate, Burro, Levi's Red and Vintage, New York
Industries, YMC, and Duffer of St George, Sportivo
is an unmissable stop. Staff are extremely helpful.

Fashion accessories

Lingerie & underwear

¡Oh, qué luna!

C/Ayala 32, Salamanca (91 431 37 25). Metro
Serrano. **Open** 10am-2pm, 5-8.30pm Mon-Fri; 11am-
2pm, 5-8.30pm Sat. **Credit** AmEx, DC, MC, V.
Map p311 J4.
Glam, sexy lingerie, negligées and dressing gowns.
It also does a line in bedlinen and swimwear.

Oysho

C/Fuencarral 124, Chamberí (91 448 83 55). Metro
Bilbao. **Open** 10am-8.30pm, Mon-Sat. **Credit** AmEx,
DC, MC, V. **Map** p309 F3.
Part of the retail group that also includes Zara, Pull
& Bear and Often, Oysho specialises in sexy but
inexpensive underwear designs for younger women.
Other locations: Madrid 2-La Vaguada, C/Monforte
de Lemos 39 (91 730 04 41).

Women's Secret

C/Velázquez 48, Salamanca (91 578 14 53). Metro
Velázquez. **Open** *Sept-June* 10am-8.30pm Mon-Sat.
July, Aug 10am-2pm, 5-8.30pm Mon-Sat. **Credit**
AmEx, DC, MC, V. **Map** p311 J4.
Quality underwear at very competitive prices, plus
swimwear and skincare products.

Jewellery & accessories

Concha García
C/Goya 38, Salamanca (91 435 49 36). Metro Goya.
Open 10.30am-8.30pm Mon-Fri; 10.30am-2pm, 5-8pm
Sat. **Credit** AmEx, DC, MC, V. **Map** p311 K4.
Concha García's two shops-cum-galleries are impor-
tant showcases for contemporary and ethnic jew-
ellery design, both national and international.

Joaquín Berao
*C/Claudio Coello 35, Salamanca & Retiro (91 577
28 28). Metro Serrano.* **Open** *Sept-July* 10am-2pm,
5-8.30pm Mon-Sat. *Aug* 10am-2pm Mon-Sat. **Credit**
AmEx, DC, MC, V
Chunky, twisted and contorted, but also fluidly elegant, Joaquín Berao's solid silver bracelets, neck-
laces, earrings and chokers are increasingly the
choice of those in the know.

Piamonte
*C/Piamonte 16, Chueca (91 522 45 80). Metro
Chueca.* **Open** 10.30am-8.30pm Mon-Sat. **Credit**
AmEx, DC, MC, V. **Map** p310 H5.
Highly desirable bags in all shapes, sizes and fab-
rics, from denim to super-soft leather.
Other locations: C/Lagasca 28, Salamanca (91 575
55 20); C/Marqués de Monasterio 5, Chueca (91 308
40 62); C/Villanueva 16, Salamanca (91 435 37 47).

Scooter
*Callejón de Jorge Juan 12, Salamanca (91 576 47
49). Metro Serrano.* **Open** 10.30am-8.30pm Mon-Fri;
10.30am-2.30pm, 5-8.30pm Sat. **Credit** DC, MC, V.
Map p311 J5.
Accessories are the focus of this French store, with
funky, chunky jewellery, Anya Hindmarch bags
and gorgeous flip flops by Dorotea. The clothes –
a mix of funky and ethnic – are worth a look too.

Shoes & leather

Spain is a major producer of footwear, with
the Valencia and Alicante areas dominated by
shoe factories. As a result, Madrid is a haven
for the confirmed shoe addict. The street to
head for is Augusto Figueroa, in the heart of
Chueca. Here you'll find a street packed with
factory *'muestrarios'* (selling samples) such as
Vime or Caligae.

Antigua Casa Crespo
*C/Divino Pastor 29, Malasaña & Conde Duque
(91 521 56 54). Metro Bilbao.* **Open** 10am-1.30pm,
4.30-8pm Mon-Fri; 10am-1.30pm Sat. Closed late Aug.
No credit cards. **Map** p309 E3.
This perfectly preserved old-fashioned store is dedicated to espadrilles of all sizes and colours.

Camper
*C/Serrano 24, Salamanca (91 578 25 60/
www.camper.com). Metro Serrano.* **Open**
9.30am-8.30pm Mon-Sat. **Credit** AmEx, DC,
MC, V. **Map** p311 I5.

Branches of the Mallorcan family firm continue to
spring up all over the city. At this one, two large
plinths display the entire men's and women's collection – brightly coloured, fun shoes and sandals.
Other locations: throughout the city.

Excrupulus Net
*C/Almirante 7, Chueca (91 521 72 44). Metro
Chueca.* **Open** *Sept-May* 11am-2pm, 5-8.30pm. *June-
Aug* 11am-2pm, 5.30-8.30pm. **Credit** AmEx, DC, MC,
V. **Map** p310 H5.
A trio of women are behind this shoe shop, which
brings together unique designs from Catalan and
Mallorcan shoe designers, including Muxart.

Farrutx
*C/Serrano 7, Salamanca (91 577 09 24/www.
farrutx.com). Metro Serrano.* **Open** *Sept-June*
10am-2pm, 5-8.30pm Mon-Sat. *July, Aug* 10am-2pm,
5.30-8.30pm Mon-Sat. **Credit** AmEx, DC, MC, V.
Map p311 I5.
Innovative and elegant leather designs from this popular Mallorcan company, with bags and shoes too.
Other locations: throughout the city.

Loewe
*C/Serrano 26 & 34, Salamanca (91 577 60 56/
www.loewe.es). Metro Serrano.* **Open** 9.30am-8.30pm
Mon-Sat. **Credit** AmEx, DC, MC, V. **Map** p311 I4.
The world-famous, elite Spanish leather goods com-
pany, selling bags, shoes, cases and a small range
of clothes. Prices are very high.
Other locations: throughout the city.

Nuevos Guerrilleros
Puerta del Sol 5, Sol (91 521 27 08). Metro Sol.
Open 10.30am-8.30pm Mon-Sat. **Credit** AmEx, MC,
V. **Map** p313 E7.
A bargain-basement store with a giant stock of
cheap and cheerful men's and women's shoes, with
occasionally wacky designs.

The ubiquitous **Zara**.
See p175.

Repairers

All markets and most streets have a shoe repairer – look out for *rápido* or *reparación de calzados* signs.

Costura

C/Príncipe 22, Santa Ana (91 524 88 24). Metro Antón Martín. **Open** 10am-1.30pm, 4.30-8pm Mon-Fri; 10am-1.30pm Sat. Closed Aug. **Credit** V. **Map** p313 F8.

This small shop sells party dresses but also has an excellent repair service for any type of clothing.

Florists

Anthurium

C/Pelayo 19, Chueca (91 522 69 29/www.anthur flor.com). Metro Chueca. **Open** 10am-2pm, 5-9pm Mon-Fri; 10.30am-2pm Sat. **No credit cards.** **Map** p310 G5.

The owners of this trendy florist's will put together an arresting arrangement with a little notice.

Martín Floristas

C/Huertas 2, Huertas (91 429 13 32). Metro Antón Martín. **Open** 10am-2pm, 5-8pm Mon-Fri; 10am-2pm Sat. **Credit** AmEx, DC, MC, V. **Map** p313 E8.

This family-run business has been going for over a century, selling a full range of cut flowers (including pretty arrangements) as well as potted plants.

Food & drink

Chocolates, cakes & sweets

Antigua Pastelería del Pozo

C/Pozo 8, Santa Ana (91 522 38 94). Metro Sol. **Open** 9.30am-2pm, 5-8pm Tue-Sat; 9am-2pm Sun, public hols. Closed last 2wks July, Aug, 1st wk Sept. **No credit cards.** **Map** 309 E7.

With the same decor and counter as when it opened in 1830, this lovely old *pastelería* is a true period piece, with cakes that live up to its design.

Convento de las Carboneras

Plaza Conde de Miranda 3, Los Austrias (91 548 37 01). Metro Sol. **Open** 9.30am-1pm, 6-8pm Mon-Sat. **No credit cards.** **Map** p313 D8.

The Carboneras nuns make a selection of speciality cakes and biscuits including *mantecados, yemas* and almond biscuits. As this is a closed convent you buy them through a grille.

La Duquesita

C/Fernando VI 2, Chueca (91 308 02 31). Metro Alonso Martínez. **Open** 9.30am-2.30pm, 5-9pm Tue-Sat; 9.30am-3pm, 5-9pm Sun. Closed Aug. **Credit** MC, V. **Map** p310 H4.

This traditional *pastelería*, dating from 1914, has featured in lots of period-piece movies. Gorgeous chocolates and cakes are up for grabs, along with *turrón* in the run-up to Christmas.

La Mallorquina

Puerta del Sol 8, Sol & Gran Vía (91 521 12 01). Metro Sol. **Open** 9am-9.15pm daily. Closed mid July, Aug. **No credit cards.** **Map** p313 E7.

Always bustling with people, La Mallorquina occupies a prime location right on the Puerta del Sol. Downstairs, the pastry shop sells great cakes and savouries, all baked on the premises. The upstairs café has a pre-war feel and a team of old-school waiters in attendance.

El Riojano

C/Mayor 10, Los Austrias (91 366 44 82). Metro Sol. **Open** Sept-June 9am-2pm, 5-9pm daily. July, Aug 10am-2pm, 5-9pm Mon-Fri; 10am-2.30pm, 5.30-8.30pm Sat. **Credit** MC, V. **Map** p313 D7.

El Riojano has been in business since 1885, selling irresistible cakes, pastries, meringues and seasonal goodies. All are made in the traditional way, with meringues a particular speciality. Enjoy one with a coffee in the café out back.

Delicacies

Magerit, stand No.20/21 in La Cebada market (*see p181*), is an excellent place to buy cheese. For olives of all varieties, **F Illanas**, stalls 33-44, in the Mercado de Chamberí, C/Alonso Cano 10 (91 446 95 89), is a good bet. Several branches of **El Corte Inglés** (*see p167*), and most **OpenCor** outlets (*see p168*) have luxury food sections called El Club del Gourmet.

La Boulette

Stands 63-68, Mercado de La Paz, C/Ayala 28, Salamanca (91 431 77 25). Metro Serrano. **Open** 9am-2.30pm, 5.30-8pm Mon-Fri; 9am-2.30pm Sat. **Credit** MC, V. **Map** p311 J4.

Probably the largest selection of cheeses in Madrid and possibly the country. Over 400 varieties of both Spanish and imported cheeses are on sale. The charcuterie section has a similarly impressive range.

González

C/León 12, Huertas & Santa Ana (91 429 56 18). Metro Antón Martín. **Open** 10.30am-3pm, 7pm-midnight Tue-Sat. **Credit** AmEx, DC, MC, V. **Map** p313 F8.

Once a local grocer's, González is now a smart deli with a fine range of cheeses, charcuterie, preserves, fruit and nuts, olive oils and more besides. The back room is now a pleasant, well-stocked wine bar.

Hespen & Suárez Mercado Contemporáneo

C/Barceló 15, Chueca (91 445 39 03/www.hespeny suarez.com). Metro Alonso Martínez or Tribunal. **Open** Sept-July 8.30am-10pm Mon-Fri; 10am-10pm Sat, Sun. Aug 8.30am-10pm Mon-Fri; 10am-10pm Sat, 10am-5pm Sun. **Credit** AmEx, MC, V. **Map** p310 G4.

This smart deli offers flavours from around the world in the form of raw ingredients and dried goods, plus prepared dishes to take away.

Trading places

Up until Madrid's promotion to capital status in 1561, and the construction of the Plaza Mayor, guilds of tradespeople and artisans had tended to cluster together in certain streets or quarters. A brief glance at a map of the higgledy-piggledy street layout in the environs of the Plaza Mayor shows this clearly: many streets are named after the guilds, *gremios*, that were concentrated in the immediate vicinity.

A little north of the Plaza Mayor, just across the Calle Mayor, is the Plaza de Herredores, 'Blacksmiths' Square', and running from there to Calle Arenal is the Calle de las Hileras, or 'Spinners' Street'. Parallel to this is Calle Bordadores, 'Embroiderers' Street', whose artisans presumably bought their supplies of *hilo*, thread, one street over. Also serving the textile trade were the *coloreros*, purveyors of dyes, who were established in the tiny street of the same name just a few yards away. To the west of Plaza Mayor is the Calle Sal, thus named because salt was sold from the royal deposits there. A few yards away is the minuscule Calle Botoneras, where buttons were sold, and close by is the Calle de los Esparteros, here mats were manufactured from esparto grass, still used nowadays to make espadrilles. To the south of the square is the Calle Latoneros, where the brassmongers traded. This street feeds into the Calle de los Cuchilleros, 'Knifemakers' Street', where Plaza Mayor butchers bought their cleavers. A little further south, what is nowadays the main drag of the Rastro, the Ribera de Curtidores, 'Tanners' Alley', was close to the city's slaughterhouse. The name 'Rastro' very possibly has its origin in the blood-stained trail, or *rastro*, left by the slaughtered animals.

As the centuries went by and Madrid expanded, these trades slowly disappeared or moved out and other commercial establishments sprang up. During the 19th and 20th centuries other shopping thoroughfares became associated with vendors of certain types of product, even

though the street names now had nothing to do with the wares on sale. Right up until the advent of the PC, if you wanted to buy a typewriter you headed for Calles Hortaleza and Hernán Cortés (a couple of shops selling Remington portables are still there). If you needed anything orthopaedic you went to the Calle Carretas, where there are still a couple of establishments selling these items. Books – both new and second-hand – you found in the Calle de los Libreros (*pictured*) and the Cuesta de Moyano, as you still do today. The Calles de la Paz and Postas have long had a tradition of shops dealing in religious artefacts and the Plaza de Pontejos still has several haberdashers and remnants shops.

More recently, specialised streets have started to deal in modern goods. Take a walk along the Calle Barquillo in Chueca, you will notice that an abundance of shops there sell hi-fi equipment, hence the nickname Calle del Sonido ('Sound Street'). From here runs the Calle Almirante, which since the '80s has been colonised by a number of designer fashion shops, earning it the moniker of 'Calle de la Moda', a title for which C/Claudio Coello in the Salamanca neighbourhood would now contend. More fashion, of the street- and clubwear variety, is concentrated along the C/Fuencarral, riding the Mercado de Fuencarral wave of the last few years. They may not be tinsmiths or button sellers any more, but many of Madrid's retailers still seem happier having their direct competitors just across the street.

Mantequerías Bravo

*C/Ayala 24, Salamanca (91 576 02 93). Metro
Serrano.* **Open** 9.30am-2.30pm, 5.30-8.30pm Mon-Fri;
9.30am-2.30pm Sat. Closed Aug. **Credit** AmEx, DC,
MC, V. **Map** p311 J4.
A marvellous selection of foodstuffs is on sale in this
shop, including meats and cheeses, wines and spirits and coffees and teas. Imports include English
mustard and cream crackers.
Other locations: Paseo General Martínez Campos
23, Chamberí (91 448 09 18).

La Moderna Apicultura

*C/Doctor Esquerdo 47, Salamanca (91 574 52 40).
Metro O'Donnell.* **Open** 9.30am-1.30pm, 4.30-8pm
Mon-Fri; 9.30am-1-30pm Sat. **No credit cards**.
Honey is the theme running through this shop, with
no less than 20 varieties, plus chocolate and jam.

Museo del Jamón

*Carrera de San Jerónimo 6, Huertas & Santa Ana
(91 521 03 46). Metro Sol.* **Open** 9am-midnight
daily. **Credit** MC, V. **Map** p313 E7.
Dotted around town, the various branches of the
'Ham Museum' are a sight to behold, with dozens of
hams dangling from the ceiling. Sample their wares
at the bar or in their restaurants.
Other locations: throughout the city.

Patrimonio Comunal Olivarero

*C/Mejía Lequerica 1, Chueca (91 308 05
05/www.pco.es). Metro Alonso Martínez.* **Open**
10am-2pm, 5-8pm Mon-Fri; 10am-2pm Sat. Closed
Aug. **Credit** MC, V. **Map** p310 G4.
Olive oil from every region of Spain that produces
the stuff is on sale here. Quantities go from two-litre
bottles to five-litre cans, and some make lovely gifts.

Health & herbs

NaturaSi

*C/Doctor Fleming 1, Chamartín (91 458 32 54/
www.naturasi.it). Metro Santiago Bernabéu.* **Open**
10am-8.30pm Mon-Sat. **Credit** AmEx, DC, MC, V.
This 'natural' supermarket sells a huge range of ecological and natural foodstuffs among them fresh
fruit and veg, cheese and herbal products.

Salud Madrid

*Paseo Santa María de la Cabeza 3, Atocha (91 527
89 29). Metro Atocha.* **Open** *Sept-June* 10am-8pm
Mon-Sat. *Aug* 10am-8pm Mon-Fri; 10am-2pm Sat.
No credit cards. **Map** p314 H10.
The huge selection of organic and macrobiotic products at this shop includes hard-to-find Japanese items
and pollen from the bees in the Sierra de Madrid.
Other locations: C/Ortega y Gasset 77, Salamanca
(91 309 53 90).

Markets

Madrid's markets are a noisy, colourful way to
get close to the locals – and stock up on cheap
food. They offer a vast range of fruit and veg,

meat, wet fish, cheese, charcuterie and offal.
Spaniards do queue (although it may not look
like it) – just ask each other *'¿Quién es el
último/la última?'* (Who's the last in the queue?)
before joining. All the following markets are
open from around 9am-2pm and 5-8pm (15 May-
15 Sept until 8.30pm) during the week, and 9am-
2pm on Saturdays.

Anton Martín

*C/Santa Isabel 5, Lavapiés (91 369 06 20). Metro
Antón Martín.* **Map** p313 F9.

La Cebada

*Plaza de la Cebada s/n, La Latina (91 365 91 76).
Metro La Latina.* **Map** p313 D9.

Chamartín

*C/Bolivia 9, Chamartín (91 459 49 48). Metro
Colombia.*
In an upmarket neighbourhood with many affluent
foreign residents, and produce to match.

Chamberí

*C/Alonso Cano, 10, Chamberí (no phone). Metro
Iglesia.* **Map** p310 G1.
Big, with lots of variety. The fruit and veg stalls in
the middle are among the best in town.

Maravillas

*C/Bravo Murillo 122, Tetuán (91 534 84 29).
Metro Alvarado.*
Madrid's biggest market, and the best for fish.

Los Mostenses

*Plaza de Los Mostenses, Malasaña (no phone).
Metro Plaza de España.* **Map** p309 D5.
A huge market with an international feel: Chinese
and Mexican products are much in evidence.

La Paz

*C/Ayala 28, Salamanca (91 435 07 43). Metro
Serrano.* **Map** p311 J4.
A very upmarket market, with a dazzling range of
quality products. It's worth a visit just for the
gourmet cheese stall La Boulette (*see also p178*).

El Rastro

*C/Ribera de Curtidores, between Plaza de Cascorro &
Ronda de Toledo (no phone). Metro La Latina.* **Open**
dawn-approx 2pm Sun. **Map** p313 D9-10.
The city's most famous market dates back nearly
five centuries. Stalls set up from 7am, with the hard-
core bargain-hunters arriving soon afterwards. In
truth, there are few real deals to be had these days,
but in among the tat are Moroccan stalls selling
lovely leather bags (though be sure to haggle hard),
and antiques stalls and shops that are worth a trawl
(*see also p168*). In any case, it's still a quintessential stop on the tourist shopping map, but do keep
an eye on your bag.

San Miguel

*Plaza de San Miguel, Los Austrias (91 548 12 14).
Metro Sol.* **Map** p313 D8.

La Duquesita. *See p178.*

This pretty market has a restored 19th-century wrought-iron façade. There's a good selection of produce, and a bustling café in the middle.

Supermarkets

Hypermarkets are mostly to be found on the main roads around the edge of the city, and are mainly accessible only by car. If you're mobile and need to stock up, look for ads for Alcampo, Continente or Pryca. Many branches of **El Corte Inglés** (*see p167*) also have (pricey) supermarkets. For information on Sunday opening, *see p167*. In town, apart from the chains listed below, look out for branches of **Día**, which has a no-frills approach to retailing, and **Lidl**, with good-quality products at unbeatable prices.

Caprabo

Lagasca 51, Salamanca (91 431 77 11). Metro Serrano. **Open** *Sept-July* 9am-9pm Mon-Sat. *Aug* 9am-2.30pm, 5-9pm Mon Sat. **Credit** MC, V. **Map** p311 J4.
Other locations: throughout the city.

Champion

C/Valencia 1, Lavapiés (91 467 42 08). Metro Lavapiés. **Open** 9am-10pm Mon-Sat. **Credit** MC, V. **Map** p313 F10.
Other locations: throughout the city.

Sabeco

C/Bravo Murillo 16, Chamberí (91 447 37 71). Metro Quevedo. **Open** 9.30am-9pm Mon-Sat. **Credit** MC, V.
Other locations: throughout the city.

Wine & drink

Bodegas Santa Cecilia

C/Blasco de Garay 72-74, Chamberí (91 445 52 83/ www.santacecilia.es). Metro Islas Filipinas. **Open** 10am-2pm, 5-8.30pm Mon-Sat. **Credit** AmEx, DC, MC, V.
This *bodega*, occupying two almost-adjacent locales, stocks a vast array of wines, beers and spirits – over 4,000 in total. They're mainly Spanish, while beers and spirits come from all over. The gourmet shop, No.72, hosts frequent tasting sessions.
Other locations: C/Bravo Murillo 50, Cuatro Caminos (91 442 35 32).

Lavinia

C/José Ortega y Gasset 16, Salamanca (91 426 06 04/www.lavinia.es). Metro Nuñez de Balboa. **Open** 10am-9pm Mon-Sat. **Credit** AmEx, DC, MC, V. **Map** p311 J3.
No oenophile should miss visiting Lavinia, which claims to be Europe's largest wine shop. In stark contrast to many of Madrid's dusty old *bodegas*, it's bright, airy and spacious, and staff are knowledgeable and helpful.

Mariano Madrueño

C/Postigo de San Martín 3, Sol & Gran Via (91 521 19 55/www.dongourmet.com). Metro Callao. **Open** 10am-2pm, 5.30-8.30pm Mon-Sat. Closed Sun & 2nd & 3rd wks Aug. **Credit** MC, V. **Map** p313 D7.
This classic old *bodega*, dating back to 1895, has a charming interior, with wrought-iron columns and carved wooden shelves. As for the booze on sale, the selection is enormous, with wines and spirits, plus the *bodega's* own (lethal) coffee and orange liqueurs.

Reserva y Cata

C/Conde de Xiquena 13, Chueca (91 319 04 01/www.reservaycata.com). Metro Chueca. **Open** 11am-2.30pm, 5.30-8.30pm Mon-Fri; 11am-2.30pm Sat. **Credit** AmEx, DC, MC, V. **Map** p310 H5.
This shop is crammed full of wines from Spain and abroad, all displayed with helpful information and often at prices lower than in the supermarkets. Tasting sessions and courses are also offered.
Other locations: C/Ramiro II 7, Chamberí (91 553 04 02).

Hair & beauty

Cosmetics & perfumes

Make Up Store

C/Fuencarral 124, Chamberí (91 593 99 54). Metro Bilbao. **Open** 10am-9pm Mon-Sat. **Credit** MC, V. **Map** p309 F3.

This chain has everything from eyeshadows in every colour to funky make-up bags. Staff are friendly. **Other locations**: C/Orense 14, Chamberí (91 555 45 94); C/Goya 19, Chamberí (91 435 85 52).

Sephora

C/Alberto Aguilera 62, Conde Duque (91 550 20 50/ www.sephora.com). Metro Argüelles. **Open** 10am-9.30pm Mon-Sat. **Credit** AmEx, MC, DC, V. **Map** p308 C3.
This popular Parisian cosmetics and perfume chain offers an A to Z of brands, including its own line. **Other locations**: Puerta del Sol 3, Sol (91 523 71 71).

Hairdressers

Jofer

C/Galileo 56, Chamberí (91 447 51 60). Metro Quevedo. **Open** 8am-10pm Mon-Sat. **Credit** AmEx, DC, MC, V. **Map** p309 D1.
A good bet if you just want a quick trim or blow-dry. Prices vary but are generally reasonable, and at most branches you don't need an appointment. Waxing, tanning and other services are also offered. **Other locations**: throughout the city.

Juan, ¡por Diós!

Pérez Galdós 3, Chueca (91 523 36 49). Metro Chueca or Gran Vía. **Open** 10am-9pm Mon-Sat. **Credit** AmEx, DC, MC, V. **Map** p310 I5.
Currently the place to get your hair cut in Madrid's trendiest quarter, this innovative place also stocks international style magazines, CDs and, rumour has it, will even be installing a wi-fi connection too.

Massages

Masajes a 1,000

C/Carranza 6, Malasaña (91 447 47 77/www. masajesa1000.com). Metro Bilbao. **Open** 8am-midnight daily. **Credit** AmEx, MC, V. **Map** p309 E3.
That's Masajes for €6 to you and me. While it tries to come up with a new and catchy euro-based name, Masajes a 1,000 (pesetas) continues to rub, knead, pluck and tweeze its way through its loyal clientele. Tanning, waxing and pedicures are also offered, all for various numbers of €6 vouchers.
Other locations: throughout the city.

Sana Sana

C/General Martínez Campos 40, Chamberí (91 310 54 24). Metro Rubén Darío. **Open** *Sept-July* 10am-10pm Mon-Sat. *Aug* 11am-10pm Mon-Fri. **Credit** AmEx, DC, MC, V. **Map** p310 H2.
An instant massage chain that offers a ten-minute workover for the harassed exec using specially designed chairs. It also offers shiatsu, sports and anti-stress massage, and beauty treatments. No booking is necessary for the short massage.

Spas

See also p242 **Getting steamy**.

Agua y Bien

C/Martínez Villergas 16, Northern suburbs (91 403 31 73/www.aguaybien.es). Metro Barrio de la Concepción. **Open** 10am-10pm Mon-Fri; 10am-3pm Sat, Sun. **Credit** AmEx, DC, MC, V.

Swine and dandy: the **Museo del Jamón**. *See p181.*

Eat, Drink, Shop

Material world

A common sight in Madrid is people running with sheets in their hands, especially around the areas of Sol, Atocha and Bravo Murillo. They're not taking part in the capital's version of the running of the bulls, but rather they are the street sellers christened 'los top manta' ('the blanket-tops'), who sell their pirated CDs and DVDs laid out on squares of material. Once a policeman is spotted, strings tied to the corners of the material are hastily pulled and running in the opposite direction is the only way to avoid trouble.

Europe's biggest and most successful pirates operate in Spain and in 2003 the Spanish music industry lost an estimated €150 million in record sales through pirating. Whereas an original CD costs up to €20, pirated copies are sold at €3 a pop. The most popular albums are measured by their presence on the sheets: you will find anything from Madonna to the latest Latin sensation, all in plastic pockets with a photocopied cover of the original album as an identifier. Through police operations and anti-pirate campaigns by the General Society of Authors and Writers more arrests have been made and more pirated CDs confiscated in Madrid than in any other Spanish city.

The copies are made with the latest software in flats around the centre of the city, and then sold mainly by African, Latin American and Eastern European immigrants, most of whom are operating without residence permits or visas. Madrid's mayor, Alberto Ruíz Gallardon, declared in 2003 that pirating was an act of 'murder against creation' and police and musicians are up in arms about the blanket sensation.

Mother and daughter's favourite Alejandro Sanz went so far as to put an anti-copy device on his 2003 album No es lo mismo. It took the pirates 24 hours to break the protection and start making copies, of which thousands have subsequently been sold.

Not content with just challenging the music industry, however, the last two years has seen the arrival of copied DVDs, with some films on the blankets before they even hit the movie screens. Costing less than a

cinema ticket, pirated blockbusters, classics and independent movies all feature in the manta charts, either copied from DVD releases in the US or filmed inside the cinema. A group of Chinese immigrants was found copying DVDs for distribution in Valencia and Madrid in May 2004, with enough software and material to burn a million pirated copies in the space of a year.

The other face of pirating that you may meet on a night out in Madrid is that of the mochilero (backpacker), usually a Chinese or Indian immigrant, selling copied CDs or DVDs in bars. Surprisingly, you will see some madrileños buying from them. Regardless of whether or not they're alcohol-induced impulse buys, pirating is a growing problem for the industries whose work is being copied, while, on the other hand, the city's escalating immigrant population continues to see the manta as a much-needed source of income. The choice is yours.

A small but extremely friendly spa, with staff who work hard to put you at your ease. A favourite is the 'thermal circuit', which offers an hour and a quarter's worth of showers, spa treatments, jacuzzi and massage. Staff are distinctly unstarchy.

Thermas Spa Center

Centro Comercial y Deportivo La Ermita, C/Sepúlveda 345, Casa de Campo (91 470 05 61). Metro Puerta del Ángel. **Open** 10am-9pm Mon-Fri; 10am-3pm Sat. **Credit** DC, MC, V.

Inside a shopping and sports centre, Thermas dishes out a range of treatments including seaweed and mud wraps and full massage. It also has a sauna, Turkish bath and jacuzzi.

Tattoos & body piercing

Factory Tattoo

C/Montera 24, Sol & Gran Vía (91 521 44 69). Metro Gran Vía or Sol. **Open** 10am-10pm Mon-Sat. **Credit** AmEx, DC, MC, V. **Map** p313 E7.
Factory is the most popular of the city's tattoo parlours, its seedy location no doubt adding to its allure. If your pain threshold is low, it's worth a visit just to see – and wince at – photos of piercings past.

Music

For wannabe DJs, **C/La Palma** and the surrounding streets are the place to be, with all genres of dance music covered in a plethora of record shops. Head to **Fnac** (*see p167*) for the best selection of DVDs and music CDs and avoid El Corte Inglés if possible, with its ineffectual classification and sprawling layout.

AMA Records

Mercado Fuencarral, C/Fuencarral 45, Malasaña (91 522 64 03/www.ama-records.com). Metro Tribunal. **Open** 11am-9pm Mon-Sat. **Credit** MC, V. **Map** p309 F5.
Super-friendly staff combined with a fantastic selection of hip hop, house, nu jazz, reggae, lounge and breakbeat, make Ama Records a hub for the city's musical community. It's also a great place for flyers.

El Flamenco Vive

C/Conde de Lemos 7, Los Austrias (91 547 39 17/ www.elflamencovive.es). Metro Ópera. **Open** 10.30am-2pm, 5-9pm Mon-Sat. **Credit** AmEx, DC, MC, V. **Map** p313 D7.
Even if you harbour only a passing interest in flamenco, the brilliant range of CDs, guitars, books and other paraphernalia at this shop will lure you in.

Madrid Rock

Gran Vía 25 (91 523 26 52). Metro Gran Vía. **Open** 10am-10pm daily. **Credit** MC, V. **Map** p313 E6.
Always a hive of activity, Madrid Rock is the focal point for all of the musical clans of the city. National and international material is on the ground floor, the basement stocks classical and DVDs, while the top floor is dedicated to dance, soundtracks and soul. Also has a box office for most concerts in town.

Up Beat Discos

C/Espíritu Santo 6, Malasaña (91 522 76 60/ www.up-beat.com). Metro Noviciado or Tribunal. **Open** 11am-2pm, 5-8.30pm Mon-Fri; 11am-2pm Sat. **Credit** MC V. **Map** p309 E4.
Soul, jazz and reggae dominate the shelves here, with a hand-picked collection of CDs and vinyl, along with a sideline in donkey jackets, Parkas,

Doctor Marten's, and so on. The shop has a fab '60s feel, with a space dedicated to scooter parts. Staff can track down rareties.

Musical instruments

Garrido Bailén

C/Bailén 19, corner C/Mayor 88, Los Austrias (91 542 45 01). Metro Ópera. **Open** 10am-1.30pm, 4.30-8.15pm Mon-Fri; 10am-1.45pm Sat. **Credit** AmEx, DC, MC, V. **Map** p312 C8.
An impressively wide range of instruments, with everything from traditional Spanish guitars to sitars. A limited range of sheet music is also stocked.

Guitarrería F Manzanero

C/Santa Ana 12, La Latina (91 366 00 47/ www.guitarrasmanzanero.com). Metro La Latina. **Open** *Sept-June* 10am-1.30pm, 5-8pm Mon-Fri. *July* 10am-1.30pm Mon-Fri. Closed Aug. **Credit** AmEx, DC, MC, V. **Map** p313 D9.
For a real taste of Spanish guitar-making, drop by at this master guitar-maker's shop, which also has a great display of old and rare string instruments. Call first to avoid disappointment.

Opticians

Grand Optical

Puerta del Sol 14, Sol (91 701 49 80). Metro Sol. **Open** 10am-9pm Mon-Sat. **Credit** AmEx, DC, MC, V. **Map** p313 E7.

Sephora. *See p183*.

Guantes Luque. *See p187.*

This high-street optician is part of the same group as the UK's Vision Express. Frames are by DKNY, D&G, Christian Dior and Cartier, among others, and there's also a wide range of contacts. Prescription glasses or sunglasses take an hour to make up.
Other locations: La Vaguada (*see p168*).

Pharmacies

For general information on pharmacies, *see p286*. The following are open 24 hours a day.

Farmacia Central
Paseo de Santa María de la Cabeza 64, Embajadores (91 473 06 72). Metro Palos de la Frontera. **No credit cards**.

Farmacia Lastra
C/Conde de Peñalver 27, Salamanca (91 402 43 63). Metro Goya. **Credit** AmEx, DC, MC, V. **Map** p311 L4.

Photocopying

Most stationers (*papelerías*) or printers (*imprentas*) also have faxes and photocopiers.

WORKcenter
Plaza Canalejas, Huertas & Santa Ana (91 360 13 95/www.workcenter.es). Metro Sevilla or Sol. **Open** 24hrs daily. **Credit** AmEx, DC, MC, V. **Map** p313 F7. For anyone who needs a CV copied in a hurry, posters printed, digital prints produced from any file format or internet access, WORKcenter is the place to go. Staff are helpful and branches centrally located, though net connection isn't cheap at €6 an hour. **Other locations**: throughout the city.

Photographic

Foto Sistema
Gran Vía 22 (91 521 20 63/www.fotosistema.es). Metro Gran Vía. **Open** 9.30am-8pm Mon-Fri; 9.30am-2pm Sat. **Credit** AmEx, DC, MC, V. **Map** p313 F6.
A good-quality one-hour developing service for colour, black and white, slides and enlargements. **Other locations**: throughout the city.

Fotocasión
C/Carlos Arniches 22, Rastro (91 467 64 91). Metro Puerta de Toledo. **Open** 4.30-8.30pm Mon; 9.30am-2pm, 4.30-8.30pm Tue-Fri; 9.30am-2.30pm Sat, Sun. **Credit** MC, V. **Map** p313 D10.
A treasure trove for photographers and camera collectors. Owner José Luis Mur is a walking encyclopedia on cameras; he also has great offers on spare parts and new and second-hand cameras.

Image Center
Plaza Santa Ana 1, Santa Ana (91 532 62 00/www.imagecenter.es). Metro Antón Martín. **Open** 9am-9pm Mon-Sat. **Credit** AmEx, DC, MC, V. **Map** p313 E/F8.

A huge branch of a well-run chain, Image Center offers processing in an hour as well as the usual range of photographic necessities, video and electronic equipment.
Other locations: throughout the city.

Speciality shops

Almirante 23

C/Almirante 23, Chueca (91 308 12 02). Metro Chueca. **Open** 5-8pm Mon-Fri; 11am-1.30pm Sat. **Credit** AmEx, DC, MC, V. **Map** p310 H5.
This curiosity shop is packed full with all manner of old stuff, including toys, tacky postcards, prints, cameras, watches, bull-fighting programmes and more. Brilliant for browsing – and buying gifts.

Belloso

C/Mayor 23, Los Austrias (91 366 42 58/ www.belloso.com). Metro Sol. **Open** *Sept-June* 9.45am-2pm, 4.45-8pm Mon-Sat. *July, Aug* 9.45am-2pm Sat. **Credit** AmEx, DC, MC, V. **Map** p313 D7.
This neighbourhood abounds in shops selling Catholic paraphernalia, but Belloso is one of the best. The gear on offer covers a huge range, including rosaries, crucifixes and statues of the Virgin.

La Casa de los Chales

C/Duque de Sesto 54, Salamanca (91 574 25 73/ www.casadeloschales.com). Metro Goya or O'Donnell. **Open** 8am-1.30pm, 5-8.30pm Mon-Sat. **Credit** AmEx, MC, V. **Map** p315 L7.
The 'House of Shawls' has a huge range of *mantones de Manila*, beautifully made fringed and embroidered shawls. Capes, handbags and feather boas complete the stock.

Casa de Diego

Puerta del Sol 12, Sol (91 522 66 43//www.casade diego.com). Metro Sol. **Open** 9.30am-8pm Mon-Sat. **Credit** AmEx, DC, MC. **Map** p313 E7.
This much-loved shop specialises in hand-painted fans, umbrellas and classy walking sticks.

Efectos Militares y Civiles G Bodas

C/Mayor 15, Los Austrias (91 365 88 00). Metro Sol. **Open** 9.45am-1.45pm, 5-8pm Mon-Fri; 9.45am-1.45pm Sat. Closed Aug. **Credit** AmEx, DC, MC, V. **Map** p313 D7.
Not everybody's cup of tea, this shop sells a mix of flags, medals, insignia and other military knick-knacks. For those that way inclined there are busts of Franco and religious figures such as the Pope.

Guantes Luque

C/Espoz y Mina 3, Santa Ana (91 522 32 87). Metro Sol. **Open** 10am-1.30pm, 5-8pm Mon-Sat. **Credit** MC, V. **Map** p313 E8.
Gloves in all sizes, colours and materials. If you can't find them here you won't find them anywhere.

M&M

C/San Agustin 7, Huertas & Santa Ana (91 429 68 01). Metro Antón Martin or Sevilla. **Open** *July-Sept* 9am-1.30pm, 4.30-8pm Mon-Fri;

10am-1.30pm Sat. *Aug* 9am-1.30pm, 4.30-8pm Mon-Fri. **Credit** AmEx, DC, MC, V. **Map** p314 G8.
The official art materials supplier to the Circulo de Bellas Artes, this shop counts Dali and Picasso among its former customers. The staff are helpful and well informed.

Objetos de Arte Toledano

Paseo del Prado 10, Huertas (91 429 50 00/ www.artetoledando.com). Metro Banco de España. **Open** 9.30am-8pm Mon-Sat. **Credit** AmEx, DC, MC, V. **Map** p314 G7.
Located across from the Prado, this souvenir shop par excellence sells traditional *españoladas* such as fans, flamenco and bullfighting dolls. A great place to find that gift for your kitsch-loving friends.

Sport

Adidas Stuff

C/Mayor 21, Sol (91 364 45 89). Metro Sol. **Open** 10am-9.30pm Mon-Sat, 11am-9pm Sun. **Credit** AmEx, DC, MC, V. **Map** p313 E7.
This is sportswear as fashion: you can't imagine customers getting the stuff sweaty or dirty, it's far too cool. Official Real Madrid kits are sold here too.

Área Real Madrid

C/del Carmen 3, Sol (91 521 79 50). Metro Sol. **Open** 10am-9pm Mon-Sat; 11am-8pm Sun. **Credit** AmEx, MC, V **Map** p313 E7.
A true emporia for the Real Madrid-inclined. On sale are, naturally, replica shirts and all manner of other stuff bearing the club's logo, from ashtrays to mouse mats, bath towels to undies. The other branch is in a shopping centre next to the Bernabéu stadium.
Other locations: C/Concha Espina 1, Esquina del Bernabéu Shopping Centre, Chamartín (91 398 43 00).

Supporters Shop

C/Goya 50, Salamanca (91 575 88 68). Metro Goya. **Open** 10am-2pm, 5-8.30pm Mon-Fri; 10.30am-2.30pm, 5.30-8.30pm Sat. **Credit** AmEx, DC, MC, V. **Map** p311 K4.
Selling shirts and other memorabilia from over 500 clubs worldwide, Supporters Shop can usually kit out fans of even the most obscure teams.

Tornal Moya Deportes

Ronda de Valencia 8, Lavapiés (91 527 54 40/ www.tornalmoya.com). Metro Embajadores. **Open** 10am-2pm, 5-8.30pm Mon-Sat. **Credit** MC, V. **Map** p313 F10.
This big, well-laid-out shop stocks the lot: top-name sportswear, trainers, walking boots, swimwear, tennis rackets, replica football shirts and bags.

Stamps & coins

Stamp & coin market

Plaza Mayor, Los Austrias. Metro Sol. **Open** *approx* 9am-2pm Sun. **Map** p313 D8.
On Sunday mornings, an avid mass of stamp and coin collectors swarm over the Plaza Mayor, buy-

ing, selling and eyeing up each others' wares. This also acts as a Sunday-morning attraction for anyone out on a stroll in town, whether or not they are really bothered about tarnished old pesetas, stamps of all nations and 19th-century share certificates. Other traders sell old magazines, second-hand books, postcards, badges and ex-Soviet bloc military regalia, you can even get phonecards nowadays, along with just about anything else that someone, somewhere, considers collectable.

Ticket agents

There are all manner of ways of avoiding queues to buy tickets (*entradas*) for shows and gigs these days, among them telesales, online purchase and cashpoints. Some of the biggest players in this game are savings banks (Cajas de Ahorro) such as the Caixa de Catalunya and La Caixa, who do advanced sales by phone, as does the all-embracing Corte Inglés.

Each of these services is associated with different venues, so check in a listings magazine such as the *Guía del Ocio* to see which of them handles the telesales for the show you want to attend. The *Guía del Ocio* itself offers online sales for cinemas and other venues via its webpage, www.guiadelocio.com. The big two record stores, **Fnac** (*see p167*) and **Madrid Rock** (*see p185*), sell rock and pop gig tickets.

El Corte Inglés
902 400 222/www.elcorteingles.es. **Open** 10am-10pm daily. **Credit** AmEx, DC, MC, V.
El Corte Inglés sells tickets for a huge range of shows and events, either by phone, online or at any of its stores.

Entradas.com
902 488 488/www.entradas.com. **Open** 24hrs daily. **Credit** AmEx (some venues), DC, MC, V.
This 24-hour ticketing service functions both by telephone and online. When dialling, depending on the type of event you wish to buy a ticket for, you get put through to a different number, and it's generally easier to book via the net. Tickets can be collected at the event box office.

Servicaixa/La Caixa
902 33 22 11/ww3.servitticket.com. **Open** 24hrs daily. **Credit** AmEx, DC, MC, V.
Servicaixa has a limited share of the theatre ticket sales market but offers versatility as you have the possibility of purchasing over the telephone, online or from ATM machines.

Tel-entradas/Caixa de Catalunya
902 10 12 12/www.telentradas.com. **Open** 24hrs daily. **Credit** MC, V.
Through the Caixa de Catalunya you can book tickets for theatres, venues and concerts, pay by credit card and pick them up either at a branch of the bank or from the venue's box office itself (depending on

the show and the venue). Some staff members speak minimal English, but don't bank on it. Online purchasing, with pages in English, is another option.

Tobacco & smoking

Estancos (tobacco shops; *see p291*) can be found all over town.

La Cava de Magallanes
C/Magallanes 16, Chamberí (91 446 28 17). Metro Quevedo. **Open** *Sept-June* 8.30am-8.30pm Mon-Sat. *July, Aug* 8.30am-2.30pm, 5-8.30pm Mon-Sat. **Credit** MC, V. **Map** p309 E1.
A temple to tobacco, La Cava de Magallanes stocks over 350 different types of cigars, all maintained at optimum temperature in a special humidified room. The knowledgeable owner speaks a little English. There is a good range of accessories too. Note that some credit cards incur a small extra charge.

La Mansión del Fumador
C/Carmen 22, Sol & Gran Vía (91 532 08 17). *Metro Sol*. **Open** 10.30am-1.30pm, 4.30-8.30pm Mon-Sat. **Credit** AmEx, MC, V. **Map** p313 E7.
Not a place to buy tobacco or cigarettes, La Mansión del Fumador does, however, stock a big range of accessories such as cigar-cutters, lighters, humidors, pipes and ashtrays.

Travel services

Forocio
Carrera de San Jerónimo 18, Santa Ana (91 522 56 77/www.forocio.com). Metro Sevilla or Sol. **Open** 10.30am-7.50pm Mon-Fri. **Credit** DC, MC, V. **Map** p313 E7.
This multi-purpose agency offers services for young foreigners, such as 'International Parties' every Thursday in the Palacio de Gaviria (*see p229*), Interrail and student cards, language exchanges, budget flights, day trips and weekend tours. The 'Tarjeta Forocio' gives a 10% discount on trips. English and other languages are spoken.

Metropolitan Viajes
C/Galileo 25, Chamberí (91 448 54 13). Metro Argüelles. **Open** 9.30am-2pm, 4.30-8pm Mon-Fri. **Credit** AmEx, DC, MC, V. **Map** p309 D2.
This small but ultra-friendly agency often has great budget deals on flights to the UK and has also been highly praised by frequent transatlantic flyers.

Viajes Zeppelin
Plaza de Santo Domingo 2, Sol & Gran Vía (91 542 51 54/www.v-zeppelin.es). Metro Santo Domingo. **Open** 9am-8pm Mon-Fri; 10am-1pm Sat. **Credit** AmEx, DC, MC, V. **Map** p313 D6.
This well-established agency with friendly service specialises in cheap European charter flights and long-haul youth fares. You can also book online. **Other locations**: C/General Margallo 20, Castillejos (91 571 82 58); C/Hermosilla 92, Salamanca (91 431 40 36); C/Gaztambide 24, Moncloa (91 544 75 34).

Arts & Entertainment

Festivals & Events

Madrid, where there's a festival every other day, and a party on all the rest.

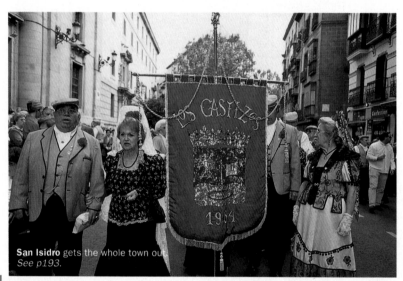

San Isidro gets the whole town out.
See p193.

Practically all year round, apart from perhaps during the late winter lull (when everybody is worn out and broke from Christmas, New Year and Reyes) and the end of the summer, anyone coming to Madrid is likely to encounter an arts festival, a music fest, a fiesta or a themed film season. There is something here to suit all tastes, though, to make sure you catch one you like, it's worth doing a little forward planning.

Events and festivals that receive official sponsorship come under the aegis of either the Ayuntamiento (city council) or the Comunidad de Madrid (regional government), and the influence of politics, inevitably, is felt in culture. Municipal events are beginning to look less tawdry and more upbeat with the new mayor, Alberto Ruiz-Gallardón, at the helm, and Comunidad cultural policy has maintained a consistently high standard in recent years.

Other events are independent and still more are semi-independent, functioning with a mix of public and private money. Visual arts events, such as the huge contemporary art fair **ARCO** and the city-wide photographic extravaganza **PhotoEspaña**, are organised this way. The alternative music festival **Festimad**, held in the dormitory town of Móstoles, makes do with

small grants from the local council and a range of private patrons, although the organisers complained bitterly about the withdrawl of their grant from the Madrid city council in 2003 owing to the festival's anti-war stance.

Fiestas usually celebrate a religious or historical event, though this is really just a pretext for dressing up, getting out and partying, something for which *madrileños* seem to have an innate talent. **Dos de Mayo**, **San Isidro**, **San Antonio de la Florida** and **La Paloma** are fiestas that people take part in with great gusto, and all are normally accompanied by good weather. Not that freezing temperatures or a few drops of rain are an impediment for the thousands who step out for **Reyes** (Three Kings' Day) and **Carnaval**.

WHAT'S ON

Advanced festival information is scarce as programming tends to be finalised close to the starting date. For information on Ayuntamiento-backed events try 010 or www.munimadrid.es, and for Comunidad-backed events, try 012 or www.madrid.org. Otherwise, listings magazines such as the *Guía del Ocio* and *Metrópoli* (a supplement of *El Mundo*), provide pull-out supplements on the Friday preceding big events and festivals. Spanish speakers should also look at www.lanetro.com, a good listings site. Events marked * below incorporate public holidays. For a full list of them, *see p295*.

Spring

See also p217 **Playing in time**, for the Música Antigua Aranjuez festival.

Día de la Mujer/Semana de la Mujer

Various venues. Route normally starts at Plaza Jacinto Benavente, Huertas & Santa Ana. Metro Sol or Tirso de Molina. **Information** Dirección General de la Mujer (91 420 85 92). **Date** 8 Mar & surrounding wk.
International Women's day is celebrated in Madrid with a march, usually from Plaza Jacinto Benavente to the bottom of C/Atocha. Some of the many other related events taking place over the week include short film seasons and concerts.

Festival de Arte Sacro

Various venues. **Information** Tourist offices & 012/www.madrid.org. **Date** Last 3wks Mar.
This three-week festival of music, dance, theatre, poetry, movies and conferences focuses on the role of religion in art over the centuries. The most recent festival looked at traditions in eastern European countries and the Levant (eastern Spain).

Teatralia

Various venues. **Information** Tourist offices & 012/www.madrid.org. **Date** Last 3wks Mar.
A regional jamboree of performing arts, including theatre, puppet shows, circus and cinema as well as workshops and other activities aimed at children and young people. In Madrid itself the main venues are the Teatros Pradillo and Triángulo, the Sala Cuarta Pared (for all, *see p249*), the Círculo de Bellas Artes (*see p81*) and the Carpa de Los Malabaristas (Jugglers' Tent) in the Casa de Campo.

Semana Santa (Holy Week)*

All over Madrid. **Information** Tourist offices & 010/www.munimadrid.es. **Date** wk leading up to Good Friday and Easter weekend (Mar/Apr).
Easter is usually a good time to be in Madrid, as many *madrileños* get out of town for the long weekend, and the weather is usually good. In Madrid and nearby towns, there are many parish processions in which hooded *penitentes* schlep figures of Christ and the Virgin around. Regarded as the most impressive is that of Jesús Nazareño el Pobre from San Pedro El Viejo and around La Latina. All over town there are organ and choral performances in churches.

Madrid en Danza

Various venues. **Information** Tourist offices & 012/www.madrid.org. **Dates** 3wks Apr.
Madrid's international dance festival always brings in an impressive range of companies from Spain and abroad. The emphasis is on contemporary dance

and there are many parallel activities: symposiums, exhibitions, video showings and workshops. The festival takes place throughout the whole region, but in town, the main venues to look for include the Teatros de Madrid, Albéniz, La Abadía, Sala Cuarta Pared (*see pp245-49*).

Fiesta del Trabajo* (May Day)

City centre & Casa de Campo. Metro Batán or Lago. **Date** 1 May.
The largest May Day march, attracting upwards of 60,000 people, is called jointly by the communist-led CCOO and the socialist UGT unions, which converge on Sol. Smaller in scale but quite animated is the anarcho-syndicalist CGT's march from Atocha to Plaza Jacinto Benavente. The anarchist purists CNT/AIT, meanwhile, march up C/Bravo Murillo

The best Trade fairs

Catch all the fun of the *feria* at the Juan Carlos I exhibition centre, out towards the airport (information 91 722 50 00 and www.ifema.es).

ARCO

An international contemporary art fair packed with gallery owners, critics and the general public. Mid February.

International Fashion Week

A bi-annual showcase for the best of Spanish and international creators. Ostensibly for professionals, but in practice blagging entry is fairly easy. Mid February and mid September.

Expo-Ocio

Dedicated to hobbies and leisure pursuits, this one always draws huge crowds. Third week of March.

Science Fair

Wonderful if you have kids in tow, with touchy-feely exhibits to stimulate all the senses. Late March/early April.

SIMO

Computer geeks unite at this huge international data-processing, multimedia and communications show. November.

Feriarte

An international art and antiques fair. Mid December.

Juvenalia

Youth-oriented sports activities, along with magic, juggling, story-telling and so on. Late December.

Arts & Entertainment

In the frame Burial of the Sardine

It doesn't get any weirder. On Ash Wednesday, the last day of Carnival, Madrid mourns the death of a sardine. In Pythonesque absurdity, his scaly little corpse, dressed in Sunday best, is somberly paraded through the streets of old Madrid by La Alegre Cofradía de la Sardina (the Happy Brotherhood of the Sardine). They carry his diminutive coffin from bar to bar, enjoying a tongue-in-cheek display of funereal ceremony along with their *cañas*. The route changes annually, but always winds up at the Fuente de los Pajaritos in the Casa de Campo.

The origins of this wacky pageant are sadly unclear. Some say that it derives from the days when abundant sardines were sold on the last day in which eating meat is permitted before Lent began; and that the ripe little fellow came to symbolise the many sacrifices that lie ahead until Easter. The fish may also have phallic implications, and its burial could be a harbinger of sexual abstinence during Lent. Other sources link it to the reign of Carlos III (1759-1788), when a shipload of rotten sardines arrived at his court and he ordered that they be buried immediately.

Despite the ritual's uncertain roots, Goya's masterful and macabre painting suggests that the custom was in full swing by the early 1800s (although the concrete date of the painting is unknown). Goya depicts a frenzied bacchanal of wild cavorting, masks and partner-swapping, overseen by a gruesome death mask. Despite the title of the painting, no sardines are in sight.

The sardine, its burial and all other carnival merriment was temporarily suppressed during the dictatorship. La Alegre Cofradía, then a small group of high-spirited friends, thought they'd chance it anyway. One Ash Wednesday in the early 1950s, they marched the fish to the Casa de Campo, singing and dancing en route. The police were summoned by a humourless priest, who felt this spectacle to be sacrilegious. The police found the

entourage to contain so many venerable old lawyers, doctors and journalists, however, that they simply joined the throng.

Nowadays, the Cofradía has more than 90 members and a sister organisation, La Peña del Boquerón (the Anchovy Club), for the widows of the dead sardine. The march usually begins at 6pm, from sardine HQ at C/Rodrigo de Guevara 4 in La Latina (you will know the building by the fish on the door). But be prepared for a mournful moment, as all of the ornately painted miniature coffins from previous years are on display at the Cofradía site, and you will be expected to pay proper respects to the dearly departed fish.

Goya's **Burial of the Sardine** *is found at the Real Academia de Bellas Artes de San Fernando, see p81.*

from Cuatro Caminos. Many of the participants then head to the Casa de Campo where the UGT organises a lively party with stalls run by the *casas regionales*, clubs representing Spain's regions.

Dos de Mayo*

District of Malasaña. Metro Bilbao, Noviciado or Tribunal. **Map** p309 E4. *Parque de las Vistillas. Metro Ópera.* **Map** p312 C8. **Information** Tourist offices & 012. **Date** 2 May.

Commemorating the fateful day in 1808 when the people of Madrid rose up against Napoleon's occupying troops and paid for their audacity by being massacred, 2 May is now the region's official holiday and kick-starts a nearly continuous series of fiestas that go on throughout the rest of the spring and summer. Things get going in the Malasaña neighbourhood – named after the uprising's teenage heroine, Manuela Malasaña – in the Plaza Dos de Mayo, where the Monteleón barracks, a main bastion of resistance, then stood. Live gigs are held in the Plaza and in the Las Vistillas park and there are other events at a number of other spots around town.

San Isidro*

Plaza Mayor, Los Austrias, & all over Madrid. **Information** Plaza Mayor tourist office & 010. **Date** 1wk around 15 May.

For six days either side of 15 May, this is the time to see *madrileños* doing what they do best: taking to the streets and having a rollicking good knees-up. The fiestas celebrate San Isidro, Madrid's patron saint, a humble 12th-century labourer and well-digger to whom all manner of miracles are attributed and whose wife, María de la Cabeza, was also canonised, making them the only sainted couple in history. The action centres on the Plaza Mayor, where the fiestas are officially declared open and where there are nightly gigs with the odd classical performance thrown in. There is more music in Las Vistillas park; music, theatre, painting workshops and more are put on for kids in the Retiro; classic *zarzuela* arias get an airing in the Conde Duque Cultural Centre; the Auditorium in the Museo de la Ciudad programmes classical music; in the Planetarium there are performances of early, medieval and baroque music, and lovers of Spanish Golden Age theatre are catered for in the Plaza de San Andrés. An associated event is the Feria de la Cacharrería, a ceramics market, held in the Plaza de las Comendadoras, close to Conde Duque. Recent additions to the programming are Documenta, a short season of international documentary films; + Arte, a mixed bag of installations, performances, hip hop, electronic music and sanctioned graffiti, and Universimad, a rock festival at the Complutense.

Throughout the week there are also numerous religious ceremonies in various churches. The 15th itself sees a procession of vintage cars in the Castellana. Possibly most fun of all is the traditional *romería* (pilgrimage) at and around the Ermita de San Isidro, in the park of the same name. There, families in their traditional *castizo* garb, looking like something

out of a Goya painting, drink from wine skins and stuff themselves with traditional *madrileño* delicacies such as chorizo, morcilla and other offal dishes.

Feria del Libro Antiguo y de Ocasión

Paseo de Recoletos, Salamanca. Metro Banco de España or Colón. **Information** 91 420 34 21. **Dates** 2wks Apr-May. **Map** p314 H6.

An old and second-hand book fair spanning a week either side of the San Isidro weekend. Here you may stumble across rare treasures, out-of-print editions or recent remainders. Don't expect much in English.

Festimad

Venue tbc. **Information** 91 522 37 87/ www.festimad.es **Dates** late May.

Despite problems with funding and various other ups and downs in recent years (including having to look for a new venue for 2005), Festimad, Madrid's biggest rock festival, is certainly still alive and kicking. Now held in a park in the southern satellite town of Móstoles, Festimad has four stages where a range of Spanish indie bands perform. In fact, rock in all its variant forms is centrestage here, along with dance music, DJ sessions and a few big names. Recent years have seen artists of the calibre of Massive Attack, Rammstein, Marilyn Manson, Asian Dub Foundation, Pixies, Korn, Ben Harper, Patti Smith and the (International) Noise Conspiracy.

Madrid EnCanto

Teatro Albéniz (see p247). **Information** (91 522 02 00/www.madrid.org). **Date** 3wks May-June.

This short festival of song in the Teatro Albéniz has taken on an increasingly Latin flavour, as singer-songwriters from countries like Spain, Portugal and Latin America feature. The big names in 2004 were Chavela Vargas, the octogenarian Mexican whose voice frequently appears in Almodóvar films, the Afro-Portuguese fado singer Mariza and veteran Catalan singer-songwriter Lluis Llach.

La Feria del Libro (Book Fair)

Parque del Retiro. Metro Atocha or Ibiza. **Information** 91 533 51 84/www.ferialibro.com. **Date** 2wks end May-June. **Map** p315 J6-9.

First celebrated in 1933, the Book Fair is now a major international event. Hundreds of publishers are present and well-known writers show up to sign copies of their works.

Summer

San Antonio de la Florida

Ermita de San Antonio de la Florida. **Information** 91 547 07 22. **Date** 13 June. **Map** p308 A4.

One of the first of the summer's biggest street parties, the San Antonio celebrations can trace their history back a very long way. June 13 is the feast day of San Antonio, the patron saint of seamstresses. Single girls used to place 13 pins in the baptismal font of the hermitage. If one stuck to her finger she would marry within a year. The main party, including events for kids, takes place across the Paseo de la Florida, in the Parque de la Bombilla.

PHotoEspaña

Various venues. **Information** 91 360 13 20/ www.phedigital.com. **Dates** June/July.
Every June since 1998, PHotoEspaña has swept through Madrid's major museums and galleries, redefining the city as an international photography epicentre. Each year has a different theme; the 2004 festival, *Historias*, tackled the interplay between fact and fiction in the visual documentation of history. In recent years, the retinue of photographic stars, many of whom give workshops and lectures throughout the festival, has included Nan Goldin, Joel Peter Witkin, Philip Lorca di Corcia, and Paul Graham. PHotoEspaña also transforms C/Huertas into an active outdoor exhibition space and puts on slide projections in Plaza Santa Ana and Centro Cultural Conde Duque.

Urban Mix

Various venues. **Information** 91 521 64 65. **Date** June.
A short festival, originally offering music, contemporary dance and art exhibitions. In recent years the organisers have lowered their sights somewhat, by concentrating almost exclusively on music. But are expecting city council funding for 2005, so a broader programme may be expected in future. James Brown, Macy Gray, Lenny Kravitz, Massive Attack, Björk, Alicia Keys and Bebo Valdés with El Cigala have all featured.

Músicas del Mundo Getafe (World Music Festival)

Various venues in Getafe. Bus 441, 442 from Atocha/train C-4 to Getafe Centro. **Information** 91 681 82 12. **Date** late June-July.
The southern industrial satellite town of Getafe organises an annual World Music Festival. For budgeting reasons this festival has had its share of ups and downs but looks set to continue. Past festivals have seen a predominance of African and Spanish fusion performers but in recent years the festival has featured music from the American continent, blues and reggae particularly, and from eastern Europe.

Veranos de la Villa

Various venues. **Information** Tourist offices & 010/ www.munimadrid.es. **Dates** July/Aug.
As part of the 'Summers in the City' festival, a goodly selection of top names have appeared at the patio of the Centro Cultural Conde Duque, which acts as the festival's main stage. Among them are Brazilians Milton Nascimento, Caetano Veloso and Carlinhos Brown, the fabulous Cape Verdean singer Cesaria Évora, many top flamenco artists, Youssou N'Dour and Femi Kuti, Cubans like Ibrahim Ferrer and some gnarled old rockers. Interspersed among them, however, there has also been a fair amount of dross. Elsewhere, *zarzuelas* are programmed in both the

Centro Cultural de la Villa and in the Sabatini Gardens beside the Royal Palace, the 'Titirilandia' puppet season for kids takes place in the Retiro, while Golden Age or more contemporary theatre productions may be seen outdoors beside the Muralla Árabe and in the Centro Cultural Galileo, and fringe venues all over town offer plenty more 'alternative' shows. Also outdoors is a two-screen cinema in the Parque de la Bombilla, down on the Paseo de la Florida.

Verbenas de San Cayetano, San Lorenzo & La Paloma

La Latina & Lavapiés. Metro La Latina or Lavapiés. **Information** Tourist offices & www.muni madrid.es/010. **Date** 6-15 Aug. **Map** p313 D/E9.
Madrid popular culture at its best – the streets and squares of the old Lavapiés, Rastro and La Latina neighbourhoods are dolled up with flowers and bunting and the locals don their *castizo* gear for some serious street partying. San Cayetano is first, on 7 August, followed by San Lorenzo on the 10th and La Paloma on the 15th. Daytime sees parades and events for kids; by night there are organ grinders, traditional *chotis* dancing, the aroma of grilled chorizo and *churros*, sangría by the bucketful and a lot of good clean fun.

Autumn

Fiestas del Partido Comunista

Recinto Ferial de la Casa de Campo. Metro Lago. **Information** Partido Comunista de España (91 300 49 69/www.pce.es). **Date** mid Sept.
In the political minority nowadays, the Spanish Communist Party still has enough resources and clout to stage a three-day fiesta. There are performances by flamenco and rock bands, theatre shows, stalls run by political groups, debates on many political and social issues and lots of regional cuisine in the *casas regionales*. Tickets are available in advance from the music store Madrid Rock.

Festival de Otoño

Various venues. **Information** Comunidad de Madrid (91 720 81 94/3), tourist offices & 012/ www.madrid.org. **Date** 4-5wks Oct-Nov.
The impressive and always enjoyable 'Autumn Festival' offers somewhere in the region of 60-odd theatre, dance and music spectacles and remains one of the city's major performing arts events. The range throughout the festival is quite wide. Acts as diverse as the Brodsky Quartet, Ballets Trockadero de Monaco, musical groups from Rajasthan, La Comédie Française, Eddie Palmieri and the Spanish Orquesta Nacional de Jazz have all popped up over the last couple of years. Events take place both in the capital and surrounding towns, making a trip out quite tempting. Around ten venues in Madrid itself have shows, among them the Teatros Albéniz and Zarzuela, the Círculo de Bellas Artes and fringe spaces such as Teatro Pradillo and Sala Cuarta Pared. *See pp245-9.*

Arts & Entertainment

All dolled up for **San Isidro**. See p193.

Winter

For **International Fashion Week** and the **ARCO** contemporary art fair (both occur in February), *see p191* **Trade fairs**.

Estampa
Recinto Ferial de la Casa de Campo, Avda de Portugal s/n. Metro Lago. **Information** 91 544 77 27/www.estampa.org. **Dates** Nov-Dec.
A firm fixture on the arts calendar, Estampa is a well-attended show that brings together galleries and collectors from around the world to exhibit prints and contemporary art editions.

Feria de Artesanía
Paseo de Recoletos, Salamanca. Metro Banco de España or Colón. **Information** www.agrupacion artesanosmadrid.org & 012. **Date** Mid Dec-5 Jan. **Map** p310 H5.
This large and crowded crafts fair is an ideal place to look for original presents and coincides with Christmas, New Year and Reyes. There are hundreds of stalls selling a range of handmade goods.

Navidad* (Christmas)
All over Madrid. **Date** 25 Dec.
Less hyped than in northern climes, Christmas begins, very reasonably, in December, and is traditionally less important than Epiphany (Reyes). Consequently you are not reminded of the number of shopping days left until Christmas at every turn and the absence of piped carols is almost eerie. Father Christmas, tinsel, flashing lights and baubles are far more evident than a few decades ago, however; all these trappings, plus masses of other cheap festive junk, are sold in the Christmas market in Plaza Mayor throughout December. The big family blow-out is usually on Noche Buena (Christmas Eve) with shrimps, red cabbage and either roast lamb, sea bream or both. Some families exchange presents on the otherwise fairly quiet Christmas Day, but the big ones are usually saved for 6 January. Worth checking out at this time are the nativity scenes (*belenes*), displayed in many places, and the many organ recitals, choral performances and chamber music concerts held in churches and other venues.

Noche Vieja (New Year's Eve)
Puerta del Sol, Sol & Gran Via. Metro Sol. **Date** 31 Dec. **Map** p313 E7.
New Year's Eve is celebrated with gusto, usually *en familia*, and involves another blow-out meal, litres of cava and the curious tradition of eating 12 grapes as the clock chimes midnight. Ever resourceful, many supermarkets now sell seedless grapes pre-packed in dozens for the occasion. The Puerta del Sol is where thousands throng if not celebrating at home – not recommended with kids or for agoraphobics. Clubs and bars organise parties, often starting at 12.30am or later. (Expensive) tickets should be purchased in advance.

Reyes* (Three Kings)
All over Madrid. **Date** 6 Jan.
On the evening of 5 January, Noche de Reyes, thousands of children and their parents line up along C/Alcalá to watch the annual *cabalgata* (parade) which is also televised. Dozens of elaborate floats pass by and the riders hurl sweets to the children. Later, most families have a big dinner, and the following day presents await those who have been good. Those who haven't get a piece of coal.

Festival de Flamenco Caja Madrid
Casa Encendida (see p87) & Teatro Albéniz (see p247). **Information** Cultyart 91 553 67 45/www.cultyart.com). **Dates** 2wks Feb.
This five-day festival brings the top names in flamenco for sessions of passionate, throaty *cante jondo*, foot-stomping and intricate guitar playing.

Carnaval
Various venues. **Date** wk before Lent (usually late Feb/early Mar).
Carnival is a very good excuse for dressing up and partying, either in the street or in bars and clubs, many of which organise carnival specials. It opens in the Plaza Mayor, followed by a parade around old Madrid. On Ash Wednesday, the last day, there is a ribald ceremony during which a fish is carted around to the strains of a marching band, before being interred (*see p192* **In the frame**). This officially marks the end of Carnival.

Arts & Entertainment

Children

Fun and games to fill the gap between siesta and fiesta.

San Isidro. *See p197.*

This is a city where children are welcome almost everywhere. *Madrileños* are, in general, a friendly bunch and if you have kids in tow their amiability is sure to go up a notch. The care of children is considered everybody's business. Waitresses will scoop your baby up to show to the kitchen staff and old ladies will happily advise you your child is wearing too few/too many clothes for the season.

Taking children to restaurants or *terrazas* (pavement cafés or bars) is considered the norm, but be prepared to adapt to Spanish meal times; lunch in Spain is eaten around 2pm and dinner from 10pm. If your kids really can't wait, then the numerous fast-food or pasta and pizza places are your best hope, and high chairs and children's menus can usually be found in these joints.

In summer, afternoon temperatures can hover around a very uncomfortable 40°C and so outdoor activities are best in the morning. After a late lunch, a siesta is the best option before venturing out into the relatively cool evening air. The city comes alive again in the hour or two before dusk when families come out to stroll, eat ice-cream and watch the world go by.

Be warned that few metro stations have lifts, and buses will only admit pushchairs if they are folded. Baby-changing facilities are limited to shopping centres, the department store El Corte Inglés (*see p167*), and the airport.

Attractions

Kids also enjoy the **Teleférico** cable-car (*see p107*) that runs from the Parque del Oeste deep into the Casa de Campo, and the dizzying **Faro de Madrid** (*see p107*).

Faunia
Avda de las Comunidades 28, Eastern suburbs (91 301 62 10/www.faunia.es). Metro Valdebernardo. **Open** *Jan-Mar* 10am-6pm Wed-Sun. *Apr, May, last 2wks Sept* 10am-8pm daily. *June-mid Sept* 10am-9pm daily. *Oct, Nov* 10am-7pm Wed-Sun. *Dec* 10am-5.30pm daily. **Admission** €18; €12 3-12s, over-60s; free under-3s. **Credit** AmEx, MC, V.
Part zoo, part theme park, Faunia recreates the world's different ecosystems in a series of domes. Best of the bunch is the Amazon jungle house, which echoes with the screech of exotic birds; an intense tropical storm is simulated every half-hour. And in

summer Penguin World, an impressive reconstruction of a polar zone, where you can see the little fellas zipping about, is wildly popular. Faunia is not a cheap day out and queues can be long.

IMAX Madrid

C/Meneses, Parque Tierno Galván, Legazpi, South of centre (91 467 48 00/www.imaxmadrid.com). Metro Méndez Álvaro. **Admission** €7; €5.90 Mon & over-65s; free under-3s. **Credit** AmEx, MC, V.
The hourly wildlife and scientific shows are only in Spanish, but the 3D and Omnimax presentations are awesome enough to be enjoyed by all children.

Palacio de Hielo

C/Silvano 77, Eastern suburbs (91 716 01 59/ www.palaciodehielo.com). Metro Canillas. **Open** Oct-May 11.30am-10.30pm Tue-Sun. **Admission** €4-€10. **No credit cards.**
The newly opened Ice Palace is a huge leisure complex dominated by a 1,800-square-metre ice rink. With a curling and skating school, a 24-lane bowling alley and a 15-screen cinema this is good option for a rainy day out with teenagers. The site, out towards Barajas Airport, also has a shopping centre and a nursery for kids aged three to 11.

Parque de Atracciones

Casa de Campo (91 463 29 00/91 526 80 30/ www.parquedeatracciones.es). Metro Batán. **Open** varies (see website). **Admission** €5.70; €9.60 incl 2 rides; Supercalco (all-inclusive ticket) €21.80; €11.50 under-6s. **Credit** MC, V.
A funfair with something for everyone. The scariest ride is the Lanzadera, which is rather like doing a sitting bungee jump. There is now a children's version too, so nobody has to miss the terror. Other new features include indoor paintball and a 4D cinema. There are long queues for some rides.

Planetario de Madrid

Parque Tierno Galván, Legazpi, South of centre (91 467 38 98). Metro Méndez Álvaro. **Shows** vary; phone to check. **Admission** €3; €1.20 2-14s, over-65s. **No credit cards.**
Close to the IMAX (*see above*), the Planetarium has seasonal exhibitions on the solar system as well as 45- minute shows. Like the IMAX, the narration here is only in Spanish and may test your kids' interest in the heavens if they are non-Spanish speakers.

Zoo-Aquarium de la Casa de Campo

Casa de Campo (91 512 37 70/www.zoomadrid. com). Metro Batán. **Open** 10.30am-dusk daily. **Admission** €13.10; €10.55 under-8s, over-65s; free under-3s. **Credit** MC, V.
An attractively landscaped zoo in the heart of the Casa de Campo. The animals look as happy as can be expected, though the big cats could do with a bit more leg-room. At the Land of Gorillas a sheet of reassuringly thick glass separates you from huge, glowering, silverbacks. Children will enjoy the walk-through the shark tank and dolphinarium. There is also a petting zoo and a train ride.

Babysitting & childcare

English-speaking babysitters can be found through local English-language magazines and newspapers (*see p288*), or at www.casalista.com. Alternatively parents can leave children aged from four to 12 for short periods at any of the following *ludotecas* (play centres).

Centro de Recreo Infantil Dinopeppino

C/Mártires de Alcalá 4, Malasaña & Conde Duque (91 559 22 04). Metro Ventura Rodríguez. **Open** 4.30-8.30pm Mon-Fri; 11.30am-2pm, 4.30-8.30pm Sat, Sun. **Admission** €5.50 hr; €42 10hr multi-entry. **No credit cards. Map** p309 D3.
A well-equipped and spacious play centre.

Chiquipark

Estación Chamartín, C/Agustín de Foxá, Charmartín (91 323 19 83/www.chiquipark.com). Metro Chamartín. **Open** 4.30-9pm Mon-Fri; noon-2.30pm, 4pm-9pm Sat, Sun. Closed Aug-mid Sept. **Admission** €11. **Credit** MC, V.
A chain of six play centres; this is the most central branch. The admission fee is valid for one session and includes a sandwich, drink and goody bag.

Gorongoro

Avda de Felipe II 34, Salamanca (91 431 06 45). Metro Goya. **Open** Sept-June 4.30-9pm Tue-Fri; 11.30am-2.30pm, 4.30-9pm Sat, Sun. *July, Aug* 6-9.30pm Mon-Fri; 11.30am-2.30pm, 6-9pm Sat. **Admission** (per hr) €5.30 over-4s; €4.60 under-4s. **Credit** DC, MC, V. **Map** p311 L5.
This well-equipped play centre is close to the Retiro and the Goya shopping area.

Imposible Aburrirse

C/Peñuelas 41, South of centre (91 474 21 99/ www.imposibleaburrirse.net). Metro Acacias or Embajadores. **Open** Sept-mid July 10am-2pm, 5-9.30pm Mon-Fri; 5-9.30pm Sat, Sun. *Mid July-Aug* 8am-5pm Mon-Fri. **Admission** (per hr) €3.30 over-4s; €3 under-4s. **Credit** AmEx, MC, V.
A vast play centre, including a gym and cafeteria.

Entertainment

Events aimed at children are dotted around the year, starting in January with a parade on the eve of **Reyes**, when Spanish children traditionally get their presents. The parade features floats from which the Three Kings throw sweets to children along the route. During **Carnaval** special kids' activities are organised, and there are also children's events during **San Isidro** and **Veranos de la Villa** (for all, *see pp190-95*). In April festivities for **El Día del Niño** (Day of the Child) are held in C/Bravo Murillo in Tetuán. The street is taken over by bouncy castles, puppet shows, foam-spraying firemen and candy floss stalls.

Look out, too, for children's theatre. **Teatro San Pol** in the Casa de Campo (C/San Pol de Mar 1, 91 541 90 89/www.teatrosanpol.com) puts on occasional shows in English. The **Madrid Players**, an English-language theatre group (91 326 24 39/www.madridplayers.org), puts on a pantomime at Christmas and hosts theatre workshops for kids in March, July and October.

In the Retiro park the permanent **Teatro Municipal de Titeres** (91 792 41 12/mobile 670 72 33 60/www.titirilandia.com), near the boating lake, has puppet shows most weekends, albeit in Spanish. **La Casa Encendida** (*see p87*) runs children's workshops on diverse subjects. In July and August storytelling sessions are held once a week and at weekends there are puppet shows in the patio.

Museums

The **Museo del Ferrocarril** (*see p113*) houses steam, diesel and electric locomotives. Children's activities include a theatre, a mini-train and a market for model train enthusiasts.

Cosmocaixa

C/Pintor Velázquez s/n, Alcobendas (91 484 52 00/ www.fundacio.lacaixa.es). Bus 151, 152, 153, 154, 156, 157 from Plaza Castilla. **Open** 10am-8pm Tue-Sun. **Admission** €3; €1.50 under-16s; €1 over-65s; free under-7s. **Credit** DC, MC, V.
Kids and adults uncover the mysteries of science via hands-on interactive exhibits. The *clik de los niños*, where processes can be tried out, is popular, as is the *toca, toca* (touch, touch) area for small children, where there are animals to stroke.

Museo de Cera (Wax Museum)

Paseo de Recoletos 41, Salamanca (91 319 26 49/ www.museoceramadrid.com). Metro Colón. **Open** 10am-2.30pm, 4.30-8.30pm Mon-Fri; 10am-8.30pm Sat, Sun. **Admission** *Museum* €10; €6 4-7s, over-60s; free under-4s. *Tren del Terror* €3. *Multivisión Diaporama* €20. *Combined ticket* €12; €8 4-7s, over-60s. **No credit cards. Map** p310 I4.
Madame Tussaud's it isn't (no queueing for starters), yet this wax museum has a certain tacky charm. Along with the usual rogues, celebs and elder states-men, there's the Tren de Terror (ghost train) and the Multivision Diaporama whips through the history of Spain in a 27-projector (count 'em) slide show.

Parks & playgrounds

Small neighbourhood parks are not Madrid's strong point; play areas have improved in recent years but are still a little tame. One of the better play areas is in the **Plaza de Oriente**, next to the Palacio Real. The **Paseo del Prado** central boulevard has safe wooden climbing frames and slides and **Dos de Mayo** in Malasaña has play areas for toddlers and

terrazas for adults, as does the nearby **Plaza de las Comendadoras**. On Sunday mornings **Calle Fuencarral** between metros Bilbao and Quevedo is closed to traffic and taken over by bike-riders and skateboarders.

The **Retiro** (*see p98*) has a boating lake, cafés around the edge, buskers, artists, puppet shows, sports facilities and a good play area by the Puerta de Alcalá entrance. To the east is the Parque del Oeste, which boasts great views, decent play areas, ice-cream parlours and the Teleférico. The huge **Casa de Campo**

Our mouse

Ask any Spanish child to name the most famous mouse in the world and few of them will come up with Mickey. By far the most celebrated rodent in Spain and much of South America is Ratoncito Pérez, the mythical mouse who sneaks into children's rooms at night to slip money under the pillow when a tooth falls out. What few people know is that El Ratón (the mouse) Pérez is actually a *madrileño*.

Stroll half a minute from the Puerta del Sol and you can see a plaque marking the house where Pepito Pérez lived in a biscuit tin in the basement of a pastry shop. The ground floor of No.8 Calle Arenal is now a small arcade of shops. Inside, you'll find a mouse-sized statue (well, hamster-sized, perhaps). There are also illustrated panels telling the story of Pepito and his creator, a Jesuit priest, Father Coloma.

Juan Coloma, who found God after nearly killing himself while cleaning his revolver as a young man, first published the story of Ratoncito Pérez in 1902. He dedicated the book to the young King Alfonso XIII, to whom he had told the story while the monarch was a sickly child. According to the story the mouse would frequently escape from the basement by means of the sewers. From this labyrinth he could find his way into the bedroom of any child from the boy-king to the poorest *niño* in the land, exchanging a lost tooth for money or a small gift. The tradition continues to this day.

In 2003 the mayor of Madrid finally unveiled the plaque to Ratoncito Pérez, announcing rather grandly that, just as the Americans have Mickey Mouse, Pepito 'deserves recognition as a symbol of the hopes and dreams of all children, and because he is *our* mouse'.

Palacio de Hielo. *See p197.*

(*see p105*) has the Zoo, the Parque de Atracciones funfair, an even bigger boating lake and the best outdoor pools in Madrid (*see p243*), with a shaded and shallow kids' pool.

Out of town

Most rides in the waterparks around town are suited to older kids, but there are usually areas for small children. For general pools, *see p243*.

Aquasur
Ctra de Andalucia (A-4), km 44, Aranjuez (91 891 60 34). Bus 423, 423A from Estación Sur/by car A-4/by train C-3 from Atocha. **Open** *Mid June-Sept* 11am-8pm daily. Closed Oct-mid June. **Admission** *Mon-Fri* €8; €5 3-9s. *Sat* €12; €9 3-9s. *Sun* €15; €10 3-9s. **No credit cards**.
The cheapest of the waterparks, with a giant, five-slide pool plus another for little kids.

Aquópolis-San Fernando
Crta de Barcelona (A-2), km 15.5, San Fernando de Henares (91 673 10 13/www.aquopolis.es/san fernando). Bus (Continental) to Alcalá de Henares or Torrejón from Avda de América/by car A-2. **Open** *June, Sept* noon-7pm daily. *July, Aug* noon-8pm Mon-Fri; 11am-8pm Sat, Sun. Closed Oct-May. **Admission** €13.80; €9.50 3-10s, over-65s. **Credit** MC, V.
Madrid's first waterpark, with giant water slides, pools for smaller and larger kids, wave pools and wilder attractions for reckless youths.

Aquópolis-Villanueva
Avda de la Dehesa, Villanueva de la Cañada (91 815 69 11/www.aquopolis.es/villanueva). Bus 627 from Moncloa/by car Carretera de La Coruña (A-6), exit 41, then M503. **Open** *mid June-mid Sept* noon-7.30pm **Admission** €15 (€16.50 Sat, Sun); €9.50 3-10s; €9.50 3-10s; €10.50 over-65s. **Credit** AmEx, MC, V.
One of the largest waterparks in Europe, run by the same company as the Aquópolis San Fernando and with similar attractions.

De Pino a Pino
Área Recreativa del Chorro, Navafría (mobile 659 45 45 68/www.depinoapino.com). By car A-6/AP-61 to Segovia (100km), then N110 to Navafría (20km). **Open** *Mid June-mid Sept* 10.30am-8pm daily. *Mid May-mid June, mid Sept-Oct* 11.30am-7.30pm Sat, Sun. Closed Nov-mid May. **Admission** €23; €21 14-18s; €15 9-13s; €10 7-8s. **No credit cards**.
A way from Madrid, but well worth the trip, 'From Pine to Pine' is a forest-based adventure park where logs, hanging bridges and tree platforms are incorporated into routes that criss-cross the pine forests. Courses are designed with varying levels of difficulty according to kids' ages and each takes an hour.

Safari de Madrid
Aldea del Fresno, Carretera de Extremadura (A-5), km 32 (91 862 23 76). By car A-5 to Navalcarnero, then M-507 to Aldea del Fresno. **Open** 10.30am-sunset daily. **Admission** €10; €6 3-10s. **Credit** V.
A drive-through safari park where giraffes, elephants, big cats and monkeys roam free. In summer there's a swimming pool, a lake with pedalos for rent, a go-kart track, mini-motorbikes and a giant slide.

Tren de la Fresa (Strawberry Train)
Estación de Atocha (902 22 88 22). Metro Atocha Renfe. **Open** depart from Atocha 10am Sat, Sun (return from Aranjuez 6pm). Closed mid Oct-late Apr, mid July-mid Sept. **Tickets** €23; €15 2-12s. **Credit** MC, V. **Map** p314 H10.
A relaxing and enjoyable steam train ride to Aranjuez (*see p268*). The 1920s train departs from Atocha station and the ticket price includes visits to the palaces and gardens. Aranjuez's famous strawberries are served by hostesses in period costume.

Warnerbros Park
San Martín de la Vega (91 821 1234/www.warner brospark.com). By car A-4 to km 22, then M-506 to San Martín de la Vega/by train C-3 from Atocha. **Open** varies (see website). Closed Nov-Mar. **Admission** *1 day* €32; €24 5-11s, over-60s. *2 days* €48; €36 5-11s, over-60s. **Credit** AmEx, DC, MC, V.
The park has five themed areas with rides to match: Hollywood Boulevard, Cartoon Village, Old West Territory, DC Super Heroes and Warner Brothers Studios. Popular rides can have long, hot queues, and. It's an expensive day out, especially as visitors are not allowed to bring in their own food.

Xanadu
Autovía A-5, km 23.5, Arroyomolinos (91 648 23 65/www.parquedenievedemadrid.com). Bus 496, 498, 524, 528 from Príncipe Pío, or 529H, 531, 531A, 536, N5 from Méndez Álvaro. **Open** 10am-midnight Mon-Thur, Sun; 10am-2am Fri, Sat. **Admission** *1hr* €10, €8 under-13s Mon-Thur; €14, €12 under-13s Fri-Sun. *2hrs* €16, €14 under-13s Mon-Thur; €21, €18 under-13s Fri-Sun. **Credit** AmEx, DC, MC, V.
Billed as 'Europe's largest destination for snow, shopping and leisure', Xanadu boasts 24,000sq m of indoor ski slopes. All the necessary equipment can be hired. There are also go-karts, a 15-screen cinema, 200 shops and around 30 restaurants.

Arts & Entertainment

Film

Madrid goes to the movies.

Madrileños and movies go together like chocolate and *churros*. Indeed, this happy foursome is all that's needed for a perfect night out. Tickets are reasonably cheap even for the plushest screens and the range of film fare is easily a match for Paris or London.

Spain has no film censorship and its movie aficionados have long indulged their considered taste for avant-garde cinema, which, in turn, has inspired the works of homegrown masters such as Pedro Almodóvar and Julio Medem. Once the *enfant terrible* of Spanish cinema, the deservedly garlanded Almodóvar now makes mature and richly textured films that are both emotionally and stylistically audacious. The metaphysical Medem, whose thrilling documentary on the Basque conflict, *Basque Ball*, made him a controversial figure in Spain, seems likely to produce his most interesting work in the years to come. Interestingly, what Almodóvar and Medem have in common is the composer Alberto Iglesias, whose exquisite soundtracks are a prime factor in their pleasure and popularity. Other names to watch for are the social realists Iciar Bollaín and Fernando León de Aranoa; the satirist Álex de la Iglesia, and the precocious maestro that is Alejandro Amenábar – director of Nicole Kidman in *The Others*. Added to this roster are veterans such as Carlos Saura, who are still going strong.

State funding was slashed under the Aznar administration, but instead of crippling the film industry the new framework of subsidies from private, national and regional television companies might provide the stability that has been lacking. Due to complex funding and distribution policies, an enormous amount of films are made in Spain when compared with the number that eventually make it into mainstream cinemas. However, a plethora of film festivals of every persuasion provide a springboard for new film-makers and the production of short films is especially booming, with art-house cinemas programming some of the best before their main features.

VENUES

Ushers still show you to your seat at the **Callao** (Plaza Callao 3, 91 522 58 01) and the **Palacio de la Música** (Gran Via 35, 91 521 62 09). If you prefer the shopping mall cinema-going experience, take the metro north to the Barrio del Pilar for **La Vaguada** (91 730 06 22) or west to Pozuelo and the 25-screen **Kinepolis** (C/Edgar Neville s/n, 91 512 70 00). For a more refined experience, try the commercially viable art-house cinemas for Spanish auteurs, documentaries, foreign films in VO (*versión original* – ie, undubbed and with subtitles), and an exhilarating variety of quirky, classic and controversial features. For film seasons and older films, both Spanish and VO, choose the grand **Filmoteca** or the **Enana Marrón**.

TICKETS AND TIMES

Daily newspapers, the weekly *Guia del Ocio* and the www.lanetro.com website have film reviews and full listings. Screenings tend to start promptly with few trailers or ads, though a brisk turnover means that credits are curtailed and latecomers are a constant hazard. Screenings (*pases*) usually start at around 4pm. The 8pm screening is the most popular, though the late screenings (*sesiones de madrugada*) at midnight and 1am can be surprisingly packed if they're showing cult films or current favourites. Read the newspapers for VO listings, and once there check whether your seating is allocated (*numerada*) before paying. Be warned of the rarity of adequately tiered seating – Spaniards are getting taller and the screens are yet to be put any higher. Monday and Wednesday are often *días del espectador* ('spectator days'), offering special discounts, though every cinema has its own policy on the when-and-why of price reductions. Internet reservations are available through www.guiadelocio.com and many cinemas will take advance bookings for busy times and popular films.

VO cinemas

Alphaville

C/Martín de los Heros 14, Argüelles (91 559 38 36). Metro Plaza de España. **Tickets** €5.80; €3.80 Mon. **No credit cards. Map** p308 C4.
This legendary four-screener was the first of Madrid's art-house cinemas and played a crucial role in the *Movida* during the '80s. The screens and sound systems are showing their age and tiering is inadequate, but the basement café is still a fashionable meeting place with a bohemian atmosphere.

Casa de América

Paseo de Recoletos 2, Salamanca (91 595 48 00/www.casamerica.es). Metro Banco de España. **Tickets** €2. **No credit cards. Map** p314 H6.
This cultural centre has its own cinema screening classic and contemporary Spanish and Latin American cinema as themed seasons and special events. Showings at 7.30pm Monday to Friday.

Cine Estudio de Bellas Artes

C/Alcalá 42, Huertas & Santa Ana (91 522 50 92/www.circulobellasartes.com). Metro Banco de España. **Tickets** €4; €2.40 members; €9 *bono* of 3 films. **No credit cards. Map** p314 G7.
Originally a theatre, this repertory cinema is part of the grand Círculo de Bellas Artes building, which celebrates 125 years in 2005. The sound system is excellent, and the programme of themed film seasons goes down well with the trendy audience.

La Enana Marrón

Travesía de San Mateo 8, Chueca (91 308 14 97/www.laenanamarron.org). Metro Tribunal. **Tickets** €4; €2.60 members. **No credit cards. Map** p310 G4.
A side street in Chueca is the hip and lively location of the strangely named Brown Dwarf microcinema, specialising in experimental films, retrospectives, shorts and repertory classics. A meeting place for movie folk, fans and students with debates and discussions, it also boasts a witty website.

Ideal Yelmo Cineplex

C/Doctor Cortezo 6, Lavapiés (91 369 25 18/www.yelmocineplex.es). Metro Tirso de Molina. **Tickets** €5.90; €4.40 Mon. **Credit** MC, V. **Map** p313 E8.
This hugely popular eight-screen multiplex is an efficient if somewhat characterless venue for international mainstream films in *versión original*.

Luna

C/Luna 2, Sol & Gran Vía (91 522 47 52). Metro Callao. **Tickets** €5.50; €4 Wed except public hols. **No credit cards. Map** p313 E6.
Though the neighbourhood used to be a bit dodgy at night, it has been improving since the Luna was reborn as a VO house. The four screens show an off-beat, idiosyncratic selection of foreign films.

Pequeño Cine Estudio

C/Magallanes 1, Chamberí (91 447 29 20/www.pcineestudio.com). Metro Quevedo. **Tickets** €5.50; €3.50 Mon except public hols and concessions 1st show Tue-Fri except public hols. **No credit cards. Map** p309 E2.
It's always worth keeping an eye on this peculiar little VO cinema because its rapid turnover means that rarely viewed classics from Hollywood and world cinema often make it on to the programme. It also hosts debates and round-table discussions.

Renoir Plaza de España

C/Martín de los Heros 12, Argüelles 91 541 41 00/www.cinesrenoir.com). Metro Plaza de España. **Tickets** €5.50; €4 concessions 1st show Mon-Fri except public hols. **Credit** MC, V. **Map** p308 C4.
The flagship of the enterprising Renoir chain, with screens on the small side and a haphazard queuing system in the cramped foyer, although good sound systems and a keen crowd of film fans ensure enjoyable viewing. The Cuatro Caminos branch is also worth a mention for its larger screens, decent bar and intelligent balance of Spanish and world cinema, while the Princesa also has an eclectic mix of Spanish, European and independent American cinema.
Other locations: throughout the city.

Verdi

C/Bravo Murillo 28, Chamberí (91 447 39 30). Metro Canal or Quevedo. **Tickets** €5.80; €4 Mon, 1st show Tue-Fri. **Credit** DC, MC, V. **Map** p309 E2.
This relative newcomer to the ranks of VO cinemas has five screens showing a lively mix of art-house, Spanish, independent and mainstream foreign films.

The Filmoteca

Filmoteca Española (Cine Doré)

C/Santa Isabel 3, Lavapiés (91 369 21 18/www.cultura.ecd.es/cine/film). Metro Antón Martín. **Open** *Bar-cafés* 2pm-midnight Tue-Sun. *Bookshop* 4.30-10.30pm Tue-Sun. **Tickets** €1.35; €10.22 10 films. **No credit cards. Map** p313 F9.

Known affectionately as *la filmo* and featured in films by Almodóvar, this chic art nouveau national film theatre was founded more than 50 years ago. The neon-lit foyer/café is a lively meeting place and the tiny bookshop is always full of browsers. A free, expansive, fold-out monthly programme features-details of its eclectic seasons of films from the Spanish National Archive and world cinema. The grand auditorium is an especially marvellous place to see silent movies, sometimes accompanied by live music. The outdoor rooftop cinema and bar are open – and popular – during the summer months.

Open-air movies

Fescinal (Cine de Verano)

Parque de la Bombilla, Avda de Valladolid, La Florida (91 541 37 21/www.fescinal.info). Metro Príncipe Pío. **Tickets** €4.50; €3.50 concessions; free under-5s. **No credit cards.**

An open-air night-time venue for catching double bills of mainstream films during the Veranos de la Villa festival from July to September. As well as the massive screen (with wayward sound), there's a smaller one for kids, plus the opportunity to munch on *bocadillos* and *cerveza* for that truly communal experience of movie-watching.

10/10 for 8½

Cinéfilos will find a mecca of moviedom at Madrid's Ocho y Medio bookshop. Rolling since 1996 and recently relocated to these much larger premises near the Plaza de España, the store's empire is growing quickly.

Stock now numbers over 15,000 books and includes titles in Spanish, English, Italian and French, and anything not on the shelves can be ordered. The DVD section is also excellent and visitors will find film posters, T-shirts, calendars and all sorts of filmic gadgets. Not surprisingly, the shop has become something of a living museum for lovers of Spanish cinema – even the carrier bags, re-designed every few months by an actor or director, have become collectors' items.

Framed posters of recent films are scrawled with thanks and blessings from cast and crew and every space on the wall sports a signed doodle or dedication from famous film folk. Frequent guest signings and launch parties have made the store the hub of the Spanish film industry and it now has a thriving series of its own publications, including a celebrated spiral-bound series of scripts.

Given its reputation, it's not surprising that Ocho y Medio's enthusiastic owners, Jesús Robles and María Silveyro, have been awarded several prestigious prizes and are constant recipients of thanks during awards ceremonies from their many friends among the film-making elite. Both of them speak English and are fonts of information – if you're lucky enough to catch them in, they're always happy to chat. It's worth signing up to the mailing list before you leave, too.

Just across the street are some of the city's best multi-screen art-house and VO cinemas – the Alphaville, the Renoir Plaza de España and the Renoir Princesa – while a range of tapas bars, *tavernas* and restaurants serves the film-going crowds. So the location is perfect for when the bookshop closes and you're turfed on to the streets... at 8.30pm, of course, hence the Felliniesque name.

Ocho y Medio

C/Martín de los Heros 23 (91 559 06 28/www.ochoymedio.com). Metro Plaza de España. **Open** 10am-2pm, 4-8.30pm Mon-Sat. **Credit** AmEx, DC, MC, V. **Map** p308 C4.

Galleries

After three decades of uncertain evolution, the Madrid gallery scene edges into a period of stable growth.

During the 36 years of Franco, few commercial galleries existed in Spain. As a result, after the demise of the dictatorship, Madrid had a lot of catching up to do – hence the ensuing gallery boom of the 1980s… followed by a disheartening bust in the '90s. Now the climate is stabilising, more collectors are buying, and galleries are more confident of the future.

This is in part due to the growing success of ARCO and PHotoEspaña, combined with a new savvy on the part of the galleries. Some of the best have grouped together as associations: in many galleries you can pick up a brochure featuring a gallery map from either the Asociación de Galerías de Arte de Madrid (www.artemadrid.com) or the association Galerías del 28012/28014 (the postcodes of some of the city's best galleries). Furthermore, provincial Madrid is slowly giving way to worldly Madrid – galleries are refining their skills in promoting Spanish artists abroad while tuning in to the most avant-garde art movements of London, New York and Paris (*see also p206* **Going global**).

In a complementary blend of institutional muscle from the big guys and spunk from the smaller galleries, the streets surrounding the Reina Sofía are gradually transforming into the city's art nexus, and major banks are creating plush new art centres in the area. Most notably, La Caixa is in the process of building a multi-million-euro cultural centre, designed by Herzog & de Meuron. Gallery owners are picking up on this creative momentum: twice a year – once at the beginning of autumn and again during ARCO – Galerías del 28012/28014 co-ordinates opening parties on the same night, resulting in something akin to a neighbourhood gallery crawl. Enhancing the artsy vibe, each June PHotoEspaña (*see p194*) adorns C/Huertas with photography in the streets and hosts popular summer slide shows in Plaza Santa Ana. Another enterprising idea in the neighbourhood is the Escaparate de San Pedro: a small window at C/San Pedro 9 shows a new photograph each month in an effort to introduce passers-by to photography. The photos can be purchased online at www.elescaparatedesanpedro.com.

Madrid's galleries generally exist in clusters, with many lining the same streets. The grandest galleries tend to be around Alonso Martínez and Colón metros, with plenty of interesting places in the environs of C/San Pedro and C/Doctor Fourquet in the Antón Martin and Lavapiés areas. As well as the association brochures, you can pick up the free monthly magazine *Guiarte* in galleries or tourist offices to see who's exhibiting where. The *Guía del Ocio* and local newspapers also provide up-to-date exhibition information.

Huertas & Santa Ana

Ángel Romero
C/San Pedro 5 (91 429 32 08/www.galeriaangel romero.com). Metro Atocha. **Open** 11am-2pm, 5.30-8.30pm Mon-Sat. Closed July-mid Sept. **No credit cards. Map** p314 G9.
A beautiful gallery with a cavernous basement, which has previously shown some of Spain's most intriguing young artists. In recent years its scope has become more international, with artists from Cuba, France and Germany. Keep an eye out for young German painter Barbara Stammel.

Galería Carmen de la Guerra
C/San Pedro 6 (91 420 03 55/www.carmendela guerra.com). Metro Antón Martín. **Open** 11am-2pm, 5-9pm Tue-Sat. Closed Aug. **No credit cards. Map** p314 G9.
Popular with young artists and collectors, Carmen de la Guerra is innovative, fun and often whimsical (its performance art being a prime example). Spanish actor Jordi Molla exhibits his painting and photography here; other interesting names to look out for include Soledad Cordoba and David Trullo. The musty downstairs cave dates from 1864; it was originally used as a bakery but now exhibits installation and video projects.

Galería La Fábrica
C/Alameda 9 (91 360 13 20/www.lafabrica galeria.com). Metro Atocha. **Open** 11am-2pm, 5-8.30pm Tue-Sat. Closed Aug. **No credit cards. Map** p314 G9.
La Fábrica is a hub of the Madrid art world, heavily involved in exhibitions such as PHotoEspaña. It exhibits major-league as well as up-and-coming artists and is known for its insights into photography. On Mondays in autumn the gallery hosts Los Lunes de la Fábrica – parties and/or book presentations attended by Madrid's arty crowd. It also publishes art books and, in collaboration with website www.notodo.com, organises art competitions.

Galería La Fábrica.
See p203.

Lavapiés

Cruce

C/Dr Fourquet 5 (91 528 77 83). Metro Atocha. **Open**
5.30-9.30pm Tue-Sat. Closed Aug. **Map** p313 F10.
More than just a gallery, Cruce is a community hub
for young Spanish artists, poets and intellectuals. In
addition to fun and outlandish exhibitions, it hosts
book presentations, concerts and poetry readings.
Pick up the monthly schedule to see what's on.

Salvador Díaz

C/Sánchez Bustillo 7 (91 527 4000/www.salvador
diaz.net). Metro Atocha. **Open** 11am-2pm, 4.30-
8.30pm Mon-Fri; 11am-2pm Sat. Closed Aug.
No credit cards. Map p314 G9.
Located just across the plaza from the Reina Sofía,
this is a lovely space to browse. It's open and spacious, and shows new talents in contemporary photography, sculpture and installation work.

Chueca

Antonio Machón

C/Conde de Xiquena 8 (91 532 40 93). Metro
Chueca. **Open** 11am-2pm, 5-9pm Tue-Sat. Closed
Aug. **No credit cards. Map** p310 H5.
Machón has long dealt with famous older artists like
Tàpies, Bonifacio and Jordi Teixidor, but also works
with new talents such as Ángeles San José, Alberto
Requera and Chema Cobo. In particular, the gallery
has a real eye for monochromes and abstract art.

Arnés y Röpke

C/Conde Xiquena 14 (91 702 14 92/www.galeria
arnesyropke.com). Metro Chueca. **Open** 5-9pm
Mon; 11am-2pm, 5-9pm Tue-Fri; 11am-2pm Sat.
No credit cards. Map p310 H5.
The owners of this gallery are a Spanish/German
duo who promote abstract and figurative art (photography is a forte). They have been successful in
bringing European contemporary art to Spain and
Spain's avant-garde to the rest of the world. If you
can, try to catch a show by Arnold Odermatt.

Edurne

C/Justiniano 3 (91 310 06 51/www.galeria
edurne.com). Metro Alonso Martínez. **Open** 11am-
2pm, 6-9pm Mon-Fri; noon-1.30pm, 6-8.30pm Sat.
Closed Aug. **No credit cards. Map** p311 H4.
In 1964, despite the controlling eyes of the dictatorship, Margarita de Lucas and Antonio de Navascues
opened Edurne, the first gallery of its kind. This
engaging pair is credited with promoting many of
Spain's top artists when they were just starting out.
Luis Gordillo, Antonio Saura and Gerardo Rueda are
among the earlier protégés; recent exhibitions include
Enrique Veganzones and Andrés Monteagudo.

Elba Benítez

C/San Lorenzo 11 (91 308 04 68/www.elba
benitez.com). Metro Tribunal. **Open** 11am-2pm,
4.30-8.30pm Tue-Sat. Closed Aug. **No credit
cards. Map** p310 G4.
Located in the courtyard of a faded old villa, this is
a pleasant gallery to wander through. Elba Benítez
promotes Spanish art abroad, although her repertoire also includes international artists. The art is
very modern, with an emphasis on photography,
video and installation pieces.

Elvira González

C/General Castaños 3 (91 319 59 00). Metro Colón.
Open Nov-May 10.30am-2pm, 4.30-8.30pm Mon-Fri;
11am-2pm, 6-9pm Sat. June, July, Sept, Oct 10.30am-
2pm Mon-Fri; 11am-2pm Sat. Closed Aug. **No
credit cards. Map** p310 H4.
One of the most distinguished galleries in Madrid,
this is an appealing enclave of contemporary art,
both Spanish and international. LeWitt, Lichtenstein,
Warhol and Picasso have all featured in the past.

Galería La Caja Negra

C/Fernando VI 17, 2° izq (91 310 43 60/
www.lacajanegra.com). Metro Alonso Martínez.
Open 10am-2pm, 5-9pm Mon-Sat. Closed Aug.
Credit AmEx, DC, MC, V. **Map** p310 H4.
Something of a leader on the local art scene, representing international mega artists in addition to
famous Spanish contemporary artists. La Caja

Negra specialises in original graphic works, photography and illustrated books. Chillida, Tàpies, Barceló, Antonio Saura, Richard Serra and even Picasso are all to be found here, while the internationals include Braque, LeWitt, Rauschenberg, Robert Motherwell and Keith Haring.

Galería Juana de Aizpuru

C/Barquillo 44, 1º (91 310 55 61/www.galeria juanadeaizpuru.com). Metro Chueca. **Open** 4.30-8.30pm Mon; 10.30am-2pm, 4.30-8.30pm Tue-Sat. **No credit cards. Map** p310 H5.
Madrid's *grande dame* of vanguard photography has been setting the standard since 1983. Juana is known and loved worldwide and represents such local photography luminaries as Alberto Garcia Alex and Cristina García Rodero. Foreign artists who grace the walls include Joel Peter Witkin, William Wegman and Sol Lewitt. Installation work, video and sculpture also feature.

Heinrich Ehrhardt

C/San Lorenzo 11 (91 310 44 15/www.henrich ehrhart.com). Metro Chueca. **Open** 11am-2pm Tue-Sat. **Credit** AmEx. **Map** p310 G4.
This contemporary gallery originally endeavoured to introduce Madrid to German artists such as Joseph Beuys and Baselitz. In the past few years, however, it has expanded its scope to include several young Spanish artists such as Ángel Borrego and Secundino Hernández.

Moriarty

C/Almirante 5, 1º (91 531 43 65/www.galeria moriarty.com). Metro Chueca. **Open** 11am-2pm, 5-8.30pm Tue-Fri; 11am-2pm Sat. Closed July, Aug. **Credit** V. **Map** p310 H5.
Established in 1981, Lola Moriarty's gallery was a prime hangout and showcase for artists on the Movida scene, and today still supports the Spanish avant-garde and contemporary art scene. Some of her current top artists are photographers: the renowned duo Walter Martin and Paloma Muñoz, the surrealist talent Chema Madoz, and Atsuko Arai.

Sen

C/Barquillo 43 (91 319 16 71/www.galeriasen.com). Metro Chueca. **Open** 11am-2pm, 4.30-8.30pm Mon-Fri; 11am-2pm Sat. Closed Aug. **No credit cards. Map** p310 H5.
Sen is another Movida-related gallery, and helped fringe artists like Costus and Ceesepe earn the respect of critics. It exhibits both established and up-and-coming names in various media – painting, sculpture and photography. Two of its top photographers include Pamela Spitz and Ouka Lele.

Salamanca

Guillermo de Osma

C/Claudio Coello 4, 1º izq (91 435 59 36/www. guillermodeosma.com). Metro Retiro. **Open** 10am-2pm, 4.30-8.30pm Mon-Fri; noon-2pm Sat. **No credit cards. Map** p314 I6.

A classic on the Madrid art scene, Guillermo de Osma specialises in artists from the avant-garde movements of 1910-40 and holds five to six shows a year, always accompanied by a superb catalogue. In the past it has worked with the crème de la crème of the art world: Picasso, Braque, Oscar Dominguez and Torres García, to name but a few.

Oliva Arauna

C/Claudio Coello 19 (91 435 18 08/www.oliva arauna.com). Metro Retiro or Serrano. **Open** 4.30pm-8.30pm Mon; 11am-2pm, 4.30-8.30pm Tue-Sat. Closed Aug. **No credit cards. Map** p311 I5.
Another empress of contemporary art, Oliva Arauna has a taste for large, bold, challenging photographs and slick minimalist sculpture. A small but impressive gallery, this is a good place to get a glimpse of Spain's most inventive photographers. Concha Prada, in particular, is one to watch.

Chamberí

Estiarte

C/Almagro 44 (91 308 15 69/70/www.estiarte. com). Metro Rubén Darío. **Open** 10am-2pm, 4.30-8.30pm Mon-Fri; 10am-2pm, 5-9pm Sat. **Credit** DC, MC, V. **Map** p310 H2.
This gallery has specialised in original graphics for 30 years and represents many big names, past and present – Miquel Barceló, Max Ernst, José María Sicilia, Eva Lootz, Calder, Chillida and Picasso.

Galería Javier López

C/Manuel González Longoria 7 (91 593 21 84/ www.galeriajavierlopez.com). Metro Alonso Martínez. **Open** 11am-2pm, 5-9pm Tue-Sat. Closed Aug. **No credit cards. Map** p310 G3.
Javier López is a well-known figure on the Madrid art circuit. The gallery originally opened in London, but moved to Madrid in 1996, and shows artists as prestigious – and diverse – as Donald Judd, Andreas Gursky, Edward Ruscha and Hiroshu Sugimoto.

Galería Soledad Lorenzo

C/Orfila 5 (91 308 28 87/www.soledadlorenzo.com). Metro Alonso Martínez. **Open** 4.30-8.30pm Mon; 11am-2pm, 4.30-8.30pm Tue-Sat. Closed Aug. **No credit cards. Map** p310 H4.
A forerunner among Madrid's galleries, this large, beautiful space shows highly contemporary installation work, video, painting and photography. The artists are primarily Spanish, and include the likes of Miguel Barceló, Tàpies and Julian Schnabel.

Marlborough

C/Orfila 5 (91 319 14 14/www.galeriamarl borough.com). Metro Alonso Martínez. **Open** Sept-July 11am-2pm, 4.30-8.30pm Mon-Sat. Closed Aug. **Credit** MC, V. **Map** p310 H4.
This luminary of the Madrid art world represents Spanish artists such as Antonio Saura, Blanca Muñoz and Luis Gordillo, and has branches in London, New York, Monte Carlo and Santiago. In the past it has also collaborated with international

artists – David Hockney and Francis Bacon, to name but two. The expansive space, designed by US architect Richard Gluckman, is a work of art in itself. Note that the gallery sometimes closes for the afternoon in summer.

ARCO

Feria de Madrid (91 722 50 00/www.arcospain. org). Metro Campo de las Naciones. **Dates** 9-14 Feb 2005, 9-13 Feb 2006. **Open** noon-9pm Mon-Sat. **Admission** €30 Thur; from €28 Fri, Sat; from €24 Sun, Mon. **Credit** varies.

While the Arte Contemporáneo (ARCO) fair has been around since 1982, it has only recently gained major international kudos. Now scores of Spanish and foreign art heavyweights pack into the city for a week each February, seeking out the latest art trends. In 2004, 274 galleries from 32 different countries set up stalls at the Parque Ferial Juan Carlos I, transforming the pavilion into a colourful sea of contemporary art. It has become so big, in fact, that a few of the local galleries that have long been involved have been booted from the line-up, creating much resentment. Regardless, ARCO has become the primary showcase to expose Spanish talents to the rest of the world.

Going global

Artistically speaking, Madrid has long had a reputation for looking inwards, for not caring for art originating outside Spain – or even outside the city, for that matter. Much of this isolationism can be blamed on the 36-year cross-cultural blockade the country suffered under Franco. Even today, many gallery owners still feel that Madrid lags about four decades behind other European capitals.

But the city is catching up. In the last few years, foreign names have begun to appear regularly in exhibitions, and many more overseas artists have moved here, stimulating a mutual flow of art awareness. There are now many local galleries working in tandem with a foreign branch: cool, contemporary **Marina Miranda** (C/Fúcar 12, 91 420 22 38), for example, fosters art *intercambios* with Portugal, and the Argentine-run **Centro de Arte Moderno** (C/Gobernador 25, 91 429 8363, www.cam.org.ar) promotes a Spanish/Latin American exchange, especially in the field of photography. The growth of the ARCO and PHotoEspaña art fairs have also given Madrid a strong push into the international limelight.

Helga de Alvear, a feisty, fashionable German gallery owner who has lived in Madrid for over 40 years and runs her eponymous gallery, is a leader in internationalising the city's art climate. Not that this is intentional: as she puts it, 'For me, art doesn't have a nationality. I don't care about nationality as long as I like it.' Nonetheless, the artists she selects tend to be international: British filmmaker Isaac Julien, Australian photographer Tracey Moffatt and Canadian artist Christine Davis, for example.

Alvear opened the gallery in 1979 when her friend, artist Juana Mordó, was struggling to

Helga de Alvear.

sell her art. In the early days, Alvear represented many of Madrid's famous local talents, and still does, even though she now has a very international scope. She explains, 'I have seen many changes in the art world here. Madrid is now much more international. People in Madrid are starting to travel; they are reading and learning about culture. Art awareness is something that has to be learned, and Madrid is only now opening up'.

Even so, change has been very slow to manifest itself. Several gallery owners maintain that a good number of local collectors will still only buy what they know and what they have seen before, and there are still those who think that painting is the only respectable art for their homes – not photography or installation work. But Alvear remains hopeful: 'The traditional mindset will start to change. People will catch on.'

Helga de Alvear

C/Dr Fourquet 12 (91 468 05 06/www.helga dealvear.net). Metro Atocha. **Open** *Sept-June* 11am-2pm, 4.30-8.30pm Tue-Sat. *July* 11am-2pm, 4.30-8.30pm Tue-Fri; 11am-2pm Sat. Closed Aug. **No credit cards. Map** p314 G9.

Gay & Lesbian

Darkrooms, cabins, golden nights and cottaging: Madrid's gay scene is not for the faint-hearted.

Smoke. *See p213.*

Chueca both is and isn't a ghetto. Given Madrid's general acceptance and support of gay life, the *barrio* is now fully embraced by *madrileños* as one of the most stylish destinations for shopping and nightlife – and simply sitting in cafés. The elitism of gay 'hoods in other major cities has faded here, and has been replaced with a mix of tolerance, individualism, innovation and old-world Spain. It might sound like a cliché, but it's not uncommon to see construction workers and black-clad old women sipping an early-morning coffee with *churros* alongside the spent and unkempt boys piling out of the leather bars. And it's not just a question of unwitting demographic integration: the turnout for Gay Pride in June 2004 hit an astounding million, meaning that heterosexuals gatecrashed the party in their hundreds of thousands.

The throbbing heart of the scene (*el ambiente*) is the Plaza de Chueca. Tightly packed around what is an otherwise nondescript square in the centre of town, it's home to a dazzling array of bars and services aimed almost exclusively at one of Madrid's most vociferous and certainly most dynamic communities. With bars, cafés, hotels, saunas, travel agencies and bookshops, the formerly run-down neighbourhood has emerged as one of the city's most vibrant and trendy areas. But Chueca has become, perhaps, a victim of its own success, its hip hangouts attracting a non-gay crowd in recent years. Now, many want their ghetto back, at least for cruising, and plenty of shag-and-go gay male-only bars have popped up all over the place. Special events aimed at specific subcultures are a growth industry too: there are camping weekends in the nearby mountains for bears, an action-packed 'Sleazy Madrid' long weekend every spring, plus lesbian raves with dykey darkrooms, body-shaving bashes and sloppy mud parties.

PUBLICATIONS

Some of the best of the free publications lying around in bars are *Shangay Express* newspaper – or its pocket-sized companion volume with listings on the gay and lesbian scene throughout Spain; *Odisea*, which deals more with social and political issues and publishes a handy map of the scene; or *Revista Mensual*, sold at news kiosks (its personal ads are riveting). Fetish fans (men only) should look out for *Phetix*, a free quarterly guide to all the sex clubs and parties.

There are also some good websites, all with guides to the scene plus nifty extra features, such as personals and access to chat. Try www.mensual.com, www.chueca.com, www.vozgay.com or www.naciongay.com and its sister site www.guiagay.com.

Cafés & restaurants

As well as the following (all of which are in Chueca), other restaurants that are noticeably popular among the gay community include **Bazaar** (*see p130*), **Suite** (*see p125*), **El Armario** (*see p130*), **La Dame Noire** (*see p134*), **Gula Gula** (*see p125*) and **El 26 de Libertad** (*see p130*). **Ángel Sierra** (C/Gravina 11, 91 531 01 26), while not a gay bar per se, is smack on the Plaza de Chueca and therefore an ideal way to start the evening.

Café Acuarela

C/Gravina 10 (91 522 21 43). Metro Chueca. **Open** 3pm-3am daily. **Credit** MC, V. **Map** p310 G5.
By day this is a quiet, mixed haven to duck into and catch your breath. Curl up with a book and sample one of the teas. After sundown, sip a cocktail, sink into a deep sofa and admire the decor – a mix of kitsch, retro glamour and exuberant baroque.

Café Figueroa

C/Augusto Figueroa 17 (91 521 16 73). Metro Chueca. **Open** *Oct-May* noon-1am Mon-Thur; noon-2.30am Fri, Sat; 4pm-1am Sun. *June-Sept* 4.30-11.30pm daily. **No credit cards. Map** p310 G5.
Madrid's original gay café is a sedate place where the lace curtains, 19th-century chandeliers and winding wooden staircase lend themselves nicely to a cosy destination for those who want gay in an old Spain way. There's a pool table upstairs.

Café La Troje

C/Pelayo 26 (91 531 05 35). Metro Chueca. **Open** 2pm-2am Mon-Thur, Sun; 2pm-2.30am Fri, Sat. **No credit cards. Map** p310 G5.
A romantic and popular stop, with friendly service and screens playing chill-out videos. It gets chockfull at weekends with an amiable and mixed crowd, who are generally on their way somewhere else.

Colby Urban

C/Fuencarral 52 (91 521 25 54). Metro Chueca. **Open** 10am-1am Mon-Thur; 10am-2.30am Fri, Sat; noon-1am Sun. **Credit** AmEx, MC, V. **Map** p310 G5.
It's red, it's urban, it's aspirational. Colby Urban is the flagship of a string of cool eateries and chilled-out cafés with a concept. We're not sure what the concept is, but the location is handy, the custom is pretty and the diner-style food hits the spot.

D'Mystic

C/Gravina 5 (91 308 24 60/www.dmystic.net). Metro Chueca. **Open** 10am-2pm daily. **Credit** DC, MC, V. **Map** p310 G5.
This den of cool is located at a strategic crosssroads, with bigger-than-average cocktails that make up for the aloof staff. Watch the real world stroll by outside or gaze at the natural world on the New Agey videos on the screens inside. Relax, listen to the whale songs and the waterfalls. Then get out and head for Eagle (*see p210*).

Diurno

C/San Marcos 37 (91 522 00 09). Metro Chueca. **Open** 10am-midnight Mon-Thur; 10am-1am Fri; 11am-1am Sat, Sun. **Credit** MC, V. **Map** p310 G5.
A minimalist and sexy film-rental café spinning all-day chill-out sounds (and occasional techno). As well as a fabulous selection of movies, there are delicious sandwiches, salads, pasta dishes and cakes. A peaceful place to start the day, upbeat and lively at night.

Laan Café

C/Pelayo 28 (91 552 68 61). Metro Chueca. **Open** 10am-1.30am Mon-Thur; 10am-2.30am Fri, Sat. **No credit cards. Map** p310 G5.
Plonk yourself on the banquettes here and you risk being smothered by the giant red cushions. This otherwise slick and somewhat stark café is great for people-watching, chatting and getting stuck into the fab chocolate cake. In the mornings breakfast and fresh juices are served, while at night the vibe segues into buzzing New York.

Mama Inés

C/Hortaleza 22 (91 523 23 33). Metro Gran Via. **Open** 10am-2am daily. **No credit cards. Map** p310 G5.
Another place to successfully combine a decent breakfast with plenty of eye candy. Chill-out and nu flamenco waft through this modern but surprisingly intimate café during the day, while at night house takes over and the T-shirts get progressively tighter.

Pink Pollo

C/Infantas 18 (91 531 16 75/www.pinkpollo.com). Metro Banco de España. **Open** 1.30-4pm, 8pm-midnight daily. **Credit** MC, V. **Map** p314 G6.
There are times when only chicken and chips delivered to your hotel room by a strippergram dressed as a gay pink rooster will do. Having filled this blindingly obvious gap in the market, Pink Pollo also provides a diner-style fast-food restaurant, fetchingly done up in pastels and chock-full of kitsch.

XXX Café

C/Clavel, corner C/Reina (91 522 37 77). Metro Gran Via. **Open** 3.30pm-2am Mon-Thur, Sun; 3.30pm-3am Fri, Sat. **Credit** MC, V. **Map** p313 F6.
Quiet until the pre-dinner crowd arrives to shake it up, this is a small and popular meeting point where the staff are gorgeous and the regulars friendly. Park yourself by the window for the best view – with any luck, you'll be snapped up in no time.

Clubs & *discobares*

A *discobar* treads the line between club and regular drinking den. Admission is generally free (exceptions are noted below), and there is normally a diminutive dancefloor to justify the pricier-than-average drinks.

As well as the venues below, **Ohm** (*see p229*) and **Weekend** (*see p229*) also have a big gay following, as does **Space of Sound** (*p238*) on a Sunday from midnight to 6am Monday morning. Unless otherwise stated, all of the following are in Chueca.

Black & White

C/Libertad 34 (91 531 11 41). Metro Chueca. **Open** 10pm-5am daily. **No credit cards. Map** p310 G5.
The grubby upstairs bar is a hit with cocky *latino* rent boys and their older prospective patrons and plays host to some of the best cabaret shows in town. Downstairs things really liven up in the heaving *discobar* that is popular with revellers of all ages and orientations. A classic.

Kapital Love

C/Atocha 125, Huertas & Santa Ana (91 420 29 06). Metro Atocha. **Open** midnight-7am Sun. **Admission** €16. **Credit** AmEx, DC, MC, V. **Map** p314 G9.
Another palace to brighten up dull Sundays. Keep your bearings as you make your way through Madrid's megaclub, and head for the gay corner of this empire of decadence and dance. *See also p231*.

Liquid

C/Barquillo 8 (91 532 74 28/www.liquid.es). Metro Chueca. **Open** 9pm-3am Mon-Thur, Sun; 9pm-4am Fri, Sat. **Credit** AmEx, DC, MC, V. **Map** p310 H5.
A cool, happening place in which to see and be seen, with a contemporary, minimalist interior. The emphasis is on watching the parade of heavenly bodies – if, that is, you can take your eyes off the megascreens showing the latest dance music videos.

Pink Flamingo

Sala Flamingo, C/Gran Via 34 (91 541 35 00/ www.tripfamily.com). Metro Gran Via. **Open** midnight-5am Thur. **Admission** (incl 1 drink) €7. **No credit cards. Map** p313 E6.
The only real gay dance club on Thursday nights really does pack 'em in. When it's really busy there's hardly room to gyrate as Madrid's top DJ Kike Boy pumps out the goods at this wild, slightly run-down venue, popular with a hip, young dancey crowd.

Pride

Palacio de Gaviria, C/Arenal 9, Sol & Gran Via (91 526 60 69). Metro Ópera. **Open** 8pm-5am 1st Sun of mth. **Admission** €15. **Credit** AmEx, DC, MC, V. **Map** p313 D7.
Be queen for a Sunday night, in the sumptuous splendour of the former palace of Isabel II's lover. This is truly one of the most incredible places to dance and cruise with style. Explore the *belle époque*

Liquid refreshment.

19th-century state rooms and hall of mirrors, then settle on your favourite *ambiente*. Drag acts, bingo and cool DJs keep things moving, and lesbians hold court in their very own chambers.

Queen Madrid

C/Barbieri 7 (no phone). Metro Chueca. **Open** 10pm-2.30am Mon-Thur, Sun; 10pm-3.30am Fri, Sat. **Admission** (minimum consumption €7). **No credit cards. Map** p313 F6.
Catering for the overflow from nearby Why Not? (*see p210*), this big, brash, fun *discobar* gets packed with a young, mixed crowd who dance the night away to an eclectic mix of bouncy hi-NRG and naff Spanish golden oldies. When this pales you can always eye up the gorgeous bar staff.

Rick's

C/Clavel 8 (no phone). Metro Gran Via. **Open** 11.30pm-6.30am Mon-Thur, Sun; 11pm-7am Fri, Sat. **Admission** (incl 1 drink) €7. **No credit cards. Map** p313 F6.
Expensive drinks and an expensive, older crowd are the hallmarks of this friendly late-night alternative to the discos. With hi-NRG beats and camp Spanish hits, it's standing-room only at weekends.

Royal Coolture at Cool

C/Isabel la Católica 6, Sol (91 542 34 39). Metro Santo Domingo. **Open** midnight-6am Fri, Sat. **Admission** (incl 1 drink) €15. **No credit cards. Map** p309 D5.
The *número uno* place to be on Friday and Saturday nights. Snarling caged gogos, preening Muscle Marys, serious shirtless studs with sweaty torsos,

Arts & Entertainment

spaced-out twentysomethings and gorgeous waiters are all part of the coolture at this slick, designerish two-floored club. Join them on the throbbing dance-floor or bop to the handbag music upstairs.

Sunrise

C/Barbieri 7 (91 523 28 08). Metro Chueca. **Open** midnight-6am Thur-Sat. **Credit** MC, V. **Map** p313 F6.

If you can make it past the menacing doormen in bad suits, a smart red interior awaits you, filled with a designer-clad young crowd.

Why Not?

C/San Bartolomé 7 (91 521 80 34). Metro Chueca or Gran Vía. **Open** 10.30pm-6.30am daily. **Credit** DC, MC, V. **Map** p313 F6.

It's almost impossible not to make new friends, or indeed to avoid grinding against them, in this packed but charming subterranean dungeon.The music's great, the mixed crowd young, hip and intent on having a good time. The drinks don't come cheap, but with free entrance it's still a good alternative to the clubs.

Exclusively male/hardcore

Bangalá

C/Escuadra 1, Lavapiés (no phone). Metro Lavapiés. **Open** 10pm-2am daily. **Admission** free. **No credit cards. Map** p313 F9.

It's sleek. It's black. It's red. Bangalá is the latest addition to the Lavapiés scene and promises to outdo its rivals with fetisho-licious nights such as Night of Tongues or Dawn of the Vampires. Behind the bar are two pristine darkrooms and a few cabins.

Copper

C/San Vicente Ferrer 34, Malasaña (no phone/ www.copperbar.net). Metro Tribunal. **Open** 8pm-3am Mon-Thur; 8pm-3.30am Fri-Sat; 5pm-3am Sun. **Admission** (incl 1 drink) €7. **No credit cards. Map** p309 F4.

The friendly guys at this sloppy, sweaty club got tired of trying to enforce the dress code so now it's nearly always naked, underwear or jock-strap fun (check the website). There's a chatty crowd out front, and popular large backroom.

Cruising

C/Pérez Galdós 5, Chueca (91 521 51 43). Metro Chueca. **Open** 6pm-3am Mon-Thur, Sun; 6pm-3.30am Fri, Sat. **No credit cards. Map** p310 G5.

A fun, sleazy cruising club that puts the 'laid' into 'laid-back'. Upstairs there's a quieter pub-like area, and a diminutive porn cinema; downstairs there's a dancefloor and a spacious public loo-like darkroom. The place could do with a lick of paint but its faded glory is part of its enduring charm.

Eagle

C/Pelayo 30, Chueca (no phone). Metro Chueca. **Open** noon-2am Mon-Fri; 6pm-3am Sat, Sun. **Admission** free. **No credit cards. Map** p310 G5.

The nerve centre of the fetish scene, where boots, chaps and handcuffs are all that the well-dressed devotee need worry about packing. The small and cramped downstairs gives way to an even tighter squeeze in the upstairs play area, where the real boys are to be found. You might chance upon Leather Night, Uniform Night or – if you really hit the jackpot – Golden Night.

Hell

C/Buenavista 14, Lavapiés (no phone/www. hellsexclub.com). Metro Antón Martín. **Open** 10.30pm-3am Tue-Fri; 11.30pm-3.30am Sat, Sun. **Admission** free. **No credit cards. Map** p313 F9.

A tiny and rough fetish club with hard cruising. Tuesday nights are nude while Saturdays are given over to kinky underwear parties. Wednesday is Noche Sport ('sneaker sex' is how they describe it), while Thursdays are for exhibitionists and those who like to watch them. Other nights are devoted to private parties or special events. Log on to the titillating website for details.

Hot

C/Infantas 9, Chueca (91 522 84 48/www.barhot. com). Metro Chueca. **Open** 6pm-3am Mon-Thur, Sun; 6pm-3.30am Fri, Sat. **Admission** free. **No credit cards. Map** p313 F6.

Hot, hairy, homo heaven at this fun bear den for hir-sute late thirty- and fortysomethings. Things get even hotter downstairs in the darkroom. Two drinks for the price of one, every day until midnight.

New Leather Bar

C/Pelayo 42, Chueca (91 308 14 62). Metro Chueca. **Open** 8pm-3am daily. **Admission** free. **No credit cards. Map** p310 G5.

The name of this big, two-floor hangout is a bit misleading as little leather is in evidence, but the crowd is raunchy, and can be found in the large darkroom or lurking in anticipation in the cabins. Check out the individual movie screens over the urinals.

Odarko

C/Loreto Chicote 7, Malasaña (no phone/www. odarko.com). Metro Callao. **Open** 10pm-4am Thur-Sat; 6pm-4am Sun. **Admission** (incl 1 drink) €7-€10. **Credit** DC, MC, V. **Map** p313 E6.

The seedy backstreets off Gran Vía make the perfect approach to this lively sex club, where chains chink, bars rattle and boots scuff the soiled floor. Dress code is strictly enforced on weekends and some of the nights are pretty full-on. Check the website in advance, lest you turn up in your crisp new Fred Perry top to find it's the Wild & Wet Piss session. Improbably, the owners also run a little B&B business upstairs.

The Paw

C/Calatrava 29, La Latina (no phone/www.thepaw madrid.com). Metro Puerta de Toledo. **Open** 10pm-6am Wed, Thur, Sun; midnight-8am Fri, Sat. **Admission** (incl 1 or 2 drinks) €11-€15. **No credit cards. Map** p312 C9.

Formerly known as Into The Tank, this louche little joint is off the beaten track but well worth the effort for dress code and fetish fans. If you forgot to pack your cop uniform, don't worry, you can go naked every night. Check out the hot underwear parties: log on to the website for all the lurid details.

Strong Center

C/Trujillos 7, Sol & Gran Vía (91 541 54 15). Metro Ópera. **Open** midnight-7am daily. **Admission** (incl 2 drinks) €8 Mon-Thur, Sun; €10 Fri, Sat. **No credit cards. Map** p313 D7.

The dancefloor at the Strong Center is a forlorn, empty place. Don't dismay, however, as no one comes here for the music, and you're just about to discover Spain's biggest and most labyrinthine darkroom, where you can lose yourself among hundreds of hot, horny men.

Saunas

Men

C/Pelayo 25, Chueca (91 531 25 83). Metro Chueca. **Open** 3.30pm-8am daily. **Admission** €9; €4 under-25s. **No credit cards. Map** p310 G5.

A small, dowdy sauna with a perplexing door policy (thought cute young guys are usually safe). Located right at the heart of the gay scene, Men is always rammed with a cross-section of gay Madrid. There's a bar, darkroom and a few cabins in which to spend a steamy hour or two.

Paraíso Sauna

C/Norte 15, Conde Duque (91 531 98 91). Metro Noviciado. **Open** noon-midnight daily. **Admission** €12. **No credit cards. Map** p309 E4.

Located in what used to be a popular flamenco club, this extensive, spotlessly clean sauna has maintained its original evocative mosaics. The young, hunky clients often seem more interested in their own well-toned pecs than in you, but there is a small pool, porn cinema, bar, darkroom and cabins as consolation. Massage and sunbeds are also available, though rarely solicited.

Sauna Príncipe

Travesía Beatas 3, Malasaña (91 548 22 18). Metro Santo Domingo. **Open** 2pm-midnight daily. **Admission** €10. **No credit cards. Map** p313 F8.

This sauna is better equipped than its rivals and caters for a varied crowd, though it's particularly popular with bears, not to mention tourists.

Gay & lesbian shops

Amantis

C/Pelayo 46, Chueca (91 702 05 11). Metro Chueca. **Open** 11am-10pm Mon-Sat; 6.30-10pm Sun. **Credit** AmEx, DC, MC, V. **Map** p310 G5.

The most discreet of the sex shops in terms of location, with a sunny small-town shop feel. It's filled with condoms, lube, improbable dildos, porn mags, videos and DVDs.

Berkana

C/Hortaleza 64, Chueca (91 532 13 93). Metro Chueca. **Open** 10.30am-9pm Mon-Fri; 11.30am-9pm Sat; noon-2pm, 5-9pm Sun. **Credit** AmEx, DC, MC, V. **Map** p310 G5.

There are books and videos in English, and staff are friendly and helpful. Browsing is encouraged and you can linger over erotica at the in-store café.

La Lupe. *See p213.*

Arts & Entertainment

Movida Marys

The sangría, the tapas, the all-night clubbing, the funky boutiques, the plaza-cruising – it's all divinely *divertido*, but where do you go when you want something a little more, well, cultural? Almodóvar only comes out with one film every couple of years, and although there's Gay Pride, there's no gay Prado. (Although there is that rather scorching Velázquez, *The Forge of Vulcan*, with gorgeous Apollo and his shirtless buddies).

So thank heavens for theatre. In recent years the Madrid stage has seen a revolution of freedom and innovation, which has given rise to a stunning explosion of gay-themed dance, narrative and comedy pieces that are selling out night after night, and not only to strictly gay audiences. Fancy sitting in a front row holding a urinal in your arms, say, while three hot young Spaniards simulate cottaging? Or hearing the heart-straining poetry of a young woman's coming-out saga as she not only undresses on stage but simultaneously peels away the layers of all that is expected of a long-imposed feminine archetype? Well, you're in luck.

And if you're worried about the language barrier, don't be. The city's foremost alternative theatre, **DT Espacio Escénico** (C/Reina 9, Chueca, 91 521 71 55), with its bold experimentation with space and narrative, is now in its fourth year of the Festival Versión Original, featuring dance and theatre works from around the world in their original language (including English). Perfectly suited to the electric and eclectic gay landscape of Madrid, it continues to offer extremely sexy and provocative pieces to the public, defying previously understood commercial theatre norms. Ground-breaking space-text-dance is successfully combined with theatre that seduces, informs, provokes and entertains all at once. Every year, to coincide with Gay Pride, the venue also holds a festival of original language, gay-themed dance and theatre pieces from around the globe.

La Sala Triángulo (C/Zurita 20, Lavapiés, 91 530 68 91) was one of the pioneers of the alternative theatre movement in the city, bursting on to the scene 16 years ago with instinct, foresight and an ear to the ground of vanguard Madrid theatre-going tastes. It has had nothing but sold-out audiences ever since. The work is characterised by mostly narrative pieces with socio-political themes and a leaning towards minorities and the marginalised. The company's aim is to place potentially charged topics in a context and stage design that an audience both young and modern in spirit can identify with.

Estudio Liberarte (Teatro Liberarte, C/Francisca Conde 7, Tetuán, 91 733 00 29) is the brainchild of two friends who started putting on plays in a tiny rented basement in 1996, until four years later when they took a risky purchase of an old car workshop in one of Madrid's working-class *barrios*, staging daring and original plays. Estudio Liberarte has become not only one of the capital's theatre companies at the vanguard of new gay theatre but also the darling of one of the less theatre-oriented parts of town, attracting long-time Tetuán denizens as well as the hip, young cosmopolitanites from the centre of Madrid. Though only eight members strong, it seems to be winning over young and old, straight and gay alike with its long-running hit comedy, *Gays Confessing at a Sausage Party*.

And if you don't happen to find anything in English, with the right frame of mind you will absorb more than you think. Theatre is the medium of gesture and emotion, of universal themes, of love and loss. It's in the air. And, hey, if you *really* don't get it, at least you might get a few scenes with sex and nudity.

City Sex Store

C/Hortaleza 18, Chueca (91 181 27 23). Metro Chueca. **Open** 11am-10pm Mon-Fri; 11am-11pm Sat; 12.30-9.30pm Sun. **Credit** AmEx, DC, MC, V. **Map** p310 G5.

Bright, shiny and well organised, City Sex Store is a veritable supermarket of porn, with merchandise spread out over two floors.

A Different Life

C/Pelayo 30, Chueca (91 532 96 52). Metro Chueca. **Open** 10.30am-9.30pm daily. **Credit** AmEx, DC, MC, V. **Map** p310 G5.

A well-stocked bookshop, with some titles in English, plus magazines and a range of cheesy gay gifts. Downstairs you'll find an eye-popping range of porn videos, which can be bought or rented.

Lambda Viajes

C/Fuencarral 43, Malasaña (91 532 78 33). Metro Chueca. **Open** 9.30am-2.30pm, 4.30-8pm Mon-Fri; 10am-1.30pm Sat. **Credit** MC, V. **Map** p310 G5.

This travel agency is aimed at a gay clientele, and can book rooms in gay hotels throughout Spain and abroad. It also offers package trips to various destinations. The helpful staff speak English.

SR

C/Pelayo 7, Chueca (91 523 19 64). Metro Chueca.
Open 5.30-10pm Mon; 11am-2pm, 5.30-10pm Tue-Sat. **Credit** AmEx, DC, MC, V. **Map** p310 G5.
Everything for the discerning leather and fetish fan.
Leatherwear, uniforms, rubber and SM gear, plus
indispensable accessories – masks, slings, chains
and handcuffs to help you turn that unused boxroom
into your very own dungeon. And no, we don't know
what the live crocodiles are for, either.

Lesbian Madrid

All those places for the boys, and barely enough
bars to make a decent pub crawl for lesbians –
what's a girl to do? Keep her eyes peeled, that's
what. Madrid's lesbian scene is growing, but it
still has a long way to go before catching up
with the gay male *ambiente*. There are lots of
one-nighters throughout the year, one organised
by the Supernenas and another by Diversité –
ask around, or look for flyers in the venues on
and near Plaza de Chueca. The square is where
you should start off, in any case: every bar
here seems to be lesbian-owned, though the
clientele is mixed.

Olivia.

Cafés, bars & clubs

As well as the following, other venues popular
with lesbians include **Café Acuarela** (*see
p208*) and **La Lupe** (C/Torrecilla del Leal 12,
91 527 50 19; *see also p232*).

El Barberillo de Lavapiés

C/Salitre 43, Lavapiés (no phone). Metro Antón
Martín or Lavapiés. **Open** 9pm-3am Tue-Thur, Sun;
9pm-4am Fri, Sat. **No credit cards. Map** p313 F9.
A quiet, relaxed café-bar in the heart of Lavapiés.
Worth a visit if you're in the area, though it rarely
gets busy. There are cards and board games for
those with a competitive streak.

Club Social de COGAM

C/Fuencarral 37, Chueca (91 522 45 17). Metro
Chueca or Tribunal. **Open** 5-10.30pm daily.
No credit cards. Map p310 G5.
A café run by the gay and lesbian association
COGAM (*see p285*), but most popular with women.
It's a nice place to go for a drink and find out what's
cooking on the political or social side of the scene.

Escape

C/Gravina 13, Chueca (91 532 52 06). Metro
Chueca. **Open** midnight-6am Tue-Sun. **Admission**
(incl 1 drink) €7. **No credit cards. Map** p310 G5.
This cavernous dancehall draped in bullfighter red
is one of the most popular destinations for women
and is filled to the brim with the sexiest *chicas* in the
city at the weekends. In fact, its popularity has spiralled to the extent that it's now one of the more boisterous clubs around Plaza de Chueca.

Íntima

Long Play, Plaza Vázquez de Mella 2, Chueca (no
phone/diversitemadrid@hotmail.com). Metro Chueca
or Gran Vía. **Open** midnight-6am 1st Thur of mth.
Admission (incl 1 drink) €8. **No credit cards.
Map** p313 F6.
The girls at Diversité event planners run this thriving monthly women-only night, which comes complete with Madrid's first and only lesbian darkroom.
Dance to the hard house and keep your raffle ticket
safe: top prizes include tattoos and piercings.

Medea

C/Cabeza 33, Lavapiés (no phone). Metro Antón
Martín or Tirso de Molina. **Open** 10pm-6am
Thur-Sat. **No credit cards. Map** p313 E9.
Though it has become a tad tatty in recent years,
this big no-nonsense women's disco is one of the
clear favourites on the lesbian scene. Men are admitted in the company of their Sapphic sisters.

Olivia

C/San Bartolomé 16, Chueca (no phone). Metro
Chueca. **Open** 10pm-3.30am Thur-Sat. **Admission**
free. **No credit cards. Map** p313 F6.
The decor's nothing to write home about but this
small, chatty den is chock-a-block with lipstick lesbians. The staff are approachable and the music fun.

Smoke

C/San Bartolomé 11, Chueca (no phone). Metro
Chueca. **Open** 8pm-2.30am Tue-Sun. **No credit
cards. Map** p313 F6.
Smoke? More like the whiff of diesel. This is not one
for the lipstick lesbian. Nonetheless, it's a really
friendly, relaxed crowd, amid the faded glamour of
an old Chueca *taberna*.

Truco

C/Gravina 10, Chueca (91 532 89 21). Metro
Chueca. **Open** 10pm-2.30am daily. **No credit
cards. Map** p310 G5.
Truco gets really crowded and with an extremely
young and loud crowd. However, this hi-octane corner joint is *the* place for gals looking for gals in the
earlier part of the evening, and a stone's throw from
the very popular girl bar, Escape.

Arts & Entertainment

Music

The high notes and low notes of a somewhat beleaguered scene.

Teatro Real. *See p216.*

Classical & Opera

Madrid's cultural clout has steadily increased over recent years and it is gradually shaking off a reputation for producing stuffy composers, ensembles with limited scope and a reactionary public. Today, while Madrid's home-grown orchestras may not be that highly reputed worldwide, credit must go to a city that depends predominantly on public funds to bring in top-class international musicians and ensembles to its worthy concert venues. Madrid has been particularly slated when it comes to contemporary music. But while this has not profited quite as much as contemporary art from the cultural interest shown by banks and businesses in recent times (thanks to the latter's sexier image), things have nevertheless been looking up with ever-increasing accessibility to concerts and recitals.

Traditionally, the scene orbits around three main venues: the modern and austere (and arguably the best-quality classical venue in Europe) **Auditorio Nacional**, the grand **Teatro Real**, hosting opera, and the **Teatro**
de la Zarzuela for a decent selection of classical concerts (as well as for *zarzuela*, Madrid's traditional operetta art form).

A word of advice for attending classical concerts in Madrid – get there early. The stereotypical Spanish tardiness is not a trait shared by classical music lovers.

ZARZUELA

Zarzuela is an ineffable part of *madrileño* culture, though tricky for the outsider to get a grip on. It was Spain's early answer to the Italian opera – shorter and funnier and incorporating elements of theatre, slapstick and dance. Golden Age playwrights Félix Lope de Vega and Pedro Calderón de la Barca were early pioneers of the genre, which was later developed by the likes of Ramón de la Cruz and the composer Federico de Chueca and, moving into the 20th century, Amadeo Vives and Jacinto Guerrero. *Zarzuela* is full of local jokes (usually rhyming and rattled off at speed) and traditional songs with which the public will sing along, so be prepared. Catch it in its home ground of the Teatro de la Zarzuela, in the Centro Cultural de la Villa in July or August, or at a summer open-air performance.

INFORMATION AND TICKETS

Check venue websites detailing current and future seasons, as well as any last-minute changes or cancellations. You can pick up leaflets from most of the venues – often quicker than trying to get through by phone – or check the *Guía del Ocio* or daily newspapers. Tickets can usually be bought via phone or internet from the venue itself (check venue listings) or from Tel-entrada or Caixa de Catalunya (902 10 12 12, www.telentradas.com). Tickets for state-run venues such as the Auditorio Nacional and the Teatro de la Zarzuela are sold at one another's box offices as well as ServiCaixa (902 33 22 11, ww3.serviticket.com).

You can get hold of Spanish classical music magazines in music and specialised record shops and main bookshops. The best are *Scherzo* (see also www.scherzo.es and go to *enlaces* and the month in question); *Ritmo* (or see www.ritmo.es and go to *vamos de concierto*), and *Ópera Actual* for opera, which is based in Barcelona but serves all of Spain.

Orchestras & ensembles

Orquesta y Coro de la Comunidad de Madrid

Madrid's state-funded regional orchestra is one of the city's most highly regarded. It provides accompaniment for the shows at the Teatro de la Zarzuela, but also performs at the Auditorio Nacional. The orchestra's artistic director, José Ramón Encinar, provides an occasionally erratic programme of mainly Spanish composers.

Orquesta y Coro de RTVE

The orchestra and choir of Spain's national state-run television and radio stations (Radio Televisión España), was originally founded for broadcasting. Its home is in the Teatro Monumental and concerts are usually Thursdays and Fridays at 8pm. Season tickets, running from October till late March, are reasonably priced and the programme is consistently good. The artistic director is Adrian Leaper.

Orquesta & Coro Nacional de España (OCNE)

A certain element of instability has hounded Spain's national orchestra and choir over the years, with numerous strikes carried out by the state-employed members when asked to practise at home outside their set paid hours. They take to the stage every weekend at the Auditorio Nacional, occasionally performing world premières of contemporary pieces. Josep Pons is the current director and is attempting to renovate programme content. He has even displayed an interest in adding jazz, tango and ethnic music to the orchestra's traditionally classical and Romantic repertoire. Lorenzo Ramos is the recently appointed director of the choir.

Orquesta Sinfónica de Madrid

The *orquesta titular* of the Teatro Real and oldest existing symphonic ensemble in Spain has a reputation within classical music circles for proposing odd, irregular seasonal programmes. The centenary year (2004) looked more stable, however, with a proposed series of chamber concerts, *zarzuelas* and symphonic concerts. At the Teatro Real the major operas are also usually complemented by related concerts put on by the orchestra and performed in a new concert space in one of the upstairs rooms.

As well as all the top Spanish conductors, the OSM has also worked with international greats such as Peter Haag, Pinchas Steinberg and Kurt Sanderling. Its artistic director is the esteemed Jesús López Cobos, but his work at the Teatro Real is so demanding that his commitment to orchestral work can sometimes play second fiddle.

Proyecto Guerrero

This is one of the more interesting ensembles covering the much ignored contemporary spectrum. Having said that, professional opinions as to its real competence are mixed. Under the artistic direction of Juan Carlos Garvayo, Proyecto Guerrero is the main component of the Auditorio Nacional's Música de Hoy programme (www.musicadhoy.com).

Venues

The **Círculo de Bellas Artes'** classical and contemporary music programme has broadened immensely over the last few years (*see p81*). The **Teatro Español** (*see p247*) occasionally holds *zarzuelas* and performances by chamber and symphonic orchestras. A handful of cafés and restaurants around town offer an opera-accompanied dining experience. Try the **Café Viena** (C/Luisa Fernanda 23, 91 559 38 28) for its Monday night sessions (dinner followed by a short *zarzuela* or opera performance, all for €30 plus wine). Also, check out the professional singing waiters at **La Favorita** (*see p139*) and **La Castafiore** (C/Marqués de Monasterio 5, 91 532 21 00). Another place to keep an eye on is the **Centro Asturiano** (C/Farmacia 2, 4°, 91 532 82 81), which runs a cycle called Lunes Musicales with concerts performed by small ensembles on Mondays. **La Fidula** (C/Huertas 57, 91 429 29 47, www.lafidula.com) is a cosy café with concerts on Fridays and Saturdays.

Auditorio Nacional de Música

C/Príncipe de Vergara 146, Prosperidad (91 337 01 00/www.auditorionacional.mcu.es). Metro Cruz del Rayo or Prosperidad. **Open** *Box office* 4-6pm Mon; 10am-5pm Tue-Fri; 11am-1pm Sat. Closed Aug. **Main season** Oct-June. **Tickets** *OCNE concerts* €9-€15. *Other concerts* €6-€28. **Credit** MC, V.
This impressive concert hall has capacity in its main auditorium for over 2,000, and a smaller chamber hall, La Sala de Cámara. As well as the OCNE, the

Auditorio hosts the Comunidad de Madrid's orchestra, ORCAM, and is the provisional home of the Joven Orquesta Nacional de España (worth checking out for their youth and enthusiasm – in contrast to the OCNE). In addition, there are ensembles such as that of the Universidad Politécnica de Madrid who invite orchestras to accompany the university's choir, performing selected Friday and Saturday evenings at 10.30pm. But the most recommendable concerts are those by invited international orchestras – which is, happily enough, something the Spanish state likes to invest its music budget in. The best seasons are the Grandes Intérpretes, the Liceo de Cámara, (Fundación Caja Madrid), Ibermúsica, Ciclo de Cámara y Polifonía and the contemporary Música de Hoy programme (*see p216* Proyecto Guerrero). Look out too for organ recitals.

One-off attendees will be joining an ageing audience, the majority of them being serious season-ticket holders, who tend to be particularly expressive. Many make their feelings known when pleased with the odd exultant cheer of '*bravo*', but more save themselves for when they want to voice their disapproval (boobings and abuse have been known in reaction to particularly offensive contemporary compositions, especially when the composer is present). Tickets for the Auditorio usually go on sale about a fortnight before the performance, and can be hard to get hold of. Tickets are generally cheaper for Sunday morning concerts.

The 2004-05 season promises a series of concerts on the theme *Viena 1900* including music by A Schönberg, Gustav Mahler, HW Henze, Bach, Schubert, Haydn and Brahms, plus two *conciertos extraordinarios* to commemorate the 400th anniversary of *Don Quijote,* featuring music inspired by Cervantes' work.

Real Academia de las Bellas Artes de San Fernando

C/Alcalá 13, Sol & Gran Vía (91 524 08 64/ www.insde.es) Metro Sevilla or Sol. Concerts *Sept-Jun* noon Sat. Admission free. Map p313 F7.
This beautiful building right in the heart of Madrid is a must for a concert experience. It hosts three or four cycles of free concerts a year, usually organised through the Radio Nacional de España for broadcast with musicians from the Escuela Superior de Música Reina Sofía. One well-reputed cycle is the short baroque season, which usually takes place in March.

Teatro Monumental

C/Atocha 65, Lavapiés (91 429 12 81). Metro Antón Martín. Open *Box office* Sept-June 11am-2pm, 5-7pm daily. July 9am-2pm Tue-Fri. Closed Aug. Main season Oct-March. Tickets €6.60-€16. Credit AmEx, DC, MC, V. Map p313 F8.
Located in slightly seedy Antón Martín, the Monumental has more character than most, but is functional rather than beautiful. Its main purpose is to record broadcast concerts by the RTVE Orchestra and Choir – consequently it may not have the glitz of the Teatro Real, but it does have excellent acoustics and high-quality performances. The principal diet here is generally concerts, with a side order of opera and *zarzuela*. The Monumental opens to the public free of charge for general rehearsals on Thursday mornings and chamber music concerts around midday on Saturdays.

Teatro Real

Plaza de Isabel II, Los Austrias (91 516 06 00/ www.teatro-real.com). Metro Opera. Open *Box office* 10am-1.30pm, 5.30-8pm Mon-Sat, from 2hrs before show Sun. *Visits* 10.30am-1.30pm Mon, Wed-Sun. Main season Sept-July. Tickets *Ballet* €7-€90. *Opera* €13-€120.*Visits* €4. Credit AmEx, DC, MC, V. Map p313 D7.
Shaped like a compressed oval, the interior of the city's opera house is breathtakingly ornate compared with its sombre façade, and one of the most technologically advanced in Europe. Productions are impressive, with complicated revolving sets and attention to detail in costume and props, and enjoy funding from some of Spain's biggest companies, as well as the Comunidad de Madrid. Projection screens at either side of the stage show the full-stage action, though this does not quite compensate for the lack of vision at the far ends of the top galleries (the *tribunas* and part of the *anfiteatro*). There is also a screen above the stage showing Spanish surtitles for non-Spanish operas. The acoustics are so good that the quality of the sound is practically the same everywhere in the hall.

The annual Festival de Verano runs alongside the theatre's regular programme in June and July but offers a more orchestra- and dance-orientated programme as well as children's shows (tickets for these events are much cheaper and easier to obtain). Guided tours run every day except Tuesday, and take visitors through the main dressing room and auditoria. Technical tours can be reserved for Sundays, lasting about an hour and a half (91 516 06 96 for all tour enquiries/booking).

Performances usually begin at 8pm, or 6pm on Sundays, with ballet and family opera matinées at noon. Tickets go on sale approximately ten days before the première, and standby tickets are available on the day. With the cheapest tickets, for rows F and G, vision is seriously reduced; check the website for a detailed plan. Season tickets offer a 60% discount.

The 2004-05 season will begin with celebrations of the OSM's centenary. The opera house is using a few ploys to try and draw in larger audiences, offering more reduced-rate and non-season-ticket seating, and staging more events in the building's Café Palacio. It is also running a variety of events, such as a cycle of forgotten Spanish operas (Los Clásicos del Real); the first 'stage creation' competition (the winning production team will then put on Benjamin Britten's children's opera, *The Little Sweep*, in June 2005) and an end-of-season concert by the OSM in the plaza outside in July 2005. Opera highlights will be Verdi's *Macbeth* (November 2004), Rossini's *Barber of Seville* (January 2005), Verdi's *La Traviata* (March 2005) and Mozart's *The Magic Flute* (July 2005).

Playing in time

Concert programmers in and around Madrid are slowly waking up to the charms of the region, taking music out of the theatres and lighting up monasteries, palaces and gardens. What could be more inviting than a soirée of Rachmaninoff, Fauré, Mozart and Schumann in one of the cool churches of the Sierra when the temperature is reaching the 40s down in Madrid?

The **Clásicos en Verano** concerts may not bring the greatest musicians but they are worth a mention, if only for their sheer range. Come July and August, it seems as if every nook and cranny – each old church and every town hall – around Madrid is filled with the sweet sounds of piano concertos, percussion groups, choirs, wind ensembles, string quartets, accompanied poetry and medieval music by local groups. The range and random aspect of the programming has led to Bach and Handel arias being performed at the San Andrés church in Rascafría (see p259), while, in nearby Alameda del Valle, a group of young men climbed stepladders and read names and numbers from the phone book as if they were poetry.

Not only are these concerts widespread and plentiful (there are nearly 100 of them in 53 different towns), they're also free. Pass by a tourist information office (see p294) or the Consejería de Cultura y Deportes on C/Alcalá 31 to pick up a full programme. Some of the more striking venues include the Castillo de los Mendoza in Manzanares el Real (see p264); and the Iglesia de San Bernabé and Iglesia de los Arroyos in El Escorial (see p255).

There are a couple of other options in historical settings that are more highly respected in classical music circles. Care for a turn about the charming gardens of the Aranjuez Palace (see p268) serenaded by *zarambeques*, *folías*, *marionas*, *fandangos* and *pasacalles*? The festival of **Música Antigua Aranjuez** (*pictured*), which celebrated its 11th edition in 2004, keeps the music live in the place that inspired Joaquín Rodrigo's haunting *Concierto de Aranjuez*, but with sounds from much earlier in the palace's history. At weekends during the months of

June and July the palace hosts concerts of medieval, renaissance and baroque music played on original instruments from the period. Many of the composers featured do not enjoy wide exposure today, although they were well known in their day. Concerts are held inside the palace (in the chapel and the Sala de Teatro), as well as in the palace grounds. The much-loved guided 'musical walks' have pauses for concerts along the way. Tickets are around €20 from Tel-entradas (902 10 12 12, www.telentradas.com).

The Fundación Caja Madrid (www.fundacion cajamadrid.es) is behind several impressive classical music cycles throughout the year in places of interest. The **Fiestas Reales** festival puts on very good concerts in El Escorial, Madrid's Monasterio de la Descalzas Reales (see p255) and San Jerónimo El Real (see p104). In 2004 they organised a series of concerts in honour of the Santiago de Compostela pilgrimage to be performed at points of interest along the route, including churches, chapels and cathedrals in towns such as Pamplona, La Rioja, Burgos, León and even Santiago de Compostela. This foundation is the most active and positively focused in Madrid and these concerts are of an excellent standard.

Sounds of the city

Madrid's villagey nature has led to many neighbourhoods developing their own flavours, and nowhere is this more evident than in the music each *barrio* creates. While the overriding sound is that of commercial radio dedicated to the usual lite Spanish pop fare – just like most countries it has been dominated by those put through the TV starmaking machinery – the fact remains that the city spits out an impressive array of talent.

You might get the impression that southern Madrid is all rock, rock, rock. It is indeed as hard rocking as you can imagine, with an entire swathe, from Vallecas to Carabanchel, being home to a kind of blue-collar, beer-drinking, dope-smoking form of full-on rock. Stars of this scene include Rosendo, and the lamented Los Enemigos, and countless hardcore bands that play a few shows and then disappear into the ether. But it's not all rock. The southern 'burbs of Madrid proper, as well as southern and eastern satellite towns like Alcorcón, Móstales and Torrejón de Ardoz have seen the emergence of rap and hip hop outfits that are more than passably good. Initially ignored by the media taste-makers, the scene has developed some quality acts over the years including people like DJ Jotamayuscula and Frank T. Recently the scene has started to go international, with records released in Puerto Rico, the US, Mexico, Chile and Argentina.

In central Madrid, Malasaña has always been home to a rockier form of modernity. While its roots lie in La Movida, the creative explosion following Spain's democratisation, these days the music is divided into two different, yet complementary, camps. One pays homage to the city's love of Spanish-language rock, with testosterone overkill being the rule of thumb. The flipside is the explosion of clubs dedicated to championing Anglo-American alternative rock and dance music. In the best of cases, bands like Femme Fatale manage to add new wrinkles to trends existing in other European capitals with wit and verve.

Northern *barrios* like Salamanca and the area surrounding the Santiago Bernabéu football stadium are rich, yuppified and dearly love their pop. In fact, it's the artists from

this scene that put Spain on the musical map. Take the locally adored Iglesias dynasty, for example. Between father Julio and son Enrique, they have shifted umpteen million CDs. Alejandro Sanz is another exponent of the *pijo* scene. He alone sold over 12 million in 2003 and won Best Latin Grammy the same year. It's interesting to note that as soon as these geezers become big, they abandon the city and their grassroots Ralph Lauren-clad fanbase for Miami's more expensive and clement climes.

Lavapiés, finally yet importantly, continues to be the multicultural melting pot of the city. Most of the successful bands closely identified with the area – La Cabra Mecánica, Amparanoia, El Bicho – specialise in *mestizaje* (cross-breeding). While the root of all continues to be traditional styles such as flamenco or rumba, they mix in rock, Latin jazz, and even electronica to fine effect. In fact, of all the musical cauldrons simmering in Madrid, this is really the one you ought to watch, as it finds itself increasingly in the sights of the international music press.

Teatro de la Zarzuela

C/Jovellanos 4, Huertas & Santa Ana (91 524 54 00/http://teatrodelazarzuela.mcu.es). Metro Banco de España or Sevilla. **Open** *Box office* noon-6pm daily (noon-8pm performance days). **Main season** Sept-July. **Tickets** €6-€54. **Credit** AmEx, DC, V. **Map** p314 G7.

The Teatro de la Zarzuela, which served as an opera house for many years previous to the Teatro Real's renovation, is now principally devoted to its *raison d'être* – staging *zarzuela*, the home-grown Spanish operetta. Despite *zarzuela*'s uncool image and lack of credibility among serious music lovers, it retains considerable popularity, drawing in audiences for daily 8pm performances from October to July. Accompanying the Teatro's packed *zarzuela* programme are performances of dance (often by the Ballet Nacional), music, plays, conferences and special family-orientated shows. The annual Ciclo del Lied, which pays tribute to the lesser-known 19th-century German song form, is well reputed.

Institutions

Institutions such as the **British Council** (www.britishcouncil.org/es), the Institut Français (www.ifmadrid.com), the **Istituto Italiano di Cultura** (www.iicmadrid.com) and the **Goethe Institut** (www.goethe.de/wm/mad) are also worth checking for classical music concerts and related activities. *See also p246* Centro Cultural de la Villa.

Centro para la Difusión de la Música Contemporánea

Centro de Arte Reina Sofía, C/Santa Isabel 52, Lavapiés (91 467 50 62/http://cdmc.mcu.es). Metro Atocha. **Main season** Oct-May. **Map** p314 G10.

Founded by Luis de Pablo, this pioneering institution boldly goes where few others in Madrid dare to go – into the dangerous world of the contemporary. The Centro gives 30 or so commissions annually to students who debut at the Auditorio Nacional, the Círculo de Bellas Artes or at the Reina Sofía museum itself. The centre also organises an interesting contemporary music festival, La Música Toma el Museo, with free concerts around the museum as well as out on the pleasant patio.

Fundación Canal

C/Mateo Inurria 2, Chamartín (91 545 15 06/www.fundacioncanal.com). Metro Plaza de Castilla. **Main season** Oct-July.

In 2002 Madrid's water company, the Canal Isabel II, set up this foundation which has become active in all areas of the arts, programming exhibitions and concerts year-round. Regular music programming really got off the ground from the beginning of 2003 and has included seasons of chamber music performed by musicians from the Orquesta de la Comunidad de Madrid and several one-off recitals by virtuosos such as the Russian pianist Alexander Moutouzkine. Non-classical music gets a look in too, the regular 'conFUSIÓN' series has featured genres as diverse as bossa nova, gospel and jazz.

Fundación Carlos Amberes

C/Claudio Coello 99 (91 435 22 01/www.fcamberes.org). Metro Serrano. **Main season** Sept-June. **Map** p311 J2.

This foundation dates back to 1594, when it was founded by a 16th-century Flemish benefactor. Today, as well as exhibitions and conferences, it hosts an average of 15 to 20 concerts per year in three cycles (at the beginning of the year, in May and at the end of the year), both in its rather dingy basement and sometimes upstairs in a converted church, which is pretty but has bad acoustics. The programme nods towards the Low Countries.

Fundación Juan March

C/Castelló 77, Salamanca (91 435 42 40/www.march.es). Metro Núñez de Balboa. **Main season** Oct-June. **Map** p311 K3.

Set up in 1955, this charitable foundation and hive of musical, artistic and scientific activity was one of few such organisations in Spain for a good many years. These days the Fundación Juan March remains a key player in Madrid's classical world, putting on around 150-200 free concerts per year. These usually consist of soloists or chamber ensembles and take place on Mondays at midday and Wednesday evenings from 7pm (the most popular slot, with better-known professional musicians and broadcast on Radio Nacional) as well as some Saturdays at midday with younger musicians. The concert hall seats 300; when it fills up a second hall with a big screen is opened, and then the bar. The programme in general is pretty much free from restrictions as it does not depend on ticket sales; there is a leaning towards Spanish composers, but with a lot of flexibility. In 2005 a programme specifically dedicated to Spanish music will celebrate the foundation's 50th anniversary.

Festivals

Fiesta season in Madrid kicks off in May with the week of merriment leading up to **San Isidro** on the 15th. The council provides annual free concerts including *zarzuela* in the Centro Cultural Conde Duque (*see p90*) as well as in parks to the west of the city and the Plaza Mayor. Classical concerts, given by ensembles such as the Banda Sinfónica Municipal, are sometimes held in the Teatro Español. See the council's website www.munimadrid.es or ask at tourist offices for a San Isidro programme.

The international **Día de la Música** on June 21 involves 12 hours of non-stop dance, musical theatre, cinema, photography and, of course, music in an increasing number of museums and other venues across the city, organised by the Círculo de Bellas Artes, and all for free. June also sees classical concerts in **Alcalá de Henares** on some Sundays performed by local orchestras in the Plaza Cervantes bandstand. For the summer festivals **Clásicos en Verano** and **Festival de Música Antigua**, *see p217* **Playing in time**.

Rock, Roots & Jazz

In the words of one Madrid concert promoter: 'On one side there's the musicians and the live music lovers, on the other, the council…' As part of the local authority's continuing crusade against what it apparently deems to be low culture, bar and venue owners continue to fight a sometimes insurmountable battle in order to put on live music. Two of the city's most cherished venues, Suristán and Sala Caracol, have had to close their doors in recent times under intense pressure from the authorities. The owners of Suristán, Madrid's only true world music venue, simply had to throw in the towel after constant licence checks, a tax on concerts (retroactive for five years) that nearly crippled them and a complete lack of support from any governing body.

The official line given by the authorities for these closures is the noise problem. However, empirical evidence suggests that the moment there is negative press about an area or a street regarding noise pollution or late-night revellers, the council covers its back by finding some licensing anomaly and shutting down at least one venue in that area. To reopen again is a bureaucratic nightmare, because as quickly as a bar may sort out its noise problems, getting the case to the top of the pile either means waiting an eternity or – some allege – handing over a wad of cash in an envelope. In another bizarre twist to the tale, as part of the anti-alcohol drive, the council has also banned under-18s from concerts, something which some lament as the beginning of the end of rock in Spain.

Surprisingly, in the face of such fervent opposition, Madrid's live music scene continues to thrive. CD sales are frighteningly low in Spain, with Spaniards buying an average of only 1.4 CDs a year. Figures suggest that there are as many pirate CDs bought off the street these days as there are in the shops. This doesn't give big acts a huge impetus to tour in Spain, but interestingly, each year seems to attract bigger names to the city, receiving a warm reception from all but the council.

VENUES

In the centre of Madrid there is not one concert venue that holds more than 2,500 spectators. Intimacy is the order of the day then, with

Getting down at **Arena**.

many big names coming to play in surprisingly small auditoriums. As well as those listed here, the bullring at Las Ventas (*see p34*) sometimes hosts gigs, and being outdoors is perfect for the concerts put on there in July. The Parque de Atracciones (*see p197*) in the Casa de Campo is another summer venue where you can catch some local rock groups.

Venues listed do not charge admission unless otherwise stated. If there is no charge on the door, there will most likely be a supplement on your first drink, which usually goes straight into the pocket of the band. Few venues will accept credit cards on the door, although we have noted those that do in our listings. To make licensing issues easier, many of these venues stay open as nightclubs after the concerts end, while some clubs in the **Nightlife** chapter (*see pp225-238*) often host live music.

FESTIVE SOUNDS

With such good weather, music festivals are understandably popular. **San Isidro** is a good place to catch free concerts in Las Vistillas park. July sees the **Veranos de la Villa** festival, which attracts names such as Dido and Gilberto Gil. Madrid's indie festival, **Festimad**, has seen its last year in the Parque del Soto due to environmental issues. However, the Mostoles council plans to find a new site and keep the event close to home. The **Carnaval** and **Dos de Mayo** holidays see live acts performing for free, as do the **Fiestas del Partido Comunista** in September and the **May Day** celebrations. For all these festivals and more, *see pp190-195* **Festivals & Events**.

LISTINGS

It's good to check out the local papers if you want information about upcoming gigs. The *Guía del Ocio, Salir Salir* and the Friday supplements of many Spanish newspapers have listings for forthcoming gigs, although they're not always comprehensive. Otherwise, concert information comes on posters, flyers and in free magazines found in bars, and music and fashion shops. Magazines to look for include *MondoSonoro, Punto H, GO* and the irregular *Undersounds*. Concert information is also available on the web if you speak Spanish at: www.lanetro.com, www.madridmusic.com and www.mondosonoro.com

Rock/world music

Al'Laboratorio

C/Colón 14, Malasaña & Conde Duque (91 532 26 69). Metro Tribunal. **Open** 9pm-3am Tue-Thur, Sun; 9pm-10am Fri, Sat. **Map** p309 F5.
Al'Lab looks like a fairly normal bar on the ground floor, albeit a mite tatty. Descend the stairs and pull back the curtain, however, and you'll find yourself in an underground bunker with stage and moshing crowd. Programming local rock and metal bands most nights, it's fun, but not for the claustrophobic.

Arena

C/Princesa 1, Argüelles (91 547 57 11/www. salarena.com). Metro Plaza de España. **Open** midnight-6am Thur-Sat (concert days opens 10pm). **Admission** varies. **Map** p309 D5.
Arena plays host to several club nights, but is also a fairly hot live music venue. The layout is not especially conducive to everyone getting a good view of

the action, but it's an intimate venue, with recent visitors including the likes of Groove Armada, the Freestylers, Jet and Sexy Sadie.

La Buena Dicha

C/Santa Hortensia 14, Chamartín (91 413 60 14). Metro Alfonso XIII or Prosperidad. **Open** 10pm-6am Thur-Sat. Closed Aug. **Concerts** 10pm-midnight Fri, Sat. **Admission** (incl 1 drink) €5 for concerts.
A medium-sized venue with a large stage and lots of smoke and light tricksiness, La Buena Dicha programmes little-known local pop and rock outfits, usually of a pretty good standard. Be warned, it can be hard to find, so allow plenty of time.

Búho Real

C/Regueros 5, Chueca (91 319 10 88/www.buho real.com). Metro Alonso Martínez or Chueca. **Open** 7pm-3am daily. **Credit** MC, V. **Map** p310 H4.
The lights go down very low in the Búho Real, and the spots come up on a tiny stage. The size limitations here dictate the acts – expect local jazz or acoustic groups, most of them just two- or three-piece bands. The name means the 'Royal Owl', which goes some way to explain the large collection of minature owls on display.

Café la Palma

C/La Palma 62 (91 522 50 31/www.cafela palma.com) Metro Noviciado. **Open** 4pm-3.30am daily. **Admission** (incl 1 drink) €5 for concerts on Thur, Fri, Sat. **No credit cards.** **Map** p309 E4.
This is a long-standing favourite amongst the Malasaña crowd. Choose from an area with tables, a chill-out zone where everyone lazes on cushions on the floor or the main room, where from Thursday to Saturday you can catch concerts from local up-and-comers such as Mojo Project.

Jazz bands jam at **Café Berlin**. See p223.

Chesterfield

C/Serrano Jover 5, Conde Duque (91 542 2817). Metro Argüelles. **Open** 1.30pm-3.30am daily. **Map** p308 C3.
For a small venue, Chesterfield has an impressive track record, as the signed photos on the wall attest. As well as smaller local acts, Mark Knopfler, Lisa Stansfield and Elvis Costello have all made appearances recently, as well as Spanish megastars David Bisbal and Alex Ubago.

La Coquette

C/Hileras 14, Los Austrias (no phone). Metro Opera or Sol. **Open** 8pm-2.30am Mon-Thur, Sun; 8pm-3am Fri, Sat. Closed Aug. **Map** p313 D7.
This basement bar, going for some 20 years now, was Madrid's first dedicated exclusively to blues. Run by a Swiss-Spanish guy called Albert, who has a large collection of old records that won't disappoint, there are live acts featuring local bluesers from Tuesday to Thursday. Can get very smoky.

La Cubierta de Leganés

C/Maestro s/n, Leganés (91 689 87 15/www.la-cubierta.com). Metro Leganés Central. **Open** varies. **Admission** varies.
La Cubierta is a bullring with retractable roof in Leganés, one of the southern suburbs of Madrid. Bullrings often double as concert venues – the only flaw in this otherwise sound plan is that the shape of a bullring is not conducive to good acoustics, leaving a crisp kick-drum distorted into a nebulous throb. That said, it's a magnet for rock and heavy metal groups, plus dance acts too, so you won't be surprised to hear that the Chemical Brothers, Deep Purple and the Corrs have all paid a visit.

Divino Aqualung

Paseo Ermita del Santo 48, Southern suburbs (91 470 24 61). Metro Puerta del Ángel. **Open** (weekday concerts) from 9pm; (club) midnight-6.30am, Fri, Sat. **Admission** varies.
It's best to catch a taxi to get to Aqualung as the walk from the metro is a bit of a hike. Distance aside, as a live music venue Divino benefits from an excellent sound system plus several elevated areas from which you can get a good view of the action. Brings diverse acts, in recent times Roots Manuva, Belle & Sebastian and Les Philippes.

Garibaldi Café

C/San Felipe Neri 4, Los Austrias (91 559 27 33/ www.salagaribaldi.com). Metro Ópera. **Open** 10pm-6am daily. **Admission** varies. **Map** p313 D7.
A roomy venue with a good sound system and a varied programme. Its staple fare is new bands doing the rounds on the local scene, but in addition there are now the almost inevitable DJ sessions at the weekend. Midweek you'll find stand-ups, storytelling, theatre and dance.

Gruta 77

C/Nicolás Morales s/n, Southern suburbs (91 471 23 70). Metro Oporto. **Open** *Sept-July* 8pm-6am daily. *Aug* 8pm-6am Mon-Sat. **Admission** varies.
A mix of local unsigned groups and touring bands from the States, Australia and Japan pass through this 300-seater *sala*. Punk, rock, ska and *mestizaje* tastes are catered for, with regular rock competitions, the prize being the chance to professionally record an album. An excellent sound system makes it worth the trip out to the 'burbs.

Honky Tonk

C/Covarrubias 24, Chamberí (91 445 68 86/
www.honkytonk.net). Metro Alonso Martínez. **Open**
Sept-June 9.30pm-5am daily. *July, Aug* 10.30pm-5am.
Admission free. **Map** p310 G3.

Honky Tonk programmes local country, blues and
rock acts nightly, and its own Gary Moore/Rolling
Stones-influenced band performs regularly. Ignore
the intimidating doormen and get here early as the
large pillars that hold up the building tend to restrict
the views of those not at the front.

Moby Dick

Avenida del Brasil 5 (91 555 76 71/www.moby
dickclub.com). Metro Cuzco or Santiago Bernabéu.
Open 10pm-3am Mon-Thur, 10pm-5am Fri, Sat.
Admission varies. **Credit** (bar only) MC, V.

With two different levels for music, Moby Dick
caters for plenty of tastes. Mainly a venue for local
groups and touring Spanish bands, it can still pull
a few surprises. Ash, the Libertines and Gorky's
Zycotic Mynky have all paid a visit, as have the sublime Fat Freddy's Drop. Warm up next door with a
pint of Guinness in its sister bar the Irish Rover first.

Palacio Vistalegre

C/Utebo 1, Southern suburbs (91 422 07 81/
www.palaciovistalegre.com). Metro Oporto or Vista
Alegre. **Open** varies. **Admission** varies.

This stadium is what the Spanish call *multi-usos*, so
it serves as a basketball stadium and a conference
hall as well as a concert venue. That doesn't make
it any less popular as a music hall, though, and big
international names pack 'em in here. Lenny Kravitz,
Linkin Park and Robbie Williams have all rocked a
crowd here in recent times.

Ritmo & Compás

C/Conde de Vilches 22, Salamanca (91 355 28 00/
www.ritmoycompas.com). Metro Cartagena or
Diego de León. **Open** *Bar* 4pm-end of concert.
Admission varies.

A music fanatic's paradise, Ritmo & Compás boasts
160 rehearsal rooms over two sites, recording studios, its own record label and courses and seminars.
As a live venue it has a programme as diverse as its
facilities, including pop-rock, reggae, northern soul,
metal, blues, funk, techno and breakbeat. The stage
and auditorium are well designed allowing a good
view from any angle.

La Riviera

Paseo Bajo de la Virgen del Puerto s/n, Los Austrias
(91 365 24 15). Metro Puerto del Ángel. **Open** *Gigs*
varies. *Club* midnight-5am Fri, Sat. **Admission**
varies. **Map** p312 A8.

This club on the banks of the Manzanares is a major
player on the Madrid music scene and is ranked by
many as the city's best medium-sized venue. It's
certainly popular, and comes equipped with an
excellent sound system. All manner of acts have
passed through in recent times, among them The
Darkness, Ice T, Ben Harper, Macy Gray, Bad
Religion, Moloko and Massive Attack.

La Sala

Avda Nuestra Señora de Fátima 42, Carabanchel
(91 525 54 44). Metro Carabanchel. **Open** 8pm-5am
daily. **Admission** varies.

The neon and neo-classical columns in the entrance,
the torch-lighting inside – it's all a bit strip joint, but
don't let that, or the suburban location, put you off.
La Sala's mixed bag of gigs mainly features Spanish
pop, but there have also been performances from the
likes of Deacon Blue and Ron Wood. There is a
concert space with room for 700 on the first floor,
while downstairs there are pinball machines, a pool
table and a loud but louche atmosphere.

Siroco

C/San Dimas 3, Malasaña (91 593 30 70/
www.siroco.es). Metro Noviciado or San Bernardo.
Open 9.30pm-5am Thur; 9.30pm-6am Fri, Sat.
Admission (incl 1 drink) €5-€8. **No credit cards.**
Map p309 E3.

Regulars at this long-established joint know just
what they want, and management are happy to provide it, programming a steady schedule of well-
established local rock, indie, pop and funk outfits
and providing a stage for young hopefuls. In addition, there are late-night DJ sessions covering a
broad range of styles. The club has its own record
label and is frequented by A&R types from others.

El Sol

C/Jardines 3, Sol & Gran Vía (91 532 64 90/
www.elsolmad.com). Metro Gran Vía. **Open** 11pm-
5am Tue-Thur; 11pm-6am Fri, Sat. **Admission** (incl
1 drink) €9. **Credit** (bar only) MC, V. **Map** p313 E7.

A steady flow of top live acts passes through El Sol,
another remnant of the Movida. The décor is not up
to much, but the vibe and the programme make up
for that. A mixture of rock, rhythm and blues, punk,
soul, and hip hop from national outfits, complemented by visits from international acts such as
Evan Dando, Chicks on Speed and The Buzzcocks.

Jazz

The **Festival de Otoño** (*see p194*) includes a
jazz section and many top names (especially
from the field of Latin jazz) appear here. Other
venues with occasional live jazz acts include
Marula (*see p226*), and the otherwise sleepy
Café El Despertar (C/Torrecilla del Leal
18, 91 530 80 95) in Lavapiés. Fair-trade café
Zanzíbar (*see p161*) has a varied programme
of jazz, blues and bossa nova, and **Anticafé**
(*see p152*) hosts a diverse blend of Latin jazz,
flamenco and jam sessions.

Café Berlín

C/Jacometrezo 4 (91 532 73 60/www.cafe
berlin.net). Metro Callao or Santo Domingo. **Open**
11pm-6am daily. **Admission** supplement varies.
No credit cards. **Map** p313 D6.

In 2003 the Berlin was another venue to fall foul of
enforced closure by the council but has since

Arts & Entertainment

bounced back impressively. While it is mainly a jazz venue showcasing local groups, bigger names such as Eddie Henderson also come to call. Upon arrival, expect to be greeted by owner Eric's very large and very friendly dog.

Café Central

Plaza del Ángel 10, Huertas & Santa Ana (91 369 41 43/www.cafecentralmadrid.com). Metro Antón Martín or Sol. **Open** 1.30pm-2.30am Mon-Thur, Sun; 1.30pm-3.30am Fri, Sat. **Admission** gigs €6-€12. **Credit** AmEx, DC, MC, V. **Map** p313 E8.

For many years now, this beautiful place with high ceilings and elegant decor, has been *the* place to get your jazz fix in Madrid. The artists that come here put it among the best of its kind in Europe. George Adams, Don Pullen, Ben Sidran and Bob Sands have all taken the stage, as well as Spanish stalwarts such as Chano Domínguez, Jorge Pardo and the oldest and greatest of them all, Pedro Iturralde.

Café Populart

C/Huertas 22, Huertas (91 429 84 07/ www.populart.es). Metro Antón Martín. **Open** 6pm-2.30am Mon-Thur, Sun; 6pm-3.30am Fri, Sat. **Admission** free. **Map** p313 F8.

Escape from the beer-crawl route that is Huertas by slipping into this superb jazz club. There's no cover charge, but the drinks are a bit pricey. A strong backer of Spanish jazz and host to many an international artist, Populart features jazz and blues every night with two shows, one at 11.30pm and the other at 12.30am.

Clamores

C/Alburquerque 14, Chamberí (91 445 79 38/ www.salaclamores.com). Metro Bilbao. **Open** 7pm-2am Mon-Thur, Sun; 7pm-4am Fri, Sat. **Admission** (concerts only) varies. **Map** p309 F3.

This emblematic jazz club opened in 1979, and for eight years served as the set for the TV programme *Jazz Entre Amigos*. Stocking what is apparently the widest range of cavas and champagnes in Madrid, it has a very varied programme these days, with tango, pop, rock, bossa, samba and folk all on the bill as well as the jazz that made its name. The live acts sprawl into late-night jam sessions on Friday and Saturday nights.

Colegio Mayor San Juan Evangelista

C/Gregorio del Amo 4, Moncloa (91 534 24 00/ www.cmusanjuan.com). Metro Metropolitano. **Open** 10pm Fri-Sun. Closed July-Sept. **Admission** varies.

This auditorium located in a student residence, and known affectionately as the 'Johnny', is actually much more important than you might think. Contrary to its appearance, it's one of the city's most discerning jazz clubs – hundreds of great names have passed through the doors here in the 30-plus years of its existence. Look out for its annual spring jazz festival and the Flamenco por Tarantos festival in April. The auditorium was due to reopen after renovation as this guide went to press.

Dizzy Jazz

C/Luz 8, Las Matas (91 635 65 54/www.musica actual.com/dizzyjazz). Trains C-8, C-10 to Las Matas/bus from Moncloa to Las Matas, N-6 Carretera de A Coruña exit Las Matas. **Open** 11pm-4am Fri, Sat. **Admission** concert nights €6.

Las Matas is a bit of a schlep from the city centre, but often worth it for great jazz and Brazilian acts. There are two shows, the first at midnight and the second at 1.30am.

Segundo Jazz

C/Comandante Zorita 8, Cuatro Caminos, Tetúan (91 554 94 37). Metro Cuatro Caminos or Nuevos Ministerios. **Open** 7pm-4am daily. **Admission** (min consumption) €5.

Founded many years ago by the owner of the legendary Whisky Jazz Club, this is Madrid's longest standing jazz joint. Nowadays, as well as jazz, the programme takes in Brazilian groups, singer-songwriters and '60s cover bands banging out Beatles and Stones songs. A great atmosphere and friendly staff make it an essential stop, but don't get there too early: concerts start at midnight.

Latin

La Bodeguita de Beny

C/Tres Cruces, 8, Sol & Gran Vía (91 521 34 82). Metro Gran Vía. **Open** 7pm-3am daily. **Admission** free. **Map** p313 E6.

This rather narrow bar, adorned with pictures of Beny Moré, specialises in Cuban cocktails and sounds. From Wednesday through to Sunday there are performances on the tiny stage. Expect to find acoustic duos and trios (there's no space for full bands), playing *son, guaracha* and Latin jazz.

Galileo Galilei

C/Galileo 100, Chamberí (91 534 75 57/www.sala galileogalilei.com). Metro Islas Filipinas or Quevedo. **Open** 6pm-3am Mon-Sat. **Admission** €6-€15 Mon-Fri; €23 Sat.

A sister club of Clamores, Galileo Galilei presents possibly the widest range of artists to be seen under one roof in all of Madrid. Whatever kind of music you like, you'll likely find it here, since all the bases seem to be covered. There's Latin jazz, flamenco, salsa, singer-songwriters and myriad types of fusion. There are also ladies-only stripshows on Saturday nights. This former cinema is spacious, though the mock-Hellenic decor can be a bit over the top.

Oba-Oba

C/Jacometrezo 4, Sol & Gran Vía (no phone). Metro Callao. **Open** 7pm-5am Mon-Thur, Sun; 7pm-6am Fri, Sat. **Admission** €8. **Map** p313 D6.

An old favourite, the Oba-Oba has been serving up ice-cold Caipirinhas and fabulous samba for 25 years or so to its good-time clientele. There are live acts jamming here several nights a week, and, given the theme, it's perhaps less than surprising that almost all of them are Brazilian.

Nightlife

Party now, sleep later.

Sleep is almost a dirty word to this most fun-loving of people: Macbeth didn't murder sleep, Madrid did. The Spanish love to party, and they have always partied harder and later than any other nationality you'd care to mention.

In recent years, however, it seems as if things have changed somewhat. The hedonistic days of La Movida – the libertine backlash against the repression of the Franco era – are gone. Instead, the scene is facing its own backlash, as the local government, and in turn, the police, crack down on the giant night-time playground that is Madrid. This is mainly due to the unwanted by-products of excess: the noise and mess left by the party people, and the political pressure brought on by consistent complaints from the city's residents. However, the crack-down has failed to quell the spirit driving the nocturnal antics that continue to make Madrid one of the finest places to go out on the town.

WHAT HAPPENS WHEN
The nightlife here has distinct stages. In the early evening, from 6pm until midnight, teenagers take to the streets. Most of them congregate in parks and squares and engage in what is known locally as the *botellón*. Thousands of litres of red wine are mixed with Coke, to make a sticky mix known as *calimocho*, the drink that launched a million teen-hangovers. Officially, the *botellón* is now illegal in Madrid, the focal point of a stand-off between the police and wannabe revellers being the Plaza Dos de Mayo, one of the most popular sites for *botellón*. However, 15 squad cars can't be there every night, nor can they cover the hundreds of other squares in Madrid, ensuring that it still goes on every weekend without fail.

At around 11, a more mature crowd will start to spill out of the restaurants and hit the bars. Generally, bars break down into several distinct categories, with *bares de copas* selling spirit-based drinks with or without a DJ in the corner. Then there are the *discobares,* which may require a cover charge and bang out a combination of international and Spanish pop, perfect for the alcohol-fuelled crowd that frequents them. Then there are the funkier pre-club bars that will often have a house DJ warming you up for a night out on the town. Thanks to recent legislation, bars are obliged to close at around 3am: precisely the moment when the clubs or *discotecas* fill.

Cool. *See p227.*

The best Pre-club bars

For pot-holing
Explore the dark underground caves of **Café Rock Corto Maltés** on a Friday or Saturday night – you'll discover a DJ and a bang-up-for-it crowd. *See p233.*

For a bit of star-gazing
Hang out with the beautiful people and play a game of spot the *famosos* at **Moma 56**, Madrid's swankiest joint. *See p237.*

For some proper sangría
Head for **Las Cuevas de Sésamo**, a traditional sangría bar complete with wise Spanish sayings emblazoned on the walls. *See p231.*

For getting your groove on
Try as you might to resist, the achingly funky selection from the DJs at **Marula** will get you moving. *See p226.*

(*Discoteca* carries none of its usual cheesy connotations in Spanish; in fact be careful what you ask for when talking to the locals – *club* in Spanish generally means brothel.)

SURVIVAL TIPS

Having changed your body clock around to suit your schedule in Madrid, there are just a few more things you need to bear in mind before you go out seeking *la marcha*, or a good time. Don't get too dolled up; with some notable exceptions, Madrid is not a town where people dress to impress. Creativity is more important than couture. Be careful with the drinks; measures poured here are such that you may, for once, actually ask them to put a little less in. The ticket you are given on the door of a club is almost always valid for a drink, so don't just toss it away.

If you're here long-term, do your best to ingratiate yourself with the *relaciones públicas* outside. It's their job to get you in, whether you pay or not. Before long you'll be swanning in on guest lists all over town. If you think you can bring a crowd down every week and you live to party, you can always try the job out yourself – foreign customers are welcomed in nightclubs in Madrid, and many promoters actively seek young foreigners to bring in more of the same.

Finally, before you head out for your night on the town, you might consider checking club websites for printable flyers that will get you in for a discounted fee.

Los Austrias & La Latina

Atenas

C/Segovia & C/Cuesta de la Vega (91 765 12 06/ mobile 650 50 67 93). Metro Puerta del Ángel/ Ópera. **Open** noon-4am daily. Closed Nov-Mar. **Admission** free. **No credit cards. Map** p312 B8.
A super-cool *terraza* set in its own small park. The plentiful tables in the front bar are filled by midnight and the overflow swells on to the surrounding gentle slope of grass. With no complaining neighbours to worry about, the crowd can enjoy the easy sounds of Latin house mixed by the DJ long after other *terrazas* have called it a night.

El Barbú

C/Santiago 3 (91 542 56 98/www.el-barbu.com). Metro Ópera or Sol. **Open** 10.30pm-5.30am Mon-Thur; 10.30pm-4am Fri, Sat. **Admission** free. **Credit** DC, MC, V. **Map** p313 D7.
A sumptuous red velvet curtain separates the chilled front bar from two spacious candlelit chambers at the back where a swirling wash of intensely coloured psychedelic projections bathe the walls and ceilings. The DJ keeps the easy-going, urbane crowd happy with a slick mixture of funk, salsa and African beats. This is more the kind of a place to give you a warm glow than to really light your fire.

Danzoo

Maxime, Ronda de Toledo 1 (information 902 49 99 94). Metro Puerta de Toledo. **Open** midnight-6am Sat. **Admission** (incl 1 drink) €13; free before 2am. **No credit cards. Map** p313 D10.
Progressive and tech-house with an edge. This is not one for the handbag housers out there, rather this is a hard session; like Spinal Tap's amplifiers, the volume here goes up to 11. The crowd is grungy and tends to be predominantly male.

Deconya

C/Don Pedro 6 (no phone). Metro La Latina. **Open** 9pm-4am Mon-Sat. **Admission** free. **Credit** AmEx, DC, MC, V. **Map** p312 C9.
This is known for being a place for artists, musicians and the in-crowd to hang out. Quieter midweek when the sounds are rock 'n' roll and blues, the weekends see the English resident DJ take the reins and bang out some funky house tracks. Mounted above the dancefloor is a mad professor's representation of the solar system, with a large glitter ball as the sun – proof that in Madrid the world revolves around gettin' your groove on.

Kathmandú

C/Señores de Luzón 3 (no phone/www.club kathmandu.com). Metro Ópera or Sol. **Open** 12.30-5am Thur; 12.30-6am Fri, Sat. **Admission** (incl 1 drink) €7 Fri, Sat; free Thur. **No credit cards. Map** p312 C7.
This basement club is cosy, friendly and nicely chilled. The DJs spin a delicious mix of funk, soul, jazz and hip hop to lure the friendly clientele on to the dancefloor by about 3am. Those who don't dance content themselves with the ample seating in the cave-like surroundings and just nod along.

Marula

C/Caños Viejos 3 (91 366 15 96/www.marulacafe. com). Metro La Latina. **Open** 11pm-5.30am Mon-Thur, Sun; 11pm-6am Fri, Sat. **Admission** €7 after 2am Thur-Sat, otherwise free. **No credit cards. Map** p312 C8.
This small venue now serves as a bar, a club and a place to hear live music. Tuesday nights are concert nights, but the place really hots up at weekends, attracting DJ sessions from local talent such as Señorlobo, Chema Ama and Javi Kalero. The summertime terrace is a big pull, filling up by midnight and staying that way until the early hours.

Sol & Gran Vía

After-Sun

Handyman Tavern, Plaza del Carmen 3 (91 521 0567). Metro Callao or Sol. **Open** 6am-9.30am Fri; 6am-10am Sat, Sun. **Admission** (incl 1 drink) €8. **No credit cards. Map** p313 E7.
After-hours are usually the preserve of house-heads who don't want to go home, but here everything is different – from the location (the basement of an Irish bar) to the music policy. Anything goes on the

Brazilian beats fill the nights at **Oba-Oba**. *See p229.*

CD decks, from break-beat to thrash metal to hip hop – even Vanilla Ice gets a look in. Always packed and, perhaps because it has a tendency to buck all the usual clubbing conventions, great fun.

Bash

Plaza Callao 4 (91 541 35 00/www.tripfamily.com). Metro Callao. **Open** midnight-6am Wed. **Admission** (incl 1 drink) €10. **No credit cards. Map** p313 D6.
Wednesday is firmly established as hip hop night in Madrid, and judging by the turnout these clubs get, Thursdays must see a massive drop in Madrid's productivity thanks to what must surely be some cracking hangovers. Bash doesn't really get going until after 1am, but once it does there's no room to move. The residents specialise in the latest R&B and hip hop and the guest DJs have featured Funk Master Flex among others.

Cool

C/Isabel la Católica 6 (91 542 34 39). Metro Santo Domingo. **Open** midnight-6am Thur-Sat. **Admission** (incl 1 drink) €15. **No credit cards. Map** p313 D6.
Cool was always too stylish to be dominated by the straight crowd. And so it has come to pass that it now has a mainly gay following. Once you get beyond the stainless steel and the sweeping ramps of the entrance, there are two upstairs lounges, one complete with wall-mounted plasma screens overlooking a large and heaving dancefloor filled with hundreds of muscle-boys. Simon & Shaker, the house producers and DJs of the moment, are regulars here, pumping out the tribal tech-house that's a mainstay of the Iberian sound.

Coppelia 101

Sala Pública, Plaza de los Mostenses 11 (no phone). Metro Plaza de España. **Open** 12.30am-6am Fri, Sat. **Admission** (incl 1 drink) €12. **No credit cards. Map** p309 D5.
A nice and grimy basement club, with two different vibes. The main room throbs with chugging techno-breaks and electro; plenty of '80s vocals are given a new lease of life here. The smaller back room plays host to anything from drum 'n' bass and hip hop to house or breakbeat. The crowd is up for it and out of it, and the atmosphere sweaty and smoky.

Hanabi

C/Muñóz Torero 5 (no phone). Metro Gran Vía. **Open** 10.30pm-3.30am Tue-Sat. **Admission** free. **No credit cards. Map** p313 E6.
This snug little *sala* has been around forever, but has seen more reincarnations than the Dalai Lama. Currently opening its doors with the subtitle 'Soulful Club', it seems like the promoters are finally on to a winner. An impressive roster of local guest DJs come to help the young crowd get their groove on before a big night out. Expect funk-fuelled house, Brazilian electro and a bit of nu jazz.

Joy Eslava

C/Arenal 11 (91 366 54 39). Metro Ópera or Sol. **Open** 11.30pm-5.30am Mon-Thur, Sun; 6.30pm-6.30am Fri, Sat. **Admission** €12 Mon-Thur, Sun; €15 Fri, Sat (incl 1 drink). **Credit** AmEx, DC, MC, V. **Map** p313 D7.
Unusual in that it retains some original trappings of its former incarnation as a 19th-century theatre, in every other respect this is an ordinary high-street

club. The vast crammed dancefloor runs the gamut from teenage tribes through housewives. Staple Spanish pop with the odd foray into flamenco.

Museo Chicote

Gran Vía 12 (91 532 67 37/www.museochicote.com). *Metro Gran Vía.* **Open** 8am-2am Mon-Sat. **Admission** free. **Credit** AmEx, DC, MC, V. **Map** p313 F6.

Famously a haunt of Hemingway, this cocktail bar is now run by Trip Family, the promoters responsible for the best gay nights in town. The crowd is *super-fashion*, and enjoys the sublime soundtrack provided by the city's coolest DJs. On Thursday nights catch Spain's answer to Gilles Peterson, DJ Sandro Bianchi, playing electro-soul, funk, hip hop and anything with a groove.

Oba-Oba

C/Jacometrezo 4, Sol & Gran Vía (no phone). Metro Callao. **Open** 7pm-5am Mon-Thur, Sun; 7pm-6am Fri, Sat. **Admission** €5-€12. **No credit cards**. **Map** p313 D6.

Live music early on gives way later to Brazilian beats. The tunes are set on auto-pilot during the week, but at the weekend expect DJ sessions. The crowd is very adept at shaking its booty samba style, though women have been known to complain about a few too many *pulpos* (octopuses – Spanish slang for wandering hands) in the place. Reputed to serve the best Caipirinhas in the city.

Ocho y Medio

C/Mesonero Romanos 13 (91 541 3500/www.trip family.com). Metro Callao or Gran Vía. **Open** midnight-5am Fri. **Admission** €10 (incl 1 drink). **No credit cards**. **Map** p313 E6.

Although somewhat anachronistic, Ocho y Medio is the perfect stop on your hedonistic tour of the town if you're looking for an alcohol-fuelled mass of party energy. DJ Smart makes it all sound very '80s and '90s, thrashing out an eclectic mix of indie, electro-clash, electro-pop, new wave and New York rock. It takes a master to weld Blur and Depêche Mode seamlessly.

Ohm

Bash, Plaza Callao 4 (91 541 35 00/www.trip family.com). Metro Callao. **Open** midnight-6am Fri, Sat. **Admission** (incl 1 drink) €10. **No credit cards**. **Map** p313 D6.

While some nights come and go with alarming frequency, Trip Family's Ohm is one that's here for the duration. Strictly speaking it's a gay night, but it's too much fun (and too central) for the straight crowd to stay away. The result is a friendly party atmosphere with soulful, vocal-driven house tracks mixed to perfection by residents Kike Boy and Tetsu.

Palacio de Gaviria

C/Arenal 9 (91 526 60 69/www.palaciogaviria.com). Metro Ópera or Sol. **Open** 10.30pm-3am Mon-Wed; 11pm-6am Thur-Sat; 8.30pm-2.30am Sun. **Admission** (incl 1 drink) €9 Mon-Thur; €15 Fri, Sat; €12 Sun. **Credit** AmEx, DC, MC, V. **Map** p313 D7.

Prepare to go large in a stately 19th-century palace. Ascend the splendid sweeping staircase, and enter a multitude of rooms with three dancefloors playing pumping dance tunes, Spanish pop and 1980s favourites. Portraits hang on the walls and frescoes adorn the ceilings… imagine the Ministry of Sound in Kensington Palace and you're halfway there. Thursdays see the International Party attracting foreign students, expats and a smattering of tourists. There are also tango and salsa classes from Monday to Friday from 7.30pm.

El Sol

C/Jardines 3 (91 532 64 90/www.elsolmad.com). Metro Gran Vía or Sol. **Open** 11pm-5am Tue-Thur; 11pm-6am Fri, Sat. **Admission** €7.50. **Credit** (bar only) MC, V. **Map** p313 E7.

To call this music joint and club 'no-frills', is an understatement – as its faded yellow walls and middle-aged bar staff attest. However, as anyone knows, it's the music and crowd that make a night, and that's where El Sol is a winner. The DJ serves up an eclectic selection of unmixed rock, soul, funk and R&B. Before long you're lured on to the floor and there you will stay, getting down alongside a varied crowd of twenty- and thirtysomethings.

Suite

C/Virgen de los Peligros 4 (91 521 40 31/www.suite cafe.com). Metro Sevilla. **Open** 9.30pm-3am Mon-Thur; 9.30pm-4.30am Fri, Sat. **Admission** free. **Credit** AmEx, DC, MC, V. **Map** p313 F7.

This is a smart pre-club bar that owes its look to many a London venue. All glass, steel and leather sofas, Suite doubles as a restaurant. Packed to the gills at the weekend, there are bouncers but normally there's no cover charge. The highlight is the upstairs dancefloor, supplying all the tunes you need to kickstart the evening.

Weekend

Bash, Plaza Callao 4 (91 541 3500/www.trip family.com). Metro Callao. **Open** midnight-5am Sun. **Admission** (incl 1 drink) €10. **No credit cards**. **Map** p310 D6.

Weekend is one of the longest standing and most successful Sunday club nights, with a funky feel. Resident DJ Roberto Rodriguez downshifts a gear from the harder revolutions of his other appearances and cruises with the vinyl set to Latin and nu jazz, taking the mixed gay and straight crowd all the way through to Monday morning.

Huertas & Santa Ana

Alhambra/El Buscón

C/Victoria 5 & 9 (91 521 07 08/91 522 54 12). Metro Sol. **Open** 11pm-3.30am Thur-Sat. **Admission** free. **No credit cards**. **Map** p313 E7.

Typically Spanish tapas bars by day, these two adjacent eateries assume a whole new identity come the weekend as DJs play a mix of everything from new flamenco and '80s pop to handbag house.

Turning the tables

Time was when Ibiza was the only place in Spain to turn up any talent behind the decks. Not so these days, with a healthy stable of DJs emerging from a maturing local scene in Madrid, many finding recognition – critical or otherwise – on the national and international circuit. **Wally López** of Weekend Records is Madrid's DJ superstar, having seen Europe-wide success with his instantly recognisable remix of David Guetta's 'A Little More Love'. Winning the Best Newcomer award at the 2002 Ibiza DJ Awards must have been a bittersweet experience for Wally, seeing as he has been plugging away tirelessly in the trade since the tender age of 13. His own productions and remixes are all brimming with funky house grooves and sparkle with inventiveness. Currently signed to the UK label Underwater, he has made guest appearances in Ibiza, Paris, Los Angeles, Tel Aviv, Barcelona and Fabrik in Madrid (*see p238*). Check out his *I'm Coming to London* live mix CD for a taster.

Simón García and his partner **Karim Shaker** (*see p227* **Cool**) are two producers responsible for defining the Madrid sound that's currently garnering perhaps even more support overseas than it is here. Under monikers including Sundayprayers, Latin Soul Drivers, Beatfreakers and plain old Simon & Shaker, they have already racked up a back catalogue of dancefloor stormers that have been given plenty of airtime by the BBC's Pete Tong, Roger Sánchez and the king of tribal beats himself, Danny Tenaglia.

Their release of *The Underground Sound of Madrid*, with their label collaborator Dimas, showcases not only their considerable mixing talents but also the style that characterises the local scene – dark, driving tribal house that hits you with deep grooves and then sets you spinning with its percussive vibes and moody instrumental breaks.

On a funkier tip is the **Hi-Top** collective, a record label founded in Madrid by New Yorker David Lapof (aka El Gran Lapofski) specialising in jazz, funk, lounge and Latin beats. As well as David's sublime selections in compilations such as the label's 2004 release *Spain is Different*, label-mate Ruben 'Watch TV' García has also dusted off a fair few rarities and put them together for his After School Special compilation series. You can catch the Hi-Top crew in venues such as Marula (*see p226*) and Hanabi (*see p227*) or

on the superb DialSoul weekend radio station on 100.4FM from 8pm until midnight on Saturday and Sunday.

Tune in to DialSoul at 4pm and you'll catch **Sandro Bianchi**, the up-and-coming Italian-born (but Madrid-based) DJ and producer. Sandro mixes up a selection of electronica fused with jazz, soul, funk and bossa, touching on hip hop and Latin grooves too. As well as his residency in Museo Chicote (*see p229*), Sandro guests all over Spain, particularly at fashion events, and is even contracted to mix the soundtrack for stores such as luxury goods vendors Loewe. And you thought the cashier just chucked on any old compilation CD.

Finally, for sheer control of a big room, the resident and promoter of Deep (*see p238*), **JL Magoya**, is the man to see. Not only does he work a crowd to perfection during his mammoth sets, José Luis is personally responsible for bringing some of the biggest international names to town. Magoya is Madrid's Mr House, and stands out as another *madrileño* who is making musical waves around the world.

Sandro Bianchi.

Heavily Andaluz, the south of Spain leaps out from every ornately tiled alcove and arch. This place pulls in all sorts, from the international crowd to pony-tailed flamenco aficionados.

Bar de la Comedia

C/Príncipe 16 (91 521 51 64). Metro Sevilla or Sol. **Open** 10pm-3.30am daily. **Admission** free. **No credit cards. Map** p313 F8.
There's nothing funny about Bar de la Comedia. Instead expect a welcome change of pace on this frenzied strip. An international crowd do their thing to a steady soundtrack of hip hop, two step and R&B dance-floor grinders. The door staff are somewhat capricious in their admissions policy.

La Boca del Lobo

C/Echegaray 11 (91 429 70 13). Metro Sevilla. **Open** 11pm-3.30am Wed-Sat. **Admission** (incl 1 drink) €8 after 1am Fri, Sat, otherwise free. **No credit cards. Map** p313 F8.
Unselfconsciously hip and unremittingly friendly, La Boca del Lobo combines live bands with a heady mix of house, breakbeats and R&B. Emerge from the sweaty downstairs dancefloor to the cramped bar area by the entrance or retire upstairs to find a seat (almost impossible after midnight at weekends) and watch the DJ spin a beguiling cocktail of music.

El Burladero

C/Echegaray 19 (mobile 670 366 903). Metro Sevilla or Sol. **Open** 8pm-4am daily. **Admission** free. **No credit cards. Map** p313 F8.
A cosmopolitan crowd, buzzing to the sound of flamenco and rumba, throngs the Moorish arches, amid Andalucian tiles and a rogues' gallery of bullfighters. Upstairs the rumba rumbles but doesn't dominate. Head up here for a respite and a chat with the languid barman, but the frenzied guitar and pistol-shot hand-clapping will eventually lure you back.

Café Ducados

Plaza de Canalejas 3 (91 360 00 89). Metro Sevilla or Sol. **Open** 11am-2.30am daily. **Admission** free. **Credit** AmEx, MC, V. **Map** p313 F7.
For many a reveller, Ducados is the place to start the evening. The ground floor is airy and relaxed. Downstairs is a basement with stars on the ceiling, and (after 1am) a crowd that's getting down, leaving barely room to move. The tunes are floor-fillers that stray towards the cheesy side of good taste, but, given that it's free to enter and bang in the centre of town, no one's complaining.

Cardamomo

C/Echegaray 15 (91 369 07 57). Metro Sevilla. **Open** 10pm-4am Mon-Sat. **Admission** free. **No credit cards. Map** p313 F8.
A firm fixture on the scene, this frenetic flamenco bar plays a mixture of flamenco and rumba tunes, often to thundering effect as the crowd dance, stamp and clap both on and off the diminutive dancefloor. On Wednesdays and Sundays there's a great variety of live flamenco and rumba acts.

Las Cuevas de Sésamo

C/Príncipe 7 (91 429 65 24). Metro Sevilla or Sol. **Open** 7pm-2am Mon-Thur, Sun; 7pm-2.30am Fri, Sat. **Admission** free. **No credit cards. Map** p313 F8.
It's easy to find this basement cavern at weekends – just look for the queue snaking out of the door. But it's worth the wait for what's inside: a sit-down affair with live piano music from 9pm (except Monday), where punters take advantage of the cheapish drinks and friendly atmosphere. A good choice to start the night rather than a final destination.

La Fontana de Oro

C/Victoria 1 (91 531 04 20/www.fontanadeoro.com). Metro Sol. **Open** noon-6am daily. **Admission** free. **No credit cards. Map** p313 E7.
As Madrid's oldest bar, this place used to be a real institution. These days, though, it's an Irish theme bar, run-of-the-mill by day, but when night falls that all changes. The crowd packs in, fuelling up for the night ahead and losing themselves to a mix of classic beer anthems and a variety of live music.

Kapital

C/Atocha 125 (91 420 29 06/www.grupo-kapital.com). Metro Atocha. **Open** *Night session* midnight-6am Thur-Sat. *Afternoon session* 6-10.30pm Fri-Sat. **Admission** *Night session* (incl 1 drink) €15. *Afternoon session* (incl 2 soft drinks) €8. **Credit** AmEx, DC, MC, V. **Map** p314 H9.
The Godzilla of Madrid clubs, with splendid views of the main dancefloor from many of the upper balconies: dance voyeur heaven. Of seven storeys, each has something different to offer: the main dancefloor and bars are at ground level; the first floor has karaoke; the third R&B and hip hop; the fourth cosy cocktail bars; the fifth is Spanish disco; the sixth has a cinema and more cool sounds, and at the top is a terrace with a retractable roof. No trainers.

Sala Stella

C/Arlabán 7 (91 523 86 54/91 522 88 26/www.meb-mondo.com). Metro Sevilla. **Open** 1am-6am Thur; 1am-7am Fri, Sat. **Admission** (incl 1 drink) €12 Thur; €13 Fri, Sat. **Credit** AmEx, DC, MC, V. **Map** p313 F7.
If you only go to one club in Madrid, make sure it's this one. Mondo, the fiendishly popular Thursday nighter, has been the champion of the Berlin-electro sound in Madrid, thanks to Gerardo Niva's skilful selection of tunes and guest DJs. On Fridays Ángel García spins a West Coast, future jazz-house set, which sounds frighteningly cool but can lack peaks. Saturdays are the intriguingly named Rubble Action, where the policy is simply 'electronic music', allowing the DJs to mix up new wave, avant-electro, disco, acid… you name it.

Souza

C/Moratín 36 (91 429 15 06). Metro Antón Martín. **Open** 8pm-2.30am Thur-Sun. **Admission** free. **No credit cards. Map** p314 G8.
If the frenzied pace of Madrid nighteries is getting a bit much, Souza offers a welcome change of scene.

The tunes are jazz and Latin beats, the crowd is late twenties and early thirties and the cocktails ease you through the evening. Bar staff mix a mean Whisky Sour, not to mention the Long Island Iced Tea and a wicked Bloody Mary to get you in the mood, for a proper night out on the town.

Torero

C/Cruz 26 (91 523 11 29). Metro Sol. **Open** 11.30pm-4.30am Tue, Wed; 11.30pm-6am Thur-Sat. **Admission** (incl 1 drink) free Tue, Wed; 10 Thur-Sat. **No credit cards. Map** p313 E7/8.

Don't be put off by the forbidding exterior, the only thing not dancing inside is the wall-mounted bull's head that stares down impassively at the mostly local crowd. The ground floor gyrates to Spanish and Latin beats, while on the floor below house reverberates off the red-brick walls. Don't wear trainers, though. They're not allowed.

Rastro & Lavapiés

See also p38 **Candela.**

Bar San Lorenzo

C/Salitre 38 (no phone). Metro Lavapiés. **Open** 5pm-2.30am daily. **Admission** free. **No credit cards. Map** p313 E9.

Also known as Taurino, or more commonly 'that bar on Salitre', the San Lorenzo has no sign. Stained-glass windows and furniture that could have been found on the street lend this intimate, candlelit venue a kooky charm. Popular with smokers, a guy with dreadlocks in a sarong puts on the CDs, switching between minimal sounds and tripped-out dub.

El Juglar

C/Lavapiés 37 (91 528 43 81/www.juglar.tv). Metro Lavapiés. **Open** 8.30pm-3am Mon-Thur; 8.30pm-3.30am Fri-Sun. *Concerts* usually start at 10pm. **Admission** *Bar* free. *Concerts* average €5. **No credit cards. Map** p313 E9.

Epitomising Lavapiés – a bohemian, cool and laid-back hangout for those who like the tempo of their evening to be energetic but not too frenetic. The bare red brick and chrome front bar provides a chilled background for the broad-based crowd and soundtrack of jazz and soul. After midnight the rhythm speeds up in the back as the resident DJ Señores de Funk spins a mix of souped-up soul, Latin and funk.

Kappa

C/Olmo 26 (no phone). Metro Antón Martín. **Open** 8.30pm-3am daily. Closed 10 days mid Aug. **Admission** free. **No credit cards. Map** p313 F9.

An unprepossessing and easily missed little hideaway, Kappa is amiable and intimate and, despite its complete lack of decor, somehow cosy. This chameleon of *locales* has built up quite a cult following among those who feel life should have an unhurried pace, and the DJ plays a bit of everything as long as it's mellow. This is an ideal pre-club launch pad or a haven where you can kick back and chill out when Madrid threatens to overwhelm.

La Lupe

C/Torrecilla del Leal 12 (91 527 50 19). Metro Antón Martín. **Open** 7pm-2.30am Mon-Wed; 6pm-3.30am Thur-Sun. **Admission** free. **No credit cards. Map** p313 F9.

Now with a sister bar in C/Hortaleza, La Lupe is a microcosm of everything that makes Madrid the city it is. The signs on the walls say it all, from the notice that welcomes gays and lesbians to the poster protesting against any law that prohibits bars staying open until whatever ungodly hour they please. A diverse and open-minded crowd enjoys Mojitos mixed to perfection in this alternative nightspot, which also hosts cabaret nights.

La Ventura

C/Olmo 31 (91 521 48 54). Metro Antón Martín. **Open** 10pm-2.30am Tue-Thur, Sun; 11pm-3am Fri, Sat. **Admission** free. **No credit cards. Map** p313 F9.

You might not know its name (there is no sign), but if you've been in Madrid a while, you're sure to have been here at least once. Lounge on full-length floor cushions while soaking up the measured sounds of trip hop and dub. Later the pace hots up a little with breakbeat, electronica and house thrown in, and the dancefloor is filled by a cosmopolitan crowd of students, ex-students and the casually hip.

Chueca

Areia

C/Hortaleza 92 (91 310 03 07/www.areiachillout. com). Metro Chueca. **Open** 1pm-2.30am Mon-Thur, Sun; 1pm-3am Fri, Sat. **Admission** free. **Credit** AmEx, DC, MC, V. **Map** p310 G4.

Once an Irish bar, Areia has been transformed beyond recognition into a chill-out that covers all the angles: by day it's a place to get lunch or a snack, in the afternoon it's a place to chill, and in the evenings the vibe hots up as a cool crowd passes through on their nightly tour of the city. The seductive Eastern decor, along with sofas and cushions on which to lounge, can make it difficult to leave.

Mito

C/Augusto Figueroa 3 (91 531 89 96/www. discomito.com). Metro Chueca. **Open** 11pm-6am daily. **Admission** free before 2am; €7 2-4.30am; €10 4.30-6am. **No credit cards. Map** p310 G5.

One of the few clubs to open every night of the week, this is one to avoid at the weekend but to take advantage of midweek if you really can't wait till Thursday for an all-nighter. A mix of older house tracks and Latin dance grooves await you, along with a crowd that doesn't know when to stop.

Pachá

C/Barceló 11 (91 447 01 28). Metro Tribunal. **Open** midnight-6am Thur-Sat. **Admission** (incl 1 drink) 12. **Credit** AmEx, DC, MC, V. **Map** p310 G4.

In a club scene that ditches the glitz, Pachá is the black sheep. The bouncers may claim it's for royal relatives and the jet set, but it mainly attracts rich kids and posers. Dress up to get in, and expect glamorous go-gos, on-stage dance routines and themed parties, enacted to a soundtrack of soulful house. Wednesdays are hip hop nights, with appearances from the likes of local rising star Jotamayuscula and Grandmaster Flash. Not on a par with its Ibiza namesake, but fun for those who like a bit of glam.

Stars Café

C/Marqués de Valdeiglesias 5 (91 522 27 12/ www.starscafedance.com). Metro Banco de España. **Open** 1pm-2am Mon-Wed; 1pm-3am Thur; 1pm-3.30am Fri; 8pm-3.30am Sat. **Credit** AmEx, DC, MC, V. **Map** p314 G6.

For a pre-club bar or a complete night out, look to the Stars Café. Hangout café, restaurant and crêperie – Stars does the lot. Later the music kicks in with the young and lovely (or not) swaying gently to some of the best Brazilian and Latin jazz fusion around. Down in the dark basement, after midnight from Thursday to Saturday, some equally dark and twisted house assumes centre stage.

Stromboli

C/Hortaleza 96 (91 319 46 28). Metro Alonso Martínez. **Open** 6.30pm-3.30am daily. **Credit** MC, V. **Map** p310 G4.

A very cool little lounge that's perfect for a mid-week drink or as a stop on your weekend tour of the town. Very much part of the hip scene around C/Hortaleza and C/Fuencarral, and a place where the club DJs of Madrid drop their big-room style and spin something a little more intimate.

Malasaña & Conde Duque

Binomio

C/Corredera Baja de San Pablo 26, Malasaña (no phone). Metro Tribunal. **Open** 10.30pm-5.30am Mon-Sat. **Admission** free. **No credit cards. Map** p309 F5. Camper than the Christmas lights with which it's decorated, this cabaret club is quite something. It's also certainly something unusual. Drag queens, magicians, bolero singers and more than a few flamenco dancers perform in the most intimate of surroundings, and audience participation is not optional. Shows start at 1am, or 2am at weekends.

Café Rock Corto Maltés

Plaza Dos de Mayo 9 (91 531 13 17). Metro Bilbao or Tribunal. **Open** 7pm-2am Mon-Thur, Sun; 7pm-3am Fri, Sat. **Admission** free. **Credit** DC, MC, V. **Map** p309 F3.

As well as a sizeable summertime terrace outside, Corto has a great vibe inside, with a troupe of guest DJs spinning a varied selection of deep house, electro and floor-fillers. When summer is over and the terrace is closed, the party doesn't end. Oh no. That's when the large barred doors leading down to the cavernous basement swing open for an underground (in every sense) house session. It's all good fun, but with a cave capacity of only a few score, you'll leave with plenty of new friends.

For non-stop dancing

Once it gets going, **El Sol**'s dancefloor is unstoppable. Escape on to the stage when the pace gets too much. *See p229.*

For catching Sesame Street

At **Siroco**, you can watch cartoons and kids' programmes while you get down to a sublime funk and soul selection. *See p236.*

For a budget night out

Live instruments alongside the DJ and no cover charge make **Tempo** a must when the euros are running low. *See p236.*

For objects of desire

Heartbreakingly gorgeous night owls steal the show at **Goldfield**. *See p236.*

For charming even the snakes

Asian influences and oriental dancers, Buddha Bar's DJ Ravin and even the odd snake-charmer are to be found at **Shabay**. *See p237.*

For a cool night out

Arctic-strength air-conditioning or an outdoor terrace are the only things that will get you through the summer months. **Ananda** is the biggest terrace, and the best. *See p236.*

For checking out the big boys

Carl Cox, Eric Morillo, Roger Sánchez, Masters at Work have all paid a visit to Madrid's true superclub, **Divino**. *See p238.*

Démodé

C/Ballesta 7 (mobile 678 50 52 37). Metro Chueca. **Open** 11pm-3.30am Thur-Sun. **Admission** free. **No credit cards. Map** p309 F5.

The flyers let you know what you're in for – an elegant figure reclines against a backdrop of flock wallpaper in a juxtaposition of the übertrendy and the super-cheesy. This pre-club joint is housed in an old brothel. Faux oil paintings still adorn the walls, but red lighting, sofas and an ample sound system have transformed it into one of the coolest nightspots of the moment. DJs spin both underground house and electro for a mixed gay/straight crowd.

Morocco

C/Marqués de Leganés 7 (91 531 51 67). Metro Santo Domingo. **Open** 11pm-5.30am Thur; midnight-6am Fri, Sat. **Admission** (incl 2 drinks) €8 Fri, Sat; (incl 1 drink) €6 Thur. **No credit cards. Map** p309 E5.

Arts & Entertainment

What Londoners take when they go out.

EVERY WEEK

Tupperware. *See p236.*

Once owned by Movida legend Alaska, Morocco has two feet firmly planted in the past. From its '80s decor and crowd, everything here smacks of days gone by. The DJ mixes mainly classic Spanish pop with today's nu flamenco. Despite all this throwback action, it's still great fun, being completely free of pretension and brimming with dancefloor energy.

Nasti

C/San Vicente Ferrer 33 (91 521 76 05/www.nasti. ws). Metro Tribunal. **Open** midnight-6am Fri, Sat. **Admission** (incl 1 drink) €7.50. **No credit cards.** **Map** p309 E4.

The remit here is simple – pack out a small and smoky *sala* with a fiercely loyal crowd, and play anything from the Sex Pistols to Joy Division to make them dance. A riotous, grungy and alternative crowd find their home here, enjoying the live acts such as Fanny Pack or Humbert Humbert and the guest DJs such as 2 Many DJs.

El No.1

C/Minas 1 (no phone). Metro Noviciado. **Open** 7pm-1am Mon-Thur; 7pm-2am Fri, Sat. **Admission** free. **No credit cards.** **Map** p309 E4.

Spacious, friendly and soothingly decorated, this is an oasis of calm in the desert storm of Madrid's nightlife. With a café-style air, the easygoing crowd partake of whatever exotic tea, coffee or *copa* takes their fancy. Downstairs hosts DJs at weekends who spin a subtle web of jazz and Latin house.

Oui

C/Marqués de Santa Ana 11 (no phone). Metro Noviciado. **Open** *Sept-June* 10.30pm-3.30am Wed-Sat. *July, Aug* 10.30pm-3.30am Thur-Sat. **Admission** free. **No credit cards.** **Map** p309 E4.

A truly unique bar, Oui is damn difficult to find but worth the search. Its bizarre shape and eclectic music policy – expect anything from early techno to

present-day electronica, along with a knowledgeable and loyal clientele, make this a gem among the sometimes mediocre bars of Malasaña.

El Perro de la Parte Atrás del Coche

C/Puebla 15 (no phone). Metro Gran Vía. **Open** 9.30pm-3.30am daily. **Admission** (minimum consumption) €6. **No credit cards.** **Map** p314 F5.

As the unusual name (it means the 'nodding dog') suggests, everything about El Perro is different. The music policy is a mix-up of everything, with hip hop, house, soul and funk from the resident DJs. The live acts take in heavy metal, so you might get Aretha Franklin one night and a Metallica tribute band the next. A crowd from all walks of life make this an eclectic mix that shouldn't work, but really does.

Radar

C/Amaniel 22 (no phone). Metro Noviciado or Plaza de España. **Open** 10pm-2.30am Thur; 10.30pm-3.30am Fri, Sat; 9.30pm-2.30am Sun. **Admission** free. **No credit cards.** **Map** p309 D4.

For those who get off on experimental electronic music, this is a must-visit venue. Small and dark, the decor – minimalist 1980s computer-game chic – forms the perfect backdrop. When the DJs hit the decks at weekends the electronica, noise and techno enthusiasts flock, and like all good venues it manages to draw you completely into its world.

Sala Dink

C/Amaniel 13 (no phone). Metro Noviciado. **Open** midnight-6am Fri, Sat. **Admission** (incl 1 drink) €12. **No credit cards.** **Map** p309 D4.

The star has fallen a bit for this once legendary venue and, despite a refit, Dink is fighting to regain a following. Resident DJ David Mariscal was a long-term fixture at The Room, so expect a similar vibe – deep West Coast house with little vocal action.

Siroco

C/San Dimas 3 (91 593 30 70/www.siroco.es).
Metro Noviciado. **Open** 9.30pm-5am Thur; 9.30pm-
6am Fri, Sat. **Admission** (incl 1 drink) €5-€8.
No credit cards. Map p309 E3.
A wonderfully creative crew run Siroco, something
that is abundantly clear from their flyers, their
programme and the visuals of the club itself.
Doubling as a live music venue, it starts to hot up
after the concerts finish at around 2am, when a
crowd composed mainly of wannabe b-boys, club
kids and beardy young students get down to the
soul, funk and rare groove seven-inchers deftly
woven together by the resident DJs.

Tempo

*C/Duque de Osuna 8 (91 547 7518/www.tempomad
rid.com). Metro Plaza España.* **Open** *Sept-June* 5pm-
3am daily. *July* 5pm-3am Mon-Sat. Closed Aug.
Admission free. **Credit** MC, V. **Map** p309 D4.
A very cool little venue that doubles as a café by day
and a venue at night for live acts and DJs. In the
pleasant upstairs café you can sit and have a bite,
but as the night wears on, head downstairs, either
to the dimly lit chill-out room or the dancefloor
bathed with psychedelic projections. The in-house
DJ often is accompanied by live percussion.

Tetería No.2

C/Pez 16 (no phone). Metro Noviciado. **Open** *Sept-
June* 6pm-3.30am Tue-Sun. *July, Aug* 7pm-3.30am
Tue-Sun. **No credit cards. Map** p309 E5.
The sister venue of No.1 (*see p235*). Visit them in the
order suggested by the names, and you'll be warmed
up nicely and ready to dance by the time you arrive
at No.2. The split-level venue is narrow but spacious
upstairs, the bar by the entrance giving way to a
large salon. The downstairs *sala* is a wonderful
arched cave, with a higher volume designed to make
you dance. Funk and soul are on the speakers, with
live acts on various nights of the week.

Tupperware

*C/Corredera Alta de San Pablo 26 (no phone). Metro
Tribunal.* **Open** 9pm-3.30am daily. **Admission** free.
No credit cards. Map p309 F4.
Truly postmodern, this place is outrageously kitsch
but with a pop art sensibility that saves it from crossing over too far into tackiness. The fake fur, *Star
Wars* pictures and the faux-cool 1970s psychedelia
hang together surprisingly well, and there's a pleasant anything-goes music policy that brings all kinds
of sounds from acid jazz to house to soul. The crowd,
slightly older and with less to prove, tend to chill out
in the easygoing vibe.

Salamanca & the Retiro

Ananda

*C/Ciudad de Barcelona 2 (91 506 02 56). Metro
Atocha.* **Open** 11pm-3am daily. Closed mid Sept-
May. **Admission** (incl 1 drink) €10 Mon-Sat; €15
Sun. **Credit** AmEx, DC, V. **Map** p314 H10.

This is the mother of all club terraces: the enormous
2,000-square-metre complex comes complete with
two dancefloors (one indoors and one out), ten bars
and plenty of cushion-strewn sofas and chairs, all of
them done up in a bit of an Eastern theme. The regular clientele generally ranges from your usual
fresh-faced clubby kids (especially on Wednesdays
and Sundays for the Sundance parties, where
sounds are vocal and tech house) to older guys in
suits out sharking for ladies. The place is not cheap,
but from June to August that's a small price to pay
to stay cool in the city.

North & west

Argüelles

DU:OM

*Sala Arena, C/Princesa 1 (91 547 57 11/www.
salarena.com). Metro Plaza de España.* **Open** 1-6am
Fri, Sat. **Admission** varies. **Map** p309 D5.
A dual-personality club night, with diametrically
opposed sounds on each floor. Downstairs Juanjo
Martin and Victor da House mix a bang-up-to-date
selection of tech and tribal house tracks with
whooshing high-level sweeps and pounding 4/4
beats that keep the crowd dancing all night long.
Upstairs it's an anything-goes policy with Spanish
pop (or *pachanga*) thrown together with commercial
hip hop, cheesy dance tracks and eurotrance.

Goldfield

*C/Ventura Rodríguez 7 (no phone). Metro Plaza
España or Ventura Rodríguez.* **Open** 1am-7.30am
Fri, Sat. **Admission** (incl 1 drink) €15. **No credit
cards. Map** p308 C4.
Where the pretty people go to dance. Spanish actress
Paz Vega is one of the promoters of Goldfield, and
as you would expect from a celluloid star, the
emphasis in her club is on glamour. Resident DJ
Jabato whacks out the sexy house tunes and the
crowd enjoy checking themselves out in the mirrors.
Thursdays are Soul 13, a hot new night showcasing
soul, hip hop, R&B and funk.

Chamberí

Low

C/Galileo 26 (91 360 57 50). Metro Quevedo. **Open**
midnight-5.45am Fri. **Admission** €10. **Credit** (bar
only) MC, V. **Map** p309 D2.
Low finds its home in a long-standing Madrid venue
(Revolver), which has, in recent years, changed its
name with alarming regularity. Still, it seems as if
this current Friday night incarnation just might be
here to stay, as it has been capitalising on the recent
mainstream interest in the more experimental side
of electronica. The DJs – resident and otherwise –
spin a varied mix, taking in everything from electro,
electro-clash, electro-pop, pop and even good, old-
fashioned rock'n'roll. The large venue doesn't fill up
until 3am, so don't rush.

Moma 56

C/José Abascal 56 (91 399 09 00/www.moma56.com).
Metro Alonso Cano or Gregorio Marañón. **Open**
11pm-6am Wed-Sat. **Admission** (incl 1 drink) €10.
No credit cards.
If it's a bit of glamour you're looking for and you
actually feel up to the challenge of getting through
the door, then you should probably check out Moma
56. Multifunctional in a New York style, the venue
is a restaurant, bar and nightclub, with stylish decor
and a semi-celebrity crowd.

Nature

Sala Changó, C/Covarrubias 42 (91 446 00 36/
www.natureclub.net). Metro Alonso Martinez.
Open midnight-6am Thur. **Admission** (incl 2
drinks, 1 drink after 3am) €10. **Credit** AmEx,
DC, MC, V. **Map** p310 G3.

Since the late '90s it has been Nature's mission to
break Madrid's addiction to house, and introduce a
different sound into the town's limited musical
scope. Nature mixes up breaks, jungle, electro and
drum'n'bass to great effect. The dancers are some of
the best to be seen in Madrid, while the regular
crowd – studenty, tattooed and dreadlocked – looks
a little less coordinated on the dancefloor.

Shabay

C/Miguel Ángel 3 (91 319 76 92/www.shabay.com).
Metro Rubén Dario. **Open** 11.30pm-5am Tue-Thur;
11.30pm-6am Fri, Sat; 9pm-3am Sun. Closed 2wks
mid Aug. **Admission** (incl 1 drink) €15. **Credit**
AmEx, DC, MC, V. **Map** p310 I2.
Full of Eastern promise, Shabay has lots of intricate
decoration and a carefully crafted atmosphere.
A once-monthly residency from DJ Ravin (he of

Notes from the underground

Ironically, most of Madrid's wildest nightlife
takes place during the day. Since the
legendary after-hours Boccacio and Midday
took the scene by storm during the '90s,
matinal clubs have been as essential to your
disco-disciple as nocturnal spots.

For the uninitiated, an after-hours can be
broadly defined as a club that opens when
nightclubs chuck out, normally at 6am. In
turn, when these clubs serve their last drinks
and spin their last tune at 10am or so, a
whole gamut of basement haunts quietly
open their doors – the after-hours to the
after-hours. For a while, there was only
minimal interference from the authorities in
these morning sessions. However, all that
changed in 1999 when the city council made
them illegal and put the regulation of such
clubs high on its agenda. From then on, after-
hours were – like many activities – technically
illegal, but for the most part tolerated.

There was more bad news for after-hours
in 2002, when several high-profile all-day
Sunday parties hit the headlines. A long-
running and extremely popular monthly fiesta,
the Goa Rave, ended up on the front page of
one of the national dailies when five clubbers
were rushed to hospital after over-indulging.
Another buzzing Monday morning after-hours
club named Still … in the Morning also made
the news when it was reported that people on
their way to work were having to step over its
comatose hedonists dozing on the pavement.

These much-publicised incidents brought
an inevitable crackdown. These days it is not
uncommon for party-goers to be confronted
by policemen making their way through an

after, checking licences and generally
freaking out the highly stimulated clubbers.
To dodge actual closure of their underground
hangouts, promoters constantly change the
name of the landlord, ensuring that any legal
process repeatedly has to go back to square
one, allowing them to continue to operate.

Despite, or perhaps because of, this
repressive climate, *afters* pop up in the most
unlikely places, like the sex shop that ran
an invite-only, all-day dance-fest. Then there
was Gimnasio, which opened its doors on
Saturday and Sunday mornings for a party
that – as the name implies – took place in
a gym, on the sixth floor of an office building.
It ran for several months until the inevitable
police raid. The promoter was quoted as
claiming that the 12-hour house sessions
'were put on for paying members of the gym,
enabling them to get together, dance and
enjoy themselves at the weekend'.

The police have squeezed promoters so
much that the mother of all Sunday sessions,
Space of Sound (*see p238*), finally had to
move to a night-time slot, after nine iconic
years of all-day Sunday madness. Happily,
after a year of keeping its head down, the
coast is clearer and Space is seeing in
Sunday again from September 2004.

How long it will last is another story.
After-hours come and go now with startling
regularity. The surest way to find them is to
look carefully at the flyers you are handed
as you leave a club or to check in the usual
places (Mercado de Fuencarral, bars, record
shops and so on). If you want to see what
hard-core partying is all about, you'll find them.

Arts & Entertainment

Buddha Bar in Paris) brings in the oriental and Afrobeat sounds that have made his name among the clubbing crowd. From Tuesday to Saturday the place functions as a nightclub, but on Sundays the pace drops a few notches for a chill-out session complete with incense, candles and a selection of treats from Indian and Thai cuisine.

Chamartín

Space of Sound

Sala Macumba, Estación de Chamartín (902 49 99 94/www.spaceofsound.net). Metro Chamartín. **Open** 10am-7pm Sun. **Admission** (incl 1 drink) €12. **No credit cards**.

After a year's absence, the city's biggest all-day party is back, and what a monster it really is. The crowd is weirdly territorial, with one area that's mainly gay, another that's predominantly straight and even a group of transsexuals claiming an area by one of the bars. The attraction is the eclectic crowd and the amazing sound. In fact, the sound system here is unmatched and, along with the resident DJs – specialists in both tech and progressive house – the promoters bring in the likes of Deep Dish and Steve Lawler. Forget the Retiro, this is what Sundays in Madrid are for.

South of centre

Deep at Divino

Paseo Ermita del Santo 48 (mobile 619 224 464). Metro Puerta del Ángel. **Open** midnight-7am Fri. Closed July, Aug. **Admission** (incl 1 drink) €10-€18. **No credit cards**.

The city's one true superclub, Divino is an enormous, amorphous venue, with hidden rooms and sections suddenly appearing when the likes of Carl Cox, John Digweed or the Masters at Work come to play. The crowd is on the young side, with a somewhat glassy-eyed appreciation of the house grooves and broken beats from the sound system.

Fabrik

Avda de la Industria 82, Ctra Fuenlabrada-Moralejos de Enmedio (mobile 699 90 96 81/www.grupo-kapital.com). Metro Fuenlabrada then bus 496, 497. **Open** 11pm-6am Sat. **Admission** (incl 1 drink) €18. **Credit** AmEx, DC, MC, V.

Fabrik is a converted warehouse kitted out with a dazzling array of disco surprises: a 60kw sound system; a huge outdoor terrace complete with a fake river and two covered dancefloors; and, in the main arena, a vertical and horizontal megatron to shoot freezing nitrogen into the crowd. It's a bit of a schlep to get here, but well worth the taxi fare.

Not too **Shabay**. *See p237.*

In **Deep at Divino**.

Sport & Fitness

Madrid is pumping it up in the hope of hosting the 2012 Olympics.

Bowling Chamartín. *See p243.*

If Madrid wins what has been a strong bid to host the 2012 Olympic Games (the IOC will decide in July 2005) the city will get the go-ahead to make widespread improvements to its sporting infrastructure. Plans have already been laid for a massive Olympic Village, powered by self-sustaining energy, linked up by a massive cycle route. The city's bid was helped by a trump-filled starting hand. Mayor Ruiz Gallardón, highly conscious of the tourist-inducing improvements Barcelona made when they hosted the 1992 Games, claims that 70 per cent of the necessary facilities for the Olympics are already in place or being built. That's not so hard to believe when you consider that the city boasts nearly 50 sports centres, covering 70 different activities.

For those who prefer spectator sports to participating themselves, Madrid is home to two successful Primera División clubs (eternal rivals Atlético and Real Madrid), and two of Spain's top basketball clubs; what's more, it hosts one of Europe's most prestigious marathons, and is the setting for the finish of the famous Vuelta a España cycling race.

Spectator sports

Athletics/*atletismo*

Estadio de la Comunidad de Madrid

Avda de Arcentales s/n, Eastern suburbs (91 720 24 00). Metro Las Musas.

Set to become the epicentre of the Olympic Village, this stadium (and indeed the whole neighbourhood) is dominated by the vast plate-shaped 'Peineta' stand (so named as it resembles a flamenco dancer's comb), while the rest is flanked by small grassy banks. If Madrid gets the Olympic go-ahead the grassy knolls will be turned into state-of-the art seating areas, and the capacity of the stadium will rise from its current 20,000 to 75,000. The public can use the track for training, and there are also other sporting facilities, including tennis courts.

Maratón Popular de Madrid

Information MAPOMA/902 210 578/ www.mapoma.es or www.maratonmadrid.org.

Madrid's marathon, on the last Sunday in April, is growing year on year, both in number of participants and prestige, and is now considered to be among the

Arts & Entertainment

Time Out Madrid **239**

world's top ten. In 2004, 13,000 athletes took part, including 3,200 foreigners. The halfway mark is in the dead centre of the city; thousands of cheery folk collect in Puerta del Sol to egg on the tiring runners; an estimated million spectators annually take to the city streets to catch the race. The previous Sunday there is another road race, the 20 Kilómetros de Madrid, organised by Agrupación Deportiva Maratón (91 402 69 62, www.admaraton.es).

Basketball/*baloncesto*

Basketball is Spain's second most popular sport, and Madrid has two of the country's top teams: **Estudiantes** is the city's best-supported club, while **Real Madrid**, affiliated to the football club of the same name, is traditionally the more successful. Both teams regularly qualify for the all-important league play-offs that run in May to eventually decide the annual champions.

Adecco Estudiantes

Palacio Vistalegre, C/Utebo 1, Southern suburbs (91 422 07 81/www.palaciovistalegre.com). Metro Oporto or Vista Alegre.
'Estu' have a fanatical group of supporters (nick-named 'La Demencia'), who travel home and away and festoon 'El Vistalegre' with colourful scarves, banners and, on special occasions, huge mosaics. The 15,000-capacity stadium, shaped like a space pod, was built on the top of the old bullring and two huge bronze bulls still guard its entrance. You can pick up tickets (€15-€50) on match days; for information on fixtures, ring the club on 91 562 40 22 or check out the website www.club estudiantes.com.

Real Madrid

Pabellón Raimundo Saporta, Paseo de la Castellana 259, Northern suburbs (902 281 709/www.real madrid.com). Metro Begoña.
Real Madrid's hoop stars have a trophy record to match that of the football team, but have fallen away in recent years. At the time of writing the team found itself homeless for the 2004/5 season, after club president Florentino Pérez sold the training ground in order to pay off the huge debts of Real Madrid FC. The relative (and unwarranted) complacency of Real Madrid's fans is compensated for by the exuberance of their professional cheerleaders.

Cycling/*ciclismo*

La Vuelta a España (www.lavuelta.com) is an enormous deal in the cycling world, with the best international cyclists competing with a ferocity and determination only surpassed by their efforts in the Tour de France. La Vuelta finishes in Madrid, where a knowledgeable crowd awaits the arrival of the time-triallers. In September 2005 Spain will host the World Cycling Championships.

Football/*fútbol*

Madrid has two top-drawer football teams, **Real Madrid** (known as 'El Real', or simply 'Madrid') and **Atlético de Madrid** ('Atleti'). El Real's policy of signing the world's top players (*'los galácticos'*) and filling up the rest of the squad with youth-teamers means that they are usually very exciting to watch. Real Madrid is the most successful European team in the history of the game, but more of the city's working-class population support Atleti (*see also p241* **Taking sides**). Try and get hold of a ticket for one of the two Derbies played every season for an unforgettable experience.

League matches are played on a Saturday or a Sunday evening, from September to May or June; one of the teams plays in Madrid every weekend. Cup and European matches are held during the week. Tickets can be very hard to come by, especially for Real Madrid games; if you can't get one at the ticket office, you might have to resort to buying a *'reventa'* ('resale') from one of the touts outside the ground. For shirts and fan-junk, *see p187* **Área Real Madrid**, or try the club shops.

Atlético de Madrid

Estadio Vicente Calderón, Paseo Virgen del Puerto 67, South of centre (91 366 47 07/www.club atleticodemadrid.com/shop 91 366 82 37). Metro Pirámides. **Open** *Ticket office* 10am-2pm, 5-8pm day before match; from 11am till kick-off on match days. **Tickets** €20-€42. **Credit** MC, V. **No credit cards**.
The Calderón stadium has a fantastic atmosphere, with thousands of singing fans whose red and white scarves, shirts and banners leave you in no doubt as to their allegiance, and who noisily back their team whatever the score. The stadium has a 57,000 capacity, and often sells out, so plan well ahead. Expect to pay upwards of €30 for a decent seat.

Real Madrid

Estadio Santiago Bernabéu, Paseo de la Castellana 144, Chamartín (91 398 43 00/www.realmadrid.es). Metro Santiago Bernabéu. **Open** *(Guided tours)* 6-9pm daily, depending on match times. **Tickets** €15-€115. **Credit** AmEx, DC, MC, V.
When Real Madrid are playing with flair and style and knocking goal after goal in against a bewildered opposition, the Bernabéu is a great place to be. The stadium holds 75,000 people, and is nearly always full for league games. But the fans, many of whom travel in from out of town for the game, have been well nourished on a diet of success, and don't concede to defeat easily, waving white handkerchiefs when their star-saturated team fails to perform. The far-right group Ultras Sur, which stands behind one of the goals, is a nasty mob who keep a barrage of singing and insult-hurling going throughout the game. Tickets can only be bought over the phone on 902 324 324.

Taking sides

In the last 50 years Real Madrid (*pictured*) have won trophies with clockwork regularity, and in doing so have picked up the support of the floating football voter throughout the country: a recent nationwide survey discovered that 43 per cent of Spaniards admitted to supporting the team they call 'El Real'. In the capital this figure extends to 70 per cent, with only 19 per cent supporting Real's city rivals Atlético de Madrid.

However, the statistics disguise a rather more complex reality. Atlético's 57,000-capacity Vicente Calderón stadium is a mere half-hour walk from Plaza Mayor, in a heavily populated working-class residential area, whereas the Santiago Bernabéu (capacity 75,000) finds itself in the swanky district of Chamartín further uptown. That means the working-class population of south and central Madrid tend to support '*los rojiblancos*' (Atleti, the 'red-and-whites') rather than '*los merengues*' (Real, the 'meringues'). While it's true to say that many Real Madrid match-going fans are from humble, local, working-class *barrios*, a good proportion of the Bernabéu faithful come in from the suburbs, from other cities in Spain, or from even further afield.

Thus the two sets of aficionados tend to behave very differently. Both teams have their nasty right-wing, flag-waving, stand-behind-the-goal-and-sing-throughout-the-match *ultras* (Real's Ultra Sur, Atleti's Frente Atlético). It's the behaviour of the average fan that is more telling. Atleti supporters, known as '*los indios*' (the Indians), sing more, wear their colours more, and get behind the team when they are losing. They pride themselves on their loyalty. In a recent spell in the depths of La Segunda (the second division, otherwise known as '*el infierno*', or hell) their stadium was virtually full every game. Atlético fans are so used to the slings and arrows of outrageous fortune that they have built the expectation of defeat into their collective personality. Their 100th anniversary song, contracted to be written and sung by hard-living singer-songwriter and Atleti fan Joaquín Sabina, rocks to the chorus '*Que manera de sufrir...*' ('what a way to suffer') ...'*que*

manera de palmar' ('what a way to lose a game we should have won').

Meanwhile Real fans ('*los vikingos*'), bloated on a diet of almost constant success, need something really special to get them off their seats. They are quicker to turn against their team when things are going wrong, bringing out their white handkerchiefs to perform '*la pañolada*' (a method of showing dissatisfaction among football crowds) or, indeed, staying away altogether when the team is in a bad patch. Real's 100th-anniversary rendition of their traditional hymn reflects the self-important nature of the club: Plácido Domingo booms '*Hala Madrid... con su bandera limpia y blanca que no empaña*' ('Hail Madrid... with its clean white flag that never gets tarnished').

All this makes for a rather different viewing experience. At the Santiago Bernabéu, you get to see more '*galácticos*' (superstars), there's more likelihood of a spectacular home win, and you even get warmed by vast gas fires in winter. At the Vicente Calderón the warmth is more natural. You're less likely to enjoy the vicarious thrill of victory, it's true, but, whatever the result, you're in for a better atmosphere and a more emotional experience. You might even, if you're that way inclined, end up jumping up and down and joining the Atleti fans in their favourite song and ultimate insult '¡*Quién no bote Madridista es, es!*'– 'Whoever doesn't pogo is a Real Madrid fan, oh yes they are.'

Alex Leith is the author of El Becks – A Season in the Sun.

Motor sports

Circuito del Jarama
Ctra de Burgos (A-I), km 27, San Sebastián de los Reyes (91 657 08 75/www.jarama.com). Bus 171 from Plaza de Castilla to Ciudad Santo Domingo.
The last time the Jarama track hosted a Formula One race was way back in 1981, but it still has a full calendar of motorbike and truck racing.

Billiards & pool/*billares*

Shooters Pool Hall & Bar
Gran Vía 31 (91 522 40 10). Metro Callao or Gran Vía. **Open** 3.30pm-2.30am Mon-Thur; 3.30pm-3.30am Fri; 4.30pm-3.30am Sat; 4.30pm-2.30am Sun. **Credit** MC, V. **Map** p313 E6.

Getting steamy

As traffic, work hours and the cost of living grows and the siesta diminishes, Madrid is turning to spas and alternative therapies with increasing frequency.

At the forefront of Madrid's current health and relaxation infatuation are the **Medina Mayrit** baths (*pictured*). An instant hit with *madrileños* from the minute they opened in 2003, the baths are still so popular you need to call weeks in advance for a weekend booking.

As clichéd as it sounds, Medina Mayrit really is an oasis of calm, located just minutes from the Puerta del Sol. A series of pools span out beneath arched ceilings, half lit by flickering lamps. One shallow pool of warm water abuts another of hot water, with a deeper pool of cold water nearby for a chilly plunge.

The company behind the hammam, El Grupo Al Andalus, prioritises historic authenticity. Masons from Andalucía were hired to lay the stone floors; which replicate the streets of Granada's Albaicín (Moorish quarter). The mosaic walls at the entrance are designed in the red, blue and green tiles found in the Alhambra. Upstairs, a tearoom/restaurant, La Colina de Almanzora, specialises in historic Arabic food.

Enthusiasts claim that the hammam provides relief for any number of ailments, from the common cold to arthritis and hangovers. The heat improves circulation, eliminates toxins and keeps the skin clean and supple. After a visit most people feel energised and refreshed, though if it's some deep relaxation you're after, book a 15-minute massage (for an extra fee).

Another good place to sweat out your sins is the **Acquaplaya** bath and spa in the basement of the Hotel Senator España. For

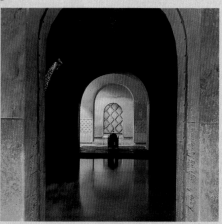

€15 you can indulge in three hours of soaking, steaming and swimming (floating oranges in one small pool are a fragrant diversion). Even quirkier is the *sala de relax* in the back, an '80s-style black room that makes your teeth glow. The hotel also provides massage, facials and other treatments, at reasonable prices.

Acquaplaya
Hotel Senator España, Gran Vía 70 (91 524 25 05). Metro Plaza de España. **Open** 10am-10pm Tue-Sun. **Admission** €15 for up to 3hrs. **Credit** AmEx, DC, MC, V. **Map** p309 D5.

Medina Mayrit
C/Atocha 14 (902 333 334/www.medina mayrit.com). Metro Sol or Tirso de Molina. **Open** 10am-2am (last entry midnight) daily. **Admission** *Baths* €18. *Baths & massage* (from 4pm & all day Sat, Sun) €25; before 4pm Mon-Fri €22.50; €15-€21 concessions. **Credit** AmEx, DC, MC, V.
Check the website for special offers.

A fashion-conscious international crowd sup Guinness while shooting American pool in this classy basement bar, with a background of hip electronic music. Tables cost €6 an hour.

Bowling/*boleras*

Bowling Chamartín

Área recreativa, Estación de Chamartín, C/Agustín de Foxá (91 315 71 19). Metro Chamartín. **Open** 10am-12.30am Mon-Fri; 10am-2am Sat, Sun. **Admission** (incl shoe hire) €3.30 before 5pm, €4.40 after 5pm Mon-Fri; €4.40 before 5pm, €5 after 5pm Sat, Sun. **No credit cards**.

A colourful 20-lane alley with a neon-lit bar, now the oldest and most central in the city. It gets crowded on Saturdays, when there's lots of whooping.

Football/*fútbol*

English Football League

Originally made up of British expats, this men's *fútbol sala* league (outdoor five-a-side) is now multinational, with many Spanish and Latin American players involved, and has two divisions. Games are played on Sundays from 2-4pm at the Colegio del Niño Jesús, just east of the Retiro (metro Ibiza or Sainz de Baranda/map p315 K8). Teams are often looking for new talent; if you're in Madrid for a while and want to get involved, contact Mike Kemp on 677 895 552 or at kempster67@hotmail.com. The standard varies; the league is well organised but played in a spirit of fun, and ages range from 16 to 40-plus.

Golf

Golf clubs around Madrid tend to be quite exclusive, and expensive, affairs.

Club de Campo Villa de Madrid

Carretera de Castilla, km 2 (91 550 08 40/www.club villademadrid.com). Bus 84 or 284 from Moncloa. **Open** 8am-sunset daily. **Rates** €12.85 club entry, plus €44.80 course fee Mon-Fri; €25.40 club entry, plus €84.70 course fee Sat, Sun. **No credit cards**.

Co-designed by Seve Ballesteros, this is considered the best and most difficult golf course near Madrid. As well as golf, there are squash and tennis courts, clay pigeon and range shooting, plus hockey pitches, polo facilities, horse riding and a swimming pool.

Horse riding/*hípica*

Indiana Parque Recreativo Natural

Apdo Correos 32, San Martín de Valdeiglesias (91 861 27 99/www.indiana-sl.com). By bus 551 from Méndez Álvaro/by car A-5 then M501 (58.5km). **No credit cards**.

Trekking here involves crossing rivers and reservoirs, and going up mountains. Beginners can also take classes in the riding school, or there's climbing, archery, and canoeing. Worth the schlep out of town.

Las Palomas

Club Hípico, Ctra de Colmenar Viejo km 28.9 (91 803 31 76/mobile 670 972 150/www.telefonica.net/web/chlaspalomas). By bus 721, 724, 725, 726 from Plaza de Castilla. **Open** 10am-2pm, 5-7pm Tue-Sun. **No credit cards**.

Offers riding courses for all levels. Courses of ten classes start at €100.

Skiing

Before heading off to the ski resorts out of town, *madrileños* like to practise their turns at the vast Xanadu indoor skiing centre just outside Madrid. *See also p199.*

Squash

Gimnasio Argüelles

C/Andres Mellado 21-23, Moncloa (91 549 0040). Metro Argüelles. **Open** *Sept-July* 8am-11pm Mon-Fri; 9am-3pm Sat, Sun. *Aug* 10am-10pm Mon-Fri. **Rates** *Squash* €16 per hr. *Gym* €7. **No credit cards**. **Map** p308 C2.

A fully equipped gym open to non-members, with a squash court for dedicated rubber-bashers.

Swimming pools/*piscinas*

Leaflets available at city sports centres have details of all the pools around Madrid or see the web page of the Instituto Muncipal de Deportes (www.imd.es) and click on '*Instalaciones municipales*'. In addition to the pools below, *see p244* Estadio Vallehermoso. For the popular rooftop pool at the Hotel Emperador, *see p43*. For waterparks around Madrid, *see p199*.

Open-air municipal pools

Piscinas Casa de Campo, Avda del Angel s/n, Casa de Campo (91 463 00 50). Metro Lago. **Open** 11am-9pm daily. Closed mid Sept-May. **Admission** €3.80; 80¢-€2.15 concessions. *Voucher for 10 admissions* €32; €9-€18 concessions. **No credit cards**.

Land-locked Madrid is stiflingly hot in the summer, so at weekends half the city seems to turn up at this beautiful leafy complex, which has three open-air pools (one Olympic, one medium, one for kids) set in green meadows. Topless bathing is tolerated, and there's an informal gay area. Of the other municipal pools, the Francos Rodríguez has a beach volleyball court, and the Barrio del Pilar and La Elipa have nude sunbathing areas; the latter has water chutes. All have the same hours and prices.

Other pools: Barrio del Pilar C/Monforte de Lemos 13-15, Northern suburbs (91 314 79 43); **Concepción** C/José del Hierro, Eastern suburbs (91 403 90 20); **La Elipa** Acceso del Parque de La Elipa, Eastern suburbs (91 430 35 11); **Francos Rodríguez** C/Numancia 1, Tetuán (91 459 98 71); **Moratalaz** C/Valdebernardo s/n, Eastern suburbs (91 772 71 00).

Arts & Entertainment

Indoor municipal pools

Piscina La Latina, Plaza de la Cebada 1 (91 365 80 31). Metro La Latina. **Open** *Sept-June* 8.15am-7pm Mon-Thur; 8.15am-6pm Fri; 10am-8.30pm Sat, Sun. *July* 10am-8pm Mon-Fri; 10am-2pm Sat, Sun. Closed Aug. **Admission** €3.80; 90¢-€2.15 concessions. *Voucher for 10 admissions* €32; €9-€18 concessions. **No credit cards. Map** p313 D9.

The city has many indoor pools, most of which are open all year except August (hours may vary). La Latina is rather tatty, but rather convenient, being the only pool in central Madrid. Chamartín, a little further out, is Olympic-sized.

Other pools: Chamartín Plaza del Perú s/n (91 350 12 23).

Canal de Isabel II

Avda Filipinas 54, Chamberí (91 533 96 42). Metro Canal or Ríos Rosas. **Open** *Swimming pool* late May-early Sept 11am-8pm daily. **Admission** *Swimming pool* €3.30 Mon-Fri; €3.60 Sat, Sun; half-price concessions; €28.10 voucher for 10 visits. **No credit cards.**

Olympic-sized and children's pools, tennis courts, and a bar and restaurant, all with good wheelchair access. Like most watering holes in Madrid, it can get very crowded at weekends.

Tennis/*tenis*

Tennis in Spain is easily accessible at reasonable prices, with numerous council-run clay and tarmac courts for hire. At municipal *polideportivos*, €4.70 gets you a court for an hour. The best city-run complex is the **Tenis Casa de Campo** in the Casa de Campo, close to the boating lake (91 464 96 17), which boasts 15 floodlit courts. The **Barrio del Pilar**, **Concepción** and **La Elipa** swimming pools (for all, *see p243*) also have tennis courts for hire, as does the **Canal de Isabel II** (*see above*; you should book in advance).

Fitness

Gyms/*gimnasios*

Bodhidharma

C/Moratines 18, South of centre (91 517 28 16/www.bodhidharma-gym.com). Metro Acacias or Embajadores. **Open** *Sept-July* 8am-11pm Mon-Fri; 9am-2pm, 6-10pm Sat; 10am-3pm Sun. *Aug* 8am-11pm Mon-Fri; 9am-2pm Sat. **Rates** €49.80 per mth; €123.80 for 3mths. **Credit** MC, V.

A well-equipped health club for men and women, with a sauna, free weights, exercise machines and aerobics classes.

Votre Ligne

C/Lagasca 88, 1°, Salamanca (91 576 40 00/www.votre-ligne.com). Metro Núñez de Balboa. **Open** 8am-9.30pm Mon-Fri; 10am-2pm Sat. **Rates** €50 per mth. **Credit** AmEx, MC, V. **Map** p311 J3.

There's a strictly-no-men policy in this classy joint, which offers gym and aerobics classes, a sauna, jacuzzis, a pool and beauticians. There are special rates for non-members in summer.

Other locations: C/Juan Ramón Jiménez 45, Chamartín (91 359 14 36).

Sports centres/*polideportivos*

Madrid has 48 city-owned *polideportivos* managed by the Instituto Municipal de Deportes. You can find more information on their website, www.imd.es or at any of the centres. Some are more basic than others, though the entrance fees are the same.

Estadio Vallehermoso

Avda de las Islas Filipinas 10, Chamberí (91 534 77 23/information 012). Metro Islas Filipinas. **Open** 8.30am-9.30pm Mon-Sat; 8.30am-3pm Sun. *Swimming pool* 11am-8pm daily June-Aug. **Admission** *Swimming pool* €3.30 Mon-Fri; €3.60 Sat, Sun. *Season ticket for 10 visits* €28.10. **No credit cards.**

This complex combines an athletics stadium and multi-purpose sports centre with an indoor sports hall, gym, football pitch, open-air swimming pool and facilities for practising golf. It's also a good place for jogging.

Parque de Ocío La Ermita – Paidesport Center

C/Sepúlveda 3-5, Virgen del Puerto, South of centre (91 470 01 11/www.paidesport.com). Metro Puerta del Ángel. **Open** *Sept-July* 9am-11pm Mon-Fri; 8pm Sat; 10am-3pm Sun. *Aug* 9am-11pm Mon-Fri; 10am-3pm Sat; 10am-3pm Sun. **Admission** *Tennis, squash* from €6 for 30mins. *Swimming pool* €11. **No credit cards.**

A slick, privately run complex down near the river, open to non-members and generally rammed with earnest hardbodies pumping iron. It has racket courts, an open-air pool, a gym and weights room and an indoor sports hall.

Polideportivo La Chopera

Parque del Retiro (91 420 11 54). Metro Atocha. **Open** 10am-8.30pm Mon-Fri; 9am-9pm Sat, Sun. Closed Aug. **Admission** varies according to facilities used. **Map** p314 I9.

Shaded by the trees of the Retiro park and close to the Prado, La Chopera is a fine place to play tennis, indoor football or basketball.

Disabled sports facilities

The city sports institute is slowly adapting its *polideportivos* to allow full access for disabled users, but this programme is not yet complete. The majority of indoor swimming pools have been adapted, and many outdoor pools have ramps and full-access changing rooms. Those at Casa de Campo and Concepción (for both, *see p243*) have the best disabled facilities.

Theatre & Dance

Musicals and blockbusters take centre stage while rebellious fringe theatres cook up trouble in the wings.

Veranos de la Villa. *See p246.*

The battle for hearts and minds of Madrid's increasingly polarised theatre-going public is perhaps best illustrated by the controversy that raged when the Círculo de Bellas Artes put on Íñigo Ramírez de Haro's *Me Cago en Dios* ('I shit on God' – a surprisingly common Spanish exclamation). Cast members were physically attacked, the Church weighed in, and the playwright's sister-in-law, President of the Madrid regional government, Esperanza Aguirre, wrote to the theatre director and asked him to cancel the play. Undaunted, Ramírez et al then took the production to the maverick **Teatro Alfil**, where it later opened and ran under a new title: *Me Cago en la Censura* – 'I shit on censorship'.

Elsewhere it's a familiar story: while Gran Vía is littered with Broadway and West End hand-me-downs, the little theatres of Madrid carry on in the face of local government and city council limits on licences and funds.

Spain's fervent passion for the blockbuster musical has not wavered; having closed on Broadway and the West End, the 22-year-old musical *Cats* opened in the Teatro Coliseum for Christmas 2003, hot on the heels of *Cabaret* and *We Will Rock You*.

Still the fighting spirit of the fringe makes up for the mainstream's old-fashioned outlook. The **Triángulo** and **Cuarta Pared** theatres, the oldest of the *salas alternativas*, always offer challenging works, and newcomer **TIS** has been a key player too. It has to be said that, to outsiders, the alternative scene here can seem to be not that alternative, really, but bear in mind that until the late '80s there was virtually no non-mainstream theatre here at all.

THE DANCE SCENE

As in the theatre world, the best thing going for the dance scene are its festivals, though these are hardly crowd-pullers. Three major companies are based in Madrid: the **Compañía Nacional de Danza**, under the direction of Nacho Duato; the state **Ballet Nacional de España**, which specialises in Spanish dance; and the **Ballet de la Comunidad de Madrid**. Duato's company has a contemporary, although far from radical style. José Antonio Ruiz took over direction of the Ballet Nacional in May 2004, but the company is hard to catch as it tours frequently. The Ballet de la Comunidad, run by director and choreographer Víctor Ullate, is a safe bet, too.

As ever, contemporary dance teeters precariously on an economic knife-edge, but spaces such as the **Pradillo**, **Cuarta Pared**, **El Triángulo**, **El Canto de la Cabra** and the **Centro de Nuevos Creadores** at the Sala Mirador continue to show good work. The two main contemporary dance companies are **10y10**, in residency at the Sala Mirador, and **Provisional Danza**, one of the pioneers of contemporary dance in Spain since 1987, led by the renowned choreographer Carmen Werner.

SEASONS AND FESTIVALS

The **Festival de Otoño** (*see p194*) is the city's biggest festival for theatre, dance and puppetry, attracting major international names and sometimes putting on shows in English. More alternative theatre and dance is showcased in January and February in the original **Escena Contemporánea**, the better-funded sibling to the marginally more avant-garde **La Alternativa** festival, while in June there's the **Festival de Teatro Alternativo de Primavera**. Also in the spring is **Madrid en Danza**, which offers a variety of dance styles, from flamenco to kathak, and is always worth seeing, as are many of the events in the misnamed **Día de la Danza** (it's actually three days, at the end of April/beginning of May). Events centre on the Teatro Albéniz and feature top names in dance. The summer **Veranos de la Villa** programme offers even more outdoor performances. The Centro Cultural de la Villa's **Apuesta de la Danza**, attracts prestigious companies such as Ibérica de Danza and Mar Gómez's company. And, for a summer trip out of town, don't miss the **Festival de Teatro Clásico** in the town of Almargo every July. The event pays tribute to Lope de Vega, Molière, Shakespeare and friends with plays, workshops and street performances (get information at C/Príncipe 14, 91 521 07 20). The **Madrid Sur** festival (91 355 58 67, www.iitm.org) takes place in the southern suburbs in the autumn with a philosophical theme such as 2003's 'Rebellion of Ethics'. For information on gay-orientated theatre, *see* **Movida Marys** *p212*).

TICKETS AND TIMES

Many of the mainstream theatres are closed on Mondays and most of the fringe venues are only open from Thursday to Sunday. Cheaper tickets are often available on Wednesdays and Sundays. Most theatres sell through telesales, and we list several in the shopping section, *see p188*. But you can also call the venue to check. The best places to find information are the *Guía del Ocio* and daily newspapers, especially in the Friday listings supplements that most of them publish.

Nuevo Ballet Español at the **Teatro Albéniz**. *See p247.*

Mainstream theatres

Other theatres to look out for include **Teatro Alcázar** (C/Alcalá 20, 91 532 06 16, www.teatro alcazar.com), which throughout summer 2004 showed flamenco fusionist Rafael Amargo's *Enramblao*, the **Calderón** (C/Atocha 18, 91 429 58 90) for *101 Dalmatians* and the like, the **Teatro Lara** (Corredera Baja de San Pablo 15, 91 522 89 04) for more family entertainment, and **Teatro de Cámara** (C/San Cosme y San Damián 3, 91 527 09 54) for heavyweight classics. It's worth noting that the Teatro Real (*see p216*) often stages dance productions, notably with the Ballet Nacional de España and the Compañía Nacional de Danza, as well as small pieces in the informal 'Café Danza'. *See also p219* **Teatro de la Zarzuela**.

Centro Cultural de la Villa

Jardines del Descubrimiento, Plaza de Colón, Salamanca (91 480 03 00). Metro Serrano. **Open** *Box office* 11am-1.30pm, 5-6pm or until performance Tue-Sun. **Tickets** €5-€21. **No credit cards.** **Map** p310 I4.

The theatre in the city's purpose-built cultural centre shows an eclectic mix of concerts, opera, *zarzuela*, cinema, drama and dance. There are also jazz performances, workshops and children's puppet shows.

Sala Mirador

C/Doctor Fourquet 31, Lavapiés (91 539 57 67). Metro Atocha or Lavapiés. **Open** *Box office* 1hr before performance Thur-Sun. Closed Aug. **Tickets** €12-€15. **No credit cards.** **Map** p314 G10.

Doubling as theatre/dance school and performance space, this is also the site of the long-running *La Katarsis del Tomatazo*, performed every Friday and Saturday night at 11pm. The deal is, the audience are given tomatoes as they enter, which they can use to express their feelings on this singing and dancing cabaret. Other less therapeutic productions are a mix of theatre and dance.

Teatro Albéniz

C/Paz 11, Los Austrias (91 531 83 11). Metro Sol. **Open** *Box office* 11.30am-1pm, 5.30-9pm daily. Closed July-mid Aug. **Tickets** €13-€25. **Credit** V. **Map** p313 E8.

The Albéniz puts on a large amount of dance along with its regular theatre programme: from humorous drag-ballet company Les Ballets Trokadero de Monte Carlo to the stunning Ballet Nacional de Cuba and Spanish two-man company Nuevo Ballet Español. It is also the principal venue for the Festival de Otoño and hosts a series of concerts, Madrid En Canto, from May into June; 2004 saw a special focus on Latin American names.

Teatro Alfil

C/Pez 10, Malasaña (91 521 45 41/www.teatroalfil. com). Metro Callao or Noviciado. **Open** *Box office* 1hr before performance daily. **Tickets** €9-€12. **No credit cards. Map** p309 E4.

Madrid's renegade theatre, the Alfil has been threatened with closure in previous years, but has battled on, and produced increasingly radical plays – both *The Vagina Monologues* and *Puppetry of the Penis* were staged here. The Alfil is also one of the few venues to host stand-up comedy – the Festival de Teatro de Humor is held here in June.

Teatro de la Abadía

C/Fernández de los Ríos 42, Chamberí (91 448 16 27/91 448 11 81/www.teatroabadia.com). Metro Quevedo. **Open** *Box office* 5-9pm Tue-Sat; 5-8pm Sun. Closed Aug. **Tickets** €12-€19; concessions apply Wed. **Credit** V. **Map** p309 E5.

Housed inside an abandoned church, the award-winning Abadía dabbles in music and dance as well as theatre. It participates in the Festival de Otoño and Madrid en Danza festivals, and brings unusual one-offs to the regular programming.

Teatro de Madrid

Avda de la Ilustración s/n, Barrio del Pilar (91 730 17 50). Metro Barrio del Pilar. **Open** *Box office* 5.30pm until performance Tue-Thur; 11.30am-1.30pm, 5.30pm until performance Fri-Sun. **Tickets** €11-€22. **Credit** MC, V.

The Teatro de Madrid specialises in bringing the highest-calibre Spanish and international dance companies to the city, staging a mixture of ballet, contemporary dance and fusion performances such as flamenco and tango. It is also home to the Nuevo Ballet Español, the company of the fiery duo Ángel Rojas and Carlo Rodríguez, and regularly stages good children's shows around Christmas, as well as a *zarzuela* in the summer.

Teatro Español

C/Príncipe 25, Huertas & Santa Ana (91 360 14 80). Metro Sevilla or Sol. **Open** *Box office* 11.30am-1.30pm, 5-7.30pm Tue-Sun. **Tickets** €3-€20. **No credit cards. Map** p313 F8.

This grand theatre on Plaza Santa Ana dates back to 1745, but that doesn't mean it's old-fashioned. In fact, its new artistic director, Mario Gas, looks set to seriously shake up its programming, and he closed the 2003-4 season with a festive selection of theatre, dance and music. The 2004-5 season will see the Royal Shakespeare Company bringing an homage to the Spanish Golden Age to this historic theatre as part of the Festival de Otoño.

Teatro Fernando de Rojas

C/Alcalá 42 (91 360 54 00/www.circulobellas artes.com). Metro Banco de España or Sevilla. **Open** *Box office* 1hr before performance. Closed Aug. **Tickets** varies. **No credit cards. Map** p314 G7.

Housed in the Círculo de Bellas Artes, and not to be confused with the unconnected Teatro de Bellas Artes next door, the Fernando de Rojas stages three or four works a season, mixing contemporary and traditional, Spanish and international. It hosts an annual festival in September showing productions by a variety of theatre groups from across Spain, and a dance festival in late November.

Teatro La Latina

Plaza de la Cebada 2, La Latina (91 365 28 35). Metro La Latina. **Open** *Box office* 11am-1pm, 6-8pm daily. **Tickets** €15-€30. **No credit cards.**

Previously known for its homespun comic theatre (plenty of star names in farcical situations and lots of banging of doors), this comfortable venue has undergone a slight shift of image in recent years. Although it still host some comedy acts each season, the programme now mainly consists of quality drama, most of it 20th-century.

Teatro María Guerrero

C/Tamayo y Baus 4, Chueca (91 310 15 00/91). Metro Colón. **Open** *Box office* noon until show Tue-Sun. Closed Aug. **Tickets** €11-€18; half-price concessions Wed. **Credit** AmEx, DC, V. **Map** p310 H5.

This beautiful late 19th-century theatre is the home of the state-run Centro Dramático Nacional (CDN). Having reopened after major renovations in May 2003, it is now ready to celebrate the CDN's 25th anniversary in style.

Teatro Nuevo Apolo

Plaza de Tirso de Molina 1, Rastro & Lavapiés (91 369 06 37). Metro Tirso de Molina. **Open** *Box office* 11.30am-1.30pm, 5pm until performance Tue-Sun. Closed mid July-mid Aug. **Tickets** €20-€30. **No credit cards. Map** p313 E8.

This venue has welcomed dancer Joaquín Cortes and the Mayumana dance-percussion troupe in recent seasons. The big show of the 2004 summer season was *El Musical de Broadway*, incorporating 30 musical greats in an intense two hours.

Teatro Pavón

C/Embajadores 9, La Latina (91 528 28 19). Metro La Latina. **Open** *Box office* 11.30am-1.30pm, 5-6pm daily. Closed mid July-early Sept. **Tickets** €8-€16. **Credit** MC, V. **Map** p313 D9.

The Compañía Nacional de Teatro Clásico moved here in 2002 while its real home, the Teatro de la Comédia, is being restored. An impressive building that sat semi-derelict for many years, it currently stages classical productions by the Compañía Nacional as well as by a number of invited companies. Here you'll usually get works by Spanish Golden Age greats along with the occasional Molière, Shakespeare or the like.

Trouble on the fringe

A love-hate dynamic seems to govern the city council's relationship with Madrid's fringe theatres. The uncertain status of some 'rebel' theatres clashes with the Ayuntamiento's proactive approach to enforcing licensing laws. Yet, because theatre is viewed as a positive cultural addition to the city, it has managed to escape the full force of council heavy-handedness (unlike cafés and bars). In general, unlicensed theatres are only asked to close if the council receives complaints about them.

When it comes to dealing with the council, the fringe theatres have two linked problems: the licensing question, and safety and soundproofing regulations that theatres see as unreasonable.

Owners and managers of some theatres that have run into trouble say that they submitted licence requests, but their papers were delayed in the bureaucratic quagmire of the Ayuntamiento. Until they obtain a licence, they are unable to receive financial backing to pay for the required safety measures and soundproofing. Theatre owners also believe they are discriminated against: most theatres in Madrid don't have licences but never face the threat of closure.

Noise complaints about Sala TIS on Calle Primavera (*pictured, and see p249*) reached the council in November 2003. When they discovered that TIS didn't have a licence, the Ayuntamiento came to assess the situation. They left without shutting the theatre down, but also didn't clear it to operate. TIS received enormous support from the press, its neighbours and cultural associations. Even the Ayuntamiento listed its productions on the council website (along with a statement that the venue had been ordered to close).

Then another theatre, Teatro Espada de Madera at 21 Calle Calvario, received a closure notice. In contrast to most similar cases, the council had received no complaints about that theatre. The theatre's administration theorised that the closure order was spurred by a newspaper article

on unlicensed theatres that had cited it as an example. Like TIS, Espada de Madera continues to put on plays at the time of writing, and has been told that it has six months to make alterations to the building.

In the face of this government pressure, nine small performance spaces have formed ANEM (Association of New Performance Spaces in Madrid), which is now lobbying for the creation of an '*espacios 99*' category for theatres with fewer than 99 seats (a category that exists in most countries). Currently, small spaces in Spain have to meet the same safety and soundproofing requirements as theatres with seating capacities of 300 or more. The group also wants a representative on the council. At present each theatre has to deal with councillors from whatever part of the city they're in, and they feel this means rules are applied inconsistently.

Madrid is sometimes accused of lacking real alternative theatre, and with such a lack of positive support from above, it's understandable why. But the situation is not without hope. If ANEM succeeds in bringing attention to the plight of small theatres, these spaces could at last receive the necessary backing to provide safe environments without compromising their independent spirit.

Fringe/alternative

The **Teatro de las Aguas** (C/Aguas 8, 91 366 96 42) occasionally has productions in English. Small, more alternative spaces include: **DT** (C/Reina 9, 91 521 71 55) for theatre, cabaret and dance productions on gay themes; **Nave de Los Locos** (C/Francisco Guzmán 28, 91 560 14 79), which has an open-air festival in July; and **Lagrada** (C/Ercilla 20, 91 517 96 98), for kitchen sink dramas and contemporary plays.

El Canto de la Cabra

C/San Gregorio 8, Chueca (91 310 42 22/www.el cantodelacabra.com). Metro Chueca. **Open** *Box office* 1hr before performance. **Tickets** €8-€12. **No credit cards. Map** p310 G5.

The 'Goat's Bleat' presents 15 to 20 companies a year, performing contemporary Spanish and international work and some dance. The indoor theatre seats 70, and popular open-air performances are given on the patio in the summer.

Cuarta Pared

C/Ercilla 17, South of centre (91 517 23 17/ www.cuartapared.es). Metro Embajadores. **Open** *Box office* 1hr before performance Thur-Sun. Closed Aug. **Tickets** €10; €5-€7.50 concessions. *Children's shows* €5. **No credit cards.**

Cuarta Pared plays a crucial role in training and as a producer. The resident company produces excellent work, it hosts visiting productions, is a major dance venue and stages acclaimed children's theatre.

El Montacargas

C/Antillón 19, Puerta del Ángel, South of centre (91 526 11 73). Metro Puerta del Ángel. **Open** *Box office* 30mins before show Thur-Sun. **Tickets** €9; €7 concessions. *Children's shows* €7. **No credit cards.**

Programming here favours contemporary Spanish work, but highlights of the year also include the International Clown Festival in September.

Sala Triángulo

C/Zurita 20, Lavapiés (91 530 68 91/www.teatro triangulo.com). Metro Antón Martín or Lavapiés. **Open** *Box office* 30mins before show. **Tickets** €8-€10. **No credit cards. Map** p313 F9.

The original, and many would argue the best, of the alternative theatres, Triángulo is fiercely independent and uncompromising. There are always several productions going at once, usually including new writing and cross-art-form collaborations. It works closely with other theatres during festivals (it takes part in the Festival de Otoño and is the force behind La Alternativa in February, the Festival de Teatro Alternativo de Primavera in June and Al Fresco in July and August).

Teatro Pradillo

C/Pradillo 12, Chamartín (91 416 90 11). Metro Concha Espina. **Open** *Box office* 1hr before performance. **Tickets** €12. *Children's shows* €7. **Credit** MC, V.

Although principally devoted to Spanish work, the Pradillo sometimes stages work in the original language, especially as part of the Festival de Otoño. Other strengths are children's theatre, particularly puppet shows, and dance. It is one of the principal organisers of the Escena Contemporánea, and runs a festival for European dance companies in December and another for flamenco in August.

TIS (Teatro Independiente Sur)

C/Primavera 11, Lavapiés (91 528 13 59/ www.galeria-tis.com). Metro Lavapiés. **Open** *Aug, Sept* 11am-2pm, 5-10pm daily. *Oct-July* 10am-10pm daily. **Tickets** € 10. **No credit cards. Map** p313 F9.

TIS has only been around a couple of years, and has yet to secure a licence (*see p248* **Trouble on the fringe**). Its alternative (and often wacky) performances meet with mixed reviews, but it has put on plays by more than 250 international theatre companies in its short and sometimes precarious lifetime. There's also an interesting gallery with constantly changing exhibitions. Look out for occasional plays in English.

Dance classes

If you take more than a passive interest in flamenco, you might want to try classes. Below are some of the more established dance centres.

Centro de Danza Karen Taft

C/Libertad 15, Chueca (91 522 84 40/www.karen taft.com). Metro Chueca. **Open** *Oct-June* 9am-10pm Mon-Fri. *July-Sept* 10am-10pm Mon-Thur. **Map** p310 G5.

This is one of the foremost dance schools in Spain, and offers classes in classical and modern dance, as well as flamenco.

Clara Ramona

Paseo de las Delicias 35, Atocha (91 468 60 38/ mobile 639 01 99 17). Metro Atocha. **Open** varies (call for information). **Map** p314 H10.

Bilingual dancer/choreographer Clara Ramona works internationally but has her *danza española* school in Madrid. She's a great teacher for all levels.

Estudios Amor de Dios

C/Santa Isabel 5, 1°, Lavapiés (91 360 04 34). Metro Antón Martín. **Open** varies (call for details). **Map** p313 F9.

The most famous flamenco school in the world celebrated its 50th anniversary in 2003 by opening at a new location (having been homeless for more than a year). It now sits (or rather stamps) above the Antón Martín indoor market building.

El Horno

C/Esgrima 11, Lavapiés (91 527 57 01/www. centroelhorno.com). Metro Tirso de Molina. **Open** 10am-11pm Mon-Fri; 10am-7pm Sat. **Map** p313 E9.

El Horno has a flamenco and *sevillana* leaning, but also covers African, jazz and capoeira as well as drama, at very reasonable prices.

Arts & Entertainment

Trips Out of Town

Getting Started

Escaping *la vida loca*.

It's a tough call. Spend the entire long weekend in Madrid in order to fit in all three of the mandatory museums? Or take advantage of one of the extraordinary day trips the city offers? Three words: change your ticket. In summer, the cool mountain air of the sierras beckons, along with excellent hiking and some of the best campsites anywhere. In winter, what better than to hole up in a traditional *mesón* in the stately cities of Toledo or Segovia, with red wine, a log fire and some suckling pig? Year round the palaces, gardens and monasteries at Aranjuez, La Granja, Riofrio and El Escorial make for a compelling visit.

The areas to the north and west of Madrid have the most spectacular landscapes, following the three main sierra ranges. The less dramatic country to the south and east – where dry tableland, tufty hillocks and fertile river basins gently intermingle – is full of fascinating towns.

By bus

Within the city details of bus services are available on 012 (or on 91 580 42 60 from outside Madrid), and you can get information from tourist offices and on the regional transport website, www.ctm-madrid.es. Most buses depart from Estación Sur de Autobuses (C/Méndez Álvaro, 91 468 42 00), but some go from Plaza Castilla (to north-west destinations), the streets around Moncloa, Conde de Casal and Avenida Mediterráneo (heading south), Avenida de America terminus (heading north-east) and Paseo de la Florida 11 (for Segovia and around). Most termini have their own same-name metro station; exceptions are Estación Sur, on the Méndez Álvaro metro and *cercanía* lines, and Paseo de la Florida 11, near Príncipe Pío metro.

By car

In 2004 many major roads changed name, and road map publishers and car-hire agencies were slow to catch up. 'National' roads, such as those formerly known as N-I and N-II, for example, became A-1 and A-2, except on toll-paying roads (*peajes*), where the prefix is now AP. The six notorious major roads, now numbered A-1 to A-6, can all be reached from the M-30 or the outlying M-40 ring road. The A-1 (Carretera de Burgos) leads to the eastern Guadarrama and

Sierra Pobre, the A-2 Barcelona road goes to Alcalá de Henares, and the A-3 Valencia road to Chinchón. The A-42 (formerly the N-401) to Toledo can be reached from either the M-30 or the A-4. The A-6 La Coruña road leads to El Escorial, Segovia, Ávila and Salamanca.

Expect bottlenecks at weekends, especially for the return trip on Sunday evenings: streets can be gridlocked until midnight. Immense traffic jams and a substantial crop of accidents are also depressingly predictable during long holiday weekends (*puentes*). Don't even think about driving at the beginning or end of August, particularly on the A-3 Valencia road. For more on driving and car hire, *see pp281-2*.

By train

The system of local trains (*cercanías*) runs to many interesting towns around Madrid; Alcalá de Henares, Aranjuez, El Escorial, Cercedilla and many more. The ageing but efficient single gauge extension line, the scenic C-9, wends its way up from Cercedilla through mountain pinewoods to Cotos, which adjoins ski slopes and a glacial lake. Services to other destinations leave from main-line stations, Chamartín and Atocha, though many trains also stop between them at Nuevos Ministerios and Recoletos stations. It's also worth noting that the high-speed AVE and Talgo trains, from Atocha to Seville and Córdoba respectively, make a weekend or even a day trip to Andalucía a possibility. Depending on when you travel, there are often very good low-price fare deals as well. Several trains a day run to both cities.

RENFE information

902 24 02 02/www.renfe.es. **Open** *Information* 24hrs. *Reservations* 5am-11.40pm daily. **Credit** AmEx, DC, MC, V.
Tickets for long-distance services can be booked by phone with a credit card. Tickets can be delivered to a Madrid address for a small extra charge.

RENFE central sales office

C/Alcalá 44, Huertas & Santa Ana (no phone). *Metro Banco de España.* **Open** 9.30am-8pm Mon-Fri. **Credit** AmEx, DC, MC, V. **Map** p314 G7.
Information and tickets for the AVE, Talgo and all other RENFE long-distance services are available from this office, which is a short walk from Plaza de Cibeles. It does not handle phone enquiries, which go through the central number above.

Trips Out of Town

North & West

Picture-postcard castles and snow-capped mountains within easy reach of the city.

Ávila

It's an impressive sight; a forbidding stronghold encircled by thick 11th-century walls rising out of a boulder-strewn landscape. Despite its elegant buildings and well-to-do market town feel, there is something slightly sinister about Ávila's fortressed isolation; plaques around town celebrate Franco's victories and point out that this was the birthplace of Isabel La Católica – the most powerful and merciless woman in the history of Spain. It is also the highest provincial capital in the country, with bitterly cold winters.

Proverbially a town of *cantos y santos* (stones and saints), it was home to Spain's greatest mystic, Santa Teresa, the 16th-century spiritualist, reformer and writer who founded 18 convents and revolutionised Catholicism, yet lived a life of spartan self-denial. As well as a statue in the town centre, there are countless other reminders of her presence. The baroque Convento de Santa Teresa (Plaza de la Santa 2, 920 21 10 30, open 9.30am-1pm, 3.30-8pm daily, admission free) stands on the plot of the house she was born in and the Convento de San José contains the Museo Teresiano de Carmelitas Descalzas (C/Madres 4, 920 22 21 27, open Nov-mid Apr 10am-1.30pm, 3-6pm daily, mid Apr-Oct 10am-1.30pm, 4-7pm; admission €1) where you can see her manuscripts and relics. Franco is said to have kept the saint's mummified arm by his bedside in his final years.

The medieval city is a timewarp of cobbled lanes, sleepy squares, family mansions and stately religious buildings. The highlight is undoubtedly the stark fortified 12th-century **cathedral** (information 920 21 10 00, closed until end 2004), embedded in the walls and rebuilt over the ages in Romanesque, Gothic and Renaissance styles. The **Basílica de San Vicente** (Plaza de San Vicente 1, 920 25 52 30 open 10am-2pm, 4-7pm daily, admission €1.40 Mon-Sat, free Sun), located outside the walls, is a similar hybrid of styles. Built on the spot where St Vincent and his two sisters were martyred in the fourth century, it has gruesome scenes of their torture depicted in relief around Vicente's tomb. Nearby, the Romanesque church of **San Andrés** stands, and the palatial but melancholy 15th-century Gothic **Santo**

Storks nesting in **Ávila**.

Tomás monastery, containing the alabaster tomb of Ferdinand and Isabella's only son and heir, Don Juan, who died at 19.

The city's wonderfully preserved **walls** (902 10 21 21, July-Sept 10am-7.15pm daily, open Apr-June 10am-7.15pm Tue-Sun, Oct-March 11am-5.15pm Tue-Sun, admission €3.50, €2 concessions), which were built after the knights had rid the city of the Moors, extend for one and a half miles and have nine gates and 88 watchtowers. For the best views go across the River Adaja to **Los Cuatro Postes**, a small Doric-columned monument perched on a knoll west of the city. The walls can be climbed at the Puerta del Alcázar just south of the cathedral and Puerta de San Vicente to the north.

Where to stay & eat

Among the major culinary delights to be found in Ávila are large steaks (*chuletones de Ávila*) from the fighting Iberian strain of black bulls,

El Escorial.

and delicious haricot beans (*judías* or *alubias*) from Barco de Ávila. Look out too for *cocido morañego*, a local variant on Madrid's famed winter stew; Ávila's own Castilian version of gazpacho, using fresh vegetables from the Tiétar Valley; roast lamb (*cordero asado*) and suckling pig (*lechona*). *Yemas de Santa Teresa* – rich sweets made from egg yolks and said to have been originally created by the saint herself in one of her rare moments of indulgence – are another of Ávila's specialities; you'll see them for sale all over town.

A good place to try them is the charming **Mesón del Rastro** (Plaza del Rastro 1, 920 21 12 19, rates €35-€41, mains €14, set lunch €14.50), which has all the trimmings of a traditional Castilian tavern (boars' heads, log fires) without the usual high prices. **El Rincón** (Plaza de Zurraquín 3-4, 920 35 10 44, rates €42-€48, restaurant closed Mon & all Feb, mains €9.50) is another to serve the same food as everywhere else, but at lower prices. **La Alcazaba** (Plaza Mosén Rubi 3, 920 25 62 90, closed Mon, mains €16) is more creative – try monkfish tournedor in Pernod sauce, or duck with caramelised apples. On the other side of the river, with a great view of the walls from its terrace, is **Mesón el Puente** (Bajada de la Losa 2, 920 21 90 51, closed Mon, mains €10.50).

Many of the town's hotels are located in converted mansions and Renaissance palaces. The delightful **Parador Raimundo de Borgoña** (C/Marqués de Canales de Chozas

2, 920 21 13 40, rates €105-€279, mains €14.50) serves an exceptional breakfast, available to non-residents as well as guests. **Hostería de Bracamonte** (C/Bracamonte 6, 920 25 12 80, rate €66, restaurant closed Tue & all of Nov, mains €14) has a seigneurial air and lots of game dishes. **Palacio de Valderrábanos** (Plaza de la Catedral 9, 920 21 10 23, rate €119) is a grander hotel located on the plaza with splendid views of the cathedral.

Getting there

By bus
Larrea (91 530 48 00) from Estación Sur has eight buses weekdays, 3 buses weekends. Journey time is 1hr 20mins. Last return is at 7pm weekdays and weekends.

By car
Take the A-6/AP-6 to Villacastín, then the N110 (113km/70 miles).

By train
There are 20 trains daily from Chamartín or Atocha, 8am-10.30pm. The last return is at 9.30pm. Journey time (Regional Exprés services) is anything between 1hr 15mins-2hrs.

Tourist information

Oficina de Turismo
Plaza de la Catedral 4 (920 21 13 87/www.jcyl.es/ turismo). **Open** *Oct-June* 10am-2pm, 5-8pm daily. *July-Sept* 9am-8pm daily.

all but two of the sovereigns who reigned over four centuries (absentees being Philip V, who was buried at La Granja, and Ferdinand VI, whose remains are in Madrid). The Basilica, with its notable *Christ Crucified* in Carrara marble by Benvenuto Cellini, has no fewer than 45 altars.

The main galleries are located on what was the lower floor of Philip's own austere rooms, above the **Basilica**. There is a small jalousie window overlooking the high altar so he could participate in Mass even if he was ill and confined to his surprisingly small bed. His cherished Hieronymous Bosch triptych was just a tiny part of a huge Habsburg art collection that includes celebrated works by Velázquez, Ribera, Alonso Cano and individual masterpieces like El Greco's *Adoration of the Name of Jesus* and Titian's *Last Supper,* concentrated mainly in the museum, chapterhouse, church and the ornate barrel-vaulted library – whose 50,000 volumes rival the Vatican's holdings.

The most refreshing section of El Escorial is the **Palacio de los Borbones**, remodelled by Charles IV in a light airy neo-classical style that contrasts with the general austerity and gloom. Highlights here are the tapestries designed by Goya and his contemporaries. Guided tours can be arranged on Friday afternoons and Saturdays. It is worth noting that it can get very cold inside the building, even on warm days.

Two other small palaces lie in the spacious gardens and parklands surrounding the monastery and can be visited with prior reservation on the palace number: the **Casita de Arriba**, or Upper House, (open Easter, July & Aug 10am-6pm Tue-Sun; admission €3.40, €1.70 concessions), and the **Casita del Príncipe** (Prince's House), with paintings by Lucas Jordan, a charming garden with 100-year-old sequoia trees, open at weekends only, from April to September. The park is open year-round from 10am-6pm Tuesday to Sunday.

Outside the monastery El Escorial is really two separate towns. Down below, next to the railway station, is **El Escorial de Abajo**, and at the top of the hill, clustered alongside the monastery, is the grander **San Lorenzo**. Look out here for Charles III's 18th-century **Real Coliseo** theatre and the parish church of **San Bartolomé**. A couple of kilometres out on the road towards the Casita de Arriba is the **Silla de Felipe**, 'Philip's Seat', from where he used to watch progress on the building, and now a great picnic spot.

El Escorial

The grand, austere monastery of San Lorenzo de El Escorial never fails to divide opinion, but is indubitably one of the most significant buildings in the history of Spain. Many people see it as the outward manifestation of its founding monarch's mind – Philip II was at once fanatically religious and wildly ambitious, and so his legacy in stone is both spartan and vast. The building is also symbolic architecturally, and it was the grey slate and spiky turrets of El Escorial that inspired decades of the 'Herreran' style (also known as Castilian baroque).

Construction was completed in record time between 1563 and 1574, initially by Juan Bautista de Toledo – who died shortly after work started – and subsequently by Juan de Herrera. Everything here is on a grand scale: collectors of statistics may care to note that its main façade is 200 metres (700 feet) long, the overhead cupola measures 92 metres (302 feet), and there are 15 cloisters, 16 kilometres (ten miles) of corridors, 86 stairways, 88 fountains, 1,200 doors and 2,675 windows.

Philip conceived the palace as a mausoleum and contemplative retreat, built as a final resting place for his father, Charles I, and to celebrate the 1557 Spanish victory over the French at St Quentin on St Lawrence's day (San Lorenzo). It's laid out to resemble the grid-iron on which the saint himself was martyred. The jasper, gold and marble **Panteón de los Reyes**, designed by Gian Battista Crescenzi in the 1620s, contains

Monasterio de San Lorenzo El Real de El Escorial

91 890 59 02/3/4/5/www.patrimonionacional.es. **Open** *Oct-Mar* 10am-5pm. *Apr-Sept* 10am-6pm Tue-Sun. *Palacio de los Borbones* Guided tours 4pm, 5pm, 6pm Fri; 10am, 11am, noon, 5pm, 6pm Sat. *Casita del*

Príncipe Guided tours 10.30am-1pm, 3.30-6.30pm
Sat, Sun. **Admission** *Monastery* €9; €4 concessions;
Wed free for EU citizens. *Palacio de los Borbones*
€3.60; €2 concessions. *Casita del Príncipe* €3.60;
€2 concessions. **No credit cards.**
Reservations are essential for the Palacio and Casita
tours, at least 24 hours in advance.

Where to eat

Fonda Genara (Plaza San Lorenzo 2, 91 890
43 57, mains €15.50) is a pretty if slightly pricey
restaurant with old theatre posters around the
walls. **Parrilla Principe** (C/Floridablanca 6,
91 890 16 11, rates €52-€58, restaurant closed
Tue, mains €20) is a small, peaceful 18th-
century palace with a hotel on the upper floors
and a blend of Castilian and seafood cuisine
available in the restaurant below. **Madrid
Sevilla** (C/Benavente 1, 91 890 15 19, closed
Mon & 2 wks Sept-Nov, mains €9.50) has
simple but reasonably priced food, while **La
Chistera** (Plaza Jacinto Benavente 5, 91 890
37 26, closed Mon night, set lunch €8, set
dinner €13.50) is principally a tapas bar.

The nicest place for a drink or snack is the
Babel Café (C/Juan de Austria 7, 91 896 04 43),
with live music, a small cinema club, exhibitions,
internet access and a garden. Up above the town
in the Monte Abantos district, **Horizontal**
(Camino Horizontal, 91 890 38 11, closed Tue,
main course €20) offers outdoor eating in
summer and a seat by the fire in winter.

Where to stay

Designed by Herrera, the **Hotel Victoria
Palace** (C/Juan Toledo 4, 91 890 15 11,
www.hotelvictoriapalace.com, rates €126-€145)
is an exquisite hotel with a charming garden
just a couple of hundred yards from the
monastery. **El Botánico** (C/Timoteo Padrón
16, 91 890 78 79, rates €119-€226) is a
beautifully renovated summer house with a
library, gardens and fine monastery views.
Right in the heart of San Lorenzo is **Hotel
Miranda Suizo** (C/Floridablanca 18, 91 890
47 11, rates €74-€82) has some rooms looking
over out the monastery and a bustling café,
and **Hostal Cristina** (C/Juan de Toledo 6, 91
890 19 61, rates €42-€46.50) is a comfortable,
good-value *residencia*.

Getting there

By bus

Herranz (91 890 41 22) buses 661 and 664 from
Moncloa (journey time 55mins), every 20mins 7am-
11.30pm Mon-Fri, every 30mins 8.30am-10.15pm Sat,
9am-11pm Sun. Last return is at 10.30pm Mon-Fri,
8pm Sat, 10pm Sun.

By car

Take the N-6 or the AP-6 to Guadarrama, and San
Lorenzo is left (south) on the M-600 (50km/31 miles).

By train

Cercanías C-8a, 26 trains from Atocha (journey time
1hr 15mins) 5.45am-11.30pm Mon-Fri; every hour
6.30am-11.30pm Sat, Sun. Last return 10.15pm daily.
Trains run to El Escorial town, from where it's a 2km
(1.25-mile) walk or bus-ride uphill to San Lorenzo and
the monastery. The bus is much more direct.

The Sierras

As Madrid becomes more and more
crowded, so its inhabitants have come to
rely on escapes to the Guadarrama and
Gredos mountain ranges to maintain their
sanity. The mountains are within easy
reach: whether by car, bus or train, one
can soon be up in alpine landscapes,
1,000 metres above sea level. Most
villages in the sierras now have some
kind of information centre, and simple
illustrated guides to a range of walks
(often signposted) are available. Town
halls are another good place to look
for further information.

In summer, take plenty of water and be
sure to wear clothes that offer protection
from the sun. In winter, wear waterproof,
warm (and breathable) gear. Be warned,
though: only experienced walkers should
try the higher walks in winter. Weather in
the mountains is notoriously changeable:
check forecasts before you go. It might be
a good idea to buy food and water in
Madrid before setting off.

Skiing around the Madrid region is a hit-
or-miss affair. Of the resorts near Madrid,
Valdesquí (91 570 12 24, www.
valdesqui.es) usually has the best snow.
La Pinilla (921 55 11 13, www.lapinilla.es)
is directly north of Madrid near Riaza; the
others are in the central Guadarrama.
The only one with accommodation is the
Puerto de Navacerrada (91 594 33 02,
www.puertonavacerrada.com). All-in
package trips to these resorts can be
booked at any travel agency in Madrid.
These ski stations offer limited skiing only
and are of little interest to intermediate or
advanced skiers, but are great for day trips
out of Madrid. Recorded information (in
Spanish only) on snow conditions at ski
resorts and on various out-of-season
activities can be found on the Atudem
phoneline (91 350 20 20).

Tourist information

Oficina de Turismo

C/Grimaldi 2 (91 890 53 13/www.turismosanlorenzo.org). **Open** 10am-6pm Mon-Fri; 10am-7pm Sat, Sun.

El Valle de los Caídos

Built between 1940 and 1959 by Civil War prisoners of the defeated Republican army, Franco's giant mausoleum, the 'Valley of the Fallen' (the fallen on Franco's side, at least) stands in a forested valley a few miles from El Escorial. It was the *generalísimo*'s grand project, and its stark, grandiose, authoritarian style is worthy of the likes of Mussolini or Ceaucescu. It is easily spotted from up to 50 kilometres (31 miles) away by a huge 150-metre (500-foot) high cross (said to weigh over 180,000 tons) which itself is placed 150 metres above the main esplanade.The monument was completed at great financial and human cost and many Republicans perished while quarrying the dense granite rock needed to build it. Ironically, and to the grief of their families, many of their bodies probably now lie close to those of their oppressors.

Its cold, atmospherically lit underground chambers, lined with eerie cowled figures, do exert a certain mesmerising aura; like it or loathe it. The mausoleum is basically a huge tunnel, driven 260 metres (867 feet) into the granite rock. At its entrance are 16th-century monoliths, 12 metres (40 feet) high, while deep in the interior you can see bright-coloured tapestries of the *Apocalypse of St John*; a cupola decorated with mosaics showing heaven-bound saints and martyrs of Spain, and an altar-bound polychrome wooden sculpture of Christ crucified. It contains a subterranean church, an ossuary of six chapels bearing the remains of Civil War dead and the tombs of two men – Franco himself and José Antonio Primo de Rivera, the rich young founder of the Falange who died in the early phases of the Civil War, thus conveniently leaving El Caudillo from El Ferrol unchallenged as leader. Both have fresh flowers placed on their graves daily, paid for by the state, to the disgust of most (though by no means all) of the Spanish population.

The views are quite staggering, especially from the base of the cross, reached via a funicular (€2.50 return).

El Valle de los Caídos

91 890 56 11/www.patrimonionacional.es. **Open** *Nov-Mar* 10am-6pm Tue-Sun. *Apr-Oct* 9.30am-7pm Tue-Sun. **Admission** €5; €2.50 concessions. **Credit** MC, V.

Getting there

By bus

Bus 660 at 3.15pm Tue-Sun from San Lorenzo del Escorial (*see p255*). Return at 5.30pm. Journey time 10mins.

By car

The Valle de los Caídos is 13km/8 miles north of San Lorenzo de El Escorial, and reached via a turn off the M-600, between San Lorenzo and the Guadarrama exit of the A-6/A-P6.

Sierra de Guadarrama

The Guadarrama range runs from El Escorial (*see p255*) in the south-west to Somosierra in the north-east, and separates the two Castilian *mesetas*, or plains: Castile to the north, and La Mancha to the south. For a selection of the many walks possible in the area, the most helpful information centre is that at Valle de la Fuenfría (*see p259*).

Until the 1970s, when a tunnel was built underneath it, the Puerto de Guadarrama pass was the only way out of Madrid to Segovia and Valladolid, and it would often be impassable for days on end in winter. Also known as the Alto de los Leones because of the lion that sits atop a plinth here (the lion is the symbol of the village of Guadarrama), the pass was the scene of bitter fighting during the battle for Madrid during

The deeply disturbing **Valle de los Caídos**.

La Granja. See p260.

the Civil War, and Hemingway set large parts of *For Whom the Bell Tolls* here. The remains of gun emplacements and bunkers from that era still litter the area.

A dirt road runs from the top of the pass, south-west for 30km (19 miles) to the charming and peaceful village of Peguerinos, from where there are buses and a fully paved road to El Escorial. Along the way there are opportunities for camping (*see below*). The track (signposted) veers off to the left from the Guadarrama direction, among a jumble of radio towers and satellite dishes. There is a restaurant called Alto de León just at the turning. Coming the other way, the track is signposted 'Valle Enmedio'.

Another breathtaking walk, taking around three hours, runs from **Tablada** station. Walk up 2km (1.25 miles) – not all the way to the pass – to a post indicating km 56, and take a well-marked forestry track on the right, marked with a stone sign, to the Peña del Arcipreste de Hita (1,527m/5,010ft). The track eventually descends again, to reach the station at Cercedilla.

Cercedilla is not an especially picturesque village, but it has managed to retain its own identity despite its popularity in summer, when the population swells from 5,000 to around 40,000. To find it at its most authentic, visit in winter, especially if you want to try any of the longer walks nearby. In summer, rooms can be very difficult to find. The village sits at the head of a valley that leads up to the Puerto de la Fuenfría (1,796 metres/5,895 feet), a pass that in turn forms a route across the Sierra dating back to at least Roman times. Along the way there is a Calzada Romana (Roman Road), which dates back to the first century AD, with two fine Roman bridges at El Descalzo and Enmedio. The pass is also an important junction of carefully developed modern footpaths.

The most leisurely excursion from Cercedilla is on the old-world narrow-gauge *cercanías* line (C-9) that runs through fine scenery up to the Cotos ski station, a charming way to get up to and beyond the **Puerto de Navacerrada**, especially when it's snowing. Alternatively, from the *cercanías* station in Cercedilla, a 45-minute walk up the M-966 (the main road in front of you) will bring you to a stretch of open alpine woodland known as **Las Dehesas**, with an information centre that's an essential port of call for visitors to the valley, with good free maps. Las Dehesas is a very popular picnic spot, with natural spring swimming pools, only open in summer, and freezing even then.

The nearby town of **Navacerrada** is a lively place with a mountain village feel, and several decent restaurants serving appropriately Alpine food (expect to be dipping your bread into lots of raclettes and fondues), making it a fun base.

Where to stay & eat

Valle Enmedio (91 898 31 76, closed Mon-
Thur Oct-June, rates €4.50 adults, €4 under-
10s, €5.20 tent, €4.50 car), 11 kilometres seven
miles) along the track to Peguerinos, is an
idyllic and well-equipped campsite with
wooden bungalows, set in a forest. In
Peguerinos itself, **La Flor** (C/Espinar 7, 91 898
30 40, rates €40 with shared bath, mains €7.50)
is a basic but friendly *pensión*. For food, try
Alto del León (91 854 12 27, main course
€13), on the crest of the pass.

Choices are much greater in Cercedilla.
Casa Gómez (C/Emilio Serrano 40, 91 852
01 46, mains €12, set lunch €8, closed Mon),
opposite the station, specialises in wild
mushrooms and game in season. **El Chivo
Loco** (C/Pontezuela 23, 91 852 34 39, closed
Tue July-mid Sept, closed Mon-Fri mid Sept-
June), meanwhile, does excellent tapas. As you
come out of the station, on the right, is **Hostal
Longinos – El Aribel** (C/Emilio Serrano 41,
91 852 15 11, rates €40). Booking is essential
in summer and at weekends.

In Navacerrada, try the **Hotel Nava Real**
(C/Huertas, 91 853 10 00, rates €64.50, mains
€12), which also has a more imaginative
restaurant than most. **Restaurante Paco**
(Plaza Doctor Gereda, 91 856 05 62, mains
€11.50, closed Wed Sept-June) has tables
outside overlooking the town square.

Getting there

By bus
The Larrea bus 684 from Moncloa to Cercedilla
leaves every 30mins (journey time 50mins-1hr)
from 6am-10.30pm Mon-Fri, hourly 8am-10pm Sat,
Sun. Last return is at 8.45pm. The Larrea bus 691
runs from Madrid to Puerto Navacerrada, leaving
Madrid at 9.25am (return 4.25pm) Mon-Fri and at
8am, 8.45am and 9.30am (return 3.45pm, 5pm and
6.45pm) Sat, Sun.

By car
A-6 to Guadarrama, then M-995 to Cercedilla,
and M-966 to Puerto de la Fuenfría (56km/35 miles)
or straight on to Puerto de Guadarrama (55km/34
miles). To Peguerinos, go via El Escorial, 23km
(14 miles) up to Santa María de la Alameda.
From Cercedilla, take the M-995 to the A-6. For
Navacerrada, take the A-6 to Collado Villalba,
then the M-601.

By train
For Tablada, there are two trains daily from Atocha
and Chamartín. For Cercedilla, take C-2, then C-9 to
Puerto de Navacerrada. There are six trains Mon-Fri
and trains run hourly Sat, Sun; the last train back
from Cercedilla is at about 10.30pm (check timetable
for the exact time).

Tourist information

Centro de Información Valle de la Fuenfría
*Carretera de las Dehesas, km 2, Cercedilla (91 852
22 13).* **Open** 10am-6pm daily.

Edificio Deporte y Montaña
*Puerto de Navacerrada (91 852 33 02/
www.puertonavacerrada.com).* **Open** 9am-6pm daily.

Valle de Lozoya

The wide, flat Valle de Lozoya runs north-east
from below the pass of Puerto de los Cotos
(1,830 metres/6,006 feet), to the main A-1
Burgos road. There is little to detain you in the
village of **Rascafría** at the western end of the
valley, which has been drearily overdeveloped,
except for the stunning **Monasterio de El
Paular** (91 869 14 25, tours noon, 1pm & 5pm
Mon-Wed, Fri & Sat, noon, 1pm Thur, 1pm,
4pm, 5pm & 6pm Sun, admission free) nearby.
This Benedictine monastery, a short way south
of the village, was founded in 1390 but was still
being added to 500 years later. It is still partly
occupied by monks, even though most of it is
now a Sheraton hotel, and it remains a
wonderful sight with its stunning backdrop
of snow-capped peaks.

One of the many rewarding walks
around here is along the GR-10 path from
the monastery up to the Puerto de los Cotos,
which winds its way through pine forests and
a picturesque roe deer habitat. Heading in the
other direction, the path runs two kilometres to
some natural swimming pools at Las Presillas.
In summer there is a small kiosk there, selling
drinks. From the town itself, it's also possible
to walk across the mountains to the palace of
La Granja (*see p260*).

Where to stay & eat

Casa Briscas (Plaza España 13, 91 869 12
26, mains €10.50, menú €7.50) is the best eating
option in Rascafría's main square, and has a
terrace that really comes alive in summer. The
44-room **Santa María del Paular** (91 869
10 11, rates €124-€175, mains €19, closed Jan)
occupies the former monastery cloister and is
delightfully peaceful. Male visitors (only)
seeking a place of contemplation can stay at the
monastery itself (91 869 14 25) for €30 a night,
full-board, for a minimum three nights' stay,
and a maximum of ten. **Los Calizos** (Carretera
Miraflores-Rascafría km 30, 91 869 11 12, rates
€120 incl breakfast & dinner, mains €19) is a
stone house by the Lozoya River, located a
short distance outside town.

Getting there

By bus

To or from Rascafría, take Continental (91 314 57 55) bus 194, which leaves Madrid from Plaza Castilla at 2pm, 6pm Mon-Fri; 8am, 6pm Sat; 8am, 2.30pm Sun. The last bus back is at 5pm Mon-Fri, 10.30pm Sat, 6.30pm Sun.

By car

For Puerto de los Cotos, take the A-6 to Collado-Villalba, M-601 to Puerto de Navacerrada, then the M-604 (64km/40 miles). For Rascafría, go via Cotos, or the M-607 to Colmenar Viejo, M-609 to Soto del Real, M-611 to Rascafría (80km/50 miles). To get here directly from Madrid, take the A-1 via Colmenar Viejo and Miraflores de la Sierra.

By train

For Puerto de los Cotos, take C-8b to Cercedilla, then line C-9 to Cotos. There are six trains daily Mon-Fri (9.35am, 11.35am, 1.35pm, 3.35pm, 5.35pm, 7.35pm). Trains run hourly Sat, Sun (9.35am-7.35pm). Last return is 8.43pm.

La Granja

Another palace to start life as a hunting lodge, later to be converted by the Bourbons, is La Granja, about 11 kilometres (seven miles) from Segovia back towards Madrid on the N-101. It was built on the site of a former shrine, San Ildefonso, by Philip V, homesick for his youth in Versailles. His wife Isabel Farnese also added some distinctive touches, not least of which are the famous fountains. The result is perhaps the loveliest of all the Bourbon palaces.

Work on the structure was carried out in record time between 1721 and 1723 by Teodoro Ardamans, and the extensive gardens over a longer period under the main supervision of René Carlier. Amid the formal hedgerows, lawns and rows of trees you'll find voluptuous statues, limpid pools and the fountains, some of which spring to life three times a week in the summer and then all of which are turned on for one memorable evening each year, 25 August. Water comes from an artificial lake called El Mar, set in a woodland at the end of the estate and backed by the dramatic sheer wall of the Peñalara, the highest peak in the Guadarrama.

The palace itself, restored after a devastating fire in 1918, is an opulent maze of elegant salons and chambers that abound in classical frescoes, dazzling cut-glass chandeliers (made in the palace's own glass factory, which still functions today) and priceless *objets d'art*. The tapestry selection, though representing only a part of the Spanish and Flemish royal collection, is among the finest you'll see anywhere. Unfortunately visits are only via guided tours of up to 45 people at a time.

The charming village of **San Ildefonso** has long been a favourite resort for escaping the oppressive Madrid summer heat; if you have your own transport it offers a relaxing alternative to staying in Segovia. Among its imposing private houses is the **Casa de Infantes**, built by Carlos III for his sons Gabriel and Antonio.

Palacio Real de La Granja de San Ildefonso

921 47 00 19/www.patrimonionacional.es. **Open** *Oct-Mar* 10am-1.30pm, 3-5pm Tue-Sat; 10am-2pm Sun. *Apr-Sept* 10am-6pm Tue-Sun. Fountains operate May-Sept at 5.30pm Wed, Sat & Sun. **Admission** *Palace* €5; €2.50 concessions. Wed free for EU citizens. *Gardens* free. **No credit cards.**

Where to stay & eat

It's essential to reserve ahead at the wildly popular **Casa Zaca** (C/Embajadores 6, 921 47 00 87, lunch only, closed Mon, mains €10); it offers home-style cuisine, so instead of the standard roast lamb or *cochinillo* there are gutsy casseroles and braised ox tongue. A reasonable, low-key alternative is **Bar Mari** (C/Valenciana 2, 921 47 03 46, mains €11) or try the tapas, in front of a roaring fire, at the colourful **La Fundición** (Plaza de la Calandria 1, 921 47 00 46, closed Wed-Fri lunch, all Mon & Tue). **Hostal Las Fuentes** (C/Padre Claret 6, 921 47 10 24, rates €97-€104) is a beautifully restored house with quiet rooms looking down

Riofrío.

to Segovia or into a flower-filled courtyard.
Hotel Roma (C/Guardas 2, 921 47 07 52,
rates €54.60-€61, restaurant closed Tue, mains
€13.50, closed Nov) is comfortable enough.

Getting there

By bus

La Sepulvedana (91 530 48 00) from Paseo de la
Florida 11 seven to ten buses daily (journey time
1hr15mins-2hrs). Last return 9pm.

By car

A 6 to Collado Villalba, then M-601 north (78km/48
miles).

Riofrío

After the death of Philip V, Isabel Farnese could
not bear to stay on at La Granja with her stepson
Fernando VI, and so had another palace built at
Riofrío. She was to survive Fernando, however,
and thus Riofrío was never completely finished.
Later Alfonso XII came here to mourn the
sudden death of his new bride, Mercedes, and the
whole palace still has a melancholy air, despite
the warm pinks and greens of its exterior.

It was built in the middle of the best deer-
hunting country near Madrid, and later
sovereigns also came to this beautiful estate to
blast away to their hearts' content. With this in
mind, half the palace has been turned into a
hunting museum – a mandatory and overlong
part of the guided tour. Unless hundreds of

antlers and stuffed animals are the kind of
thing that turns you on, it is probably best
admired from outside, with a picnic.

Palacio de Riofrío

921 47 00 19. **Open** *Oct-Mar* 10am-1.30pm,
3-5pm Tue-Sat; 10am-2pm Sun. *Apr-Sept* 10am-6pm
Tue-Sun. **Admission** €5; €2.50 concessions. Wed
free for EU citizens. **No credit cards**.

Getting there

By car

The palace is south-west of Segovia, on the SG-724
side road between the N110 and N603 (90km/56 miles
from Madrid).

By train

Segovia trains (*see p265*) stop at La Losa-Navas
de Riofrío, about 2km (1.25 miles) from Riofrío.

Segovia

Segovia combines beautiful architecture with
visual warmth in a region more associated with
austerity. In contrast with the traditional grey
chill of Castile it glows, radiant and mellow.
Make the approach by road across vast plains
and it appears as if by witchcraft, rising on a
burnished hillock like an acropolis or ship in
full sail. The scene is dominated by the
Alcázar fortress, with its sharply angled
ramparts, spiky towers and high gables; a
fantastical fairytale vision.

Trips Out of Town

Segovia

Convento de los Carmelitas Descalzas

Iglesia de Vera Cruz

Casa de la Moneda

Monasterio de El Parral

Alameda del Parral

PASEO DE LA ALAMEDA DEL PARRAL

C/LOS MOLINOS

C/PARRAL

C/SAN MARCOS

CAMARQUÉS DE VILLENA

C/MONEDA

Rio Eresma

C/CHAPITERA

PASEO DE SANTO DOMINGO DE GUZMÁN

Hospital de la Misericordia

C/PUERTA DE SANTIAGO

Monasterio de Santa Cruz la Real

C/DOCTOR VELASCO

C/CARDENAL ZÚÑIGA

Jardín de Mauricio Fromkes

PLAZA DE REINA VICTORIA EUGENIA

Iglesia de San Esteban

Iglesia de San Quirce

Iglesia de San Nicolás

PASEO DEL OBISPO

C/NELARE

Alcázar

Iglesia de San Andrés

RONDA DON

C/DIADIZ

C/SANTO

Casa Museo de Antonio Machado

Museo del Palacio Episcopal

Ayuntamiento

CUESTA DE SAN BARTOLOMÉ

C/SAN NICOLÁS

C/TARAY

San Juan de los Caballeros

Torre de Hércules

Iglesia la Trinidad

PLAZUELA DE COLMENARES

C/POZO

Museo de Segovia

Casa del Sol

C/SOCORRO

C/JUAN II

Cathedral

PLAZA MAYOR

Iglesia de San Miguel

C/SAN FACUNDO

C/COLON

C/SAN AGUSTIN

Casa de las Cadenas

C/LOS GASCOS

CUESTA DE LOS HOYOS

C/MARQUÉS DEL ARCO

Torreón de los Arias Dávila

Museo de Esteban Vicente

C/JUDERIA

VIA DE ROMA

Iglesia de San Sebastián

Rio Clamores

Convento del Corpus Christi

C/LEOPOLDO MORENO

C/SAN VALENTÍN

C/JOSE CANALEJAS

PASEO DE LOS TILOS

El Torreón de Lozoya

C/SAN JUSTO

Iglesia de San Justo

Iglesia de San Martín

Palacio del Conde Alpuente

C/OBISPO GANDASEGUI

Casa de los Picos

C/CERVANTES PLAZA DEL AZOGUEJO

Aqueduct

PLAZA DE SAN JUSTO

C/OCHOA ONDATEGUI

C/SAN MILLÁN

C/CAIMEN

PLAZA DE DÍAZ SANZ

C/MON ALMIRA

PASEO DE EZEQUIEL GONZÁLEZ

C/LAS CARRETAS

AVENIDA DE FERNANDEZ LADREDA

Iglesia de San Clemente

C/SAN FRANCISCO

C/PIEDAD

Iglesia de San Millán

C/SANTO DOMINGO DE SILOS

Academia de Artillería

C/INDEPENDENCIA

C/SAN ROQUE

Bus Station

Jardincillos de San Roque

C/LOS COCHES

C/ROBLE

C/LARMIN BOTÁNICO

C/CAPRICHO

To Train Station

0   400 m
0   400 yds

© Copyright Time Out Group 2004

CARRETERA DE ÁVILA

CARRETERA DE MADRONA

Jardín Botánico

C/SANTO TOMÁS

Trips Out of Town

Impregnably poised on the edge of a hair-raising abyss into which a negligent nurse once accidentally dropped a 14th-century heir to the throne and then flung herself after him to avoid punishment, it was originally built as a modest stone fort 200 years earlier, and underwent radical changes over the centuries. Most of the world-famous fairy castle architecture seen today is a brilliant work of restoration carried out after a disastrous fire in 1862. Though owned by the army, the bastion's purpose is now purely commercial and its chambers are open daily for the paying public to inspect the weapons, armour, tapestries and artworks on display.

Close by is the huge, airy and very light Gothic **cathedral** (C/Marqués del Arco, 921 46 22 05, open Oct-Mar 9.30am-5.30pm Mon-Sat, 1.30-5.30pm Sun, Apr-Sept 9.30am-6.30pm Mon-Sat, 1.30-6.30pm Sun, admission €2). The current structure was built to replace a predecessor destroyed in a 1521 revolt. Inside

there's a tiny museum that holds an interesting collection of tapestries, paintings and a wonderful 16th-century grandfather clock.

Very different, but just as extraordinary as the Alcázar, is the 728-metre- (2,426-feet) long Roman **aqueduct**, made of gleaming Guadarrama granite in rough-hewn blocks that mesh perfectly without mortar, though it no longer brings water from the Riofrío as it first did over 2,000 years ago. The **Plaza del Azoguejo** below, where markets are now held, was a rendezvous for thieves and vagabonds in Cervantes' day. Steps rise up the wall at the place where the aqueduct merges into the rising hill, or you can spiral up the streets channelling traffic up and down. A warren of intricate lanes criss-crosses the old town like a demented spider's web, weaving you past squares, gardens, mansions, palaces and museums. The town is never short of tourists but is still resolutely traditional: in the Plaza Mayor the

Segovia.

atmosphere of the past blends with real-life bustle and you can still find plenty of bars and cafés filled only with locals.

Of its dozen or so churches and convents, all built between the 12th and 16th centuries, **San Esteban**, noted for its striking bell tower, and **San Millán**, with its Moorish-influenced decor and elaborately carved wooden ceiling, stand out. Among its secular buildings the **Casa de los Picos**, with waffle-iron studs on its façade, can be found amid the shopping streets downhill from the cathedral. Also not to be missed is the **Monastery of El Parral**, founded by Henry VI and now a national monument. One of the best views is from 13th-century **Iglesia de Vera Cruz** built by the Knights Templars with spoils from the Crusades,

Alcázar de Segovia

Plaza de la Reina María Cristina (921 46 07 59). **Open** *Oct-Feb* 10am-6pm daily. *Mar-Sept* 10am-7pm daily. **Admission** €3.50; €2.30 concessions. Tue free for EU citizens. **No credit cards**.

Where to stay & eat

The **Méson del Duque** (C/Cervantes 12, 921 46 24 87, main course €17) is a long-standing favourite with colourfully decorated dining rooms on several floors serving excellent Castilian fare. **Restaurant José María**

(C/Cronista Lecea 11, 921 46 11 11, main course €14.50) is a traditionally styled *mesón* serving first-rate *cochinillo* (suckling pig) and probably the best lamb in town. It also has a good tapas bar. The **Tasca La Posada** (C/Judería Vieja 19, 921 46 21 71, main course €9.50) is an atmospheric bar with great tapas, a lively dining room and excellent-value food. **Cuevas de San Esteban** (C/Valdelaguila 15, 921 46 09 82, mains €13) is another place to avoid the tourist-trap market with reasonably priced Castilian food. For something different, **Narizotas** (Plaza Medina del Campo 1, 921 46 26 79, mains €15) has a selection of good risottos and salads, as well as the usual hit parade of roast meats.

Los Linajes (C/Dr Velasco 9, 921 46 04 75, rates €85-€104) is an atmospheric 13th-century palace close to San Esteban church with beams, antiques and a lush patio, while the **Acueducto** (C/Padre Claret 10, 921 42 48 00, rate €85) is a comfortable, established hotel where some of the rooms overlook the Roman aqueduct. Alternatively, try **Las Sirenas** (C/Juan Bravo 30, 921 46 26 63, rates €65-€76), a homely hotel in the old town near San Martín church. **Hostal Taray** (Plaza San Facundo 1, 921 46 30 41, rates €32) is useful for those on a budget, as is the very central **El Hidalgo** (C/José Canalejas 5, 921 46 35 29, rates €40-€43).

Patones de Arriba. *See p266.*

Getting there

By bus

La Sepulvedana (91 530 48 00) buses run from Paseo de la Florida 11, every 30mins (journey time 1hr 15mins). Last return 9.30pm daily.

By car

Take the A-6/AP-6 to Guadarrama, then the N603 (90km/56 miles); or the Navacerrada road from Guadarrama (a slow mountain road).

By train

There are eight trains daily from Atocha or Chamartín, but be warned: it's a slow journey (2hrs).

Tourist information

Oficina de Turismo

Plaza Mayor 10 (921 46 03 34/www.turismocastillayleon.com). **Open** *July, Aug* 9am-8pm Mon-Thur, Sun; 9am-9pm Fri, Sat. *Sept-June* 9am-2pm, 5-8pm daily.

Manzanares el Real & La Pedriza

La Pedriza is a rocky crag crisscrossed with paths. Birthplace of the Manzanares river, it is home to the Sierra's biggest colony of griffon vultures, protected in the Parque Regional de la Cuenca Alta del Manzanares. The area fills up on Sundays, but don't be fooled – many experienced climbers still get lost in La Pedriza, and fatalities have been known. The starting point for a hike is the town of **Manzanares el Real**, dominated by the almost cartoonish vision of a perfect 'Spanish' castle, the 15th-century **Castillo de Manzanares el Real**, once the stronghold of the Mendozas, one of the most powerful aristocratic clans of medieval Castile. Much of its interior is the product of recent restoration work, but the castle retains a fascinating mix of late Gothic and Mudéjar features, especially in the courtyard and the beautiful upper gallery, which has a spectacular view over the valley.

Castillo de Manzanares el Real

91 853 00 08. **Open** *Oct-June* 10am-5.10pm Tue-Sun. *July-Sept* 10am-5.10pm Tue-Fri; 10am-6.40pm Sat; 10am-5.40pm Sun. **Admission** €1.80; 80¢ concessions. **No credit cards.**

Where to stay & eat

A kilometre or so out of town on the path to El Yelmo is the small but well-appointed **Hostal El Tranco** (C/Tranco 4, 91 853 04 23, rates €37-€52, mains €10). Nearby are a couple of lively bars with terraces. Another option is

La Fresneda campsite on the Carretera M-608 in Soto el Real (91 847 65 23, Sept-June open weekends only, rates €6 per person, including tent and car).

Getting there

By bus

Colmenarejo 724 from Plaza Castilla, buses approx hourly 7am-11.30pm Mon-Fri, 8am-11.30pm Sat, Sun. The last return is at 10.20pm.

By car

Take the M-607 to Colmenar Viejo, then the M-609 to Soto del Real. Turn west on to the M-608 for Manzanares el Real (53km/33 miles).

Sierra Norte

In contrast to the majestic alpine landscapes of the Guadarrama, this tract of rolling hills some 60 kilometres (37 miles) north-east of Madrid toward Guadalajara at first seems decidedly the poorer relative. Isolated until the 1980s, the Sierra Norte suffered from depopulation, with many villages being abandoned, until it was 'discovered' by *madrileños* looking for a more authentic, and cheaper, weekend retreat. The Sierra Norte is also host to the region's finest deciduous forests. Even at the height of summer the area is never crowded.

The gateway to the area is **Buitrago de Lozoya**, just off the A-1. What remains of its walled medieval centre shows traces of Arab times, and its cool and dignified Gothic 15th-century **Iglesia de Santa María**, recently restored after fire swept through it in 1936, is also worth a visit. The real charm of Buitrago, however, is the quirky little **Museo Picasso** in the basement of its town hall (Plaza Picasso 1, 91 868 00 04, open 11am-1.45pm, 4-6pm Tue, Thur, Fri, 11am-1.45pm Wed, 10am-2pm, 4-7pm Sat, 10am-2pm Sun, admission free), consisting of some 60 works, especially centred on bullfighting themes, and mostly from his later years. Picasso donated the pictures to his hairdresser and friend Eugenio Arias, a native of the town who met Picasso in Toulouse, where they were both living in exile. For 26 years Arias cut Picasso's hair in return for his paintings and sketches, and on his return to Spain donated them to the town.

Among the first places of interest after Buitrago is **Montejo de la Sierra**, 16 kilometres (ten miles) to the north-east, and a good central point for excursions on foot. It has an interesting Renaissance church, but the jewel in its crown is a magnificent beech forest, eight kilometres (five miles) away at **El Chaparral**. It can be visited with guided tours, run from the **Centro de Recursos de Alta Montaña** information centre (C/Real 64, 91 869 70 58, open 9am-6pm Tue-Fri, 9.30am-9pm Sat, Sun). It's a good idea to book places well ahead, especially from October to December. This is also popular mountain biking country, and the same centre has information on hiking routes.

An easy-to-follow bike route from Montejo, taking about three and a half hours, but which can also be walked in about twice the time, is along a dirt track that cuts off the road to La Hiruela uphill towards the signposted Puerto de Cardoso and Cardoso de la Sierra, in the province of Guadalajara, before turning back to descend again to Montejo. On the way there are inspiring views north to the Ayllón mountains, and the 2,129-metre (6,985-foot) Peña Cebollera. Further south, at the bottom of a magnificent valley in the very heart of the Sierra Norte, lies **Puebla de la Sierra**. With a population of less than 100, this mountain hamlet has been almost entirely restored, and probably looks better now than it ever has. There are many houses to rent at weekends, and it makes an ideal base for walks to the surrounding reservoirs. Information on walks is available at the Parador de la Puebla – not an official parador– in the centre of the village.

About 25 kilometres (16 miles) south-west of Puebla (as the crow flies, not as the road winds) is **El Berrueco**, with a 13th-century church and the huge El Atazar reservoir. **El Atazar** village is the starting point for more walks, and a range of water sports are yours for the asking at the reservoir. The picturesque villages of **Patones de Arriba** and **Patones de Abajo** sit on the southern edge of the Sierra, and are reached via the Torrelaguna road off the A-1 from Madrid. The former is a cluster of slate houses and narrow, cobbled streets, reached by a steep, twisting road, though most live in the latter. A restoration project in recent years has been a mixed blessing, saving many of the villages' ancient houses from decay, but attracting rich second-homers from the city. Patones (as they are collectively known) is thought to have once been a peculiar enclave within Spain, a diminutive Visigothic kingdom which held its independence until the 18th century. A road north-east from Patones leads seven kilometres (four and a half miles) to the vast **Cueva del Reguerillo**, with prehistoric cave paintings around its underground lakes. The cave is unmarked, so be sure to ask directions before setting off, and a torch is helpful when you get there.

Where to stay & eat

Buitrago has the **Hostal Madrid-Paris** (Avda Madrid 23, 91 868 11 26, €30), an old stone house with 25 bargain rooms and a great-value restaurant. For old-fashioned food in surroundings to match, try **Asador Jubel** (C/Real 33, 91 868 03 09, closed Tue, mains €9). **Mesón del Hayedo** (C/Turco, 91 869 70 23, rates €40, restaurant closed Sun dinner and all Mon, mains €20) is small, with a crowded and lively restaurant, especially on Sundays. **Taberna de Teo** (Plaza de la Constitución 10, 91 868 0512, June-Sept closed Wed, Oct-May closed Tue & Wed) is a beautifully restored wine bar with excellent tapas.

In Puebla de la Sierra, the **Parador de la Puebla** (Plaza Carlos Ruiz 2, 91 869 72 56, rates €48-€54 incl breakfast, closed Tue) only has five rooms, so make sure that you book well in advance. However, staff will recommend other houses in the village that let rooms if you're out of luck. In upmarket Patones the restored five-room country house **Hotel del Tiempo Perdido** (Travesia del Ayuntamiento 7, 91 843 21 52, weekends only, closed Aug, rates €181) is as good as it gets. And for food, you can't beat the old-world charm of **El Rey de Patones** (C/Asas, 91 843 20 37, closed dinner Mon-Tue, Thur, Sun, closed lunch Fri, Sat, all Wed & Aug, main course €13).

Getting there

By bus

Continental bus 191 runs from Plaza Castilla to Buitrago (6.15am-9.30pm Mon-Fri; 8am-8.30pm Sat, Sun). Last bus from Buitrago back to Madrid is at 8pm Mon-Fri, 6pm Sat, 10.45pm Sun. The 196 also goes to Buitrago and Acebeda via El Berrueco on Sat and Sun; it leaves Madrid at 8am Sat, returning at 1pm; on Sun it leaves Madrid at 9am, returning at 7pm. The 199 to Montejo de la Sierra via El Berrueco leaves Madrid 8am on Sat and Sun, returning at noon on both days. Many local microbus services run from Buitrago.

By car

Take the A-1 north direct to Buitrago de Lozoya (75km/47 miles), or turn right in Venturada (51km/32 miles; signposted to Torrelaguna) for Patones, or just north of La Cabrera (62km/39 miles) for El Berrueco.

Tourist information

Centro de Turismo de la Sierra Norte

Avda del Generalisimo 36, La Cabrera (91 868 86 98/www.sierranortemadrid.org). **Open** 9am-6pm daily.

The tourist office for the whole area is in La Cabrera, 18km (11 miles) south of Buitrago. Buitrago town hall (91 868 00 04, www.buitrago.org) also has a lot of information on activities in the Sierra above the Picasso Museum.

South & East

Heading east towards Alcalá de Henares and south towards Toledo, the dramatic views and charming villages inspire.

Alcalá de Henares & around

After the horrific terrorist attacks of March 2004, Alcalá de Henares was descended upon by the world's camera crews and catapulted to fame for all the wrong reasons. Centuries before the terrorist attacks of 2004, all eyes were on Alcalá as Spain's centre of learning and culture, its superb university was founded in 1498, and it was the birthplace of Cervantes. As far back as Roman times Complutum, as it was known then, was a large and important city.

The university moved to Madrid in the 19th century, but there is still a strong sense of the city's educational history here today. The streets in the old quarter are lined with **Colegios Mayores** – student halls of residence in the 16th and 17th centuries, now converted into hotels and restaurants. One of the most impressive is the **Colegio de San Ildefonso**, famous for its stunning Plateresque façade and three-tiered patio, which is still the setting for the solemn opening of university terms and the presentation of the Cervantes Prize for Literature.

The main square, named after the city's most famous literary son, is a great spot to relax over a coffee and admire the buildings that line it, such as the **Casa Consistorial** (town hall) and the **Capilla de Oidor**, a 15th-century chapel now used for exhibitions. If you want to know more about the creator of Don Quixote, head to the author's birthplace, now the **Museo Casa Cervantes** (C/Imagen 2, 91 889 96 54, open 10am-5.30pm Tue-Sun, admission free). On the city's west side are the **Catedral Magistral** and the **Museo de Esculturas al Aire Libre**, an open-air museum with 50 or so sculptures.

One of the most entertaining ways to get to Alcalá is via the Tren de Cervantes (which runs weekends in autumn and spring, leaving Atocha station in Madrid at 11am, and returning at 7pm). Guides in Golden Age costume ply passengers with information about the city, and, on arrival, give them a tour of the town.

From Alcalá you can take a short excursion 17 kilometres (9.5 miles) down the M-204, to **Nuevo Baztán**. A peaceful little place, it was founded by a banker in the early 18th century and the entire village was designed by renowned architect José de Churriguera, giving it a wonderfully harmonious feel.

Alcalá de Henares.

Nuevo Baztán.

Chinchón's galleried Plaza Mayor.

Where to eat

Alcalá's best-known restaurant is the **Hostería del Estudiante** (C/Colegios 3, 91 888 03 30, closed 2wks Aug, mains €21.50, set lunch €26), which occupies a stunning 16th-century *colegio* and specialises in hearty Castilian food – roast lamb and suckling pig, garlic soup and the Alcalá dessert speciality, *costrada*, which is something like a sweet millefeuille. At the back of the *hostería*, and across a garden is the **Cafetería El Restaurado** (Plaza San Diego s/n, 91 885 41 40, lunch only, closed Sat & Sun, all Aug, set menu €6.50). It's handy and popular with students for a quick and cheap lunch. **Mesón Don José** (C/Santiago 4, 91 881 86 17, closed Mon dinner & 3wks Aug, mains €9.50, set lunch €8) is cheap and relatively atmospheric. For good tapas washed down with draught *vermut*, try the attractive, tiled bar **Cervecería El Hidalgo** (C/El Bedel 3, mobile 627 215 706, closed Wed).

In Nuevo Baztán, the **Mesón El Conde** (Plaza la Iglesia 5, 91 873 53 27, mains €9.50, set lunch €7.50) is a reasonably priced, traditional place with balconies over the square and tables outside in summer.

Getting there

By bus

Continental Auto (91 356 23 07) bus 223 leaves from Avda de América every 5-10mins, 6.15am-11pm Mon-Fri, less frequently Sat & Sun. Journey time approx 35 mins.

By car

On the A-2 it's approximately a 25min drive (31km/19miles).

By train

Cercanías C-2; approx every 10mins (15-20mins weekends), 5.20am-11.50pm daily. Journey time 35mins. From the station it's a 10min walk to the centre (go straight down Paseo de la Estación).

Tourist information

Oficinas de Turismo

Callejón Santa María 1 (91 889 26 94/www.alcala henares-turismo.com). **Open** *Oct-May* 10am-2pm, 4-6.30pm daily. *June, Sept* 10am-2pm, 5-7.30pm daily. *July, Aug* 10am-2pm, 5-7.30pm Tue-Sun.
Plaza de los Santos Niños s/n (91 881 06 34). **Open** *Oct-May* 10am-2pm, 4-6.30pm daily. *June, Sept* 10am-2pm, 5-7.30pm daily. *July, Aug* 10am-2pm, 5-7.30pm Mon, Wed-Sun.

Chinchón & around

Out of season Chinchón is a sleepy little town, famous for its *anís* liqueur and its pretty, arcaded Plaza Mayor, overlooked by wooden balconies all the way around, and occasionally used for bullfights. This is where you'll find the town hall, tourist office and, most importantly, plenty of balcony restaurants and bars, where the traditional lunch is lamb cooked in a wood-burning oven, washed down with red from the *cuevas* (cellars) and finished off with a glass of the famous local brew.

The neo-classical **Iglesia de la Asunción** overlooking the plaza houses Goya's depiction of the Assumption. Just next door is the **Teatro Lope de Vega** where the playwright wrote *El Blasón de los Chavos de Villalba* and which now doubles as a cinema. Just outside the town is the 16th-century castle, built on the site of the original 12th-century fortress. Sadly, only the ground floor remains, and it's home to sheep and the local *botellón* scene.

Chinchón hosts an open-air folk festival in the plaza at the beginning of June, and during the fiestas in August the bulls run up and down the Avda del Generalísimo (or C/Huertos as some residents prefer), and there are fireworks, a fairground and bands performing near the castle.

It's worth driving to **Colmenar de Oreja**, five kilometres (three miles) away on the M-311. A quiet, untouristy place, it has an unspoilt Plaza Mayor, again ringed with wooden galleries, though on a smaller scale than Chinchón's, and a handsome 13th-century church, the **Iglesia de Santa María**. The tower is by Juan de Herrera.

Where to stay & eat

The balcony restaurants lining the Plaza Mayor all offer similar Chinchón fare – garlic soup and roasted red peppers, roast lamb and suckling pig. **La Casa del Pregonero** (Plaza Mayor 4,

Aranjuez.

91 894 06 96, www.lacasadelpregonero.com, closed Tue, mains €15), is slightly different – it uses local ingredients with some interesting twists, and has an attractive patio at the back. The **Mesón Cuevas del Vino** (C/Benito Hortelano 13, 91 894 02 06, www.cuevasdel vino.com, closed Tue & 2wks Aug, mains €14.50) is an atmospheric place, with an ancient oil press and some old carriages. For accommodation, try the delightful **Parador de Chinchón** (Avda Generalisimo 1, 91 894 08 36, www.parador.es, rates €122), in a 17th-century former Augustinian convent, or the slightly less luxurious, but still very comfortable **Hostal Chinchón** (C/José Antonio 12, 91 893 53 98, www.hostalchinchon.com, rate €40).

Getting there

By bus

La Veloz (91 409 76 02) runs from Conde de Casal metro station. Buses leave every 30mins, 7am-11pm Mon-Fri; every hour, 8am-midnight Sat; and every 1hr 30mins, 9am-11pm Sun. Last return 10pm weekdays and Sun, 11pm Sat. Journey time approx 1hr.

By car

Take the A-3, then the M-311, or the A-4/M-404 (45km/28 miles).

Aranjuez

Aranjuez was the official spring residence of the Spanish monarchy and its hangers-on from the 17th to the 19th century. It was probably originally chosen for its setting and lush countryside – it is an oasis in the arid plains of central Spain, situated in a wide valley formed by the Jarama and Tajo (Tagus) rivers. The royals have long gone, but the **Palacio Real** is still the principal tourist attraction, along with the town's famous asparagus and strawberries.

Originally built as a hunting lodge for Charles I (Charles V of the Holy Roman Empire), the palace took its current shape under Philip II in the 1560s, and was extended in the 1770s by Charles III. It's a charming mix of baroque and classical, and typical of the Bourbon palaces, with a sumptuous **throne room** and a cosy **ballroom**. It is the gardens, however, that are the real attraction, particularly the 16th-century-designed **Jardín de la Isla** and **Jardín del Príncipe**. The gardens inspired Rodrigo's famous *Concierto de Aranjuez* and the musical tradition continues today with a summer season of mostly open-air concerts and musical promenades, principally featuring baroque music (*see p217* **Playing in time**). It is in the garden that you'll find the delightfully over-the-top **Casita del Labrador**, which was built for Charles IV. Half-hourly tours of this early 19th-century folly – complete with painted ceilings, tapestry-lined walls, and porcelain and marble floors – are available, though you must book in advance (91 891 03 05).

In the town itself, **Museo del Toro** (Avenida Plaza de Toros s/n, 91 892 16 43, open 10am-6pm Tue-Sun, admission €3, €1.20-€1.80 concessions) aims to re-create the atmosphere of the bullfight and the traditions and entertainments of the court. If you're so inclined you can travel to Aranjuez on the Tren de la Fresa steam train, with hostesses in period costume plying you with cheery historical facts (*see p199*).

Palacio Real de Aranjuez

91 891 07 40/www.patrimonionacional.es. **Open** *Palaces* 10am-6.15pm Tue-Sun. *Gardens* Oct-Mar 10am-6pm daily. Apr-Sept 8am-8.30pm daily. **Admission** *Palace* €4.90; €2.40 concessions. *Casita del Labrador* (guided tours only) €3; €1.50 concessions. *Casa de Marinos* €3; €1.50 concessions. *Gardens* free. Free to EU citizens Wed. **No credit cards**.

Where to stay & eat

Casa Pablo (C/Almibar 42, 91 891 14 51, closed Aug, mains €20) has superb seafood, while, for traditional ingredients cooked in a more imaginative way, **Concierto** (C/Real 1, 91 892 47 04, closed Mon, mains €18) is a good choice, especially if you catch one of the jazz or classical music sessions.

La Posta (C/Postas 23, 91 891 8074, closed Sun & 2wks July, mains €11.50, set lunch €8.60-€14) is a good cheap and cheerful option.

In the frame El Greco's Toledo

Born Domenikos Theotocopoulos in 1541 on the island of Crete, El Greco originally trained as a painter of religious icons. As the island was then a Venetian colony, Venice was the logical place for an ambitious young man to seek his fortune and Il Greco (as he styled himself) spent ten years in Italy adding the influences of Titian, Tintoretto and Michaelangelo to his Byzantine roots. The result was a love-it-or-hate-it style that was to influence painters from Picasso to Pollock. Trademark features include figures with elongated limbs and heavy-lidded heroin eyes, psychedelic colours and such distorted perspective that some critics have suggested that El Greco suffered from an ailment that affected his vision.

The painter was attracted to Spain by rumours that Philip II was seeking artists to decorate his El Escorial palace, but the conservative king was horrified by El Greco's freakish, ghostly figures. The artist eventually wound up in Toledo, where he remained until his death in 1614, at the age of 73. Much to the regret of the tourist office, nobody is sure which of the city's numerous churches holds his remains.

In Toledo he found great success and charged such extortionate fees for his work that several clients took him to court, although El Greco claimed that, 'As surely as the rate of payment is inferior to the value of my sublime work, so will my name go down in posterity as one of the greatest geniuses of Spanish painting.' Even so, he died a pauper after blowing all his money on an extravagant home and outlandish whims, such as hiring musicians to play as he dined.

El Greco painted several portraits of his adopted city, the most famous being *View of Toledo*, in New York's Metropolitan Museum of Art. As distorted as his human figures, they are more like spiritual impressions of the city than topographically accurate paintings – for instance, he would move the cathedral and the Alcázar closer together to symbolise the marriage of church and state. Not surprisingly, Toledo became something of a muse for El Greco and as well as taking centre stage in these landscapes the city also featured in the background of several religious paintings, including *Laocöon, Christ in Agony on the Cross* and *The Immaculate Conception*.

His masterpiece, the enormous *Burial of the Count of Orgaz*, is one of Toledo's major crowd-pullers, and it remains in the arched alcove of the Santo Tomé church where it was originally painted. It includes a self portrait: El Greco is the seventh mourner on the left and the only figure to look directly at the observer. His son, Jorge Manuel, is the little lad holding the hanky that bears El Greco's signature, which he signed in Hellenic script to the end of his days.

To stay the night, the sleek **Príncipe de la Paz** (C/San Antonio 22, 91 809 92 22, www.nh-hotels.com, rates €105-€136) has stylish rooms overlooking the palace, while the **Hostal Rusiñol** (C/San Antonio 76, 91 891 01 55, rates €24-€39) is a budget *pensión*.

Getting there

By bus

Buses run from Estación Sur every 30mins, 6.30am-11.30pm Mon-Fri; every hour 7am-11pm Sat; every hour 8am-11pm Sun. Last return 11.30pm Mon-Fri, 11pm Sat & Sun.

By car

Take the A-4, then the M-305 (47km/29 miles).

By train

Cercanías C-3 from Atocha, trains every 15-30mins 5.40am-11.55pm. Last return 11.30pm. For those who want more attention and love kids, the steam-powered 'Strawberry Train' (Tren de la Fresa) runs on summer weekends and holidays (*see p199*).

Tourist information

Oficina de Turismo

Plaza de San Antonio (91 891 04 27). **Open** *Oct-Mar* 10am-6.30pm daily. *Apr-Sept* 10am-7.30pm daily.

Toledo

Once the imperial capital of Spain (1087-1561) and still the ecclesiastical heart of the country, 'Holy Toledo' holds two millennia of history and incomparable cultural riches. Its impregnable hilltop position, tremendous fortified walls and the natural moat formed by the River Tagus have made this an important strategic stronghold for everyone from the Romans to the Visigoths, Muslims and Christians.

During the Middle Ages, Toledo was known as 'the city of three cultures' when the Jewish, Muslim and Christian population lived in a uniquely heterogenous society; many religious buildings still bear a strange palimpsest of crucifixes, stars of David and Arab script. Over time, these religions blurred into each other, creating the Mozárabes (Christians who lived under Muslim rule with a semi-Arabic liturgy), and later the Mudéjares, Muslims who did the reverse after the Christian conquest. This air of tolerance also attracted many world-class scholars, and Toledo became a famous centre of learning with prominent schools of science, mathematics, theology and mysticism.

Now enjoying a Golden Age of tourism, Toledo is by far the most popular daytrip from Madrid, and the steep, cobbled streets are mobbed with tour groups until the buses depart at sundown. The city is absolutely gridlocked during the Corpus Christi processions, during which the route is marked by white awnings over the streets and the cobblestones are strewn with rosemary, thyme and rose petals. Incense and chanting give the town an eerie medieval air, as do the period costumes and the priceless Flemish tapestries hung on the cathedral walls.

THE BISAGRA TO THE CATHEDRAL

If you come from Madrid by bus, car or train, the main point of entry to the old walled city is the imposing **Puerta de Bisagra**. This was built at the end of the reign of Emperor Carlos V to replace the original 11th-century Moorish gate and bears his imperial crest of the two-headed eagle, the symbol of Toledo. Before going into the old city proper, pick up a map from the tourist office opposite and walk back a little way down the main street to the **Museo Duque de Lerma** (C/Cardenal Tavera 2, 925 22 04 51, open 10.30am-1.30pm, 3.30-6pm daily, admission €3). Housed in the 1541 **Hospital de Tavera**, with a fine chapel and Renaissance courtyards, it has works by Tintoretto, Zurbarán and the city's adopted son, El Greco.

To avoid the steep climb from here to the city, take the free escalator (7am-10pm Mon-Fri, 8am-10pm weekends). Alternatively, behind the gate, the superb Mudéjar church of **Santiago del Arrabal** stands out, with an impressive brick tower and horseshoe arches. Part of it was once a mosque, but after the Christian conquest it was rebuilt as a church. The maze of streets on either side as you head up C/Real del Arrabal was (as the name implies) the Arrabal – an area originally outside the Christian city. Off to the right on C/Cristo de la Luz are the gardens and stunning latticed brickwork of the **Mezquita Cristo de la Luz** (925 25 41 91, open Apr-Oct 10am-2.30pm, 3.30-7pm daily, Nov-Mar 10am-2.30pm, 3.30-6pm daily, admission €1.50, €1.20 concessions) built in 999, this mosque is the oldest surviving building in Toledo. According to legend, its name came from the fact that as Alfonso VI entered Toledo after the reconquest, his horse knelt at the door of the mosque, where, behind a stone in the archway, stood Christ, illuminated by the light of an oil lamp.

Dominating the skyline is the grim, black-turretted **Alcázar**, an enormous fortress built on the highest point of Toledo where Roman, Visigothic and Muslim forts stood before. Its armoury museum is closed until 2006 while it is extended to house the sizeable collection of the Museo del Ejército in Madrid. Using the Alcázar as a landmark, head up C/Real de Arrabal and C/Cuesta de Armas to the social nerve centre of the city, **Plaza de Zocodover**. Originally known as the *suk-al-dawad*, or animal market,

Trips Out of Town

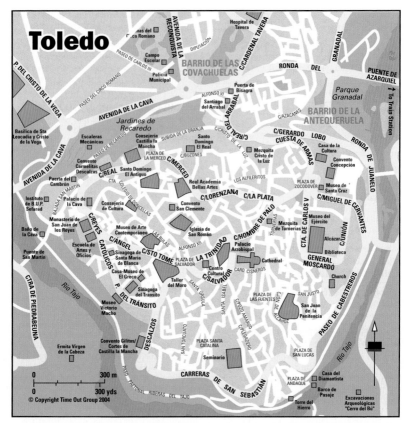

Toledo

it became the site for *autos-da-fé* after the reconquest, but is now lined with restaurant and café terraces serving everything from partridge to Big Macs. Nearby, the Renaissance **Hospital de Santa Cruz** (C/Miguel de Cervantes 3, 925 22 10 36, open 10am-6.30pm Mon-Sat, 10am-2pm Sun, admission free) is now a museum housing tapestries, and works by El Greco and Ribera.

C/Comercio, the old town's main street, leads from the Zocodover to the Plaza Mayor, where the **Palacio Arzobispal** (the Archbishop's Palace) and the jaw-dropping **Cathedral** (C/Cardenal Cisneros 1, 925 22 22 41, open 10.30am-6.30pm Mon-Sat, 2-6pm Sun, admission €5.50) dominate.

Spain's second-largest cathedral (after Seville) but for many the more beautiful of the two, Toledo's cathedral was completed in 1493 after 250 years of construction. A Christian church is said to have been founded here in the first century AD by Saint Eugene, the first

Bishop of Toledo. Mainly Gothic in style with touches of Mudéjar, neo-classical and baroque, the cathedral has 750 stained-glass windows, 70 cupolas and five naves, and is supported by 88 columns with 22 side chapels. You could easily spend a whole day exploring its dark interiors but some of its most extraordinary features include the sacristy's prestigious art collection (including El Greco's *The Disrobing of Christ*) the lavishly carved central choir and, behind the main altar, Narciso Tomé's unique 16th-century *Transparente,* a baroque frenzy of bronze, stucco, coloured marble and painting lit by beams of light via a circular 'sunroof' dripping with alabaster putti.

SANTO TOME AND THE SYNAGOGUES

Just around the corner from the cathedral, the narrow alleys that lead to **Plaza del Salvador** are the most visited parts of Toledo. They are lined with shops selling Toledo's artisan products: Toledan steel has been famous for its strength since Roman times and C/Santo Tomé is packed with shops selling everything from flick-knives to sabres and plumed helmets. Equally ubiquitous is *damasquinado* – the Damascus style of decoration brought over by the Moors, in which fine threads of gold and silver are hammered into blackened metal – which covers everything from chess sets to knife handles and jewellery. For the sweet-toothed, Toledan marzipan is sold in all shapes and flavours.

The first major building en route is the **Taller del Moro**, a Mudéjar workshop housing exhibitions of Toledo craftsmanship; it is closed for renovation until late 2005. Behind the Taller, down C/San Juan de Diós, follow the crowds to the Mudéjar church of **Santo Tomé** (Plaza del Conde 4, 925 25 60 98, open Oct-Feb 10am-6pm daily; Mar-Sept 10am-7pm daily; admission €1.50, €1.20 concessions), which holds only one painting: El Greco's masterpiece, *El Entierro del Conde de Orgaz*. Around the corner lies the **Casa-Museo de El Greco** (C/Samuel Leví s/n, 92 522 40 46), although, despite the fanfare, it has never actually been confirmed that the artist lived here. The house – a reconstructed 16th-century Toledan home – is closed indefinitely for restoration, but it's worth checking out the museum (open 10am-2pm, 4-9pm Tue-Sat, 10am-2pm Sun, admission €2.40) for its impressive collection of El Greco's later works, along with other paintings and sculptures.

In medieval times this area was Toledo's *judería,* the Jewish quarter, once the world's most important centre of Jewish scholarship. Many of its finest works of Jewish-Mudéjar architecture were restored in 1992 as an act of atonement for the 500th anniversary of the expulsion of Jews from Spain. The most recent beneficiary of the makeover is the **Sinagoga del Tránsito**, reopened in late 2003, a richly decorated multicultural blaze of Hebrew inscriptions, Gothic carvings and Moorish columns. It was built in 1357 and its immense size is a testimony to the huge Jewish population that once lived in Toledo. Today there is not even the minimum number of adult males (ten) to hold a service. After 1492 the synagogue was used as a church, but it now pulls in large crowds with its fascinating museum of Sephardic Jewish culture, the **Museo Sefardí** (C/Samuel Leví s/n, 925 22 36 65, open Mar-Nov 10am-2pm, 4-9pm Tue-Sat, 10am-2pm Sun, Dec-Feb 10am-2pm, 4-6pm Tue-Sat, 10am-2pm Sun, admission €2.40, free under-18s and over-65s) where displays include silver and crystal circumcision instruments and a 2,000-year-old ossuary.

The second of the surviving medieval synagogues, the **Sinagoga de Santa María la Blanca** (C/Reyes Católicos 4, 925 22 72 57,

Toledo.

open Oct-Mar 10am-5.45pm daily, Apr-Sept 10am-6.45pm daily; admission €1.50, €1.20 concessions) lies at the opposite end of narrow C/Judería. Its small, plain interior, dominated by horseshoe arches, is extremely beautiful, in spite of the gaudy baroque altar that was added later. Behind it, at C/Ángel 15, is a lovely bookshop dedicated to all matters Jewish, the Casa de Jacob.

The main street of the *judería* is now, ironically, called C/Reyes Católicos, and is topped by the very Catholic **Monasterio de San Juan de los Reyes** (C/Reyes Católicos 17, 925 22 38 02, open Oct-June 10am-5.45pm, July-Sept 10am-6.45pm daily, admission €1.50). Built by Ferdinand and Isabella, it was originally intended to be the royal pantheon and has a dramatic Gothic cloister and an exterior garlanded with grim black chains; during the reconquest, these chains were supposedly taken from Christian prisoners and then used to hang Jewish dissidents.

Trips Out of Town

The recycled cathedral

You may think you're doing your bit for the environment with that weekly trip to the recycling bins, but the average person's attempts at recycling pale into insignificance compared to the efforts of Justo Gallego, a pensioner in the small town of Mejorada del Campo, to the east of Madrid.

Back in the early 1960s, Justo took it upon himself to start building a cathedral, using mostly stuff that other people had thrown away. Neither builder, architect nor engineer, he was a farmer before entering the Convento de Santa María de Huerta, a Trappist monastery in Soria, northern Spain. He stayed there for seven years until he fell ill with TB and the other monks politely if rather selfishly asked him to leave.

He was at something of a loose end after that, until 12 October 1961 – the feast day of Our Lady of the Pillar – when it suddenly came to him that he had been put on this earth to construct a cathedral in his home town. Justo flogged his belongings and started right away, on a patch of land he had inherited from his parents. Unsurprisingly, the money raised did not go very far, and soon he was using whatever he could scavenge. More than 40 years later, he is still at it. Local firms sometimes donate supplies they no longer need, but otherwise he has recycled the most unlikely of materials, helped along by occasional contributions.

It's a curious sight, but the structure does somehow resemble a cathedral, and mass has even been held there. It is, however, a long way from completion. Now in his 70s, Justo is desperate for more funds and materials to complete his mission while he is still able to do so. Local builders and architects are reluctant to take the project on because it never had planning permission – or, indeed, any kind of official authorisation. In fact, Justo himself readily admits he never drew up any sort of plans and there is no guarantee it won't fall down at any minute.

The structure could be described as neo-Romanesque, and is 40 metres (131 feet) high with 12 towers. It has a large nave, partly covered by a dome with a diameter of almost 12 metres (39 feet). There is also a crypt, cloisters, a library and various other as yet unspecified spaces. Columns are made from oil drums, arches constructed from piles of old tyres and towers built with bits of bricks and piping. Bicycle wheels have been transformed into pulleys to get materials up the structure. The main entrance is approached by mosaic steps and spiral staircases link different levels. The structure has become a symbol of the town and has attracted media attention from all over the world. If and when it will ever be completed, though, only God knows.

Catedral de Nuestra Senora del Pilar

C/Antoni Gaudí, Mejorada del Campo.
By bus: from Conde de Casal every 30mins weekdays, every 90mins Sat, Sun.
By car: A-3, then M-203 (21km).

Next to the monastery is a long stone balcony with impossibly romantic views over the River Tagus, the San Martín bridge and the typical *cigarrales* (Toledan country homes) on the opposite hill. For another great view, back over the whole city, head out of town over the River Tagus by the San Martín bridge, and turn right along the Carretera de Piedrabuena.

Where to eat

As Toledo province is the hunting centre of Spain, hearty game dishes dominate. Partridge (*perdiz*) is the most typical dish, and is usually served *a la toledana* – cooked slowly with onion, garlic and bayleaf – or else with *pochas* (succulent white beans) or pickled and eaten cold. Venison and wild boar stews are another speciality, along with roast suckling pig and *cuchifrito* (fricassee of lamb with egg and wine) and *tortilla a la magra* (cured ham omelette).

All these and more are on offer at traditional restaurants such as **La Abadía** (Plaza de San Nicolás 3, 925 25 07 46, mains €25, set lunch €12) where a labyrinth of bars and dining rooms fill a 16th-century palace. If a whole pig seems a bit much, try their *pulgas* (bite-sized rolls). **Restaurante Aurelio** (C/Sinagoga 6, 925 22 20 97, closed Wed, mains €20) is in the heart of the Jewish quarter and filled with ancient farming tools. After more than a century serving food, **Venta de Aires** (Paseo Circo Romano 55, 92 522 52 90, closed dinner Sun, mains €16) must be doing something right. Particularly good at lunchtime when it's packed with locals feasting on excellent cod dishes and, naturally, partridge, is **La Perdiz** (C/Reyes Católicos 7, 92 525 29 19, closed dinner Sun, all Mon & 2wks Aug, mains €16, set lunch €21). For a sophisticated twist on these local staples – quail fried with ginger and lemon or duck breasts with grapefruit sauce – **Los Cuatro Tiempos** (C/Sixto Ramón Parro 5, 925 22 37 82, closed Sun dinner, mains €18, set lunch €20) is located in a charming 16th-century National Heritage building. For a real treat, the famous **Asador Adolfo** (C/Granada 6, 925 25 24 72, closed dinner Sun, all Mon & 2nd half July, mains €23) is worth a visit for its impeccable service, fantastic wine list and light cuisine such as tempura courgette flowers with saffron.

Shamelessly overpriced tourist feeding troughs prevail around the cathedral and Plaza de Zocodover but you can get a good, basic menú del día with the locals in the shady courtyard of **Alex** (C/Amador de los Ríos 10, 92 522 39 63, closed Mon, mains €9, set lunch €13.50), the crowded **Santa Fe** (C/Santa Fe 2, 925 22 10 17, set meals €9-€23) or, if you're handy with a map, the bars and restaurants

dotted around the **Corral de Don Diego**, a shady patio set back from the street through a narrow archway.

Bear in mind that most of Toledo's restaurants close for a fortnight in July or August.

Where to stay

Rooms in the old city can be hard to come by in the high season, so it's best to book ahead, especially for Corpus Christi. With unbeatable views of the city, the luxury **Parador Conde de Orgaz** (Paseo de los Cigarrales, 925 22 18 50, www.parador.es, rates €129-€181) is about ten minutes' cab ride from the city. The splendid pool and top-notch restaurant make it worth allowing a day just to spend in the hotel. Right next to the Casa El Greco, the charming **Hotel Pintor El Greco** (C/Alamillos del Tránsito 13, 92 528 51 91, www.hotelpintor elgreco.com, rate €110) occupies a converted 17th-century bakery that combines an original façade and patio with mod cons such as satellite TV. More economical is the new and very central **Hostal Santo Tomé** (C/Santo Tomé 13, 925 22 17 12, www.hostalsantotome.com, rate €48) with ten comfortable rooms in an old Toledan townhouse. The **Hostal Descalzos** (C/Descalzos 30, 925 22 28 88, rates €48-€60) is also great value with en-suite, air-conditioned rooms around a sunny patio with swimming pool and jacuzzi.

Getting there

By bus

Continental Auto (902 330 400, www.continental-auto.es) runs from Estación Sur every 30mins from 5.30am (6.30am Sat, 8.30am Sun), last return at 10pm (11pm Sun). Journey time is around 1hr 15mins.

By car

Take the A-42 off the M-30 (70km/44 miles).

By train

There are 5 trains a day from Atocha, with the last return at 6.40pm. Journey time is around 1hr 15mins (with completion of AVE in 2005 it will become 30mins). From the station, take bus 6 to the Puerta de Bisagra, or you'll face a long uphill walk.

Tourist information

Oficina Municipal de Turismo

Plaza del Ayuntamiento (925 25 40 30). **Open** 10.30am-2.30pm Mon; 10.30am-2.30pm, 4.30-7pm Tue-Sun.

Oficina de Turismo

Puerta de Bisagra (925 22 08 43/www.jccm.es). **Open** *Oct-June* 9am-6pm Mon-Fri; 9am-7pm Sat; 9am-3pm Sun. *July-Sept* 9am-7pm Mon-Sat; 9am-3pm Sun.

Trips Out of Town

Directory

Features

Directory

Getting Around

By air

Madrid's **Barajas Airport** is 13km (8 miles) north-east of the city on the A2 motorway. Thanks to the new Richard Rogers-designed terminal T-4 – to open in 2005 – the total airport capacity is expected to reach 700 million passengers per year. All airlines that are members of the OneWorld network (including BA, Iberia, Aer Lingus and American Airlines) will share T-4 with Spanair for both national and international flights. The rest of the traffic will be distributed between the three existing terminals: non-Spanish airlines and flights on Spanish airlines from non-Schengen-area countries (such as Britain and the USA – *see p294*) use Terminal 1 (T-1); most domestic flights and Spanish airlines' flights from Schengen countries use T-2; some local flights and the Madrid-Barcelona air shuttle use T-3. In T-1 and T-2 there are 24-hour exchange facilities and ATM machines, hotel booking desks. In T1 there is a tourist office (*see p294*) and a rail reservations desk.

For airport information, call 902 35 35 70 or 91 393 60 00, or check website www.aena.es, which includes updated flight information. All phone lines are open 24 hours daily.

Airport bus

Plaza de Colón terminal (91 431 61 92/information 91 406 88 10). Metro Colón or Serrano. **Map** p310 I4.
This special bus service runs between T1 and T2 at Barajas and the Plaza de Colón, and takes between 30mins and 1hr, depending on the traffic. There are six stops en route, including one at Avda de América, which provides a useful metro and bus connection. The Colón bus terminal is down some steps underneath the square, and has a taxi rank; to get from there to Colón metro, go up to street level and cross the Castellana by the underpass at the corner of C/Goya. First buses of the day leave Colón and Barajas at 4.45am; they run every 16-18mins, 6.15am-11.30pm, and about every 20mins at other times. Last buses leave Barajas at 2am daily, and Colón at 1.30am. A single ticket costs €2.50 and can only be bought on board. The airport buses are not accessible to wheelchairs.

Aerocity

91 747 75 70/www.aerocity.com. Provides shuttle services between the airport and city-centre hotels, on request. Quite handy for small groups and cheaper than taking several taxis. Prices go from €17 up to €38 depending on the size of the group (from one to a maximum of seven), the location of the hotel (city centre or outskirts) and the number of pieces of luggage in some cases. The company has two reservation desks at the airport (arrivals at T-1 and T-2); phonelines are open 24hrs.

Metro from the airport

The metro is the cheapest means of getting to central Madrid. Bear in mind that the Aeropuerto metro station is between T-2 and T-3, which means that if, as is very likely, you arrive at T-1, you have a 10-15min walk to get there. From the airport it's four stops on metro line 8 (pink) and 12mins to Nuevos Ministerios. On outward journeys, if you are flying with Iberia, Alitalia and some other airlines you can also check in here. From Nuevos Ministerios it's around another 15mins into the centre of Madrid. You can save money by buying a Metrobús ticket at the airport station (*see p281* **Tickets please**).

Taxis from the airport

The taxi fare to central Madrid should be around €17-€19 (depending on traffic), including a €4.20 special airport supplement (no luggage supplement). There are further supplements after 10pm and on Sundays (for both, 18¢ per km). There are lots of taxis at Barajas, but ignore any drivers who approach you inside the building, just use the ones at the ranks outside the terminal. Check the meter is at the current minimum fare (€1.55) when you begin the journey; it's a good idea to check a map first, and to have a landmark in mind in the area to which you should be going. For more on taxis, *see p280*.

Airlines

Aer Lingus
91 541 41 16/902 22 00 05/
www.aerlingus.ie.
Air Europa
902 40 15 01/www.air-europa.com.
American Airlines
902 40 15 01/www.aa.com.
British Airways
902 11 13 33/
www.british-airways.com.
easyJet
902 29 99 92/www.easyjet.com.
Iberia
902 40 05 00/www.iberia.com.

By bus

Almost all international and long-distance coach services to Madrid terminate at the Estación Sur de Autobuses, C/Méndez Álvaro to the south of central Madrid (information 91 468 42 00/91 468 45 11 from 6.30am to midnight; bus companies also have their own information lines). It's next to metro (line 6) and *cercanía* (local train lines C5, C7 and C10) stations, both also called Méndez Álvaro. Bus 148 also runs from there to the city centre (Plaza del Callao and Plaza de España). Taxi fares from the bus station carry a €2.20 supplement.

By train

Spanish national railways (RENFE) has two main stations in Madrid. Trains from France, Catalonia and northern Spain arrive at **Chamartín**, on the north side of the city, some distance from the centre. High-speed AVE trains from Andalucía and Valencia, express services from Lisbon and trains from southern and eastern Spain arrive at **Atocha**, at the southern end of the Paseo del Prado. There are exchange facilities at both stations, and a tourist office at Chamartín (see p294). Atocha is also the main hub of RENFE's local rail lines (cercanías) for the Madrid area (see p280).

Metro line 10 is the fastest from Chamartín to the city centre, and Atocha RENFE (the train station; not the same metro as Atocha) is four metro stops from Sol on line 1. A taxi fare to the centre from Chamartín should be around €13, including a €2.20 station supplement. There are extra supplements at night and on Sundays (18¢ per km). The same need for caution with cabs at the airport (see p280) applies to drivers touting for fares at main rail stations.

For more information on all rail services, see p252.

RENFE Information

902 24 02 02/www.renfe.es. **Open** information 24hrs daily. Reservations 5am-22.30pm daily.

Estación de Atocha

Glorieta del Emperador Carlos V. Metro Atocha Renfe, Salamanca & the Retiro. **Map** p314 H10.

Estación de Chamartín

C/Agustín de Foxá, Chamartín. Metro Chamartín.

Maps

Metro and central area street maps are included at the back of this guide. Metro maps are also available at all metro stations: ask for 'un plano del metro'. The Consorcio de Transportes, the regional transport authority, publishes good free maps, especially the Plano de los Transportes del

Centro de Madrid, from which the maps in this guide are taken. It should be available at tourist offices (ask for a transport map, rather than the inferior street map tourist offices often give out). For good shops to buy maps, see pp170-71.

Public transport

To really get to know Madrid, it's best to explore on foot. Most of the main attractions are within walking distance of each other and for orientation purposes think of Puerta del Sol as the centre. Street numbers in Madrid all run outwards from Sol. Public transport is cheap and efficient – both bus and metro will get you where you want to go within half an hour, although it's best to avoid the buses during rush hour.

For transport outside Madrid, see p252. For transport for disabled travellers, see p284.

Note: all transport and taxi fares are subject to revision each January.

Metro

The metro is the quickest and simplest means of travelling to most parts of the city. Each of its 13 lines (including the new Metrosur and Ramal lines) is identified by a number and a colour on maps and at stations. Metro stations also make essential reference points, and 'metro Sevilla', 'metro Goya' and so on will often be given to you as tags with addresses.

The metro is open 6am-2am daily. Tickets are available at all stations from coin-operated machines and staffed ticket booths. Trains run every three to five minutes during weekdays, and about every 10-15mins after 11pm and on Sundays. The metro can get packed in rush hours (7.30-9.30am, 1-2.30pm, 7.30-9pm).

The newly elected government of the Madrid

region (Comunidad de Madrid) is studying the possibility of keeping the metro open all night on Friday and Saturday.

Metro information

C/Cavanilles 58, Salamanca & the Retiro (902 44 44 03/www. metromadrid.es). Metro Conde de Casal. **Open** 6am-1.30am daily. There are also customer service points at the airport, Atocha, Chamartín, Avenida de América, Nuevos Ministerios and Alto de Arenal stations.

Buses

Run by the Empresa Municipal de Transportes (EMT). For fare and ticket information, see p281 **Tickets, please**.

Most run from about 6am-11.30pm daily, with buses every 10-15mins (more often on more popular routes). Night buses then take over. You board buses at the front, and get off via the middle or rear doors. The fare is the same for each journey (€1.15), however far you go. Officially, there is a limit to how much luggage you can take on city buses, and trying to board with luggage during rush hours is almost impossible. Drivers are not obliged to give you the change if they don't have it (and if what you give them is more than five times the price of the ticket), nor will they allow you to travel for free. But they must write down your contact details for the bus company to send you the change later on.

For tourist buses, see p59.

Useful routes

2 From Avda Reina Victoria, above Moncloa, to Plaza de España, then along Gran Via to Cibeles, the Retiro and Plaza Manuel Becerra.

3 From Puerta de Toledo up Gran Via de San Francisco and C/Mayor to Sol, then up C/Hortaleza to Cuatro Caminos, C/Bravo Murillo; ends close to the Estadio Bernabéu.

5 From Puerta del Sol via the Plaza de Cibeles, Plaza de Colón and the Castellana to Chamartín station.

14 From Conde de Casal along Paseo Reina Cristina to Atocha, then along Paseo del Prado, Recoletos and the Castellana to Chamartín.

Directory

27 A frequent service all the way up and down the Castellana from Embajadores via Atocha to Plaza Castilla.

C The 'Circular' route runs in a wide circuit around the city, via Atocha, Embajadores, Plaza de España, Moncloa, Cuatro Caminos, Plaza Manuel Becerra and the Retiro.

Night buses

Between midnight and around 5am there are 20 night routes in operation – N1 to N20 – called Búho (Owl) buses. All begin from Plaza de Cibeles and run out to the suburbs, and are numbered in a clockwise sequence; thus, N1 runs north to Manoteras, N2 a little further east to Hortaleza, and so on. The N18 runs along the Gran Via to Moncloa and Tetuán; the N20 along the length of the Castellana to Fuencarral. They run every half hour between midnight and 3am and every hour or so after that. Tickets and fares are the same as for daytime services.

EMT Information

C/Cerro de la Plata 4, Retiro (902 50 78 50/91 406 88 10). Metro Pacífico. **Open** 8am-2pm Mon-Fri.
There is also an EMT kiosk at the Plaza de Cibeles, Retiro.

Cercanías/ local trains

The highly efficient *cercanías* or local network of railways for the Madrid area consists of 12 lines converging on Atocha, several of which connect with metro lines along their routes. They are most useful for trips to the suburbs, or to the Guadarrama and towns near Madrid such as Aranjuez or El Escorial. Also, lines C-7a and C-7b combine (with one change at Príncipe Pío) to form a circle line within Madrid that is quicker than the metro for some journeys, and the RENFE line between Chamartín and Atocha is the fastest link between the two main stations. *Cercanías* lines run from 5-6am to 11pm-midnight daily, with trains on most lines about every 10-30mins. Fares vary with distance, but the lines are included in the monthly season ticket (*see p281* **Tickets please**). For a map of the *cercanías* network, *see p319*.

Taxis

Madrid taxis are white, with a diagonal red stripe on the front doors. The city has over 15,000 taxis, so they are rarely hard to find, except late at night at the weekend or when it's raining heavily. When a taxi is free there is a '*Libre*' (free) sign behind the windscreen, and a green light on the roof. If there is also a sign with the name of a district in red, it means the driver is on his way home, and not obliged to take you anywhere that isn't near that route. There are taxi ranks, marked by a blue sign with a white T, throughout the centre. At the airport and rail and bus stations, it's always best to take a taxi from the official ranks; within Madrid, however, those in the know flag cabs down in the street, to avoid both the risk of scams, and station supplements. To avoid being swindled by a non-official taxi, make sure they have their licence number visible on the front and a meter, and always ask for the approximate fare before getting in.

FARES

Official fare rates and supplements are shown inside each cab (in English and Spanish), on the right-hand sun visor and/or the rear windows. In 2004 the minimum fare was €1.55, which is what the meter should show when you first set off. The minimum fare is the same at all times, but the additional charge increases at a higher rate at night (11pm-6am) and on Sundays and public holidays, and there are extra supplements for trips starting from the bus and train stations (€2.20); to and from the trade fair complex (€2.20), and to and from the airport (€4.20). Also, the fare rate is higher for journeys to suburban towns in the outer tariff zone (zone B). Drivers are not officially

required to carry more than €12 in change, and very few accept credit cards.

RECEIPTS AND COMPLAINTS

To get a receipt, ask for '*un recibo, por favor*'. If you think you've been overcharged or have any other complaint, insist the receipt is made out in full, with details of the journey and the driver's signature, NIF number and licence plate, and the date. Make a note of the taxi number, displayed on a plaque on the dashboard. Take or send the receipt, keeping a copy, with a complaints form to the city taxi office at the address below. The form is included in the Taxi Information leaflet available from tourist offices.

Sección de Autotaxi y Vehículos de Alquiler

Ayuntamiento de Madrid, C/Vallehermoso 1, Chamberí, 28015 (91 588 96 32). **Open** 9am-2pm Mon-Fri. **Map** p309 D3.

PHONE CABS

You can call for a cab from any of the companies listed below. Operators will rarely speak much English, so if you aren't at a specific address give the name of the street and a restaurant or bar that makes a suitable place to wait, or position yourself near a street corner and say, for example, 'San Agustín, *esquina* Prado' (San Agustín, corner of Prado). The operator will also ask your name. Phone cabs start the meter from the point when a call is answered. Very few cabs will take credit cards.
Radio-Taxi Asociación Gremial *91 447 51 80.*
Radio-Taxi Independiente *91 405 12 13/91 405 55 00.*
Radio Teléfono Taxi/Euro Taxi *91 547 85 00/91 547 82 00.*
Teletaxi *91 371 21 31/91 371 37 11.*

Cycling

Cycling in Madrid is only for the truly experienced (or mad) in view of the heavy traffic and lack of cycle lanes on any of

Tickets, please

Compared to transport ticketing systems in many other capital cities, Madrid's is simple and effective – just €1.15 for any single journey (*un sencillo*) on the bus or metro within the capital, no matter how long the journey. And on the metro you can change any number of times as long as you don't get off. The only exceptions to this are trips to the stations Rivas Urbanizaciones, Rivas Vaciamadrid, La Poveda and Arganda del Rey (all on Line 9), and all stations beyond Puerta del Sur on the new MetroSur line, which circles the southern suburbs.

However, it's easier and more economical to buy a ticket for 10 journeys (*billete de diez/Metrobús*), which can be used on the bus and metro, available at all metro stations and some *estancos* and *kioskos*, but not on the bus. You can share the ticket between two or more people and keep it for as long as you like (or until the prices go up). The current price of a Metrobús is €5.35.

On the metro, you simply insert the ticket into the machine at the gate that leads through to the platform, which cancels one unit for each trip – remember to collect it afterwards – and will reject expired tickets. There is no checking or collection of tickets at station exits. On buses, the Metrobús should be inserted arrow downwards into the blue and yellow machine just behind the driver.

Abonos – season tickets

If you're planning on staying much longer than a fortnight, a monthly season ticket is a good idea. Unlike the Metrobús, it is valid for *cercanías* trains as well as the metro and city buses, allowing you to use it on some trips out of town. Your first *abono* must be obtained with an identity card, available only from *estancos*, for which you will need two passport-size photos and must fill in a brief form. In succeeding months you can buy tickets to revalidate the card from metro stations and EMT kiosks as well as *estancos*. Note, though, that an *abono* is valid for an actual calendar month, not for 30 days from date of purchase, so that if your stay runs across two months, buying one may not be particularly economical, unless you qualify for one of the different age discounts. Also, if you can, buy your *abono* before the start of the month to avoid the nightmare queues on the first of the month.

Unless you are planning to travel a lot outside the city, Zone A should cover everywhere you need to go. A standard one-month Zone A *abono* currently costs €34.55, and there are substantial reductions for young people or over-65s. Note that the *abono* cannot be used on the airport bus.

the city's central streets (there are a few in parks and by the river). However, bikes are a great idea for trips to the larger city parks (Retiro, Casa de Campo) and especially the Madrid Sierras. Bikes can be taken free of charge on some *cercanías* lines and on the metro at weekends. Cycle hire shops often ask that you leave proof of identity (take a photocopy to avoid having to leave your passport) as well as a cash deposit. For cycling tours out of town, *see p252*.

Driving

Driving in the city is rarely a quick way of getting anywhere thanks to traffic jams, and finding a parking space is

another headache. However, a car is an asset for trips outside the city. If you do decide to drive, bear these points in mind:

● You can drive here with a valid driving licence from most countries, but an international licence, available in Britain from the AA or RAC, is also useful.
● Keep your licence, vehicle documents, passport and insurance papers with you at all times.
● It is compulsory to wear seat belts and carry two warning triangles, spares and tools to fit them, a reflective jacket, spare headlight bulbs and spare glasses if you wear them.
● Children under 12 may not travel in the front seats of a car.
● The speed limit is 50kmph in towns, 90kmph on most highways and 120kmph on motorways – although many drivers ignore this. Speeding fines imposed on motorways (*autopistas*) and highways are paid on the spot.

● Spanish drivers often drink and drive, but the legal alcohol limits are similar to those in most EU countries.
● Do not leave anything of value, including a car radio, in your car, and do not leave bags or coats in view on the seats. Foreign numberplates are particularly tempting.
● In general drivers go as fast as they can, irrespective of the speed limit. At traffic lights many will follow through on the amber light as it changes between green and red. Do not stop sharply when you see a light begin to change, as you may be hit from behind.
● When oncoming drivers flash lights at you it means they will not slow down (contrary to the British practice). On main highways, the flashing of lights is usually a helpful warning there's a speed trap ahead.

Signs & terms

cede el paso – give way
usted no tiene la prioridad – you don't have the right of way
unico sentido – one way

cambio de sentido – indicates a junction that allows you to change direction
recuerde – remember
cinturón de seguridad – seat belt
ronda de circunnavegación – ring road (around major towns and cities)

Car & motorbike hire

Car hire can be pricey, so shop around; there are often good weekend deals. Most companies have a minimum age limit (usually 21) and require you to have had a licence for over a year. You will also need a credit card (as opposed to a debit card), or leave a big cash deposit (sometimes up to €500). Check if IVA (VAT), at 16 per cent, and unlimited mileage are included. All the companies listed require you to take out a *seguro franquicia* – a fixed amount you have to pay in the event of an accident or any damage caused to the vehicle, and which is put on your credit card when you take the car (usually around half the hire cost – it is only charged if you return the vehicle damaged).

Avis
C/Agustín de Foxá 25, Chamartín (91 733 32 30). **Open** 8am-7pm Mon-Fri; 9am-1pm Sat, Sun. **Credit** AmEx, DC, MC, V.

Easycar
www.easycar.com. **Credit** AmEx, MC, V.
Booking and payment is done online. Rates can be low, but conditions are pretty complicated.

Econocar
C/Felix Boix 2, Chamartín (91 359 14 03/econocar@econocar.net). *Metro Plaza Castilla.* **Open** 9am-2pm, 4-8pm Mon-Fri; 9.30am-1.30pm Sat. **Credit** AmEx, DC, MC, V.
Local company with good rates.

Europcar
Avda del Partenón 16-18, Eastern suburbs (91 722 62 26/reservations 902 10 50 30). *Metro Campo de las Naciones.* **Open** 8.30am-2pm, 4.30-8pm Mon-Fri. **Credit** AmEx, DC, MC, V. **Other locations** (open 8am-9pm Mon-Fri): Barajas airport (91 393 72 35); Atocha station (91 530 01 94); Chamartín station (91 323 17 21); C/San Leonardo 8, Malasaña (91 541 88 92); C/Orense 29, Tetuán (91 555 99 30); Nuevos Ministerios metro (91 411 8054).

Motoalquiler
C/Conde Duque 13, Malasaña (91 542 06 57). *Metro San Bernardo.* **Open** 8am-1.30pm, 5-8pm Mon-Fri. **Credit** AmEx, DC, MC, V. **Map** p309 D4.
Motorcycle specialists.

National-Atesa
Paseo de la Castellana 130, Chamartín (91 782 01 30/902 10 01 01). *Metro Santiago Bernabéu.* **Open** Sept-July

9am-2pm, 3.30-6pm Mon-Thur; 9am-3pm Fri. *Aug* 9am-3pm Mon-Fri. **Credit** AmEx, DC, MC, V. **Other locations:** Barajas airport (91 393 72 32).

PlanCar
C/Embajadores 173, South of centre (91 530 27 23). *Metro Legazpi.* **Open** 9am-2pm, 4.30-8.30pm Mon-Fri; 9am-1.30pm Sat. **Credit** AmEx, V.
A local agency that's convenient for those in the south of the city.

Breakdown services

If you are planning to take a car to Spain it's advisable to join a motoring organisation such as the AA or RAC, which have reciprocal arrangements with their Spanish equivalent, RACE.

RACE (Real Automóvil Club de España)
Assistance freephone 902 300 505/information 902 40 45 45/www.race.es.
The RACE has English-speaking staff and will send immediate 24hr breakdown assistance. If you are outside Madrid, call the emergency freephone number, but you will be referred on to a local number. Repairs are carried out on the spot when possible; if not, your vehicle will be towed to the nearest suitable garage. Members of affiliated organisations abroad are not charged for call-outs, but non-members pay around €99 for the basic breakdown service.

Parking

For car-owning *madrileños* parking is a daily trauma. The city police (Policia Municipal) give out tickets readily (many locals never pay them). Be careful not to park in front of doorways with the sign *'vado permanente'*, indicating an entry with 24-hour right of access. The ORA system (Operación Regulación Aparcamiento) now applies (*see below*) to the whole city centre (roughly between Moncloa, C/José Abascal, C/Doctor Esquerdo and Atocha). Residents park for free if they have an annual sticker.

ORA
Non-residents must pay to park in zones painted in blue or green from 9am to 8pm Mon-Fri and 9am to 3pm Sat (9am to 3pm Mon-Sat in August). Pay-and-display machines are located on pavements. Maximum validity of tickets is two hours in blue zones and one hour in the green, after which a new card must be used, and the car parked in a new spot. Cars parked in the ORA zone without

a card can be towed away (*see below*). In the blue areas, tickets cost up to €1.60 for two hours and in the green areas, €1.30 for one hour. All streets in this zone that do not have additional restrictions posted are ORA parking areas.

Car parks
Central car parks *Plaza de las Cortes, Plaza Santa Ana, C/Sevilla, Plaza Jacinto Benavente, Plaza Mayor, C/Descalzas Reales, C/Tudescos, Plaza de España.* **Open** 24hrs daily. **Rates** 85¢ for every 30mins, then €17 from 9½ to 24hrs.
There are some 50 municipal car parks around Madrid, indicated by a white 'P'-on-blue sign. It's especially advisable to use a car park if your car has foreign plates. Car parks have disabled access.

Towing away
Information 91 345 00 50. **Main pounds** *Plaza del Carmen. Metro Sol.* **Map** p313 E7. *Plaza Colón. Metro Colón.* **Map** p310 I4. *C/Velázquez, 87. Metro Nuñez de Balboa.* **Map** p311 J2. **Open** 24hrs daily.
If your car seems to have been towed away, call the central number and quote your number plate to be told which pound it has gone to. It will cost €84.14 to recover your car. You'll have to pay 78¢ for the first half-hour and 69¢ per half-hour after that, timed from the moment it was towed away. For each complete extra day in the pound it's €13.91.

Fuel stations

Unleaded petrol is *sin plomo*; regular is *súper*, and diesel fuel is *gas-oil*.

24-hour petrol stations
Atocha
Repsol, junction of Paseo de Infanta Isabel & Avda Ciudad de Barcelona, next to Atocha station. **Credit** AmEx, MC, V. **Map** p314 I10.
24hr shop on site.

Campsa
Paseo de Santa María de la Cabeza 18, on southward exit from Glorieta del Emperador Carlos V. **Credit** AmEx, MC, V. **Map** p314 H10.
24hr shop on site.

Avda de América
Repsol C/María de Molina 21. **Credit** AmEx, MC, V. **Map** p311 K1.

Salamanca
Repsol C/Goya 24, junction C/Núñez de Balboa. **Credit** AmEx, DC, MC, V. **Map** p311 J4.

Cuatro Caminos
Carba C/Ríos Rosas 1, by C/Bravo Murillo. **Credit** AmEx, MC, V. **Other locations:** C/Montera 32 (91 532 90 73).

Resources A-Z

Addresses

Individual flats in apartment blocks have traditionally been identified by the abbreviations '*izq*' (*izquierda*, left) or '*dcha*' (*derecha*, right) after the floor number (C/Prado 221, 5ª dcha) and occasionally '*int*' (interior, or inwardly facing) or '*ext*' (exterior); in newer buildings they may be shown more simply (C/Prado 223, 4B). If a building has no street number (usually because it's too big, like a station or hospital), *s/n* (*sin número*) is written.

Age restrictions

In Spain, you have to be 18 to drive a car, 16 to smoke or drink, and 18 to get married, while the age of consent is a startling 13.

Business

Administrative services

A *gestoría* is a very Spanish institution, combining the functions of lawyer, accountant, business adviser and general aid with bureaucracy. They can be very helpful in seeing short cuts that foreigners are often unaware of. English is spoken at these *gestorías*.

Gestoría Calvo Canga

C/Serrano 27, Salamanca (91 577 07 09). Metro Serrano. **Open** 9am-2pm, 5-8pm Mon-Fri. **Map** p311 I4.

A general *gestoría* that deals with the areas of labour law, tax and accounts, and residency.

Gestoría Cavanna

C/Hermosilla 4, Salamanca (91 431 86 67). Metro Colón. **Open** Sept-June 9am-1.30pm, 5-7.30pm Mon-Fri. July, Aug 9am-1.30pm Mon-Fri. **Map** p310 I4.
Cavanna specialises in tax and employment law.

Work Manager

Edificio CTM, Oficina 201, Ctra Villaverde a Vallecas, km 3,5, South of centre (91 786 6277/wmanager@arrakis.es). Metro Legazpi then bus 88. **Open** 9am-2pm, 4-8pm Mon-Fri.
This *gestoría* gives advice on all kinds of legal and bureaucratic problems, at decent rates.

Conventions & Conferences

IFEMA/Feria de Madrid

Recinto Ferial Juan Carlos I, Northern suburbs (902 22 15 15/www.ifema.es). Metro Campo de las Naciones. **Open** Office 9am-5pm Mon-Fri.
Madrid's lavish state-of-the-art trade fair centre has ten main pavilions, a 600-seater auditorium, a brand-new 10,000sq m convention centre and many smaller facilities, plus 20 catering outlets and no less than 14,000 parking spaces. By the entrance is the Palacio Municipal de Congresos, a 2,000-capacity conference hall.

Oficina de Congresos de Madrid

C/Mayor 69, Los Austrias (91 588 29 00/www.munimadrid.es). Metro Ópera or Sol. **Open** Oct-May 8am-3pm, 4-6pm Mon-Thur; 8am-3pm Fri. June-Sept 8.30am-2.30pm Mon-Fri. **Map** p312 C8.
An office of the city council that assists those planning to hold a conference or similar event in Madrid. The Oficina de Congresos will facilitate contacts with venues and service companies.

Palacio de Exposiciones y Congresos

Paseo de la Castellana 99, Tetuán (91 337 81 00/www.madrid conventioncentre.com). Metro Santiago Bernabéu. **Open** 9am-2.30pm, 4.30-7pm Mon-Fri.
Longer established than the Feria (*see above*) and used for several major international conferences. It has conference rooms and galleries of all sizes; facilities are excellent.

Recintos Feriales de la Casa de Campo

Avda de Portugal s/n, Casa de Campo (91 588 93 93). Metro Lago. **Open** Sept-July 8am-3pm Mon-Fri. Aug 8am-2pm Mon-Fri.
An attractive site with three halls and open-air space.

Courier services

DHL

902 12 24 24/www.dhl.com. **Open** Phoneline 24hrs daily. Pick-ups & deliveries 9am-7pm Mon-Sat. **No credit cards.**

MFR Distribución Urgente

Avda del Manzanares 202, Southern suburbs (91 476 71 61/www.motorecado.com). Metro Laguna. **Open** 8am-7pm Mon-Fri. **No credit cards. Map** p312 A9-10.

RUM

C/Galileo 91, Moncloa (91 535 38 16). Metro Quevedo. **Open** 9am-7pm Mon-Fri. **No credit cards. Map** p309 D1.

Trébol

C/Esperanza 3, Lavapiés (91 530 32 32). Metro Lavapiés. **Open** Sept-July 9am-8pm Mon-Fri. Aug 9am-3pm Mon-Fri. **No credit cards. Map** p313 F9.

Travel advice

For up-to-date information on travel to a specific country – including the latest news on safety and security, health issues, local laws and customs – contact your home country government's department of foreign affairs. Most have websites that are packed with useful advice for would-be travellers.

Australia
www.dfat.gov.au/travel

Canada
www.voyage.gc.ca

New Zealand
www.mft.govt.nz/travel

Ireland
www.irlgov.ie/iveagh

UK
www.fco.gov.uk/travel

USA
http://state.gov/travel

Directory

Office & computer services

Bitmailer

C/Juan Bravo 51, Salamanca (91 402 15 51/www.bitmailer.com). Metro Diego de León. **Open** 9am-7pm Mon-Fri. **No credit cards.** **Map** p311 K2.

An internet service provider with a helpful and efficient back-up service. There is also software for sale.

Data Rent

C/Mesena 18, Northern suburbs (91 759 62 42/www.datarent.es). Metro Arturo Soria. **Open** Sept-June 9am-2pm, 4-7pm Mon-Fri. July, Aug 8am-3pm Mon-Fri. **Credit** MC, V.

PCs, printers, OHP projectors and other equipment for rent by the day, the week or the month.

Translators

Bowneglobal Solutions

C/Orense 69 1º, Tetuán (91 567 54 00). Metro Nuevos Ministerios. **Open** 9am-6.30pm Mon-Fri.

A professional translation service.

Traductora Jurada (Official translator)

Concepción Pardo de Vera
C/Costa Brava 20, Northern suburbs (91 734 23 31). Bus 134 from Callao.
Polidioma
C/Cea Bermudez 6, 6º izq, Chamberí (91 554 46 20/polidioma@ polidioma.com). Metro Islas Filipinas.

In Spain, official and other bodies often demand that foreign documents be translated by legally certified translators. Call for an appointment; rates are higher than for other translators. Some consulates (*see p285*) also provide these services or they can put you in contact with other translators.

Useful organisations

Bolsa de Comercio (Stock Exchange)

Plaza de la Lealtad 1, Retiro (91 589 26 00/902 22 16 62/www.bolsa madrid.es). Metro Banco de España. **Open** 9am-5pm Mon-Thur, 9am-2pm Fri. **Map** p314 H7.

Cámara de Comercio e Industria de Madrid

C/Ribera del Loira 56, Campo de las Naciones (91 538 35 00/ www.camaramadrid.es). Metro Campo de las Naciones or Mar de Cristal.

Has a useful information service for foreign investors in Madrid. You must make an appointment first.

Instituto Español de Comercio Exterior

Paseo de la Castellana 14-16, Salamanca (91 349 61 00/902 349 000/www.icex.es). Metro Colón. **Open** Oct-May 8am-5pm Mon-Fri. June-Sept 8am-3pm Mon-Fri. **Map** p310 I4.

The state-run ICEX (Spanish Institute for Foreign Trade) has an excellent information service to aid small- to medium-sized businesses.

Complaints

If you have a complaint, ask for an official complaint form (*hoja de reclamación*), which most businesses, shops, bars and so on, are obliged to have available for customers. Fill out the form, leaving the colour copy with the business. Then take this, and any receipts or other relevant paperwork, to the official consumer office, listed below.

Oficina Municipal de Información al Consumidor

C/Mayor 83 2º, Los Austrias (91 211 18 51). Metro Sol. **Open** 10.30am-1.30pm Mon-Fri. **Map** p312 C8.

The official centre for consumer advice and complaint follow-up. You need to make an appointment first.

Customs

If tax has been paid in the country of origin then EU residents do not have to declare goods imported into Spain from other EU countries for their personal use. However, customs officers can question whether large amounts of any item really are for your own use, and random checks are made for drugs. Quantities accepted as being for personal use include:

● up to 800 cigarettes, 400 small cigars, 200 cigars or 1kg of loose tobacco

● 10 litres of spirits (over 22% alcohol), 20 litres of fortified wine or alcoholic drinks with under 22% of alcohol, 90 litres of wine (under 22%) or 110 litres of beer

Limits for non-EU residents and goods brought from outside the EU:

● 200 cigarettes or 100 small cigars or 50 cigars or 250g (8.82oz) of tobacco

● 1 litre of spirits (over 22% alcohol) or 2 litres of any other alcoholic drink with under 22% alcohol

● 50g (1.76oz) of perfume

● 500g coffee, 100g tea

There are no restrictions on cameras, watches or electrical goods, within reasonable limits, and visitors are also allowed to carry up to €6,000 in cash. Non-EU residents can also reclaim Value Added Tax (IVA) paid on some large purchases when they leave Spain. For details, *see p167*.

Disabled travellers

Madrid is still not a city where disabled people, especially wheelchair users, can get around easily. However, the situation is steadily improving as new buildings are constructed with accessibility in mind and old ones are gradually adapted: technically all public buildings should have been made accessible by law, though in practice much remains to be done. Access to public transport is also patchy.

There is an excellent guide, *Guía de Accesibilidad de Madrid*, published by the Ayuntamiento (city council) in collaboration with disabled association FAMMA. It is available from the FAMMA office at C/Galileo 69 (91 593 35 50/ www.famma.org).

Access to sights

Some of the city's wheelchair-friendly venues are listed below.

Centro Conde Duque
Centro Cultural de la Villa
Museo de América
Museo de Cera
Museo de la Ciudad
Museo del Libro
Museo Nacional Centro de Arte Reina Sofía
Museo del Prado
Museo Real Academia de Bellas Artes de San Fernando
Museo Romántico
Museo Tiflológico
Museo Thyssen-Bornemisza
Palacio Real
Planetario de Madrid
Real Fábrica de Tapices
Santiago Bernabéu stadium

Buses

There are seats reserved for people with mobility problems behind the driver on most of the city's buses. Buses on many routes are now of the *piso bajo* (low floor) type, with low doors and spaces for wheelchairs. These are identified by the red on white stripes at the front and back of the bus and the slogan '*piso bajo pensado para todos*'.

Metro

All new metro stations have been built with access in mind, and so those on newer lines (Line 8 to the airport, the Gregorio Marañón interchange, Line 7 to Pitis, some others) have good lifts. However, older stations in the city centre generally have a lot of steps, and although you may get on at a station with a lift, it may turn out to be impossible to get off at your destination. The metro map on p320 of this guide and the free maps available at metro stations indicate stations with lifts.

RENFE & *cercanías*

Of the mainline rail stations, Atocha, Chamartín, Nuevos Ministerios and Príncipe Pío all have good access. Cercanías trains have very limited access, but some newer stations such as Méndez Alvaro (by Estación Sur coach station) have lifts connecting metro, train and bus stations. There are also good interchanges at Moncloa and Plaza Castilla.

Taxis

Special taxis adapted for wheelchairs can be called through Euro-Taxi on 91 547 82 00/91 547 86 00 and Tele-Taxi on 91 371 21 31. Make it clear you want an adapted model (ask for a Euro-Taxi). The number of such taxis in Madrid is very limited (although it rose by 100 in 2004) and waiting time can be up to 30mins. Fares are the same as for standard cabs, but the meter is started as soon as a request is received, so the cost can be quite high.

Drugs

Many people in Spain openly smoke cannabis, but its possession or consumption in public is illegal. It's theoretically OK to smoke cannabis in private, but not to possess it, although this law is rarely enforced. There's been a recent crackdown in bars, however.

Electricity

The standard current in Spain is now 220V, but a few old buildings in Madrid still have 125V circuits, so it's a good idea to check before using electrical equipment in older hotels. Plugs are all of the two-round-pin type. The 220V current works fine with British 240V products, with a plug adaptor. With US 110V appliances you will need a current transformer.

Embassies

For a full list look in the local phone book under *embajadas*.

American Embassy

C/Serrano 75, Salamanca (91 587 22 00/www.embusa.es). Metro Rubén Darío. **Open** *Phoneline* 24hrs daily. *Office* 9am-6pm (9am-1pm passports) Mon-Fri. **Map** p311 I2.
The general switchboard will put you through to the consulate.

Australian Embassy

Plaza del Descubridor Diego de Ordás 3, Chamberí (91 441 60 25/ visas 91 441 93 00/emergency phoneline 900 99 61 99/www.spain.embassy.gov.au). Metro Ríos Rosas. **Open** 8.30am-4.30pm (visas 10am-noon) Mon-Fri.

British Embassy

Paseo de Recoletos 7-9, Chueca (91 308 06 18/91 700 82 00/ www.ukinspain.com). Metro Alonso Martínez. **Open** *Sept-June* 9am-1.30pm; 3-5.30pm Mon-Thur; 9am-3pm Fri. *July, Aug* 8.30am-3pm Mon-Thur; 8.30am-2.30pm Fri. **Map** p310 H3.
General commercial, economic and other information about the UK.

British Consulate
C/Marqués de la Ensenada 16, Chueca (91 308 52 01). Metro Colón. **Open** 8am-2pm (until 6pm for emergencies) Mon-Fri. **Map** p310 H4.
For queries relating to passports, visas and legal problems.

Canadian Embassy

C/Núñez de Balboa 35, Salamanca (91 423 32 50/www.canada-es.org). Metro Velázquez. **Open** *Sept-July* 8.30am-5.30pm Mon-Thur; 8.30am-12.30pm Fri. *Aug* 8.30am-2.30pm Mon-Fri. **Map** p311 J4.
Emergency number for citizens (reverse charge calls accepted) is 1 613 996 8885.

Irish Embassy

Paseo de la Castellana 46, Salamanca (91 436 40 93). Metro Rubén Darío. **Open** 10am-2pm Mon-Fri. **Map** p310 I3.

New Zealand Embassy

Plaza de la Lealtad 2 (91 523 02 26). Metro Retiro or Banco de España. **Open** 9am-1.30pm, 3-5.30pm Mon-Fri. **Map** p314 H7.

Emergencies

Madrid has a general number – 112 – to call for the emergency services (you also dial this number from GSM mobiles). Some staff speak English, French and/or German.

However, you can be kept on hold for a long time; it's usually quicker to call direct. For more on the police, *see p290*.
Ambulancia (Ambulance) *061/092/91 335 45 45.*
Bomberos (Fire service) *Madrid capital 080. Whole comunidad 085.*
Policía Municipal (City Police) *092.*
Policía Nacional (National Police) *091.*
Guardia Civil *General 062/ Madrid capital 91 534 02 00/ Traffic police 91 533 53 00.*

Emergency repairs

Electricity

Unión Fenosa *901 38 02 20.*
Iberdrola *901 202 020.*
The company you need to call will be indicated on the electricity meter as well as your bill. Both phone lines are open 24hrs.

Gas

Butane gas: Repsol Butano *901 12 12 12.*
Gas Natural *900 75 07 50.*

Water

Canal de Isabel II *901 51 25 12.*

Gay & lesbian

COGAM

C/Fuencarral 37, Chueca (91 522 45 17/91 523 00 70/www.cogam.org). Metro Chueca or Tribunal. **Open** 10am-2pm, 5-9pm Mon-Fri. **Map** p309 F5.
The largest gay and lesbian organisation in Madrid, COGAM is one of the main organisers of Gay Pride and campaigns on various issues. The on-site café is a great place to chill and find out what's new on the scene.

Fundación Triángulo

C/Eloy Gonzalo 25, 1 ext dcha, Chamberí (91 593 05 40/ www.fundaciontriangulo.es). Metro Quevedo. **Open** 10am-2pm, 6-9pm Tue; 6-9pm Thur. **Map** p309 F2.
A gay cultural organisation that campaigns on equality issues. It also runs a helpline (91 446 63 94, same schedules as above) and offers legal help and health and AIDS prevention programmes.

Health

All visitors can obtain emergency care through the Spanish national health service. EU citizens are entitled to basic attention for free

Directory

if they have an E111 form (if you get one sent or faxed within four days, you will still be exempt from charges) or an E128 form, which is designed for people working or studying abroad for an extended period of time. Many medicines are charged for, however. In non-emergency situations, it's usually quicker to use travel insurance and private clinics (*see p287*) rather than the state system. The European Commission is planning to issue an European Health Insurance Card (due to be launched in 2004), which is to replace the E111 form and therefore speed up all the paperwork.

Accidents & emergencies

In a medical emergency go to the casualty department (*urgencias*) of any of the city's major hospitals (*see below*). All are open 24 hours daily. The Clinico or Gregorio Marañón are the most central. If you have no E111 or insurance, you can still be seen at any casualty department (you'll have to pay on the spot but be reimbursed back home by presenting the invoices and medical reports). In a non-emergency, pharmacists are very well informed and can often offer advice for minor complaints and injuries.

For an ambulance call **061**. You can also try the Red Cross (Cruz Roja, 91 522 22 22) or the SAMUR service (reached via the Municipal Police on 092).

AIDS/HIV

Centro Sanitario Sandova

C/Sandoval 7, Chamberí (91 445 23 28). Metro Bilbao or San Bernardo. **Open** 9am-noon Mon-Fri. **Map** p309 E3.
An official clinic that carries out free, confidential HIV tests.

Médicos del Mundo

C/Juan Montalvo 6, Moncloa (freephone 900 11 10 00/91 536 15 00). Metro Guzmán el Bueno. **Open** 10am-8pm Mon-Fri.
Support and advice on HIV and AIDS.

Hospitals

Ciudad Sanitaria La Paz

Paseo de la Castellana 261, Chamartín (91 727 70 00). Metro Begoña.
Near Plaza Castilla in the north of the city.

Hospital Clínico San Carlos

C/Profesor Martín Lagos, Moncloa (91 330 30 00). Metro Moncloa.
The entrance for the accident and emergency department is from Calle Isaac Peral, just off the Plaza de Cristo Rey.

Hospital General Gregorio Marañón

C/Doctor Esquerdo 146, Salamanca (91 586 00 00). Metro O'Donnell.

Complementary medicine

Instituto de Medicina Integral

Plaza de la Independencia 4, Salamanca (91 576 26 49). Metro Banco de España. **Open** 9am-1.30pm, 5-7.30pm Mon-Fri. **No credit cards**. **Map** p314 H6.
There are several English-speaking practitioners at this clinic, which offers treatments including homeopathy and acupuncture.

Contraception & women's health

Condoms (*profilácticos, condones* or *preservativos*) are available from most pharmacies, and vending machines and supermarkets.

Asociación de Mujeres para la Salud

Avda Alfonso XIII 118, Chamartín (91 519 56 78). Metro Colombia. **Open** 10am-1pm, 4-8pm Mon-Thur.
A feminist medical association offering free advice and counselling.

Clínica Duratón

C/Colegiata 4, Los Austrias (91 429 77 69). Metro Tirso de Molina. **Open** Sept-July 9.30am-1.30pm, 4.30-8.30pm Mon-Fri. Aug 4.30-8.30pm Mon-Fri. **Map** p313 D8.
Family-planning centre run by women doctors and staff.

Dentists

Dentistry is not covered by EU reciprocal agreements, so private rates apply.

Clínica Dental Cisne

C/Magallanes 18, Chamberí (91 446 32 21/24hr emergencies mobile 661 857 170). Metro Quevedo. **Open** Oct-May 10am-1.30pm, 3-8pm Mon, Tue, Thur; 2-8pm Wed; 9am-3pm Fri. June-Sept 10am-1.30pm,

3-8pm Mon, Tue, Thur; 9am-3pm Wed; 9am-3pm Fri. **Credit** MC, V. **Map** p309 E2.
British dentist Dr Ian Daniel is based at this clinic. Hours may vary in summer, and the clinic sometimes closes in August.

Doctors

Centros de salud are local health centres with three or so doctors and various specialised clinics. Waiting times can be long and consultations brief, but if necessary you will be referred to a hospital. Usually open 8am-9pm Mon-Fri and 9am-5pm Sat. These are some of the most central:

Centro de Salud Alameda

C/Alameda 9, Huertas & Santa Ana (91 420 38 02). Metro Atocha. **Map** p314 G9.

Centro de Salud Argüelles

C/Quintana 11, Argüelles (91 559 02 23). Metro Argüelles. **Map** p308 C3.

Centro de Salud Las Cortes

C/San Jerónimo 32, Huertas & Santa Ana (91 369 04 91). Metro Sevilla. **Map** p314 G7.

Opticians

For Grand Optical, a centrally located optician's, *see p187*.

Pharmacies

Pharmacies (*farmacias*) are signalled by large, green, usually flashing, crosses. Those within the official system of the College of Pharmacies are normally open 9.30am-2pm, 5-8pm Mon-Sat. An order when a duty rota operates. Every pharmacy has a list of the College's *farmacias de guardia* (duty pharmacies) for that day posted outside the door, with the nearest ones highlighted (many now show them using a computerised, push-button panel). Duty pharmacies are also listed in local newspapers, and information is available on the 010 and 098 phonelines (*see p294*) and at www.canaldefarmacia.com. At night, duty pharmacies may look as if they are closed, and you may have to knock on the shutters to be served.

Currently there are also two 24-hour pharmacies in Madrid, open every day of the year; *see p187*.

Private health care

Unidad Médica Anglo-Americana

C/Conde de Aranda 1-1º izq, Salamanca (91 435 18 23). Metro Retiro. **Open** *Sept-July* 9am-8pm Mon-Fri; 10am-1.30pm Sat. *Aug* 10am-4pm Mon-Fri. **Credit** AmEx, MC, V. **Map** p314 I6.
A British-American clinic with a full range of services, including dentistry. Staff make house and hotel calls.

Helplines

Alcoholics Anonymous

C/Juan Bravo, 40 2º (91 309 19 47). Metro Diego de León. **Map** p311 L2.
English-speaking group meets 8pm Mon-Fri; 6pm Sat; 7pm Sun.

Narcotics Anonymous

C/Doctor Piga 4 (902 114 147). Metro Lavapiés. **Map** p313 F9.
English-speaking meeting every Sunday at 5.30pm.

ID

Foreigners should carry national ID or a passport, although a photocopy is usually OK. You will be asked to show the passport itself or a driving licence when paying by credit card in shops.

Insurance

EU nationals are entitled to use the Spanish state health service, provided they have an E111 form, which in Britain can be obtained from post offices, health centres and Social Security offices. This will cover you for emergencies, but for short-term visitors it's often simpler to avoid dealing with the state bureaucracy and take out private travel insurance before departure, particularly as this will also cover you for stolen or lost cash or valuables.

Some non-EU countries also have reciprocal healthcare agreements with Spain, but, again, for most travellers it will be more convenient to have private travel insurance for all eventualities before arriving in the country. For more on all health services, *see p285*. For information on car insurance, *see p282*.

Internet

Internet access options keep evolving, but the basic choice is between internet service providers

(ISPs) that offer free basic access, such as Wanadoo (902 01 19 02, www.wanadoo.es) or those that charge a fee for relatively better service, such as Auna (902 50 00 90, www.iddeo.com). Gonuts4free (807 51 70 45/www.gonuts4free.com) is an Anglo-Spanish free ISP. In both cases you pay for your internet time in your phone bill.

Madrid has plenty of cybercafés and internet centres, particularly around Puerta del Sol. For other computer services, *see p282*.

BBiGG

C/Alcalá 21, Sol (91 521 92 07/ www.bbigg.com). Metro Sol. **Open** 24hrs daily. **Credit** V. **Map** p313 E/F7.
300 PCs, with the latest flat-screen technology and CRT for games.
Other locations: C/Mayor 1, Sol (91 531 23 64).

Cibercafé Alamo

C/El Alamo 7, Malasaña (91 542 82 62). Metro Noviciado. **Open** 8am-2am Mon-Fri; noon-2am Sat, Sun. **Map** p309 D5.
A real café with music, friendly staff and a pleasant atmosphere.

EasyInternetCafé

C/Montera 10, Sol (91 523 55 63). Metro Sol. **Open** 24hrs daily. **Map** p313 E7.
Access prices depend on demand – at peak hours a euro gets you 40mins on the net, late-night it's more like 2hrs.

WORKcenter

C/Alberto Aguilera 1, Malasaña (91 121 76 00/902 11 50 11/ www.workcenter.es). Metro San Bernardo. **Open** 24hrs daily. **Credit** MC, V. **Map** p309 E3.
An office centre where you can send or receive faxes and emails, access the net, print from a disk, make copies or get ID photos. Internet access is pricey, though (from €1/10mins or €3/hour).
Other locations: Paseo de Castellana 149, Salamanca (91 121 76 30); C/Conde de Peñalver 51, Salamanca (91 121 56 60); C/Maria de Molina 40, Salamanca (91 121 56 80).

Local access numbers

BT *91 270 60 00.*
Compuserve *91 395 65 00/ 908 274 255.*

Left luggage

Barajas airport

Terminals T-1 & T-2. **Open** 24hrs daily. **Rates** €2.65 first 24hrs; €3.30 (small locker) & €4.65 (big locker) per day thereafter.

Estación Sur (buses)

Open 6.30am-11.30pm daily. **Rates** €1.25 per case per day. A staffed office.

RENFE train stations

Open *Chamartín* 7am-11pm daily. *Atocha* 6.30am-10.30pm daily. **Rates** €2.40-€4.50 depending on size of locker.

Legal help

ARE 2

C/Princesa 3, 12 (902 44 77 22/ www.are2consulting.com). Metro Velázquez. **Open** 9am-9pm Mon-Fri (by appointment). **Map** p309 D4.
This Spanish firm can help with residency and work permits, accidents, tax and so on. English is spoken here.

Libraries

Madrid has many municipal public libraries, but few are in the centre of the city and they generally have limited selections of books in English. For a full list of libraries, check *'bibliotecas'* in the local *Páginas Amarillas* (*Yellow Pages*) or call 010.

Ateneo Artístico, Científico y Literario de Madrid

C/Prado 21, Huertas (91 429 74 42/ www.ateneodemadrid.com). Metro Antón Martín. **Open** 9am-12.45am Mon-Sat; 9am-9.45pm Sun. **Map** p313 F8.
A literary and philosophical club founded in 1820, Madrid's Ateneo has often been a focal point in the city's cultural life. It also has the second largest library in Spain, and has the advantage of being open when others are closed. Membership costs €90 to join, then €36 every three months, and members have access to talks, cultural events and other activities.

Biblioteca Nacional

Paseo de Recoletos 20, Salamanca (91 580 78 00/91 580 77 19/ ww.bne.es). Metro Colón. **Open** 9am-9pm Mon-Fri; 9am-2pm Sat. **Map** p310 I5.
Spain's national library has early books and manuscripts on display (in the Museo del Libro), and is also the home of the Hemeroteca Nacional, the national newspaper library (*see p288*). To use the library regularly you need accreditation from a university or similar institution, but a one-day pass is quite easy to obtain (you need to take a passport or residency card).

Biblioteca Pedro Salinas

Glorieta de la Puerta de Toledo 1, La Latina (91 366 54 07). Metro Puerta de Toledo. **Open** *Oct-June* 8.30am-8.45pm Mon-Fri; 9am-1.45pm Sat. *July-Sept* 8.30am-8.45pm Mon-Fri. **Map** p312 C10.

The most attractive and convenient of Madrid's public libraries. Books can be taken out on loan.

British Council

Paseo del General Martínez Campos 31, Chamberí (91 337 35 00/ www.britishcouncil.es). Metro Iglesia. **Open** *Oct-June* 9.30am-6.45pm Mon-Thur; 9.30am-5.45pm Fri. *July-Sept* 9am-2pm Mon-Fri.

The library in the British Council study centre has a massive selection of books and videos in English, as well as CD-Roms, internet access and daily newspapers. Membership rates are €30 for three months, €45 for six months or €50 per year.

Hemeroteca Municipal

C/Conde Duque 11, Conde Duque (91 588 57 71). Metro Noviciado. **Open** *Sept-July* 9am-8.30pm Mon-Fri. *Aug* 9am-2pm Mon-Fri. **Map** p309 D4.

If you just have to track down that essential piece of information, the city newspaper library in the Centro Conde Duque is the place to do it. You need to obtain a researcher's card to get in, for which you must provide a copy of your passport and two ID photos.

Lost property

Airport & rail stations

If you lose something before check-in at Barajas Airport, report the loss to the Aviación Civil office (AENA) in the relevant terminal, or call 91 393 61 19. If you think you've mislaid anything on the RENFE rail network, look for the Atención al Viajero desk or Jefe de Estación office at the main station nearest to where your property went astray. For information by phone on lost property call 91 300 70 53 (Chamartín) or 91 506 69 69 (Atocha).

In all cases, ask for *objetos perdidos.*

Sección de Taxis del Ayuntamiento

C/Vallehermoso 1, Chamberí (91 588 43 48). Metro San Bernardo. **Open** 9am-2pm Mon-Fri. **Map** p309 D3.

EMT (city buses)

C/Cerro de la Plata 4, Salamanca (91 406 88 43). Metro Pacífico. **Open** 9.30am-2pm Mon-Fri.

The lost-property office for items that have been lost on Madrid's city or airport buses.

Negociado de Objetos Perdidos (Madrid City Council)

Plaza de Legazpi 7, South of centre (91 588 43 46/44). Metro Legazpi. **Open** *Oct-June* 9am-2pm Mon-Fri. *July-Sept* 9am-1.30pm Mon-Fri.

This office mainly receives articles found on the metro or in taxis, but if you're lucky, something lost in the street may turn up here.

Media

Newspapers

Spanish newspapers may come in tabloid size, but they are far from light-hearted, preferring heavy political commentary. Sensationalist, celeb-dominated stories are reserved for the *prensa de corazón* (press of the heart), such as *¡Hola!, Diez Minutos* or *¡Qué me dices!.* The free daily papers *Madrid y Más* and *Metro,* are handed out outside most central metro stations.

ABC

Despite its conservative outlook, *ABC*'s journalists have the highest professional reputation. Read by Madrid's most respectable citizens.

Marca & As

Sports-only (in fact mostly football-only) papers. *Marca* is usually the country's bestselling daily paper.

El Mundo

This centrist, populist paper made its name by unearthing many corruption scandals under the Socialists during the 1990s. Friday's 'La Luna de Metrópoli' supplement is a good source of listings and information on the cultural agenda.

El País

The liberal *El País* is the established paper of record, and also carries good daily information on Madrid, with Friday's 'Tentaciones' supplement great for music and popular culture.

La Razón

Right-wing and sensationalist daily with much of its editorial coming from ABC.

English-language

Foreign newspapers are on sale in **Fnac** (*see p167*), all **Vip's** stores (*see p168*) and at most kiosks around Sol, Gran Vía, Calle Alcalá and the Castellana.

The Broadsheet

A glossy free monthly with articles on all aspects of life in Madrid and Spain, along with useful classified ads pages.

InMadrid

A free monthly aimed at English-speaking residents – you can pick it up in pubs, bookshops, universities, language schools and tourist offices. Good articles on the Madrid scene, plus listings information, events, reviews and small ads.

Listings & classifieds

Local papers carry daily film and theatre listings, and the Friday supplements of *El Mundo* (Metrópoli) and *El País* (Tentaciones) give fuller information, reviews and so on. For monthly music listings look out for the Barcelona-based magazines *Mondo Sonoro* and *Go* (in bars and music shops).

Segundamano

'Second-hand' comes out three times a week and is the best place for small ads of all kinds.

Guía del Ocio

A weekly listings magazine with cinema, arts, entertainment, concerts, nightlife and restaurant listings, and a good galleries section. It's handy, but can be inaccurate.

Music & style mags

Undersounds, Rockdelux, the Spanish version of *Rolling Stone* and the new *MTV* magazine are mainly sold in kiosks or music shops and at festivals. A few free mags to look out for are the clubbers' zine *AB* and the smarter monthly *Cartel.*

Radio

The Spanish are avid radio fans; you'll hear radios blaring out in bars, cafés, buses and taxis.

Radio Nacional de España stations to listen for include RNE-2 (96.5 FM, classical music) and RNE-3 (93.2 FM, an excellent and eclectic mix of rock and world music). There are dozens of other local stations.

The main commercial broadcaster is **SER** (Sociedad Española de Radiofusión), which controls four networks: SER, a news network, and two music channels.

One specific English-language programme to look out for is Radio Círculo's Madrid Live on Tuesdays from 8.30pm to 9pm (repeated on Friday at 10pm), which can be found on 100.4FM. Produced and presented by radio journalist Ann Bateson, it focuses on the city's arts, entertainment and social scene.

The BBC World Service can be found in the evenings on 12095 kHz short wave.

TV

There are five main channels, which pump out an endless diet of tacky game shows, talk shows, really bad imported *telenovelas* (soaps) from South America and badly dubbed American movies. Just about the only redeeming feature is the news, although **Canal 2** does show some good documentaries and films.

Non-Spanish films and shows on some channels can be seen in undubbed versions on stereo TVs; look for VO (*versión original*) in listings and a 'Dual' symbol at the top of the screen.

TVE 1 (La Primera)

Flagship channel of state broadcaster RTVE, consequently the news can be very pro-government. This too-obvious symbiosis between media and politics resulted in the dismissal of its programme director after the 2004 elections.

TVE 2 (La Dos)

The least commercial of all the TV channels, La 2 is good for documentaries and late-night movies (often in VO).

Antena 3

A private channel with an emphasis on family entertainment mixed with late-night salaciousness.

Tele 5

Another private channel. This celebrity-obsessed station is the one to blame for the Spanish version of Big Brother, *El Gran Hermano*.

Telemadrid

Madrid's own station. Good for live football on Saturday and the Megahit movie on Sunday nights.

Canal +

A subscriber channel with a good selection of sport, movies and US hits. Many hotels, bars and cafés now receive it.

Money

Spain is part of the euro zone. One euro is made up of 100 *céntimos*. One thing to remember is that the

---

A matter of courses

There are plenty of learning opportunities for foreign adults at Madrid's universities and private institutions. Unsurprisingly, many of these are Spanish-language courses.

Language schools offer intensive summer courses in general Spanish (from beginner level to advanced) lasting from one week to four months or more. EleMadrid (www.elemadrid.com), Alba Language Consulting (www.albalanguage.com) or International House (www.ihmadrid.com) also run specialised courses for job-related Spanish (in fields including medicine, law, commerce and hotel management) and for those who plan to become Spanish teachers. Many of the schools, such as Acento Español (www.acentoespanol.com), Academia Contacto (www.academia contacto.com), Academia InHispania (www.inhispania.com) or Idiomas Plus (www.madridplus.es) balance the tuition programme with leisure activities aimed at allowing students to learn about the city and Spanish culture. Schools can also help with accommodation.

For those who already have a reasonable level of Spanish, there are plenty of other interesting programmes around. Universidad Complutense de Madrid's prestigious summer lecture series have been taking place for the last 17 years in the mountain town of El Escorial. Lecturers have included luminaries such as poet Rafael Albertí, film-makers Pedro Almodóvar and Carlos Saura, and sculptor Eduardo Chillida, along with international artists, politicians, economists and scientists. Subjects are usually related in some way to current events, and have drawn on disciplines as varied as economics, politics, art, literature, psychology, sociology and environmentalism. Places on the lecture series are limited and fees are quite high (for programme details and fees, see www.ucm.es/info/cv). Students can apply for a scholarship that covers the costs of accommodation (in shared rooms) and meals.

The Madrid Chamber of Commerce offers a good selection of vocational courses. There are classes throughout the year in subjects ranging from business Spanish for foreign executives to Spanish wine-tasting and oenology (you'll need a good level of Spanish for the latter). These courses have a very good reputation, both in Spain and abroad. Tuition fees are reasonable and class sizes are limited, which means there can be some competition for places. Check out www.camaramadrid.es for more information (click on 'formación' and 'monográficos'). Or phone the Chamber of Commerce (91 538 38 38, 8.30am-8.30pm Mon-Fri).

Cooking courses are popular too. Club Cooking (www.club-cooking.com) is a fun and friendly school with classes in cookery for all standards (there are even courses for children). Courses cover topics including cooking with cod, rice cooking, Moroccan food, and cakes and pastry.

Directory

British/US practice on decimal points and commas is reversed (so 1.000 euros means one thousand euros, while 1,00 euro is one euro). There are banknotes for €5, €10, €20, €50, €100, €200 and €500, in different colours and designs. Then there are three copper coins (five, two and one *céntimo*), three gold-coloured coins (50, 20 and 10 *céntimos*) and large coins for one euro (silver centre, gold rim) and two euros (gold centre, silver rim).

Banks & exchange

Banks and savings banks (*cajas de ahorros*) readily accept cash and travellers' cheques (you must show your passport). Commission rates vary, and it's worth shopping around before changing money (although banks usually give the best rates); also, given the rates charged by Spanish banks, it's often cheaper to get money from an ATM machine by credit or debit card rather than with travellers' cheques. It is always quicker to change money at larger bank offices than at local branches.
There are many small bureaux de change (*cambio*), particularly on the Gran Vía and Puerta del Sol. Exchange rates are usually worse than in banks.

BANK HOURS
Banks and savings banks normally open 8am-2pm Monday-Friday. From October to May many branches also open from 9am to 1pm on Saturday. Hours vary a little between different banks, and some have branches that stay open until around 5pm one day a week (usually Thursday). Savings banks often open late on Thursday afternoons, but are less likely to open on Saturdays. Banks are closed on public holidays.

Out-of-hours services

Outside normal hours you can change money at the airport (terminals T-1 and T-2, open 24hrs daily), at main train stations (Atocha, 9am-9pm daily; Chamartín, 8am-10pm daily), in El Corte Inglés (*see p167*), in hotels, at private *cambios* and at the places listed below. At the airport, Chamartín and outside some banks in Gran Vía and Puerta del Sol there are automatic cash exchange machines that accept notes in major currencies, in good condition (be careful of using these at night).

American Express
Plaza de las Cortes 2, Huertas (902 37 56 37). Metro Banco de España. **Open** 9am-7.30pm Mon-Fri; 9am-2pm Sat. **Map** p314 G8.

The usual AmEx services, and an ATM for AmEx cards. Money can be transferred worldwide in 24 hours. **Other locations:** C/Juan Ignacio Luca de Tena 17 (902 37 56 37).

Western Union Money Transfer
Change Express, Gran Vía 16, Sol & Gran Vía (91 542 81 80/900 63 36 33). Metro Gran Vía. **Open** 9.30am-3pm, 4.30-10pm daily. **Map** p313 F6. Change Express is the local Western Union agent: the quickest if not the cheapest way to have money sent from abroad.
Other locations: Gran Vía 25, 46 & 53.

Chequepoint
Plaza de Callao 4, Sol & Gran Vía (91 532 29 22). **Open** 9am-midnight daily. **Map** p313 D7.
An international exchange company.

Credit cards

Major credit and charge cards are accepted in most hotels, shops and restaurants, and for many other services. You can also withdraw cash with major cards from most bank ATM machines, which provide instructions in different languages. Exchange rates and handling fees often work out to be more economical than exchanging cash or travellers' cheques. Banks will also advance cash against credit cards over the counter, but they prefer you to use an ATM.

Lost or stolen cards
American Express *freephone 900 99 44 26.*
Diners Club *902 40 11 12.*
Mastercard *freephone 900 97 12 31.*
Visa *91 519 60 00; freephone 900 99 12 16.*

Tax

There are different rates of sales tax (IVA): for hotels and restaurants, the rate is seven per cent; in shops, it's most commonly 16 per cent, but four to seven per cent on some items. IVA is generally included in listed prices – if it's not, the expression '*mas IVA*' (plus tax) must be stated after the price. In shops displaying a 'Tax-Free Shopping' sticker, non-EU residents can reclaim tax on large purchases (*see p167*).

Eating, drinking and shopping all happen late in Madrid. The siesta has faded to a myth, but *madrileños* do operate to a distinctive schedule. Most shops open from 10am to 2pm, and 5-5.30pm to 8-8.30pm, Monday to Saturday, although many stay closed on Saturday afternoons. Food markets open earlier, around 8am. In July and especially in August most shops and services (such as the Post Office and administrations) close in the afternoon. August is also the time when most shops, bars and restaurants close for their annual holidays (from two weeks up to the whole month). Major stores and malls are open from 10am to 9pm without a break, Monday to Saturday (for the vexed question of Sunday shopping, *see p167*). Big supermarkets (Al Campo, Carrefour) open from 10am to 10pm Mon-Sat and the first Sunday of each month.
Madrileños still eat, drink, go out and stay out later than their neighbours in virtually every other European country. Most restaurants are open 1.30-2pm to 4pm, and 9pm to midnight, and many close on Sunday nights and Mondays, and for at least part of August. Many businesses finish at 3pm in the summer. Most museums (state ones) close one day a week, usually Monday.

Police

Spain has several police forces. In Madrid the most important are the local Policía Municipal, in navy and pale blue, and the Policía Nacional, in darker blue and white uniforms (or all-blue combat gear). Each force has its own responsibilities, although they overlap. Municipales are principally concerned with traffic and parking problems and local regulations. The force with primary responsibility for dealing with crime are the Nacionales. The Guardia Civil, in green, are responsible, among other things, for policing inter-city highways, and customs.

Reporting a crime

If you are robbed or attacked, you should report the incident as soon as possible at the nearest Policía Nacional station (*comisaría*), where you will be asked to make an official statement (*denuncia*). It is extremely unlikely anything you have lost will be recovered, but you need the *denuncia* to make an insurance claim. Very few officers speak any English.

Comisaría del Centro
C/Leganitos 19, Sol & Gran Vía (91 548 79 85/902 10 21 12). Metro Santo Domingo or Plaza de España. **Map** p313 D6.
The Policía Nacional headquarters for central Madrid, near Plaza de

España. Some other police stations in the city centre are listed below; all are open 24hrs daily.

Puerta del Sol

Inside metro Sol, by C/Carretas exit, Sol & Gran Vía (91 521 09 11). Metro Sol. **Map** p313 E7.

Huertas/Retiro

C/Huertas 76-78 (91 322 10 17). Metro Antón Martín. **Map** p314 G8.

Chamberí

C/Rafael Calvo 33 (91 322 32 78). Metro Iglesia. **Map** p310 H2.

Postal services

If you just need normal-rate stamps (*sellos*), it's easier to buy them in an *estanco* (*see below*). Post offices now have automatic stamp dispensing machines (with a weighing system) but they do not always work.

Palacio de Comunicaciones

Plaza de Cibeles, Salamanca & Retiro (902 19 71 97/www.correos.es). Metro Banco de España. **Open** 8.30am-9.30pm Mon-Fri; 8.30am-2pm Sat (from 2pm to 9.30pm, service is given at Puerta N, in the C/Montalbán). **Map** p314 H7.
In the magnificent central post office, all manner of postal services are available at separate windows around the main hall. Faxes can be sent and received at all post offices, but rates are expensive, so it's better to use a private fax bureau. There is an information desk near the main entrance. Note that not all services are available at all times during the general opening times. Mail sent poste restante should be addressed to Lista de Correos, 28000 Madrid, Spain. To collect it, go to windows 17-20 with your passport. For express post, say you want to send *a 'carta urgente'*.

Other city centre post offices are located in El Corte Inglés, C/Preciados 1-4, Sol & Gran Vía; Carrera de San Francisco 13, La Latina; C/Mejía Lequerica 7, Chueca; C/Jorge Juan 20, Salamanca, and at Terminal 1 in the airport.

Postal rates & postboxes

Letters and postcards up to 20g cost 27¢ within Spain, 52¢ to Europe and North Africa, and 77¢ to the rest of the world. Note that you will pay more for 'irregular' shaped envelopes (basically, ones that are not rectangular). Cards and letters to other European countries usually

arrive in 3-4 days, those to North America in about a week. Normal postboxes are yellow with two horizontal red stripes. There are also a few special red postboxes for urgent mail, with hourly collections.

Postal Exprés

Available at all post offices, this efficient express mail service offers next-day delivery within Spain of packages up to 1kg (2.2lb), for €9-10, according to distance and dimension.

Estancos

The main role of the tobacco shop or *estanco* (identified by a brown and yellow sign with the word '*tabacos*') is, as the sign suggests, to supply tobacco-related products. But they are also places to buy stamps, phonecards and Metrobús and monthly *abono* tickets. *Estancos* are also the only places where you can obtain the official money vouchers (*papel de estado*) needed for dealings with Spanish bureaucracy. Some also have photocopiers and fax facilities.

Queuing

Despite appearances to the contrary, Spaniards have a highly developed queuing culture. People don't always bother standing in line, but they generally know when it is their turn. Common practice is to ask when you first arrive, to no one in particular, '*¿Quién da la vez?*' or '*Quién es el último/la última?*' ('Who's last?'); see who nods back at you, and follow on after them. Say '*yo*' (me) to the next person who asks.

Religion

Anglican

St George's (British Embassy Church)
C/Núñez de Balboa 43, Salamanca (91 576 51 09). Metro Velázquez. **Services** *Sept-June* 7.30pm Wed; 10.30am Fri; 8.30am, 10am, 11.15am Sun. *July, Aug* 8.30am, 11.15am Sun. **Map** p311 J3.

Catholic (in English)

Our Lady of Mercy
Avenida Alfonso XIII 165, Chamartín (91 416 90 09). Metro Pío XII. **English Mass** 11am Sun.

Jewish

Sinagoga de Madrid
C/Balmes 3, Eastern suburbs (91 591 31 31). Metro Iglesia. **Prayers** 8am, 8pm Mon-Fri; 9.15am Sat; 9am Sun. **Map** p310 G1.

Muslim

Centro Cultural Islámico de Madrid
C/Salvador de Madariaga 4, Eastern suburbs (91 326 26 10). Metro Barrio de la Concepción. **Open** 10am-8pm Mon-Thur, Sat, Sun; noon-4pm Fri.

Renting a flat

The price of flats to rent in Madrid varies wildly, so it pays to shop around. A room in a shared flat costs upwards of €300 a month, while a one-bedroom flat is around €600 or more. Places to look for flat ads are the papers *Segundamano* and *Anuntis* and the English language magazine *InMadrid* (for all, *see p288*). Another option is to look around for '*Se alquila*' (to rent) signs.

Contratos de alquiler (rental agreements) generally cover a five-year period, within which a landlord can only raise the rent each year in line with inflation, set in the official price index (IPC). Landlords usually ask for the equivalent of one month's rent as a *fianza* (deposit) and a month's rent in advance. Details of contracts (especially with regards to responsibility for repairs) vary a lot; don't sign a *contrato* unless you're fully confident of your Spanish and/or a lawyer or *gestor* has looked at it.

Safety

As in most major cities, street crime is a problem in Madrid and tourists are often targeted. One plus point is that pickpocketing and bag-snatching are more likely than any violent crime. Places to be especially on your guard are the Puerta del Sol, Gran Vía, the Plaza Mayor, the Plaza Santa Ana and, above all, the Rastro and Retiro park; watch out, too, on the metro. The area around the junction of Gran Vía and Calle Montera is a centre of street prostitution, and can feel uncomfortable at night. Most recently, the Lavapiés district has acquired a bad reputation for street crime, which has developed alongside the growth in racial tensions in the area, as robberies are often attributed to young, homeless North African illegal immigrants, though most thefts reported by *Time Out* readers and local media appear to involve small groups of teenage eastern European or gypsy girls.

Street criminals prey very deliberately on the unwary, and their chances of success can be limited greatly by the following simple precautions.

Directory

● When sitting in a café, especially at an outside table, never leave a bag or coat on the ground, on the back of a chair or anywhere you cannot see it clearly. If in doubt, keep it on your lap.

● Give the impression of knowing what's going on around you, and – without getting paranoid – be alert and watch out to see if you are being followed.

● Wear shoulder bags pulled to the front, not at your back, especially in the underground. Keep the bag closed and a hand on top of it.

● Avoid pulling out large notes to pay for things, especially in the street at night; try not to get large notes when changing money.

● Be aware that street thieves often work in pairs or groups; if someone hassles you for money or to buy something, or pulls out a **map** and asks for directions, keep walking, as this can be a ruse to distract you so that the thief's 'partner' can get at your bag. This is often done pretty crudely, and so is not hard to recognise.

● Be extremely careful when you withdraw money from ATMs. Don't let anyone distract your attention while putting in your PIN code.

● Beware of fake policemen: if someone asks to see your ID, ask to see their identification first.

Smoking

Spaniards smoke – big time. It's not unusual for a bank cashier to serve you while puffing on the first of the day. Likewise, it's unusual to find non-smoking areas in restaurants or bars, although smoking bans in cinemas, theatres, the airport and on mainline trains are generally respected. Smoking is officially banned throughout the metro system, but many people take this to mean on trains only, and not station platforms.

Study

Foreign students from the EU staying more than three months require a residency permit (Tarjeta de Residencia Para la Realización de Estudios); non-EU students may also need a visa. For more details, *see p294.*

Accommodation

RoomMadrid

C/Conde Duque 7, Malasaña (91 548 03 35/91 548 10 21/ www.roomeurope.com). Metro Plaza España. **Open** noon-3pm, 5-8pm Mon-Fri. **Map** p309 D4.

This agency specialises in finding rooms in shared flats, with a minimum stay of one month in summer and three months from September to June. Commission starts at €60.

Madrid Sal y Ven

C/Recoletos 11, 1° B, Salamanca (91 435 22 62/www.salyven.com). Metro Retiro. **Open** 9.30am-2pm, 3.30-7pm Mon-Fri. **Map** p310 5I. Sal y Ven finds rooms in shared flats with a minimum stay of one week. The agency charges €25-€50 as commission.

Language learning

Todo Español

C/General Díaz Porlier 1, Salamanca (91 435 42 38). Metro Goya. **Open** 10am-7pm Mon-Fri. **Map** p311 K4. A very efficient and friendly school, with five students per class. Staff can help students to find accommodation in Madrid.

Carpe Diem

C/Fuencarral 13, 1°, Malasaña (91 522 31 22/www.carpemadrid.com). Metro Gran Vía. **Open** 10am-7pm Mon-Fri. **Map** p313 E6. A young, funky Spanish-language academy, with small groups and enthusiastic teachers.

Academia Actual Plus

Gran Vía 71, 1° izq, Sol & Gran Vía (91 547 56 08). Metro Plaza de España. **Open** 9.30am-2pm, 4-8.30pm Mon-Fri. **Map** p309 D5. A central and highly recommended school. There are no more than eight students per class.

Escuela Oficial de Idiomas

Avda de los Caños 2, Chamberí (91 636 19 36/www.eoidiomas. com/eoi/eoi.html). Metro Cruz del Rayo. **Open** 10am-1pm, 4-9pm Mon-Fri. Closed July, Aug. This government-run school offers courses in Spanish and several other languages throughout the academic year (there are no summer courses). The school has are several other centres in the Madrid area; call for a full list. Registration is in August/ September and April/May, and competition for places is so stiff that a lottery system dictates who gets in.

International House

C/Zurbano 8, Chamberí (91 310 13 14/ihmadrid.com). Metro Alonso Martínez. **Open** 9am-8.30pm Mon-Fri. **Map** p310 H3. This branch of the well-known International House offers Spanish courses at all levels.

Universidad Complutense de Madrid

Secretaría de Cursos para Extranjeros, Facultad de Filosofía y Letras, Ciudad Universitaria, 28040 Madrid (91 394 53 25/www.ucm.es). **Open** Sept-June 10am-1pm, 3-6pm Mon-Fri. July 10am-1pm Mon-Fri. Closed Aug.

Three-month Spanish courses for foreigners are held during the academic year. Higher-level students can study linguistics, literature and culture; there are also intensive language courses.

Universities

Erasmus, Socrates & Lingua programmes

Information in the UK: UK Socrates & Erasmus Council Building, The University, Canterbury, Kent CT2 7PD (01227 762 712/ www.erasmus.ac.uk).

The Erasmus student-exchange scheme and Lingua project (for language learning) are the main parts of the EU's Socrates programme to help students move freely between member states. To be eligible you must be studying at an exchange institution. Prospective students should contact their college's Erasmus co-ordinator.

Universidad de Alcalá de Henares

C/Escritorios, 4, Alcalá de Henares (91 881 23 78/www.uah.es). **Open** *Office* 9am-2pm, 4-7pm Mon-Fri. Offers Spanish courses for foreigners.

Universidad Autónoma de Madrid

Ciudad Universitaria de Cantoblanco, Ctra de Colmenar km15, 28049 Madrid (91 497 46 33/www.uam.es). **Open** *Office* 9am-2pm, 4-6pm Mon-Fri.

The UAM now competes in prestige with the Complutense.

Universidad Carlos III

C/Madrid 126, Getafe, 28903 Madrid (91 624 95 00/91 624 98 39/www.uc3m.es). **Open** *Office* 9am-2pm, 4-6pm Mon-Fri.

One of Madrid's newest universities, with campuses in Getafe and Leganés.

Universidad Complutense de Madrid

Avda de Séneca 2, Moncloa (91 452 04 00/www.ucm.es). **Open** *Office* 9am-2pm, 4-6pm Mon-Fri; 9am-1am Sat.

Carrying the card

A new ruling, made in March 2003, effectively exempts many EU citizens living in Spain from the obligation to apply for and carry a resident's card (*tarjeta de residencia*). Students, along with contracted workers, freelancers, business owners or retired people who have already made Spanish Social Security contributions, are entitled to live in Spain and use their own country's ID card, or passport, for all dealings or transactions. Not all branches of the administration are aware of the ruling but it is clearly stated both on the British Embassy's website (www.ukinspain.com) and the Ministry of the Interior's (www.mir.es/dgei/documentos/residencia.htm).

Everybody in Spain, both nationals and foreigners, however, is obliged to carry a valid form of ID. In the case of those foreigners who do not have a national ID card, this means carrying your passport, which is risky. Technically not legal, but usually acceptable, is to carry a photocopy of the relevant pages. Alternatively, you can apply for a resident's card voluntarily, at the foreigners' police station, the Comisaría de Extranjería. First you must still obtain the NIE (*número de identificación de extranjeros* – foreigners' identity number). The process is simple – go to the Comisaría de Extranjería or a police station that deals with foreigners' affairs with your passport and a photocopy of the important pages, fill out an application form and you will be sent your number by post. The number is used for all financial dealings and is necessary for opening bank accounts, tax declarations and so on. For the residency card, you will then need three passport photos, along with your passport and a photocopy. Proof of income and medical insurance are no longer necessary.

Non-EU citizens have a tougher time. While in Spain on a tourist visa you are technically not allowed to work, though many do. If you are made a job offer while in Spain you must return to your home country and apply for a *visado de residencia* (residence visa). Without this you may not enter Spain to work. The process can take some time and applications are not always successful. Once the visa has been issued, you can travel to Spain, take up the job and begin the lengthy application process for a resident's card and work permit (*permiso de trabajo*). On making the application, the following documents must be submitted along with the official application form: photocopy of a valid passport; a police certificate from your home city stating that you have no prison record (officially translated into Spanish by a sworn translator); an official medical certificate (obtained upon arrival in Spain); three identical passport photographs; where applicable, documents proving why you are more capable of performing the job than a Spaniard or EU citizen; where necessary, proof that you have the qualifications or training required for the job. Work permits and resident's cards, once issued, are initially valid for one year, the second for two, the third for three. After five years you will be granted a permanent work permit, which, though valid indefinitely, must be renewed every five years. Good legal advice is recommended throughout the process.

Comisaría de Extranjería

C/General Pardiñas 90 (91 322 68 13/14).
Metro Núñez de Balboa. **Open** 9am-2pm,
4-7pm Mon-Thur. **Map** p311 K2.

The prestigious Complutense is Madrid's main university. The largest and oldest in Spain, it is home to 98,000 students, 3,000 of them from abroad.

Telephones

Since the Spanish national phone company (Telefónica) was privatised, other companies – such as Jazztel and Auna – now compete with it in certain areas. Nevertheless, Telefónica remains the main player in the field as far as infrastructure is concerned, though its prices remain relatively high.

Dialling & codes

It is necessary to dial provincial area codes with all phone numbers in Spain, even when you are calling from within the same area. Hence, all normal phone numbers in the Madrid area are preceded by 91, and you must dial this whether you're calling within Madrid, from elsewhere in Spain or from abroad. Numbers beginning 900 are freephone lines; 901, 902 or 906 numbers are special-rate services and can be very pricey. Spanish mobile phone numbers have six digits and begin with a 6.

International & long-distance calls

To call abroad, dial 00 followed by the country code, then the area code (omitting the first zero in UK numbers) and number. To call Madrid from abroad, dial the international code (00 in the UK, 001 from the USA), then 34 for Spain.

Australia *61.*
Canada *1.*
Irish Republic *353.*
New Zealand *64.*
United Kingdom *44.*
USA *1.*

Directory

Mobile phones

The Spanish are mobile (*móvil*) mad and just about everybody has one (or two). You can pay each month or use rechargeable pre-paid cards. Call costs depend on the type of contract you have. Mobile phones from other countries can be used in Spain with a 'roaming' system, which you need to activate before leaving home.

Spain Cell Phone

687 558 529/www.puertade madrid.com/rentacellphone.
This company offers short- and long-term mobile phone rental in Spain and Europe. Call rates are low and incoming calls are free.

Phone centres

For making international calls it's often worth using a call centre (*locutorio*). You don't need change (you are charged when you've finished your call), the booths keep out noise, and many offer international call rates cheaper than Telefónica's. There are many phone centres around Lavapiés, Huertas and Malasaña. Often other services – fax, internet, currency exchange and money transfer – are available.
There is a directory of *locutorios* at www.ociolatino.com.

Envio Latino

Plaza Dos de Mayo 22, Malasaña (91 448 14 11). Metro Tribunal. **Open** 10.30am-midnight daily. **Map** p309 E4.

Money Exchange

C/Infantas 1, Chueca (91 532 75 35). Metro Gran Via. **Open** 10am-10pm daily. **Map** p313 F6.

Public phones

Payphones are relatively plentiful in the city, although due to the traffic noise, it's often worth using a phone in a bar or café, even though they often cost 50 per cent more than regular booths. Most models of payphone take coins (from five *céntimos* up), phonecards and credit cards, and have a digital display with instructions in English and other languages.
The first minute of a daytime local call costs around 11¢ *céntimos*; to a mobile phone around 35¢; to a 902 number, around 18¢. You are usually given credit to make more calls without having to insert more money.
Kioskos and *estancos* sell €5 (up to 70 minutes of communication) and €10 (up to 140 minutes) phonecards by various companies. Many of the cards give you a free number to call;

an operator or automatic system then connects you with the number you want and can tell you how much is left on your card.

Operator services

Usually, operators will only speak Spanish, though most international operators speak basic English.
National directory enquiries 11818
International directory enquiries & operator 11825
National operator 11822
Telephone faults service 1002
Time 093
Weather 11822
Wake-up calls 096. You key in the time when you want to be woken, using the 24hr clock, eg 0830 if you want to be woken at 8.30am.
General information 098. Although less comprehensive than the 010 line, this Telefónica local information service is open 24hrs.

Time

Spain is one hour ahead of UK time, six hours ahead of US EST and nine ahead of PST. Daylight saving time runs concurrently with the UK. So, when it's 6pm in Madrid, it's 5pm in London and, usually, noon in New York.

Tipping

In Spain there are no fixed rules or percentages for tipping and in general Spaniards tip very little. It is usual to leave around five to ten per cent for a waiter in a restaurant, rarely over three or four euros, and people often leave a few *céntimos* of small change in a bar. It's also usual to tip hotel porters, toilet and cinema attendants. In taxis the norm is around five per cent; more for longer journeys, or if a driver has been especially helpful.

Toilets

Public toilets are rare, although there are some with an attendant in the Retiro, by the lake; at Chamartín and Atocha stations; and in the Paseo del Prado. However, proprietors usually don't mind if you pop into a bar or café (better, though, if you ask first), and big stores such as El Corte Inglés or fast-food restaurants are a good bet.

Tourist information

City and regional authority (Comunidad de Madrid) tourist offices all provide similar basic information on Madrid and its

region, plus free maps (*see also p279*). The city also runs a phone information line for locals, 010, that can be useful to visitors. Tourist offices do not make hotel bookings but can advise on vacancies; for booking agencies, *see p41*.
Full information on what's on is in local papers, listings magazines and local English-language magazines (*see p288*). For useful websites, *see p297*.

Oficina Municipal de Turismo

Plaza Mayor 3, Los Austrias (91 588 16 36). Metro Sol. **Open** 10am-8pm Mon-Sat; 10am-3pm Sun. **Map** p313 D8.
The city office is also the departure point for walking tours.

Oficinas de Información Turística

Mercado Puerta de Toledo, Ronda de Toledo 1, stand 3134, La Latina (91 364 18 76/902 100 007). Metro Puerta de Toledo. **Open** 9am-7pm Mon-Sat; 9am-2.30pm Sun.
Other information offices on the general 902 number are located at: C/Duque de Medinaceli 2, Huertas; Barajas Airport Terminal 1; Chamartín Station, near platform 20. Hours vary slightly between offices.

Summer information officers

During July and August pairs of young information guides, in bright yellow and blue uniforms, are sent by the city tourist board to roam the central area ready to answer enquiries (8am-8pm daily). They also staff information stands at Puerta del Sol, Plaza del Callao, Plaza Mayor, by the Palacio Real and by the Prado.

010 phoneline

Open 8am-9pm Mon-Fri; 9am-2pm Sat.
A city-run information line that will answer enquiries of any and every kind on Madrid, and particularly on events promoted by the city council. Calls are accepted in French and English, but you may have to wait for an English-speaking operator. From outside Madrid, call 91 540 40 10/40. There is also a tourist information line, 901 30 06 00, which usually has more limited information.

Visas & immigration

Spain is one of the European Union countries that is party to the Schengen Agreement (which includes all of the EU except the UK, Ireland or the countries that joined in May 2004. These countries share immigration policies and have reduced border controls between each other. To enter Spain nationals from countries that are party to the agreement need only show their national ID card, but British, Irish, those from the new EU countries and all non-EU citizens must have full passports.

Additional visas are not needed by US, Canadian, Australian, New Zealand or Israeli citizens for stays of up to three months. Citizens of South Africa and some other countries do need a visa to enter Spain and the Schengen area. They can be obtained from Spanish consulates in other European countries as well as in your home country (or from those of other Schengen countries you visit).

For long-term stays, *see p293* **Carrying the card**.

Water

Madrid's tap water is good and safe to drink, with less of the chlorine taste that you get in some Spanish cities. There are occasional water shortages during the summer, and signs posted in hotels urge guests to avoid wasting water. If you want tap rather than bottled water in a restaurant specify that you want *agua del grifo*.

When to go

It's not for nothing that the climate of Madrid has been described as 'nine months of winter (*invierno*) and three months of hell (*infierno*)'. Many people can't cope with the summer heat, while others love it. Climate aside, the city is great fun during the fiestas. *See also pp190-95*.

Climate

Winter in Madrid can be very cold, although there's often bright, crisp sunshine and most rain falls in autumn and spring. Spring is unpredictable – February can often be freakishly warm, while in April, rain is likely. Summer temperatures range from hot to unbearably hot, although it's a dry heat with little humidity. In July and August it doesn't really cool down at night, making partying in the street great fun, but sleeping less so. Traditionally there's a mass exodus in August. Autumn weather is usually bright and warm and it's often possible to eat and drink outside well into October. *See also below* **Average monthly climate**.

Holidays

On public holidays (*fiestas*), virtually all shops, banks and offices, and some bars and restaurants, are closed. There is a near-normal public transport service, though, except on Christmas Day and New Year's Day, and many museums are open, with Sunday hours. When a holiday falls on a Tuesday or Thursday many people take the day before or after the weekend off as well, in a long weekend called a *puente* (bridge). Many places are also closed for the whole of Easter Week. For the city's festivals, *see pp190-95*. The usual official holidays are:
New Year's Day/Año Nuevo 1 Jan; Three Kings/Reyes Magos 6 Jan; Good Friday/Viernes Santo; May (Labour) Day/Fiesta del Trabajo 1 May; Madrid Day/Día de la Comunidad de Madrid 2 May; San Isidro 15 May; Virgen de la Paloma 15 Aug; Discovery of America/Día de la Hispanidad 12 Oct; All Saints'

Day/Todos los Santos 1 Nov; Virgen de la Almudena 9 Nov; Constitution Day/Día de la Constitución 6 Dec; Immaculate Conception/La Inmaculada 8 Dec; Christmas Day/Navidad 25 Dec.

Women

Instituto de la Mujer

C/Condesa de Venadito 34, La Concepción (91 363 80 00). Metro Barrio de la Concepción. **Open** 9am-2pm, 4-6pm Mon-Thur; 9am-2pm Fri. A government organisation that acts as an umbrella for many other bodies, with a useful information service. The Institute has a legal office at C/Génova 11, Chueca (91 700 19 10/www.mtas.es/mujer).

Working

There is a huge number of foreigners living and working in Madrid. Ninety-five per cent of those from the EU are teaching English. To get a job in one of the academies with better pay and conditions, it's advisable to have a relevant qualification such as TEFL. Private classes are also available, but bear in mind that work often dries up over the summer and holiday periods.

There is a lot of red tape involved in working in Madrid; you can ignore the bureaucracy for a while, but in the long run it's best to sort things out. If you come here contracted from your country of origin, papers should be dealt with by your employer. The quickest way to deal with the Spanish state's love of form-filling is to resort to one of the agencies called *gestorías* (see p283).

For information on working visas and long-term residency, *see p293* **Carrying the card**.

Average monthly climate

	Max temp (c/f)	Min temp (c/f)	Rainfall (mm/in)	Rain (days)
Jan	9/48	2/36	39/1.5	8
Feb	11/52	2/36	34/1.3	7
March	15/59	5/41	43/1.7	10
April	18/64	7/45	48/1.9	9
May	21/70	10/50	47/1.8	10
June	27/81	15/59	27/1.0	5
July	31/88	17/63	11/0.4	2
August	30/86	17/63	15/0.6	3
Sept	25/77	14/57	32/1.2	6
Oct	19/66	10/50	53/2.0	8
Nov	13/55	5/41	47/1.8	9
Dec	9/48	2/36	48/1.9	10

Directory

Vocabulary

Like other Latin languages, Spanish has different familiar and polite forms of the second person (you). Many young people now use the familiar *tú* form most of the time; for foreigners, though, it's always advisable to use the more polite *usted* with people you do not know, and certainly with anyone over the age of 50. In the phrases listed here all verbs are given in the *usted* form. For help in making your way through menus, *see p122 and p144*.

Pronunciation

c, before an **i** or an **e**, and **z** are like **th** in thin.
c in all other cases is as in cat.
g, before an **i** or an **e**, and **j** are pronounced with a guttural **h**-sound that does not exist in English – like **ch** in Scottish lo**ch**, but much harder.
g in all other cases is pronounced as in **g**et.
h at the beginning of a word is normally silent.
ll is pronounced almost like a **y**.
ñ is like **ny** in ca**ny**on.
A single **r** at the beginning of a word and **rr** elsewhere are heavily rolled.

Basics

hello *hola*; **hello** (when answering the phone) *hola, diga*
good morning, good day *buenos días*; **good afternoon, good evening** *buenas tardes*; **good evening** (after dark), **good night** *buenas noches*
goodbye/see you later *adiós/hasta luego*
please *por favor*; **thank you** (very much) *(muchas) gracias*
you're welcome *de nada*
do you speak English? *¿habla inglés?*
I don't speak Spanish *no hablo español*
I don't understand *no entiendo*
what's your name? *¿cómo se llama?*
speak more slowly, please *hable más despacio, por favor*
wait a moment *espere un momento*
Sir/Mr *señor* (sr); **Madam/Mrs** *señora* (sra); **Miss** *señorita* (srta)
excuse me/sorry *perdón*
excuse me, please *oiga* (the standard way to attract someone's attention, politely; literally 'hear me')

OK/fine/(or to a waiter) **that's enough** *vale*
where is... *¿dónde está…?*
why? *¿porqué?*; **when?** *¿cuándo?*; **who?** *¿quién?*; **what?** *¿qué?*; **where?** *¿dónde?*; **how?** *¿cómo?*
who is it? *¿quién es?*
is/are there any... *¿hay…?*
very *muy*; **and** *y*; **or** *o*
with *con*; **without** *sin*
open *abierto*; **closed** *cerrado*
what time does it open/close? *¿a qué hora abre/cierra?*
pull (on signs) *tirar*; **push** *empujar*
I would like... *quiero…* (literally, 'I want…'); **how many would you like?** *¿cuántos quiere?*
I like *me gusta*
I don't like *no me gusta*
good *bueno/a*; **bad** *malo/a*; **well/badly** *bien/mal*; **small** *pequeño/a*; **big** *gran, grande*; **expensive** *caro/a*; **cheap** *barato/a*; **hot** (food, drink) *caliente*; **cold** *frío/a*
something *algo*; **nothing** *nada*
more/less *más/menos*
more or less *más o menos*
the bill/check, please *la cuenta, por favor*
how much is it? *¿cuánto es?*
do you have any change? *¿tiene cambio?*
price *precio*; **free** *gratis*
discount *descuento*
bank *banco*; **to rent** *alquilar*; **(for) rent, rental** *(en) alquiler*; **post office** *correos*; **stamp** *sello*; **postcard** *postal*; **toilet** *los servicios*

Getting around

airport *aeropuerto*; **railway station** *estación de ferrocarril/estación de RENFE* (Spanish Railways);
Metro station *estación de Metro*
entrance *entrada*; **exit** *salida*
car *coche*; **bus** *autobús*; **train** *tren*
a ticket *un billete*; **return** *de ida y vuelta*; **bus stop** *parada de autobús*; **the next stop** *la próxima parada*
excuse me, do you know the way to...? *¿oiga, señor/señora/etc, sabe como llegar a...?*
left *izquierda*; **right** *derecha*
here *aquí*; **there** *allí*
straight on *recto*; **to the end of the street** *al final de la calle*
as far as *hasta*; **towards** *hacia*
near *cerca*; **far** *lejos*

Accommodation

do you have a double/single room for tonight/one week? *¿tiene una habitación doble/para una persona para esta noche/una semana?*
where is the car park? *¿dónde está el parking?*

we have a reservation *tenemos reserva*
an inside/outside room *una habitación interior/exterior*
with/without bathroom *con/sin baño*; **shower** *ducha*
double bed *cama de matrimonio*; **with twin beds** *con dos camas*
breakfast included *desayuno incluido*
air-conditioning *aire acondicionado*; **lift** *ascensor*; **swimming pool** *piscina*

Time

morning *la mañana*; **midday** *mediodía*; **afternoon/evening** *la tarde*; **night** *la noche*; **late night/early morning** (roughly 1-6am) *la madrugada*
now *ahora*; **later** *más tarde*
yesterday *ayer*; **today** *hoy*; **tomorrow** *mañana*; **tomorrow morning** *mañana por la mañana*
early *temprano*; **late** *tarde*
delay *retraso*; **delayed** *retrasado*
at what time...? *¿a qué hora...?*
in an hour *en una hora*
the bus will take 2 hours (to get there) *el autobús tardará dos horas (en llegar)*
at 2 *a las dos*; **at 8pm** *a las ocho de la tarde*; **at 1.30** *a la una y media*
at 5.15 *a las cinco y cuarto*;
at 22.30 *a veintidós treinta*

Numbers

0 *cero*; 1 *un, uno, una*; 2 *dos*; 3 *tres*;
4 *cuatro*; 5 *cinco*; 6 *seis*; 7 *siete*;
8 *ocho*; 9 *nueve*; 10 *diez*; 11 *once*;
12 *doce*; 13 *trece*; 14 *catorce*;
15 *quince*; 16 *dieciséis*; 17 *diecisiete*;
18 *dieciocho*; 19 *diecinueve*;
20 *veinte*; 21 *veintiuno*; 22 *veintidós*;
30 *treinta*; 40 *cuarenta*;
50 *cincuenta*; 60 *sesenta*; 70 *setenta*;
80 *ochenta*; 90 *noventa*; 100 *cien*;
1,000 *mil*; 1,000,000 *un millón*

Days, months & seasons

Monday *lunes*; **Tuesday** *martes*; **Wednesday** *miércoles*; **Thursday** *jueves*; **Friday** *viernes*; **Saturday** *sábado*; **Sunday** *domingo*
January *enero*; **February** *febrero*; **March** *marzo*; **April** *abril*; **May** *mayo*; **June** *junio*; **July** *julio*; **August** *agosto*; **September** *septiembre*; **October** *octubre*; **November** *noviembre*; **December** *diciembre*
spring *primavera*; **summer** *verano*; **autumn/fall** *otoño*; **winter** *invierno*

Directory

Further Reference

Art & architecture

Hugh Broughton *Madrid* The capital's architecture analysed for a lay audience.
Jonathan Brown *Velázquez: Painter and Courtier* The most comprehensive study in English.
JH Elliott & Jonathan Brown *A Palace for a King: The Buen Retiro and the Court of Philip IV* A vivid reconstruction of the life, culture and spectacle of the Habsburg Court, and the grandest of Madrid's palaces.
Francisco de Goya *Disasters of War; Disparates, or the Proverbs; Los Caprichos* Dover Books publish good-value, high-quality reproductions of Goya's three most remarkable series of etchings.
Robert Hughes *Goya* A dynamic new biography of Madrid's favourite son.
Michael Jacobs *Madrid Observed* A lively survey by one of the best current foreign writers on Spain. A good walking companion.
Angus Mitchell *Spain: Interiors, Gardens, Architecture, Landscape* Lavishly illustrated.

Food & drink

Alan Davidson *Tio Pepe Guide to the Seafood of Spain and Portugal* An excellent pocket-sized guide with illustrations, to Spain's fishy delights.
Sam and Sam Clark *Moro* The best modern cookbook in English for reproducing the tastes of Spain.

History, politics, culture

Phil Ball *Morbo* A fascinating history of Spanish football, with a good section on Real Madrid.
JH Elliott *Imperial Spain, 1469-1716* The standard history.
RA Fletcher *Moorish Spain* Varied account of a little-known period in European history.
Ronald Fraser *Blood of Spain* An oral history of the Spanish Civil War, the most vivid and human account of Spain's great crisis.
Juan Lalaguna *A Traveller's History of Spain* A handy introduction to the country.
Ian Gibson *Fire in the Blood* Idiosyncratic vision of modern Spain by Lorca's biographer.
David Gilmour *Cities of Spain* With an informative, impressionistic chapter on Madrid.

John Hooper *The New Spaniards* The best survey of post-1975 Spain, updated to cover changes in the 1990s.
Paul Preston *Franco, Comrades!, Doves of War* Exhaustive portraits of the key players on both sides of the Spanish Civil War. The same author's *The Spanish Civil War* is a good concise account of the war.
Rob Stone *Spanish Cinema* A fascinating history of Spanish film through the Franco years and beyond.
Hugh Thomas, ed *Madrid, A Traveller's Companion* A great anthology of writings on Madrid from the Middle Ages to the 1930s, by authors as varied as Casanova, Pérez Galdós and the Duke of Wellington.

Literature

Pedro Almodóvar *Patty Diphusa Stories and Other Writings* Frothy, disposable, but full of the sparky, sexy atmosphere of the Madrid of La Movida.
Camilo José Cela *The Hive* Nobel-prizewinner Cela's sardonic masterpiece on Madrid in the aftermath of the Civil War.
Miguel de Cervantes *Don Quixote* The Golden Age classic, and still an entertaining read. Now available in an excellent and lively new translation by Edith Grossman.
Antonio Múñoz Molina *Prince of Shadows* A psychological thriller based on the legacy of the recent past in modern Madrid.
Benito Pérez Galdós *Fortunata and Jacinta* The masterwork of Spain's great 19th-century novelist, a story of love and class of great depth set amid the political conflicts of 1860s Madrid.
Arturo Pérez Reverte *The Fencing Master, The Flanders Road* and *The Club Dumas* (also published as *The Dumas Club*) Elegant, unconventional mystery novels by one of the most lauded of current Spanish writers.
Francisco de Quevedo, & anon (Penguin edition) *Two Spanish Picaresque Novels* The anonymous *Lazarillo de Tormes* and Quevedo's 1626 *El Buscón* (translated as 'The Swindler'), an earthy masterpiece and an essential Golden Century text.
Benjamin Prado *Not Only Fire* Examination of post-Civil War intergenerational relationships by one of Spain's bright young hopes.

Plácido Domingo *Romanzas de Zarzuelas* One of his several recordings of lush tunes from the *zarzuelas* that have played a big part in the revival of Madrid's own comic operas.

El Gran Lapofsky *Spain is Different* A fantastic selection of Latin, bossa, nu-jazz and funk-infused tracks – some of which are unavailable rarities – interspersed with skits from Spaniards telling us just why Spain is different.
Ray Heredia *Quien no corre, vuela* One of the most original new-flamenco performers.
Los Jóvenes Flamencos Several CDs in this series, bringing together all the best *nuevo flamenco* artists of the last 15 years, have been issued by the Nuevos Medios label. One at least is available outside Spain with the title *The Young Flamencos*.
El Lebrijano, con la Orquesta Arábigo Andaluza *Casablanca* Fascinating crossover recording by flamenco *cantaor* El Lebrijano, accompanied by Moroccan musicians and using traditional themes from Muslim Andalusia.
Carmen Linares *Antología* Classic flamenco themes sung by one of the best younger *cantaoras*. Another CD, *Carmen Linares, Cantaora*, may be more widely available outside Spain.
Corazón Loco *40 Joyas del Pop Español* Excellent intro to the perky, occasionally daft and sometimes pretty cool soundtrack of modern Madrid.
Paco de Lucía *Luzia*, or any of the many recordings by the greatest of modern flamenco guitarists.
José Mercé *Del Amanecer* Fine performances by *cantaor* Mercé, with Vicente Amigo on guitar.
Joaquín Sabina *Pongamos que hablo de Madrid* Sabina is a cool and witty *chanteur* of modern Madrid.
Tomatito *Guitarra Gitana* An exceptional Gypsy flamenco guitarist, former accompanist of Camarón.

www.munimadrid.es The Madrid Ayuntamiento's functional website, with some information in English.
www.madrid.org Equivalent site of the Comunidad: practical information on local services, in Spanish only.
www.ctm-madrid.es Madrid transport information.
www.lanetro.com A useful online listings magazine, with concerts, clubs films and reviews.
www.lecool.com Weekly round-up of the city's quirkiest, coolest events.
www.renfe.es Spanish Railways' site, with online booking.
http://madrid.lanetro.com The hippest and best of the local Spanish-language events and listings sites, with news on music, clubs, restaurants, films and more in and around Madrid. It's often hard to access, though.

Index

Note: page numbers in **bold**
indicate section(s) giving key
information on topic; *italics*
indicate photos.

Index

Advertisers' Index

Please refer to the relevant pages for full contact details

Key to Symbols

 Metro entrance

20 Bus Route

145 End of bus route

 Night bus terminus

 Airport bus route

 Coach depot

Mainline rail station

Cercanías local rail station

AVE high-speed train

i Tourist Information

Maps

Trips out of Town

© Copyright Time Out Group 2004

Madrid by Area

AVDA MONFORTE DE LEMOS

M30

NORTHERN SUBURBS

Chamartín Station

PLAZA DE CASTILLA

TETUÁN

AVDA PÍO XII

M30

PLAZA DE CUZCO

CHAMARTÍN

ARGÜELLES & MONCLOA

Dehesa de la Villa

C/OFELIA NIETO

C/BRAVO MURILLO

C/ORENSE

PASEO DE LA CASTELLANA

Santiago Bernabéu Stadium

AVDA RAMÓN Y CAJAL

C/SERRANO

C/RDO. FDEZ VILLAVERDE

C/MURILLO

C/BRAVO MURILLO

PASEO DE SAN FRANCISCO DE SALES

C/CEA BERMUDEZ

C/JOSÉ ABASCAL

CHAMBERÍ

C/SANTA ENGRACIA

C/JOAQUÍN COSTA

Auditorio Nacional

C/MARÍA DE MOLINA

AVENIDA DE AMÉRICA

C/FRANCISCO SILVELA

Parque del Oeste

C/PRINCIPE DE VERGARA

Las Ventas Bullring

CASA DE CAMPO

C/PRINCESA

Centro Cultural Conde Duque

C/FUENCARRAL

C/HORTALEZA

PASEO DE RECOLETOS

PLAZA DE COLÓN

C/SERRANO

C/VELAZQUEZ

SALAMANCA & RETIRO

MALASAÑA & CONDE DUQUE

C/GOYA

Príncipe Pío Station

PLAZA DE ESPAÑA

SOL & GRAN VÍA

CHUECA

C/ALCALÁ

C/O'DONNELL

CALLE DOCTOR ESQUERDO

Campo del Moro

Palacio Real

GRAN VÍA

Puerta del Sol

Museo Thyssen

AVDA MENÉNDEZ PELAYO

Parque de la Elipa

C/ARENAL

C/BAILÉN

C/MAYOR

PLAZA MAYOR

HUERTAS & SANTA ANA

Parque del Buen Retiro

PASEO DEL PRADO

LOS AUSTRIAS & LA LATINA

C/HUERTAS

Museo del Prado

C/TOLEDO

C/ATOCHA

RASTRO & LAVAPIÉS

RONDA DE TOLEDO

Centro de Arte Reina Sofía

Atocha Station

AVDA DEL MEDITERRÁNEO

AVDA CIUDAD DE BARCELONA

Vicente Calderón Stadium

PASEO SANTA MARÍA DE LA CABEZA

PASEO DE LAS DELICIAS

C/MÉNDEZ ÁLVARO

M30

SOUTHERN SUBURBS

SOUTH OF CENTRE

Planetario

Rayo Vallecano Stadium

Parque de Tierno Galvan

VALLECAS

0   800 m

0   800 yds

© Copyright Time Out Group 2004

307

This is a map page showing a section of Madrid, with streets, landmarks, and metro stations including:

Landmarks and places:
- Museo Sorolla
- Delegación Gobierno Madrid
- Rubén Darío
- Gta. de Emilio Castelar
- Gta. de Rubén Darío
- Iglesia
- Gta. Pintor Sorolla
- Pza. de Chamberí
- J.M.D. Chamberí
- Iglesia San Fermín de los Navarros
- Bilbao
- Alonso Martínez
- Pza. de Alonso Martínez
- Tribunal
- Museo Romántico
- Museo Municipal
- Soc. Gral. de Autores
- Colón
- Pza. de Colón
- Pza. de la Villa de París
- Museo de Figuras de Cera
- Palacio de Justicia
- Pza. de las Salesas
- Centro Cultural de la Villa
- Bus Aeropuerto
- Biblioteca Nacional
- Recoletos
- Convento Mercedarias Descalzas
- Pza. de Chueca
- Chueca
- Teatro Mª Guerrero
- Palacio Mqués. de Salamanca

Street names (selection):
García, Paredes, Viriato, Gral. Martínez Campos, Rafael, Calvo, Dato, Eduardo, Arrando, Jenner, Españoleto, Caracas, Zurbano, Zurbarán, C. Blanca de Navarra, Montesquinza, Fernando, El Santo, Sagasta, Calle de Génova, Orellana, C. Alcalá Galiano, Castaños, Campoamor, Sta. Teresa, Argensola, Belén, Barquillo, Piamonte, Prim, Almirante, Bárbara de Braganza, Paseo de Recoletos, Paseo de la Castellana, Fuencarral, Hortaleza, San Lorenzo, San Mateo, Farmacia, Figueroa, Augusto, San Marcos, Gravina, C. Libertad, Pza. del Conde, and others.

Metro/bus route numbers shown: 7, 16, 61, 147, 40, 5, 37, 21, 149, 3, 150, 45, 27, 14, 19, 51, 74, 53, 9

Street Index